An Age of Crisis

AN AGE OF CRISIS

Man and World in Eighteenth Century French Thought

by LESTER G. CROCKER

The Goucher College Series

THE JOHNS HOPKINS PRESS
Baltimore and London

TO

Arthur O. Lovejoy

"maestro di color che sanno"

ACKNOWLEDGMENTS

WITHOUT the John Simon Guggenheim Fellowship and the Fulbright Research Fellowship, which were granted to me for the academic year 1954–1955, the research required for this book could not have been undertaken. For these opportunities, I am deeply grateful.

I am indebted to the Institute for Advanced Study, and in particular to Dr. J. Robert Oppenheimer, for the privilege of membership in the Institute this year, an appointment which has enabled me to complete this volume and to advance the preparation of the one that is to follow.

An enlightened administration at Goucher College, headed by Dr. Otto F. Kraushaar and Dean Elizabeth Geen, has fostered and encouraged my efforts in every possible way.

To Dr. Arthur O. Lovejoy, who listened to every word in this book, save only the chapter on the novel and the notes, I owe a special debt, for his infinite patience and for the wisdom of his vast philosophical culture. It is in appreciation for the friendship he has shown me that I have dedicated the book to him.

My sincere thanks to Professor George R. Havens, of the Ohio State University, who read the entire volume with care and made many valuable suggestions; to my faithful friend, Raymond P.

Hawes, professor emeritus of philosophy at Goucher College, who read the first section and most of the third; to Professor Albert Hammond, of the department of Philosophy of The Johns Hopkins University, who made helpful comments in regard to the chapters on freedom; to Professor René Girard, of The Johns Hopkins University, who read the chapter on the novel; to Professor Robert R. Palmer, of Princeton University, whose observations on the concluding chapter were most constructive; and to my constant friend, Professor Alexandre Koyré, on whose wisdom and encouragement I have come to rely.

Finally, to my wife this book owes more than I could possibly convey in words.

Lester G. Crocker

CONTENTS

PREFATORY NOTE

IN UNDERTAKING to write a synthetical study of French ethical thought during the Age of Enlightenment, I am not unaware either of the difficulties of such an enterprise, or of my own deficiencies. As it is a subject of crucial importance for an understanding of our cultural history, as well as for the eighteenth century—one, moreover, that has never been essayed—it has for several years attracted me. In the loss of the metaphysical fundament of values and the consequent ethical confusion and uncertainty, I believe we can observe the opening chapter of the moral crisis of the modern world, which has come to such a critical pass in the twentieth century. This study, of which I am now offering the first part, is bound to have many shortcomings. My hope is that scholars and students will find in it enough of merit to make of it withal a useful instrument, and to justify the labors of which it is the fruit.

The general plan of the work involves three parts. The first, which is now before the reader, examines the metaphysical and psychological assumptions and problems which form, as it were, the sub-structure and the building blocks prerequisite to ethical theory. It will be followed, I hope, by a study of theories relating to the genesis of moral experience and the nature of moral judgments; and finally, by an analysis of the ethical systems and value concepts which were evolved in an effort to solve the problems of the moral life.

Having used the adjective "synthetical," I should like to emphasize that it is not equivalent to "exhaustive." It would be idle, even in a work of this considerable dimension, to pretend to a complete treatment of each of the main questions that will be taken up, or of the ethical philosophy of the great authors of the age, about whom separate volumes are readily available. It is rather hoped that each writer, and each problem, will be seen in truer perspective, as they take their proper place in the complex, interacting currents of eighteenth century intellectual history.

It is this picture of interrelationships, within the living matrix of a moment of cultural history, rather than exhaustive detail, that is the proper aim of a synthetical treatment. For this reason, too, I have given a large place to the lesser authors. To conceive a faithful picture of the intellectual climate, it is necessary to see not only the peaks, but the whole area out of which they grow. T. S. Eliot has wisely observed that "we can touch the life of the great works of literature of any age all the better if we know something of the less." It is the minor writers who form the chain and the tradition.

It will be my general plan to give lengthiest consideration to the most important and influential figures. As other criteria must also be allowed due weight, there will inevitably be some distortion in this regard. These criteria include intrinsic originality and depth of thought, which are not invariably to be found in the most famous writers; and the fact that certain men, now all but forgotten, may have exercised notable influence in their time, or have been peculiarly representative of a widely held view. It will not, of course, be my primary purpose to trace sources in the case of individual authors, although some apparent filiation of ideas may be evident. A particular author's thought will rather be seen to arise from a certain context, under its influence or in reaction to it. It will, however, be necessary to give some attention to important thinkers of the seventeenth century who exercised a direct and continuing influence on the later writers. Furthermore, I shall not hesitate to leave the confines of France to bring in illuminating parallels and contrasts from England or elsewhere.

The structure of the book will be much like that of Cassirer's *Philosophy of the Enlightenment;* that is to say, a series of problems will be examined successively, and chronology will be followed within each topic, rather than as in the conventional history, which pursues a single chronological line, treating all subjects simultaneously. I believe that this method will lead to clearer and more fruitful generalizations. Furthermore, while in a general way ideas were what they were because of temporal relationships, often, in the eighteenth century, we witness a complex and contradictory interweaving, with the important phenomenon less that of novelty than wider diffusion or more intensive probing. Some of the most radical ideas are announced in the earliest years of the century. The increasing momentum of rational criticism is then countered by an ever stronger defence. Ideas and currents of thought eddy and ebb in dynamic whirlpools. Chronology, in such instances, is more valid as a point of reference and control than as a sure guide to the inner nature and meanings of the ideological conflicts.[1]

There is, to be sure, a definite evolution in eighteenth century French ethical thinking, although it moves in concentric circles rather than following a straight path. While centers of interest evolve, nothing is really left behind. The same problems and arguments recur. At the outset of the century, writers are concerned primarily with secularizing moral ideas, and with restoring the legitimacy of the natural claims of human nature, particularly in regard to pleasure and the passions. The problem of evil is one principal focus of debate. At this stage, we see Leibniz and Bayle as the two opposing figures, though the influence of Spinoza is also considerable. By and large, pessimism about man, both theological and secular, is dominant. The question of human nature comes even more into the foreground in the second quarter of the century, with Mandeville and Shaftesbury the leading champions influencing the indigenous developments in French thought. The analyses of cynicism and optimism each point to different paths, the one later bearing fruit in Helvétius, the other in Rousseau (though equivocally) and in Bernardin de Saint-Pierre. As clandestine manuscripts multiply and thrive, the prob-

---

[1] For the same reason, it becomes vain and delusive, more often than not, to attempt to attribute an idea to a particular source or influence.

lems of free will and natural religion assume greater importance.

But now a new and decisive element enters French thought. The sensationist philosophy of Locke corresponds to the experimentalist, scientific mood of the time. As developed by Condillac, it becomes the guide both to an analysis of human nature and motivation, and to an ethical program which will be the *philosophes'* answer to the challenge to create a secular morality that will both satisfy that nature and control it. Now pessimism about man's nature deepens and the means of coping with it becomes the principal problem. Ethics is necessarily enlarged to embrace the social and political reformation of the community. Ostensibly empirical and scientific, the new programs are fundamentally rationalistic and even Cartesian. But they no sooner come into being than they evoke their own antithesis—not only in the Christian writings, which run parallel to the new developments, not unmodified by them—but particularly in a group of writers, ranging from Rousseau to Saint-Martin and Bernardin de Saint-Pierre, who revolt against the physical, analytic explanations of man. Their own view of man is in many ways quite different, and they look to other resources within him; but so powerful is the analysis of their opponents, that Rousseau, at least, will rely to a large extent on the same psychological mechanisms, although he would utilize them differently. Furthermore, there is almost perfect unity on all sides both in the continuing emphasis on happiness in this life and in the simultaneous, ever-increasing enshrinement of the Christian virtue of *bienfaisance*. The latter virtue was gradually assuming a more social garb under the heading of "good citizenship"—an ideal that was to become dominant and repressive during the French Revolution. As the Revolution approaches, few new ideas are advanced. It is rather a matter of sharpening one's position and of drawing from it the ultimate conclusions. Some of these hold fearsome nihilistic or totalitarian possibilities, which the Revolution, and the later course of Western history, will unfortunately bring true, truer than anyone would then have dreamed.

Lastly, it would be well, at this starting point, to define as clearly as possible several words that will occur frequently throughout the book.

By *philosophes,* it is well known by now, we designate that group of eighteenth century French writers who, refusing to abide by Christian doctrines and dogma, and by the authority of the Church, searched for the truth in the light of reason and experience. They were not (excepting Condillac) systematic philosophers in the usual sense, but were primarily combative social and moral thinkers, usually with a strong tinge of scientific dilletantism.

By "law," the eighteenth century meant either that regularity of behavior, or that normative rule of behavior which was thought to inhere in the nature of things, or in their relationships. When the capitalized phrase, "Natural Law," is used, it refers to that doctrine which conceived of a higher law, prior to all human laws, which was presumed to arise "from the fact of God's providential government of the world and from the rational and social nature of human beings"; a law which is "ultimately rational, universal, unchangeable and divine, at least in respect to the main principles of right and justice." [2] It refers also to the moral content or prescriptions of that law. However, it must also be remembered that there arose variant concepts of Natural Law, which will be analyzed in their proper place. Other meanings of the word "law," such as the laws of a State, will either be obvious in the context or will be designated by such an expression as "positive law."

The word "nihilism" is always to be taken in the ethical sense, as the denial of the validity of all distinctions of moral value.

The words "humanism, humanist, humanistic" will also appear from time to time. The humanist (if I may quote a definition I have used elsewhere) holds that man, although he is within nature, has distinctive characteristics which set him apart from other natural forms. He holds this distinctiveness to be definitive, to override, in metaphysical and ethical importance, the common realm of nature he shares with other living things. Inasmuch as this is so, he believes that choice of action, and evaluation of action, lie properly within the sphere of human power and judgment. Humanism, ultimately, implies a certain belief and faith in man.

The concepts of "reason" and "nature" are more difficult to define, and yet they are the most important of all. These words

[2] G. H. Sabine, *A History of Political Theory,* p. 164–170.

were the guideposts of eighteenth century thought. The relation of these concepts to ethics, and to each other, constitutes one of the crucial problems.

By the naked word "reason" (unless otherwise qualified by adjectives or the context), the processes of logic and ratiocination, or of abstraction and theorizing will not necessarily be implied. The reader should rather take it to signify "rational self-evidence," or the enlightened (i.e., unprejudiced) use of the faculty of ordinary reflection. The expressions "the natural light of reason," "right reason," were often used. Reason was frequently opposed to the passions, on the one hand, and to deductive reasoning, on the other. What Père Buffier remarks about common sense, in his *Traité des premières vérités* (1724), is pertinent to this concept of reason: "I understand then here by common sense, the disposition which nature has put in all men, or manifestly in most of them, in order that they may make, when they have attained the use of reason, a common and uniform judgment of the different objects of the intimate feelings of their own perception. . . ." [3] Reason, in this sense, was consequently often deemed to be universal and natural. It is this "natural reason" which Burke held up in attacking the "artificial reason" of rationalists who plan societies: the latter have made reason "fight against itself." [4] It is "artificial" reason which Rousseau also damns in the name of "Nature," or intuitive reason, as the "philosophy of a day." [5] "Natural" reason is by definition universal; the principles of happiness and right living, wrote Louis de Beausobre, "are the same; nature and reason dictate them to all men." [6] As Ernst Cassirer has put it, "The eighteenth century is imbued with a belief in the unity and immutability of reason." [7]

When Cassirer asserts, however, that reason is "the unifying and central point of the century, expressing all that it longs and strives for, and all that it achieves," we must make an essential reservation. "Nature," and the "natural," represent a co-equal center of force and a co-equal target. It is obvious from what we have just said that reason and nature, as they were conceived, had

[3] Par. 33 (1822 ed., p. 26).
[4] *A Vindication of Natural Society* (1756), in *Works*, I, 37.
[5] *Lettre à M. d'Alembert sur les spectacles*, p. 110–111.
[6] *Essai sur le bonheur*, p. 206.
[7] *The Philosophy of the Enlightenment*, p. 5.

a certain area of coincidence. This is especially true for methodology. Rational law was held to inhere in phenomena; consequently it was sought in the facts of observation and experiment.[8] Despite the empirical and inductive intent of a Montesquieu or a Quesnay, the real aim was not to formulate hypotheses but to derive absolute laws, as satisfactory to the reason as those of mathematics or logic.

But "nature" had many other implications, which were in some instances at variance with right reason; so many, in fact, that we cannot hope to give a simple definition of this concept. As Bayle commented, "There is scarcely a word that is used in a vaguer way than that of Nature; it enters into all kinds of discourse, now with one sense, now with another, and one is scarcely ever dealing with a precise idea." And he goes on to say, "But above all, the conclusion is not certain, *this comes from nature, therefore this is good and right*. We see in the human species many very bad things, although it cannot be doubted that they are the work of nature . . . Nature is a state of sickness." [9] There is no doubt that in ethical thinking, part of the confusion came from the failure to distinguish what is *right* by nature from that which is according to nature. And then, what *is* "according to nature"? For Diderot and Rousseau, it is sometimes sexual freedom; for Montesquieu, and for Diderot and Rousseau (at other moments), it is modesty. Hume points out that some writers, in their use of the word "natural," took it in the sense of "common," in contrast to "rare" or "unusual." He criticizes the word as unphilosophical and meaningless; both vice and virtue are equally natural; or, with as much justification, "equally artificial and out of nature." [10] And Grimm threw up his hands. "What devilish nonsense! What is nature? Is it not all that is? . . . How can what is be contrary to nature?" [11]

---

[8] Cassirer also makes far too sharp a separation between seventeenth century reason, as a body of eternal truths revealing the essence of things, and eighteenth century reason as an energy guiding the discovery of truth.

[9] *Réponse aux questions d'un provincial*, in *Oeuvres diverses*, I, 74 ff, 95 ff. At the other end of the century, Dupont de Nemours accuses the innumerable meanings of the word of having thrown modern philosophers into confusion. *Philosophie de l'univers* (1792), p. 217.

[10] *Treatise of Human Nature*, in *Hume's Moral and Political Philosophy*, ed. Aiken, p. 46–48.

[11] *Correspondance litteraire*, IX, 49 (juin 1770).

Our best guide to the meanings of the word "nature" is in the studies by Arthur O. Lovejoy and George Boas.[12] Of the various meanings that were especially current in the eighteenth century, one may be said to have been basic and general, especially when "nature" was not coupled with "reason," but rather set off against the products of human reason, such as art and culture. Nature, in this sense, is what is prior to reason; what, in Montaigne's vocabulary, was "naïve," and in the eighteenth century vocabulary, "original." It is also what is spontaneous. "Such is the pure impulse of nature," writes Rousseau in the *Discours sur l'inégalité,* "anterior to all reflection." The Age of Enlightenment witnesses a growing emphasis on the idea of nature as the non-rational and the non-moral, as the designation for the objects and processes of the sensible world.

In this latter sense, "nature" is opposed to custom and positive law, which were called "artificial." By some it will also be opposed to morals, as it was well known that traditional moral laws are subject to frequent change and wide diversity; they therefore seemed man-made. This use of the word was usually accompanied either by ethical scepticism or by an endeavor to find anew objective and universally valid moral criteria.

However, as Dr. Lovejoy has demonstrated in the article referred to above, the word "nature" easily, almost inevitably took on a normative meaning, in addition to these descriptive uses. This was a psychological transference due to the approval that went with the word in its connotation of the norm of value or excellence. Thus the same word designated both the purely organic or physical, and, as in the phrases "Natural Religion" and "Natural Law," that which was moral and acceptable to the reason, and so, quite often, in flat contradiction with the first sense. As "natural" also designated what is original, it became attached to the various notions pertaining to the currents of primitivism, and was used to condemn various aspects of civilized societies that were decried as "artificial."

The confusion between these two connotations led, then, to the conception of the natural as a formal criterion of validity. It did

---

[12] See *Primitivism and Related Ideas in Antiquity,* p. 447–456; and A. O. Lovejoy, " 'Nature' as Norm in Tertullian," in *Essays in the History of Ideas,* p. 308–338, to which I am greatly indebted in the present discussion.

not, however, dictate substantive constructs, but merely said, "What is objectively right is objectively right." The substantive content of the "natural" remained an open question. It could imply what derives from instincts common to men and other animals, the rule of the strong, or (as in Aristotle and Spinoza) the use by the individual of his natural powers. It could, on the contrary, imply what realizes the most distinctive attributes of human nature (e.g., conscience, altruism, moral judgments); and by extension, natural political rights. It could even, as we have seen, be transformed into a kind of rationalism, referring to self-evident truths "arising either out of the nature of the good or the nature of the relations in which moral agents stand to one another." [13] This is nature as right reason, the rationalistic element in the soul, and "ethical naturalism as rationalistic intuitionism in morals."

This exposition of the diverse meanings of the idea of "nature" must be qualified by the apt comment of Basil Willey: "Nevertheless in our period it was not the ambiguity of 'Nature' which people felt most strongly; it was rather the clarity, the authority, and the universal acceptability of Nature and Nature's laws." [14] This was true in general, despite the fact that a few careful thinkers were disturbed by the vague and contradictory meanings given to the word. It was true, also, because still another meaning of "nature" opposed it to the supernatural, and thus expressed the most fundamental viewpoint of the new philosophy. However it is not quite correct to make this further generalization: "The laws of Nature are the laws of reason; they are always and everywhere the same." More accurately, we could say that this was rather the hope and aspiration, and sometimes the belief. But an opposition between the two norms was also evident to both Christians and rationalists.

This distinction brings us to our final and most important consideration. The uncertainties and confusions we have just observed were not essentially a semantic problem or deficiency. They were the result of profound uncertainties and confusions in basic concepts themselves, all of which were being challenged and re-explored. Thus the question we noted before will in-

[13] Lovejoy and Boas, *loc. cit.*, def. 55.
[14] *The Eighteenth Century Background*, p. 2.

evitably return to confront the moral philosophers of the eighteenth century. Is nature one thing, and the moral life another? If so, we are saying that what is and what ought to be are not identical; for if only some of what is is right, then we are interposing a supra-natural, or rational criterion. But if, on the other hand, nature and the moral life are one, why are they empirically divergent? If we accept the first answer, what are the relative claims of each, and can they be reconciled? Here is the great problem that characterizes the ethical writings we are about to investigate. It is equivalent to asking, Is an ethics possible, and if so, on what basis? This is the whole sense of the eighteenth century investigation, and of our inquiry.

Editorial Note: All quotations are translated into English, except poetry.

Man in the Universe

One

MAN'S RELATION TO GOD

DESPITE their professed scorn for metaphysics, eighteenth century French writers, having a deep concern with ethical problems, found themselves involved in metaphysical disputations at each step. It is obvious that as soon as one penetrates to the depth of ultimate questions this must indeed be so, for any ethics rests on a metaphysical position. Regrettably, French writers of the time, carried away by the rise of experimental science and the fashionable outcry against rationalistic systems, often approached metaphysical questions in a superficial, common-sense or cavalier way—even while they were constructing their own rationalistic systems. But they inevitably found that they could not limit themselves to a mere empirical code of obedience to law and custom, for the individual would assuredly ask, "Why *their* rules, and not mine?" and endeavor to elude the shackles of such tyranny.

Involvement with metaphysics was all the more inescapable because eighteenth century thinkers were caught in the conflicts of an age of profound cultural crisis. The dominant, inherited Christian world-view, having with some difficulty survived the challenge of the Renaissance (and having to some extent absorbed or blunted it), found itself assailed by the second tide of the Renaissance, a flood-tide of such great driving force that it soon put the prevailing religious outlook into a desperate plight, from which it never completely recovered. This second tide was the development and the wide cultural penetration of a mechanistic physical and biological science. It was aided and abetted by a variety of intellectual factors, including the influence of the seventeenth century English empirical philosophers and certain aspects of Descartes' and Spinoza's writings, and by the unrest generated by a deteriorating social and economic establishment. The play of life and of ideas forms an inextricable pattern of interaction. We need only recall the bare fact that there is an obvious moral breakdown in certain sectors of French society, which is reflected brilliantly in the literature of the time, both in the form of extreme moral freedom and in desperate efforts to preach the traditional Christian virtues. If it is necessary, as history seems to show, that the question of man be raised ever anew, it is also necessary that the answers grow authentically from the soil of contemporary experience. They cannot be simply borrowed from the past generations. "Ideas count in the story of civilization insofar as they correspond to conditions of fact and to the genuine requirements of the situation in a given epoch." [1] In the epoch which we are about to study, a complete reassessment of human nature and destiny had to be undertaken, in the light of the collapse of the Christian hegemony and the rise of naturalism.[2]

The challenge to the inherited order was complete and critical. Christian ethics was assailed both in its formal structure and its metaphysical basis. "Man," writes Alexandre Koyré, "lost his place in the world, or more correctly perhaps, lost the very world in which he was living and about which he was thinking, and had to transform and replace not only his fundamental concepts and attributes, but even the very framework of this thought." A cosmos ordered according to a hierarchy of value was replaced by an indefinite universe in which all components "are placed on the same level of being. . . . At the end we find nihilism and despair." [3] We shall in the course of this study survey the spectrum

---

[1] Corrado Rosso, "Il paradosso di Robinet," p. 57.

[2] Cf. Gilbert Chinard's perceptive remark: "The eighteenth century realized that the 'science' or rather the knowledge of man continued to remain almost stationary, while discoveries were being multiplied with overwhelming speed. Consequently, it seemed proper that we devote all our efforts to the search for man. . . . 'The proper study of Mankind is Man.'" (In Morelly, *Code de la nature*, p. 158–159 n.)

[3] *From the Closed World to the Infinite Universe*, p. 2, 43.

of problems that were explored by eighteenth century writers in their effort to absorb the new currents of thought and to establish a new and viable ethics; a span of reactions that extends from unshakable traditionalism, through compromise, to revolt and utter nihilism.

The Christian edifice, metaphysical and ethical, rested on the firm cornerstone of God's existence. It provided a solution to the ultimate problem in any ethics. The value of our acts, it is clear, depends on their meaning (if any), as well as on their consequences. This meaning is to a significant extent determined by our relation to the universe of which we are a part, that is, by the meaning (or meaninglessness) of human destiny and of the universe itself. The existence of a God as Christianity conceived him—the infuser of order, meaning and value throughout his creation—erected a firm ethics on the basis of imperatives that were unchallengeable by God's lowly and utterly dependent creatures.[4] Compliance was enforced by the awesome sanction of Hell and the tantalizing perspective of life eternal in Paradise. Here then was a settled concept of a structured cosmos, with a guaranteed destiny and authorized values for men. It was to be attacked and challenged in each and every thread of its fabric.

This Christian outlook was, however, stoutly and ably defended in the eighteenth century, not only as a vested institutional interest that was essential to all the institutions of the Old Régime, but by many who sincerely thought that the Christian metaphysic was the best basis, indeed the only possible basis for an ethics that could be functionally operative among creatures such as men are. Against all attacks and would-be compromises, the defenders upheld, in the first place, the necessity of God's existence, as a metaphysical postulate. The argumentation of this phase of the controversy is not of direct concern to us here. But if we accept the postulate of a personal God, wise and beneficent, then men's relationship to him must be of a certain character that will determine their entire moral life. It is these determinative rela-

---

[4] A clear picture of man's complete dependence on God, and the touchstone of obligation that derives from it, is given by Malebranche, in the second part of his *Traité de morale,* especially p. 149–151, 153–154. Also p. 161: "Certainly man is not wisdom or light unto himself. There is a universal Reason which illuminates all minds. . . . For all minds can, so to speak, embrace the same idea at the same time and in different places. . . ."

tionships that were most severely challenged, even by many who accepted God's existence as a metaphysical and ethical necessity.

The Christian concept places man directly under the thumb of God, our chastiser and our protector, and the provider of ethical directives. These directives are both general, imprinted in our heart and reason, and specific, as revealed in the Gospel and developed by the Church. What disposition the eighteenth century made of the Christian code will gradually emerge from our discussion. The atheists and deists took attitudes that varied considerably. But all the atheistic writers, in their denial of God's existence, obviously attacked the supposed relation between man and God that provided the structure for ethics. The concepts of Heaven and of eternal punishments, depending on a fictitious immortal soul, were ridiculed, and man was reduced to a mortal and material animal. The consequences for the new ethics will be apparent in the hedonistic, utilitarian and nihilistic directions that developed.

The atheistic writers took special pains to deny the existence of final causes in the universe. The new science of Galileo and of Newton (although Newton himself maintained his Christianity) had no use for final causes and simply excluded them. Descartes and Spinoza were powerful reinforcements to this view. Various manuscript works, secretly circulated in the early part of the eighteenth century, attacked the anthropomorphism of such doctrines as final causes, universal order and the beauty of the universe which provided some of the arguments for God's existence.[5] The rise of a mechanistic biology again reinforced this tendency, for it conceived of organic matter as possessing an intrinsic power to unfold its own patterns and developments.[6] All of these tendencies are fused in the work of the later atheists.

The idea of final causes was linked with that of an orderly uni-

---

[5] For instance, the *Traité des trois imposteurs*, the second chapter of which is largely a development of the Appendix to Part One of Spinoza's *Ethic*. For a study of the struggle to free science from theology, see D. Mornet, *Les Sciences de la nature en France au XVIIIe siècle*, Pt. 1, ch. 3.

[6] See A. Vartanian: "Trembley's Polyp, La Mettrie, and Eighteenth-century French Materialism"; L. G. Crocker: "Diderot and Eighteenth Century French Transformism," in *Forerunners of Darwin*. Curiously, Leibniz, an upholder of final causes, aided the development of this view by his concept of the monads as self-sufficient sources of their activities and changes. (*Monadology*, par. 11, 18, 22.)

verse. Order was never denied by these mechanistic determinists, in the scientific sense of inevitable cause-effect. They knew that science requires faith in the constancy and intelligibility of the natural order; and if they were moral determinists, it was because they believed that this was equally necessary and true in human behavior.[7] But the Christian concept of order, the preconceived plan of an intelligent and beneficent Creator, was of course ruled out. The point is nowhere made more effectively than in one of Diderot's earlier writings, the *Lettre sur les aveugles* (1749), where the blind Saunderson points to himself as a proof that order and final causes are man's fond illusions.[8]

Even Vauvenargues, who was not a mechanist, but an outstanding analyst of human behavior, and who believed that men could establish order through reason and virtue, agreed that the universe they live in is blind, senseless and devoid of moral order.

> Among kings, among people, among individuals, the stronger assigns himself rights over the weaker, and the same rule is followed by animals and inanimate beings; so that everything in the universe is done by violence; and this order which we reprove with some appearance of justice is the most general, the most immutable and the most important of nature.[9]

But another time he writes that the universe is "under God's hand. . . . None can free himself from the yoke of him who, from high above, commands all the peoples of the earth. . . ." This is the cry of Vauvenargues' anguished heart. "Ah! if it were true, if men depended only on themselves, if there were not rewards for the good and punishments for crime, if all were limited to this earth, what a lamentable state!" Vauvenargues is clearly struggling with

[7] "If the course of nature were not ruled by general and uniform laws, by universal causes, if the same causes were not ordinarily followed by the same effects, it would be absurd to propose a way of living." (Diderot, art. "Induction" in the *Encyclopédie*; also in Diderot, *Oeuvres*, xv, 214.)

[8] See this whole development. (*Lettre sur les aveugles*, éd. R. Niklaus, p. 39-44.) Diderot's earlier *Pensées philosophiques* (1746) had proposed the finalism evident in organisms as an incontrovertible argument against atheism. This was the trend of biological writings until the middle years of the 1740's as seen in the popular works of Pluche, Derham, Nieuwentyt, Bonnet and others. In his *Pensées sur l'interprétation de la nature* (1754), Diderot again attacked finalism as scientifically harmful as well as absurd. (*Oeuvres*, ii, 53-55.)

[9] *Réflexions, Oeuvres morales* (1746), iii, 38 (par. 183). Réflexion 65 adds "the most absolute, the most ancient."

despair, pushing away the nihilism he saw lurking in a non-moral universe.[10]

One year after the *Lettre sur les aveugles,* Maupertuis, in his *Essai de cosmologie,* went to some pains to examine the question in a cooler and more dispassionate way. He finds that living bodies have parts whose utility escapes us, and that some are not nearly so perfect as others. Similarly, some beings are useless, or even harmful. What does it prove to point out the perfect construction of a poisonous snake? And Maupertuis mocks the finalistic apologetics of the recent books on insectology. The earth itself does not appear to have been particularly designed for life, especially for human life. Besides, design and finalism are in themselves insufficient, unless we know and approve of the motive of the Maker: it might all be the work of a demon.[11]

The belief that physical nature is reducible to rational laws of motion implied, for Newtonians like Voltaire, that the universe is orderly and rational. It did not have this implication for thinkers like Maupertuis and Diderot. They were impressed by the constant creation and destruction, by the disorderly dynamism of infinite diversity. This was true of the physical universe, and even more obviously of the biological world. All life is war and disorder, creating a precarious balance. And in the realm of life, man, above all, is a disorderly element, because he is free to escape the fixed limits and set harmonies that rule the life of animals.

La Mettrie, and later d'Holbach and other materialists concurred in opposing the concept of a rationally ordered universe. La Mettrie suggests that God may not be the only alternative to a universe of chance; that nature may be inherently self-organizing; "that the sun is as natural a production as electricity; that it was no more made to warm the earth and all its inhabitants, whom it sometimes scorches, than rain to make grain grow, which it often rots." Nor was the eye "really made on purpose" for seeing; rather it sees "only because it happens to be organized and placed as it is; given the same rules of motion that Nature follows in the generation and development of bodies, it was not possible that this marvelous organ could be organized and placed otherwise." [12]

---

[10] I, 280–298.
[11] *Oeuvres,* I, 14–16.
[12] *L'homme machine,* ed. Solovine, p. 108–110.

Actually, La Mettrie's contention involves a rather un-rigorous chain of reasoning. There is no chance, and everything is necessary according to natural laws; these laws embody no purpose or finality; therefore (but this is the part La Mettrie does not state), if things as they exist are favorable to life, that is only *chance*. Ultimately, there is little difference between blind necessity and chance. La Mettrie's concept is essentially the one which Diderot was to develop in *Le Rêve de d'Alembert*. In his *Système d'Epicure* (1750), La Mettrie was even more outspoken in his assertion of the blind necessity of everything and the insignificance of man.[13]

D'Holbach, as would be expected, denounces our idea of order in the universe as anthropomorphic and relative.[14] Nature's order, according to this famous atheist, is merely "the chain of causes and effects necessary to its active existence . . . merely a way of looking at the necessity of things." "Disorder" is an equally necessary state of change, in consonance with the inalterable "general order of nature," and quite necessary to "the maintenance of the whole." D'Holbach states this dual view explicitly. "The order and disorder of nature do not exist"—they are attitudes determined by our own existence and its conservation. "Yet everything is in order in a nature none of whose parts can ever diverge from the certain and necessary rules which flow from the essence they have received; there is no disorder in a whole to the maintenance of which disorder is necessary, whose general course can never be upset. . . ." D'Holbach seems blissfully unaware of the ethical implications of his metaphysics, particularly of his last phrases. That they underlie the ethics of the absurd, or moral anarchism, as developed particularly by the marquis de Sade, is made even clearer in the following lines:

We cannot too often repeat [that] relatively to the great whole, all the movements of beings, all their ways of acting, can only be within the order and in conformity with nature. . . . Even more, each individual always acts within the order; all his actions, the whole system of his movements are always a necessary consequence of his permanent or temporary way of existence.

[13] Cf. p. 216–227.
[14] *Système de la nature*, I, 65–70.

The ethical consequences d'Holbach does infer are, as we shall later see, an attempt to establish ethics on a social basis, divorced from metaphysical considerations.

The utmost radical consequences of the metaphysical and ethical position of the eighteenth century atheist are reached in the work of the marquis de Sade, whose important place in the thought of his age has been shamefully neglected.[15] In his attacks on religion, Sade reads like an amalgam of Fréret, La Mettrie and d'Holbach, whose spiritual son he frequently acknowledges himself to be.[16] Sweeping away the entire structure of Western culture, from roof to cellar, he declares man to be completely free of moral constraint because he is living in an absurd and meaningless universe, utterly deprived of purpose and moral value. "Causes are perhaps useless to effects, and all of us, by a force as blind as it is necessary, are only the inept machines of vegetation, whose mysteries, explaining all movement here below, also reveal the origin of all actions of men and animals." [17] The intricacies of the Sadian ethic will be developed in due course. But first, and throughout his work, Sade takes pains to paint the universe as un-moral and meaningless. Sade's greatest heroine, Juliette, learns this lesson early in her amazing career. "I am convinced that crime serves nature's intentions as well as wisdom and virtue; let us sally forth into this perverse world . . ." [18] But this is only a

[15] "One can leaf through compact and detailed 'works on 'ideas in the eighteenth century' without finding his name mentioned a single time." (Simone de Beauvoir, "Faut-il bruler Sade?" p. 1002). Exception must be made for an unpublished dissertation by Prof. Robert E. Taylor, of New York University; however I have not consulted unpublished scholarly writings. Since Sade cannot be accorded any *more* than his just place, I shall largely limit my references, with certain exceptions, in this first part, at least, to two of his most typical works, *Les Infortunes de la vertu*, written in 1787 (ed. M. Heine), and *Histoire de Juliette, ou les prospérités du vice*, written in 1791. Mme de Beauvoir points out that Sade, like the *philosophes*, considered himself the spokesman for mankind, though self-justification and release from guilt may have been his unconscious motives. "To hide from men such basic truths, whatever may be their consequences, is not to love them well." And, "I shall have contributed something to the progress of enlightenment and I shall be glad." (Quoted by de Beauvoir, *op. cit.*, 1178.) Mme de Beauvoir, in her analysis of Sade's literary technique, has not noticed the essential structural resemblance between his "novels" and the *conte philosophique*. We have a series of situations rather than a plot; each is composed, as it were, like a tableau, and held as long as interesting; then rapidly liquidated by a sudden event, often involving change of place.

[16] The *Histoire de Juliette* contains an atheistic discourse that is an excellent summary of this aspect of the century (1, 40 ff.).

[17] *Ibid.*, IV, 197.

[18] I, 139.

beginning, and Juliette does not as yet suspect the amplitude of her future career. The picture of a non-moral universe gives way to an immoral one, in which "crime" and destruction are the essential processes. Disorder is the only order of the world. "All of this is within the order of things, my daughter," answered Noirceuil, ". . . the weak must be the food of the strong. Cast your eyes on the universe, on all the laws that rule it . . . tyranny and injustice, as the sole principles of all disorder, must be the first laws of a cause that acts only by disorder." [19] In destroying we partake fittingly in the universe of which we are a part.[20] In fact, the more atrocious our crimes, the more harmonious is our conduct with the universal order.[21]

Man, then, finds himself in a meaningless, absurd and cruel world. God, if he existed, could only be treacherous, evil, a monster. The world everywhere shows the hand of the opposite of what a God would be. It is not too much to say that the crisis of modern culture is crystallized in Sade. In reading him, we think, for instance, of the revolt of Ivan Karamazov. Ivan could not accept the universe which God has supposedly created, when he considered the torture and sufferings of innocent children. But as soon as he repudiates divine order, and tries to establish his own rules of life, he recognizes the legitimacy of murder, and everything becomes permissible. We can perhaps begin to understand why Sade, through the character of Mme Delbène, proclaims that this monstrous chimera of a God which man has established is the sole injustice for which mankind cannot be forgiven, all the more since it has led them to self-renunciation and the surrender of their autonomy.

Sade only draws the ultimate conclusions, as he himself indicates, from the radical philosophies developed earlier in the century.

Assuming the nature of the universe to be what the *philosophes* pronounced it to be, the next step was to uncover and to proclaim

[19] I, 274–275.

[20] II, 137.

[21] I, 231. Sade comments on his own character's words: "*Aimable* La Mettrie, profound Helvétius, wise and learned Montesquieu, why then, so penetrated with this truth, have you only hinted at it in your divine books? O century of ignorance and of tyranny, how you have harmed human knowledge and in what slavery you confined the greatest geniuses of the universe! Let us dare then to speak today, since we can, and since we owe men the truth, let us dare to unveil it completely."

the truth about man's place in it. The direction of thought was to free men from tutelage to God and accountability to him. Only in this way, thought Diderot, d'Holbach and Helvétius, could a truly human ethics be constructed, what d'Holbach called "the morality of nature, founded on the essence of man in society." [22] Many of the deists shared in this desire to release man from the unwanted protection and directives. This phase of the assault on Christianity involved three principal propositions, which were closely intertwined: that man is cosmically unimportant, not a specially privileged creature; that he belongs entirely within the natural order; and that the doctrine of providentialism is absurd. We shall devote the remainder of this chapter to an examination of these issues, reserving special aspects of them for the following two chapters of this section.

Bayle, Pope and a host of writers, early in the century, continued the down-grading of man, which had run throughout the sixteenth and seventeenth centuries, laughing at the pride with which he puffs up his own importance. There was indeed a fundamental inconsistency in the Christian concept of an ordered universe and that of the ever-ready hand of a beneficent God, prompt to interfere with the workings of his own laws, for his specially favored creation, man. Fontenelle pointed out that "all is included in a physical order, in which the actions of men are the same things to God as eclipses, and in which he foresees both according to the same principle." [23]

This issue was brought to a sharp focus in the prolonged discussion over suicide. This act was quickly seen by both sides to be a crucial test of man's freedom or his dependence on a superior force. "Petty and weak creature that he is, he has been able to convince himself," writes Bayle, "that he could not die without disturbing all of nature and without obliging all of Heaven to go to great trouble to illuminate the pomp of his funeral. Stupid and ridiculous vanity! [24]

The problem of suicide was one of those abstract questions,

---

[22] *Op. cit.*, II, 268. The whole ethical sense of Diderot's *Lettre sur les aveugles* is that our moral notions derive from our bodies and not from anything existing outside of us (p. 12–14).

[23] *Traité sur la liberté de M . . .* , in *Nouvelles libertés de penser* (1743), p. 151. The attribution to Fontenelle is not certain.

[24] *Pensées sur la comète, Oeuvres diverses*, III, 55.

beloved of eighteenth century minds, whose history reached back into a long past, and which took on fresh actuality in the new ferment of ideas. Like the others, its ramifications extended deeply into the fields of ethics, politics and metaphysics, and called for a re-examination of certain of their basic assumptions.[25] But its original focal point was the question with which we are dealing, the relationship of man to God. The inherited Christian orthodoxy had transmitted an aversion to self-murder that goes back, in literature, to Plato. Its purport was to deny that we are absolute owners or masters of ourselves. An owner must be superior to what he owns, and only God stands in this relation to us. Nor have we a right to end what we did not begin; or to dispose of what we did not acquire but received only for temporary use. In general, this was the line adhered to by the eighteenth century apologists, including orthodox lay writers such as Formey and Jean Dumas. It received its fullest and most brilliant development in Rousseau's *La Nouvelle Héloïse*.[26]

Some of the humanistic writers contented themselves with tangential refutations of the Christian view. They proposed, for instance, that it is possible to feel certain that God has given us a valid reason to take our quietus. The more radical thinkers denied the entire concept of dependence. Voltaire and Hume, d'Alembert and Maupertuis, harking back to the Renaissance writers and to the ancient Stoics, proclaimed that the dignity of the human condition lay in part in the evaluation we can make of ourselves, and the consequent right to end our lives when we feel there is due cause. To Hume this involved the denial of any significant relation with God. "For my part, I find that I owe my birth to a long chain of causes, of which many depended upon voluntary actions of men." [27] Voltaire argued that man's reason

[25] In our discussion, we shall exclude the psychological and political phases of the prolonged controversy. See L. G. Crocker, "The Discussion of Suicide in the Eighteenth Century," for a more complete analysis and more precise references.

[26] Pt. III, Letters, 21, 22. The first of these letters constitutes the best summary of the humanistic arguments in favor of suicide. The second, containing Rousseau's intended refutation, is far less convincing. Its chief force against the dispassionate logic of the preceding letter is its impassioned eloquence. Rousseau does allow suicide in cases of incurable physical suffering, on the ground that the afflicted person has actually ceased being a man. In his mind, the defense of suicide epitomizes the whole outlook of his enemies, the encyclopedist group, and one feels that they are his real target.

[27] *Essay on Suicide*, published posthumously in 1789.

stands in lieu of God's reason.[28] He frequently has the characters of his plays proclaim their mastery over their own ultimate destiny.

Despite different approaches, the defenders of man's right to self-extinction were united on one basic point: "that life does not intrinsically possess a transcendent, mystic value, before which all purely human motives, no matter how significant, are nullified." [29] On the actual evaluation of justifiable motives, there was considerable variation. But the real issue lay in placing the decision in the realm of individual prerogative, where it could be a pragmatic decision. Among the proponents of this humanistic position, d'Holbach asserted with particular vigor the eudaemonic basis of life, and the resultant right to leave it.[30]

The upholders of Christianity, for their part, did not remain purely on the defensive. Their opponents' criterion of conduct seemed to them to sever ethical judgment from any sure, objective basis. The ultimate logic of the *philosophes*—it was pointed out by Bergier, Delisle de Sales and others—was to condone murder, as well as suicide. The humanists countered that killing is sanctioned in many circumstances of life. But Holland replied that if we follow the views of the *philosophes*, doing away with unhappy people becomes a social duty. Bergier seems almost to open the door to Sade, by arguing that if the hedonic criterion were valid, there is no vicious action it would not sanction.[31]

It was Bayle's position that was destined to triumph, in its widest implications of man's contingency and insignificance. The writers of anonymous manuscripts were not long in taking up his cue. All beings are equal to the Creator, writes the unknown author of the *Traité des trois imposteurs;* man does not cost him

[28] *Oeuvres*, xx, 302.

[29] L. G. Crocker, *loc. cit.*, p. 55.

[30] *Système de la nature*, I, 327–336.

[31] Holland, *Réflexions philosophiques sur le "Système de la nature,"* Pt. I, p. 214. In this regard, see Albert Camus' significant *reprise* of the subject in the Introduction to *L'homme révolté*. He refers to nihilism, according to which life has no particular value, as "that monotonous order, installed by an impoverished logic, in the eyes of which everything becomes of equal value. This logic has pushed the values of suicide to their extreme consequence, legitimized murder." In the logic of the absurd, "murder and suicide are one and the same thing, and must be accepted or rejected together. Thus absolute nihilism, which agrees to legitimize suicide, runs even more easily to logical murder . . . Suicide and murder here are two faces of a single order, that of an unhappy mind which prefers, to the suffering of a finite status, the black exaltation in which earth and heaven are annihilated." (p. 17–18.)

more to produce "than a worm or a flower," nor does he care more about man than about a worm, a lion or a stone.[32] We see here the germ of Sade's statement, that the total destruction of the human race would afflict the universe so little "that it would no more interrupt its course than if the entire species of rabbits or hares were extinguished." [33] La Mettrie gives us the most succinct summary of this dominant trend in eighteenth century thought. "Man is not fashioned out of a more precious clay; Nature has used only one and the same dough, in which she has only varied the leaven." [34]

This declaration of independence, often coupled with the integration of man into an indifferent natural order, runs its course throughout the century, in numerous printed works of both atheists and deists. Even supposing God as universal cause, writes Fréret, that cause "neither loves, nor hates, nor punishes, nor rewards, but always acts in conformity with eternal and invariable laws," while all beings "constantly execute these same laws." [35] Voltaire unleashed the sharpest barbs of his irony, in *Candide* and elsewhere, against the idea that God has arranged things, or rearranges them, for the welfare and benefit of mankind. Nothing seemed to Voltaire more typical of man's absurd pride than prayer, in which he begs an immutable God to reject the wisdom of his unvarying laws in order to make an exception for an insignificant creature.[36] So widespread was the acceptance of this attitude, that even a moderate *philosophe* like the chevalier de Jaucourt joined the chorus.

> As man is led to believe himself the most perfect of all beings, he also believes himself the final cause of all creation. The

[32] Fol. 195–197.

[33] Sade, *op. cit*, I, 93, and note; III, 188.

[34] *L'Homme machine*, p. 99.

[35] *Lettre de Thrasibule à Leucippe, Oeuvres complètes*, III, 133. Fréret goes on to say that there is no need to suppose such a universal cause (p. 141).

[36] *Dictionnaire philosophique*, "Providence." See also Robinet, in C. Rosso, "Il paradosso di Robinet," p. 56. Locke's influence on Voltaire is well known. In his *Essay concerning human understanding*, Locke had written, "He that will consider the infinite power, wisdom and goodness of the Creator of all things will find reason to think it was not all laid out upon so inconsiderable, mean, and impotent a creature as he will find man to be, who in all probability is the lowest of all intellectual beings." (Ch. 3, par. 23.) The idea was common in the seventeenth century, as a corollary of the chain-of-being concept, and is found in Descartes, Spinoza and Leibniz. See A. O. Lovejoy, *The Great Chain of Being*, p. 187–189.

reputedly orthodox philosophers in all centuries have taught
that the world was made for man, the earth for his habitat, and
all luminous bodies to serve as a spectacle to him. Kings do not
do as much, when they imagine themselves to be the final cause
for which all societies have been formed and governments instituted.[37]

When the author of the *Traité des trois imposteurs* asserts that
"to God there is nothing that is beautiful or ugly, good or evil,
perfect or imperfect," his obvious intent is to free men from all
supra-human imperatives. This was, in the mind of many eighteenth century thinkers, a necessary prelude to a humanistic outlook on values and behavior. Morelly, for instance, emphasizes
the complete divorce between human ethical judgments and the
existence of God. "There is in nature neither physical nor moral
evil in relation to the Divinity, that is to say, that there is between him and created beings no relation that can be disagreeable to him." [38]

But most of these would-be humanists did not foresee the Pandora's box they were opening, in freeing men from external,
supernatural directives. How free is man—completely free? La
Mettrie proudly proclaims man's independence, in a passage that is
very close to our first quotation from Sade. "Besides, who knows
whether the reason for man's existence may not be his existence
itself? Perhaps he was casually thrown upon a point of the earth's
surface without our being able to know how or why; but only that
he must live and die, like those mushrooms that come out over-
night, or those flowers that border ditches and cover walls." [39]
Independence is achieved, but only at the cost of meaninglessness
and what the twentieth century was to call "the absurd." Having
our independence, where do we go from there? It was not foreseen
by most that a small group, radical in their logic, would proclaim
a philosophy of moral nihilism, seeing in cosmic meaninglessness
that of all human actions, and consequently, the complete sub-
jectivity of values.

[37] *Encyclopédie*, "Téléologie." Mention should be made of the deistic anarchist,
Dom Deschamps, for whom the sole reality of providence is that of a human
psychological need and a political weapon of exploitation. (*Le vrai système de Dom
Deschamps*, p. 203.)
[38] *Code de la nature* (1755), éd. Chinard, p. 253.
[39] *Op. cit.*, p. 105.

Nihilism is not only of the left. There were a few *fin de siècle* writers at the other extreme, absolutists like Rivarol and Sabatier de Castres—one might call them proto-totalitarians—whose views tally on several significant points with those of the earlier materialists. Thus on the question we are discussing, Sabatier reminds us that the insects that feed on us would have a different opinion as to which animal is the favorite of nature. Then he addresses man. "Weak, vain animal! Learn that Nature is no more concerned with you, than with the mites to whom you serve as lodging and food during your life, and with the worms who devour you after your death. . . . But if there is a species whom she has favored, it is certainly not the human, destructive of almost all others, and the only one that destroys itself."[40] Sabatier and Rivarol, while wishing to safeguard religion in order to repress the people, consider it only as a tool of social discipline, a tyranny necessitated by human nature and justified by the lack of a divine basis for ethics. Without doubt, their thinking, though anti-*philosophe,* was in large part a consequence of the ideas of the *philosophes.*

Most of the *philosophes,* moved by humanistic motives, fought hard to avoid the possibility of nihilistic consequences. Their purpose was only to clear the ground for the erection of a new edifice. Perhaps none expressed it so naïvely as Morelly. "God has permitted that alongside of his immutable laws, human reason, that created deity, should raise its own, and that it should be itself the creator of a moral world whose mechanism would run sufficiently well for the present passing state of humanity. . . ." [41]

It is only too obvious, in these lines, that the idea of providence is slipping in through the back door. Again we are brought back to the same dilemma, which beset the eighteenth century humanist, and in greatest degree, the humanist who felt it necessary, for metaphysical or ethical reasons, to cling to a belief in God. If man is free from cosmic directives, how can we avoid the conclusions of absolute relativism, even of subjectivism and nihilism, with its counterpart of social tyranny? The problem for a large group of writers, probably the most representative of the

[40] *Pensées et observations morales et politiques,* p. 14–15.
[41] *Op. cit.,* p. 261; see also p. 166.

century, was, then, to rid themselves of the Christian complex
of supernatural ideas and valuations, and yet retain a sure, objective basis for ethics. Man, they thought, had to be free to build
a moral statute that would fulfill his natural drives and desires,
including those of his moral nature. Such a statute must also
satisfy his reason, which saw the universe, and man's relation to
other men, in a new empirical and scientific context. But reason
did not always justify man's natural demands; and it also required
that the statute possess the sanction of objective validity.

The less radical *philosophes* endeavored, then, to throw up a
rampart around a middle position. They wished to alter man's
relation to God, in the way we have seen, but desired with equal
urgency to hold to their belief in God and in a universe of physical and moral order expressed in the "Natural Law." Montesquieu
and Voltaire both put justice on the ultimate basis of God's law.
"God," writes the latter, "manifests himself to their [men's] reason: they need justice, they adore in him the origin (*le principe*)
of all justice." [42] The laws, which reason prescribes to us, according to Condillac, "are then the laws which God himself prescribes
to us." [43]

There was another type of cosmic moral order envisaged by
several thinkers, including Leibniz, Malebranche, Formey and
others. It was not merely ordained by God, in his power and
wisdom, but rather inherent in the nature of things. Even God
could not change it, any more than he could change the sum of
the degrees of the angles in a triangle. But the difference between
the two concepts is theological or metaphysical; for ethics, one
will serve as well as the other. In both concepts, all has its place
in a meaningful universe. And in the second case, it was always
assumed that a good and all-wise God stands behind the moral
nature of things, and supports it. God remains the guarantor of
moral value. The clash between these two views, which are ethically one, and the outlook that stemmed from materialism, can
easily be illustrated by a somewhat dramatic example. The deists
will argue that, in the very nature of things, and by the will of
God, it is wrong to torture an innocent child. The marquis de
Sade, however, will urge us to torture innocent children—and

[42] Voltaire, *Questions de Zapata, Oeuvres*, XXVI, 189.
[43] *Traité des animaux*, in *Oeuvres philosophiques*, p. 370.

(in his books) he does. His justification is, precisely, the denial of meaning or value either existing in things, or established by a superior will. There remains only the will—or the whims—of the sentient individual.

The deist who wished to combine the scientific need for inalterable law and the belief in God was obliged, then, to have recourse to the kind of "providence" we have noted in Morelly, one which imprinted the moral nature of God in the totality of his original creation, rather than a capricious *ad hoc* interventionism that supervised the destiny of each human individual. This viewpoint led at once to another Pandora's box, the problem of evil.[44] The order, if not understood, had to be believed in. "Is everything then chance?" asks Erasmus in one of Fontenelle's dialogues. "Yes," replies Charles V, "provided we give that name to an order we do not know." [45] The universe may not be made for man, explains Bayle, but it was made by God for "a far vaster and more sublime end," one in which man has his due and proper place.[46] In other words, there is a general providence, or rational structure in the universe, but we are not its particular or uniquely favored objects. This was the view of Pope, whose *Essay on Man* had a wide influence in France, especially during the first half of the century. Voltaire imitated him in the sixth *Discours sur l'homme:*

> Ouvrages de mes mains, enfants du même père,
> Qui portez, leur dit-il, mon divin caractère,
> Vous êtes nés pour moi, rien ne fut fait pour vous. . . .
> Rien n'est grand ni petit; tout est ce qu'il doit être.

As a Newtonian, Voltaire believed that the universe, from its very creation, was arranged, once and for all, in an orderly way.

Montesquieu opened his great work, *De l'esprit des lois* (1748), by affirming that there is a divine reason, and that laws are "the relationships that obtain between it and the various beings, and the relationships of these various beings among themselves. God has relations with the universe as creator and as conserver. . . ." Man is governed by these laws. As an intelligent being, he also

[44] So that we also may preserve some order and clarity, we shall postpone discussion of this complex question until the second chapter.

[45] *Dialogues des Morts,* "Charles V et Erasme."

[46] *Pensées sur la comète, loc. cit.*

violates them.[47] But human reasoning is "always subordinated to that supreme cause, who does all it wishes, and uses all it wishes," for its own ends.[48] Montesquieu quotes Plato to the effect that an impious man is one who holds that the gods do not concern themselves with the things of this world.[49] This is approximately the position of d'Alembert, who was a follower of Newton and Locke. "We cannot doubt," he asserts, "that all the bodies of which this universe is composed make a unified system, whose parts depend on each other, and which have inter-relations that result from the harmony of the whole." [50]

A very typical member of this moderate group of *philosophes* was Saint-Lambert. His *Commentaire sur le catéchisme universel* is a deistic work, preaching a "softened" Christian virtue without the Christian religion. The world is a moral order; but this does not mean that God supervises all of man's acts, or confines his reason in its freedom of judgment. "If I have properly assigned him his place in the universe, he will not believe himself an important enough being to deserve special attention from the Power which rules the immensity of worlds; he will not waste his time trying by prayers, sacrifices, macerations, to make the Great Being change his eternal laws, to cure him of a tooth-ache, or to correct the bad temper of his wife." [51] Closing the period, Volney summarizes this whole outlook by affirming, on the one hand, the harmony, order and objectivity of relationships—man being no exception—yet discovering, within this impersonal natural law, purpose and final causes.[52]

Somewhat apart from the others, the Physiocrats formed a rather coherent group in the second half of the century. The principal members were Quesnay, Turgot, Le Mercier de la Rivière, Dupont de Nemours, Baudeau and Roubaud. The dis-

[47] Livre I, ch. 1.
[48] Livre XVI, ch. 2.
[49] Livre XXV, ch. 7.
[50] *Encyclopédie,* art. "Cosmiques (qualités)." D'Alembert's idea apparently has some relation to the harmony of Leibniz. But Leibniz's concept of the independence of monads was generally not understood, or at least not accepted, since it seemed contradictory to that of universal harmony. Even Wolff, through whom Leibniz was largely interpreted, had modified his master's concept.
[51] II, 326. See also Marmontel: *Leçons d'un père à ses enfants sur la métaphysique, Oeuvres,* XVII, 103.
[52] *Les Ruines,* in *Oeuvres complètes,* I, ch. V, VI; *La loi naturelle,* I, 251–56.

tinctiveness of their economic theory—as well as its distinction—
was its implantation in a general theory, in a "field theory," as
it were, of metaphysical, political, psychological and moral law.
Economics, in their doctrine, was not separated from the whole
of human and natural realities. Its basis was, precisely, the postulate of a uniform and all-pervasive natural order. "The march of
nature," writes Quesnay, "is uniform, and its laws are general";
and this idea is echoed by all the rest. A further assumption was
made, namely, that this natural order, when followed by men
(who are entirely a part of it and in no way transcendent), works
to their good and to their happiness. It is the best possible order,
declares Quesnay; and Dupont affirms that "good is brought about
by itself." Behind the natural order is God; as Mirabeau puts it,
a "supreme theocracy which institutes the natural order, whose
immutable laws mark out our duties and designate our crimes."
Quesnay also speaks of a "theocracy that has fixed invariably, by
weights and measures, the rights and duties of men united in
society." But although this Divinity is sometimes personalized by
the Physiocrats, more often it appears to be immanent in the
natural order, rather than prior to it or transcending it, and its
legislation is only "the code of nature." Providence, consequently,
also becomes fused with the natural order, and loses its Christian
meaning. It is clear that the Physiocrats had absorbed the new
scientific outlook of their time, and were close to the central body
of deistic thinkers.[53]

It would be deceptive to conclude from such an agreement on
providence and final causes that these deists represented a homo-
geneous viewpoint. The whole matter was far too vague, indefinite
and impenetrable for any deep unity to be possible. Thus Bayle,
Fontenelle, Voltaire and others held that the ultimate moral nature of the universal order does not correspond to the lights of
human reason—with Voltaire making a notable exception for
"Natural Law." Others, like Montesquieu, Marmontel, Volney
and the Physiocrats, while not pretending that man could penetrate God's designs, insisted far more on the all-pervasiveness and

[53] For further details, and references, see G. Weulersse, *Le mouvement physiocratique en France*, II, 111–118. Weulersse refers to such earlier eighteenth century
writers as Boisguillebert, d'Argenson and Herbert as sources for the notion of a
just and good natural order.

obvious rationality of God's moral order, which is in accord with
the human understanding and is readily understood by it. There
is no apparent difference between Montesquieu's position and
that of Thomas Aquinas, who says that "all things partake somewhat of the eternal law, in so far as, namely, from its being imprinted on them, they derive their respective inclinations to their
proper acts and ends." [54] These deists did not emphasize, at least
from the viewpoint of man's relation to God, the discrepancy
between that law and the empirical order of things. But this again
leads us to the problem of evil. There was an important third
group of deists, whom we shall discuss shortly, headed by so great
a figure as Rousseau, a group that was much closer to the Christian view of an immediate, personal providence. These deists, like
those of the first group (headed by Voltaire), were deeply involved in the problem of evil, and determined to justify the ways
of God to man. So intricate and interdependent was the complex
of questions faced by the writers of the Enlightenment, that any
one problem, dominant in the mind of an individual, could bend
all the rest to its focus. The mystical Saint-Martin, for instance,
eager to dissociate God from evil, simply denies that the universe
has any more to do with God than the things we create have to
do with us. The universe bears everywhere the marks of disorder
and deformity. How stupid to assimilate this universe of disorder
and chaos to God! [55]

But Saint-Martin is a character apart. The trend on all sides
was to see an orderly universe. Only "order," as we have already
seen, may involve quite different notions of man's relationship
to the universe in which he dwells. The Christian held to a hi-
erarchically structured moral order imposed by God. The deist
might settle for a vaguer original directive—more or less com-
prehensible to reason, but the certainty of which was obvious in
a Newtonian universe whose design and law revealed the mind
and hand of a divine intelligence. The materialist, on the other
hand, saw a totally different kind of order, one of matter and its
determined interactions, devoid of moral implications. The deist,

[54] Quoted by C. L. Becker, *The Heavenly City of the Eighteenth Century Philosophers*, p. 3.
[55] *Tableau naturel des rapports qui existent entre Dieu, l'homme et l'univers*
(1782).

who could not help being affected by the scientific spirit of his time, tended to absorb this last notion of order. Thus Condorcet (who is also a most typical representative of the moderate "philosophic" group), believes in God, freedom of the will, and God's natural moral law; but as a scientist he maintains a universe of rigid cause and effect. "When one knows the laws, one can predict the phenomena. . . . The only foundation for belief in the natural sciences is this idea, that the general laws, known or unknown, that govern the phenomena of the universe, are necessary and constant."

Unfortunately, it is not so easy to fuse the notion of an impersonal material order with that of a divine or simply a moral order. What should a Voltaire, deist and would-be humanist, do, when his reason told him that God was the only guarantor of moral law and value, but told him also that there was no immortal soul and no free will in a necessary and material world? Such an order took no cognizance of man's moral needs and did not allow him the freedom necessary for moral responsibility. How could this order have given us natural desires, whose satisfaction (contrary to the Christian ethics) was inherently right, and at the same time, a moral reason that frequently contravened these legitimate strivings? Here was a contradiction which mystics or ascetics could try to resolve in favor of the second, and certain materialists, by eliminating the second in favor of the first. The eighteenth century deist, believing both nature and reason to be God-given and normative, endeavored above all to unite them, or to find at least a *modus vivendi*. But the problem will turn out to be well-nigh insoluble.

The perplexities of the eighteenth century deist are seen in clearest focus in Voltaire. As we follow his thought over most of the century's course, we are struck by his uncertainty about man's relation to God. There is no immortal soul and no eternal reward or punishment—of this he grows more and more certain. But we are punished, none the less, by conscience, nature or society, and these sanctions may be the result of God's planning.[56] He reaches the unexpected conclusion that not having a soul, we are even more dependent on God than if we had one, as a mechanism de-

[56] Art. "Théiste."

pends on its maker.[57] We can "mériter ou démériter" in God's eyes, "be punished or rewarded." [58] Voltaire wavers, but feels that man is not entirely free from the eye of God.

So much for punishment. Does God protect us? Not by providential interventions, according to Voltaire's most frequent decision. But God's hand is everywhere visible in the fabric of the universe, down to the last detail. "Everything in my body is means and end." [59] All things are God's blind instruments; our ideas and our instincts come from his plan. Thus if we have a "social instinct" of compassion (*bienveillance*), God has put it into us as he has given every animal its particular instinct.[60] Voltaire's wonder grows with the years, and he persistently refuses to abandon final causes.[61] This "general providence," however, was to become more remote and vague, in Voltaire's evolving outlook, as the incubus of the problem of evil placed the finger of blame on God, or disculpated him only at the price of a terrible renunciation: our mind must give up trying to penetrate the meaning of the universe, trying to discover consonance and relationship between *it* and *us*. And then where is the metaphysical basis of ethics? [62]

Voltaire was perfectly aware of the danger. This is dramatically revealed as early as his *Traité de métaphysique* (1734). First, after separating man from dependence on God's protection, he is led,

---

[57] *Oeuvres* (XXVIII: 458, 1771). (Page references to Voltaire's works will be to the Moland edition, unless otherwise noted.) The logic is doubtful, since the mechanism, once made, is no longer dependent on the maker for its process.

[58] XXII: 77, 1766.

[59] XXVI, 61–63. See "Providence" (1771): "I believe in general providence . . . but I do not believe that a particular providence changes the economy of the world for your sparrow or for your cat." In *Candide* the dervish tells Pangloss that God doesn't care whether there is good or evil on earth. "When His Highness sends a vessel to Egypt, does he worry whether the mice in the ship are comfortable or not?" The Ingénu tells us that we are completely under God's power, like the stars and the elements; "that we are little wheels of the immense machine of which he is the soul; that he acts by general laws, and not by particular views."

[60] *Traité de métaphysique* (1734), éd. H. T. Patterson, p. 55–58.

[61] In a letter to Helvétius, for instance, he admits that matter has necessary and "blind" relations, such as distance and shape; but, "as for relations of design, I am sorry: it seems to me that a male or a female, a blade of grass and its seed, are demonstrations of an intelligent being which was prior to the work."

[62] Voltaire was more and more affected by the materialism of his time. "Destiny," he wrote in 1755, "plays with men who are only atoms in motion, submitted to the general law which scatters them in the great clash of the events of the world, which they can neither foresee, nor forestall nor understand." (XXXVIII: 494.) When Voltaire is at this pole of his thought, man seems to be adrift, but not free.

by the force of logic, to a picture of the world which is precisely
that of the materialistic extremists:

> God has put men and animals on earth, it is up to them to get
> along the best they can. Too bad for the flies that fall into the
> spider's web; too bad for the bull attacked by a lion, and for
> the lambs met by wolves! But if a lamb were to say to a wolf:
> 'You are violating the moral good, and God will punish you';
> the wolf would answer, 'I am accomplishing my physical good,
> and it doesn't seem that God cares whether I eat you or not.'
> What the lamb should have done was not to stray from the
> shepherd and the dog who could have defended him.[63]

But then Voltaire proceeds at once to shore up the dikes, before morality is swamped by the wave of nihilism.

> If some one infers from all this that he has only to abandon
> himself headlong to all the furies of his unchained desires, and
> that, there being no absolute virtue or vice, he can do anything
> with impunity, that man had better see first whether he has
> an army of a hundred thousand soldiers devoted to his service;
> and even then, he will take a great risk by declaring himself
> an enemy of the human race. But if this man is only a private
> citizen, if he is at all reasonable, he will see that he has made
> a bad decision, and that he will be infallibly chastised, either
> by the punishments so wisely invented by men against the
> enemies of society, or by the very fear of punishment, which
> is a rather cruel torture in itself.

How well has Voltaire shored up the dikes? He has no other
defence than that of *prudence,* and none against the man who *can*
"get away with it." [64]

But the coin had another face. If man is not the object of God's
extraordinary solicitude, he has no special debt, and no special
dependence. The earth is not particularly favorable to life, or to
man. The God who made this world is removed from human
value judgments of good and evil, and man cannot offend him—
"it is only towards man that man can be guilty." [65] From this
viewpoint, then, we are free to create ethical standards that are
pragmatically valid and responsive to our human needs and reali-

---

[63] For Hume's brilliant exposition of this problem, see his *Enquiry concerning
human understanding,* Sect. xi; in E. A. Burtt, *The English Philosophers from
Bacon to Mill,* p. 672–677.
[64] P. 62.
[65] XVII: 576–581.

ties—and this was an important part of what Voltaire desired. Yet—and this is a belief in which he never wavers—the basis of all moral judgment is an aprioristic "Natural Law," a moral "instinct" or responsiveness built into us by God—who thereby becomes the origin and guarantor of value. God has given us a certain kind of reason, which *naturally* generates certain universal ideas, even as the body has a certain development. Both unfold along fixed modes of behavior.[66] In this situation, value judgments are not ours to create. Consequently, Voltaire attacks Pufendorf's theory of moral entities—modes we attach to objects and acts to secure order, propriety or social control.[67] This is because our essential value judgments are created by God and put into us for all time by him.[68]

Voltaire's task, and his problem, will be to reconcile these conflicting perspectives on man in the universe, with their consequences for value-creation, and for placing the locus of ethical judgment in experiential and pragmatic or in aprioristic (or "instinctual") standards. Reason and nature must be fused to one purpose, and we shall later follow him in this pursuit.

Voltaire's intellectual perplexities were shared by many another, but in no other writer do we get so clear a picture of the torment and the swaying. Montesquieu, who belonged to the same generation, was more reticent, and more interested in political philosophy. In his *Pensées* we see him clinging to providentialism. "This providence that watches over us is extremely powerful." God would be imperfect if he had created us and then withdrawn; he can make us happy, and he must will it—or be more imperfect than men.[69] But in another *Pensée*, he refers with apparent approval to the idea that "God is attached only to the conservation of species and not at all to that of individuals." [70] And in another unpublished piece, (perhaps his first), he seems to adopt a somewhat intermediary course, affirming that God has provided men with all they need, and approving finalism as demonstrated by the organs of the body.[71] Montesquieu's great constructive work

[66] XXVI: 78.

[67] XVIII: 426.

[68] This part of the discussion is based on my article, "Voltaire's struggle for humanism."

[69] *Oeuvres*, éd. Masson, II, 342.

[70] P. 274.

[71] *Essai touchant les lois naturelles, Oeuvres*, III, 192–3 *et passim*.

excludes providentialism from its own fabric. In all these statements, however, he is clearly safeguarding moral law by preserving man's dependence on God's wishes and intentions.

Buffon, along with other emancipated scientific thinkers, rejects final causes as notions that are sterile of any scientific use or validity. "Is it not obvious that these final causes are only arbitrary relationships and moral abstractions, which deserve less weight even than metaphysical abstractions?" [72] However Buffon also considers man an exception in nature, and God's chosen creature.[73] And he concludes his "Première Vue" with an exordium to God, who maintains the harmony of the universe, "God of kindness . . . God our benefactor," who rules the world in all its movements with his "paternal oversight." [74]

If the deist was beset with dilemmas, the atheist was not free of them either, in his picture of man's relation to the universe. All species of providentialism and final causes are, as we have seen, abruptly dismissed, usually with heavy ridicule.[75] Man finds himself cut loose from cosmic strings, left face to face with himself, with his own nature. Again we ask, how free *is* man? From the viewpoint of determinism, not free at all. Was he then submitted to nature, or could he in some way rise above it? If the first alternative was embraced, then was the "nature" to which he was yoked the "nature" of all beings, or a particular "nature" of his own? Nor were these the only decisions to be made. Lacking an external standard, was the "nature" of each individual the ultimate moral criterion, or could the free creativity of our moral reason surpass this *nature* and operate as a social collectivity? This would be to substitute a new external standard by which to measure individual actions, and give morality a firm new ground. But what could assure its validity and authority? Obviously, the questions we have raised evoked a variety of attempted solutions, and these form a large part of the body of eighteenth century ethical speculation. That the enigma was not untied is evidenced by the prolongation of the same perplexities into the cultural crisis of

[72] *Histoire naturelle* (1749), in Buffon, éd. Corpus général des philosophes français, p. 258.
[73] *Ibid.*, p. 33, etc.
[74] *Ibid.*, p. 35.
[75] Diderot's Jacques quips, "One never knows what heaven wants or does not want, and it probably knows nothing about it itself." (*Oeuvres*, VI, 100.)

the twentieth century. It seemed that the materialists, and many deists, freed man from God only to plunge him into another kind of servitude, or into anarchy. The result was a desperate struggle for those (and they were the larger number) who desired to be humanists, and to make man a moral being, the master of his destiny.

Let us turn now to the orthodox Christians, to whom the weakness of this position was transparently clear. Moral values, they were convinced, could not be justified except by man's submission to an external or higher authority, and none could be set up except a personal, provident God. Let us look at a development in Le-Franc de Pompignan, even though it carry us somewhat beyond this chapter of our investigation. It is typical of what we find in Bergier, Gauchat and the host of Christian polemicists. Attacking La Mettrie, Le Franc quotes his assertion that truth and virtue "are entities that are valid only insofar as they are useful to him who has them; there is no intrinsic virtue or vice, no moral good or evil, no just or unjust." Le Franc first points out that even d'Holbach had rejected La Mettrie. But d'Holbach, he continues with complete accuracy, had not realized that his own ethics was—when reduced to its fundamental basis—the same. (Le Franc's criticism could be applied with equal justice to Diderot, who, however, unlike d'Holbach, was aware of the impasse.) For La Mettrie to be wrong, continues Le Franc, for there to be a real distinction between virtue and vice, between just and unjust, three conditions are necessary. The second of Le Franc's conditions, freedom of choice, does not concern us at this point. The first condition is the existence of a supreme, universal law, without which values can only be either arbitrary conventions or something which "each person would be justified to judge by their unique relation to himself." In the latter case, moral values would constantly change with interests; in the former, they would have an even more arbitrary and evanescent foundation. The third condition is that of "an infallible reward for virtue and an inevitable punishment for vice." Without this consequence, the distinction between vice and virtue becomes meaningless.[76]

For similar reasons, the Christian could not accept the too

---

[76] *La religion vengée*, 1772, p. 201–207. The formulation seems to come from Leibniz, "On the Notions of Right and Justice," *Monadology*, p. 292–4, 269–70.

remote providence of a Voltaire. Pope had earlier expressed, in the *Essay on Man,* a like view. God sees hero and sparrow fall with equal indifference, a bubble burst or a world. Crousaz, in his commentary on Pope, assailed this outlook. If everything is indifferent in relation to God, he retorted, and all beings have the same value, then everything should be indifferent to man likewise. If I can kill a sparrow, because it is to my interest, I can kill a man. Crousaz's criticism is significant. In it we can see a phenomenon we shall observe several times in the course of this inquiry. The Christian apologist lays open weaknesses and possible implications in the metaphysics or ethics of the would-be humanists, deist or atheist; while other atheists will actually carry out the apologist's prediction by reaching a philosophy of moral nihilism.[77]

According to an outstanding twentieth century Protestant theologian, Reinhold Niebuhr, the Christian view of man is distinguished by three ideas: man's spiritual self-transcendence in the doctrine of "the image of God"; man's weakness, dependence and finiteness (a unity, then, of God-likeness and creatureliness); the evil in man stemming from his unwillingness to acknowledge his dependence and accept his finiteness.[78] Although these ideas receive no such convenient a formulation in the eighteenth century, they permeate the apologetic writings, and we shall encounter them in their proper place. In connection with our present complex of problems, the dependence of man on God was, for the devout Christian, part of his concept of a universe suffused with God's providence. It was, of course, the theme of Sunday sermons and pious homilies (including former *philosophe* Marmontel's *Leçons d'un père à ses enfants*); but, excluding these, we find it also to be the active defense of the polemicists. What would man gain, cries the abbé Boudier de Villemaire, if he were not submitted to the government of God? "Thrown then into a corner of the universe, *pêle-mêle* with the beasts, having the same end as they, his intelligence would distinguish him from the vilest of them only by his awareness of his ills." Under God's management, however, we are illumined by a beautifully planned universe. Nor

[77] *Examen de l'Essai de M. Pope* (1737), p. 61 ff. Later, Bergier attacks d'Holbach, and Delisle de Sales fumes against Morelly on the same grounds.
[78] *The Nature and Destiny of Man,* I, 150.

is it pride, as the unbelievers assert, that leads us to think God has arranged things for us, but God's own attributes.[79] Vauvenargues (who was not a Christian polemicist) had earlier included a discourse, in his *Traité sur le libre arbitre,* designed precisely to confirm our dependence on God. "Will man's indocile pride dare to murmur against his subordination?" We should rather be proud to be part of an orderly structure, in which everything works according to law. It is true that Vauvenargues' ensuing argument is not quite orthodox, for it excludes providential intervention and seems close to mechanism.[80] We shall witness other instances of Christians becoming "infected" with the new philosophy. But he then returns to his theme. "Man's excellence is in his dependence," he assures us once again; for through it we participate in the infinity of God's being "by so beautiful a union." Man, independent, without God, has weakness and wretchedness as his only lot. "The feeling of his imperfection," concludes Vauvenargues in a phrase that calls to mind both Pascal and Niebuhr, "makes his eternal torture." [81]

In reply to the arguments of the sceptics, the apologists found it convenient to admit the impenetrability of God's order. The quaint abbé Pluche, who constantly saw God's ever-protecting hand, urges us not to try to enter his sphere and explain his work, but to attend to ours. And ours is not to investigate those operations which God has reserved to his own knowledge, but to rule our conduct "by the warnings of experience and the external testimony" which instruct us sufficiently of the natural order and of revelation.[82] Of course we cannot understand God, Mably assures us—and consequently must not judge him; but we must none the less rely on him, since he gives us his blessings. The most obvious sign of this is his uniting all men "through the link of morality and virtues, on which the happiness of each citizen and of society is founded.[83] Rouillé d'Orfeuil also assures us we need

---

[79] *L'irréligion dévoilée* (1774), p. 46–54.

[80] "Thus outside objects form ideas in the mind, these ideas feeling, these feelings volitions, this volition [forms] actions in us and outside of us."

[81] *Oeuvres,* I, 347–349.

[82] *Le spectacle de la nature* (1746), v, 124–134. Compare the opinion of *philosophe* and deist Dupont de Nemours, about the unity and intelligibility of God's natural order. "It must not be, in the parts we cannot see, submitted to other laws than those which are manifest to us in the parts perceptible to our senses." (*Philosophie de l'univers* (1792), p. 13–14).

[83] *Oeuvres,* VIII, 352.

entertain no doubt that God governs all and keeps order. "Concentrated in the imperceptible point that he occupies, man cannot penetrate his immutable decrees . . . the order of events is directed by providence. . . . Let us admire in silence the wisdom of this order . . . and await with confidence what providence destines for us." [84]

It does not fall within our province to analyze in detail the eighteenth century Christian portrayal of divine providence. Its naïve extremes have often been ridiculed. As Bernardin de Saint-Pierre explains with some ecstasy, the harmony of animals, plants and man is all designed for man's convenience. "It is not due to chance." The last comment—and perhaps also the idea of harmony—would have found approval among the scientific materialists; but they would have sneered at Bernardin's complete anthropomorphizing of nature. Here is a complete inversion, they would have exclaimed; the harmony derives from *man's* adaptation to environment, from his learning to utilize what he has found. For Bernardin all is placed here by God, perfectly adapted to man's needs, including those of thirst, hunger, transportation, shelter and a variety of pleasures, such as perfume for his sense of smell. The first volume of the *Etudes* is a long exposition and defense of providentialism. Moths, for instance, are designed to prevent "monopoleurs" from hoarding the cloth needed by the poor. Nowhere in the eighteenth century does man seem closer to God or less able to escape his decrees. God, "who had abandoned him to his own lights, still watched over his destiny." [85]

As I have already suggested, a number of deists hewed close to the Christian line—far closer than Voltaire—in their acceptance of an active providence. Thus Dupont de Nemours, while admitting that God has given men resources for happiness, asserts that this is all we can say with positive knowledge. Yet he refers to such phenomena as miraculous escapes from danger which cannot be due to chance—(the science he accepts admits no chance, all results from physical laws or "the active power with which intelligent beings apply these laws to their acts")—and

---

[84] *L'Alambic moral . . .* (1773), p. 470.

[85] *Oeuvres*, v, 358. Cf. a similar statement in Barbeu du Bourg, *Petit code . . .*, p. 234. For other typical expressions of naive providentialism, see Christian Wolff, in Leibniz, *Monadology*, p. 167–8; Pluche, III, 3–4; Bernardin de Saint-Pierre, *Etudes de la nature*, I, 343 ff., II, 425–428, *Harmonies de la nature, Oeuvres*, IX, 80 ff., 200 ff. Formey, *L'Anti-Sans-Souci* (1761), I, 46–54; *Le philosophe chrétien* (1752), III, 449–462.

concludes that "it is by no means impossible, it is not even unlikely, that [God] has assured them [even] greater succor; we are
surrounded by facts that can be explained only by this supposition." After all, there is nothing to prevent the Supreme Intelligence from doing what he has given intelligent beings the power
to do—to apply the laws of nature in certain ways. Even more:
as we favor good animals, so does an Intelligence superior to ours
favor good men.[86]

In this development, Dupont may well be under the influence
of Rousseau. Both his unshakable religious emotions and his increasing opposition to the entire direction of the philosophy of
the encyclopedists led Rousseau to a firm belief in God's direct,
continuing providence. In his readings at Les Charmettes, he
had early absorbed the lessons of Nieuwentyt's *L'existence de Dieu
démontrée par les merveilles de la nature* (1727) and Pluche's
Spectacle de la nature (1732)—lessons he was never to forget.
In the *Lettre à d'Alembert* (1758), he implicitly embraced finalism. Personifying nature, he attributes modesty, blushing and
similar phenomena to "the voice of nature," directing the sexes
to their proper actions and ends.[87] Two years earlier, in a famous
letter to Voltaire ("Lettre sur la Providence," 18 août 1756),
written in reply to the latter's *Poème sur le désastre de Lisbonne,*
Rousseau had first expressed himself on the question of providence. The whole matter of providence and evil, he asserts, has
been the subject of confused thinking on the part of both priests
and philosophers. The error of the former is to read God's intervention into purely natural events, attributing to providence what
would have occurred without it. The error of the philosophers
is to blame God for whatever happens or fails to happen. "Thus
whatever nature has decided, providence is always right with the
dévots, always wrong with the *philosophes.*" Actually, in all these
cases, only law is involved. "It is probable that particular events
are nothing in the eyes of the master of the universe; that his
providence is only universal; that he limits himself to preserving
genuses and species, and presiding over the whole, without worrying about the manner in which each individual spends this brief
life." In this fashion (which was in no way original), Rousseau

---

[86] *Op. cit.,* p. 120–121; 138–139.
[87] Ed. M. Fuchs, p. 113–115.

believes he can free God from the onus of evil and yet preserve a moral universe. But he none the less concludes, "All the subtleties of metaphysics will not make me doubt for a moment the immortality of the soul and a beneficent providence." [88]

In *La Nouvelle Héloïse*,[89] Rousseau is no longer concerned with justifying God or conciliating Voltaire. Julie d'Etanges thanks God for directing all of her steps in moments of darkness. "Eternal Providence, who make the insect crawl and the heavens roll, you watch over the least of your works!" [90] Julie wishes to be virtuous, in order to be in harmony with the order of nature established by God and the rules of reason he has given her. Now Rousseau has his heroine forewarn Saint-Preux against the illusion of "general laws"; he need not worry that God will get tired from watching over each individual.[91] She contrasts her attitude with her husband's, during their walks: "the one admiring in the rich and brilliant adornment which the earth displays the work and the gifts of the Author of the universe; the other seeing in all these manifestations only a fortuitous combination where nothing is linked except by blind force." Near the close of her life, Julie passionately proclaims her confidence in her God, "God of peace, God of goodness," benevolent father.[92]

These ideas all receive more objective development in *Emile*. "Of all the attributes of an all-powerful Divinity," writes Rousseau, "goodness is the one without which he can least be conceived." [93] The Author of things not only provides for the needs he has given us, "but even for those we give to ourselves," [94] by modifying our tastes accordingly. "I do not know," says the Vicaire, "what is the purpose of the whole; but I see that each piece is made for the others; I admire the worker in the detail of his work, and I am sure that all these gears function thus in harmony only for a common end which I cannot perceive." [95] And he, too, expresses a deep gratitude for God's protection.

[88] *Correspondance générale*, II, 324.
[89] Published in 1761, written and revised over a period of the four or five preceding years.
[90] *La Nouvelle Héloïse*, éd. D. Mornet, III, 65–66.
[91] *Ibid.*, IV, 229. Rousseau's distrust of "general laws" is developed in the *Profession de foi*. Cf. *Emile*, éd. Richard, p. 332.
[92] *La Nouvelle Héloïse*, IV, 268.
[93] *Emile*, p. 48; also *Profession de foi, ibid.*, p. 347.
[94] P. 165.
[95] P. 332–333.

Rousseau's determination to cling to providentialism, I have suggested, was due partly to his emotional needs, partly to his desire to contravene the tendencies of the materialists. Better than most materialists, he realized the possible ultimate implications of some of their own ideas. He was certain there can be no metaphysical foundation for ethics, other than God. Getting to the heart of the question, he attacks the definition of virtue as "love of order," as insufficient in itself. Which order is to be loved? If there is no God, one order has the same value as another; there is no hierarchy of value. Some order there always is. We can make an order in relation to the whole, into which the ego is integrated; or we can order the whole in relation to the ego. Without God, there is no reason to override the self. "If the Divinity does not exist, only the evil man reasons, the good man is insane." [96] Here we see another of the many instances of anti-*philosophes* who open the back door to the most extreme doctrines they are opposing. For some were bound to say, the Divinity does *not* exist! And the rest of the ship goes down with the pilot.

For Rousseau, then, as for the other deists—whatever their shade of opinion in regard to providence—the establishment of God's interest in man is especially important in setting unshakeable bases of ethics. This is accomplished directly by divine rewards and punishments—although Voltaire and some other deists rejected those that come after death; and indirectly, by "Natural Law" and conscience. Thus Rousseau, justifying his *Emile* in the famous *Lettre à M. de Beaumont,* asserts the incomprehensibility of the idea of Creation, but declares that this matter of pure speculation does not affect his duties: "for after all, what matters to explain the origin of beings, as long as I know how they subsist, what place I should fill among them, and in virtue of what this obligation is imposed on me?" The obligation is imposed, and by higher authority. Doubt, scepticism and relativism are thereby excluded. The world is an order, a moral order, a beneficent order. It contains a hierarchy of values, laid out by God's wisdom. All is set and given. Right and wrong are clearly made known, now and for all time.

Like all other periods, the eighteenth century was dynamic and cannot be regarded as a static unit. However (as has been noted

[96] P. 356.

in the Introduction), the sweep of the years brought comparatively little change in the consistency of the arguments on this issue. What time did bring was rather a change in the popularity or diffusion of the various attitudes. As the century advances, personal providence tends to become a general or original providence, and simultaneously, the radical materialistic conclusions achieve more widespread acceptance. Then, as a reaction, and partly due to the growing influence of Rousseau, providentialism is proclaimed anew, in its most extreme form, and unashamedly. To a certain extent, this evolution was a phase of the question of evil, to which we now turn.

Two

THE PROBLEM OF EVIL

OF THE MANY abstract questions that exercised the curiosity of eighteenth century thinkers—happiness, luxury, progress, man and beast, truth and falsehood, and so on—none evoked more universal and heated debate than the problem of evil, with the possible exception of freedom of the will. As Diderot wrote in his article "Manichéisme," "It must be admitted, of all the questions that occur to the mind, it is the most difficult and thorny." Voltaire, anguished by it, cried, "Here is the most difficult and important of questions. All of human life is involved." [1] What was really involved was a direct attack on the existence of God, to begin with, and an assessment of his nature. Beyond these primary issues, the relation between man and God, the doctrines of providence and moral freedom, and ultimately, the Divine sanction for ethical values were inseparable parts of the debate. [2]

The dilemma of God's goodness and omnipotence, set off against a world of ills, evils and injustice, was not new to the Age of Enlightenment. As far back as men have reflected on themselves

---

[1] *Oeuvres*, XVII, 576–581.

[2] The discussion has been analyzed with great acumen—but not completely, nor adequately from the viewpoint of this study, by Paul Hazard: "Le Problème du mal," and by André Morize, in his critical edition of *Candide*.

and the world they live in, they have speculated about their relation to the superior powers they conceived to have created the universe and to direct it. When they reached a point of rational maturity at which they could objectify both themselves and their world in somewhat abstract terms, they began to be tormented by the problem of evil. In two ancient cultures it found lofty expression—with a diversity of answers—in the Book of Job and the Greek tragedies. Christianity had tried to resolve the problem, at least in part, by the doctrine of the Fall, which made evil an obstacle, incurred freely by man, that he had to overcome.[3]

The eighteenth century, precisely because it was an age of enlightenment, had to re-examine and thrash out anew the age-old problem. In a period of independent and rebellious rationalism, no authoritarian answers could be accepted without questioning. As mastery over the physical world seemed more and more a certainty, many no longer felt the need to fall back on faith to explain their misery. In the new scientific and secular outlook, the Fall became a myth, unrelated to known phenomena. The obsession with happiness that characterized the eighteenth century, and the change in the social and moral climate after the death of Louis XIV also helped turn people away from the traditional Christian patience with suffering on this earth. Besides, as we have seen in the first chapter, many important questions could not be solved without taking the problem of evil into account. The eighteenth century, as Pope clearly acknowledged, felt obliged "to vindicate the ways of God to man." [4]

---

[3] See Basil Willey, *The Eighteenth Century Background,* p. 46–47.

[4] Note also, Chubb, *A Vindication of God's Character* (1726). These pressures affected the pious, those who believed in a personal God, as well as deists.

Pascal, according to Cassirer (*op. cit.,* p. 137 ff.), was a constant challenge to the *philosophes* (just as Bayle was to the apologists). Pascal had tried to show that the duality and paradox of man cannot be explained within nature or by reason, but only by the incomprehensible mystery of the Fall, that is, by a transcendental reference. This much, of course, is true. What Cassirer fails to see (and what Bayle did see), is that there is no justification of God in this, only an evasion that critical reason cannot tolerate. Nor does Cassirer seem to grasp the principal cause of Pascal's having been a torment to the *philosophes.* The real effect of Pascal's "apology" was to change the whole direction and to open a new chapter: the analysis and explanation of *man* (to which subject we shall devote the third section of this volume). It was on this ground that Pascal was an endless challenge to the *philosophes,* to explain man in natural terms and to "defend" him. As a result, Cassirer is led to include in his discussion such matters as Maupertuis' hedonistic calculus of pleasure, which is unrelated to the problem of theodicy. He does not recognize the independence of the analysis of human nature made from the view-

The discussion was, then, an inevitable one. Two men may be said to have started the debate on its new course by their clear statement of the opposing views, Bayle by his challenge, Leibniz by his defense. The heart of Bayle's argument is the contention, taken from Vanini and ultimately from Epicurus, that God either lacks the power to eliminate evil (and so is not God) or does not will to do so (and so is evil). Bayle's thunderous broadside was in part triggered by William King's *De origine mali* (1702). One of King's main arguments was the time-honored Christian defense that to have made man good, God would have had to deprive him of the inestimable gift of freedom. Bayle seeks to demolish this bastion. All God had to do, he counters, was to make souls predisposed to good; it would have been enough to give his grace to all, instead of to a few. To nullify King's assertion that men could not be happy without freedom, Bayle refers to the happiness of the angels and saints in Paradise. In fact, men could get along well without freedom, for "It is an imperfection to be able to make a bad choice." Freedom is only a source of unhappiness, especially since God has not made us so that we make good use of it. From the question of moral evil, Bayle passes to that of physical ills. The human reason cannot understand why such ills are absolutely necessary. Matter is said to be imperfect, but the compound of matter and pain seems to have been decided by an arbitrary will, not by a cause supposedly omnipotent and good.[5]

points of economics, politics and morals, but attempts to see these analyses as forms of a theodicy problem. But it is difficult to believe, for instance, that Rousseau's principal aspiration is not to free man from hopeless evil and despair, rather than to exonerate God. On the other hand, the question of evil, in its metaphysical aspects, was developed by the *philosophes*, as we are about to see, in directions quite unrelated to Pascal's argumentation. Cassirer's failure to mention Bayle is significant; for his discussion makes no real effort to explore the characteristic and original developments in France, but is slanted *backwards*, so to speak, from the viewpoint of late eighteenth century developments in Germany.

[5] *Réponse aux questions d'un provincial* (1704–1707), *Oeuvres diverses*, III, 664–675. Bayle also puts forth a logical argument not taken up by later writers. Moral evil is not necessary, since it results from the *free* choice of the human will. Adam did not *have to* make the wrong choice. Evil is therefore contingent, foreseen by God but not caused by him. Bayle then demolishes his own argument. If everything that was possible had to be (cf. Spinoza), then moral evil is not contingent but necessary, and it is therefore false that men are free! It is necessary that they make a bad choice, so that, once again, God is the author of evil and sin, as the creator of souls condemned to sin.

Bayle also refutes King's arguments, that evil is merely absence of good, inevitable in created beings, and that an imperfect creation is better than none. Cf. Paul Hazard, *loc. cit.*, p. 148–149.

Time and again Bayle develops his theses, sharpening his knives, but adding only a few important associated ideas. He points out that his own paradoxes could well lead to the "Spinozist" concept of God as "a nature that exists and acts necessarily, without knowing what it does," a God who is intelligent only inasmuch as "the thought of creatures are his modifications." Reason, he concludes tantalizingly, is unable to cut this Gordian knot, and the question of evil remains unsolvable.[6]

Bayle's paradoxes are of supreme importance in the reassessment of the metaphysical foundations of values and morals. The most obvious doubt he raises is whether God and the universe are good (moral), or evil, or simply indifferent. If there is no consonance between human ethical notions and universal being, then the former have no non-psychological, or ontological ground. Bayle himself spells out some of the ethical consequences. Since God connives in evil, "you will conclude that common notions had miserably deluded you in signifying to you as a perfection or imperfection, absolutely speaking, what is not so at all in regard to God." They are only *our* ideas of just, perfect, etc. Since our moral judgment tells us it is a wrong to allow those whom you can make happy and virtuous to fall into the opposite states, there is no doubt that God has acted against the common notions of right and goodness; so that "what is bad for man, may be good for God." [7] Bayle also implicitly eliminates any absolute order (thereby opposing Malebranche and Leibniz), and rests all on God's will. Still another corollary is that happiness is the highest value. Bayle constantly insists on this theme in his studies of evil: God's goodness must equal man's happiness. It is a rather curious distinction that is implied: the highest value, for man, is taken to be happiness; but for God, it is goodness.

Bayle's contentions were echoed time and again by later writers, by atheists and deists who wished to establish a purely human, non-authoritarian ethics, one based on universal, "common-sense reason" (what was later termed "une morale laïque").[8] We shall

[6] *Dictionnaire*, "Pauliciens," IV, 528–540; see also "Manichéens," IV, 92–94, "Marcionites," IV, iii; *Réponse . . . , Oeuvres diverses*, III, 796–802.

[7] "Entretien de Maxime et de Thémiste," *Oeuvres diverses*, IV, 19–24.

[8] In particular, the dilemma of God's power and goodness is repeated by practically every anti-Christian writer. One has only to think of its recurrence in Voltaire's writings. Diderot, although concerned less than the deists, uses it in a letter to Damilaville (Oct. 1760): "My friend, the devil doesn't want the good to prosper;

avoid these repetitions and only mention briefly some of the developments of ethical significance.

A number of writers expand on Bayle's echoing of Job's complaint, that in this world the wicked prosper and the righteous are punished. We find it in Meslier's diffuse disquisition,[9] and later in Diderot's *Neveu de Rameau*. Further along in the century, it is developed, at about the same time, by two strangely differing writers, Sade and Delisle de Sales. Delisle relates the melodramatic history of Jenny, who sacrifices her virtue to the wicked Colonel Kirke in order to save her husband, only to learn the perfidious colonel has hanged him anyhow. The wicked triumph. And Delisle comments, "Is it believable that it is in England that the system of optimism was born?" Even if there were only one person like Jenny, "the induction against the Divinity is as terrible . . . the world is the work of an evil principle, providence is a chimera and God is the most horrible of tyrants." Delisle, however, is not ready to embrace such a despairing conclusion. There is one way out: immortality. Without this ultimate reparation, this is only a blind universe; with it, what matters the here and now? "God remains, and the problem is explained."[10]

The deist busied himself hunting for a way out of his dilemmas. To the atheist, however, nothing remained but the resignation to a universe that is at best empty of moral value, at worst, positively evil. In either case, the moralist faced a choice among several alternatives: he might proclaim a radically different base for ethical values; he might admit their arbitrariness and support them as a necessary tyranny; or he might proclaim our freedom from all moral bonds, by the utter denial of value. We shall see all three positions expounded.

Moral nihilism, already implicit in the second alternative, becomes overt in the third. Consequently, we are not surprised to find it adopted by the marquis de Sade, who at the other end of

God does—according to what they say; Martin [possibly a reference to *Candide*] could say, all that is true, but the devil is the stronger. When I think about it, I find Milord Brioché, the great puppeteer, the fellow who pulls the strings attached to our heads, caught between impotence and bad will as in a mouse-trap." (*Correspondance*, éd. G. Roth, III, 183).

[9] *Le Testament de Jean Meslier*, éd. Charles, III, 43–46.

[10] *Philosophie de la nature*, II, 317–373. For a similar story in Sade, but much more gruesome, see *Histoire de Juliette*, VI, 199 ff. We shall later note this idea in Duclos' novel, *Mme de Luz*. For Raynal's comments on the lack of relation between honesty and success, see H. Wolpe, *Raynal et sa machine de guerre*, p. 61.

the eighteenth century from Bayle, developed the nihilistic implications that had always been latent in its materialism, but which
most of the radical *philosophes,* in their struggle for humanism,
had sought to avoid. At the heart of Sade's novels is his intention
to demonstrate that in the world of nature and men, the good
(or synonymously, the weak) are destined to be the wretched victims of the vicious (or the strong). The *Justine* novels recount
the miserable fate of its virtuous heroine. The *Histoire de Juliette*
(Justine's sister) is properly sub-titled "The Prosperities of Vice,"
and the episodes of both are calculated by Sade, with greatest
relish, to demonstrate his thesis.[11] The very beginning of the first
novel in the series makes it clear how his theme was derived from
the problem of evil, inspired by Duclos' *Mme de Luz,* by the
novel, *Thérèse philosophe* (often attributed to d'Argens), possibly too by reaction against a passage in *Zadig:* "The wicked, replied Jesrad, are always unhappy. They serve to test a small
number of just men scattered over the earth, and there is no ill
from which a good is not born." Two other ideas are simultaneously present in Sade's mind: the balance of good and evil, and
the indifference of nature, or the "general plan," to the triumph
of the wicked.[12]

Sade, as we saw in the last chapter, does not neglect the metaphysical background. As if the discourses of his characters were
not sufficient, he takes pains to tell us in a footnote that evil is a
universal law of nature, increasing in gradation with the sensitivity of beings; the more sensitive they are, "the more the hand
of atrocious nature bends them under the invincible laws of
evil." [13] But he goes even further. He makes the deduction that
Delisle de Sales had foreseen and turned aside. One of his char-

[11] The climactic termination of both the Justine and the Juliette stories comes
at the very end of the latter novel. Noirceuil sends Justine out into the storm,
promising to be converted if she is spared. Juliette agrees to the test. Justine is
struck down by lightning, and the spectators shout, "Come and contemplate the
work of heaven, come and see how it rewards virtue!"
Albert Camus makes this incisive comment: "Noirceuil triumphs, and man's
crime will continue to respond to divine crime. Thus we have here a freethinker's
wager which is the reply to Pascal's wager." (*L'homme révolté,* p. 55.) It is significant that Sade has been called, "that Pascal abandoned by God."

[12] *Les Infortunes de la vertu,* p. 2–3. In fairness to Voltaire, we must remember
that he had immediately made Zadig object, "But, suppose there were only good
and no evil."

[13] *Histoire de Juliette,* V, 24 n.; see also the speech of Cardinal Bernis (IV, 105),
and VI, 172.

acters, the infamous Saint-Fond (the only one of Sade's heroes who, purely for the sake of argument, believes in God), declares that evil is necessary to God.

> I raise my eyes over the universe, I see evil, disorder and crime ruling everywhere as despots . . . what ideas result from this examination? that what we improperly term evil really is not evil, and that this mode is so necessary to the designs of the being who created us that he would cease being the master of his own work if evil did not exist universally over the earth . . . [God's hand] has created [the world] only for evil, it takes pleasure only in evil, evil is its essence . . . It is in evil that he created the world, it is by evil that he maintains it, it is for evil that he perpetuates it, it is impregnated with evil that the creature must exist . . . this mode being the soul of the Creator as it is that of the creature. . . .[14]

Therefore, to please God we too must be evil. If there were such a thing as a good person (there is none, except in relation to our own interest), he would be displeasing to God and to his ends. God is "the most wicked, the most ferocious, the most frightful of all beings. His works cannot be anything else but the result, or the movement of wickedness." [15]

Sade's extreme espousal of evil as the law of being went beyond most of his contemporaries, although an outlook fringing upon it can be seen in the novels of Laclos and Rétif de la Bretonne, and occasionally in Diderot. While the reality of evil impressed itself more and more on the minds of eighteenth century thinkers, especially after the Lisbon earthquake and the fiasco of "optimism," two other alternatives were sought out by the deists and the atheists who were trying to save a humanistic ethics despite their inability to accept the orthodox disculpation of God.

The first was to admit evil as a co-equal principle in the uni-

---

[14] *Ibid.*, ii, 260–268. For an earlier and more direct expression of the idea that God is evil, and its connection with the problem of evil, see Sade's *Les Infortunes de la vertu* (1787), p. 170, 175.

[15] Cf. the phrase of a twentieth-century novelist: "Often the injustice of some one of his acts aroused in him a sort of enthusiasm; it is the pleasure that God feels when he contemplates the Creation." (Henri de Montherlant, *Les jeunes filles*, p. 232).

Sade, however, probably does not literally mean, as Camus thinks possible, that an evil God or démiurge exists; for there is no good or evil in an absurd universe. I take him to mean that as the universe is in disharmony with human moral experience, it is, from our viewpoint, evil; and God, if he existed, would be all-powerful and evil (the second horn of Bayle's dilemma).

verse. Although we find it in several deists, this ancient solution was not really popular in the eighteenth century. To the scientifically minded it smacked of mysticism, while to the Catholic it was the condemned Manichean heresy. But a tincture of this doctrine can be found in Calvinist and Jansenist theology, which hold evil to be co-existent with, though not co-equal to good. A twentieth-century adherent has stated that part of "the Christian view of man" involves the belief in a principle or force of evil antecedent to any evil human action. Before man fell, the devil fell.[16] It is not surprising, then, that there is a current of Manicheism in the Protestant Bayle.[17] The "system of two principles" was also embraced by Deslandes, and it is visible in d'Argens and Dupont de Nemours.[18] Traces of it occur in numerous other writings, including the *Lettres persanes, Zadig* and *Candide.*

Even more interesting is the system of Robinet, who set forth a curious mélange of mysticism and the scientific spirit in his famous *De la nature* (1763–1766). Robinet endeavors both to disculpate God and to establish the necessity of evil. Embracing Spinoza's principle, that all "possibles" exist, he attacks Leibniz by asserting the consequence, that there can be only one world and that God had no choice.[19] Robinet's thesis, developed at length throughout Part I of his work, is that good and evil are objectively real and stand in a necessary and inalterable equilibrium. Behind the apparently random distribution of pleasure and suffering lies a fluid but fixed order. "The physical economy is such that good and evil are engendered with equal fecundity. They flow naturally from the depth of essences." If God freely exposed man to sin and misery, there is no way of clearing him of guilt. But God can in no way remove evil, for omnipotence

[16] Niebuhr, *op. cit.,* I, 150.

[17] He states, for instance, that evil is necessary if there is to be virtue which is resistance to evil (*Oeuvres diverses,* IV, 92). Bayle, however, is as usual sceptical of his own scepticism, and he also shows why the doctrine of Manicheism is untenable. Diderot's long article in the *Encyclopédie,* "Manichéisme," is an important summary of the debate between Bayle and his adversaries, Jaquelot and Leibniz, slanted for Diderot's own propaganda purposes, laden with irony and innuendo. Diderot uses Manicheism to attack the apologists' positions; however, from another viewpoint, he also believes in the necessity of evil and the impossibility of a perfect world.

[18] *Histoire critique de la philosophie* (1737), I, 257, 266, 277; d'Argens, *Lettres juives,* 1738, III, 155 ff.; Dupont, *Philosophie de la nature,* p. 15–36.

[19] "God no more had the power to modify the nature of the world than his own nature." (III, 180–184.)

does not extend to impossibles or contradictions. Since the suppression of evil implies contradiction—good without evil would be infinite—there is no problem of evil. In all of nature, then, each degree of good is allied with an equal degree of evil, and the total quantity of each is at every moment equal. Thus the harmony of the world is always the same, and progress is a myth or an illusion.[20] Robinet takes great pains to distinguish his theory from Manicheism, which he derides as trying to explain phenomena by a mysterious, unknowable principle; his own theory places evil in nature, leaving God as "a wholly good cause."[21] Nonetheless, the ethical consequences of one theory or the other may possibly be interpreted as leading to similar conclusions.

Although Robinet might be classified among the apologists, I have treated him here because his admission of the insuperable metaphysical necessity of evil impairs the support of ethics in a moral universe corresponding to human ethical values and aspirations.

The materialists adopted a second alternative. They denied the metaphysical reality of evil, and the very existence of a "problem of evil," inasmuch as the universe is simply empty of moral value.[22] This view is basic to La Mettrie, Helvétius, d'Holbach, and Diderot. The materialist's answer to the disaster of Lisbon was superficially like that of the Christian optimist; more profoundly, it was quite different. This *is* the best of all possible worlds, they granted, because it is the only possible world. The materialists did not approve of Robinet's equilibrium, however. Good and bad are variables. Yet all is as good as it can be, because all is necessarily determined. Good and evil are realities, but only,

---

[20] Rétif de la Bretonne was strongly influenced by Robinet. In his little known work, *L'Ecole des pères*, he declares the harmony of nature to lie in the proportion between what we call good and evil. It is "childish and vain" to judge nature by human moral standards. Balance of good and evil is also found in Sade, e.g., *Histoire de Juliette*, I, 187. In *Les Infortunes de la vertu*, he avers that the balance of good and evil makes it indifferent whether we as individuals are one or the other (p. 168).

[21] Robinet, affirms Paul Vernière, denies the immanence of God in *natura naturata*. (*Spinoza et la pensée française*, II, 651–652.) See Corrado Rosso, "Il paradosso di Robinet," p. 52–55, for an excellent discussion of the complexities and contradictions of Robinet's theory. Rosso holds that Robinet escapes from the optimism-pessimism antithesis and rises above it (p. 62–63); he also brings out Pope's and Voltaire's precedence of Robinet in the idea of an equilibrium of good and evil (p. 57–58).

[22] This was true for Sade, too, although he projects what we, in our subjective experience, call evil, into a cosmic reality.

as Spinoza had said, in terms of an individual's experience. It is not true that evil, as certain optimists claimed, is a mere appearance, an error in the human mind, or that partial evil gives rise to universal good. But it is true, as many apologists contended, that physical evil is a result of the laws of matter, and that moral evil stems from self-love—which, however, is necessary to preservation, and so a good. Hunger, said Diderot, is necessary, and so are passions (which result from sensitivity). While for the Christian optimist this evil was necessary in the best of possible worlds, for Diderot it was necessary because this is the only possible world. "All is good" is false; but we may say, "All that is, is necessary," or "All is the best it can be." [23]

The principal point, and the deep distinction, is that from the *metaphysical* viewpoint, the materialist proclaimed there was no question of good or evil. Spinoza's influence on this line of thought was deep; it runs throughout the radical writings of the time. In the important Appendix to the First Part of his *Ethic,* Spinoza had written that experience daily confirms the fact that "both the beneficial and the injurious were indiscriminately bestowed on the pious and the impious." It is convenient and comforting, warns Spinoza, for the human mind to shelve the problem by claiming that the judgments of the gods far surpass our comprehension. But this is only a *reductio ad ignorantiam.* In nature there is no right or wrong, no final causes, no awareness of man's needs, desires or judgments. Another important influence was Mandeville's *The Fable of the Bees,* which maintained that "all actions in nature, abstractly considered, are equally indifferent," cruelty and malice being words applicable only to our own feelings.[24]

[23] "Pope has well proved, after Leibniz, that the world could not be anything but what it is; but when he concluded from this that all is well, he said an absurdity; he should have been content to say that all is necessary." (*Introduction aux grands principes,* II, 85, nb.) There is a more explicit statement in the article "Laideur" (xv, 410), quoted by Fabre (*Neveu de Rameau,* p. 143, n. 61). See also *Neveu de Rameau,* p. 15, and *Le Rêve de d'Alembert, Oeuvres,* II, 138. Also, "Good and evil are without distinction in the universal arrangement" (*Lettres à Sophie Volland,* éd. Babelon, III, 288–289). For d'Holbach, see *Système de la nature,* Pt. 1, ch. 5. It may also be recalled that in England, Hume was approaching the question from another viewpoint, that of his empiricism. The gods "possess that precise degree of power, intelligence and benevolence which appear in their workmanship," and we can ascribe to them no attribute "but what can be found in the present world." All efforts to account for evil are therefore fruitless. (*An Enquiry concerning human understanding,* ed. cit., p. 671–672.)

[24] Quoted by Leslie Stephen, *English Thought in the Eighteenth Century,* II, 39.

For the eighteenth century materialist, then, the universe is not moral, and our purely human evaluations have no meaning in reference to it, no status in being. Voltaire was wrong to apply moral categories in his consideration. Certainly, if there is a "problem of evil," then it is impossible to avoid metaphysics and theology; and so Voltaire, who hated metaphysics, became embroiled in it, as did Rousseau. Diderot's contribution lay in pointing out that there is no such problem. There can be none, unless we postulate, first, design in the universe, and second, that man is the *telos* of that design. Diderot and his fellow materialists rejected both. The universe is only nature, and nature knows only survival. "In nature, all species devour each other; in society, all classes devour each other." [25]

Against this assault the optimist and the Christian set up a stout defense. We must now examine their arguments and counterarguments. As Bayle may be said to have put the siege guns into firing position, so Leibniz set up the breast-works of the defense. His *Théodicée* (1710) was an answer to Bayle's *Dictionnaire*. But whereas Bayle's strategy remained operative throughout the years ahead, the defenders of the opposing camp found it necessary, about the middle of the century, to beat a hasty retreat from Leibniz's positions and to set up new defenses.

Even as the materialists interpreted Spinoza's reasoning as substantiating a non-moral universe, so it is possible that Leibniz, by another interpretation, found in it the seed for his system of optimism. Spinoza had written that the eternal order of nature, "wherein man is but a speck," is not that of human reason. Evil is an appearance resulting from our ignorance of "the order and interdependence of nature as a whole." What reason holds to be evil "is not evil in respect to the laws of nature as a whole, but only in respect to the laws of our reason." [26]

Leibniz's system is based on the proposition that God is ultimately the sufficient reason of all particular things.

> Now, as in the Ideas of God there is an infinite number of possible universes, and as only one of them can be actual, there must be a sufficient reason for the choice of God, which leads him to decide upon one rather than another.

[25] *Neveu de Rameau* (éd. J. Fabre), p. 37–38.
[26] *Tractatus-theologico-politicus* (1670), p. 202.

And this reason can be found only in the *fitness* (*convenance*), or in the degrees of perfection, that these worlds possess, since each possible thing has the right to aspire to existence in proportion to the amount of perfection it contains in germ.

Thus the actual existence of the best that wisdom makes known to God is due to this, that his goodness makes him choose it, and his power makes him produce it.[27]

In this way Leibniz seeks to invalidate simultaneously three explanations of evil: the permissive doctrine of the scholastics, that God's will merely cooperates with ours; the Cartesian principle that God's will is the sole cause or agent in the universe; the Hobbesian thesis that God is a despotic or arbitrary power. Leibniz's optimism is entirely *a priori,* founded on "sufficient reason" and the excellence of the cause, and cannot therefore be combatted by experience. If the evil that individuals complain about were suppressed, this would no longer be the best of possible worlds, for "all is linked." [28] God wills only the good; but when he compares goods, he can will them only as they are compatible and as, in unison, they produce the greatest good possible; and evil, precisely, is one of the conditions of this greatest good. Therefore, "God wills the good antecedently, and the best consequently." [29] It is true that God is the real cause of everything positive in his creation, but none the less, he is not the cause of evil, which is a deficiency or limit.[30] To put it differently, evil has no efficient cause, being only a privation, inherent in the condition or limits of the created.[31]

The second great champion of optimism, and the most popular, was Alexander Pope. He was inspired by Shaftesbury through Bolingbroke, as well as by King and Leibniz. In particular, he favors Shaftesbury's theory, that apparent evil is the result of our insufficient knowledge of the whole.[32] Actually, Pope's optimism differed in many ways from that of Leibniz. The English poet's

---

[27] *Monadology* (1714), par. 53-55; also *Théodicée* (1710), par. 7.

[28] *Théodicée,* par. 9.

[29] Par. 23. Diderot points out that Leibniz takes away God's freedom ("Manichéisme").

[30] Par. 30.

[31] Par. 20. Paul Hazard emphasizes two other arguments of Leibniz consequent to these: that evil may be a good in the general order, and that each thing must occupy its place in the chain of beings (*op. cit.,* p. 151-153).

[32] See *An Inquiry Concerning Virtue,* Bk. I, Part 2, etc. Shaftesbury's writings are practically contemporaneous with those of Leibniz.

system was in essence *a posteriori,* founded on effects. "What can we reason, but from what we know?"—that is, from our own world.[33] Furthermore Pope tends more strongly to diminish, if not to deny, the reality of evil; in fact, the harsh appearance of evil is dissolved into the reality of positive good. "Whatever wrong we call, may, must be right, as relative to all." Man is "perfect in his sphere." "All partial evil, universal good." And of course, "Whatever is, is right." God acts not by partial but by general laws.

> All this dread ORDER break—for whom? for thee?
> Vile worm! Oh Madness! Pride! Impiety! (I, 257–258)[34]

The optimism of Leibniz and Pope seems to have acted as an opiate until the middle of the century. True, there was some resistance from theologians who did not admit original sin as a necessary part of God's best world, or who saw in optimism the denial of providence; and there was a dawning realization that this "optimism" consecrated our ills *in perpetuum.*[35] Père Castel, for instance, wrote in the Jesuit *Journal de Trévoux,* "They do not criticize providence, but they annihilate it all the better by pretending to applaud it. *All is good, all is best, all is very good, evil is not evil,* since it is the necessary cause of good . . . optimism is only a disguised materialism." [36] Optimism, declared the Catholic apologist Alès de Corbet, is a fatalism.[37] We have, precisely, seen this apparent conjunction of the materialistic and optimistic views. The system of optimism was none the less widely expounded, even by *philosophes* like Morelly, whose *Code de la*

---

[33] *Essay on Man,* I, 18. There is, however, some basis for Pope's principles in Leibniz, e.g., an evil may be the cause of a good [for Pope it *must* be], and two ills may make a great good (*Théodicée,* par. 10); it is not true there is more evil than good (par. 13). Leibniz also argues that if the wicked prosper, the remedy will come in the next life (par. 17). We need not cavil as to whether Pope's doctrine expresses the literal meaning of optimism; it was taken as a doctrine of optimism.

[34] Pope thus disculpates God by retreating to the deistic position of a remote or original providence. His ideas on providence are somewhat confused. In one place, he affirms that all was made for man (I, 131–140), elsewhere that man is just another item in Creation (III, 25–48)—he is not the object of God's particular favor (IV, 113–130).

[35] Morize, *op. cit.,* p. 170 ff. Crousaz, *op. cit.,* p. 61 ff.

[36] Quoted by Morize, p. xxiv, n. 6. One of the most vigorous of these pre-Lisbon attacks on optimism was contained in the abbé Duhamel's *Lettres flamandes* (1753), p. 24–25, 60–74 *et passim.*

[37] *Op. cit.,* p. 170 ff.

nature appeared the year before the Lisbon earthquake.[38] This system was aided and abetted, at various times during the first half of the century, by the chorus of theological naturalists referred to in the first section of this chapter—Haller, Nieuwentyt, Derham, Pluche and company. Not even the shock of the Lisbon earthquake could choke it off completely. In the second part of the century, it is still preached by the poet Saint-Lambert and the apologist Bergier.[39] Bernardin de Saint-Pierre revives, with new romantic fervor, the tradition of the theological naturalists. Most important of all, optimism underlies the outlook of Rousseau.

Rousseau's views on this subject were first expounded in his letter to Voltaire, generally called "Lettre sur la Providence." He later reaffirmed them in three separate letters of the *Nouvelle Héloïse*. In the first of these, Saint-Preux writes to Bomston about Wolmar's philosophy. Wolmar, though an atheist, is a Leibnizian. "Everything concurs to the common good in the universal system. Every man has his assigned place in the universal order of things. . . ." [40] A little later, however, it is Saint-Preux who is arguing with Wolmar in favor of the thesis that not only is there no absolute or general evil, but that particular ills are far exaggerated and far less in sum than existing good.[41] Finally, in the third of these letters, the unfortunate Julie herself, reviewing her life, points out how apparent evil yields unsuspected good.[42] The reasons underlying Rousseau's optimism, a complex of personal and philosophical motivations, cannot be analyzed at this point. It suffices to realize that for his ethical doctrine it was necessary to postulate that all is good in leaving the hands of the Creator, who, guided by the intent of realizing the maximum of welfare for his creatures, fashioned a universe permeated with moral value.

The denial of the reality of evil was not good Catholic doctrine.

---

[38] *Code de la nature*, p. 239–243. Also de Vattel: "If we took evil away from the world, and sin and crimes, it would no longer be the best . . . therefore *tout est bien*."

[39] Saint-Lambert, *Les Saisons* (Janet et Cotelle, p. 23), p. 179–180; Bergier, *Examen du matérialisme* (1771), III, 65–73.

[40] IV, 66. It is of peculiar interest that Wolmar's Leibnizianism is really a mask for political conservatism.

[41] IV, 116.

[42] IV, 311–312.

Consequently, those adherents of optimism who pushed their doctrine so far as to deny, or almost to deny its reality were generally
of deistic tincture. Toussaint is a good example. Man just likes
to complain, he writes. Physical evil—earthquakes, floods, famines,
plagues, etc.—he dismisses with a derisive "so what?" "Are you
the less overwhelmed with blessings, because Lima is submerged?
Have the fires vomited by Mt. Gibel or Vesuvius hurt you?" And
if they do reach you, you can at worst die and go to a better life
—if you've been careful. Those ills we term "needs" are blessings;
they prevent us from working too hard and their satisfaction provides pleasures. From there Toussaint goes on to defend passions,
the source of moral evil.[43] In a word, what seems disorder is only
an order not understood.

Morelly was another writer who denied the reality of physical
evil, "even in regard to us." [44] His dismissal of moral evil rests
on different grounds; it is a reality, but a purely relative and unnecessary one, due only to the perversions of the passions caused
by the institution of property, and therefore inexistent in the
state of nature.[45] And Louis de Beausobre, even after the Lisbon
earthquake, dismisses Lisbon, wars and cruelties—"those are dec-
lamations that prove nothing—for *tout est bien.*" [46]

In contradistinction to this group of deistic optimists, Maupertuis, also a firm deist, urges defenders of God to look elsewhere for their weapons. He attempts, in interesting fashion, to
draw together the problems of evil, finalism and the wisdom of
God. He paints a graphic picture of a world filled with physical
and moral evil, accuses Leibniz of diminishing God's power and
Pope of a mere "act of faith." The universe, he goes on, presents
patent instances of a plan, and of wisdom in its execution. But
is this sufficient? Maupertuis thinks there is another question we
must ask. Is there wisdom and goodness in the ultimate purpose
of these plans? The answer is perhaps beyond the scope of human
ken. Certainly, it is not in such details as the structure of an insect
that we can hope to find the evidence we need. We must seek it
rather in universal, unexceptional phenomena, such as mathematics and basic physical laws.[47] Maupertuis' arguments, however,

[43] *Les Moeurs* (1748), p. 27–50.
[44] *Code*, p. 241–242.
[45] P. 253–254, 250.
[46] *Essai sur le bonheur* (1758), p. 12, 78.
[47] *Essai de cosmologie* (1750), *Oeuvres*, I, 16 ff.

seem to have had no influence on his contemporaries, partly because he eludes the definite answer they were demanding, partly
because he was, in this matter, running counter to the dominant
trend of interest in biology.

The orthodox, who even in the high tide of optimism had
doubts about the strategy of denying the reality of evil, openly
denounced the deistic optimists after the Lisbon earthquake.
"Fatal blindness!" cries Formey. "Does the infuriated lion who
tears a traveler to pieces in the vast forests of Libya seem to you
then a good in the physical order?" And are adultery, infamy,
injustice, murder, rape, good? If evil is prevalent in nature, should
it not be so in guilty man? Should I say that my suffering is only
an increase in happiness? No, our suffering is the very proof of
God's continuing providence and justice.[48] Other apologists similarly abandon Leibnizianism and thus they free God from responsibility on other grounds, which we shall shortly examine.[49]

As is well known, the Lisbon earthquake, which occurred in
that most Catholic of cities, on All-Saints' Day, November 1,
1755, was a "crise de conscience" for the eighteenth century.
There was, it has been seen, a growing, though a minority opposition to the Leibniz-Pope types of optimism even before that
event.[50] In the preceding year the Academy of Berlin had announced its essay contest for 1755, on the distinction between
Pope's "Tout est bien" and "the system of optimism or the choice
of the best." It was won by A. F. Reinhard whose essay rejected
optimism. The general good, argued the author, foreshadowing
Voltaire's *Poème sur le désastre de Lisbonne,* is no consolation
to me; suppose the general good required me to be forever unhappy? [51]

After the shock of the earthquake, optimism crumbled, less,
perhaps, because of the increased attacks upon it, than of its own
dead weight. Actually, the sceptics and non-believers, even from
the beginning, had leveled powerful assaults directly against the
logic of the system of Leibniz and his followers. Bayle had early
asserted that there must have been a better universe, in the infinity of possibles, than one which inevitably brought about the

[48] *L'Anti-Sans-Soucy* (1761), p. 5–7, 46–54.
[49] Guidi, *Entretiens . . .* (1772), p. 295–300; Bergier, in a later work, *Principes
de métaphysique* (1780), 95 ff.
[50] See Morize, *Candide,* p. xxv ff, xxxvii ff.
[51] *Histoire de l'Académie royale . . . de Berlin,* 1755.

unhappiness of sensitive creatures. And if there was only one possible universe—then, what is God? Isn't there a Paradise? And wasn't there a Garden of Eden? Surely, these are better possibles! [52] But if you take the opposite stand and argue that all possibles must be, then God had no freedom, had to choose evil and is its author. Thus runs Bayle's logic through all his writings, putting the faithful on a hook from which they struggled helplessly to free themselves. He had stated the case so well, that later *philosophes*, even after the Lisbon disaster, could do little but work the same substance into a new shape. One example, that of d'Alembert, will suffice. In the article "Optimisme" in the *Encyclopédie*, he opens up a frontal attack. Objecting to Leibniz's asseveration that the rape of Lucretia produced Rome's freedom and virtue, he inquires why virtues had to be produced by a crime. He, too, tries to show that it is impossible to reconcile optimism with God's freedom. Having posed the question, "how many men kill each other in the best of possible worlds?" he goes on to demand why, if this is the best, God created it.[53] In the article "Fortuit," d'Alembert states bluntly that if God made the physical order, he is equally responsible for the moral order, even if contingent, that results from it.

As the earthquake renewed the problem of evil in acute form, demolishing the rampart of optimism on the one hand, and sharpening the pens of anti-Christians on the other, new defenders sprang into the breach. Shortly after the earthquake, the Academy of Rouen made it the subject of a prize essay (1757). The winner, Antoine Thomas, strives to demonstrate that the disaster was providential, a warning to make the impious tremble. Rousseau, in his reply to Voltaire's *Poème sur le désastre de Lisbonne* ("Lettre sur la Providence," August 18, 1756), contends that the fault is man's for living unnaturally in large cities—an argument also advanced by the abbé Pluquet the following year.[54] Why should the quake have taken place in a desert, as Voltaire sug-

[52] *Réponse aux questions . . . Oeuvres diverses*, III, 657–683.
[53] See also Fréret, *Lettre de Thrasibule*, p. 133–137; Meslier, *op. cit.*, III, 43–75, 118–142; d'Holbach, *Christianisme dévoilé*, p. 78–91.
[54] *Examen du fatalisme* (1757), I, 122. Alès de Corbet (*De l'origine du mal*, 1758) also justifies the earthquake according to the designs of providence. On the Lisbon earthquake, see also the following recent publications: W. H. Barber, *Leibniz in France*, Theodore Besterman, "Voltaire et le Désastre de Lisbonne," p. 7–24, and I. O. Wade, *The Search for a New Voltaire*, p. 42–48.

gests? Should the order of the world, counters Rousseau, echoing Pope, change to suit men's caprice?

The chorus of protests and counterattacks from believers and Christian apologists grew louder and stronger. It was as if there were a deepening realization that the fortress of optimism had fallen, and that unless they acted swiftly to close the breach, the *philosophes* would have a clear road to their three ultimate objectives: the dissolution of an ethical bond with God, "secular morality," and deism or atheism. In assessing their defenses systematically, as we shall now do, it is to be noted, then, that relatively few of the writers referred to belong to the first half of the century.

There were seven principal arguments, or rather lines of argument, advanced by the apologists. One was to assert that we exaggerate the amount of evil, and that the sum of good is actually greater. This type of argument may be considered as a prolongation, with some deviations, of the earlier optimism. It had considerable diffusion, chiefly among a group of moderate deists and unorthodox Christians. Thus we find it in Dupont de Nemours,[55] in Bonnet, Vauvenargues, Rousseau and Bernardin de Saint-Pierre —but also in the apologist Alès de Corbet. For the scientist Bonnet, the universe is a harmony and a unity having all the perfection it can have; consequently every evil is an effect inseparable from the existence of some good.[56] Rousseau, in his "Lettre sur la Providence," asserts his conviction that God has picked the economy with the least amount of evil; "if he has done no better, it is because he could do no better." Besides, let us not delude ourselves intellectually, he urges; life is far from unbearable, and being alive is itself so precious that it should make us overlook our ills. Philosophers (meaning Voltaire) forget in their calculations "the sweet feeling of existence, independent of all other sensations." The individual, Rousseau avers, is less important to God than the whole; and we must not forget there may be people on other planets, too. It is true that an individual may find scant consolation for his death, as Voltaire says, in the prospect

[55] *Philosophie de la nature* (1792), p. 15–36. Marmontel in his posthumous *Leçons sur la métaphysique* (p. 138–146) has even more difficulty than Dupont in convincing himself that the sum of evil is less.

[56] *Contemplation de la nature* (1781), p. 3–5. Alès had advanced similar arguments, *op. cit.*, p. 159 ff. Also Bergier, *Principes de métaphysique*, p. 95–109.

of his nourishing plants or wolves. But if it is necessary for the "conservation of mankind that there be a circulation of substances among men, animals and vegetables, then the particular hurt of an individual contributes to the general good." In all this we can observe the common eighteenth century theme of *concordia discors*, which, though related essentially to the problem of theodicy, was also to have ethical extensions and analogies.

Bernardin de Saint-Pierre, as might be expected, is more naïve, in *Pluchean* fashion, in explaining all apparent evils as real goods.[57] We are again reminded of Vauvenargues, who, writing in the period of "optimism," had found God's justice working mysteriously, through apparent ills.[58] It is obvious that we are here dealing with deists, and mostly with very sentimental deists, who cling to providentialism and Leibnizianism after the fashion has gone.

Not far from the first argument was the second, that physical suffering is necessary and useful. However it was more limited in scope, more easily proven, and consequently even more widely diffused. It is to be found early in England, in King and in Wollaston.[59] As King had put it, unpleasant sensations are inevitable, under the penalty of non-existence. Or as Dupont de Nemours was to phrase it, no pain, no pleasure; no death, no love, paternal, filial or conjugal.[60] Our physical ills are the particular effects of wise and necessary general laws—this truth seems patent and incontrovertible to a number of later apologists.[61] An earlier writer of minor category, Lesage de la Colombière, was even willing to abridge providence and unwittingly approaches the naturalistic position, by arguing that our ills prove only "that in this there is no exception for them [i.e., men] in the general laws of nature." [62] And the greater the sensitivity, the greater the

---

[57] *Etudes* . . . I, 343 ff. *et passim.* Thus storms refresh the air, volcanoes purify sea water, and rats clean the earth of human excrement, etc.

[58] The poor is solaced by his privation, the rich driven to despair by possession. *Discours sur l'inégalité de richesses,* in *Oeuvres morales,* I, 291 ff. This is an equipoise of a different kind, one of qualities and defects.

[59] Wollaston, *The Religion of Nature Delineated* (1726), p. 71. King's work (1702), already referred to, is summarized at length in the *Encyclopédie,* in the article "Mal" by Jaucourt.

[60] *Op. cit.,* p. 64–66.

[61] Denesle, p. 224–226; Polignac, II, 298–299; Para du Phanjas, *Principes,* p. 107 ff.; Marmontel, *loc. cit.*

[62] *Cours abrégé,* p. 255. The early date of this work (1711) is perhaps an explanation of the concession.

hurt—this is inevitable, Volney later points out, according to natural laws.[63] Again, advantage is counterbalanced by disadvantage.

The Physiocrats were the most important group of writers to utilize this explanation. A corollary of their integration of economic, social and moral law into the order of nature was the goodness of nature. They did not try to deny evil, but explained it in the fashion of Quesnay:

> If we examine the rules of nature attentively, we shall at least perceive that the physical causes of physical evil are themselves the causes of physical goods; that the rain which inconveniences travelers fertilises the earth; and, if we calculate without prejudice, we shall see that these causes produce infinitely more good than evil, and that they are instituted only for good; that the evil they cause incidentally results necessarily from the very essence of the properties by which they produce the good.[64]

In this view, the natural world is good, not as a result of balances and cancellations, but because a good world (whether it is the best world possible is a useless metaphysical question) must also contain evil. What matters is that the natural world, like the entire creation of God, is, by *concordia discors*, inherently good.

A third line of reasoning sought to disculpate God on the purely metaphysical grounds of his nature. St. Augustine had said that vice is only a lack (of order), and what is nothing can have no cause.[65] (The conclusion is not drawn that in this case, men are not responsible either.) Knowing that evils are necessary but that God is perfect, we should have complete trust in his goodness and work on our own perfection, which is the way to reduce our personal ills.[66]

The most common variety of this metaphysical argument was to point to the necessity of finite or created things having a lesser degree of perfection than their infinite creator. This rather ancient defense is repeated by many writers; among them, Wollaston (1726), Lesage de la Colombière (1749), Jaucourt (article "Mal"), Sulzer (1754), Rousseau ("Lettre sur la Providence,"

[63] *Les ruines* (1791), p. 29–33. For Volney, consequently, evil is not a "mysterious problem."

[64] *Droit naturel*, III, *Oeuvres*, éd. Oncken, 1888, p. 359 ff.

[65] Alès, *loc. cit.* Also Bergier (*loc. cit.*) says that some types of evil are only privation, a state relative to other beings. The argument is in Leibniz.

[66] Sulzer, "Essai sur le bonheur," *Histoire de l'Académie de Berlin* (1754), p. 399 ff.

1756), Robinet (1766), Bergier (1780), Bonnet (1781), Dupont (1792). Dupont, for instance, states that God's goodness is necessarily limited, since it cannot change the essential character of matter nor give it his goodness.[67] To ask why man is not more perfect, asserts Bonnet, is to ask why he is not an angel; we might as well ask why a deer is not a man, or why grass is not a man. "Each being has the perfection that suits its end." He refers to the principle of plenitude: each place in the chain of being must be filled, or the Universal Harmony will be destroyed. "All beings are perfect, considered in themselves." [68] Finalism is thus reaffirmed by evil itself. To this list we should add the mystic, Saint-Martin, who completely severs the imperfect nature of created things from the essence of God—for else they would be changeless and co-eternal.[69]

To some, all evil is thus explained. To others, the nature of the finite creation accounts especially for physical ills. Moral evil must be laid directly to the doing of man himself. To his shortcomings and neglect, according to Wollaston; to his malicious character, according to Lesage de la Colombière, who calls him a "bad citizen"; to his excesses and cruelty, according to Vauvenargues; to his pride, according to Pope and many others. Most apologists joined in the condemnation. We must also note the significant adherence to this group of several deists who condemned the ways of man. Throughout his writings, and despite his involvement with the metaphysical aspect of the problem, Voltaire makes it clear that man's misery comes less from his betrayal of God than from his betrayal of his own reason. Rousseau also held that man had spoiled God's good creation. But his condemnation was less directly of man himself than of society, progress and his way of life. The "Lettre sur la Providence" makes this point explicitly. "I do not see that we can look for the source of evil elsewhere than in man, free, perfected [i.e., having made progress] and therefore corrupt." Cities are one evidence of an unnatural way of life. Worse still, people refused to flee from the earthquake, because their perverted values made them fear to lose their property more than their lives. "Do we not know that the person of each

[67] *Op. cit.*, p. 49–50.
[68] *Op. cit.*, p. 2–5, 23–28. They are imperfect in relation to other particular beings, but the whole, in its harmony, is again good.
[69] *Loc. cit.*

man has become the least part of him, and that it isn't worth while to save him when all the rest is lost?" A few years later, in *Emile*, Rousseau returned to his basic theme.[70] His disciple, Bernardin de Saint-Pierre, was to echo his ideas in a more naïve way.[71]

There is a logical connection between this inculpation of man and a more specific argument (the fifth in our list), one which was old, yet enjoyed widest diffusion. It proposed that evil is a necessary result of free will. This was doubtless the most powerful argument of the theological apologists, and Bayle had knowingly sought to turn it aside. But the finesse of his logic was largely disregarded, and the point was made again and again that since God wanted man to be a moral being, he had to give man the choice of good and evil, and thus allow evil. For all moral good is done freely.[72]

This argument leads in turn to another. The sixth argument, then, rests on the belief in an after-life, in which justice will be done for all eternity. In order that God may mete out his rewards and punishments, he must give man the occasion to have merit or fault. Thus what is wrong here, wrote Wollaston, may be rectified later.[73] Our temporary wretchedness may become the source of eternal bliss; but we must remember there is merit only in proportion to the difficulty.[74] Only Bergier asks the question, why God does not reward good and punish evil in this world. *"Voilà le scandale de tous les siècles."* He doubtless wishes to strike back at Meslier and other atheists who insisted that God [if he exists] must protect and reward the good. Bergier justifies God by asserting that if he did this, then virtue would not be disinterested— it

[70] P. 5, 341–342.

[71] *Etudes.* 343 ff., 434–473. The developments are long and repetitious. We note only the following exclamation: "Certainly, to have thus fallen below the beasts, he must have wished to raise himself to the level of Divinity. Unhappy mortals! seek your happiness in virtue and you will not have to complain of nature. Despise that vain knowledge and those prejudices that have corrupted the earth." The echoes of Pope are still sounding.

[72] See Ladvocat, *Entretiens,* p. 339–342, Nonnotte, *Dictionnaire de religion,* III, 228–282; Joly, *Dictionnaire de morale,* II, 44–45; Richard, *Défense . . . ,* p. 219–220; Polignac, II, 293; Denesle, p. 123–128; Bergier, *loc. cit.;* Rousseau: *Lettre sur la Providence; Guidi, loc. cit.* The abbé Guidi is naive in his reasoning: God made Adam and Eve perfect, and that was all his responsibility; it was their fault if they decided to be wicked.

[73] *Loc. cit.*

[74] For similar reasoning, see Abbadie, *Traité de la vérité de la religion chrétienne,* I, 112–116; Para du Phanjas, *loc. cit.;* Joly, *loc. cit.;* Sisson de Valmire, *Dieu et l'homme* (1771), p. 152–155; Polignac, *loc. cit.;* Bernardin de Saint-Pierre, p. 434 ff.

is not clear why it would be disinterested in view of a future reward)—the wicked could not be freely converted, conscience would be useless, and there would be no confidence among men.[75] Condillac, Rousseau and Delisle de Sales go so far as to point to the predominance of evil on earth as proof of the immortality of the soul—for otherwise God would be unjust, the universe amoral.[76]

Such an argument leaves a neat opening to the atheist. This was clear to several philosophical apologists, and their anguish is apparent. It is visible to some degree in Rousseau's "Lettre sur la Providence." Affirming his faith in providence, according to which each material being is made in the best way "in relation to himself," he cautions that this rule is valid only when applied to the "total duration of each sensitive being." This in turn "shows how much the question of providence hangs on that of the immortality of the soul." In this Rousseau has faith, without however accepting eternal castigation. He sums up by saying that the entire complex of questions comes down to that of God's existence. If he exists, my soul is immortal, all is well. Thus it is either yes or no on this first proposition, and the rest follows. Again, this either-or proposition was not to the atheists' dislike.

We have seen that Vauvenargues, ten or more years before Rousseau, had shown himself to be obsessed, and even more anguished, by the same torment. He sounds a note of despair that makes his pronounced belief in providence seem like the drowning man's clinging to the last spar. And Marmontel, near the close of his life, strikes a not dissimilar note. Struggling for optimism, but admitting man undergoes unmerited evil "from this whole of which he had to be a painful and suffering part," he tells us to prefer Job's "Surrecturus sum" to Pope's drivel. Without life immortal, thinking man "would be too harshly sacrificed to the rest of nature; and if God had made him to be

---

[75] *Loc. cit.*

[76] Condillac, *Traité des animaux, Oeuvres philosophiques,* I, 371; Rousseau, "Lettre sur la Providence"; Delisle de Sales, *loc. cit.* The relationship had been brought out by Malebranche. Good people, he admits, are happy in good only because "a great recompense is awaiting them in heaven." God must make them happy, or else there would be no justice; consequently, they will be. (*De la Recherche de la vérité,* éd. Boullier (1880), I, 427 f.) Ten years later (1684), Malebranche put the matter more succinctly. "There is no God, if the soul is not immortal and if the universe doesn't change its face some day: for an unjust God is a chimera." (*Traité de la morale,* p. 263).

annihilated, after suffering patiently and without complaint, God would be cruel towards him." No one has a right to benefit from my suffering, not even God. But if this life is only a test, then all is clear and justified. Evil, then, is proof of the soul's immortality.[77]

One can scarcely help feeling that the desperate recourse to an ultimate setting right of wrongs is, in many cases, the signature to Bayle's victory and the defeat of rational defenses against his pyrrhonism. This impression carries over to the seventh and final line of resistance, which is again, in a sense, logically connected with the preceding one. The surest way for the apologist to overcome his insecurity in meeting Bayle's logical challenge was to surmount it, or to by-pass it. A "moderate" way of doing this was to affirm the mystery of what Abbadie termed God's infinite and orderly plan, of which we see only a tiny corner. After all, Pharaoh's bad dream led to the birth of Christ and the reign of God, and yet a man would have blamed God for the injustice done to Joseph.[78] We cannot, urges Bergier, reduce God to the limits of our minds.[79] Rousseau concurs: our place in the harmony of the whole is beyond our knowledge—except by deduction from God's perfection.[80]

A stronger—and more dangerous—way of by-passing Bayle, one that was even more common, was to affirm that God's ways are quite alien to those of men. This tactic has its ultimate source in Pascal, who tried to justify God and Christianity by proving that the injustice of the world is the justice which man deserves, that evil (from man's relative view) is good (from God's absolute view), and is willed by God. What deceives you, cries the abbé Guidi, is "the false idea that God should do the best he can for his creatures." But it is madness to want God to do what he can rather than what he wills.[81] God, says Para succinctly, "does not have our way of seeing and feeling." [82] Our delusion, adds Richard, is that it is a question of man's interest, when really it is one only of God's. If God had to follow justice, he would not be free! [83] "Censor of the universe," exclaims Polignac, "do you then think it

[77] *Op. cit.,* p. 146–159.
[78] *Loc. cit.*
[79] *Loc. cit.;* also Nonnotte, *loc. cit.*
[80] "Lettre sur la Providence." Cf. Voltaire's *Zadig.*
[81] *Op. cit.,* p. 295–310.
[82] *Op. cit.,* p. 107.
[83] *Op. cit.,* p. 220–222.

is made for you?" [84] Alès goes still further, affirms that God can love only himself.[85] Malebranche was wrong to confine his absolute freedom; following Malebranche, one can indeed end up only in the Manichean heresy. But our happiness cannot be God's end, or else he would no longer be his own end. To God, all things are only means, and so, utterly indifferent to him.[86]

This type of defense, we have said, was a dangerous one. In the first place, it tended to a denial of the very providence asserted by these same writers. It dissociated God from men, and removed the transcendent base of values. Diderot, in criticizing the theory that all is for the best, had pointed out that Leibnizian optimism limited God's freedom. This group of apologists restore God's freedom, and use it to place him beyond good and evil. Bayle, moreover, had foreseen this line of counterattack and its inevitable consequences. "All is lost," he wrote, "if divine conduct is not in conformity with our common notions of goodness and holiness." [87] Later the eccentric apologist Le Guay de Prémontval pointed out (as Meslier and the anonymous writers of anti-religious manuscripts had done before him!), that our ideas of God are naturally anthropomorphic; for Le Guay, this results from the fact that we are made in his image.[88] Consequently, if the real order of things is different from our judgments, then God has deceived us. Or else, as d'Holbach urged, there is simply no relation, and God cannot be the model for our justice.[89] Nor can he punish us for not following his laws, which we do not know.[90] Voltaire summarized the difficulty. Either God rewards or punishes, or there is no God, because God cannot be unjust. (Compare the marquis de Sade.) The justice of God must be ours, as two plus two equals four is true for him as well as for us.[91]

In the second place, this defense was dangerous because the diminishing of man in the universe opened the way to naturalistic viewpoints, or perhaps reveals their already successful infiltration.

[84] *Loc. cit.*

[85] The argument, ironically, is supplied by Bayle himself (*Oeuvres diverses*, III, 820).

[86] *Op. cit.*, p. 180 ff. See also Denesle, Bergier, *loc. cit.*

[87] *Oeuvres diverses*, IV, 23. Bayle also asserted that if God didn't owe a just universe to us, he owed it to himself.

[88] *Vues philosophiques*, p. 228 ff.

[89] D'Holbach, *Christianisme dévoilé.* p. 78 ff.

[90] The argument stems from Fréret, *Lettre à Thrasibule.*

[91] *Oeuvres*, XXVI, 321–322.

Polignac's argument, for instance, is basically the same as those of Voltaire and Hume in support of determinism and suicide. And Robinet, arguing to a quite different purpose, also denounces the anthropomorphic absurdity of saying God is good, or that God acts for his glory.[92]

The clearest realization of many of these implications is to be found in the work of an English philosopher, in the tenth and eleventh parts of Hume's *Dialogues on Natural Religion*. The discussion is not only a résumé of a large section of the controversy, but is significant in showing that the same argument used by the Christian apologist was used, and turned against him, by the naturalist. Starting from a criticism of Leibniz and an assertion of universal agreement on the prevalence of human misery, Hume has Demea (the most orthodox of the three disputants) pose this query: "And why should man . . . pretend to an exemption from the lot of all other animals? The whole earth, believe me, Philo, is cursed and polluted. A perpetual war is kindled amongst all living creatures." There follows a tableau of human misery, completed by Philo, the most radical of the three interlocutors. While Philo emphasizes man's imaginary enemies, the creatures of superstition, Demea stresses social warfare; both agree on natural ills. Turning then to Cleanthes, the third speaker, Philo questions him:

> And is it possible, Cleanthes, said Philo, that after all these reflections, and infinitely more, which might be suggested, you can still persevere in your anthropomorphism, and assert the moral attributes of the Deity, his justice, benevolence, mercy, and rectitude, to be of the same nature with these virtues in human creatures? . . . Epicurus's old questions are yet unanswered.

There is indeed a finality in nature, continues Philo, but it is purely biological and non-moral: the preservation of the individual and the propagation of the species.[93] (It will be useful to note the

[92] Cf. Vernière, *op. cit.*, II, 646–648.

[93] In Part XI, Philo declares, "The whole presents nothing but the idea of a blind nature, impregnated by a great vivifying principle, and pouring forth from her lap, without discernment or parental care, her maimed and abortive children." This concept, which is that of modern naturalism, grew out of biological developments between 1745 and 1760. It was also evolved in the writings of Maupertuis and La Mettrie, and especially in the *Lettre sur les aveugles* and the *Rêve de d'Alembert* of Diderot.

ethical import of the word "nature" here). Now Cleanthes replies briefly. He accuses Philo of having revealed his real, anti-religious intention. "If you can . . . prove mankind to be unhappy or corrupted, there is an end at once of all religion. For to what purpose establish the natural attributes of the Deity, while the moral are still doubtful and uncertain?" Not so, intervenes Demea; the pious divines have proven that "this world is but a point in comparison of the universe; this life but a moment in comparison of eternity. The present evil phenomena, therefore, are rectified in other regions, and in some future period of existence." Cleanthes, however, objects on the grounds of logic: no cause can be known but from its effects, no hypothesis proved but from the apparent phenomena. The only way to prove divine benevolence is to embrace the system of optimism, to deny the misery and wickedness of man—which he proceeds to do. Now Philo intervenes, warning Cleanthes that it is he who is heading into total scepticism, by allowing no foundation for religion without the happiness of human life (that is, without the accord of human and divine wills and concept of justice). Besides, even if there is more happiness than misery, the essential question is untouched: Why is there any misery at all in the world? Nothing can solve Epicurus's dilemma, except the assertion "that our common measures of truth and falsehood are not applicable to [these subjects]. There is no view of human life or of the condition of mankind, from which, without the greatest violence, we can infer the moral attributes [of God], or learn that infinite benevolence, conjoined with infinite power and infinite wisdom, which we must discover by the eyes of faith alone." In Part XI Philo again concludes, "we have no more reason to infer that the rectitude of the Supreme Being resembles human rectitude than that his benevolence resembles the human. Nay, it will be thought that we have still greater cause to exclude from him moral sentiments, such as we feel them, since moral evil, in the opinion of many, is much more predominant above moral good than natural evil above natural good."

The key is given in the closing words of Demea.

Hold! hold! cried Demea: Whither does your imagination hurry you? I joined in alliance with you, in order to prove the incomprehensible nature of the Divine Being, and refute the principles of Cleanthes, who would measure everything by a human rule and standard. But I now find you running into all the topics of the greatest libertines and infidels; and betraying that holy cause, which you seemingly espoused. Are you secretly, then, a more dangerous enemy than Cleanthes himself?

And Cleanthes adds, "And are you so late in perceiving it?"

In view of all this perplexity, it is not surprising that a few writers, on both sides, threw up their hands and declared the problem insoluble. Saint-Martin and Delisle de Sales admitted this final *reductio*. Of course, this was also Bayle's "conclusion," but doubtless not his ultimate intention.[94]

It was also Voltaire's conclusion, and his sincere one. Probably no one, in the eighteenth century, was more greatly tormented by the problem of theodicy. This is to be expected, in view of his great uncertainties about providence. For many, the question was a problem in logic or polemics. Bayle enjoyed the logical game, the pleasure of tormenting his opponents. Voltaire felt a genuine metaphysical anguish. Once again, we can observe in the course of his thought the terrible perplexities that beset the eighteenth century humanist. Voltaire's Natural Law ethics needed a moral universe for its ground, in order to avoid the equivocality inherent in the word "natural." In his earlier years, he had preferred to shrug off the problem. A facile optimism reveals itself in the extrapolation from his own pleasurable life to a generalized belief in the preponderance of good and the benefits of progress (*Le Mondain*, 1736). By 1738 he is admitting the reality of evil and its equilibrium with good: "Le malheur est partout, mais le bonheur aussi." [95] In the *Traité de métaphysique* (1734), he had worked hard to free God from the onus of evil. His attempt only forced him into a moral relativism that divorces God from all our human concepts.[96] *Le monde comme il va* (1746) is still optimistic, though the doubts are more insistent. In *Zadig* (1747) we see him struggling, desperately now, to maintain his confidence. The parable of the angel Jesrad, explaining apparent or partial evil

---

[94] *Oeuvres diverses*, III, 683, IV, 17.

[95] *Discours en vers sur l'homme*, Premier Discours.

[96] *Ed. cit.*, p. 16. Much later, in the *Questions sur l'Encyclopédie* (1777), he expressed a similar view, but not from the optimistic position. Our error, he writes in the article "Bien," is to attribute human qualities of goodness and justice to God (XVII, 567–581). A moral universe is then merely an anthropomorphic projection. This later pessimism contrasts sharply with his previously quoted assertion, that God's justice must correspond to ours.

as ultimate good in God's unrevealed design, seems directly inspired by Abbadie, whose writings Voltaire knew well. Zadig's
final "but" may be interpreted as a conclusion of prudent scepticism, or as something akin to Job's intellectual refusal, even as
he bows to the fact that God is God. Voltaire has not gone so far
as the rebellion of Ivan Karamazov's "even if." Even if he were
wrong, even if Father Zossima's way were the way of salvation, Ivan
would not accept salvation at the price of evil, suffering and wrong
done to the innocent, and in exchange for implied acceptance of
such a world of God. Voltaire will finally have to choose (to use
Camus's phrase) between the realm of grace and the realm of
justice. As a humanist, his decision, despite his agony, could not
be in doubt. But it was complicated and obscured by his desire to
retain the sacred (a moral world of God) as a support and guarantee for the human. Thus Zadig both accepts the divine plan and
protests against it. Why should it have to be done this way? Why
should good and justice have to be brought about through evil
and injustice? These agonizing questions are the implications of
Zadig's "but," to which Voltaire knows there can never be an
answer.

The conclusion to *Memnon* (1750) shows him to be further
shaken. The world is *not* exactly an insane asylum, "mais il en
approche." One may have the best intentions, and still everything
may go wrong. Yes, *tout est bien,* if we speak of the universe as a
whole, an angel reassures Memnon. And the latter's reply, which
closes the story, cannot help recalling the speech of Diderot's
Saunderson, in the *Lettre sur les aveugles,* which Voltaire had
read the year before even though he had refuted it in his letter of
acknowledgement. "Ah!, I shall believe that only when I am no
longer one-eyed."

For many reasons—personal, political, historical and philosophical—Voltaire was compelled to abandon optimism in the fifties,
even as a decade or so earlier, he had found himself forced to renounce moral freedom. As early as 1751, in the mischievous
epistle, "Les deux tonneaux," he portrays God as a capricious
being, needing to do something to keep from boredom, arranging
and disarranging his little system.

> Il met la fièvre en nos climats,
> Et le remède en Amérique.

God has two barrels, containing good and evil, and both rain down on all.[97]

Although Voltaire was already cutting loose from optimism before the Lisbon earthquake, that event had a compelling and dramatic effect on him, provoking his *Poème sur le désastre de Lisbonne* (1756), which in turn aroused Rousseau to make an earnest and detailed rejoinder in his "Lettre sur la Providence." The central theme of the *Poème* is that providence may well exist, but it certainly ignores the well-being of man on earth. He urges us to pity men, the eternal butt of "useless pains." Bayle's paradox has won:

> Direz-vous: C'est l'effet des éternelles lois
> Qui d'un Dieu libre et bon nécessitent le choix?

What has happened in Lisbon is not just. The Leibnizian optimist not only insults human pain, but condemns us to a despairing philosophy of necessity. "We are then only wheels that make the great machine run; we are no more precious in God's eyes than the animals who devour us." [98]

Voltaire is torn. He asserts that man does not have an exceptional status, and yet condemns optimism because it implies that he does not. In the evolution of his thinking, he inclines more and more to a kind of materialistic naturalism in which he insists on making room for God, guarantor of value, shield against nihilism. As a believer in God and a humanist, he cannot join the atheistic materialist in his intellectual acceptance of evil in the universe. He opposes both philosophies (atheism, optimism) that accept evil, whence the impasse. At the same time he takes something from each: God from the optimist, an impersonal world-machine from the materialist; and the two are irreconcilable.

Voltaire is further tormented because he cannot conceive how evil can be of no concern to this God he must intellectually admit. The materialist can point to an indifferent universe, but an indifferent God seemed to Voltaire like none, so far as our living and

---

[97] Epître LXXXIV, *Oeuvres*, X, 360–362. Cf. the abbé Dulaurens, who bitterly accuses God of treating us as his toys. (*Portefeuille d'un philosophe*, 1770, I, 135).

[98] This is not literally correct. What Leibniz affirms is that "the happiness of reasonable beings is God's unique purpose," and that "God's affection for any created thing is proportioned to the value of the thing." (*Théodicée*, par. 120, 124.)

our values are concerned. He later admitted precisely this in his *Histoire de Jenni* (1775).[99]

> I care no more about him than he does about me. . . . He has no more jurisdiction over me than a canon of Windsor has over a member of our Parliament. Then I am a god to myself; I'll sacrifice the whole world to my fancies, if I have a chance to; I am without law, I consider only myself; if other beings are sheep, I'll make myself a wolf, if they are chickens, I'll make myself a fox.

The opening to the viewpoints of atheistic materialism and moral nihilism is ready made, and Voltaire practically falls into it, in his picture of a universe with no law except violence and the survival of the strong.[100] He does not embrace the outlook he paints—he will always have to struggle not to—but others in his time will.

Here Voltaire borders on a profound tragic perception—man is a stranger in a world not made for his categories. The ultimate question in Voltaire's writings, one which comes to a notable focus in *Candide* (1759), is what basis men can have for action, in a world which Pascal had correctly painted as one of uncertainty, folly, vice and injustice—and from which he, unlike Pascal, excludes the realm of grace, which alone had saved Pascal from the nihilism he, too, had sensed with fear and anguish. In *Candide* Voltaire gives up the hope of finding a rational explanation of what happens here. Intent, action and result are not logically related. Neither the Gods nor men favor the good. The virtuous Jacques is drowned in Lisbon harbor; but the scoundrel (and he alone, aside from the two heroes) is saved, because he is strong. True, when another ship goes down, its wicked captain is punished; but Martin asks whether it was necessary for the innocent passengers to die, too.

This feeling of waste and irrationality is close to the tragic perceptions of a Sophocles or a Shakespeare. But Voltaire does not despair. The quixotic realm of justice, like that of grace, is

[99] XXI, 572–573. This is in contrast to his position in the *Traité de métaphysique* (1734) in which, determined to exculpate God, he had argued that we cannot put ourselves in God's place, and say he is just or unjust, any more than we can say that he is square, or blue; we have no idea of God's justice. (Ch. 2, *réponse*.)

[100] *Poème sur le désastre de Lisbonne, Oeuvres*, IX, 474; also article "Guerre." Sometimes Voltaire seems to make a policeman of God; this, too, fails to satisfy the difficulties of the problem of evil or of God's goodness and justice.

an illusion. Yet a limited realm of virtue and justice, one relative to our human condition, is within the compass of man's creative powers. This is Candide's garden. Voltaire's irony, the mark of man's transcendence over the world which crushes him, saves him from the abyss which he has skirted. It allows Voltaire to re-affirm man's true dignity: self-awareness, a power of thought which enables him (as *Micromégas* and *Lisbonne* had already affirmed) to measure the world in which he is lost, a limited ability to create his own destiny in cooperation with others. The area of coincidence with Pascal, and the ultimate, complete divergence, are clear.

The *Poème sur le désastre de Lisbonne* is Voltaire's crucial statement on these issues, and perhaps his most significant philosophical work. After this, we need not follow him in detail, as his pessimism deepens with the years. There are variations, as there are also with his hope for an immortality that will rectify matters.[101] He may state absolutely that God is the author of evil;[102] or write, "I shall always remain somewhat embarrassed about the origin of evil; but I shall suppose that the good Orosmane, who has made everything, was not able to do better." [103] But always this problem hovers over him like a dark cloud, affecting not only his humor but the shape of his thinking. In his last years, Voltaire tends to accept a pronounced "fatalism": all is necessary, my life, my thoughts, my will, all that exists, evil, and even God. "I cannot escape from this circle." There is no other explanation for evil; God is responsible, but not to blame.[104] Partly out of the need to cope with this metaphysical problem, Voltaire, the mocker of metaphysics, is driven to deprive man of autonomy and responsibility.[105] Yet he realizes the danger of his own conclusions, and warns that a system of necessity must not lead to atheism, which is destructive of human society.[106]

---

[101] *Oeuvres*, XXVI, 319–322 (1765), XVIII, 459–460 (1771).

[102] *L'Ingénu* (1767), XXI, 274.

[103] *Il faut prendre un parti* (1772), XXVIII, 539. In *L'Histoire de Jenni* (1775) he goes back to the idea of inevitable effects of general laws, but admits this does not entirely excuse God.

[104] *Lettres de Memmius à Cicéron* (1771), XXVIII, 450–451. Also XXX, 473 (1777); *Dictionnaire philosophique*, article "Puissance."

[105] *De l'âme* (1774), XXIX, 340–341.

[106] *Fragments sur l'Inde* (1773), XXIX, 170. I have already referred several times to Morize's excellent account of Voltaire's change of heart towards optimism, in his *Introduction to Candide*. Morize emphasizes that Voltaire's change was gradual, but already in progress during Mme du Châtelet's lifetime, in spite of her

We can summarize the debate by recalling the principal positions. For some, there is no real evil, or only partial and apparent evil. For many more, evil is real, but caused by man, and by necessary and good physical laws. This was the most widespread attitude, in the second half of the century. It allowed the possibility of "progress." For Rousseau, however, evil was, paradoxically, the very result of progress. From the Newtonian viewpoint, this position answered the question, why, if there is order and harmony in the world of nature, they are lacking in the world of men. "The answer seemed clear," writes Alexandre Koyré; "disorder and disharmony were man-made, produced by man's stupid and ignorant attempt to tamper with the laws of nature or even to suppress them and to replace them by man-made rules. The remedy seemed clear: let us go back to nature, to our own nature and live and act according to its laws." [107] We must, of course, distinguish the radically different concepts of "going back to nature" of Rousseau, on the one hand, and of a Diderot or a Morelly, on the other. "Nature" could so easily mean different things, to different men. The important point is that the new "scientific" outlook, favorable to a return to the laws of nature as a solution to human problems, really involved another type of "optimism." As our exploration of eighteenth century ideas progresses, it will become apparent that to a certain extent the philosophy of optimism, defeated in its metaphysical and theological forms (though destined to be revived near the end of the century), is transmuted into a disguised secular shape. It will appear as a faith in the goodness of nature, or of natural laws, and form a sharp dichotomy with distrust of nature, or at least of human nature. We see it already in Mandeville, whose belief that apparent evil produces good might almost be termed a secular theodicy, were he not too cynical

adherence to the doctrine. Morize should be supplemented by the briefer but more philosophical analysis of J. R. Carré, in "Voltaire philosophe," p. 544 ff. Carré points out that Voltaire borrows from both Bayle and Leibniz, and combats both. God exists, but is unknowable. He accepts both the contingency of the world (the source of evil) and finalism (the hand of God). He refuses to reduce evil to moral evil, or sin, which, inaccessible to observation and reason, is not a part of philosophy.

I have been reminded that Voltaire was still treated as an optimist by Alès as late as 1758. This may well have been the crowning blow, adding to Voltaire's exasperation.

[107] "The Significance of the Newtonian Synthesis," *Archives internationales d'histoire des sciences*, XXIX: 309.

to believe that all is good. The economists, following Montesquieu, try "to oblige minds to see in social phenomena movements depending on a determinism which, when its secret is discovered, will allow the beneficent construction of a social art." [108] We have only to adapt our institutions to natural laws. One of the outstanding exponents of this secular optimism was the marquis de Chastellux. In his widely read *De la félicité publique* (1772), we see how the Newtonian heritage favored this kind of "naturalistic optimism." All in nature is part of a cosmic harmony; evil and error, consequently, are the necessary antecedents to good. D'Holbach also assures us that nature, "through unforeseen causes and hidden relations, draws concord from discord, happiness even from unhappiness . . . By dint of falling the child learns to support himself, to walk, to avoid dangers: by suffering from his errors, man becomes wiser and succeeds in curing himself of them." [109] Not that d'Holbach's optimism really trusts nature; at least, not that of men living in society. The power of formative, even repressive institutions is necessary to keep nature from spoiling herself! None the less, statements such as these resemble the outpourings of sentimental deists who revived providentialism. Volney, for instance, opens his *La loi naturelle* (1793) by defining the law of nature as a uniform order according to which God regulates the universe: "the order which his wisdom presents to the senses and reason of mankind," to lead them "towards happiness and perfection." That such a philosophy had its moral applications, and that it led to moral difficulties, is already obvious from these two chapters.

But the controversy over evil did not stop here. It grew more subtly logical, the efforts to disculpate God became more complex. And so we have seen that a third group of writers accepted evil as a necessary and independent reality; a fourth gave up the riddle as beyond our understanding. On the other side, materialists either denied the cosmic existence of the categories of good and evil, and thereby denied the significance of the entire problem, or else tried to pin complete responsibility on God, the First Cause. In both cases, the ethical bond between man and God is dissolved.

---

[108] G. Leroy, *Histoire des idées sociales*, p. 10.
[109] Quoted by Charles Frankel, *The Faith of Reason*, p. 68. See *ibid.*, p. 57-74, for an excellent discussion of optimism in relation to the idea of progress.

We are left in an amoral universe, liberated from supra-human imperatives.

For the Christian and for the moderate deist, the problem of evil was a thorn and a torment. The faith of the one and the moral world of the other could not triumph in men's minds while this challenge remained unanswerable. In professing that the world is rationally ordered, they were obliged to accept the corollary, that it is so ordered as to meet the needs of reasonable beings. This could not be established, and they were ultimately forced to admit as much. For the atheists and materialists, on the other hand, the problem of evil was an unsurpassed weapon which they used to demolish the bonds that linked man in servitude to God, and prevented him from creating his own destiny, in accordance with reason and nature.

It was, in fact, the radical members of this group who, replacing God by nature, called upon mankind, far more literally than the adherents of the second attitude I have summarized above, to reverse man-made rule (or God-made rule) and to go back to nature. A very few proclaimed and carried out the consequence that Bayle had earlier foreseen. If God is the author of evil, Bayle had queried, why should we not find authorization in the model, and follow suit? [110] And Montesquieu, also in the early years of the century, had written, "If there is a God, my dear Rhédi, he must necessarily be just; for, if he were not, he would be the worst and most imperfect of all beings." [111] Power, without justice, can only be evil. Both these statements were warnings of trouble ahead for the eighteenth century humanists. Without a just God, they warn, there can be no metaphysical basis for ethics.

There was none left then, for the atheist. But at least men were free to build one to their own measure. This was the very object of their campaign. But could they? This was the great challenge that the anti-Christian *philosophes* took up, and which they failed to meet.

[110] *Oeuvres diverses*, III, 307.
[111] *Lettres persanes* (1721). *Lettre* LXXXIII.

Three

MAN'S PLACE

"In doubt to deem himself a god or beast;
In doubt his mind or body to prefer."—POPE

FOR THE purpose of analysis and discussion, we are obliged to separate into semi-discrete units questions which were closely related in the minds of eighteenth century thinkers. In treating the problems raised in the two preceding chapters, we were, of course, dealing with man's place in the universe. But this question also posed itself in these more direct terms: Is man an exception in the natural world? From most ancient times, through the Greeks and the Middle Ages, man had endowed nature with his own modes of feeling. From Galileo on, the separation begins. Materialism recognizes only matter and motion. For Berkeley and Hume, as Whitehead says, the scents of the rose exist only in the poet's mind. It is a dull world, indifferent to man. But the eighteenth century discovery of man's situation was ambivalent. Although for some it meant precisely this existence as an alien in a world without values, for many more (including, paradoxically, the first group), it signified his removal from an exceptional status and his total absorption into the natural world—that is, into the order of physically existing things and the laws which determine their existence and action. Paradoxically again, it was in part through this natural world that they hoped to justify a value system that (according to the more radical thinkers) did not exist in the world.

For the "extreme" providentialists, the query, "Is man an exception in the natural world?" was already answered, as it was in the Catholic orthodoxy. For others, a belief in the "general" providence of God, or disbelief in either of the terms of this phrase, easily entailed the refusal to make man an exception to the order of things, created or eternal. At the same time, this refusal did not necessarily imply a denial of man's superiority, as determined by his position in the chain of beings.

It is difficult to determine to what extent the particular problem of providence, and the attitude one took towards it, fostered the more general conclusion, and to what extent the attitude toward providence (or man's relation to God) was, conversely, a consequence of a general change in the Occidental outlook upon man and his destiny. Doubtless cause and effect are inextricable. The march of physical and astronomical science had overthrown the Christian cosmos with its hierarchy, and opened up an infinite universe, ordered by laws universally and uniformly applicable.[1] The development of the biological sciences, in the 1740's notably, revealed in dramatic fashion the inherent dynamism of matter, the possibility of organic evolution and the intimate relation between various forms of animal life.[2] In addition, the growing resistance to the Christian reading of human destiny led, by a pendulum effect, to the proclamation of contrary positions on as many points as possible.[3] The resultant movement of ideas tended strongly to the integration of man within the general fold of nature, and within the animal kingdom in particular. This shift in the view of man's position was fraught with momentous ethical consequences. Shaftesbury foresaw this clearly. "For if once we allow a subordination in his [man's] case; if Nature herself be not for man, but man for Nature; then must man, by his good leave,

[1] See A. Koyré, *From the Closed World to the Infinite Universe*, Preface and Introduction.

[2] A. Vartanian, "Trembley's Polyp, La Mettrie and eighteenth century French materialism;" B. Glass, "Maupertuis and the Beginning of Genetics;" and L. G. Crocker, "Diderot and Eighteenth Century French Transformism."

[3] As one apologist wrote, "Such is the hatred of our *philosophes* for religion, Monsieur, that they would rather degrade themselves and recognize between themselves and beasts only an accidental difference, than not to combat the Revelation which so clearly establishes the essential superiority of man over the brute." (Hayer, *La religion vengée*, VI, 288 ff.)

submit to the elements of Nature, and not the elements to him." [4]
Man becomes an accident of nature's productivity, unimportant,
contingent, doomed to extinction. His actions are as much events
in the natural world as an eclipse of the sun. He is not, in consequence, qualitatively differentiated from the rest of nature.

The pattern for the naturalistic outlook had been furnished to
the eighteenth century by Spinoza—a writer whom few took
the trouble to understand, but from whom many borrowed according to their taste.

> Most persons who have written about the affects and man's
> conduct of life seem to discuss, not the natural things which
> follow the common laws of nature, but things which are out-
> side her. They seem indeed to consider man in nature as a
> kingdom within a kingdom. For they believe that man disturbs
> rather than follows her order; that he has an absolute power
> over his own actions; and that he is altogether self-determined.
> They then proceed to attribute the cause of human weakness
> and changeableness, not to the common power of nature, but
> to some vice of human nature, which they therefore bewail,
> laugh at, mock, or, as is more generally the case, detest. . . .[5]
> It is impossible that a man should not be a part of nature and
> follow her common order. . . .[6]
> . . . But the laws of nature have regard to the common order
> of nature of which man is a part. . . . As I said in the Preface
> to the Third Part, I consider human affects and their properties
> precisely as I consider other natural objects. . . .[7]

It is not difficult to see how the eighteenth century materialist,
reading passages with such broad implications, could find every
type of conduct equally justified by *nature;* he had then the choice
of stopping there, or of seeking other moral criteria.

The revival of a naturalistic conception of man created deep
problems for the eighteenth century ethical humanist. While the
few amoralists could embrace it wholeheartedly, and the many
Christians could denounce it with equal fervor, the liberal and
humanistic *philosophes* were again caught in an anguishing
dilemma. They wished to construct a humanistic ethics on the
basis of Natural Law, or man's moral nature and needs—all of

[4] *Characteristicks,* II, 302.
[5] *Ethic,* p. 204–5.
[6] *Ibid.,* p. 354.
[7] *Ibid.,* p. 337.

which are singular and distinguishing traits of mankind; and yet they also wished to assure his re-entry into the common realm of nature and his submission to the rule of its laws. We shall, in the course of this study, observe the conflicts that arose in consequence of this dilemma and the efforts to reconcile its two horns. In the case of Diderot, as we shall see, it produced a split or dual ethical philosophy that is understandable only in the light of this general background.

The problem also involved human reason. No one could deny that man's reason enables him, to an extent, to control natural events and environment. But is his reason something unique in kind, partaking more of the nature of God than of animals? This the naturalist and the materialist were reluctant to admit, because it led to the disruption of the post-Newtonian world-machine and the imposition of supernaturalism (therefore of Christianity) in all spheres of human life. The dilemma is clear. The more we study ourselves, writes a modern biologist, Hans Zinsser, the more we discover "emotional, ethical desires, and moral impulses—love, justice, pity—that have no obvious relation to mere animal existence." Even if man is unique in certain ways (a proposition generally accepted in the eighteenth century except for a few extreme materialists), does this take him outside of the natural and the animal realm, into one which is his alone? Do his unique traits place him under a law—descriptive, if not normative —that is quite separate from the other laws of nature, belonging to a distinct realm of spirituality and moral freedom? To many *philosophes* this seemed a dangerous notion, since it again involved admission of non-physical, even of a supernatural realm of being. To make man an exception would be to destroy the hope, the intellectual outlook and direction, the basic assumption of the new philosophy. Just as there are universal rational laws which determine the physical world, so it must be with the social and moral world. While man has some laws peculiar to his activities, these are specialized forms of a body of general laws governing all of nature. A rational (therefore natural) society and life would be indicated by discovering these laws—though not many really believed that man could in this way alone become the complete master of his fate, for as Rousseau and others said, natural phenomena are rigorously necessary and identical, human phenomena are not.[7a]

A good example of the dilemma can be seen in Montesquieu. In the *Esprit des lois,* he reduces human law, in political and social realms, to a special phase of natural law. Laws are "the necessary relationships that derive from the nature of things." Yet he recognizes in man a unique understanding of political processes, free will and foresight, and allows the human law-maker some power to swerve natural processes to his chosen ends. However in Montesquieu nature ultimately triumphs over human will and intent, so that one may properly speak of his "pessimism." [8] This caused him to misinterpret the essential character of the differences, which he ably perceived, between cultures. "Instead of explaining their history by reference to human reason," writes R. G. Collingwood, "he thought of it as due to differences in climate and geography. Man, in other words, is regarded as a part of nature, and the explanation of historical events is sought in the facts of the natural world." History becomes anthropology, a natural history of man, in which institutions appear not as the free events of reason in the course of its development, "but as the necessary effects of natural cause." Human life is treated much as the life of plants, and historical change becomes merely "the different way in which one single and unchangeable thing, human nature, reacts to different stimuli." [9] There is probably a larger measure of truth in Montesquieu's view than Collingwood admits; but he is basically correct in stating that Montesquieu overemphasized external conditions and diminished the power of reason *in* human nature. In this matter, the Physiocrats followed closely Montesquieu's initial assumptions, but their firm optimism gave hope for the rational ordering of society within the ample and beneficent law of nature.

The controversy over suicide is of peculiar value to us in that

[7a] Grotius was among the first to develop the view that the world is governed by objective laws, which are intelligible and independent of divine will. The latter fact makes them understandable to human reason, since human reason is a part of the system, and there are no supra-rational directives. Hobbes maintained that the social world is subject to mechanical laws, similar to those of physical nature.

[8] See Gilbert Chinard, "Montesquieu's historical pessimism," *Studies in the history of culture,* p. 161–172.

[9] *The Idea of History,* p. 78–79.

it posed the problem of man's place in two distinct, yet conjoined ways: his relation to the totality of things (which we examined in the first chapter), and to nature around and "below" him. In our earlier analysis, we observed the conflict that ensued for the humanistic *philosophe*. We noted that the course of argumentation induced him to justify suicide by denying any special relation between man and God, and also any special status or value of human life in the cosmos. His conclusion was that we are subject to the same laws and evaluations as all other natural creatures.

But precisely on this score there developed the most interesting of reversals. As the controversy unfolded, it was the apologists who insisted on the propriety of man's following the general law of nature, from which he had no right to make himself an exception. The universal natural law of all sentient beings is self-preservation, not self-slaughter. It is unnatural for us to hate our lives, and so it is wrong. Suicide, they contended, takes man outside of the law of nature, makes him a law unto himself. On the other side, the ethical humanists had to struggle hard in their endeavor to keep the act of suicide within the general laws of nature from which they constantly refused man exemption. To save the situation, they tried to show that man's occasional exceptions to these laws are, in a larger sense, within them. Man knows laws, can therefore use them, and escape from them. But in another sense, then, man *is* a law unto himself. Only vaguely did they perceive the confusion between "law" in the sense of an empirical generalization and "law" in the normative sense, as used in the term "Natural Law."

Montesquieu's Usbek (in the seventy-sixth of the *Lettres persanes*) puts all of man's acts within the order of things. "Do I disturb the order of providence when I change the modifications of matter, and when I make a ball square that the first laws of motion, that is to say, the laws of creation and conservation had made round? . . . I may disturb all of nature as I please without anyone being able to accuse me of opposing providence." The universe, then, will have as much order and perfection after his death as before. Hume also maintains that man is an intimate part of the order of things, which tolerates no exceptions to its universal laws. But then he goes on to argue, like Montesquieu, that animals (and man in particular) are constantly interfering with the operations of nature. Therefore whatever we do must be within the order of nature, or of God. Suicide is no more impious than agriculture. Whatever is, is natural whether it follows nature's own operations or violates them. Helvétius declares that the basic motive—pleasure and pain—can lead either to life or death, with equal naturalness. La Mettrie, despite his opposition to suicide, concedes that under certain conditions, it is, precisely, "unnatural" to want to go on living. D'Holbach asserts that since all our acts are necessary and determined, this one, too, cannot be outside the determinacy of nature.[10]

There is obviously the seed of moral nihilism in the positions of Montesquieu and Hume. All acts are reduced to equivalence and justified, at least from the viewpoint of nature and God. The reasoning as to naturalness may be used to justify murder as well as self-destruction. Montesquieu's statement about a man's death not disturbing the universal order or perfection tallies exactly with Sade's defense of murder—thus carrying out the prediction which Bergier had made. Montesquieu seeks to elude the consequence by positing a providential order. However, since we may freely change it, as the atheists, including Sade, pointed out, it loses meaning.

The logical virtuosity required by the effort to include suicide in the non-human natural order is of great significance. The materialists preferred to overlook what was purely human (moral valuation, will or free will) in men's actions, in order to avoid the creation of a unique and distinct human realm which, they feared, would counter their naturalism and lend comfort to mystical outlooks. They would not see that while refusing to make man an exception in nature, they none the less did so, by giving to him alone mastery of his fate. They would not acknowledge that if man does have and is entitled to this autonomy, it can only be because he is the one exception to the mechanical laws of nature, and, though he is within the natural order, transcends it. In fact, it is because of this uniqueness that he has not only the right, but the *power* to escape from fixed, instinctual patterns of behavior.[11]

[10] Here again, Bergier's refutation points out that if evil is natural and necessary, then all crimes are equally justifiable.

[11] L. G. Crocker, *loc. cit.,* p. 71. Also, p. 72, n. 73: "Alone among the materialists La Mettrie was logically consistent; having reinstated man in nature, like Hume, he also refused to give him the special moral dignity of being privileged to decide his own fate."

Still another consequence of this dichotomous position was the paradox we noted earlier: those who wished to exalt man's dignity by making him the measure of ethical judgment, decried and depreciated his significance in the universal scheme. Like Hume, Montesquieu had written, in defense of suicide, that only our pride makes us think we are important in the universe. "We imagine that the annihilation of an object as perfect as we would degrade all of nature, and we cannot conceive that one man more or less in the world—what do I say?—that all men together, a hundred million heads like ours, are only a subtle and fine atom, which God perceives only because of his knowledge." [12] The Christians, on the other hand, in denying man autonomy, claimed that his acts were of exceptional significance and might disrupt God's plans, the order of things and the cosmic harmony.

Although the uniqueness of man was the ultimate import of the *philosophes'* position, only the most moderate of their group dared avow it. It ran counter to their general view of man's place, and would have led them right into the jaws of their enemy. This we can again clearly see in Voltaire's defense of determinism. It was part of his life-long struggle against the Christian hegemony, a struggle that involved, precisely, depriving man of such an exceptional rank. As a Deist, he puts us under the hand of God, but in an indifferent status. "Poor marionnettes of the eternal Demiurge, who do not know either why or how an invisible hand moves our springs, and then throws us and piles us up into the box." [13] "We are under the power of the eternal Being like the stars and the elements . . . we are little wheels of the immense machine of which he is the soul; he acts by general laws, and not by particular views." [14] It is understandable, then, and logical,

---

[12] *Lettres persanes* (éd. Adam), p. 198. The refutation, in the following letter, was added much later, from motives of prudence and increasing conservatism. (Cf. *ibid.*, p. X, 199 nb.) It is most curious that Sade quotes this passage at length (*Histoire de Juliette*, IV, 241), and in doing so, changes several words and phrases, notably the end, which he makes read, ". . . are only subtle and fine atoms, indifferent to nature." Since none of the editions of the *Lettres persanes* has this reading, the changes were doubtless willful.

[13] *Oeuvres*, XX, 181 ("Passions"). The analogy with Omar Khayyam is striking:

'Tis all a Chequer-board of Nights and Days
Where Destiny with Men for Pieces plays:
Hither and thither moves, and mates, and slays,
And one by one back in the Closet lays.

[14] *L'Ingénu*, XXI, 274.

that among Voltaire's arguments against freedom of the will, we should encounter this crucial sentence: "By what privilege might it be that man is not submitted to the same necessity as stars, animals, plants and all the rest of nature?"

For the *philosophes,* then, an avowal of man's uniqueness, in the sense of his transcending the common realm of nature and operating under a law peculiar to himself, was a conclusion not to be relished. We have only to read Hayer's refutation of Voltaire's last question, to see where the danger lay. Voltaire, says Hayer, should have pushed his inquiry further, and asked why man "should have *the privilege* of writing pretty verse, while horses cannot; why he should have the privilege of seeing and hearing, while stones do not. All of physical nature has a uniform course. . . . Wouldn't M. de Voltaire blush to pretend that a similar uniformity reigns in his actions?" [15] Voltaire may wish to lower himself to the condition of stones or beasts—this is Hayer's parting shot—but feeling and evidence rise up to defend Voltaire against himself.

Certain scientific, or quasi-scientific ideas were also of particular importance in directing the thinking of the *philosophes.* We must make brief mention of three of these.

One was the Condillacian psychology, which reduced mental activity to the faculties of sensation and memory, with the added processes of attention and comparison. It was pointed out that animals possessed these, as well as men (though with an important difference of degree). The materialists did not accept Descartes' belief that the mind can generate its own ideas, nor did they admit innate "structures" for utilizing sense-data in peculiarly human fashion, such as the self recognized by Locke, or the Kantian categories. Thought was reduced to physical operations.[16]

A second idea was the chain of being concept, which enjoyed almost universal currency in the eighteenth century. It could be used by the apologists and optimists to claim a special relationship with creatures higher than man, who finds himself between animal and angel, "placed on this isthmus of a middle state." But, as Arthur O. Lovejoy has amply demonstrated in his classic study, its chief implications tended "to lower man's estimate of his

[15] *Op. cit.,* VIII, 291–292.
[16] We shall return to this subject in our discussion of determinism.

cosmic importance and uniqueness." [17] Writers of naturalistic bent used it, then, to emphasize that we are part of the general order of nature, higher than other beings, but of the same clay. Maupertuis, for instance, describes the natural realm as that of a series of species blending into each other.[18] La Mettrie, Bonnet, Robinet and other scientists and scientific speculators (such as Diderot) found ever stronger reasons for integrating the human species into a dynamic and unfolding universe. The materialistic doctrine could exist on no other assumptions. Even Voltaire, who held God to be the creator of motion, remarked that existence depends on it, and that we are not the author of motion or its laws.[19] But if all is matter in motion, and its laws, then man possesses nothing distinguishing, like spirit or soul. Our constitution is *au fond* identical with the constitution of other beings.

The inevitable result of all this was the actual formulation of a theory of transformism, which, however, sprang more directly from the biological developments of the 1740's. Transformism is suggested by Maupertuis and de Maillet, perhaps by La Mettrie and Buffon, and sketched more dramatically by Diderot, in his *Pensées sur l'interprétation de la nature* (1753), as well as in unpublished writings. To quote Diderot only briefly: it is possible to conjecture

> that these elements [of animality] happened to unite, because it was possible for them to do so; that the embryo formed from these elements has passed through an infinite number of organizations and developments; that it has acquired, successively, motion, sensation, ideas, thought, reflection, consciousness, feelings, passions, signs, gestures, sounds, articulated sounds, a language, laws, sciences and arts. . . .[20]

The effect of this revolutionary notion was to derive man from *below*, rather than from *above*. To quote La Mettrie's phrases

[17] Dr. Lovejoy studies four immediate corollaries of the chain of beings concept: the equal importance of all links as opposed to anthropocentrism; man's relatively low position in the scale; the separation from animals by degree only (but Dr. Lovejoy does not develop the opposition to this idea); the tragi-comic discord in man, a dual being. *The Great Chain of Being*, ch. 6.

The theory of continuity, writes René Hubert, implied that "there was a real continuity among all living beings, that man was not endowed with exceptional faculties, heterogeneous to those of other beings, which might have led to treating him as an empire within an empire." (*Les sciences sociales dans l'Encyclopédie*, p. 168.)

[18] *Essai de cosmologie, Oeuvres*, I, 35.

[19] "Les veilles du comte de Chesterfield," *Oeuvres*, XXI, 584.

[20] *Oeuvres*, II, 57–58.

again, "nature has used only a single and same dough, in which she has merely varied the yeast," and "natural law establishes a resemblance among them [man and animals] rather than a difference."[21] Maupertuis expatiates on the varieties of men, and concludes that apes may be among these.[22] In one of the notes to his *Discours sur l'inégalité*, Rousseau also suggests that the ape may be a "savage man"—an idea later taken up by Monboddo, in England.[23] This line of thinking led inevitably to the later conclusions of Lamarck.[24] The danger of an evolutionary theory was immediately grasped by the Christian apologists. It did away with the notions of final causes and divine creation of man, and they attacked it with the weapon of ridicule.

Against this background of reality, the materialists attempted to erect a new ethics—human, clear-eyed, and without illusion—one that took into account, or reconciled, the conflicting demands of nature and of reason. Not so the moral nihilist. The nihilistic doctrine recognizes no anti-natural rational or moral claims of "human nature." Sade's "ethics" was to rest on a quasi-complete submergence into "nature."

> If it is true [he asks] that we resemble all the productions of nature, if we are not worth more than they, why persist in believing ourselves moved by different laws? Do plants and beasts feel pity, social duties, love of their neighbor? And do we see in nature any law except the supreme law of egoism? . . . what respect do you expect a man to have for laws that contradict all that nature has engraved in him?[25]

> The man who is sexually excited must be as free as an animal.[26]

[21] *L'Homme machine*, p. 99–100, 142.

[22] *Oeuvres*, II, 100. Evolution, based on scientific evidence as distinct from philosophical considerations, originated with Maupertuis. Cf. previously cited articles, and A. O. Lovejoy: "Some Eighteenth-Century Evolutionists," p. 238–251, 323–340.

[23] Cf. A. O. Lovejoy: "Monboddo and Rousseau," *Essays in the History of Ideas*, p. 38–61. It is not certain that this idea was connected with a theory of transformism.

[24] Lamarck concludes ". . . that man is entirely subjected to the laws of nature in his physical being; that he acts in conformity with these laws and by them; . . . that he is linked to the animals by organization, and that in this respect he offers . . . the term of perfection that nature has succeeded in giving to animal organization. . . ." (Quoted by Hastings, *Man and Beast in French Thought of the Eighteenth Century*, p. 171–172.)

[25] *Histoire de Juliette*, v, 128–129.

[26] *Ibid.*, v, 193. Man has no laws "other than those imprinted on minerals, plants and beasts" (v, 176–177). He does not have to follow nature's procedures—in this

The *philosophes*, a group with deeply humanistic inclinations, were often repelled by the extreme conclusions that were drawn from the logic of some of their ideas, or of similar ideas. We have already had occasion to observe how some of the consequences pointed out by the apologists as being implicit in their propositions, and angrily denounced by them as calumny, were indeed proclaimed by the most radical figures of the time. Consequently, many were shocked not only by their enemies, but also by some who must be said to have been in the same camp, fighting against Christianity and for naturalism. The road they were searching for, however, was one that would reconcile man's inclusion into nature with his possession of peculiar powers that were his alone.

Thus, Montesquieu, writing on suicide, finds that man is an exception, but that this is cosmically insignificant. Yet he later cries out against Spinoza, for making man an insignificant modification of matter. "I no longer know where to find this self which interested me so much; I am more lost in space than a drop of water in the sea. Why glory? Why shame? . . . [This modification] is in no way distinguished from being, and, in the universality of substance, the lion and the insect, Charlemagne and Chilperic have come and gone without distinction." [27] In this vague *malaise*, Montesquieu seems to have a premonition of the moral crisis of the twentieth century, which indeed has its roots in the eighteenth century re-evaluation of values.[28]

The conflict is even more striking in Diderot. To Sophie Volland he writes, "I like a philosophy which exalts mankind. To degrade it is to encourage men to vice." Yet this was precisely one

---

he is a free being—but it is only better to satisfy the profound motives of nature: egoism, passion, pleasure. Seen in this light, many of the so-called laws of nature, such as love of one's parents, are not such at all (v, 39). There is a paradoxical element in Sade's ethics, since he justifies his nihilism by an appeal from the "artificial" to the "natural," yet several times insists that we are free, and in no way bound by nature or her laws (IV, 231, 234, 250). The conflict is solved if we realize his meaning to be that the particular developments nature has worked out are null beside the particular forms we may wish to give her basic impulsions. Compare Hume on suicide.

[27] *Pensées, Oeuvres*, II, 343.

[28] Compare with Montesquieu's *Pensée* the words of the hero of a twentieth century novel: "Idiot, he said to himself, there you are getting into their filthy heroics, now! What difference can it make whether you are brave or a coward? And in whose eyes?" (Robert Merle: *Week-end à Zuydecoote*, n.d., Collection Pourpre, p. 122–123.)

result of the eighteenth century ethical revolution.[29] In the
very next line he adds, "When I have compared men to the immense space which is over their heads and under their feet, I
have made them ants that bustle about on an ant-hill. It seems to
me that their vices and their virtues, shrinking in the same proportion, are reduced to nothingness." [30] Both Voltaire and Diderot
were all their lives repelled by the extreme, and somewhat brutal
ideas of La Mettrie. Yet a significant part of their work accomplished the same reduction of man, and the radical side of Diderot,
which culminated in his great unpublished dialogues, is scarcely
distinguishable from the ethical viewpoints of La Mettrie. The
most significant challenge came with the publications of Helvétius'
De l'homme (1758), to which we shall return later in this chapter.

The general question of human distinctiveness tended to assume
concrete form around two great debates. We have already examined the discussion of suicide. The second controversy was far
more widespread and complex. It dealt in specific terms with the
relationship of man and animal. This controversy had begun in
the seventeenth century, as an attack against human vanity and
vices, and as an idealization of animals that was soon sharply
counteracted by the Cartesian automatism. The fortunes of these
phases of the man-animal debate need not concern us here. It
suffices to recall that the argument over the Cartesian theory of
animal automatism waxed strong in the first half of the eighteenth
century; then tapered off sharply as the advancing ideas of scientific
thinkers and materialists gave the whole subject a new direction and consistency, and a new importance. The distinctive
contribution of the eighteenth century was to weave the controversy into the more general conflict between naturalism and
Christianity, by making it a part of the larger question we have
been discussing in this chapter. Doubtless there was still some
desire to reprove man for his vanity, and also to advance the cause
of brutes; but this was peripheral to "the great debate." The two
opposing sides may be characterized as the detractors of man (in
varying degrees), and the defenders of man.[31]

[29] This statement of historical fact is not intended as a judgment as to where
man's dignity really lies.
[30] *Lettres à Sophie Volland*, I, 51.
[31] The most important eighteenth century writer who still was interested in the

The "detractors" started, then, with a common basic motive. Its accomplishment involved the repudiation of finalism, particularly the contention that animals (like all else) were designed for human benefit and use. It also denied the dogma that man is made in the image of God. The first thesis, which had been advanced by the optimistic providentialists, was ridiculed by Voltaire and a dozen other writers as a delusion of human vanity. The second was assailed by the general tactics of lowering man and raising the beasts. Human traits, such as love, loyalty, thought and foresight, were attributed to beasts; and it was argued that human conduct is often as instinctive as that of animals, and less efficient.[32]

In this process, the soul of the beast was one main issue. It was made clear that if we attributed thought to the beasts, then it followed that they, too, must possess an immortal soul.[33] If, on the other hand, they were judged to be purely mechanical, then there was every reason to affirm that man also was a machine. La Mettrie was the leader in this phase of the argument. Like La Mettrie, the more extreme materialists held this to be literally

subject largely in order to satirize man's smugness and the Cartesian theory was Voltaire. But behind his satire was his aversion to optimism, providentialism and Christianity. La Mettrie also delighted in satirizing and lowering man. "In what vile insects is there not almost as much *esprit* as in those who spend a learnedly puerile life observing them? . . . Their whole kingdom is, in truth, only a composite of more or less clever monkeys, at the head of whom Pope has placed Newton." (*Système d'Epicure*, p. 227–229). For a judicious (though incomplete) history of the entire discussion, see Hester Hastings, *Man and Beast in French Thought of the Eighteenth Century*. Some of the basic philosophical issues regarding the soul of man and animal receive deeper consideration in the study of Leonora Cohen Rosenfield, *From Beast-Machine to Man-Machine*. I shall, as far as possible, emphasize authors not treated by Dr. Hastings, and the general course of my analysis is rather different.

[32] *L'Homme machine*, p. 88 ff. La Mettrie insists on the many respects in which men are inferior to animals, though there is a certain part of paradox in this, and the desire to make a point. Dom Deschamps also explains how man's moral uniqueness is illusory, and reduces his advantages to the physical. (*Le vrai système*, p. 106, 145–146.) Both La Mettrie and Dom Deschamps say that it is proper to classify man as a plant (cf. *Système d'Epicure*, p. 234–235, *Vrai Système*, p. 188). Typical of the older tradition of deprecating man is J.-Fr. Bernard's dialogue, "Neptune et Saint-Antoine" (*Dialogues critiques et philosophiques*, 1730, p. 380–385). Man is pictured as inferior to fish, less free, and less enlightened in that fish do not err in choosing what is useful to them. However the new philosophical direction is also evident, in Bernard's view that man is an indistinguishable part of nature, to be judged in reference to nature, not to new aspirations, and is in no way privileged.

[33] Bayle, *Dictionnaire*, "Rorarius," Remarque E.

true; others merely made the point in order to put man and beast on the same footing.[34]

Most of the *philosophes,* however, admitted man's superiority, for this was not the *real* matter at issue. The nub of the conflict was, again, whether man is unique or whether he is but a somewhat differentiated item in nature's productions; and also, whether he has an unprivileged status in being or enjoys a special relation with God. Ultimately, the basis of values and ethics was implicated. Hume wrote that the life of a man "is of no greater importance to the universe than the life of an oyster." [35] Diderot also wrote, "The oyster who vegetates at the bottom of the seas is as perfect and as dear to nature as the arrogant biped who eats him!" Yet man, for Diderot, stands at the head of the animal world, and we shall have ample occasion to observe his dilemmas. "Reason, armed with a stone and a stick, is by itself stronger than all the animal instincts." [36] To degrade man and to magnify animal was, then, the tactics used for bringing them closer together.

It should be made clear that the so-called detractors of man were often, at least in their own minds, his defenders. It was characteristic of their humanism to assume that man would have more dignity if he were independent of God, and of supernatural directives or sanctions, than he would have if he enjoyed a "favored" status that made of him a means, and not an end. This is, after all, the crux of the eternal conflict between naturalism and supernaturalism. To achieve this purpose, it was necessary to integrate man completely into nature, to deprive him simultaneously of his uniqueness, yet—and here is where there was great variation— to maintain his superiority.

Let us look more closely at the effort of the materialists, which, as I have said, was towards a minimizing of this superiority. A whole line of writers, from those who, early in the century, penned anonymous manuscripts, through La Mettrie, Voltaire and Diderot, proposed ideas of this kind. Sabatier de Castres, a nihilistic anti-*philosophe* who wrote near the end of the period, was typical. Except for language and perfectibility [!], he declares, men

---

[34] For the intricacies of the argumentation, see Hastings, p. 19–63; Rosenfield, *op. cit.,* Part II, chap. 2.

[35] *Essay on suicide,* p. 10.

[36] *Oeuvres,* IV, 94–95.

are not superior to animals. There is more distance between a brilliant man and a stupid one, than there is between the highest animals and men. "The mind of animals differs from ours only by a little more or a little less." Both have sensitivity, memory and judgment; therefore both have reason.[37] Sabatier's development is, significantly, only an echo of Voltaire's, in the much earlier *Traité de métaphysique* (1734).

To maintain this viewpoint, the most powerful weapon of the materialists was the reduction of all our mental faculties to physical activity. To deny the soul or spirit or mind was to strike a fundamental blow at the supposed human uniqueness. Thus d'Argens gives man and beast similar "soul," but uses the equivalence to prove that matter, properly organized, can think.[38] There are, of course, degrees of complexity in material organization—this will be the central thesis of the greatest materialistic piece of the century, Diderot's *Le Rêve de d'Alembert* (1769); but these differences, which are of degree only, not of kind, account for all of nature's variations. La Mettrie's *L'Homme machine* (1748) advances the same view as that of d'Argens, but with much stronger scientific background, and also denies the uniqueness of our moral experience. La Mettrie pointed the way to Hartley, Diderot, and d'Holbach by reducing thought to motions of the brain, and explaining moral and mental activity in this fashion.[39]

In this type of argumentation, the materialists fell into a not uncommon logical fallacy. Thought may indeed be impossible without the physical activity of specialized nervous tissue. An indispensable antecedent to the occurrence of thought may be the motions of particles of the cerebral cortex. The next step, however, the reduction of thought, in its nature, to physical action and physical laws, is not implied in the premise. The materialists confused the cause of an effect with the nature of the effect; they mistakenly concluded that when you described the one, you were also describing the other. Thus if any perception or thought were described in purely physical terms to a creature unfamiliar with

[37] *Pensées et observations morales et politiques* (1794), p. 26–31.

[38] *Philosophie du bon sens* (1737), II, 76 ff.

[39] For Meslier's interesting contribution see *Testament*, p. 326–352. Many of his views can be found in the anonymous ms., "L'âme mortelle." D'Holbach defines human nature as that which distinguishes the species, but the traits he lists are (perhaps intentionally) not distinguishing. The superiorities he admits are of degree. (*Morale universelle*, 1820, I, 5–8.)

them, he could not possibly conceive them as they exist in our consciousness. Oddly enough, in another regard Diderot himself accused Helvétius of a similar logical error. As we shall shortly see, he blamed Helvétius for confusing the conditions of motivation with the actual nature of motivation.[40]

None the less, the reduction of the mental or spiritual activities of man to the level of physical motion which he shared with all other living beings was a cardinal point in the materialists' arsenal. "Man," writes d'Holbach, "is a purely physical being; moral man is only physical man considered from a certain point of view, that is to say, relatively to some of his ways of behaving, due to his particular organization. But isn't this organization the work of nature? Are not the movements and the behavior it is capable of physical?" Whether men are living in the most highly developed culture, or wandering like animals in the forest, they are no less submitted to the common laws of nature—it is still "the same animal," just as a butterfly changes its outer forms. Man, animal, vegetable: all follow the same inviolable laws of the recombinations of matter. These recombinations, in man, are such that he does have needs and laws peculiar to himself (very much as any higher animal is distinguished from a lower one). "Let us conclude that man has no reasons to think himself a privileged being in nature, he is subject to the same vicissitudes as all its other productions. His supposed prerogatives are founded only on an error." [41]

Logically, then, it was part of the tactics of this group to argue that man's superiority, which lies in his reflective powers, was only a matter of superior organic (therefore material) equipment. Bayle, Maupertuis and La Mettrie were among the early proponents of this idea.[42] For some, especially materialists like Diderot, the essential difference was in the brain itself. Our vaunted mind is only the functioning of specialized nerve cells.[43] Bonnet emphasized the sensual receptory apparatus, as well as the brain's finer organization.[44] For others, the difference lay in such

[40] See also his denial in *Pensées sur l'interprétation de la nature, Oeuvres*, II, 44.
[41] *Système de la nature*, I, 1–4, 86–7, 95–6.
[42] Cf. Rosenfield, p. 150, *et passim*.
[43] *Le Rêve de d'Alembert, passim*; see also La Mettrie, *L'Homme machine*, p. 74.
[44] *Palingénésie philosophique*, in *Oeuvres d'histoire naturelle et de philosophie*, VII, 133–137. Like Buffon, and against Rousseau, Bonnet declares that speech distinguishes man. Animals do remember and do compare sensations, but cannot

organs as the hands, the skeleton and the vocal instruments. The second viewpoint obtains in Bayle, La Mettrie and in Helvétius; the latter remarked that if we could give hands to horses, they would be as clever as men, and that if man had only hooves, he would still be a wild beast. La Mettrie claimed that if higher animals could not talk, it was for lack of organs of speech; and he did not despair of our being able some day to impart this gift to monkeys.[45] In either case, the result is the same. You may call animals machines, says Diderot, but then you will also have to say the same of men; actually, neither one is. The point is that both must be considered as like beings; and the developments of which matter—dynamic and self-patterning—is capable, are quite sufficient to explain the differences in degree.

The strongest foe of the detractors of man—strongest because of his scientific prestige—was Buffon. He not only removed man from the animal kingdom because of his immortal soul, but in particular assailed the theory that physical organization constitutes his difference. His comparison with the orang-outang was, in this regard, most effective. To be sure, man is an animal, but only in his physical organization. Buffon endeavors to demonstrate that in all other regards he must be deemed non-animal. It is by the internal qualities that we must judge, and here we encounter a complete separation. Man differs in the nature of his passions, joys and loves, though superficially they may seem alike. Furthermore, while animals have more feelings and sensations, they cannot compare them; they are conscious of present existence, but of that only. They have no memory, for memory is a succession of associated ideas, not just a recurrence of sensation. Language depends not on our unique organs, but on "a sequence of thoughts"; parrots speak words, but conceive no meaning. Alone

generalize in abstractions. If they could generalize they would not all do things in the same way. It is true that animals also have some signs, and can perform *"abstractions sensibles,"* but these produce no notions, or concepts. The failure lies in lack of power of attention, which depends on the organization of the brain. In the *Essai analytique* (VI, 130, etc.), Bonnet states that animals can develop what we now call conditioned reflexes, as when they learn to connect sounds and letters; but there is never any meaning.

[45] So in *L'Homme machine*, p. 77 ff. In *L'Homme-plante*, La Mettrie affirms that the human "soul," "which results visibly from organization" makes man "the king of animals," for it enables him alone to have language, social laws and morals. (Ed. Rougier, N. Y., p. 148–150.) J.-L. Carra attributed human superiority to a combination of posture, speech and brain. (*Système de la raison*, 1782, p. 113–115.)

man can use other animals, "because he has a reasoned project, an order of actions and a succession of means." Alone man makes progress from generation to generation, for the operations of animals are mechanical, while for us imitation is more difficult than originality, "because our soul is our own," and our body is all we have in common with others. Buffon's concept of *homo duplex* clearly divides the animal and the mental in man. He insists on the distinguishing moral and rational qualities of human societies, and derides the writings of Lesser and Réaumur on insects.[46] Finally, in the later *Epoques de la nature* (1778), he significantly points out that the present state of nature is "as much our work as its own."

The Christian apologists, of course, persistently attacked the *philosophes* for degrading man, frequently accumulating quotations from their works, quotations which may be epitomized by the following one: "There is nothing inside of man that distinguishes him from other animals."[47] The Christians were obliged, then, to demonstrate that there are such differences. Their analyses of human distinctiveness were clever and not devoid of truth. The most common argument, and the most acceptable to the large majority of the *philosophes* themselves, was moral experience. There is no apologist of man's distinctiveness who does not play upon this theme. Toward this claim it was possible to take several attitudes. Some *philosophes* insisted that animals also have a moral life, on their own plane. Others tried to evaporate the elements of uniqueness in our moral experience by reducing it to non-moral forms of motivation (self-preservation, interest, etc.); in other words, to make this distinctively human experience a special result of general natural laws. Extreme anarchists, like Sade, openly rejected the reality of moral experience itself, except, perhaps, as a form of induced illusion or habituation. But for most, the moral experience was real, and, at least in the form in which we know it, unique. Pufendorf had earlier made this clear, in a forceful statement of man's exclusive power to *produce* "moral entities." This, he says, is man's addition to things, for "moral entities" have no subsistence in themselves. They are

---

[46] *Oeuvres* (Corpus général), p. 10, 295–297, 329–350 (1749, 1753).

[47] Quoted by Hastings (p. 165) from the anonymous *Sentiments philosophiques sur la nature de l'âme*. Also Moreau, *Nouveau Mémoire pour servir à l'histoire des Cacouacs* (1757); Guy de Saint-Cyr: *Le catéchisme des Cacouacs* (1758), etc.

"certain modes, which intelligent beings attach to natural things or physical movements, with the view of directing and restricting the freedom of men's voluntary actions, and in order to put some order, propriety and beauty into human life." [48] And many, like Marmontel, claimed that moral experience constitutes a difference of kind, as well as of degree.

For the rest, the range of argumentation was wide. Often these defenders of man denied the supposition that his superiority is due primarily to the possession of hands or vocal organs—and thereby showed greater scientific accuracy than some of their opponents. By some, the animal was denied anything that resembled human faculties.[49] In England, Wollaston had emphasized the brutes' momentary perception, cut off from the past and the future, from causes and circumstances, and claimed their suffering was different from ours. "Time and life without thinking are next neighbors to nothing, to no time and no life." [50] Shaftesbury does not admit animals to be moral beings, and in making his exclusion, gives us a significant clue to his concept of virtue; moral creatures are those only that "can have the notion of a public interest" and an idea or feeling of right and wrong in relation to it.[51] Others, however, granted some thought, feeling and will to beasts, but insisted on a difference in kind that made man distinct in essence.[52] Burlamaqui agrees that both men and animals act necessarily according to their ideas of what is good and useful for them, but claims sole possession for man of (abstract) reason, comparison, judgment, awareness of past and future, cause and effect, and consequent freedom from the limitation to instinctual behavior.[53] Mendelssohn distinguishes animals, as more perfect for their functions, from men, who are perfectible.[54] This is perhaps a modification of Montesquieu: animals, affirms the latter, are governed by the invariable laws of the physical realm, to which man is also subject in his physical being. But man is sub-

[48] *Le Droit de la nature et des gens* (1672), I, 3–4. Pufendorf does not deny a "natural moral state," but sets up an "accessory" one beside it.
[49] Cf. Polignac, *L'Anti-Lucrèce*, Livre VI; Haller (Hastings, p. 52, also p. 128–129).
[50] *Religion of Nature Delineated* (1726), p. 34–35.
[51] *Characteristicks*, II, 31, 96–97.
[52] Cf. Boullier (Hastings, p. 34–36); Condillac (beasts lack morality, religion and an immortal soul, but have ideas, memory and judgment, *ibid.*, p. 53). See also p. 134 (Quesnay), p. 145 (Le Roy), p. 146–7 n (Grimm), p. 148–9 (Rivarol).
[53] *Principes du droit naturel* (1748), I, 4–5, 70.
[54] *Phédon*, 1772, p. 252–253.

ject to error, inasmuch as he lives partly in the variable world of intelligence.[55]

One of the keenest observers of animals at the time was Georges Leroy, a philosophically inclined game-warden. He was particularly concerned with replying to Buffon. While that great naturalist had lowered animals in order to exalt man, Leroy raises animals, without, however, lowering man. By precise observations he shows their intelligent adaptability, capacity to learn from experience, and power to form abstract ideas, "which are subject to rectification," concerning the "relations of certain phenomena among each other. Often, because they see, they judge what will follow." Leroy, to a certain extent, confuses simple association with abstraction. He similarly asserts that animals are conscious of the past: they learn to avoid traps where they have been caught before. They have an idea of time, since they foresee periodic recurrences. (This, again, is probably a sensitivity to the effects of time, rather than an idea of time.) Leroy reassures his readers, however, that by showing the spiritual to exist in animals, he is also preserving man from a mechanistic reduction. Man is distinct from beasts. The two marks of his separateness are compassion and its derivatives: the awareness of the rights of others and repugnance for their violation. Animals follow only self-interest.

[55] *Esprit des lois,* Bk. I, ch. 1. Several other points of view may be noted briefly. Pierre Fabre, for instance, claimed that man differs from beast by his freedom to abandon the motivations of sensation and desire, which are determined by his physical organization (Hastings, p. 119, n.1). Formey speaks of a "superior level" in the human mind, in which the ideas of sensation are "purified" and become abstract. Man thus succeeds "in making himself in a way independent of objects and impressions . . . and in placing himself in a superior region." Man alone has "universal ideas." (See Formey's Introduction to Père André: *Sur le beau,* 1767, p. 3-4.) Formey's remarks look towards a theory of man's power of objectifying the world. A much longer development, with emphasis on human liberation from impressions and impulses, is to be found in his *L'Anti-Sans-Soucy* (1761, I, 207–227). Delisle emphasized man's power of imagination, his ability to create beings "that exist only in himself," and his ability to "build a bridge to infinity" via abstractions (*op. cit.,* p. 260–261). Only one writer claimed for man the unique impulse to reproduce space and form. (Gerdil, *Recueil,* p. 106–120.) Gerdil also refers to the pleasure of knowing, and the sensitivity to non-sensible attractions. He lists other distinctions and concludes that the difference is not one of degree. He admits the gradual gradation of intelligence in the animal world, and the determinacy of organization, but says that only man can rise above the sensual world. No one, so far as I have discovered, claimed for man the equally unique ability to laugh—"a specifically human form of expression" (Alverdes, *Psychology of Animals,* p. 131). A particular aspect of man's moral uniqueness that was frequently emphasized was a group of ideas clustered around the concept of approbation. We shall study this concept in a later chapter.

"In man, the faculty of being moved by another's torment, and the suffering that we feel because of it, introduces the morality of actions." [56]

Later in the century, it was a Scotsman, Adam Ferguson, who contributed one of the most interesting discussions of man's distinctiveness. We can mention only a few of the ideas in his lengthy treatment. The one respect in which man is unique, "not only in measure or degree, but totally, and in kind . . . [is] his intelligence or mind, intimately conscious of itself, as it exists in thought, discernment and will." (Ferguson's idea is Cartesian— self-consciousness as part of the definition of mind.) Also, brutes are directed by instinct to the use of means, prior to any knowledge of end. Man is similarly directed to ends; but he chooses, invents and diversifies the means. He can escape instinctive motives through his power of generalization, and by self-training and habituation. Human society differs from animal society in not having a determinate form, and also in its giving rise to new criteria by which to judge individuals. But there is a brute in man; and Ferguson predelineates Frankenstein's monster and the twentieth century Nazi when he writes that a human creature, without reason and remorse, would be a monster: ". . . even the Yahoo is not an overcharged description of an ungoverned brute in the shape of man." [57]

In all this argumentation, little direct use seems to have been made, by French writers, of Leibniz' distinction between perception and apperception, or of his notion of the degrees of appetition.[58] But these ideas are perhaps influential wherever the concept of self-conscious thought, and of needs derived from foresight, enter the discussion.[59]

It is obvious that the Christian apologists did not stand alone. Some *philosophes* of more conservative stamp, Fontenelle, Montesquieu, Bonnet, Quesnay, Dupont and Delisle de Sales, for instance, would not accept the loss of distinctiveness. Fontenelle, despite vacillations and ambiguities, reestablishes natural con-

[56] Leroy: *Lettres sur les animaux* (1768), p. 237–270.
[57] *Principles of Moral and Political Science*, 1792, I, 21–62, 120–131.
[58] *Monadology*, 28, 29, 30.
[59] For further treatment, from the apologists' side, see Le Franc de Pompignan, *op. cit.*, p. 246–251; Gérard, *Valmont*, 1774, I, 530–533; Pey, *Entretiens*, p. 59 ff.

tinuity between man and animals, but emphasizes a discontinuity in value. Both have instinct, passion, mechanism; but human intelligence is of a different order from that of animals.[60] For Delisle, our distinctiveness lies in our ability, as free and intelligent beings, to violate the laws of nature—a general statement, of which we have seen a particular application in the position taken by the *philosophes* toward suicide. Even God cannot escape his own causation, and neither God nor angels can destroy themselves.[61] Dupont contends that the qualities of intelligence are quite unlike those of matter. Intelligence has different laws, acts on matter differently than matter acts on matter. Our will and passions move matter in a way that has nothing to do with the laws of gravitation, mechanics or geometry.[62] Man—Delisle and Marmontel agree—has faculties far beyond his needs.[63]

It is of interest to observe Montesquieu once again overriding the naturalism which he follows when it is ethically and politically innocuous. His humanistic and probably religious sentiments led him to seek out the traits which mark an unbridgeable cleavage between man and beast. The definition of man which is implicit in his remarks (as it is also in Rousseau's *Discours sur l'inégalité*) is that of a dissatisfied animal. Beasts act uniformly and with no urge to change; their needs are limited to the biological. Man is envious, restless, aggressive, ambitious, never content. He craves the superfluous, and ever invents new needs for himself. It is not enough for him to eat; he must introduce art into his cookery and flatter his palate.[64] Probably the only writer who made man's distinctiveness consist partly in his depravity was Morelly. Only man *needs* morality, and laws, because of his wickedness towards his fellow-men.[65] At the close of the century, Marmontel con-

[60] J. R. Carré, *La philosophie de Fontenelle* (1932), p. 101–102.

[61] *Philosophie de la nature*, I, 5–6.

[62] *Philosophie de l'univers*, p. 41 ff.

[63] Delisle, *op. cit.*, p. 154; Marmontel, *Leçons de métaphysique*, p. 106–114. An idea similar to the last was expressed, in the nineteenth century, by Alfred Russel Wallace.

[64] "Essai touchant les lois naturelles," *Oeuvres*, III, 182 (not published in the eighteenth century). La Mettrie accounts for man's needs by his more advanced physical organization. Cf. Johnson's *Rasselas*.

[65] *Code de la nature*, p. 175. It could be argued that Rousseau had done this in the *Discours sur l'inégalité*, and even in the *Discours sur les sciences et les arts*; but he does not explicitly include moral depravity among the distinctively human traits.

tributed a kind of summary of the qualities that were considered basic to the claim for man's uniqueness.[66]

Rousseau was frequently attacked for his degradation of man in the *Discours sur l'origine de l'inégalité*. His case, however, is a special one, and he cannot properly be classed with the other *philosophes*. Rousseau's purpose was none of those we are discussing. In order to prove man fundamentally unsocial, and in order to paint the state of nature as he wished it, Rousseau had to deprive him of almost all the qualities that make him the being we know as "man," and reduce him to an animal state (in some respects a state inferior to that of other animals). It was the possession of inherent and distinctive spiritual virtualities that (unfortunately) made possible the rise to human status. These potentialities were freedom and perfectibility—intelligence, at the early level, not being noticeably superior. In "Note J," Rousseau emphasizes that it was not language that led to man's rise (or fall), but "perfectibility," of which language was one result. The other quality was freedom. An animal is a self-operating machine, in which nature performs all the operations. Although man is also a self-operating machine, the difference is that he cooperates, as a free agent, in the operations. His distinctiveness does not lie, then, in his intelligence; all animals think, and man, in this regard, has only a superiority of degree.[67]

Rousseau's conclusion is that man was in some ways better off before his distinctive faculties became effective in changing his way of life. His aim, then, in painting man as originally bestial, was not to lower him, but to show the superiority of an earlier state to the conditions in which he now lives. A subsidiary purpose is to depreciate reason in favor of sentiment and instinct (what is "natural").[68] Rousseau was under Diderot's influence at this period (1755), and his philosophy was comparatively undeveloped. In the *Lettre à d'Alembert sur les spectacles* (1758), he has become aware of an entirely different perspective. He now understands the critical importance of the man-beast controversy in the conflict of ideas and the reevaluation of man. He immediately takes sides,

[66] *Leçons de métaphysique*, p. 103–114.

[67] *Discours sur l'origine de l'inégalité*, in Vaughan, *The Political Writings of Rousseau*, I, 149.

[68] An echo of Rousseau's distrust of reason can be seen in the abbé Yvon's article "Amour" in the *Encyclopédie*, and in Robinet, *op. cit.*, I, 21–22.

and will maintain his stand with constancy. "Man is not a dog or a wolf. It is only necessary in his species to establish the first social relations to give to his feelings a morality forever unknown to beasts. Animals have a heart and passions; but the holy image of the honest and the beautiful will never enter into any hearts except those of man." [69] At the same time, Rousseau insists that animals do have many traits commonly denoted as "human." Among these, he includes shame and love.

In *La Nouvelle Héloïse* and the *Contrat social,* Rousseau develops a further distinction. For animals, the only right is might. For men, might and right are entirely separate categories, and might is all too often the violation of right.[70] Finally, in the *Profession de foi* (1762), he clearly indicates his distaste for those who degrade man by lowering him to the animals—for now Rousseau is in open warfare with the Encyclopedists. He has no doubt that man's will and intelligence, his spiritual and moral nature, and his immortal soul, make him unique.[71]

Voltaire, a typical deist, fought against anything that would take man out of the realm of physical nature—the soul, free will, the idea that he is not an animal like all the others. In defending determinism he refuses man any exemption from the universal laws of "lower beings," and cheerfully puts man and dog under a common law. In moments of pessimism, he gives up the hope of men ever living by any other law except the natural law of the strong. Man, Voltaire writes in the *Traité de métaphysique* (1734) is an animal "less strong than others of his size, having a few more ideas than they, and a greater facility in expressing them; subject, besides, to all the same needs, born, living and dying like them. . . . Thus I judge that the same cause acts in beasts and in men in proportion to their organs." The advance of years brought to Voltaire only stronger confirmation of this conviction. As a humanist, however, Voltaire always insisted that man is

[69] Ed. M. Fuchs, p. 116–117.
[70] *La Nouvelle Héloïse,* ii, 194; *Contrat social,* p. 67–8.
[71] He also proposes other arguments; e.g., man has "superfluous" faculties, beyond those that are needed for his self-preservation.

No French writer was able to reach so striking a formulation as Kant's. "The primary characteristic of the human species is the power as rational beings to acquire a character as such." (*Anthropology,* Academy ed., vii, 329.) The things of nature are "just there"; their action can be described and calculated. Only man is called on, by himself, to make something of himself.

unique in his feelings of benevolence (that is, non-selfish motivation) and in his "natural" moral life, as embodied in a universal "Natural Law." Only man possesses abstract reason and
God-given categories of moral judgment. The question (which
Voltaire was never able to resolve successfully) is how this uniqueness fitted in, or harmonized, with subjection to undifferentiated,
universal laws. To put it another way, how can the "natural"
which moral reason condemns live with the "natural" which
moral reason approves? Voltaire was fundamentally a humanist;
but the facts of the world, as his observation noted them and as
the new science interpreted them, pulled him in a different direction, towards the pessimistic degradation of man.

Even an atheist, with moralistic and humanistic inclinations,
was subject to the same stress. Both d'Holbach and Diderot are
excellent examples, and they stand in opposition to other, amoral
atheists, like La Mettrie and Sade. Leaving the analysis of d'Holbach's theories until later, let us briefly turn again to Diderot.
The author of *Le Rêve de d'Alembert* and the *Réfutation
d'Helvétius* frequently expressed opposing opinions on the subject of the man-animal relationship, according to whether he was
in his materialistic or his moralistic mood. We have noted how
he derides the idea of man's distinctiveness or unique value, yet
insists on the great distance that separates him from other animals. His sensationalism and transformism, his materialism and
belief in the determinacy of physical organization all are consistent. But in the article "Chasteté" of the *Encyclopédie,* he
speaks ambiguously of that sentiment as something that has happened "among men, that animal *par excellence,*" something that
"has never been seen among other animals." Diderot could not
bear to see the same reduction of human conduct to self-interest
and pleasure which he himself had performed time and again.
He cried out in wrath and indignation against the reduction of
mental and emotional life to physical sensitivity, and the diminishing of man to parity with other animals. Man is something
special in nature, and cannot be explained merely by what he
has in common with other animals. "Was there a time when man
could be confused with beast? I do not think so: he was always
a man, that is, an animal combining ideas. . . . We must make
a distinction between man and animal. . . . I am a man, and I

must have causes peculiar to man." Organization is necessary to sensation, and sensation to action, but these primitive conditions are not our actual motives. Only men may have completely non-sensual motives. Only men live in time.[72]

Diderot does not only insist that the influence of the senses on the mind has been exaggerated. Still more significantly, we are obliged, on reading him, to ask ourselves when difference of degree is so great that it becomes difference in kind. In the *Salon de 1767*, for instance, he tells us that to know what good and evil are, we must know the nature of man. "What is a man? An animal? Of course; but a dog is an animal, too; a wolf is an animal, too. But a man is neither a wolf nor a dog. . . . How many philosophers, failing to make such simple observations, have made for man a morality of wolves, as stupidly as if they had prescribed for wolves the morality of men!"[73] Here then, the differences between man and animals override all similarities, and are determining.

On the distinction of man from beast depended not only the security of the Christian religion, but in a broader view that struck many *philosophes,* a secure morality. This accounts for the insistence on the uniqueness of the human moral realm that not only pervades the works of the apologists, but is to be found among moderate *philosophes* who did not feel obliged to deny spiritual faculties—notably Condillac, Buffon and Rousseau. For the ultimate ethical import of the whole controversy, though not always stated explicitly, was most certainly evident to all. If man were unique, it could not easily be denied that judgment of right and wrong inhered in him as part of his uniqueness. A case could be made for a basic universal moral code, and even for its derivation from God, in the form of moral sense or Natural Law. Without this distinctiveness, there was the danger that logic might seek out the ultimate implications; for instance, that might is right (at the very least, in the relation of State or social group to the individual). "Follow nature," might become the cry, and the Christian saw morality as the transcending of nature. Thus Wollaston had warned, precisely in this regard, that it is all right to follow "the nature of things," but not human nature, since part

---

[72] *Réfutation d'Helvétius, Oeuvres,* II, 397, 302; XVIII, 176–179.
[73] XI, 124.

of man's nature he has in common with brutes.[74] Boullier and
Chaumeix warned more specifically against sexual license which
might be justified by the confusion of human and animal. Their
fears were well founded.

The larger number of *philosophes* were content, however, to
superimpose a unique human moral realm upon the common
realm of nature shared by man and animal, and to emphasize the
uneasy partnership, rather than the primacy of the human. This
compromise seemed to them a way out of the dilemma. As Voltaire put it, "Hunger and love, the physical principle for all animals; *amour-propre* and *bienveillance,* the moral principle for
men. These prime wheels move all the others, and the whole
machine of the world is governed by them." [75] In other words, all
are subject to the same law, but man has an additional law. In
the minds of moderate *philosophes,* this conserved the "natural"
(therefore valid) character of ethical judgments. Many, notably
Voltaire and moderate deists such as Bonnet and Delisle de Sales,
conceived this moral life as taking the form of a "Natural Law,"
virtual in all men and developed by experience. Others, like
Diderot, threw aside the abstract notion of a universal Natural
Law, but held man to be naturally and necessarily moral in his
reactions to experience. (Diderot, however, is a man of complex
and contradictory moods.) The difficulty in this compromise—
and it accounts for the many divergences of opinion—lay in a
decision that could not easily be avoided. Did this "additional"
human law supersede the more basic, common law? That it was
often in contradiction to it was only too apparent. The "compromise" actually settled nothing. It merely pushed the problem
to one further remove. The decision had to be made: either the
human law supersedes the common "natural" law, or it should
be submitted to it; or else, a way must be found to reveal (or to
create) their ultimate and effective harmony.

The Christians chose the first alternative, with no need for
hesitation, despite the infiltration of the new naturalistic views,
which they tried to absorb. The majority of the *philosophes,*
struggling for a humanistic morality, sought to realize the third

---

[74] *Op. cit.,* p. 22–23. Wollaston is aware of the ambiguities of the word "nature."
[75] *Notebooks,* ed. Besterman, II, 374–375. By *amour-propre,* Voltaire means vanity
and the human desire for prestige, as distinguished from the common animal law
of self-love, or the desire to avoid pain and extinction.

way. The more radical materialists chose the second of these alternatives. La Mettrie, Helvétius, Diderot and several others were not content with demanding freedom from specially designed and revealed imperatives originating outside of man and above him. They boldly drew the conclusion that the basic laws of behavior are identical in all animals, including man, and that they may be reduced to one—pleasure. "Moral judgments" are reactions to sensation. Even the moderate Le Roy wrote that "the morality of wolves could cast light on that of men." [76] Their conclusion involved the classifying of any particular moral judgment as conventional, a result of need; relative, but valid inasmuch as it suits us. La Mettrie went even beyond this. He was one of the first to proclaim the "licentious" conclusions that worried the apologists. Reducing mental and moral life to that of bodily organs, he concluded the same standards must apply to man and animal. Pleasure and happiness are the only goods, and all sexual freedoms are thereby justified.[77] Diderot followed La Mettrie in his more radical, unpublished dialogues. The strange Benedictine monk, Dom Deschamps, was not afraid to publish his opinions.

We shall later refer to the development and expression of these attitudes in several eighteenth century novels. Nowhere were they pushed to such absolute finalities as in the works of the marquis de Sade, for whom everything is indifferent and without price in nature's blind productivity. The blade of grass, he had said, is worth as much as the man whose body nourishes it. Consequently, all we do is also indifferent. Sade's revolt is against man's pretensions to existing in a sphere apart, a sphere of reason and morals. There is only one law, the law of instinct, which makes us seek pleasure and happiness. No other law obtains, despite our self-delusion. Declaiming against parent-child moral ties or responsibilities, he demands, "See whether animals know them; of course not, and yet it is always they we must consult when we wish to learn about nature." [78] The question, what is man's place in the universe, is ultimately meaningless for Sade. It is like asking what is the place of a point on the circumference of a circle.

In this phase of their argumentation—just as in the conclusions

[76] *Lettres sur les animaux*, p. 10.
[77] *Système d'Epicure, L'Anti-Sénèque, L'Art de jouir, L'Homme machine.*
[78] *"La Philosophie dans le boudoir*, p. 223. See especially *Histoire de Juliette*, I, 60, 69; IV, 229–241, 250–251.

they drew in the debate over suicide—most eighteenth century
writers fell into a serious confusion of meanings. It involved both
terms of the phrase, "law of nature." In the first place, "Nature"
was of course a multivocal word; in the Introduction, I have summarized its most important uses. The impulse to incest and the
aversion to it; the impulse to free love and also to jealousy and
possessiveness; the impulse to do wrong and the moral judgment
of right and wrong—all may be spoken of as natural. By "nature,"
then, some meant one, some the other, some both. In the second
place, the word "law" was constantly used in two quite different
senses, the descriptive and the normative. In the first sense—as
we see it in Sade or the reference to the natural law of self-preservation—it merely summarizes the totality of phenomena, physical
or psychical, conceived as taking place in accord with certain descriptive generalizations. From this universality, eighteenth century writers frequently made a further deduction which is not
logically necessitated: that such modes of action were also normative, that is, self-evidently true, right and obligatory for men. This
is to confuse the question of the way people behave with the question of the way they should behave, to equate universal propensities with moral duties. It is as if one said, men everywhere beat
their wives, therefore wife-beating is right.

The confusion was perhaps inevitable, in view of the intellectual and moral crisis in which eighteenth century thinkers were
caught. Occasionally they became aware of it and were disturbed
by it. Thus Formey wrote that nature is indeed our guide to the
moral life and to happiness. Then he quickly added: but not
nature in the sense of "the gross inclinations that are common to
us and to animals. . . . The natural law I pose is that rule of the
beautiful, the right, the honest, that reason deduces from the consideration of our nature (*notre être*) and our situation in the universe." [79] Formey's words express the very heart of the ethical
problem of the eighteenth century: the search for a basis for
values, the desperate need to reconcile the valid claims of nature
(in its opposing senses), or of nature and reason. For if we assume
that man has certain unique traits and possessions, we are next
obliged to ask whether they conflict with those he shares with all
animal life. And if we find they do conflict, we must, as I have

[79] "Essai sur la perfection," *Mélanges philosophiques*, II, 222.

said, either override this "nature" with a new and higher law, or accept it as the sole real and ultimate authority (always lifting its head, never to be crushed)—or else—in desperation—search for a way to reconcile the contraries, the eternal foes. The moral crisis of Western man thus takes concrete form in the consciences of the eighteenth century. It is the central problem of their time, and of ours, and the thinkers of the Enlightenment were fully engaged in it.

Note. HUMAN AND ANIMAL LOVE

It was almost inevitable that the experience of sexual love should have developed into a tangential issue of the man-beast controversy. That both man and beast are impelled by a powerful urge to the act of copulation was evident to all Frenchmen. That this drive was not only irrational, but destructive to man's rational orderings, had been clearly recognized by Bayle, quite appropriately in his article on Helen of Troy, as well as in his article on Eve. As the materialistic currents of thought evolved, there appeared a tacit assumption, in some of the writings of this school, that love was a merely physical act, an indulgence in physical pleasure, for biological (i.e., racial) ends. Pleasure, writes La Mettrie in his rhapsody "La Volupté," is man's finest apanage. "Pleasure, sovereign master of men and gods, before which all disappears, even reason itself, you know how much my heart adores you. . . ." A reader of La Mettrie's writings can have no doubt about the kind of pleasure he means. Diderot, in moments of cynicism, defines love as "the voluptuous rubbing of two membranes," and as "the voluptuous loss of a few drops of fluid." [80] Sade conceived one of his main goals to be stripping the idol of love of all its false attractions, restoring it to its true status as animal pleasure in which we have the desire and right to wallow, to any excess. In Sade's mind, this was one way of uncovering the true man, man the animal, underneath the pretentious self-imposed halo of a being made in the image of God.[81] Sade's writings

[80] Compare Toussaint: "To this tender union of souls we can never apply the words of Democritus, that 'the pleasure of love is only a short epilepsy.'" (*Les Moeurs*, Pt. 3, ch. 1.)

[81] Cf. *Les Infortunes de la vertu,* Introduction de M. Heine, p. xlv–xlvii.

respond to the desire he expressed, in an essay on the novel, to reveal man not only as he shows himself, "but such as he may be, such as the modifications and all the shocks of the passions may possibly make him." It is this exploration which leads Sade to the great discovery that the vitalities in human life are destructive as well as creative, and in fact are essentially destructive when they are not chained and diverted into other channels. Sade, then, destroys the notion of love as something pure and lovely; it is, rather, much worse than merely bestial; it is cruel, and its freest and fullest expression is in torture and death. While it is not correct to assert, as Simone de Beauvoir does, that Sade was the first to see the tragedy and ugliness hidden in the sexual instincts, or that he was "the only one to discover sexuality as egoism, tyranny, cruelty," what is true is that he was the first to present sex as necessarily, inherently and essentially evil.[82]

But it was Buffon, long before Sade, who aroused opposition by an open discussion of the question, in his "Discours sur la nature des animaux," which headed the fourth volume of his *Histoire naturelle,* published in 1753. Buffon marks the difference between human and animal passions. The former are, precisely, accompanied by moral effects, though these too are produced by body, not by soul. Essentially, then, our passions are physical, like those of animals, but our soul is affected by them. This, in Buffon's opinion, is most unfortunate, at least in the passion of love. He pens a romantic apostrophe to love that begins with the exclamation, "Love! innate desire! soul of Nature!" and ends with the question, "why do you cause the happy state of all [other] beings, and the unhappiness of man?" By "moral effects," Buffon understands the concomitants of physical desire, notably vanity (in conquest, techniques and exclusive possession), and jealousy. But man, not content with nature, trying to heighten his pleasure, "has only spoiled nature; by trying to exaggerate his sentiment, he only abuses his being and hollows out in his heart an emptiness that nothing afterwards is capable of filling." [82a]

Only two years later, Jean-Jacques Rousseau followed Buffon

---

[82] "Faut-il brûler Sade?", p. 1208.
[82a] *Oeuvres,* p. 341. Buffon's opinions are quoted by Sade, in *La Philosophie dans le boudoir,* p. 139.

with an even more resounding piece, the *Discours sur l'origine de l'inégalité*. Rousseau's aim—to lay bare the "original" man underneath the civilized, or artificial man—was quite different from Buffon's, and in a way, closer to that of Sade. But the conclusion was similar. The so-called spiritual aspects of love are artificial adjuncts, based on vanity and jealousy. Their effects have been disastrous. The originals of our species "coupled fortuitously, according to chance encounter, opportunity and desire, without words being a very necessary interpreter of the things they had to say; they left each other with the same *facilité*." [83] Love was, and therefore is essentially, a physical pleasure, like that of animals, and as long as it is only this, it can produce only pleasure pure of discord or pain.[84] Rousseau's ideas were inspired by his reading of Buffon, but they take on a much wider meaning, with moral and sociological implications.

While Rousseau was openly attacked and made the object of derision, Buffon was granted more respectful dissents. D'Alembert, in his article "Courtisane" in the *Encyclopédie*, tried to "explain away" any offensive connotations of Buffon's remarks. "This philosopher did not claim that the moral pleasure does not add to the physical—experience would be against him; nor that the moral side of love is only an illusion—which is true, but does not destroy the vivacity of pleasure . . . Doubtless he meant that this moral element is what causes all the evils of love, and in that we cannot agree with him too heartily." D'Alembert's modification, it is clear, still makes the physical pleasure of love the only reality!

A minor writer, G. L. Schmid, took a stronger stand. Summarizing Buffon's opinion, he comments, "This cynical opinion degrades mankind and puts us in the rank of beasts. Fortunately it is belied by the inner feeling of every well-born and unprej-

---

[83] *Ed. cit.*, I, 154.

[84] *Ibid.*, p. 164–165, 169. The lack of a spiritual content, in Rousseau's concept, is revealed even more strikingly in his assertion that there was no reason for a man to remain with a woman during her pregnancy (p. 215–216). He refers, of course, to man's original "state of animality." In the *Lettre sur les spectacles* (1758), Rousseau affirms a contrary view, that animals share the characteristics of human love, including capriciousness and flirtatiousness, (p. 116–117).

The more radical materialists naturally concurred with Buffon's thesis. Thus Diderot: ". . . the passion of love, reduced to a simple physical appetite, did not produce any of our disorders there." (*Supplément au Voyage de Bougainville, Oeuvres*, II, 240.)

udiced man." [85] Delisle de Sales called Buffon's idea "dangerous."
He protests that "man can do more than enjoy, he can love," and
his love can become "the food of the most sublime souls." Even
more, the desire to merit one's mistress may be a spring of virtue.[86]

Voltaire protested several times against the identification of human and animal love. "Take your examples from animals," he
has the German tell the polygamous Turk, in the dialogue and
article "Femme" of the *Dictionnaire philosophique;* "resemble
them as much as you wish; as for me, I wish to love like a man." [87]
In *L'Ingénu,* the primitive hero teaches a Jansenist that love is
not a sin of the flesh—but a feeling "as noble as tender, which
can exalt the soul as well as soften it, and even at times produce
virtues."

Voltaire was in several regards a disciple of Shaftesbury, who
had, in his *Enquiry concerning Virtue,* placed the spiritual side
of love far above the physical. Through this affection, he declared,
"the greatest Hardships in the World have been submitted to,
and even Death itself voluntarily embrac'd, without any expected
Compensation." [88] Here was a sacrifice of self that seemed strictly
human. Doubtless Shaftesbury's idea impressed Diderot, too, for
he had translated the *Enquiry* in 1745. When, in later years, Diderot was in a mood to exalt human dignity and distinctiveness
above all else in nature, he sometimes thought of love as one of
the noblest, and most ennobling emotions. True, the thought
could occur to him while he was himself yearning for his mistress'
charms and urging her to reciprocate his feeling, and to conceive
of love as "an *entrepreneur* of great things, a sublime and powerful sentiment." And he gives concrete examples of what men
do out of love, almost as an explication of the Shaftesbury passage.[89] More thoughtfully, in his protest against Helvétius' level-
ing of man and animal, he cries, "Is there only physical pleasure
in possessing a beautiful woman? Is there only physical pain in
losing her by death or inconstancy? Is not the distinction between
physical and moral as solid as that of the animal who feels and

[85] *Essais sur divers sujets* . . . , p. 62 (quoted by Hastings, p. 153, n. 4).
[86] *Op. cit.,* III, 356–361. Delisle may well have *La Nouvelle Héloïse* in mind.
[87] *Oeuvres,* XIX, 104.
[88] *Characteristicks,* II, 105–106.
[89] *Lettres à Sophie Volland* (1938, II, 268).

the animal who reasons?"[90] And while it is true that Diderot's
essay *Sur les femmes* is not entirely laudatory of what the French
call "le sexe," he is just as likely, at another moment, to lift his
voice in a paean to womankind. "He who does not love woman
is a kind of monster, he who seeks her only when he is alerted
by need, leaves his species and joins the ranks of brutes."[91] Diderot, finally, follows his usual bent and generalizes. The nature
of pleasure is not the same for a man as for an animal. If we had
to choose between "pleasures of the soul" and physical pleasures,
few would prefer "the happiness of an oyster to the fate of an
intelligent being."[92]

There were other, lesser voices. A writer in Robinet's *Dictionnaire* argued that a deeper satisfaction grows out of the fading of
the first fiery passion.[93] Saint-Lambert's famous poem, *Les Saisons*
(1769) contains these verses:

> Tout désire et jouit: l'homme seul sait aimer.
> Il est souvent des sens l'esclave involontaire;
> Mais à son coeur sensible un coeur est nécessaire.

And in his notes, Saint-Lambert pens a long justification. Because
of womanly modesty and the length of conjugal association and
family life, there is necessarily in human love "more of the moral
than in animal love." In the heart of an enamored youth spring
up virtues, courage, friendship, generosity. The spiritual pleasure
enhances the physical; the lover enjoys possessing a woman, and
also possessing the object of his admiration. "His love is a kind
of enthusiasm that gives his soul energy and breadth." It represses
self-love, augments the value of public approbation. In a word,
love is an antidote to the barbarous, and, precisely, to the animal
in man.[94]

More unexpectedly, perhaps, we find d'Holbach, in his *Morale
universelle* (1776) expressing similar thoughts about the unique
needs that transform love in human beings. "Love in an intelligent, fore-seeing, reasonable being, must not be approached in

[90] *Oeuvres*, II, 302–303. Also, the very interesting passage, *ibid.*, p. 338–339.
[91] *Oeuvres*, IV, 95.
[92] Article, "Plaisir," *Oeuvres*, XVI, 300. Compare Voltaire's tale, *"Le bon bramin."*
[93] "Amour de soi," in *Dictionnaire universel* (Londres, 1777–1783).
[94] *Les Saisons* (1823), p. 48, 70–71. See also Roucher's poem, *Les Mois*, notes to
Chant III.

the manner of brutes." [95] Is d'Holbach trying here to free himself from the dilemma of his materialism, trying to reach a spiritual and moral level, a uniquely human level? This is undoubtedly the sense and direction of his ethical writings. But he is not really so inconsistent as he seems at first blush. If we read the complete passage, we see what it is that conjoins the "spiritual" to the physical sensations in man—and it is only his selfish need to be taken care of by a woman and to enjoy her companionship! This passage affords us one more glimpse into the dilemmas and difficulties of the eighteenth century materialist who longed to be a humanist and a moralist. [96]

[95] *La morale universelle* (1820), III, 4–5.

[96] There is, of course, in the eighteenth century French novel, a variety of viewpoints on love. It may be pictured as degrading (e.g., *Manon Lescaut*), or as ennobling (e.g., the novels of Duclos, Mme de Tencin, Bernardin de Saint-Pierre). In Rousseau's *La Nouvelle Héloïse*, we see love having alternately both effects, the hero and heroine torn between good and evil. The decision is uncertain, and varies with Rousseau's own moods during the composition of the work; but the ultimate course of their history makes it probable that Rousseau considers love the most dangerous (if also the most exalting) passion. There is no doubt that it is essentially a "moral" passion, though not separable from physical expression. In many other novels, love is treated as a mere instrument for ruthlessly securing physical pleasure, prestige or power. The latter viewpoint corresponds to the materialistic view, that love is essentially physical, a mechanism in the life struggle. Prévost's picture of Des Grieux would correspond to the traditional Christian view, and to that of Buffon and of Rousseau in his *Discours*. See the chapters on the novel and on the passions in the third section of this study.

Freedom and Determinism

$\mathcal{F}our$

THE ACTIVITY OF THE MIND

WITH THE rise of scientific materialism the question of "free will" became a sharp point of issue. It had been brought into dramatic focus in the seventeenth century, by Hobbes' and Spinoza's brilliant exposition of determinism. In the eighteenth century, the new sensationist psychology drove the defenders of freedom to the wall. The revaluations of human nature and of the bases of the ethical life also impelled this issue to the forefront. On no other was there more incessant, or more acrimonious debate, or was such ingenious subtlety of argument displayed.

On the one side, it was realized that man's uniqueness in the natural world was at stake; and also (to put the matter in the words of a modern philosopher) that, "unless ethics is to be dismissed as nonsense, a man must be free to do his duty, for if he were not, it would, as Kant pointed out, be nonsense to say that it was his duty." [1] On the other side, such supposed freedom was derided as a delusion which lifted man outside of nature and its universal modes of functioning. For the materialist there could be "only one being and one form of law." [2] Spinoza had scoffed at those who explain men's behavior by things which are outside

[1] C. E. M. Joad, *A Guide to Philosophy*, p. 532.
[2] Cassirer, *op. cit.*, p. 65.

"the common laws of nature," and who believe "that he has an absolute power over his own actions; and that he is altogether self-determined." [3] "We have rejected the word and the idea of chance," wrote Dupont de Nemours, "as empty of meaning and unworthy of philosophy. Nothing happens, nothing can happen, except in conformity to laws." [4] Furthermore, to eighteenth century reformers, to the theorists who wished to condition men by laws and by education, it seemed necessary to eliminate the indeterminate from human behavior. Or else, how could they count on a specific result?

We shall attempt, without the needed help of Ariadne's thread, to find our way through this labyrinth, and to bring out the main lines of argument, as well as the principal arguments, that were used in this interminable debate. We shall not enter into the vexed question of God's freedom, or into the even thornier subject of the relation of human freedom to God's omniscience and omnipotence.[5]

One of the difficulties, in the eighteenth century discussion, was lack of agreement on the substantive meaning of the concepts referred to. In order to avoid a similar confusion, it may prove useful to set up brief definitions at this point, even though these must inevitably be incomplete, and unsatisfactory to some. By "fatalism" I understand the doctrine that man is wholly led by forces outside of himself. "Determinism," on the other hand, maintains that an important part of behavior is caused by an individual's consciousness of his own goals, motives and drives, as well as by his recollection of past experience. Over these, how-

---

[3] *Ethic,* Third Part (Introductory Statement).

[4] *Op. cit.,* p. 215–216.

[5] The first question requires us to answer, for instance, whether God could have established other laws of mathematics and morals, or whether he was bound as to their nature and free only in creating their actuality. Could God make matter think? On the second question, Bossuet had submitted man's freedom to God's prescience—for else, he argued, man could make himself better than God had made him. We are free, but "the actions of our freedom are included in Divine providence." (*Traité du libre arbitre,* in *Oeuvres philosophiques,* p. 236–247). Others suggested different ways out of the dilemma. Bergier, for instance, claims that God does not foresee the future, since all time is present to him, and so the contingency of future events is not affected, any more than our knowledge of a present action affects the freedom of the person who has done it. (*Principes de métaphysique,* p. 99 ff.) Or, as the poet Louis Racine put it, "Dans l'instant que je veux il fait ma volonté, / Sans qu'à mon choix réel ce grand coup puisse nuire." (*La Grâce,* chant II). This example is enough to show the slippery depths we are avoiding.

ever, he has no control, except as he may weigh, compare, manipulate them in his mind, in a process which results in actuation by the strongest impulse. Every state of the self, including its projected goals, is wholly determined by its preceding states. Behavior, like all other natural phenomena, is therefore theoretically predictable, at any given moment, from a sufficient set of data which are "fed" into the cerebral mechanism. In opposition to determinism, or self-determinism, the theory of freedom, in one of its applications, asserts a universe in which chance, uncertainty and novelty inhere; in its moral reference, it assumes such novelty, or creativity, in the mind. It postulates a self which is free to modify character and to act morally despite accumulated influences, which is free, in other words, to make a chosen final cause the efficient cause of action.

There is a further distinction to be made. To be free, a person obviously must be free to do what he wants to do. This type of freedom, which I shall denominate "freedom of action," is not "moral freedom"; that is to say, it is not sufficient to establish right or wrong, merit or blame, responsibility and morality—although a necessary condition of any such judgments is of course that the act be one which is willed by the person judged, and not compelled. It must be assumed that a person's act is what he wants most to do (although we must take care not to confuse the word "want" with simple desire or impulse, or with the idea of pleasure).[6] This is merely to assert that he acts in accordance with his strongest volition. For moral freedom, the question then becomes, Are our volitions free? Here, then, the meaning of the word "volitions" is crucial. If by "volitions" we were to mean "desires," the answer, it is obvious, would be negative, since we cannot help desiring what we value, and not desiring what we do not value. This kind of freedom is not, however, necessary or even relevant to "moral freedom," which refers rather to motivation of action and to valuation itself. What is required for freedom is the power to control the transition of desire or impulse into motive, actuating volition, or efficient cause. This is equivalent to the power to *make* one desire or impulse the most powerful one, or to make

[6] It may be further argued that the volition which results in action is in some way productive of greater pleasure than any other. But, aside from the fact such a proposition may confuse motive and result, it is not essential to the preliminary concepts I am here attempting to set up.

it the spring of action. It involves a creative process in which something is added to what is given, and value is created.[7] Thus a person may not "want" (i.e., desire) to pay taxes, and this desire to escape pain is in itself unavoidable; but an intellectual recognition of the needs of social living and of his own responsibility may lead him to place an entirely different value on the act of paying taxes. His volition is then to pay taxes, even though the painfulness of the act is not a whit diminished thereby.

This brief introduction should make it clear why the central issue in the eighteenth century polemic over free will was the nature of the mind, or more exactly, its degree of passivity or activity. Jean-Paul Sartre has written that Frenchmen, following Descartes, understand by free will "the practice of independent thinking . . . and [their] philosophers have finally come, like Alain, to identify freedom with the act of judging." [8]

The attitudes toward this question had already been built up over the preceding hundred years or more. The developments of eighteenth century French thought will be clearer, if we keep in mind tendencies and opinions of the earlier period, in France and elsewhere. Giordano Bruno had considered the senses to be merely occasions for cognition, or stimulants to the reason, in whose activity truth originated and resided solely.[9] Hobbes and Gassendi, on the other hand, had both claimed that there is no essential difference between imaginative representation and the reasoning intellect. Descartes labored to establish the independence of the intellect. According to his doctrine, the essence of the mind is thought; the mind, therefore, always thinks. Since the senses are not always stimulated, the mind must produce thoughts itself. One of the main purposes of Descartes' so-called innatism was to free the mind from bondage to sense. However Descartes makes a further distinction. Our understanding is finite, and also passive, in the sense that it cannot help having the ideas it has. Will, on the other hand, is infinite, and it gives us the power to reject false ideas, as well as to control our passions. "Only its volitions are actions." [10]

---

[7] Such a process does not imply election of the "right," "moral," or "rational" motive.

[8] "Cartesian Freedoms," in *Literary and Philosophical Essays*, p. 169.

[9] *The Infinite Universe and the Worlds*, quoted by A. Koyré, *From the Closed World to the Infinite Universe*, p. 45–46.

[10] *Oeuvres*, ed. Garnier, IV, 143.

Jean-Paul Sartre has written an illuminating essay on Cartesian freedom, in which he concludes that "Descartes realized perfectly that the concept of freedom involved necessarily an absolute autonomy, that a free act was an absolutely new production, the germ of which could not be contained in an earlier state of the world and that consequently freedom and creation were one and the same." [11] This freedom, Descartes says, is "known without proof and merely by our experience of it." It can neither be increased, nor limited. Contrary to Locke's assertion that to be free is to be able to do what one wants (freedom as power), it is to want what one can do, for "There is nothing that is entirely in our power, save our thoughts. . . ." Man's power is limited, but his freedom is not. We can abstain from the will to perform an act that is not within our power. More positively, Descartes' method calls for the free creation of rational orderings and hypotheses, by which truth is sought and judged, and experience is anticipated.[12]

Spinoza, in his *Ethic* (1677), disagreed with Descartes' separation of the mind and the will. He maintains that we can affirm only what the understanding represents to us: "The power of the mind is . . . determined by intelligence alone." [13] Spinoza, however, agrees with Descartes that the mind generates its own ideas, and that there is a real, subsistent "self," independent of experience. Ideas are not "dumb pictures on a tablet," but are active affirmations or negations. The essence of man is realized when he frees himself from passive dependence on things, and acts upon adequate ideas, or free and rational self-expression. To be free, for Spinoza, is to act from the necessity of one's own nature.[14] This freedom is, then, the freedom of self-expression, or self-causation. Spinoza's attack against free will is an attack against the arbitrariness and irrationality of Descartes' concept of will— a subject we shall shortly return to under the name, "freedom of indifference." For Spinoza, all thought is active, but thought itself involves judgment and will, so that there cannot be an act without a reason. Spinoza's reasoning also involves this further proposi-

---

[11] *Op. cit.*, p. 183.
[12] For the complex question of negative and positive freedom in regard to abstract truth, see *ibid.*, p. 174–180.
[13] Fifth Part, Preface; also Preface to Third Part.
[14] Part I, Prop. XVII, cor. 2, and Part II, Prop. XLVIII, XLIX.

tion, which goes back to much earlier writers: since thought and will are not distinct, knowing the good and willing it are identical. This is a limit of supposed rationality imposed by Spinoza on the autonomy of the self. This autonomy is rationally necessitated; that is to say, freedom is a necessity which springs from the self.

Malebranche, in his *De la recherche de la vérité* (1675), anticipates Locke's position, even as he foreshadows Hume's criticism of causation. For Malebranche, feeling, perception and thinking are essentially the same, all a modification of the mind.[15] "Judgments and reasoning are only pure perceptions," and sensations are nothing but "modifications of the mind . . . for it is the same thing to the soul to perceive an object as to receive the idea that represents it. I understand, by the word *understanding,* that passive faculty of the soul by which it receives all the different modifications of which it is capable." [16] Included in "pure perceptions" are those of simple things, of relations between things, and of relations between relations. Malebranche, however, sustains Descartes' separation of the intellect and the will. It is the will, not the intellect that judges. The self is consequently active and creative, a mixture of passive necessity and active freedom. It is necessarily determined insofar as it must seek its good (or happiness); it is free, insofar as it cannot be constrained. Therefore we are principally free in our false judgments and criminal acts, where knowledge of the good is insufficient.[17] Malebranche thus combines some elements from Descartes (the independence of the will) with an idea also adopted by Spinoza (the necessity of willing what is conceived to be good). His criticism of our idea of causation probably injured the doctrine of free will, inasmuch as it asserted that our impression, that our willing to move our arm is the cause of its motion, is a prejudice based only on a repeated experience of sequence.[18]

In England, meanwhile, Locke and the empirical school were breaking with the tradition of Bruno and Descartes. Under the influence of Newton, the associationist psychology, or psychological atomism, was developed. It "explained (or explained away) mind as a mosaic of 'sensations' and 'ideas' linked together by

[15] *De la recherche de la vérité,* p. 281 ff.
[16] *Ibid.,* p. 21 f.
[17] *Ibid.,* p. 26–27.
[18] *Ibid.,* p. 318.

laws of association (attraction)." [19] There were, to be sure, degrees of difference. Locke admitted a kind of innate faculty that enabled us to profit from sense experience in a way that animals cannot. He clung to a unitary self, as one individual and immaterial substance. Hume, in his *Treatise on Human Nature,* later subjected this concept to a corrosive analysis. "When I enter most intimately into what I call myself, I always stumble on some particular perception or other, of heat or cold, light or shade, pain or pleasure. I never catch myself at any time without a perception and can never observe anything but the perception." Hume's last conclusion, however, is not a certain deduction. I do observe myself observing; and, as Niebuhr has said, the reality of the "I" of Hume's first phrase challenges the validity of his interpretation of the ego.

For Locke, however, the important fact is that the mind is active, in the sense that it can recombine the data of experience, and, when stimulated by pleasure or pain, direct our thoughts. Although Locke did not give the mind the power to originate ideas, he did allow it the true power of originating action:

> But to be able to bring into view ideas out of sight at one's own choice, and to compare which of them one thinks fit, this is an active power . . . when I turn my eyes another way, or remove my body out of the sunbeams, I am properly active; because of my own choice, by a power within myself, I put myself into that motion.[20]

An important consequence of this concept is that free will, for Locke, has no meaning if we seek to apply it to volition; it exists only in the sense of what I have termed freedom of action, that is, in our power to do what we will to do, in our power to motivate our acts, or to act according to our motives. Desires are necessitated, and so is the preference we make among them. But since Locke admits that we may either carry out or forbear from carrying out our preference into action—a power he calls free— it is not clear what this power is, since Locke denies it the name of volition, which in his view is determined and not free.[21]

Samuel Clarke developed Locke's theories in his own way. In his rebuttal of Collins, he emphasized the view that to be a "nec-

---

[19] Koyré, *op. cit.,* p. 310.

[20] *Essay Concerning Human Understanding,* Book II, 21, par. 72.

[21] There will be further discussion of Locke's views in the following chapter.

essary agent" is a contradiction in terms. A balance scale, moved by weights, is not an agent. "To be an Agent signifies, to have a Power of beginning Motion." [22] It also implies a power of not acting. Collins, following Descartes' distinction of an arbitrary will, had argued that if we were free, we would not have to assent to the truth. To this Clarke retorts that to see the true and the false is not an action, and has nothing to do with the will. Judgment, assent and approbation are not efficient causes of action, for they are passive, as well as necessary, and can at best be occasional causes. The will, however, is a self-moving power, which may reject the last approbation. For Clarke, then, as for Malebranche, the self is split between passive faculties of thinking and desiring, and an active will. The self is unable to confer value, or create it, but it can carry out or reject what it values, and in this lies its freedom. Here, as with Locke, we are reduced to a situation in which motives and reasons do not absolutely determine action. Freedom of indifference, or an arbitrary will, is rejected. Yet it is difficult to see on what basis the self-determining, active will of Locke and Clarke operates, since it is neither determined by necessary motives nor is it arbitrarily free.

With Leibniz, on the other hand, we have a strong emphasis on the spontaneity of the mind and its independence from the contingency of the senses. No monad can be purely passive. The mind is not a void, gradually filled from the outside; it is a force, spontaneous in its activities, which produces knowledge from within itself.[23] We shall reserve the further developments of Leibniz's theory until a later point of our discussion.

With this background, we may turn now to eighteenth century France, where Condillac's extension of the Lockean psychology resulted in a dissolution of the self into a mere sum of the perceptions and the mental acts which follow them. But Condillac represents a terminus of earlier developments in French thought. As so often happens in eighteenth century intellectual history, the directional lines were marked out in the seventeenth century, or at the very outset of the eighteenth, and the writers of the later years were left to exploit the fuller consequences, to make firmer and more daring application to specific questions.

[22] Clarke: *A Collection of Papers* (1717), p. 6–42.
[23] *Théodicée,* par. 62–66, *Monadology,* par. 11, and Clarke, *ibid.*

An examination of early eighteenth century clandestine manuscripts reveals a considerable penetration of the new ideas.[24] In one of these we read that the judgment is a mechanical process of material organs, "produced only by the meeting of all that has struck our senses." Reasoning consists "only in the varying location of some small bodies which move themselves about in our heads." [25] Another manuscript reminds us, in support of the passivity of mental activity, that ideas come despite ourselves, and that we are powerless to change their course. "So this puts an end to freedom of reflection. . . . The judgment only acquiesces and agrees that this is unlike that; and the soul cannot change this agreement and make it seem other than what it seems to it from the proposition it is examining." The inevitable conclusion is "the necessity of human actions." [26] The following argument is offered in the anonymous manuscript, *Recherche de la vérité:*

> The first idea that offers itself to a man when he consults himself on the freedom of his will is to believe that he is the absolute master to think as he wills. It is, he says, my will alone that makes my soul apply itself to the objects it presents to it. . . . There is no middle ground, it must be one or the other, either we have free will and are absolute masters of our wills, our thoughts and our actions, or we are obliged and forced by agents independent of ourselves to want to do only what they order.[27]

The same absolute choice is offered in a manuscript (later printed) which is probably the work of Fontenelle.[28] Either the soul (in modern terms, the self) can absolutely determine the brain to choose, or it cannot. If so, it can determine the brain to act virtuously "even if it is its material [i.e., predetermined] disposition to think viciously that will win out." But if choice depends solely on one of two material dispositions of the brain winning out, the soul has no power, and the stronger motive will necessarily, or automatically, determine action.

In these discussions, it is the nature of thought that is seen to be at the root of the problem of freedom. Fontenelle states spe-

---

[24] Dupuy complains in 1717 of the large number of materialists. See *Dialogues sur les plaisirs* . . . p. 14–15.

[25] *L'Ame matérielle,* fol. 152–169.

[26] *Essai sur l'âme,* fol. 6–18. The author admits having borrowed ideas from the Collins-Clarke dispute.

[27] Fol. 8 ff.

[28] *Traité de la liberté par M* . . . In *Nouvelles libertés de penser* (1743), p. 112–151.

cifically that it is fallacious to separate thought from will, and to consider the former as only raw material for the latter. Will is also thought; and no one would maintain that madmen and dreamers are free to choose.

Bayle posed the question bluntly. Is man a passive subject, or is he active? Admittedly, we have a keen sentiment of the activity of our soul. However, we are passive in our sensations, and consequently in our ideas. A created being, moreover, cannot be a principle of action and of continuous creation.[29]

Boulainvilliers denies that the mind possesses a creative power. Man is an automaton, "moving his body according to certain determinations . . . a machine-like being determined by external causes," who has learned to "excite and apply his organs according to the same determinations." All perceptions, affections and actions depend on external stimuli; only the *conatus* to persevere in being is original with the individual. It is absurd to say that the will is moved by no other cause than itself, for such a property belongs only to a necessary and not to a modal being. The mind, in actuating the will, is itself passive. It perceives ideas, but has no "real power of inventing and forging reasons at will. . . ." The memory is involuntary. And desire (which may be actuated by a representation in the mind) is also necessarily caused by objects. Freedom is an illusion. It results partly from confusing the consent derived from sensation with a free act, partly from an awareness of desire and action that is not accompanied by awareness of cause.[30]

One of the most interesting pieces on the subject of freedom, and an excellent example of the dialectic that was brought to bear upon it, was presented to the Academy of Berlin by J. B. Merian.[31] He denominates "passion" any state whose principle is external to oneself, "or which is so attached to a preceding state that the latter's existence requires its existence." Action, accord-

[29] Réponse aux questions d'un provincial," *Oeuvres Diverses*, III, 177; *Dictionnaire*, Art. "Pauliciens."

[30] Boulainvilliers, *Réfutation des erreurs de Benoît de Spinosa* (1737), p. 130–279. This work had earlier been circulated in ms. form; see Wade, *op. cit.*, p. 176 ff. For similar arguments, see also the famous ms. work, *Le Testament de Jean Meslier* (éd. Charles, III, 306).

[31] "Dissertation ontologique sur l'action, la puissance et la liberté," in *Histoire de l'Académie de Berlin*, VI, 1750, p. 459–516. Merian was a Swiss philosopher and philologist who was drawn to the court of Frederick and who became active in the Academy of Berlin.

ing to Merian, must be a state independent of those which precede it. Man is an agent only if he can produce such acts. The
power to act necessarily involves the power not to act; for if it
were only the former, it would be *powerless* not to act, and thus
be a mere force. "Either freedom is this power to act or not to
act . . . or it is nothing at all." Either there is this real difference between action and passion, or else "all is equally fatal and
necessary." We shall shortly return to Merian's *exposé*.

Still before Condillac, we have the writings of Morelly, whose
political system rested on a belief in the total, and one may say,
the totalitarian conditioning of men's minds. Since all ideas derive
from the senses, he reasons, they depend on the organs, and an
exact knowledge of the mechanism of the latter is all that is
needed "to perfect education." [32] The mind is determined in its
attention and impressions "by organic motions occasioned by sur-
rounding objects . . . and by the greater or lesser degrees of intensity of these motions . . ." The action is twofold: on our
mental faculties (imagination, memory, judgment), and on the
emotions (pleasure, pain). The mind is, therefore, "the combined
motions of the organs insofar as they act on the intellect." The
mind is impelled to give its attention to its acquired ideas (over
which it has no power) by "organic motions." The "heart" is "the
combined motions of the organs, insofar as they act on the will."
We are not surprised to see Morelly defining education as "the
art of forming good habits in man early . . . we are habituated
to willing just as we are habituated to thinking." However he
does stress differences in reaction due to inherent organic differences, far more than Helvétius was to do.

The sensationalist psychology was popularized and developed
by d'Alembert and by Condillac. Actually these writers were, in
one sense, less radical than some of their predecessors, and closer
to Locke. They considered the higher intellectual functions to be
active powers of the mind. Thus d'Alembert separates "direct
knowledge," or impressions which "we receive immediately and
without any operation of our will," from reflective knowledge,
which "the mind acquires by operating on the direct knowledge,
combining and uniting it." [33]

[32] *Essai sur l'esprit humain,* 1743, p. 2–30.
[33] *Discours préliminaire* (1751), ed. Picaret, p. 18. Also, *Eléments de philosophie,*
in *Oeuvres,* I, 133.

As for Condillac, he had affirmed, in his early *Essai sur l'origine des connaissances humaines* (1746), that memory gives man the power to govern imagination and to awaken ideas, to fix attention where he so desires.[34] To be sure, attention depends on passions, needs, the temperament and *amour-propre*. But after memory and the imagination are formed, the soul, "master to recall things seen, can direct or turn away its attention from what it sees. It can then return it to these, or only to a few of them, or give it alternately to some and to others. . . . The soul governs itself, draws out ideas it owes only to itself, enriches itself from its own fund." In fact, we dispose of our perceptions "just about as if we had the power to create them and to annihilate them." The mental faculties are given, then, a substantial existence beneath that of the soul, and above that of sensations. In the *Traité des systèmes* (1749), Condillac criticizes Malebranche for holding the mind to be entirely passive. It is absurd, he declares, to say that ideas come "toutes faites," and that the mind does not form them. Experience proves "that the understanding is passive only in regard to the ideas which come immediately from the senses, and that the others are its work." Similarly, it makes no sense for Malebranche to argue in favor of freedom of the will, when the will is moved by God.[35]

When we come to 1754, and the *Traité des sensations*, these views are partly changed by Condillac's new and original thesis, that the mental faculties, from which our concepts derive, are themselves developed *a posteriori* from our sensations. Once this step is taken, and innate faculties follow the way of innate ideas, the self dissolves into states of consciousness that result from the grouping of sensations. "Far from dominating the perceptive life from the height of its immateriality, it [the soul] suffers with servility the vicissitudes of the sensations."[36] The mind is then "active" only in the sense of being "operative"; it is not spontaneous or creative, or superior to its own operations. None the less, Condillac tries to save the self from Hume's dissolution. He does maintain the separate existence of the soul, basis of "the unity of the sentient being."[37] The soul is above the intellectual

[34] *Oeuvres*, 1798, I, 85–92.
[35] *Ibid.*, II, 112–113.
[36] G. Lyon, introduction to *Traité des sensations*, 1886, p. 6.
[37] *Traité des animaux*, ch. 2.

faculties. It is the soul that knows and that analyzes. We are free, because the soul can deliberate and decide among the actions that the will proposes. Attention, Condillac insists in the *Traité des sensations,* is a chosen sensation, "chosen" because it affects and dominates us as a result of pleasure or pain. These two sensations are the irreducible facts which produce attention, memory, reason, and our freedom in choosing. Since pleasure and pain do not depend on us, freedom means only the power to choose what is pleasurable and avoid what is painful. As G. Lyon has put it, Condillac derives all the forms of our activity from our essential passivity. A passive and empty self thus wins a victory, "the victory of being over nothingness." [38]

The materialistic determinists during the second half of the century followed the theories expounded by their predecessors. Voltaire's attitude divides into two periods. At first a defender of free will and of the creativity of the mind, he gradually reverses his stand, in the late 1730's, after a lengthy epistolary debate with Frederick the Great. From now on his view on the mind is that which he summarized in the article "Idée" of his *Dictionnaire philosophique.* We do not make our ideas. They are like our hair, which grows and falls without our doing anything about it; all we can do is to curl and powder it. Malebranche was correct in attributing everything to God as its ultimate cause. We can give ourselves no sensations nor imagine any new ones. "We can therefore do nothing purely by ourselves." All of nature—motion, sensation, ideas, can be "nothing else but the remarkable effects of hidden mathematical laws." All our actions are necessary consequences of necessary ideas. Voltaire was particularly concerned, as we saw in an earlier chapter, with denying to man any privilege that made him an exception to the fixed laws of the natural world, and took him outside of that world. [39]

For Helvétius and for La Mettrie, there is no essential difference between men and animals. The mind is shaped by experience. Helvétius, however, in *De l'Esprit* and *De l'Homme,* also reduces physical differences to insignificance. Allowing maximum play to external, formative influences, he makes man an almost completely modifiable creature. Attention, and the activity of the

[38] *Traité des sensations,* p. 11.
[39] See especially, "Il faut prendre un parti" (1772), *Oeuvres,* XXVIII, 517 ff., in which man is made a thinking machine.

mind, depend entirely on the passions, which are prompted by pleasure. This is so because judgment requires attention, which being an effort (*"peine"*), will not be performed without the motive of self-interest, which, in turn, is reducible to physical sensitivity. Utilizing this mechanism, education and laws can mold men into any shape. The action of the "soul" is always passive and necessary, determined eventually from outside, reducible to sensations. There is, consequently, no faculty of judgment distinct from that of feeling. "To feel is to judge."

D'Holbach also incorporates the sensationist theory of ideation into his determinism. If the mental powers of men are superior to those of animals, he argues, this is due to "different degrees of mobility" of the physical apparatus.[40] D'Holbach makes it clear that

> our soul cannot act by itself or without cause at any moment of our existence; it is conjointly with our body submitted to the impressions of beings which act in us necessarily and according to their properties. . . . If there existed in nature a being truly capable of moving itself by its own energy, that is to say, of producing movements independently of all other causes, such a being would have the power to halt by himself or to suspend the motion of the universe, which is only an immense and uninterrupted chain of causes, linked to each other, acting and reacting by necessary and immutable laws. . . . The hidden movements of the soul are due to causes hidden within ourselves; we think it moves itself, because we do not see the springs that move it. . . . It is only as a result of motions imprinted in our bodies that our brain is modified or our soul thinks, wills and acts.[41]

The association of our ideas, our reflection and judging, is then neither free nor even voluntary. Reason is powerless to deal with passion, as it is powerless when we are intoxicated. "In a word, our soul is not mistress of the movements which are excited in it, nor of calling up the images or ideas that could counterbalance the impulses it receives from elsewhere." [42] The error of the pro-

[40] *Système de la nature,* I, 119–120.

[41] *Ibid.,* I, 175–179. Also, *La morale universelle,* I, ch. 3.

[42] *Système de la nature,* I, 214–216. D'Holbach's reasoning had been anticipated by Vauvenargues. When the will is determined by a passion, we cannot even will to use the reason. The process is automatic. There is no self which transcends motives, which decides between passion and reason. (*Oeuvres,* I, 311 ff.)

See also the following summary by d'Holbach (p. 219): "Man then is not free at any instant of his life: he is necessarily guided at each step by the real or

ponents of free will, then, is to assume that the will is "the first motive force of its acts," whereas it is caused, independently of itself.

The extreme conclusions about the unimportance of inherited structure, which had been proposed by Helvétius, were not accepted by the majority of eighteenth century thinkers, not even by those who were confirmed followers of Locke and Condillac. One of the most dramatic episodes of the unpublished intellectual life of the period was Diderot's rebellion against the extreme and rigid materialism of Helvétius (even as he refused to accept some of La Mettrie's logic). In 1758, Diderot's *Réflexions* on Helvétius' first book, *De l'Esprit,* betrays no opposition to its theses, even though his approval is lukewarm. He does not, at all events, take any objection to the key phrase, "to feel is to judge." But in 1773, he seems to have been thunderstruck by the full force of the psychological and moral implications of Helvétius' posthumous *De l'Homme.* Some of these we have already mentioned, and we shall leave others until the third section of this volume. In regard to the present subject, we find Diderot taking most vigorous exception to two of his friend's central propositions: that to feel is to judge, and that differences in the inherited "organization" of the body are consequently of slight importance for the operations of the intellect. Diderot replies that sensation goes beyond the eye, to the brain, which alone confirms and denies, reflects and judges, and which links and interprets the evidence of all the senses. The senses are therefore relatively unimportant, and the quality of intellect is determined by that of the inherited cerebral structure. Self-interest and physical pleasure cannot, then, determine absolutely the work of the mind, not in men, at least, though it may in animals. We must beware of taking "primitive, essential and distant conditions for immediate causes." [43] If "I feel, therefore I judge" were a satisfactory proposition, we should be able to carry it back one step further, and say "I exist, there-

fictitious advantages which he attaches to the objects which excite his passion. These passions are necessary in a being who ceaselessly tends toward happiness; their energy is necessary, since it depends on their temperament; their temperament is necessary since it depends on the physical elements which compose it; the modifications of this temperament are necessary, since they are infallible and inevitable consequences of the way in which moral and physical beings ceaselessly act upon us."

[43] *Réfutation d'Helvétius,* in *Oeuvres,* II, 335-337.

fore I judge." The passage from sensation to thought involves a jump, declares Diderot, which has not as yet been adequately explained.[44] We must feel to be a poet or a philosopher, but we are not poets or philosophers because we feel.[45] The understanding, dependent though it is on the senses, transcends them. "It is a judge who is neither corrupted nor subjugated by any of the witnesses; it conserves all its authority, and it uses it to perfect itself; it combines all kinds of ideas and sensations, because it does *not* feel anything strongly." [46]

If Diderot's thinking were to be halted at this point, one would be justified in assuming that he believed in the spontaneous activity of the mind, and in connecting it with the theory of moral freedom. But we must consider the fact that Diderot is primarily interested, in this work, in establishing the importance of structural differences (which are necessary to his materialism), and in demolishing Helvétius' theory that men are subject to unlimited conditioning, inasmuch as he holds the opposite to be true. In other words, the "organization" of the body is determinative not only in regard to the sensations producing knowledge and the psychic processes, but also in regard to the character and quality of those processes. If this is to be true, then the mind must be distinct from and transcend the senses which inform it. Its functioning and end-products are not, and cannot be the same in all men, because it is not reducible to the senses. Identity of sensations would produce identity of perceptions or ideas in the *tabula rasa,* but not identity of thought or judgment.

On the other hand, while Diderot thus considers the sensational life of man to be only the occasional cause of a mind which operates on a different level and according to its own laws and processes, and while he gives it an activity peculiar to itself, he did not intend to take Rousseau's position, against the trend of eighteenth century psychology, and give the mind a creative autonomy, or freedom. The status of the mind, as Diderot expounds it, enables it to evolve new types of causation, which are moral and nonphysical, and which are not reducible to the physical. What

[44] *Ibid.,* p. 301.
[45] *Ibid.,* p. 318.
[46] *Ibid.,* p. 323, italics added.

we have, however, is a higher level of psychic determinism.[47]

Diderot had been preoccupied, from his early days, with the great problems of eighteenth century metaphysics, knowledge and the self. In the *Lettre sur les aveugles* (1749), he emphasized the mind's dependence on sensations, which it combines; it is, he says, an "internal sense," a phrase remindful of the "sensorium commune" of the scholastics. Two years later, in the *Lettre sur les sourds et muets,* he doubts that a deaf-mute, deprived of sound (or spoken language), can grasp the abstraction involved in verbal tenses; but the "soul," he affirms, is something quite above the senses. His idea is conveyed in a concrete image. The brain is a bell, the nerves are threads that ring it. "Construct on this bell one of those little figures with which we ornament the top of our clocks; let it have its ear cocked over it, like a musician listening whether his instrument is well tuned: that little figure will be *the soul.*" [48] If several of the cords are pulled at once, the figure will "hear" several sounds at once. The sounds have harmonic resonances which form chords with others that follow. The "attentive little figure compares them and judges them to be consonant or dissonant." Judgment is the formation of chords. But this process is determined by certain laws. "And this law of connection, so necessary in long harmonic phrases, this law, which requires at least one common sound between a chord and the following one, could it fail to apply here?"

The *Apologie de l'abbé de Prades* (1752) continues this sensationalism, with a Lockean insistence that mathematical truths are rational constructs, existing only in the understanding, not in nature.[49] Then, in *Le Rêve de d'Alembert* (1769), Diderot develops his ideas further. He takes up again the idea of vibrating strings (which had originally been suggested to him by his reading of La Mettrie's *L'homme machine*) . Vibrating strings, he now proposes, have the property of making other strings vibrate, sometimes with astonishing jumps; and that is how the ideas of the

[47] Whether Diderot keeps within the bounds of materialism, or surpasses it, is a question that has often been discussed, but not resolved. It is certain, at any rate, that he intends to remain within its bounds, or thinks he does.

[48] *Oeuvres,* I, 367.

[49] *Ibid.*, p. 456. Like others in his time, Diderot fails to make a similar judgment about "scientific laws."

meditating philosopher are awakened and linked.[50] This process is obviously, by the physical analogy, an automatic one, over which the mind has no control. However, while there is only a difference of physical organization between the "sensible soul" and the "reasonable soul," there is a vast difference between a musical instrument and a "philosophical instrument." This difference lies, according to Diderot, in self-consciousness and in memory. We are an instrument that learns to play itself, but only when it is moved by some "impression that has its cause within or outside of the instrument." [51] The brain (*sensorium commune*) and its memory "constitute the unity of the animal . . . and its self." [52] In a healthy man, it commands the nervous network, and so is master of itself, except in moments of passion, panic or delirium.[53] By "master of itself," Diderot explains, he means the power to select among ideas that are necessarily aroused; "I would say that among these ideas there is choice." [54] This would seem to imply freedom of the will. However Diderot is careful to explain that the choice is not really a free choice, but only "the last impulse of desire and aversion, and the last result of all one has been from his birth until the present moment." [55] So that, as far as will is concerned, there is no difference between a man who dreams and a man who is awake. In all we do, in either state, we never really will.

> Can one will, by himself? Will is always born of some internal or external motive, of some present impression, of some past reminiscence, of some passion, of some future project. After that I shall say only one word about will, that the last of our acts is the necessary effect of a single cause: ourselves, very complex, but one. To assert that I could do anything else but what I do is to assert that "I am I and that I am another."

Finally, the *Eléments de physiologie* (1774–1784) confirms this concept of a necessary, if self-directed mental process. Memory is corporal; it is a book that reads itself.[56] The work of our intellect is necessary and automatic, like the linking of cause and effect in

[50] *Le Rêve de d'Alembert,* éd. Vernière, p. 21.
[51] *Ibid.,* p. 23–24.
[52] *Ibid.,* p. 94.
[53] *Ibid.,* p. 115, 120.
[54] *Ibid.,* p. 144–145.
[55] *Ibid.,* p. 136–138. The phrasing of this idea recalls Hobbes.
[56] *Oeuvres,* IX, 368, 374.

nature.[57] "There is nothing free in intellectual operations. . . ." [58] The soul, Diderot now says, is a subaltern, less powerful than pleasure, pain, the passions or wine.[59] Thus the *Eléments de physiologie* concludes what is an expanding, but essentially consistent view of the psyche. It allows to man some conscious self-direction; but freedom, or creativity, are only illusions covering the necessary and largely automatic processes of complex convolutions of specialized nervous tissue.

It is obvious that the word "active," referring to the mind, is ambiguous. No one denied that the mind had "activities"; what was denied by the determinists was the spontaneity or creativity of these activities, its autonomous activity, or capacity of self-actuation.[60] The word "creativity" must also be carefully qualified. Determinists would not have denied that the mind is creative, in the sense of forming new combinations from perceptions or simple ideas; infinitesimal calculus is not given in the simple perceptions of quantity. What they would have denied (although most often this distinction was not explicit) is that the mind can freely determine value, or in other words, exercise choice. They would also have made this process a mechanical one, contrary even to Locke, who had insisted on the unique and active character of the mind's operations. It was precisely this power that the upholders of freedom were called on to defend. Consequently, they had to argue (at least, those among them who did not avoid this phase of the problem) that the intellect is not completely reducible to the perceptions of sensation and its consequences. If this were not so, they believed, the possibility of a rational world, of humanly created values, and of human distinctiveness would vanish. We have already seen Diderot, impelled by his humanism, reach precisely this position, yet, confined by his materialism, elude the consequence of a unique human freedom.

Let us first note that Bayle, who was not a defender of freedom, refused, in some of his writings, to concede the mind's complete

[57] *Ibid.*, p. 372.
[58] *Ibid.*, p. 379.
[59] *Ibid.*, p. 377.
[60] The difference is often in a phrase, as when Hutcheson attributes to the mind the power of comparing relations and proportions, and of "enlarging and diminishing its ideas *at pleasure*." (*An Inquiry into the Original of our Ideas of Beauty and Virtue* (1725), p. 2–3.)

dependence on the senses. This is his principal argument: "Since then the imagination has for its object things that we perceive through some sense, if our soul has any knowledge which is not imagination, it is evident that there is something in our soul that has never been perceived by the senses." Bayle suggests several instances of such knowledge: God, our own thought, propositions lacking sensible quality ("I think, therefore I am" requires only thinking and being, and the ideas of thought and of being were not in the senses first).[61]

Defenders of this thesis do not seem to be numerous in the early years of the century. Ladvocat suggests that man can direct his thoughts to whatever he wishes. His freedom "consists in precisely this, that, having the power to prefer the presence of an act to its absence, he effectively produces it." [62] Voltaire's defense of free will, in his earlier years, was largely based on the autonomy of our reflective faculties. We have the power, he asserted, to look ahead and to form ourselves for future trials and eventualities. It may be assumed that for Voltaire this signified the ability to create and select the motives of volition. "It is not that we are the absolute masters of our ideas; far from it; but we are not absolutely their slaves." [63]

Towards the middle years of the century, Burlamaqui expounded the view that the mind is "a *look* of the soul on the object it desires to know." He applies this theory to freedom. The active principle of the soul determines action after knowledge. He defines the will as "that power of the soul by which it determines itself, in virtue of a principle of activity inherent to its nature, to seek what is suitable to it . . . always in view of its happiness." [64] The position of Buffon was quite similar. He

[61] "La métaphysique," in *Oeuvres diverses*, IV, 485–486. Bayle at times *"se combat lui-même."* He goes on to say that without the senses, there would probably be no knowledge. He also maintains, in Cartesian fashion, that knowledge and volition are different kinds of thought (p. 517–519).

[62] *Entretiens sur un nouveau système de morale* (1721), p. 345–348.

[63] *Oeuvres*, XXXIII, 184 (1728).

[64] *Principes de droit naturel* (1748), I, 10–11, 19. An argument of similar nature had been proposed by Cudworth, in his posthumous *Treatise concerning eternal and immutable morality* (1731). He asserts that sensations are not knowledge, or "intellections." We seek intellectual comprehension beyond them. To know or to understand requires "some inward anticipation of the mind." Knowledge is "an inward and active energy of the mind itself" *upon* the external world, and not a stamp or impression. Ideas about wisdom and morality, about cause and end, and about sense itself, are originated by the mind.

also emphasizes the power of the mind in ideation, and especially in imagination. There is a self, whose essence is in being and in thinking, independently of our senses and all other faculties.[65]

One of the factors of Rousseau's ideological break with the Encyclopedists was his refusal to reduce the activity of the mind to a series of necessary operations on sensations. Like Diderot, he found himself aroused by Helvétius' theories, but he intended his rejection of them to be far more complete and fundamental. The essence of his position is that the mental life does not merely "take place" within us; we have a unitary self and a self-subsistent mind, both of which we know intuitively, and which it is beyond the reach of discursive reason either to prove or to disprove. We are, then, actively determining personalities, not a mass of accidental, external accretions.

In *La Nouvelle Héloïse* Rousseau ridicules the notion that education (or environment) causes all differences in intelligence. If this were true, we should not wait to find out the shape of a child's mind and character, but quickly form them the way we wish. And he mocks the idea that we could "condition" a child according to a model of an honest and rational man, or that minds could be molded "according to a common model." [66] Proceeding a little later to an attack on the determinists, he selects as the heart of their argument the supposition that an intelligent being is passive. He declares this to be nothing more than a supposition, and of no more weight against our intuition than Berkeley's demonstration that bodies may not exist. The whole question is "whether the will is determined without cause, or what is the cause that determines the will." [67] Rousseau's answer is given in *La Profession de foi*. The cause is our judgment; judgment is "active" (i.e., self-actuating), and it is, therefore, free. As other writers put it, we are agents, and not merely actors.[68]

[65] *Oeuvres*, Corpus général, xxv, 337, 340. Buffon is split between Cartesianism and sensualism.

[66] *La Nouvelle Héloïse*, ed. cit., IV, 67–71. Strictly speaking, this development is not consistent with Rousseau's theory of education as expounded in *Emile*.

[67] *Ibid.*, p. 246–248.

[68] In a marginal note in *La Nouvelle Héloïse*, which he crossed out before printing, Rousseau had written that if man has any soul (i.e., non-physical mode), it must be "active and capable of producing by itself a will . . ." (IV, 247, n.2). In the *Discours sur l'inégalité*, he had written, "It is not so much the understanding

As proof of his point, Rousseau first establishes that judgment cannot be reduced to sensation. "To judge and to feel are not the same thing." The act of comparison (and so of judgment) is not automatically called forth and necessitated by perception, but originates in the mind, and is quite distinct. To see several objects at a time is not the same as judging their differences or similarities, or as to count them. This is precisely why a judgment may be erroneous. "According to me, the distinctive faculty of the active or intelligent being is to be able to give a meaning to this word *is.* . . . Without being the master to feel or not to feel, I am the master to examine more or less what I feel." [69] Rousseau's concept of the self, then, goes beyond sensationalism, to insist on its reality as an original, spontaneous activity. "No material being is active in itself, but I am. . . . My will is independent of my senses."

Returning to the question a few pages later, Rousseau distinguishes between the passive and the active movements of his body. "I consent or I resist, I succumb or I conquer, and I feel clearly in myself when I do what I want to do, or when I only yield to my passions." Rousseau considers the passions to be impulses deriving from external objects, as if the self were essentially rational. "I am a slave by my vices, free in my remorse." Again he links the will to the intellective processes: "When you ask me what is the cause that determines my will, I ask in turn what is the cause that determines my judgment: for it is clear that these two causes are only one." If man is active in his judgments, he is in his will. He chooses the good as he judges the true; choice is judgment.

But what determines a man's judgment?

It is his intellective faculty (*"la faculté intelligente"*), it is his power to judge; the determining cause is in himself. Beyond that, I understand nothing. Of course I am not free not to will

that makes, among animals, the specific distinction of man, as his quality of a free agent." (*Oeuvres*, I, 89.) Rousseau errs in making freedom the cause of the development of intelligence, instead of its result. Actually, he speaks of "consciousness of freedom," without realizing that this phrase implies a mental superiority over animals—one which is, precisely, necessary to freedom. By freedom Rousseau means our ability to live outside of fixed instinctual patterns. But we could not do this without consciousness of our freedom to do so, and this, in turn, requires a superior and unique mental equipment.

[69] *Emile, ed. cit.*, p. 325-327.

my own good, I am not free to will my harm; but my freedom consists in the very fact that I cannot will anything that doesn't suit me, or that I so judge, without something outside of myself obliging me to. Does it follow that I am not my master, because I am not free to be another but myself? The source of all action is in the will of a free being; beyond that we cannot go. It is not the word freedom that is devoid of meaning, it is necessity. To suppose some act, some effect which does not derive from an active principle is really to suppose effects without a cause . . . any first impulse has no prior cause. . . .[70]

Rousseau's thinking may appear a bit confused. On close reading, we find that he is much closer than would be expected to Diderot's analysis. Diderot, however, pushes the process one step further, and establishes the necessity of judgments. Rousseau, on the other hand, declares this matter impenetrable, and insists on the ultimate freedom of the judging and willing self. It seems reasonable to assume that Rousseau would not have limited this freedom to willing what we judge to suit us, but would extend it to the determination of what suits us (which is required for true moral freedom), inasmuch as he has described the judgment (on which will depends) as a spontaneous and creative process. Yet there is, in one passage of *La Nouvelle Héloïse,* a curious phrase that echoes one of Diderot's and makes Rousseau seem to approach determinism, despite himself. It is when Saint-Preux writes, "Happy are children who are fortunately born!"[71] He explains that when a child is born with a bad character or nature, education can do little to change him. Physical heredity is an unalterable limit on the power of conditioning, and simultaneously, it would seem justified to add, on the freedom of the individual to create an ego-image of himself and to remake himself accordingly.

Rousseau's defense of freedom is closely tied in with the body of his philosophy. The reform of the individual requires him to possess the freedom to act according to conscience and to overcome passions. This is precisely the meaning of freedom in *La Nouvelle Héloïse.* As we shall see in the following section of this study, Rousseau criticizes society bitterly for decreasing moral

[70] *Ibid.,* p. 340.
[71] *La Nouvelle Héloïse,* IV, 73. "Heureux les enfants bien nés!" Diderot's phrase is "On est bien né, on est mal né."

freedom by certain pressures and patterns of behavior. The relation between free will and political freedom is equally clear. Men use their free wills, on entering into the social compact, giving up personal freedom in exchange for political liberty. Rousseau wishes to give men a maximum of freedom in determining their own destiny. He carries this forward consistently—even when it involves free renunciation of individual freedom for that of the whole.

It should be noted again that naturalists who consider man to be free from the fixity, or destiny, of hereditary determinism avoid the contrary position of moral freedom. They consider that man can be indefinitely conditioned, only because he is not free, but subject to necessary cause and effect. They must, however, remove the self-determinism of heredity from the process, since it would limit the power of conditioning. The proponent of moral freedom, however, admits at least the limited possibility of an individual to escape from both forms of compulsion, and to create a character and a destiny.

As the century grows older, a few other writers take up similar positions. The abbé Dulaurens, in rebuttal of Collins, formulates his ideas quite effectively:

> But if matter can think, it can produce its thoughts, arrange them, order them, direct its appetites, rule them, turn them towards objects which surround them, wherever it cares to; and it is in this that freedom consists. The soul does not have the faculty of creating, but it can produce its own modifications, add to or change its being, and give itself new degrees of being . . . and that in virtue of its peculiar active force.
>
> The motives . . . which make it act are really only its own thoughts, its own determinations; so that, although it always acts in consequence of these motives, it is none the less free, because it is itself that makes these principles and motives of its acts, taking them where it pleases, either in its inclinations, in its passions, or in the intrinsic beauty of order, or in the reasonable love of its true interests.[72]

The basis of Dulaurens' argument is, then, a self which is distinct from and superior to its perceptions, desires and thoughts.

---

[72] *Le Portefeuille d'un philosophe* (1770), v, 108–113. Whether this is Dulaurens' genuine opinion is open to doubt, in view of his support of determinism, which we shall see at a later point.

Frederick the Great, in refuting d'Holbach (he too has changed sides since his correspondence with Voltaire!) insists on the novelty of what the mind does with what it receives. Newton was a creator. We can *allow* ourselves to be dominated by our necessary impulses and disposition; but we can use our reason to control these impulses and, after deliberation, make a free choice.[73]

Bonnet protested against the tendency of the materialists to make of the mental life a mechanical product of sensational data. He argues, first, that sensation cannot be explained on the level of matter in motion. Further, the mechanism of the nervous system is only the occasional cause of the activities of the intellect. Contrary to Hume, Condillac and Diderot, he considers the unity of consciousness to be a sufficient proof of a substantial mind.[74]

For Rivarol, finally, any animal is power (*"puissance"*). We have in us a principle of active energy which is prior to any sensation. And any being that determines itself is *"puissance."* Our ideas are independent of our consent, but we have the power of "stopping at the one that pleases us." We can freely choose between a reason and a passion. To obey our will is to obey our own ideas, or our passions, or any other motive we choose. Man is a mixture of *"puissance et impuissance,"* of freedom and necessity. This freedom is not in violation of nature; we may initiate movement, but it does not escape nature's laws.[75]

[73] *Examen critique du Système de la nature,* in *Oeuvres,* IX, 158–160.
[74] *Essai analytique sur les facultés de l'âme, passim,* et *Analyse,* Art. 4, 5, 12, 13, 19.
[75] *De l'Homme,* p. 89, 206 ff.
Saint-Martin "restores the idea that man can know the principle of his being, an active and intelligent cause. He establishes the distinction between sensations and knowledge." (Monod, *De Pascal à Chateaubriand,* p. 496.)
Robinet's ideas are not easy to disentangle. He supports, to a certain degree, the creative activity of the mind, but also says that all volitions are necessary and physically determined. The soul can only will what it is made to will. But he also claims that man has free will, and can choose between good and evil, because "it can will either absolutely. . . . We have the real power to make the strongest interest yield to the least caprice, to forge our own motives for action, or to wish for no other than the desire to exercise our freedom." (*De la Nature,* 3ᵉ éd. (1766), I, 300–302, 104–105.)
Space does not permit our examining the defensive formulations, often very effective, of the Christian apologists. See Pichon, *Cartel aux philosophes à quatre pattes,* n.p., n.d., p. 2–4; Roussel, *La Loi naturelle* (1769) p. xv. Ilharat de la Chambre follows Aristotle's distinction between the voluntary and the free, and argues that the soul gives birth to its own operations; it is superior to its activities (*op. cit.,* I, 418 ff., 291). Holland emphasizes the difference between the brain and the mind. "The effect I experience on hearing the *sound* of a violin has nothing that resembles the trembling of a string, the vibrations of the air, the shaking of

In conclusion to this phase of the discussion, it may be of interest to note statements by three twentieth century writers which support, in modern terms, the theory of the activity of the mind. The first of these writers, a scientist, asserts that animals have a high degree of spontaneity and are not obliged to follow sensual stimuli.[76] Sense impressions are only guides to it, but it "may act spontaneously in a manner which cannot be predicted . . . spontaneity may lead an object to suddenly assume the character of a goal, or finally, likewise to lose it again." Biological factors (food, enemies) may compel attention. "But beyond this, it is spontaneity which decides in the case of animals whether anything in their surroundings shall acquire actuality or lose it; the direction of attention towards any object is not a reflex process, but a higher intra-central act."

The second writer, Jean Piaget, is a renowned child psychologist. "The child," he writes, "draws things as he knows them to be, not as he sees them. Of course such a habit is primarily proof of the existence and extent of that rationalism that belongs to all thought and which alone can adequately account for the nature of perception. To perceive is to construct intellectually, and if the child draws things as he conceives them, it is certainly because he cannot perceive them without conceiving them." His drawing is a reification, or exteriorization of intellectual processes, an illegitimate fixation of each moment of the constructive movement.[77]

the ear-drum, nor any motion of the brain. If it were the brain that felt, it would feel its own motion." A thinking being is conscious of its own modifications, but the brain is not. There is no mechanical relation between a motion and an idea. Ideas derive from the mind reflecting on its own states; there are no sensual qualities corresponding to hope, doubt, thought, or moral judgment. (*Réflexions philosophiques sur Le Système de la nature* (1773), p. 104–108, 161 ff.) Bergier also distinguishes mental action from physical motion (*op. cit.*, I, 16–24, 164 f.). Lelarge de Lignac defends the substantiality and spontaneous activity of the self. (See summary in R. R. Palmer, *Catholics and Unbelievers in Eighteenth Century France*, p. 143.)

For the eighteenth century German rejection of the sensationist psychology, and its support of the activity and autonomy of the mind, see Cassirer, *op. cit.*, p. 120–133. In England, a strong reaction to the sensationist psychology is found in the two series of *Essays* of Thomas Reid (1785, 1788). His criticism ranges over the entire field. It stresses the difference between perception and conception, and the view that judgment, not an isolated sensation, is the unit of knowledge, though sensation is a necessary condition, or "suggestion."

[76] F. Alverdes, *The Psychology of Animals in Relation to Human Psychology*, p. 143.

[77] J. Piaget, "The Child and Moral Realism," p. 428–9.

Herbert Dingle, a philosopher of science, confirms this analysis from a different viewpoint. He emphasizes subjective reason as "the active agent, bringing rational order into the passive chaos of experience." Experience is passive, because it is the "dead memory of experience when reason begins to operate on it. Out of that chaos of past experience reason constructs myself, you . . . and the rest of the world. . . ." Thus light is not a sense datum; the sensation of light is the sense datum, and "light is the agency which we postulate in order to 'account' for it." The elements of experience are such sense data which we cannot change, "because the passage of time removes them immediately from our control." The elements of reason, however, are ideas "which we form and transform at our discretion." Thus, in the changing concepts which the physicist has entertained about mass, he never looked at mass; "he changed it spontaneously by his own rational act, in order to connect experiences together." [78]

[78] *The Scientific Adventure,* p. 238–245.

ſive

FREEDOM OF INDIFFERENCE.
INTUITION

IN THE discussion of freedom and determinism, the debate over the spontaneity of the mind inevitably connected itself with the so-called "freedom of indifference." This subject has again come to the fore in recent approaches to the problem, and is now spoken of as "the ultimate arbitrariness" of the act of choice. In the eighteenth century, however, the question was conceived in a somewhat different fashion. Freedom of indifference was held to signify *action* without motive. On that ground it was rejected not only by the determinists, but also by many of the supporters of freedom, as a form of insanity.[1] The question, as posed in more modern terms, is whether choice is impossible without some pre-existing value, or whether value is created by choice. The eighteenth century freedom of indifference would thus have to be distinguished from moral freedom, in some way analogous to our distinction between determinism and fatalism. From the viewpoint of moral freedom, choice is not unrelated to motives; but the problem is put back one further remove, and the choice

[1] Thus an early manuscript claims that determinism humiliates man much less than blind whim, without motive, which would make of him "a monster of unreason." *Recherche de le vérité*, fol. 8–33. The author argues that the motives of our will are absolutely foreign to us and independent of us, deriving from temperament and habit, a chain with necessary links.

between or among motives is deemed to be itself not necessarily motivated, or in other words, it is deemed to be within the arbitrary power of the self.

The issue can be traced back to Epicurus and Lucretius, who, in order to escape mechanism, added a spontaneous "swerve" to Democritus' necessary motion of atoms. Epicurus thus denied the universal truth of cause; psychological freedom was related to metaphysical chance, as uncaused occurrences. In the seventeenth century, Descartes conceded the existence of a freedom of indifference. "We are so certain," he writes "of the freedom and indifference that are within us, that there is nothing we know more clearly." [2] However Descartes did not hold this to be necessary to freedom; but on the contrary, thought that we are never more free than when we have a clear reason for willing, in the rational perception of the good and the true.[3]

In the eighteenth century, the determinists condemned and mocked freedom of indifference, resolutely considering it to be the sole form or meaning of freedom.

Bayle's writings on the subject were of great importance, influencing later writers directly, and also indirectly, through Anthony Collins. He approached it often, but somewhat gingerly. "There are few matters as muddled (*embrouillées*) as that of man's free will: affirm its existence or deny it, you fall equally into a labyrinth from which you do not know how to escape. The only convincing proof of human freedom that can be given is that men are wicked and unhappy." That is, Bayle continues, men must be justifiably punishable, since God cannot punish without a cause; and if they were not free, God would be responsible for evil. That God is responsible for evil is, of course, precisely what Bayle wishes to establish.[4]

Freedom of indifference, declares Bayle, would be an imperfection. Man cannot be disciplined unless we know he will

[2] *Principes,* par. 41.

[3] See the Fourth Meditation. It was a common doctrine, both before and after Descartes, that we are free only when we act in accord with reason, not free when we act pursuant to passion. This contradicts the theory of arbitrary choice, if it assumes (as Descartes did) that the clear idea of the good entails assent. If it does not, it is self-contradictory, as the free choice of not being free (i.e., of not following the rational good) would not be freedom.

[4] "Entretiens de Maxime et de Thémiste," *Oeuvres diverses,* III, 42–43, 65–67, 821–822. Bayle at one point declares that God's responsibility makes freedom of indifference impossible.

follow the last decision of his judgment, in which case "it is sufficient to enlighten his mind on his true interests." [5] Otherwise you may convince his mind, and "nevertheless his will will proudly rebel. . . ." (It is clear that in these words we already have the basis of that "faith of the enlightenment" which characterizes its more optimistic aspect. There is also a contradiction with Bayle's pessimistic concept of man as an irrational being, led by passion and pleasure, and quite "undisciplined.") In his article "Hélène," Bayle had issued the famous (though unoriginal) comparison that was destined to be repeated countless times in the eighteenth century. "Man's will is a balance scale that is at rest when the weight of its two pans is equal, and which inclines on one side or the other, according as one of the two pans is more heavily weighted." [6] Replying to Jaquelot's criticism of this analogy, he stresses the mechanical determination of behavior: the will is determined by the judgment, which is determined by its necessary ideas. There is no place, in such a process, for freedom of indifference, since equilibrium of forces can only signify inaction. In a sense, this avoids the question, as when Bayle elsewhere writes that indifference can come only from lack of knowledge, in which case "the will is not determined." [7]

Vauvenargues attacked the concept of freedom of indifference with a type of reasoning that was clear, if not original. [8] Any act must have a motive, even when we do the opposite of what we wish to do in order to prove our freedom. Vauvenargues does not answer the question: what makes the motive of proving our freedom stronger than the motive of avoiding a painful action? If we then ask Vauvenargues whether the motive is necessarily the effective one, he will reply: "It is true that the will also has the power of stimulating ideas, but it must first be determined itself by some cause. The will is never the first cause of our actions, it

[5] "Réponse aux Questions d'un Provincial," *Oeuvres diverses,* III, 679.

[6] The idea of the scale first occurs in Cicero (*Academic Questions,* Bk. 2, par. 4), and was taken up again by Gassendi.

[7] In an earlier work Bayle had argued in a different direction. "It is not more true," he wrote, "that we are successively capable of all sorts of ideas and feelings, than that we can will new objects without end or cease . . . We have the power to apply or to stop our will." But Bayle's thought was to evolve, and it was the later phase that influenced the eighteenth century so profoundly. *Oeuvres diverses,* III, 119–120; *Nouvelles de la république des lettres, ibid.,* I, 671.

[8] "Discours sur la liberté" and "Traité du libre arbitre," in *Oeuvres,* I, 311–339.

is the last spring." [9] As for the classic example of choice without motive—and that is the essential formulation, according to the definition of freedom of indifference we have given above—the choice between heads or tails, or even and odd, Vauvenargues tells us: "if I choose even, it is because the necessity of making a choice offers itself to my thought at the instant that 'even' is present in it."

All these arguments were becoming commonplace, and working their way into the mainstream of eighteenth century thought. Little if anything is added to them by the host of later writers, and we shall limit ourselves to brief mention of several of the most important. Voltaire, in piece after piece, affirms that the only "freedom" is to do as we will, and that will is absolutely determined by the strongest motive—with the added implication that the strongest motive is necessarily the strongest. "My hunting dog is as free as I." The only difference between man and dog is a wider range of action. "You cannot wish without a reason," he says, rejecting thereby the Cartesian freedom of negation.[10] As for freedom of indifference in the choice of odd or even, he disposes of it with Vauvenargues' argument.[11] Elsewhere Voltaire writes, "Every present event is born of the past, and is father to the

---

[9] It is curious that none of the defenders of free will, except Marmontel, attempted a rebuttal of this common refutation of freedom. In reply to the argument that when we do something in order to prove we are free, we are still necessitated by the strongest motive, Marmontel writes: "To will for the sole pleasure of willing freely, without any other motive, and even in opposition to urgent motives, is to be free in the highest degree; it is to be free at least as much as we need to be in order to depend only on ourselves." (*Leçons . . . de métaphysique, Oeuvres*, XVIII, 139.)

Vauvenargues' statement points up the importance of distinguishing "motive" from "cause." Motives are not necessarily determining, but are stimuli which occur to the agent (or opportunities which his mind entertains), when he is about to make a decision. Vauvenargues' word, "determined" implies a necessary cause; the statement would therefore acquire an entirely different meaning had he used the word "awakened," or "aroused." The will would still be "the last spring," but in a different sense.

[10] "My freedom consists in not doing a bad action when my mind pictures it necessarily as bad, in subjugating a passion, when my mind makes me feel the danger of it. But we are not any more free in restraining our desires than in yielding to them"—we only follow the last of a sequence of necessary ideas. (*Le philosophe ignorant* (1766), *Oeuvres*, XXVI, 55–57.) In "Franc Arbitre" (XIX, 196–199), Voltaire repeats and develops Locke's ideas. He concludes that a man with his mistress in his arms has the power to enjoy, but not the power to abstain, unless a stronger motive overcomes his will.

[11] "Liberté, (De la)," *Oeuvres*, XIX, 578–583.

future, without which this universe would be absolutely another universe, as Leibniz has well said. . . . The eternal chain cannot be broken or entangled"—not by God, and certainly not by man. Again, he conceives of freedom only as freedom of indifference, or action without a cause. This he declares is impossible. Freedom of indifference is "a word without an idea, an absurdity, for it would be to determine oneself without reason, an effect without a cause." Even God does not have the absolute autonomy of creativeness which is freedom.[12] Then we are machines, Voltaire cheerfully admits: "We are only wheels in the world-machine." [13]

Voltaire has himself left us ample evidence of his intellectual and emotional torment over this question. "The ignorant man who thinks this way," he writes in *Le philosophe ignorant,* referring of course to himself, "has not always thought this way; but he is finally obliged to surrender." And even more touching is this confession in a personal letter, made in 1749; "I had a deep desire for us to be free; I have done what I could to believe it. Experience and reason convince me that we are machines, made to run for a certain time, and as God wills." [14] There is no doubt that Voltaire's early reluctance to accept determinism, despite his belief in a uniform natural world, was due to the problem of moral responsibility, and to his persistent humanistic desire (all too often defeated by the evidence of reality) not to lower man.

D'Holbach was typical in his denunciation of freedom of indifference as dementia, which is the only type of behavior free of motive. The deliberation of uncertainty he explains as only a temporary alternation between two motives: "I weigh the different motives that alternately stimulate (*poussent*) my will. . . . I am finally determined by the most probable motive, which takes me from my indecision and necessarily impels my will . . . this motive is always the present or future advantage I find in the

---

[12] "Philosophie," xx, 212. This is the contrary of Descartes' view; cf. Sartre, *op. cit.,* p. 183.

[13] "Franc Arbitre." Cf. "Somnambules," and also Notebooks, i, 493: "I have then while dreaming said things that I would scarcely have said while awake. I have then had thoughts despite myself, and without myself having the slightest to do with it. I had neither will nor freedom, and yet I combined ideas sagaciously, and even with some genius. What am I then but a machine?" Cf. Helvétius: "Man is a machine who, set into motion by physical sensitivity, must do what it performs. He is the wheel who, moved by a torrent, raises the pistons. . . ." (*De l'Homme,* VIII, 8–9.)

[14] *Oeuvres,* xxxvi, 565.

action to which I am resolved." [15] D'Holbach's use of the passive voice ("I am determined . . .") is significant. Our soul is not mistress "of the motives which are excited in it." The will is not itself a motive, it is only moved. We are not free for one instant in the process of deliberation; our good or harm "are necessary motives of momentary volitions." The deliberation is necessary, the uncertainty is necessary, and the resultant decision is necessarily that which weighs in our mind as the most advantageous. The word "weighs" is to be taken literally, as d'Holbach, in keeping with the other determinists, pictures the mind as a kind of scale. If the balance is equal, no action is possible. Uncertainty is a painful state, because the rapid modifications of the nervous tissue are fatiguing to the brain. If human behavior is not completely predictable, it is only because of the complexity of our conflicting motivations. Choice, then, is only hesitation, necessarily resolved. "For a man to be able to act freely, he would have to be able to will or to choose without motives, or to prevent motives from acting on his will." But no one will deny, he assures us, that action is determined by will, and that will is determined by a motive, which is independent of our control. Some have thought that we are free, because we have the power, through reason, to bring ideas (about the past or future) to bear, in order to counteract impulse. But this, too (as we saw in the preceding chapter), is an automatic association of ideas. In the following passage, d'Holbach makes his most rigorously logical statement on this issue:

> Am I the master not to desire an object which seems to me desirable? No, of course not, you will say; but you are the master to resist your desire, if you reflect on the consequences. But am I the master to reflect on these consequences, when my soul is carried away by a very strong passion which depends on my natural organization and on the causes that modify it? Is it in my power to add to these consequences all the necessary weight to counterbalance my desire? . . .[16] You should have learned, it will be said, to resist your passions and form the habit of putting a brake on your desires. I will readily admit this. But, I will reply, has my nature been susceptible of being thus modified; my hot blood, my impetuous imagination, the fire that runs

---

[15] *Système de la nature*, I, 207–222.
[16] Compare Bayle and Vauvenargues, *supra*.

in my veins, have they permitted me to make and to apply true experiences at the moment when I needed them? And even if my temperament had made me capable of it, have education, example, the ideas instilled in me at first been suitable to making me form a habit of repressing my desires? [17]

Diderot's ideas, at least in a large part of his writings, are identical with those of d'Holbach. A passage in one of his letters to Landois reveals again the continuity and uniformity of the determinist's argumentation, from Bayle, Collins and the manuscript writers down through the century. It will be seen that freedom of indifference is the essential point at issue.

Look at it closely and you will see that the word "freedom" is a word devoid of meaning; that there are not and cannot be free beings; that we are only what fits in with the general order, with organization, with education and the chain of events. That is what disposes of us invincibly. We can no more conceive of a being acting without motive than of one of the arms of a balance scale acting without the action of a weight; and the motive is always external and foreign to us, attached to us either by nature, or by some cause which is not we. What deceives us is the prodigious variety of our actions, joined to the habit we have developed from birth of confusing the voluntary with the free. . . . There is only one kind of cause, properly speaking, physical cause. There is only one kind of necessity; it is the same for all beings.[18]

Diderot returned to the theme time and again, adding fresh lights, and an increased emphasis on self-determinism, but nothing essentially new. He declares that behavior, theoretically, is entirely predictable from the past; one hundred thousand men, conditioned in the same way, presented with the same object, would experience the same volition.[19] As for freedom of indifference, it does not exist, because there never is a situation of perfect equilibrium between two motives; otherwise the choice would take place without a cause and behavior would be irrational.[20] In the article "Liberté" of the *Encyclopédie,* he ridicules the idea that the soul has an activity of its own. "There is no difference be-

---

[17] *Ibid.,* I, 216–217.
[18] *Correspondance,* éd. Roth, I, 213–214 (1756).
[19] "Volonté," *Encyclopédie.*
[20] *Rêve de d'Alembert,* II, 20, "Liberté," xv, 503 ff. This is, of course, a *petitio principii.*

tween the automatic man who acts in his sleep and the intelligent man who acts and is awake, except that the understanding is more present." [21] At the end of a day, he wrote later, a geometrician has thought and acted, "but he has acted no more freely than an inert body, than a wooden automaton which might have executed the same things as he." [22] As René Hubert has said, transcendent moral freedom is excluded by Diderot's conception of man as "an animal with power to combine ideas." [23] Mind is a special function of the material body, and everything physical obeys (in the view of eighteenth century science) mechanical laws. The decision of the will, desire, and the causal determination of the body are one and the same thing. All of this is developed by Diderot in *Le Rêve de d'Alembert*.

We shall return to Diderot shortly. Let us first look at a group of writers who were partisans of free will, and who spurned freedom of indifference as a trap or a spurious bait that did not represent their theory honestly. We shall see that their criticism is close to that of the determinists.

Even in the seventeenth century, Ameline, a disciple of Descartes, had rejected freedom of indifference as irrelevant. Its origin, he remarks shrewdly, is the fact that the will overflows the limits of understanding, in that we decide for things that are unknown, unexamined or bad. He defines indifference as irresolution, the lack of a reason to decide, and declares that *therefore* our freedom does not depend on it. It would only make our freedom imperfect and despicable, because it would make freedom simply not knowing what to decide. On the contrary (as Descartes had said), we are never more free than when there is least indifference, and when our choice is motivated by reasons and clear understanding. For Ameline, freedom is the power to decide "by an internal determination of the will," which, however, is naturally bound to seek a good and to avoid a non-good.[24]

Let us now examine Leibniz's views, although his qualifications for belonging in this group of the defenders of freedom are rather

[21] *Oeuvres*, xv, 481–482. For an analysis of this interesting article, see J. E. Barker, *op. cit.*, p. 118–123. See also "Ethiopiens," xv, 531. In "Machinal," men are again made automatic machines, despite a transparent cover of protective irony (xvi, 33–35), and in "Providence," (xvi, 453.)

[22] *Eléments de physiologie*, ix, 273.

[23] *Op. cit.*, p. 270–271.

[24] *L'Art de vivre heureux*, 1667, p. 156–161, 166 f.

dubious.[25] His opinions are formulated both in the *Théodicée* and, in more interesting fashion, in the epistolary debate with Clarke.[26] The latter maintained that God has the power of choosing between two absolutely identical cases, and that he can place particles with absolute arbitrariness, in one order or another. Leibniz could not accept this freedom of indifference, because of his principle of sufficient reason. To Clarke, Leibniz's position was equivalent to disregarding the distinction between a truly self-determining agent and a mere mechanism.

> This Notion leads to universal *Necessity* and *Fate,* by supposing that *Motives* have the same relation to the *Will of an Intelligent Agent,* as *Weights* have to a *Balance;* so that of *two* things absolutely indifferent, an Intelligent Agent can no more choose *Either,* than a Balance can move itself when the Weights on both sides are Equal.

Against this charge, Leibniz defended himself by differentiating "between a *motive,* which inclines the will without compelling, and thus preserves the spontaneity and the freedom of the subject, and a real cause, which necessarily produces its effect"; and also by distinguishing the moral, or "free necessity of a fully motivated action and the unfree or passive necessity of a mechanism." [27] Freedom, then, is not senseless arbitrariness, or acting without a motive, but doing what one freely decides is best, or right. This is in accord with Leibniz's principle that nothing happens without a sufficient reason.[28] Thus Leibniz combats both freedom of indifference, on the one hand, and the mechanical, cause-effect necessity of determinism, on the other. We have a false impression of determining ourselves without a preceding reason, due to unawareness of unconscious perceptions and appetitions. But our actions are not necessary, either, because the contrary is not absurd.[29] Action is determined by a motive; but it is also con-

---

[25] See A. O. Lovejoy, *The Great Chain of Being,* p. 167–182.

[26] See S. Clarke, *A Collection of Papers* (1717), p. 371 ff., and A. Koyré, *op. cit.,* p. 246–260.

[27] A. Koyré, *op. cit.,* p. 259–260. For a fuller treatment of freedom of indifference, see *Théodicée,* par. 48–49. According to Leibniz, if the hypothesis of Buridan's ass were meaningful, the ass would indeed die of hunger; but the hypothesis is absurd, since such absolute equalities do not exist.

[28] *Théodicée,* par. 44–45.

[29] According to Leibniz's principle of contradiction, that only is necessary, of which the contrary is absurd. His argumentation is largely metaphysical. Thus intelligence, spontaneity and contingency are the three conditions of a free act.

tingent on the spontaneous, or self-willed decision of an intelligent being. This statement must, however, be qualified by Leibniz's further conclusion that "everything is certain and determined in advance in man"; and that, though everything depends on the activity of the soul itself, the following state comes "from it and from the preceding one." [30] This is similar to the doctrine often called "self-determinism," to which we shall shortly return. In Leibniz's mind, however, volition is not absolutely necessitated; it may act from a probable or sufficient reason, not because we must do this or that (in the sense that to do the contrary is impossible); but according to what we perceive is the fitness of things, which is a "moral necessity." [31]

Towards the middle of the century, the prolific and widely read secretary of the Academy of Berlin, Samuel Formey, was to revive Leibniz's argumentation, but with an admixture of his own ideas that makes it rather confusing in places.[32] He blames those who, frightened by absolute necessity, have gone to the other extreme of leaving the soul "floating, undetermined, and receiving no impression from motives." The faculty of choosing freely does not mean that we can determine without regard to reasons for preference. On the other hand, the principle of sufficient reason implies only a hypothetical necessity. A glass of wine excites my desire, but does not force my will. I remain the master to deliberate and to determine what action to take. Freedom such as this cannot be attributed to beings without reason or consciousness. Even when the equilibrium seems most perfect [presumably in a situation like the choice between odd and even], there is some tiny perception, suitability or unconscious motive—else choice would be impossible. "If the soul could determine itself once without a reason," inquires Formey, "why wouldn't it do so regularly?" But then he adds, "I know that I can resist powerful motives, and whatever their weight, make the scale lean on the other side." This

Spontaneity is assured by his doctrine of monads and pre-established harmony (cf. par. 62). The doctrine is close to Aristotle's.

[30] *Ibid.*, par. 52, 62. The monad merely unfolds its virtualities. Consequently, the self is determined as of the moment God created it.

[31] Thus in the *Nouveaux Essais*, Leibniz says that the strongest single motive does not necessarily prevail. The mind may combine others, to overcome it; it may make "now one now another set of tendencies prevail. . . ." (*Monadology*, p. 143, nb.)

[32] "Réflexions sur la liberté," in *Mélanges philosophiques* (1754), I, 83–126.

is so because the understanding presents motives to the will, but these motives do not force it. They are impulses, to which we have the choice of yielding and resisting. As Descartes has said, indifference is only the lowest degree of freedom. "Let us then conclude that indifference applies only to the soul, which in a thousand cases is not determined by its nature to one side or the other." Thus Formey, while rejecting freedom of indifference, implies acceptance of the modern idea of the ultimate arbitrariness of choice.

The author of an article in Robinet's *Dictionnaire* claims, in refutation of freedom of indifference, that to deny motives is to deny the faculty of evaluation, and therefore to deny both freedom and the will, which must be acted on in order to will. The motive comes from the outside, but the decision whether to follow a motive, or which of several to follow, may be made by the faculty which mediates between motives and decision.[33] This same viewpoint is expressed by Dupont de Nemours.[34] The defect in the logic of these writers is visible in the last statement, which implies precisely the ultimate arbitrariness of choice (among motives) that they do not wish to admit.

Rivarol, who had defended the activity of the self, seeks a middle course.[35] Freedom of indifference he declares to be meaningless; it is not freedom at all, but rather the will "chained by indecision," or blind choice.[36] Does man, he asks, hold the scale, or is he the scale? "I reply that he is the scale itself, but an animated scale which is aware of what it weighs and which adds to the side it prefers the infallibly decisive weight of its consent."

The position of the writers in this group may be summarized as follows: it is absurd to say that because an act has a motive, we act necessarily. A motive is a quality on which we deliberate, and we are, therefore, not determined by it. As Frederick the Great put it, "Doubtless nothing happens without a cause, but not every cause is necessary."[37] It was perhaps not realized that an

---

[33] "Droit naturel," in *Dictionnaire universel,* xxv, 465–6 n.

[34] *Op. cit.,* p. 78. See also J. Dumas, *Traité du suicide* p. 309: actions are not independent of motives; free will is our ability to modify necessary impulse (desire) by internal motives that are independent of that impulse.

[35] *Op. cit.,* I, 206–208.

[36] It is scarcely necessary to point out that this type of argumentation, of which we have now seen several instances, merely eludes the questions.

[37] "Examen critique du *Système de la nature,*" *Oeuvres,* IX, 161. Frederick, like

ultimately arbitrary, or creative choice was involved in this position.

Only a few writers, and most of these Christian apologists, insisted that freedom of the self *is* freedom of indifference. Clarke, after Malebranche and before Hume, attacked the idea that we have an experience of causation: a motive followed by an action does not prove a cause-effect relation, that is, the necessity of the action. He then goes on to a crucial point, one that was often neglected by eighteenth century thinkers. Contrary to what many philosophers said, freedom does not consist in behaving according to reason, rather than according to emotion (or passion). A free being who is reasonable will do what is reasonable, but he can also do otherwise.[38]

One of the few defenders of freedom of indifference who were not clerics was the economist, Quesnay. Freedom was an essential part of his economic system, and he defends it in one of the best reasoned pieces that were written on that subject.[39] The gist of his argument is contained in this sentence: "The freedom of man, then, does not consist simply in the power of acting or not acting [as Locke and others had argued]; it consists also in that of examining and learning the motives that we should prefer to determine us." In other words, as Quesnay explains, the will acts *upon* motives (i.e., does something *to* them). The operations of the mind "not only bring new motives into being which would not have come up without them, but also change the state and power of all these motives. . . ."

Turning now to the French apologists, we find that Chaudon likewise maintains that choice is ultimately arbitrary, and not necessarily required by anything previously in the self. "We do not have only the faculty of willing, but that of willing freely, with a full and efficacious will, and even sometimes of willing without any other reason but our will." The latter event occurs when the understanding pronounces no preference (either because there are no motives, or because they are evenly balanced). This is freedom of indifference, in which the will itself becomes the

some others, has had his fill of the question. "The more we cavil over this matter, the more mixed up it gets; by dint of reasoning we finally make it so obscure that we can't understand ourselves any longer."

[38] *Op. cit.,* p. 25.

[39] *Oeuvres économiques et philosophiques, ed. cit.,* p. 747–754.

motive. According to Chaudon's reasoning, then, it is not correct to say that situations of equilibrium do not exist, or that action in them would be, as Buridan had proposed, impossible, since the self, through its will, is active and self-determining. Such action is not insane, or action without motive.[40]

According to another apologist, Para du Phanjas, freedom is a complete power of the will "to determine itself as it wills and to what it wills, without anything requiring it to act, without its needing anything for action: so that to act or not to act, really and effectively, the determination of the will itself is alone needed, a determination which comes from itself, without being forced or necessitated." [41] Our will may act prior to the operation of the understanding, and it does not have to follow the judgment of the understanding.[42]

The abbé Lelarge de Lignac, after insisting on the metaphysical reality of possibles, bases freedom of indifference on this principle: although our self necessarily loves its well-being, no sort of well-being is absolutely necessary to it.[43] No motive is rigorously compelling to our will; therefore "the reason for our volition is in our activity." Fréret had written (*Lettre de Thrasibule à Leucippe*) that the will must choose the greatest pleasure, that "it has only the force of willing, that is, of being moved." To this de Lignac replies that we often choose the lesser pleasure and the lesser good; "we will what it pleases us the most to will." [44] In this process, we can easily distinguish between what is passively felt and what comes from our own activity. Therefore all comparisons with automata are false.

[40] *Op. cit.*, II, 1–5. As for the question of reconciling freedom with the divine prescience (a question we have not discussed), Chaudon cavalierly says that it is God's problem, not ours.

[41] *Eléments de métaphysique* . . . , 1767, p. 181–190.

[42] This last argument refers again to a subsidiary controversy (to which we have already alluded) among the partisans of free will. Some of these argued that freedom is an act of enlightened intelligence, in contrast with an automatic, or a passionate act. Cf. S. Maréchal, *Examen des critiques du livre intitulé "De l'Esprit"* (1760), p. 95–96. Many Christian apologists refused to accept this limitation. Cf. the criticism in the *Journal de Trévoux* (*ibid.*, p. 113–114).

[43] *Le Témoignage du sens intime et de l'expérience* . . . (1770), I, 86–200.

[44] There is occasionally some confusion, in writers of the eighteenth century (and of other periods), between a pleasant idea and the idea of pleasure. To put the difference clearly: that idea which, as a proposed course of action, is now most pleasurable, may involve future pain, and this consequence may be perfectly clear at the moment of choice, The implication of de Lignac's argument is that the self actively determines what it is its pleasure to will.

In a passage that brings William James to mind, Ilharat de la Chambre poses the case of a man choosing one street or another in order to reach his destination. "If the soul on these occasions makes a choice, either with the lack of external determining motivations or with a perfect equilibrium of reasons that might determine it, it chooses only because it has command and dominion over its actions." [45] Certainly, freedom is limited, in a way, by the sensual apparatus of the body which produces necessary impressions, but these do not impose on the will the necessity of "attaching itself to these objects." It is also limited, in the same fashion, by ignorance, since one can will something only if it is known. But within the sphere of its existence, "the soul has a total, perfect and entire dominion over itself." This derives from *"un fond d'activité"* which is peculiar to it. This activity may be necessitated by a motive it cannot combat, and the action is then "voluntary"; but if the motive is one it can accept or reject, it is free. Since we must, in general, choose what we hold to be the good, freedom lies in determining what is good. But in a concrete case, we do have the freedom to choose evil.

We have already referred to Merian's interesting treatment of the free will problem. Turning to the question of "freedom of indifference," he begins by specifying the meaning of volition. The will is not the last judgment of the understanding, because the latter is passive. The will is rather "the exercise of the self-motivating principle which is entirely active," that is, something which "breaks the chain." It cannot be mere *perception* (of a necessary willing), as if a falling stone had consciousness. It is, then, freedom of indifference, the power to will or not to, and this not only when the alternatives are equal. Locke, he declares, misunderstood the problem. The absurdity does not lie, as Locke had written, in adding one faculty to another, freedom to willing; it lies in the fact that, since they are the same faculty, "to ask whether the will is free is to ask whether freedom is free." Collins had said that when we are given a choice, we are necessitated to an act of volition, and so are not free. But this can only mean, "we are not free to be free, because we must be free."

The defenders of freedom of indifference were, then, endeavoring to counteract the assertion that it signified senseless or

[45] *Abrégé* . . . p. 418-466.

irrational action. Approaching a modern formulation, they denied that this arbitrariness implied a complete dissociation of act and motivation. Motives are the grounds upon which the self operates in the act of choice; and when none are present, the will to act, they claimed, is itself a motive.

Merian's criticism of Locke brings us next to the important question of self-determinism. We have seen that the more naïve determinists emphasized the mechanical necessity of volition and of causation "outside of ourselves." But Spinoza, Locke, Malebranche and Leibniz placed "freedom" in causation by the self.[46] If we examine this carefully, we shall see that despite semantic differences, there is a large area of agreement between some thinkers who held man to be free—according to this definition—and many who proclaimed themselves determinists. In the problem of choice, we are dealing with a process that has three steps: (1) the competition of motivations, of whatever kind (2) volition (or the selected motive that will be transferred into action) (3) action. The crux of the matter must be in the relation between steps one and two.[47] Both groups referred to here agree that step two is necessitated by step one, but emphasize that the second step is none the less an "action" of the self, taken in the consciousness of the self. This really amounts to saying that in the turmoil of competing motives, the self is consciously observing a process, the outcome of which is necessarily determined by what the self has been (any future projection being also the result of what it has been); an outcome

[46] Locke, it will be remembered, states that the mind determines the will, or "the agent itself exercising the power that it has that particular way." (*Essay,* Part II, ch. 21, par. 29.) I am free, he adds, in the power to move my hand, or not to; but my decision is necessitated by my judgment. I am not free if I am determined by anything but my own desire and judgment. (*Ibid.,* par. 71.) Locke admits that the greatest and most pressing motive does *not* always determine the will. The mind has the power, in most cases, to suspend actions, to consider and weigh objects of desire. "In this lies the liberty man has." But this is *improperly called free will,* since we must act according to the last result of the examination. (*Ibid.,* par. 47.) Locke thus leaves open the crucial question, whether the "last result of the examination" is necessarily determined and theoretically predictable.

Self-determinism is also the essence of Spinoza's theory. "And so I am altogether for calling a man so far free, as he is led by reason; because so far he is determined to action by such causes, as can be adequately understood by his unassisted nature, although by these causes he be necessarily determined to action." (*Tractatus politicus,* ch. 1, par. 11.)

We have seen that Bayle and others followed this view of a necessary judgment necessarily determining volition.

[47] We omit here as extraneous to the present point the fact that Locke placed freedom in the relation between steps two and three.

which it must confirm, since the self cannot, at any point, escape from itself. This is "self-determinism," or "freedom," if one chooses to define the word in that way.

Other partisans of freedom, however, and inevitably those few who upheld freedom of indifference, took a position which amounts to the assertion that the second step is not necessitated by the first; that on the contrary, the self, by a self-transcendence, controls both the process and the outcome, and thus is creative. An example will make this point clearer. At this moment, I can go on writing, or I can stop. The conflicting motives are fatigue and the desire to finish this chapter. Does the self merely observe the conflict of motives and act only to confirm the stronger motive, which necessarily becomes the volition, and so, in reality, actuates the action of the self? Or does the self, by an arbitrary decision, effectively determine which is the stronger motive, the one it chooses to actuate it? In the latter view, one still does not escape from the self; but the self is deemed to have a power of self-creation.

This is precisely the point of Merian's criticism of self-determinism. Locke, he reminds us again, had said it is absurd to ask whether a man is free to will which of two acts will please him, for it is to ask, can he will what he wills. But this "will" is not volition, only a judgment. And we must still ask whether it determines volition. Locke says that to be determined by one's own judgment does not destroy freedom; but he also says that judgment is necessitated by uneasiness. There is no freedom, declares Merian, in such a chain of causes. To say that the motives are internal and self-engendered is merely to say they come from the necessity of our own nature. And in treating responsibility and punishment, Locke himself must come back to the freedom of volition which he has mocked. For Locke says that we have the power to suspend our choice until riper deliberation, and so we are responsible even though the actual volition is necessary. But to suspend judgment, Merian points out, requires an immediate act of will, and like any other act of will, this one is not free! [48] The matter is simple, argues Merian in summation. Either volition *b* is necessitated by motive *a*, or there is no connection. Can we

[48] The same applies to Leibniz's theory that the will tends in several directions, but acts only where there is least resistance—the soul does not depend on itself.

then not say that a substance is free simply because it produces the motives of its volitions from its own depths? No, answers Merian, because it produces them by volitions, and we are back to the same ultimate question. The same happens with all other by-passes, such as the argument that we can change the force of motives by bringing other motives to bear—as d'Holbach was also to note.

In short, concludes Merian, "the only way of accommodating the analogy of the balance scale to true freedom would be to add to it a power of putting on or taking off weights, but a power whose exercise would not be determined by other weights." There is freedom, then, only when volition is detached from motive, when the soul "determines without being determined." This still allows the play of motives: the self "may determine itself on stronger or weaker motives; but motives never determine it. Their prerogatives are enclosed within the limits of the understanding; and the morality of actions, their merit or demerit, consists only in our acting with full freedom on reasonable or unreasonable motivation." [49]

The theory of self-determinism, however, became widely accepted. Bayle had referred to it only briefly, but was inclined to favor it.[50] Fontenelle (if we assume him to be the author of the anonymous *Traité de la liberté par M . . .*) also considers it reasonable, but takes great care to warn against confusing self-determination with freedom. "What one does because he wills to is voluntary, but it is not free, unless one can really and effectively prevent oneself from willing it . . . The soul is necessarily determined in its brain to will what it wills." [51] According to Crousaz, the fact that I may choose the worse of two possibilities, solely in order to prove my freedom, shows that I owe my decision only to myself. This is because thinking substances may be their own objects, and find "intrinsic motives within themselves." [52]

[49] Merian anticipates the erroneous comparison of some modern writers between free will and the indeterminacy of sub-atomic particles, in his rejection of the comparison of freedom of indifference with the Epicurean deviation. "Can an atom of matter, devoid of intelligence and will, turned aside from its path without any cause, be put in parallel with an intelligent substance which foresees, deliberates and chooses by the active power with which it is endowed . . . ?" In the first case, we have an effect without a cause, which leads, he says, to absolute fatalism; in the second, an event produced by a cause, the self.

[50] *Oeuvres diverses*, III, 780–1, IV, 265.

[51] *Op. cit.*, p. 137–142.

[52] *Examen de L'Essay de Monsieur Pope* (1737), p. 33–38.

For Crousaz, however, all this is a proof of *freedom*. D'Holbach, on the other hand, proclaimed self-determination with vigor, as a denial of freedom.

> When we say that man is not free, we do not intend to compare him to a body moved simply by an impulsive cause; he contains within himself causes inherent to his being; he is moved by an internal organ *which has its own laws and which is necessarily determined as a result of ideas, perceptions, sensations which it receives from external objects.* . . . It is true that we are told that the soul enjoys an activity of its own; I admit it; but it is certain that this activity will never exert itself, if some motive or cause does not enable it to do so. . . . Gunpowder doubtless has an activity of its own, but it will never exercise it if one does not bring to it the fire that will force it to.[53]

Despite d'Holbach's assertion that he does not intend to compare man to an inert body, he ends up by so doing; this is inevitable, since the "active" power he grants to the self is not a creative power, or the ability to create motives. It is only the power to move after being moved.

Diderot, like Voltaire, was intellectually tormented by the problem of freedom. Unlike Voltaire, he did not change sides and content himself thereafter (save for a few moments of doubt) with a simple deterministic formula. We have seen how he pushed the logic of determinism to its inevitable conclusion, that man is a conscious automaton who hesitates, or deliberates. In several other pieces, however, and despite the denial of a substantial self, Diderot insists on the active, though necessary determination of the will by the self. He speaks favorably, in the article "Liberté," about Leibniz's theory of moral necessity, which is opposed to physical, or "fatal" necessity; however, he does not seem to have an exact understanding of that theory.

> Of this kind is that [freedom] which makes a man who has the use of his reason, if he is offered the choice of good food and poison, decide for the first. Freedom in this case is complete, and yet the contrary is impossible. Who can deny that the wise man, when he acts freely, necessarily follows the decision that reason prescribes to him?

This is precisely the theory which Diderot develops in the *Rêve de d'Alembert*. The brain is normally the master of the nervous

[53] *Système de la nature*, I, 224–225. Italics added.

system; it perceives, remembers, recalls, and enlarges on ideas. The will, to be sure, can act only by a motive, and has no alternative; the least of actions is the necessary effect of one cause: ourselves. By this Diderot means that ideas are determinants of the will—which is to say that mind finds its causation within its own ideas. Diderot's analogy between ideation and "vibrating strings," which he develops in the *Rêve,* implies that the process of association of ideas, although not under the free control of the will, is not one of predictable cause-effect, either. There are jumps, and there is "randomness." [54] Self-determinism, though broadened in this fashion, is not self-creation, since it limits us to an elaboration of the past. It does conceive of man as an active collaborator in his own destiny. Voltaire had written that if we were free, we could change our character.[55] Diderot believes in the determinism of heredity and environment. But some event may stimulate a child who is "badly born" to struggle against his evil character.[56]

We have the impression that Diderot was ill at ease within his own theory. Its logic appeared to him inescapable and irrefutable. But Diderot was humanist enough to recognize that logic is not a satisfactory way of accounting for human behavior. He knew that his "automaton" made moral judgments and created beauty. Even in 1749, he had written to Voltaire, admitting that the most convinced determinists were enthusiastic about beauty and the moral good, and distinguished between being hit by a tile and by a man.[57] To a certain extent this was camouflage, and it does not necessarily imply, of itself, more than self-determinism. In the much later *Eléments de physiologie,* Diderot does admit the possibility of the freedom of indifference. "If there is freedom, it is in the ignorant person. If between two things to do one has no motive for preference, it is then that one does the one which one

[54] We may take the liberty of supplying a hypothetical example to illustrate the implications of Diderot's theory. Suppose that by a process of sensations and memory, we have the idea of a roast chicken, and a desire for it. This idea may, by a "harmonic," awaken the idea of money, and we may perform an act related to the latter. The pattern may, of course, be still more complex. From the idea of the chicken we could never predict the sequence of ideas or the ultimate determinant of the will, since these follow unpredictable jumps rather than a necessary cause-effect relation.

[55] *Notebooks,* I, 298.
[56] *Lettres à Sophie Volland,* II, 279.
[57] *Oeuvres,* XIX, 422.

wills." [58] But it is in his novel, *Jacques le Fataliste* (1773), that Diderot brings out clearly the opposition between his unshakable logical conviction and his equally invincible intuition of human reality.[59] Between Jacques, the determinist, and his master, who believes he is free, the dialogue continues inconclusively throughout the novel, and Diderot never interrupts it to decide between them. Jacques, despite his Spinozist theory, and his belief that man is "a thinking and living machine," moved only by causes, becomes angry "against the unjust man." Jacques denies the value of foresight, yet tries to forestall evil. He denies virtue, but practices it. He mocks his master's statement, "I feel within myself that I am free, as I feel that I think," answering that freedom from motivation [i.e., freedom of indifference] would be "the true characteristic of a maniac." But he also says, "I think in one fashion, and I can't help acting in another"—a phrase that reminds us of a line in one of Diderot's letters to Sophie Volland: "I rage at being entangled in a devil of a philosophy that my mind can't help approving and my heart belying."

The manifestations of moral life, Diderot feels, cannot be reduced to a mechanical play of causation. Diderot's own absolute arbitrariness in breaking up his narration, and Jacques' arbitrariness in postponing a promised tale, may be more than a play of technique inherited from Marivaux and Sterne, may be the "proof" in action which cannot be given in terms of discursive logic. Here is a work suffused with contradiction and whimsy, a work in which the human factor remains incalculable, and in which the leading character tells us that behavior is an orderly, certain matter of cause and effect, as with any machine. But logic and life are simply inconsistent. Professor Jean Fabre has admirably summarized Diderot's dilemma: "Diderot's quest ends up at this *impasse:* a necessarily determined universe; an individual who refuses to submit to this determinism, who obstinately clings to his illusion of freedom." [60]

[58] *Ibid.,* IX, 375. This is also admitted in the abbé Dulaurens' defense of determinism, in *Le Compère Mathieu* (1770, III, 208). See Otis E. Fellows and A. G. Green, "Diderot and the abbé Dulaurens," p. 79–82.

[59] See J. R. Loy's important study of this work, *Diderot's Determined Fatalist,* and L. G. Crocker, *Two Diderot Studies.*

[60] Introduction to *Le Neveu de Rameau,* p. lxxx. As Dr. Johnson commented to Boswell, "All theory is against the freedom of the will; all experience for it."

This turn in Diderot's thinking leads us to the third important phase of the debate: the "intuition" of our freedom. A remark of Lord Kames sets the issue directly. Admitting that the arguments of reason are on the side of necessity, he adds that, despite this, "they fail in accounting for man's moral powers, and struggle in vain to reconcile to their system the testimony which conscience clearly gives to freedom." [61]

In the argumentation that we have followed thus far, the greater logical subtlety was exercised by the upholders of free will. This was because of the difficulty of refuting the determinists' argument (which, despite all its variations, was really a simple one: there can be no effect without a cause, or *vice versa*). On the matter of intuition, and in the question of moral responsibility, which we shall come to next, the shoe was on the other foot. The argument of the libertarians was equally simple and equally difficult to refute.

There was practically no defender of free will who did not propose the "proof" of intuition, and the variations are purely verbal. The apologist, Bergier, was one of those who were candid enough to admit that it is the only positive "proof" of freedom.[62] Formey, after much logical maneuvering, also adds, "I admit that it is to the proof of feeling that we must have recourse, to convince ourselves of the difference we have just established." [63] He insists that this kind of proof is more valid than any other. "That which makes man say that he thinks, makes him say equally that he determines himself to act or not to act. To contest his spontaneity is to destroy his thought." And Ilharat de la Chambre expresses this view as forcefully as any other writer of his time:

(Quoted by G. R. Havens, *The Age of Ideas*, p. 338.) Cf. Cassirer's comment: "Diderot saw and expressed clearly all the antinomies into which the system of fatalism finally leads. . . . He admits a vicious circle but he transforms this situation into a grand jest . . . The novel *Jack the Fatalist* endeavors to show that the concept of fate is the alpha and omega of human thinking, but it also shows how thought time and again comes into conflict with this concept, how it is forced implicitly to deny and revoke the concept even while affirming it. There is no alternative but . . . to extend our very idea of necessity so as to include that idea of inconsistency. . . ." (P. 71–72.)

[61] *Essays on the Principles of Morality* (1751), p. 201. Kames would therefore accept both: man is "a necessary agent," but one who must suffer the consequences of a natural conviction that he is free.

[62] *Apologie* . . . p. 296 f.

[63] *Op. cit.,* p. 95 ff.

In vain would one endeavor to prove that it [i.e., the will] is really endowed with this power: this doctrine is above all logic-chopping. Each of us feels that he acts when he wants to, and that he abstains from acting when it pleases him; this internal feeling is so keenly perceived in all times and ages, in all conditions, that it is not possible to fail to recognize it. . . .[64]

Rousseau's statements on this score were no different from a hundred others. Saint-Preux writes to his beloved Julie against the "sophists" who deny our freedom:

. . . because a reasoner proves in vain that I am not free; internal feeling, stronger than all his arguments, belies him constantly, and whatever choice I make in any deliberation, I feel with certainty that it is only up to me to make the contrary choice. All these scholastic subtleties are vain . . . because whether freedom exists or not, they may still prove that it doesn't exist. . . . They begin by supposing that every intelligent being is purely passive, and then they deduce from that supposition consequences that prove he is not active. . . . We do not suppose ourselves active and free; we feel that we are.[65]

The formulations of this idea in the *Profession de foi* are even better known.[66]

Voltaire's attitudes, both before and after his conversion to determinism, were predominantly pragmatic and utilitarian, and this passage from an early letter to Helvétius (1738) is significant of his *tournure d'esprit*, and of his early doubts.

I shall confess to you that after wandering very long in this labyrinth, after breaking my thread a thousand times, I've come back to the view that the good of society requires that man should believe himself free. We all act according to this principle; and it would seem to me a bit strange to admit in practice what we would reject in speculation. Once more I am beginning, my dear friend, to esteem happiness in life higher than a truth; if fatalism were unfortunately true, I should not want such a cruel truth. Why couldn't the Sovereign Being, who has

---

[64] *Op. cit.*, I, 418.

[65] *La Nouvelle Héloïse*, IV, 247-248.

[66] "You will ask me next how I know that there are spontaneous movements; I will tell you that I know it because I feel it. I want to move my arm and I move it, without the movement having any other immediate cause but my will. In vain would you try by reasoning to destroy this feeling in me; it is stronger than any evidence; you might as well prove to me that I do not exist." (Ed. cit., p. 328-329, 330, 339.)

given me an intellect which cannot be understood, have also given me a little freedom? Would he have deceived us all? Those are silly arguments. I've come back to feeling, after getting lost in reasoning.[67]

Diderot, as we have seen, was to reach an attitude not too distant from that of Voltaire's letter. Most often he had derided the proof of intuition: ". . . What is this internal feeling of our freedom? the illusion of a child who does not reflect about anything. Isn't man different then from an automaton? Not at all different from an automaton who feels." [68] Yet in the *Salon de 1767*, a work not written for publication, he had admitted that "by a natural and almost invincible inclination, we suppose in this machine will, intelligence, plan and freedom." [69] And to Falconet he wrote that "truths of feeling are more unshakeable in our soul than truths of rigorous demonstration, although it is often impossible to satisfy the mind completely about them. All the proofs adduced for them, taken separately, may be contested, but the bundle is more difficult to break." [70]

The argumentation on the side of the determinists consisted in a search for subtle or forceful formulations of a single idea: the feeling of our freedom is an illusion.[71] Bayle, for instance, admits the feeling, but argues that it is a chimera, because the soul, being a spiritual substance, cannot be an efficient cause of physical motion.[72] Fontenelle asks, Why do we *feel* free? And he replies that the error has two sources: the fact that we do only what we will to do, and the fact that we often stop to deliberate. The slave doesn't feel free, because he knows he acts on another's orders. But he would think himself free if he did not know his master, if he executed his ideas without knowing it, and if these orders were always in conformity with his own inclination. For Fontenelle, this is precisely the case with man: the brain is his master, and its orders always conform to his inclination, "since they cause the

---

[67] Besterman, *Voltaire's Correspondence*, VII, 30–31 (Best. 1368).

[68] Article "Liberté."

[69] *Oeuvres*, XI, 103.

[70] *Oeuvres*, XVIII, 125 (1766).

[71] I have found only the author of the ms. *Recherche de la vérité* who denies the intuition itself. He claims that, on the contrary, we know that we obey the stronger motive and are not free.

[72] *Oeuvres diverses*, III, 729–730, etc. For Ilharat's clever refutation, see *op. cit.*, p. 421–426. It is an intuition of volition, he says, not one of the efficient cause.

inclination itself." Deliberation is deceptive; we do not realize that we hesitate only until one side has the greater weight, and the equilibrium is broken by "material dispositions." [73]

Argumentation of this type makes Rousseau's criticism, in *La Nouvelle Héloïse,* seem quite understandable.

The most cogent phrasing of this argument was formulated by Hume. In his *Treatise on Human Nature,* Hume grants man a liberty of spontaneity which is equivalent only to Locke's concept of freedom; but he concedes that we have "a false sensation, or experience even, of the freedom of indifference." [74] Later, in the eighth section of the *Enquiry concerning Human Understanding,* Hume sought to account for this false but powerful conviction, by relating it to our experience of causation. We have the illusion of grasping a causal connection between physical events, he proposes, and do not enjoy that illusion in regard to human actions; whence the further illusion of escaping causation, or of freedom. The truth, according to Hume, is that we can never grasp a causative connection intellectually—in either case, though philosophers think it exists uniformly, in both cases.

It would be tedious, except for the reader who is interested in the play of dialectical logic, to pursue the argumentation further. Little else of substance, if anything, would be uncovered.[75]

---

[73] *Op. cit.,* p. 142–151.

[74] Aiken, p. 18.

[75] For those wishing to pursue further the history of this controversy, the following references will be of use. (1) On the side of determinism: A. Collins, *A Philosophical Inquiry concerning Human Liberty* (1717); Fréret, Lettre de *Thrasibule à Leucippe, Oeuvres,* III, 99–104; Hume, *Moral and Political Philosophy,* ed. Aiken, p. 11–22; d'Argens, *Lettres cabalistiques,* Lettre XXIII, XXXIV; *id., Songes philosophiques,* p. 31; *id., Thérèse philosophe,* I, 118–119, II, 56–58; Meslier, marginalia in Fénelon, *Oeuvres philosophiques,* p. 177–178, 225–234, 291, 553; La Mettrie, Histoire naturelle de l'âme (1745), p. 291–293; Hartley, *Observations on Man,* I, 500–508; Jaucourt, art. "Désir," *Encyclopédie;* Helvétius, *De l'Esprit,* p. 36–38; Bonnet, *Essai sur les facultés de l'âme, Oeuvres,* VI, ch. 12, 16, 18; J. Priestley, *A Free Discussion of the Doctrines of Materialism,* p. 125–149; Marat, *De l'Homme,* I, 188–189, 286–288; Sade, *Histoire de Juliette,* I, 22, IV, 106–109. For manuscripts, see *L'Ame mortelle,* fol. 70–74; *Examen de la religion,* fol. 116–117; also Ira O. Wade, *op. cit.,* p. 60 f., 225.

On the side of free will: ms. *Difficultés sur la religion,* fol. 40; Abbadie, *op. cit.,* p. 104 f.; La Placette, *Eclaircissements sur quelques difficultés . . . ;* Wollaston, *The Religion of Nature Delineated,* p. 63–64; Pufendorf, *op. cit.,* I, 60 ff.; Buffier, *Traité des premières vérités* (1843), par. 58–60, 415–419; *id., Traité de la société civile* (1726), p. 30–31; Crousaz, *La Logique* (1720), I, 219–234; Saint-Lambert, *Commentaire sur le catéchisme universel, Oeuvres philosophiques,* An IX, II, 328 f.; Burlamaqui, *op. cit.,* I, 22–39; Maupertuis, *Essai de philosophie morale,* I, 216 f.; Voltaire, *Traité de métaphysique,* p. 42–51, 61–63, *Discours en vers sur l'homme,*

Let us instead turn our attention to the ethical import of the controversy, which was focused on the question of imputation and responsibility.

2ᵉ Discours, *Eléments de Newton, Oeuvres,* XXII, 411–417, and especially XXXIV, 324–334, 368–370, 394–397, 412–417, 432–435, 454–456; Père André, "Discours sur la liberté," *Oeuvres,* I, 279–310, II, 258–262; *id., Documents inédits,* II, 304; anon., art. "Evidence," *Encyclopédie;* Yvon, art. "Action," *Encyclopédie;* d'Alembert, art. "Futur contingent," "Fortuit," *Encyclopédie; id., Elémens de philosophie, Oeuvres,* I, 209–210; Th. Reid, *Essays on the Active Powers of the Human Mind, Works,* D. Stewart, III, 173–195; Condillac, "Discours sur la liberté," *Oeuvres,* III, 423–432; R. Price, *A Review of the Principal Questions in Morals,* p. 181–183, 244 ff.; d'Aguesseau, *Oeuvres,* II, 458–460; Delisle de Sales, *op. cit.,* III, 382–394; Dupont de Nemours, *op. cit.,* p. 199–213; A. Cloots, *La république universelle,* p. 31; Hemsterhuys, *Oeuvres philosophiques,* I, 160–165; A. Ferguson, *Principles of Moral and Political Science,* I, 152–154; Rivarol, *De la philosophie moderne,* p. 50–53; *id., Pensées inédites,* 1836, p. 84–85; Marmontel, *Leçons . . . sur la métaphysique, Oeuvres,* XVII, p. 113–139.

The following Christian apologists are among the defenders of free will: P. S. Régis, *Système de philosophie,* I, 217–219; Denesle, *Examen du matérialisme,* II, 100 ff.; Boullier, *Discours philosophiques,* p. 176–258, in part a refutation of the *Traité de la liberté par M . . . ;* L. Lefrançois, *Oeuvres complètes,* I, 65–72, 785; Pluquet, *Examen du fatalisme,* I, 446 ff., and esp. III, Section 2; Hayer, *La religion vengée,* VI, 354–367 (against Helvétius), VIII, 222–287 (against Voltaire), XI, 1–23 (against art. "Fatalité"); Camuset, *Principes contre l'incrédulité,* p. 27–29, 62–69 (against d'Holbach); Sisson de Valmire, *Dieu et l'homme,* p. 123–130; Guidi, *Entretiens philosophiques,* I, 166 ff, II, 301 f.; G. J. Holland, *Réflexions philosophiques,* I, 167–173 (ag. d'Holbach); Gérard, *Le comte de Valmont,* I, 34–36, 438–443; Boudier de Villemaire, *L'irréligion dévoilée,* 73 ff; N. Bergier, *Principes de métaphysique,* p. 126–139; Paulian, *Le véritable systéme de la nature.*

Six

THE MORAL CONSEQUENCES

THE CONTROVERSY over free will was more than a debate over an abstract issue of psychology or metaphysics. It was obvious to everyone that the foundation and the nature of the ethical structure was really at stake.[1] The heart of the matter was the question of moral responsibility, and a consequence of the answer one gave to it was to define the nature of a morally good or right act. Perhaps a quick way to grasp the difficulties involved is to glance at the somewhat confused conclusions of Louis de Beausobre, who was trying to see his way through the problem. Actions, he tells us, are not good or bad in themselves, but only in relation to consequences and to motives. Motives ought to be the reason for rewards and punishment; but consequences are what make an act good or bad. Therefore, concludes de Beausobre, "we are wrong to think that what we call crime is really so, outside of its consequences, and that we should punish it, other than for the motives."[2]

Here again the supporters of free will had a strong bastion, and their opponents were hard put to it, either to attack or to outflank

[1] It will be recalled that another aspect of the controversy, the desire of the devout to exculpate God from responsibility for evil, was treated in the second chapter of the first section of this book.
[2] *Le pirrhonisme du sage,* p. 80–81.

it. Without moral freedom, they argued, duty disappears; for, as Lord Kames put it, "we can have no concept of moral obligation without supposing a power in the agent over his own actions." [3] A corollary is the disappearance of moral imputability, of merit or blame, unless we can say, I blame you for being what you are, and for doing what you must do. Referring to Spinoza, Montesquieu comments ironically that "He takes away the motive of all my actions and relieves me of all morality. He honors me to the point of wishing that I should be a very great scoundrel without crime and without anyone having the right of finding it bad. I am very grateful to that philosopher." [4] Many writers (including Diderot) reminded their readers that we distinguish the brick, or tile, which hits us, from the man who does. Formey protested to the determinists that legislation is universally built on the fact that man has the power to do or to abstain from doing certain acts. One never condemns a man who is in delirium, but all condemn a premeditated murder. If Collins is right, continues Formey, we must find the reasons of a willful parricide as valid as those of an insane person who commits the same crime.[5]

Von Haller indicated that a further consequence of this dilemma was a contradiction with the Natural Law theory. "M. de Voltaire holds the ideas of right and wrong to be general and innate; but how will he harmonize this idea with absolute necessity, to which he believes all things submitted? All imputation ends as soon as man finds it impossible to act differently without breaking what M. de Voltaire considers the absolutely necessary chain of events." [6]

According to Para du Phanjas, determinism is an ineluctable consequence of materialism, and so is its equally unavoidable corollary: there is no law of obligation for men, but only self-interest, for there cannot be a moral principle in necessarily determined matter. Natural Law is, then, only a prejudice.[7] Denesle

---

[3] *Op. cit.,* p. 206.

[4] *Pensées,* in *Oeuvres,* ed. Masson, II, 343.

[5] "Réflexions sur la liberté," *op. cit.,* p. 83 ff.

[6] A. von Haller, *Lettres de feu Mr. de Haller contre M. de Voltaire,* p. 261–262.

[7] Then you can understand, "how the hateful assassin who robs you and cuts your throat is no more guilty than the gravitating tile which falling from a roof splits your skull; or than the fierce sparrow hawk who, diving suddenly through the air, carries away and devours your dove." (*Les principes de la saine philosophie,* 1774, II, 439–440.)

brings home the point that as a result of the materialistic system, not only is a person not to blame for his viciousness, but he cannot even be vicious, except from the viewpoint of those whom he hurts. "All that can be said of those who are called good people is that they are fortunately born for society; and by this same principle, scoundrels are ill-fated men." Denesle sees the moral nihilism which is latent in a philosophy in which "every cause is an effect and every effect a cause; because everything is infinite, and nothing has begun to be, and nothing will end." [8] Remorse becomes then a stupid prejudice, and punishment a matter of protecting the majority, like the cutting off of a bad limb from a tree. Bergier also glimpses the implicit nihilism, and ironically advises the wicked man to multiply crimes and enjoy them—which is precisely what Sade, without the irony, will also advise.[9]

Marmontel, in a well written passage, declares in similar fashion that a good man "would only be a clock better constructed or more regular than another." [10] If this is so, who can deny that vice and virtue, right and wrong are purely conventional? And who can tell me that my duty is really such? [11]

Argumentation of this tenor runs throughout the history of the free will controversy. On the other side, the majority of determinists sought a logical rejoinder. Anthony Collins set the pattern for them. He boldly argued that the necessity of men's actions, quite contrary to the dictum of his opponents, is the very cornerstone of morality and laws. If man were not the necessary agent,

> determined by pleasure and pain, there would be no foundation for rewards and punishments. . . . But if pleasure and pain have a necessary effect on man, and if it be impossible for men not to choose what seems good to them, and not to avoid what

[8] This last passage again recalls William James. Denesle, *op. cit.* (1754), II, 22–24.
[9] *Op. cit.,* p. 298.
[10] *Op. cit.,* p. 214.
[11] An interesting modern statement of responsibility is given by Reinhold Niebuhr (*The Nature and Destiny of Man,* p. 255). Starting with the assertions that the fact of responsibility is attested by remorse, and that determinism holds sin to be the consequence of previous temptations, he continues: "But the interior view does not allow this interpretation. The self, which is privy to the rationalizations and processes of self-deception which accompanied and must accompany the sinful act, cannot accept . . . the simple determinism of the exterior view. Its contemplation of its act involves both the discovery and the reassertion of its freedom. It discovers that some degree of conscious dishonesty accompanied the act, which means that the self was not deterministically and blindly involved in it."

seems evil, the necessity of rewards and punishments is then evident . . . and rewards and punishment will frame those men's wills to observe and not to transgress the laws. . . . If man was not a necessary agent determined by pleasure and pain, he would have no notion of morality, or motive to practice it.[12]

Punishments may be justly inflicted on a man, concludes Collins' counterattack, even though he is a necessary agent. In the first place, he may be cut off from society as a vicious limb is cut from a tree. In the second place, punishment is a cause, which a voluntary agent, unlike a blind mechanism (such as a tile), must necessarily take into account.[12a]

Following Collins, Hume insisted that unless there are laws of behavior, there can be no meaningful system of punishments and rewards, no notion of ethical responsibility.[13] It must be pointed out, however, that the opposite position which Hume here has in mind is that of freedom of indifference, as it was commonly conceived, or action utterly divorced from motive.

A group of supporters of freedom were somewhat impressed by the form of this argument. Montesquieu, though he did not accept psychological determinism, urged that if a religion establishes that doctrine, punishments must be more severe, "so that men, who would otherwise yield to themselves, may be determined by these motives; but if the religion establishes the dogma of freedom, that is another thing." [14] D'Alembert took a similar stand. The moral justice of laws is dependent on freedom; but if we were not free, he concedes, laws and punishments would be no less useful, "as an efficacious means of conducting men by fear, and of giving, so to speak, the impulsion to the machine." If men were not free, laws and punishments would be necessary; if men are free, "they are necessary and just." [15]

Quite naturally, however, it was the determinists who pressed this argument home. In his *Portefeuille du philosophe,* Dulaurens also says that if men are not free, punishments are still useful, even though he admits they are unjust. Since men are susceptible to

[12] *A Philosophical Inquiry Concerning Human Liberty* (1717), p. 11, 87–90.
[12a] Leaving evaluation of Collins' argument to eighteenth century writers, we may, at the least, comment on his terminology. It is obvious, from our discussion in the preceding chapter, that he confuses "cause" with "motivation."
[13] Aiken, XVII, 20–22.
[14] *De l'esprit des lois,* Livre XXIV, ch. XIV.
[15] *Elémens de philosophie,* p. 210.

pleasure and pain, "that suffices to found rewards and punishments, without worrying always whether they have really deserved them." The punishments are not really related at all to the past act, but serve as a social control for the future.[16] In his more radical work, *Le Compère Mathieu,* Dulaurens made what he thought to be a vigorous effort to rescue moral imputation. This is his reasoning:

> Since man's freedom consists in *his doing what pleases him,* it follows that he can be regarded quite properly as the author of his actions, although he is not the author of the springs of his decision. . . . Whence comes the difference in Peter's and Paul's affections? It comes from different circumstances which do not originally depend either on Peter or on Paul, but derive from a chain of causes and effects. . . . But Peter and Paul are no less free in the judgment they make of things and became what they are no less freely. From this there results . . . that the good or the evil a man does . . . is to be imputed to him in view of the power, more or less great, that he will have had to forestall, avoid, break or weaken, *on time,* the concourse of circumstances which determine him. . . . The freedom which every reasonable man always has to reflect *more or less,* before the causes or motives of his decisions become irresistible, is no less dependent on the chain of causes and effect of which I have just spoken. . . .[17]

Unfortunately, Dulaurens' own "chain" of reasoning is a logical jumble, and fails to establish *moral* accountability. His "freedom" at no point takes him outside the line of necessary causation; it only allows him—also by necessary causation!—to attempt to halt one necessary motive by another. He is not master of the final decision.

In many of his writings, Diderot followed this same line of reasoning. In the *Rêve de d'Alembert,* he deems punishments to be "means to correct the modifiable being we call wicked and to encourage the one we call good." [18] The letter to Landois, and a passage in *Jacques le Fataliste* express similar ideas.[19]

In like fashion, Voltaire declares that punishments are justified only insofar as the will is not free, and must respond to the effect

[16] *Op. cit.* For a similar view in Formey, quite contradictory to his free will statements elsewhere, see his *Le bonheur, ou nouveau système de jurisprudence naturelle,* p. 94. The same can be found in Condorcet's *Vie de Voltaire,* in Voltaire, *Oeuvres,* IV, 325.
[17] *Le Compère Mathieu,* III, 212–213, 216–218. Italics in original text.
[18] *Oeuvres,* II, 176.
[19] *Jacques le Fataliste, Oeuvres,* III, 180–181.

of a cause.[20] Bonnet is in essential agreement.[21] D'Holbach, on the other hand, broadens his viewpoint to include two somewhat different conclusions. On the one hand, he agrees with the group of writers we are discussing. Our social institutions, he affirms, are founded on necessity, although it is claimed that men are free. What we really suppose is that certain motives have the power necessarily to affect and to determine men's wills, or to modify them. Education, laws and religion—all the institutions that "condition" men—rely on this determinism. Why else does a father punish his child? "Education is, then, only necessity shown to children. Legislation is necessity shown to the members of a body politic. . . ."[22] D'Holbach now proceeds to attack directly the argument of the proponents of freedom, who maintained that if actions are necessary, we cannot legitimately be angry with men or punish them. His rebuttal involves an effort to meet the challenge by proposing an ethical concept that is not contradictory to determinism.

I reply that to impute an action to someone is to attribute it to him, it is to know him as the author of it; thus even if we supposed that action to be the effect of a *necessitated* agent, the imputation may be made. The merit or blame that we attribute to an action are ideas founded on the favorable or pernicious effects that result for those who experience it; and even if we supposed the agent to have been necessitated, it is no less certain that his action will be good or bad, praiseworthy or despicable for all those who will be affected by it, in a word, of a nature to arouse their love or their anger. Love or anger are in us ways of being suitable to modifying the beings of our species. . . . Besides my anger is necessary. . . . Whence we see that the system of necessity does not change the state of things, and is not such as to confuse the ideas of vice and virtue.[23]

[20] "Franc Arbitre," xix, 199.
[21] *Op. cit.*, ch. xvi.
[22] *Système de la nature*, i, 232–236. Also, p. 245–246: "Penal laws are motives that experience shows us to be capable of containing or annihilating impulses that passions give to men's will." If the legislator goes about it properly, he is sure of success. "On decreeing gallows, tortures, various punishments for crimes, he does nothing different from the person who, in building a house, places gutters to prevent the rain water from eating away the foundations of his dwelling."
[23] *Ibid.*, p. 243–245. For a modern *reprise* of the argument of the eighteenth century determinists, see G. A. Wells, "Herder's Determinism," 108 ff. According to Professor Wells, "responsibility is susceptibility to what are called normal incentives. . . . A responsible person is thus someone who is sufficiently sensitive to certain socially

To this argument of d'Holbach's Le Franc de Pompignan replied: "If you had to consider actions that displease us as necessary, your indignation would be the wrath of a child who gets angry with his doll, and your condemnations the caprices of an iniquitous and barbarous despot." Such actions do necessarily cause anger, but *not* blame, or moral disapproval. Le Franc's reply to the argument of necessary modifiability was the one generally used by the supporters of free will. The desired modification, he points out, is not at all certain. A stone can be more surely modified by physical means than a man by moral means; and the extent to which he is, or is not modified, is also *necessary*.[24] Crousaz had similarly written: "if they do not have the freedom to reflect on these threats, and to pay attention to the idea of future punishments, rather than to present interests," then punishments are no deterrent—as experience proves.[25]

The second aspect of d'Holbach's defense leads us into that bolder view which was adopted by only a few of the most radical materialists of the eighteenth century. This was to acknowledge the logical consequence proposed by their opponents, and to accept the fact that moral responsibility is destroyed by determinism. This admission was doubtless made inevitable by irrefutable arguments such as those we have just seen. D'Holbach goes on to admit, then, that man is in the hands of nature like an inert sword in the hand of man, without effective power or responsibility: "It can fall from it without our being able to accuse him of breaking his engagements or of showing ingratitude to the one who holds it." [26] And later d'Holbach satirizes deists who, like Voltaire, assert that although men have no freedom, God punishes us justly.[27] Reference to the passages from d'Holbach which we quoted in the two preceding chapters will confirm his lucid realization that the argument of "modifiability" is insufficient to establish moral responsibility. It is surprising that some recent

approved motives that these rather than others determine his conduct." And Thomas Mann: "But determinism would never succeed in doing away with the conception of guilt. It could only add to its authority and its awfulness. . . . The evil-doer is filled with his guilt as with himself. For he is as he is, and can't and will not be otherwise—and therein lies his guilt." (*The Magic Mountain,* p. 582 f.)

[24] *Op. cit.,* p. 224–227.
[25] *Op. cit.,* p. 226–227. Also, Hayer, *Loc. cit.*
[26] *Op. cit.,* I, 329.
[27] *Ibid.,* II, 230 n.

defenders of d'Holbach (and the same may be said of some recent writings on Diderot) persist in blithely overlooking his admission that moral responsibility cannot be justified within the system of necessary cause and effect, and his frank acceptance of social sanctions. Arguing that our reason becomes the determining force in our acts, they insist that self-determinism is, consequently, freedom. But aside from the fact that d'Holbach himself denies this very assertion, such an explanation overlooks the materialists' concept of the reason as passive.[27a] Our ideas and judgments are all necessitated; and we do not have the power to modify action by bringing new motives to bear on a situation. This they proclaimed. And if a hundred thousand men, conditioned in the same way, will act in the same way, what value can we give to *self-determinism?*

The attitude of frank acceptance, with all its consequences for morality, and without apologies, is found in several writers before d'Holbach. Vauvenargues—who can be quoted, like Scripture, on both sides of almost any question—does indeed try to sketch a vague defense: "a thing is good or bad in itself, and not at all because it is necessary or not"—in fact, the most necessary and unavoidable things are the worst. Consequently—and here Vauvenargues comes to the point—vicious men are sick men; we must kill them if the health of the social body needs it, as we cut off a limb.[28]

Moral responsibility is then cheerfully discarded, and replaced by the social criterion of the results of acts. According to Fréret, "if man is not free not to do evil, the men around him are in turn not free not to hate him for the harm he does them, and . . . society, for its own conservation and happiness, has evidently the right to get rid of the one who is in the unfortunate necessity of hurting it." [29] With La Mettrie, we have the most rigorous, consistent and uncompromising system of materialism in the eighteenth century, prior to Sade's, though lacking in the breadth and resourcefulness of Diderot's philosophy. In his "Discours

[27a] Diderot unites the two ideas clearly. "In a man who reflects, necessary chain of ideas; . . . in a man who acts, chain of incidents, of which the most insignificant is as obligatory as the sunrise. Double necessity, inherent to the individual, a destiny woven from the beginning of time until the moment of my existence." (*Oeuvres*, II, 373.)

[28] "De la nécessité," *Oeuvres*, II, 13–14. See also Godwin, in Willey, *op. cit.*, p. 229.

[29] *Lettres à Eugénie*, in *Oeuvres*, III, 90–91.

préliminaire," La Mettrie expresses his theory that the inherited organization, if "fortunate," will make a necessarily virtuous man.[30] But it is developed most fully in the *Anti-Sénèque* (1748), which was generally known (and flayed) in the eighteenth century under the name, *Discours sur le bonheur*. Here La Mettrie charitably tells us that people are not to blame for not being better: "let us excuse this inhuman tendency of humanity." Men, like plants, depend on the seeds they spring from and the soil they grow in.

> Man vegetates, according to the same laws. . . . Thus depending on so many external causes, and even more on so many internal ones, how could we help being what we are? . . . When I do good or evil; when, virtuous in the morning, I am vicious in the evening, it is my blood that is the cause of it. It is what thickens it, stops it, dissolves it or hastens it. . . . Yet I think I have chosen, I congratulate myself on my freedom. . . . How mad we are! and unhappier madmen because we constantly reproach ourselves for not having done what it was not in our power to do.[31]

La Mettrie is sceptical of the claims for the necessary modifying power of education. We easily forget what has been learned, he says, and the original demands of our nature reassert themselves. "One is not even the master to profit from his education as much as he would like to. . . . I see that Cartouche was made to be Cartouche, as Pyrrhus to be Pyrrhus; I see that the one was made to steal and kill with a hidden weapon, and the other with an open weapon." Advice is utterly useless to those who are born with a criminal intent. "They may listen to it, and even applaud it; but will not be able to follow it." So, we must be indulgent, and regret having to punish the wicked, and do what we can to reward virtue. For the rest, public interest comes first: "we must certainly kill mad dogs and crush snakes." Since conscience and religion are useless, we have the gallows. "That is the origin of the necessity of strangling part of the citizenry, in order to preserve the rest, as we amputate a gangrened limb, for the health of the body." [32]

The assertion, in *L'Homme machine,* that crime is punished by

---

[30] *Oeuvres philosophiques* (Berlin, 1764), I, 36–38.
[31] *Anti-Sénèque*, in *Oeuvres philosophiques* (1774), II, 136 ff., 174–178.
[32] Some of these ideas appear again in *L'Homme machine* (1748), p. 101–103, 141–142. La Mettrie suggests medical treatment of criminals.

remorse, and virtue rewarded by the approval of conscience, is to be taken as a limited empirical judgment. La Mettrie's real opinion is that such reactions are unnecessary prejudices, harmful to happiness. Elsewhere he speaks of the philosopher in the following terms:

> Too enlightened to think himself guilty of thoughts and acts which are born and done despite himself; sighing over man's fatal condition, he does not let himself be gnawed by that executioner, remorse, bitter fruit of education, which the tree of nature never bore. . . . We are no more criminal, in following the imprint of the original impulses that govern us than the Nile is for its floods and the sea for its ravages.[33]

La Mettrie is indubitably one of Sade's closest spiritual fathers. The same reasons for which Sade admired La Mettrie caused Diderot to express aversion and disgust for him and his philosophy, whenever he spoke of him. Torn all his life between a humanistic rationalism and a rationalistic materialism, Diderot sensed the utter nihilism hidden in La Mettrie's uncompromising system. He was too much the lover of man, and of moral virtue, to accept it, as Sade was to do. He rebelled against it, as he rebelled against Helvétius—even though both had done no more than to formulate the extreme conclusions of materialism, even as he also had done, in his secret and most radical dialogues. Diderot too, sooner or later, in his habit of following ideas down to the very end of the road over which they led, was bound to admit the failure of the determinists' logical effort to solve the problem of moral responsibility. He was bound to see through his own logical fallacies, in the passages we have referred to above, on "necessary modifiability." He knew that if a man could not help being modified, it was also true that he could not help *not* being modified. Furthermore, he was on the same side as La Mettrie, and against Helvétius, in the question of the relative importance of heredity and environment. While he realized the importance of laws and education in shaping and modifying men's behavior, he also believed, as we have observed in an earlier chapter, that the conditioning of behavior was sharply limited by human nature in general, and by individual heredity.

---

[33] *Système d'Epicure, ibid.,* III, 239–240. The subject of remorse and shame will be treated in a later section of this study.

In the article "Liberté," Diderot speaks warmly of the view that, freedom being a childish illusion, men cannot be called virtuous or vicious, but only fortunate or unfortunate, doers of good or evil-doers. If I am more indignant at the man who hurts me than at the tile, "it is because I am unreasonable, and then I resemble the dog who bites the stone that has struck him." The words, "rewards" and "punishments," should be banished from morality. We do not reward, we encourage; "we do not punish, we stifle, we frighten." This is no different from the opinion Diderot had expressed in the article "Droit naturel," [34] and he will repeat it in the letter to Landois: one cannot stop being evil *à volonté;* the only difference between men is *bienfaisance* and *malfaisance,* and the former disposition is *"une bonne fortune,"* not a virtue. The same theory recurs in *Le Rêve de d'Alembert:*

—And vice and virtue, what are they?
—*De la bienfaisance ou de la malfaisance.* We are fortunately or unfortunately born . . .
—And self-esteem, shame, remorse?
—Puerilities based on ignorance and the vanity of a being who imputes to himself the merit or blame of a necessitated moment.

We need not trace similar statements in the *Introduction aux grands principes, Jacques le Fataliste* and the *Réfutation d'Helvétius.*[35] The same theories suffuse *Le Neveu de Rameau.* In the latter three works, the limits to the effectiveness of preaching and examples are pointed out, and modifiability is held to be limited by the inherited possibilities. The logical conclusion is again the substitution of utilitarian social control for moral responsibility. "If earthly justice punishes unlike machines equally," Diderot writes in answer to Helvétius, "it is because it cannot calculate these differences nor take them into account." [36] If there is no moral justification or logic in feeling remorse, there is none in punishing criminals, any more than animals or inanimate ob-

---

[34] Without free will, "there will be neither moral good nor evil, nor just nor unjust, nor obligation nor right." (*Oeuvres,* XIV, 297.)

[35] *Oeuvres,* II, 78, VII, 15, 25, 180.

[36] *Réfutation d'Helvétius,* II, 456. This explains why Diderot assured his readers, in the article "Humanité," that determinism is not socially dangerous: "The things that corrupt men will always have to be eliminated." And, as far as that goes, Diderot was right. Cf. further passages in P. Hermand, *Les idées morales de Diderot,* p. 85–6, 201–202.

jects, though we may contend there is a social justification. Diderot and the others were finally bound to admit this.

With Helvétius, who discards the importance of heredity, necessary modifiability (or the certainty of the conditioning process) is equivalent to the certainty of cause and effect. So-called virtues and vices are due only to "the different manner in which personal interest is modified." And they are so called only because of public interest.[37] Let us go now to a later chapter in Helvétius' book, and assume a person's character has been formed. Since all action is motivated by pleasure, the only question is where he finds his pleasure. If we change the expression *malheureusement né* into *malheureusement formé*, we shall find the remaining terms in Helvétius precisely like those of Fréret, La Mettrie or Diderot. "In vain would we try to hide it from ourselves; one necessarily becomes the enemies of men, when he can be happy only by their misfortune." [38] This extreme and rigorous consequence of materialism will be one of the bases of Sade's nihilism. But let us follow Helvétius to the end. Virtue—a chance conformity with public interest due largely to the esteem motive—is fragile since it must yield to the most powerful interest. Whether or not this takes place depends on how men are "modified," or conditioned. It is true that Helvétius does say, "There are men so unfortunately born as not to be able to be happy except by actions that lead them to the gallows." [39] We must consider this either a slip or a reference to rare congenital abnormalities; for he annotates the line with Pascal's phrase, "habit is a second and perhaps a first nature"; and just before that he has said that each person may try to behave the best he can, "his character and habits once formed." This conclusion is further justified by a passage in *De l'Homme*. Having repeated his conviction that men are determined by education and not by inherited organization, he asserts that responsibility is dependent on this fact.

> Indeed, if the mind, character and passions of men depended on the unequal perfection of their organs, and if each individual were a different machine, how could the justice of heaven,

[37] *De l'Esprit*, p. 52–53.
[38] *Ibid.*, p. 373 ff.
[39] *Ibid.*, 574.

or even that of the earth, require the same effects of dissimilar machines? [40]

This is the passage to which Diderot replied, in a line we have quoted above. And indeed, he was bound to refute it, for the matter it contains is of crucial importance. Helvétius evidently saw the failure of the deterministic logic, its inability to answer the argument that we may not be "sufficiently modified." He saw only one way of overcoming it. That was to postulate essential similarity of organization, and an unlimited, but sure capacity of being conditioned in one's pleasures and passions, consequently in one's behavior. If this is true, then law and punishments are entirely justified (although in practice they may be insufficient and ineffective, and fail to achieve what is in their power). There will be a few pathological cases, a few who are born so they can find their happiness in such a way only that leads them to the gallows. The rest will, and must, respond to the proper formative pressures. Unfortunately, Helvétius has escaped one logical trap only to fall into another. His theory establishes the responsibility of *society,* but not that of the individual. For if the individual, who "must" respond to the modifying causes nevertheless does not, we can only blame either society or a pathological condition beyond the individual's control. That is one reason why Diderot refused to be enticed by his friend's proposition, and realized, with rigorous logic, that ethics, based on materialism and determinism, would have to be justified, somehow, without the benefit of moral responsibility.

And this is precisely the upshot of eighteenth century determinism. Either on the system of La Mettrie and Diderot, or on that of Helvétius, we are always forced back to the "pathological" individual who cannot respond to "inevitable modifications"; who cannot be conditioned in the mold of a socially desirable pattern of behavior; who cannot help this "unfortunate" inability; and who must—charitably and indulgently, of course—be expunged. As Voltaire phrased it: "Vice is always vice, as sickness is always sickness. It will always be necessary to repress the wicked: for if they are determined to evil, we shall reply to them that they are predestined to punishment." [41]

---

[40] P. 149.
[41] "Il faut prendre un parti," *loc. cit.*

All this is, of course, quite different from the theory of the proponents of free will. Assuming the freedom of the self to create itself, by conferring value and by determining its own motivation, there is no problem of imputation. As Merian formulated their position, imputation is founded on, and limited to, the foresight of what is to be done or omitted. Consequently, "morality resides in the intent, and intent cannot go beyond foresight." Nor are we responsible, morally, for the failure of the desired effect, nor for actions under the influence of a "force majeure," such as alcohol, or an uncontrollable passion. (For the determinists, as their opponents pointed out, there would logically be no difference. The causes would be different, but the result is equally necessary and not under the control of the individual.) However Merian realizes the difficulties of legal justice, which, in contradistinction to moral justice, must "rule itself rather on the welfare of society than on the intrinsic value of moral acts."

The philosophy of materialism leads, then—at least, if we follow its real history—to an ethics deprived of moral responsibility. Good will is replaced by social pressure, and the moral experience by habit and habituation. Those who defended freedom were trying to save the basis of human ethical life. The others, or at least those who had the courage to face the ultimate consequences of their logic, gave up the possibility of a genuine moral philosophy, and of a genuine moral life, and accepted the substitutes of pleasure motivation and social necessity. On their view, punishment becomes, admittedly, a naturalistic self-protective measure, or a social tyranny of the many over the few. As one Christian apologist, Le François, naively wrote, if free will were not a self-evident truth, people would be treated as machines, manipulated, and the authorities would not try to illuminate them about their duties.[42] Here is, to be sure, the philosophical question. Do education and law operate on the assumption that they enlighten men and stimulate their emotional reactions, as "materials," so to speak, for free choice? Or do they attempt to provide the sufficient and necessary "modifying" factors to condition behavior? The same question must be asked in regard to the eighteenth century

[42] *Examen des faits,* in *Oeuvres complètes,* I, 65 f.

theory of enlightened self-interest. Finally, is legal punishment based on freedom of choice and moral responsibility, as it usually claims, or is it a method of social hygiene, tyrannical and arbitrary, but necessary? This was precisely the question involved in the eighteenth century controversy. The import of the determinists' answer was clear. As Professor Jean Fabre has put it (referring to Diderot's letter to Landois),

> A frightening phrase, which summarizes, in a blinding clarity, what ethics becomes in a materialistic system conscious of its dignity and its power: an annex of politics. At least as long as the entire species is not molded so as to serve its own development spontaneously, [a development which requires] the individual to fuse with the common interest, this morality will be necessarily tyrannical. Utilitarianism, on which mankind, sole master of its destiny, rules itself, requires the substitution of proletarian eugenics for the traditional ethics.[43]

Ernst Cassirer's conclusion is the same. "The doctrine of the absolute necessity of the events of nature gets caught in the net of its own reasoning. For on the basis of this doctrine what right have we to speak of norms at all, what right to demand and evaluate? Does not this doctrine see in every 'ought' a mere delusion which it transforms into a 'must'?"[44]

But there was still another consequence that could not be eluded. Given the deterministic answer to these questions, the only measurable, or valid ethical standard lay in the social utility of the effect of an act. Both formal value and intentional value become excluded. This consequence will, in effect, direct and dominate the major part of eighteenth century ethical doctrine. At the same time, it posed the principal problems for ethical speculation. Where is the moral realm in man, if he is not free? In what sense is he a moral agent? Most urgent of all, flowing logically and inexorably from materialistic determinism, there was the dual problem of the validity of a moral code and of the sanctions taken to enforce it. Was it not inevitable that some great rebel should arise and call upon men to free themselves from both the pattern and the tyranny? What was there to prevent some

[43] Diderot, *Neveu de Rameau,* Introduction, p. lxxvi–lxxvii.
[44] *Op. cit.,* p. 71.

courageous, even if mistaken soul from crying out, What man can tell me what is right, and what man has the right to make me obey his idea of right rather than mine? This it was the marquis de Sade's destiny to accomplish.[45]

[45] Although this is not the place to examine the extensive and complex effects of this end result on contemporary Western thought and culture, the following ironical dialogue from Salacrou's play, *Les Nuits de la colère,* is typical.

"In life, there are those who know how to get what they want, and those who do not, preach morality."

"But, my dear Cordeau, if man is no longer responsible, there is no longer any morality."

Human Nature and Motivation

Seven

THE THEORY OF HUMAN NATURE

THE ABBÉ DULAURENS, a defrocked monk, noting man's unhappiness and the failure of his vaunted reason, expostulated on the enigma of his being: "O you, who can guess those secrets the understanding of which God has reserved to himself, show me how that wretched animal can be the work of a being good in his very essence. Where are the traits of that infinite wisdom of which you speak to me in such grandiloquent terms? Is it so very wrong to go astray, and to suppose that the world is a production of chance?" [1]

In the abbé's enigma, we perceive the intimate relation of the evaluation of human nature—which was the necessary core of the process of ethical reformulation—to the general metaphysical background we examined in the first section of this study. We see, too, the age-old problem of the Christian, who must explain why man, the noblest earthly creation of a good and omnipotent God, made in his own image, should be the most wicked of all creatures, rebellious against the very good which God has privileged him to know. The answer to this problem, in the terms proposed by the Christian, was simultaneously a solution of the moral problem. Consequently, when the one came to be doubted, and often rejected

[1] "Lettre sur Dieu, sur l'homme et sur les brutes," *Portefeuille* . . . I, 132–135.

as mythical, the other was simultaneously lost. The result has been the ethical chaos of the modern world, which reached its first critical focus in the eighteenth century.

The eighteenth century understood aright the necessary relation between human nature and ethics. Whether the *philosophes* were mistaken in their central thesis, that Christianity had ignored this relation, is a question open to debate, and dependent largely on what we consider "human nature" to be. Nor do we need to enter into the thorny and abstract controversy over the relation of the "ought" to the "is." In general terms, and as regards the human species as a whole, it seems impossible to divorce entirely the "ought" and the "can." At any rate, it was so assumed in the eighteenth century. Contrary to some recent schools of psychology and anthropology, eighteenth century thinkers never doubted that the establishment of values or norms for human life is indissolubly connected with an understanding of human nature.[1a] If we do not know the nature of man, we cannot know what is good or bad for him, or what we can legitimately propose to him as ideals or goals. Neither is it possible to discover the best means to reach the selected ends. To put it succinctly, the question, for the eighteenth century, resolves itself into this interrogation: What have we a right to expect of man?

In this basic inquiry, the Age of Enlightenment does not divide itself, cleanly and conveniently, into Christian and anti-Christian. The Christian view remained strong, and often found a welcome in the camp of the *philosophes* in disguised forms. Its adherents were composed of a large group of writers who held to the proposition that man has dignity, being made in God's image and with an immortal soul. The paradox of man's nature is explained, in the Christian scheme, by his Fall, which has imprinted in him the permanent, though redeemable stain of depravity and sin. Man still has the possibility of good, but good must be made out of evil.[2] A second group of thinkers, throwing over this inherited

---

[1a] As Diderot wrote in the *Salon de 1767*, "What precise notion can we have of good or of evil, of the beautiful or the ugly, without a preliminary notion of man?" (XI, 124.) There has been a strong reaction in this direction within the last decade or so. Clyde Kluckhohn, for instance, speaks of a growing insistence that "psychological fact and theory must be taken into account in the dealing with ethical problems." ("Ethical Relativism: *sic et non*," p. 666.)

[2] We need not concern ourselves with the vexed theological problem of the concurrence of grace and free will.

interpretation, undertook a more empirical or naturalistic exploration; here the results were no unified account, but disagreement, and a variety of positions. Still a third group, developing a primitivist, romantic outlook, claimed that since God was good, all his creation, man included, reflected this essential goodness.

"Is man by nature good?" This was the most generalized formulation of the problem. But before we approach it in the next chapter, there are some basic considerations we must enter upon first. Our question, brief though it be, contains three undefined abstractions. The first is "man." Does it involve a generic essence, or a supposed "typical man," or all individuals? In most instances, we feel the writer to be thinking of a generic essence. But this is a complex problem; it forms the subject of the present chapter.

The second abstraction is "nature." Does it relate to man in isolation or in social relationship with his fellows? If the latter, is it in the primitive or civilized state? And again, if this relationship is that of the civilized state, must we assume that the original "nature" is therein covered up, so to speak, and distorted? Most writers, I should say, had in mind a social man, but attempted to get beneath the warping layers of acculturation to the hypothetical "original man." The eighteenth century thinkers were obsessed with the notion that by going back to the "origin" of things we can explain their "nature." There is, they believed, a universal human nature which is prior—logically or historically—to society. This fund of basic universality remains indestructible in the social state.[3] The question is, of what does it consist?

The third abstraction is "good." The eighteenth century meanings of that term will be developed in due course. For the present, a fairly safe generalization would be that "good," in the sense of our question, implies the notion of "non-egoistic," of motivation by concern for others, or for the welfare of the community.

A final semantic problem lies in the word "is." Does "is" imply an absolute predicate or one that indicates a partial qualifier? Does it imply that man is exclusively good (or evil), or rather that he is good, along with other qualifications? The answer to this latter

---

[3] It is for this reason that the genetic method, of reconstituting the origin or genesis of ideas and institutions, remains valid for social men. (Hubert, *Les sciences sociales dans l'Encyclopédie*, p. 171.)

question will best grow out of the discussion in the ensuing chapters.

Let us now return to the first, and basic problem raised by the question, "Is man by nature good?" Can one properly speak of "a human nature," and if so, what does it mean? According to René Hubert, the Encyclopedists' theory of human nature "rests entirely on the principle of the unity of the species and the identity of constitution of all individuals." [4] This statement is a correct one, as far as it goes; however the matter was not so simple as it would suggest. Nor does it bring out some of the most important implications of the problem.

The development of scientific rationalism, insofar as it affected the question of "a human nature," laid out two opposing routes. On the one hand, the regularity and predictability of the laws of nature, in all domains, was receiving constant re-affirmation and ever wider application. If man was to be integrated into the purely natural realm, it was not to be supposed that he constituted an exception to this regularity and predictability. To what degree various eighteenth century writers sought to integrate man into nature has been brought out in our earlier discussion. On the other hand, the development of an empirical historicism, the dawning conception of what we might call social or cultural facts, and the growing emphasis on moral relativism indicated that, quite to the contrary, human behavior testified to few if any absolute uniformities. From this dilemma eighteenth century thinkers sought an issue by conceiving of several types or degrees of universality in human nature.

Furthermore, there is no doubt that these thinkers were well aware of the moral and social implications of the stand they took on this issue. The affirmation of a universal human nature admitted the possibility of a correspondingly uniform conscience and moral law. Those who wished to hold to such a view were indeed compelled to find an invariant human nature in some shape or form. For the moral relativists, the problem presented itself in a quite different light. The new social, utilitarian ethics was to place considerable reliance for its effectiveness on the possibility of molding or conditioning men to a type of behavioral response that, in accordance with some rational determination, was considered

[4] *Ibid.*, p. 167.

desirable. This depended partly on the theory of psychological determinism, and partly on invariable universals (of psychological motivation, but not of substance), in the human character. D'Holbach writes, "one can do with men what one wishes"; and Raynal declares: "Mankind is what we want it to be; it is the way [man] is governed that makes him good or evil." [5] Helvétius, Morelly, Sabatier de Castres and several more concurred. Other writers, like Rousseau, believed in a lesser, but still considerable degree of modifiability.

If one can do with men whatever one wishes, then there is a conclusion we cannot escape. Human nature does not include ethical norms, responses or ideas. These all derive from experience, that is to say, from the effect of social institutions, conceived in the broadest sense of the term, upon our judgments. There is no "human reserve," inherent in our constitution, to prevent a total change in moral responses, a change, or revolutionary reversal, such as in our own time the Nazi and Communist ideologies have attempted to impose. There is no irremoveable resistance to what is generally conceived to be evil.

A detailed investigation of this problem in eighteenth century thought would reveal that, as usual, many *philosophes* were not rigorously consistent, but were attempting to conserve a humanistic attitude, while responding to non-humanistic trends of thought in the new currents of scientific materialism. We shall glimpse this even in our brief discussion.

It is in Voltaire that this conflict, in all its phases, is most clearly crystallized. As a would-be scientist, he is impressed by the differences between men; and as a philosopher, he believes all our ideas depend on experience writing itself upon the passive wax of our minds. The logic of both these views does not favor the concept of a uniform human nature. Occasionally, Voltaire does express such a conclusion; and we find it particularly in the *Traité de métaphysique* (1734). Between white man and negro, he there asserts, as great a difference exists as between negro and monkey, or between monkey and oyster.[6] But whenever Voltaire, the moralist, is writing, he has no doubts about a universal human nature, since he believes that man is in *essence* a moral being, and possessed

[5] D'Holbach, *op. cit.*, ch. 2; Raynal, *op. cit.*, 1774 ed., VII, 240, quoted by Wolpe, *op. cit.*, p. 88.
[6] *Traité de métaphysique*, ed. Patterson, p. 32–33, 4–5.

of the basic, eternal moral code of Natural Law. From this viewpoint he will write, "There are goitres in the Tyrol, long noses in
Venice; but the nature of man is always the same." [7] And, even
more significantly, "God has given us a principle of universal
reason, as he has given feathers to birds and fur to bears; and
this principle is so constant that it subsists despite all the passions
that fight it. . . ." [8]

By and large, this is Voltaire's basic view. The character of such
a concept of human nature is that it is substantive. It states not
only that there are tendencies and forms of behavior that are
biologically inherent in the species, but that there are also ideas
and opinions, "common to all men, which serve to make them
sociable." [9] This prolongation of the traditional form of the
Natural Law theory is, on the whole, in logical harmony with the
Cartesian psychology, which Voltaire strongly rejected. His belief
is that men, having an identical organism and, particularly, an
identical reason, generate a common store of ideas and judgments
through an essentially common experience. (Descartes, of course,
did not believe that experience was a requisite of the process.) Our
notions of the justice or injustice of any act can come only from
experience; but we should not make this distinction were we not
all equipped with a rationality that enables us to apply such a
category of judgment to the data of experience. Consequently,
Voltaire can write, without inconsistency, "I have always been
astonished that Locke . . . while refuting innate ideas so well,
has asserted that there is no notion of good or evil which is
common to all men." [10] As Voltaire's thought matured, he reached
a depth of understanding about the relation between human
nature and culture which was probably unequalled in his time.
This is evident throughout his *Essai sur les moeurs,* and especially

[7] *Notebooks,* II, 395.

[8] *Essai sur les moeurs,* XI, 23.

[9] *Oeuvres,* XX, 118. Of course, this concept also includes the universality of
passions and tendencies. Cf. the verses in his tragedy *Les Scythes* (VI, 310):

> L'univers vous dément, le ciel sait animer
> Des mêmes passions tous les êtres du monde.
> Si du même limon la nature féconde,
> Sur un modèle égal ayant fait les humains,
> Varie à l'infini les traits de ses dessins,
> Le fond de l'homme reste, il est partout le même,
> Persan, Scythe, Indien, tout défend ce qu'il aime.

[10] *Eléments de Newton,* in Patterson, p. 64, n.12.

in chapter CXCVII ("Résumé") . We shall return to this chapter at a later point. At present let us note this conclusion: "From this tableau, it ensues that everything which is intimately linked to human ˜nature is similar from one end of the world to the other. . . ."

Fontenelle, who was a Cartesian, also believed that human nature held a common substance. The principal argument in his *Digression sur les anciens et les modernes* is based on the constancy of human talents and the absence of racial differences. Reason is everywhere the same; although its content changes somewhat with progress, some things, he tells us in his *Sur l'origine des fables,* are never touched. "All men resemble each other so closely that there is no people whose follies should not make us tremble." Deslandes, some fifty years later (1737), also affirms that there are certain primitive and fundamental truths that are universal, "whether these truths were at first very easy to discover and were obvious to the mind, or whether there is a fixed point from which our thoughts must begin, a point independent of our caprices and uncertainties." [11]

Boulanger, a pioneer in anthropological history, discards the notion that man, in his origins some six thousand years ago, was different from men today. The only differences are in the superficial acquisition of knowledge.

> In regard to certain natural feelings or prejudices, and certain ideas which are almost identified with the mind and character of man, and which seize him despite himself on certain occasions, we may be sure that the ancients were the same as we; they thought, they felt like us, and as our descendents will think and feel thousands of centuries from now, if they find themselves in circumstances proper to awaken those ideas and feelings.[12]

The majority of advanced thinkers in the eighteenth century gave up the idea that human nature can be described in terms of any particular content, especially in regard to moral judgments. This does not mean, however, that even the most radical materialists necessarily renounced the idea of a universal human nature. What they did was to change the elements to which they

[11] *Op. cit.,* I, 46–47.
[12] *Recherches sur l'origine du despotisme, Oeuvres* (1794), III, 28.

granted the character of universality. What they were willing to concede to all men in common was something more elementary, basic and structural: senses, mental faculties, desires, passions and needs. Such a theory was admirably suited to their purpose. The uniform structure provided, as we shall see in ensuing chapters, the elements that could be worked with and relied upon in a deterministic cause-effect process of conditioning. But they were only broad tendencies or behavioral directions, without the rigidity of fixed judgments.

There were, however, several degrees of difference in the possible formulation of such a theory. Thus d'Alembert admits that "there are notions which are common to almost all men, and which they have in their minds with more clarity than speech can give them." [13] D'Alembert was a mathematician, and it is doubtless such ideas that he has in mind. Probably no one would have denied the universality of logical and mathematical truths. This was in agreement with Lockean sensualism. Locke, in fact, following his theory of archetypes in the fourth book of his *Essay Concerning Human Understanding,* concludes that there are certain moral as well as mathematical propositions which are eternal truths of the human mind. But this refers only to abstract knowledge, and (as we have seen in Voltaire's remark) not to concrete situations, nor to the actual determinants of behavior. Condillac and the materialists rejected Locke's idea of archetypes, and his belief in universal moral (and perhaps other abstract) ideas;[14] but not in the invariability of mathematical and logical notions. Several philosophers, however, expressed a view that is rather hard to distinguish logically either from that of Locke or from the traditional outlook. They held that while the mind has no specific content, its operations and functioning are innate and universal.

Hume expressly affirms a uniformity, or "universal principle" in human minds, proven by a study of languages. He extends this to human nature in general. "Human nature remains still the same, in its principles and operations. The same motives always produce the same actions; the same events follow from the same causes. Ambition, avarice, self-love, vanity, friendship, generosity, public spirit: these passions . . . have been, from the beginning

[13] *Discours préliminaire, Oeuvres,* I, 95.
[14] *Traité des sensations,* IV, ch. 6, par. 7.

of the world, and still are, the source of all the actions and enterprises, which have ever been observed among mankind." The use of history, in fact, is only "to discover the constant and universal principles of human nature" and "the regular springs of human action and behavior."

> Should a traveler, returning from a far country, bring us an account of men, wholly different from any with whom we were ever acquainted; men, who were entirely divested of avarice, ambition, or revenge; who knew no pleasure but friendship, generosity, and public spirit; we should immediately, from these circumstances, detect the falsehood, and prove him a liar, with the same certainty as if he had stuffed his narration with stories of centaurs and dragons, miracles and prodigies.[15]

Turgot, certain though he is that all ideas derive from sense experience, declares that (abstract) truths and errors are ever the same.[16] Condorcet rejects the multilinear evolution of peoples; we must, he says, synthesize all differing observations into a hypothetical *"peuple unique."* [17] Nevertheless, this still leaves an opening to the molding powers of education and government. Universally held ideas, on this theory, result from identity of senses and reason reacting to similar stimuli. If the situations and stimuli were changed, opinions and judgment might also be changed, at least to a large degree. If there were an absolute, inherent moral law of right and wrong, then indeed, little could be done with men's abstract judgments, except, of course, to bring them to a closer accord with that law. If, however, right and wrong did not inhere in fixed judgments or in absolute relations, but depended on a varying social utility, there was more play. Montesquieu, for instance, held certain moral judgments to be immutable laws of the relations between things; but he also provides a wide field of relative good and evil within which the legislator could function. Turgot also allows ample room for education to change the sensuous stimuli from which the mind gets its ideas.[18]

There is one phase of eighteenth century thought of which we

---

[15] *Enquiry*, in Burtt, *op. cit.*, p. 597, 633–639. Hume adds that this uniformity admits of diversity, and of "irregular and extraordinary action" not connected with any known motives.

[16] Turgot: *Oeuvres*, I, 139–140, 217.

[17] *Esquisse* . . . , Introduction, p. 11.

[18] *Loc. cit.;* see also Burlamaqui, *op. cit.*, I, 46–47.

must take note parenthetically. It applies to England, far more than to France. In that country there was an important group of writers who accepted Locke's elimination of innate ideas, and gave up the hope of deriving an objective ethical system from a universal human moral judgment. They, too, assumed that all men have the same basic constitution, but utilized it to the same end as the Natural Law theorists, that is, to affirm an immutable code of moral judgments about specific acts. This was the "moral sense" school, headed by Shaftesbury and Hutcheson. Their purpose was to establish a non-egoistic ethics of benevolence. And although the moral sense theory was rejected by Hume and other writers of the "sympathy" school, the result of their efforts, too, was in many ways similar.

The more widespread movement of thought attempted rather, as I have indicated, to find a universality in human beings which would not produce a fixity of opinions and behavior, and which could be manipulated. Such a unity was available in the basic motives and needs of all men, and particularly in self-interest. The latter phrase embraced all the ego-directed impulses. A realistic view of human nature, which recognized their universality and supremacy, might be able to work with them, since they were flexible and without a pre-determined consistency. Nor did this exclude—in the eyes of several writers, at least—the possibility of a Natural Law; not one that inhered in eternal relations of things, outside of man himself, but one that developed necessarily out of his needs and desires. Such a law might, for instance, include the search for happiness, and as a consequence, the obligation of parents to care for their children. It might even be so construed as to include a universal condemnation of murder; however we shall see that both religious apologists and moral nihilists claimed that, on the contrary, it justified murder and destroyed all moral certainty. There were, at all events, many paths to the same goal, and we must not look for consistency and uniformity in what was a diverse and inchoate body of thought.

Although the psychology of Locke and Condillac gave fresh impetus to an organic theory of human similarity, there was ample precedent for it among Cartesians. Thus Fontenelle, while he believed in a uniformity of conceptual content in the mind, insisted no less strongly on the motive of self-interest as an invariable constituent in all men. "The fashion of being disinterested will never come"; manners change, but not the human heart.[19] Bayle clearly eliminates any uniformity in opinions; but he insists that "all peoples are alike in their passions, because the principle of the actions is the same"; and this principle "is nothing else than disposition, the natural inclination to pleasure." [20] Montesquieu's opinion is identical, as is that of Mandeville.[21] If it were not for a common fund of emotions, the sympathy which Hume and others postulate as the basis of moral feelings would be impossible.

Helvétius was one of a group of writers who conceived of human behavior and opinions as almost completely modifiable, within the broad limits of self-interest. As he says, "I have proved that the same actions, successively useful and harmful in different centuries and countries, were esteemed or scorned in turn. It is the same with ideas as with actions." [22] But Helvétius never doubts the essential identity of all men. Opinions in morals, politics and metaphysics may differ endlessly, but "the operations of the human mind are always the same. . . . Men, necessarily perceiving in certain sciences the same relations between the objects they compare, must necessarily perceive the same relations in all objects." [23] If men, then, have different opinions in certain matters, it is because their interest, their passions and their education prevent them from making identical use of an intrinsically identical intellectual and affective apparatus. It is this apparatus, and these motives of pleasure and pain that constitute the true "universal human nature" on which reformers can count, and which they can manipulate.

D'Holbach was equally consistent with the Lockean psychology. He quotes Voltaire: "I shall believe that there is vice and virtue, as there is health and sickness." [24] This implies, as Voltaire also

---

[19] *Dialogues des morts* (1683), "Socrate, Montaigne."

[20] *Pensées sur la comète* (1682), *Oeuvres diverses*, III, 87.

[21] Montesquieu, *Essai touchant les loix naturelles*, *Oeuvres*, III, 188; Mandeville, *Fable of the Bees*, I, 229.

[22] *De l'esprit*, p. 176.

[23] *De l'Homme*, p. 119–120. Cf. *De l'Esprit*, p. 191–192, where Helvétius distinguishes a kind of *esprit* that varies with momentary utility and prejudices, and an immutable *esprit*, which, "independent of different manners and governments, depends on the very nature of man. . . ."

[24] *La morale universelle*, I, xvii.

held, that there is a constant norm in value judgments, which constitutes health, all deviations being pathological. There are universal moral criteria. Unlike Voltaire, however, d'Holbach derives these criteria not from an innate, God-given moral disposition, but from the mechanical operations of an immutable psychological and physiological structure.

> Whatever the prodigious variety we find in the individuals of the human race, they have a common nature which is never belied. There is no man who does not propose some good for himself at each moment in his life; there is none who, by the means he considers best, does not strive to obtain happiness and to protect himself from pain. . . . This granted, we shall call *nature* in man the collection of properties and qualities which constitute him what he is, which are inherent to his species, which distinguish him from other animal species or which he has in common with them . . . every man feels, thinks, acts, and seeks his well-being; these are the qualities and properties that constitute human nature. . . .[25]

The materialism of Diderot follows the same direction, as one reference will suffice to show. "At birth we bring only a similitude of organization with other beings, the same needs, attraction to the same pleasures, a common aversion for the same pains: which constitutes man as he is and should be the foundation of the morality that is proper for him." [26] But Diderot's ethical thought is particularly diverse and complex; in him, as in Voltaire, the struggle between a humanistic rationalism and a materialistic rationalism is particularly acute. We shall find that he also believes in a universal natural law and a universal conscience, postulating a formal distinction between good and evil, and their immediate recognition in the mind. There is in men a uniform reason, "which, being common to all men, would always and

[25] *Ibid.*, p. 4–5. Compare the following statements: "Ethics supposes the science of human nature." "The needs of men are everywhere the same." "His way of acting is in general the same in all individuals of his species, notwithstanding the nuances that differentiate them." (*Ibid.*, 1, 19, xiv.)

[26] *Supplément au Voyage de Bougainville*, éd. Chinard, p. 181. For a similar view at the end of the century, see Volney's *Les ruines*, ch. V: "just like the world of which he is a part, man is ruled by natural laws, regular in their course, consequently in their effects, immutable in their essence . . . everywhere and at all times they are present to man. . . ." Volney affirms that all these human laws are similar to the physical in their functioning.

everywhere have pointed out to them the same road, prescribed the same actions"; so that to be moral, man needs "no other knowledge than that he had received from nature." [27] The objective morality Diderot conceives in such works as the *Fragments échappés du portefeuille d'un philosophe,* and many other writings, is based on a structural unity among all men. Diderot does not deny the value of education and law—far from it. But he insists even more on the importance of heredity and of an unchangeable, basic human nature. This appears in his *Réfutation d'Helvétius,* his article on Natural Law in the *Encyclopédie,* and elsewhere. Men are susceptible to only a limited amount of conditioning. This is the sense of the thought he expressed in a conversation with his friends: "I argued that men were about the same everywhere, that you had to expect the same vices and the same virtues." [28]

Rousseau, believing in the radical difference that separates civilized man from the "original man," and believing, too, in the profound effects of education and government on the personality, postulates a universal human nature only in the structural sense of the materialists. His theory, however, followed different lines. The "original man" had only two traits that distinguished him from animals: freedom, and "perfectibility." By perfectibility, Rousseau does not mean the capacity for moral or physical perfection, or even improvement. Perfectibility has reference to the latent powers of abstract reason that were to enable men, contrary to other animals, to vary almost without limit their modes of behavior and living. But there is also another part of human nature: that which man possesses in common with other animals. This common stock of animal behavior includes the desire for self-preservation, the need to seek certain pleasurable satisfactions and to avoid pain, all of which Rousseau summarizes under the term, *amour de soi.* Taken all together, man is a Protean and unpredictable creature; but this, precisely, is what makes it possible to change him. "Do you know how far men differ from each other; how much their characters are opposed to each other? How much manners, prejudices vary according to the times, the places,

---

[27] *Oeuvres,* I, 223, 261, 269, etc.
[28] *Lettres à Sophie Volland,* I, 117.

the ages? Who would dare to fix the exact boundaries of Nature, and say: that is how far man can go, and not beyond?" [29]

Thus we again encounter, in Rousseau, the combination of a universal motivation and a capacity for variation; but the element of determinism, therefore of predictability and constancy, is discarded—at least in this aspect of his theory.

The important point is that this original nature, the sole universal, basic human nature, which has been subjected to artificial accretions and changes, does not include any moral ideas or judgments. A quite different story is told us, however, in the *Profession de foi*. In that work, Rousseau's only systematic exposé of ethics, we are assured that there is an immutable Natural Law, and that we are endowed with a conscience to intuit its directives.

Many ideas which are only vague and latent in Rousseau were to be clearly developed by Kant. The self is not merely a given nature, a potentiality awaiting only to be fulfilled. Through the will, each man must himself create the structure of his existence. Kant and Rousseau, however, bifurcate at several important points, one of which may be mentioned here. For the former, the imperative of morality is not only a law; it is, even more, the principle of law, man's unique power to transcend natural modes of expression and to give himself a law. While Rousseau doubtless believes in something like this, however vague the concept in his mind, he also believes there is a model to guide him, beyond the projection of an ideal concept, or intellectual construct. Furthermore, in his political writings, he places the power and responsibility of moral regulation and self-creation partly outside of the self, and in the formative organs of constituted society. Here Rousseau was, to be sure, following the ideology of his milieu.

Charles Leroy, of whom we have already had occasion to speak, was in many ways one of the more original thinkers among the lesser writers of the second half of the century. Leroy was greatly concerned by the question of a human nature. He develops two distinct theories. In one part of his work, he dismisses moral and cultural relativism as a theory based on superficial growths which conceal an underlying uniformity. [30] Man, like all other feeling

---

[29] *La Nouvelle Héloïse*, Seconde Préface, IV, 342–343; see also *Emile, Oeuvres*, II, 5–6, 52, 60, 182.

[30] *Lettres philosophiques* (1768), p. 292–324.

beings, "is forced to obey his nature, that is to say, the tendencies which arise from his needs, his relations and his means." Leroy refuses to accept the prevalent notion, that we can best understand this underlying nature by going back to the origins, and by comparing civilized with primitive peoples. He suggests that it would be more sound to compare peoples, of different cultures, who are at the same cultural level. "This is the only way to distinguish what man derives immediately from nature from what the exercise of his intelligence and reflection has caused him to acquire successively in the different periods of his history." We must, urges Leroy, observe and catalogue identities or similarities in inventions, arts, religion, etc. These will tell us to what degree "the entire race obeys a uniform *disposition* which, in the same circumstances, always produces about the same effects." Borrowing what facts he can from De Brosses, and from travellers' accounts, he examines artifacts, languages, and political, social and religious institutions. He finds that among all primitive peoples, the arts have developed in the same order of progress. Whereas others in his age were captivated by the differences among cultures, Leroy is struck by the surprising repetition of civil institutions and customs, of religious and moral ideas. He concludes that the intelligence of men everywhere functions in a like manner, so that "the ensemble of the principal tendencies and actions of mankind is everywhere alike, that the peoples most separated by centuries and by distance meet each other in the most bizarre inventions." But it is not reason that is "the point of common meeting"; or else reason would eventually rectify the judgments of the entire race. It seems rather that error belongs to the species, and that it reproduces itself in a finite number of forms. From this pessimistic judgment, Leroy excepts reason as applied in the positive sciences. But human behavior, and the failure of all the arts and sciences that pertain to it, show that the underlying nature of man is a system of "purely mechanical impulses." Leroy, we may reasonably say, despite certain prejudices characteristic of the *philosophes*, had the true spirit of the anthropologist, at a time when that science was scarcely dawning.

Earlier in his book,[31] Leroy offers a remarkably different exposé of the problem. Here he emphasizes the difficulty of finding any

[31] *Ibid.*, p. 160–167.

distinctive characteristic belonging to all individuals; seeing the
diversity of actions, one is tempted to suppose the same of motives. Yet philosophers must study, through men's natural motives,
the ways of making them better and happier in this life. If we
are going to follow the sensualist psychology, argues Leroy, we
must be consistent. Organs vary. Consequently,

> our judgments and our choices, being only the result of a com-
> parison between the different impressions we receive, would be
> as little alike from man to man as the impressions themselves.
> From that one might conclude that the knowledge of man is
> something impossible, that each individual has a measure which
> cannot be applied to the entire species, that the judgment we
> make of another's conduct is always unjust. . . . My reason
> must be foreign to that of a man who does not feel as I do.

All that men have in common is the desire for well-being, born
of needs, and giving birth to desire. We all have passions; and to
know what man is capable of, we must study him in his moment
of greatest passion—just as we study a hungry wolf, not a satisfied
one. Such a study will not lead to a perception of identities.

> Man has, therefore, no particular characteristic which distin-
> guishes him. He is always what his needs make him; and as
> needs, especially in the social state, vary infinitely from indi-
> vidual to individual, and in the same individual . . . we must
> find numberless contradictions in him, which are all produced
> by the common desire of well-being. . . . He seems to be less
> the product of his inclinations than of the circumstances which
> surround him. If he is not cruel by character, he needs only a
> passion and obstacle to excite him to spill blood, and habit or
> prejudices may afterwards make cruelty necessary to him.

Leroy, then, does not here consider common needs as sufficient
to constitute a common human nature. No "need" of moral judgment is included in his view. Following Rousseau, he finds our
needs so variable, and so varying in the actions they lead to, that
he cannot speak of a "human nature."

Mably also rejected relativism, but without the strikingly new
approach advanced by Leroy in the first theory we have discussed.
He attacks contemporary philosophers who erect what is done
into what should be done. Montesquieu is his chief target. Happiness does not vary with time or clime, reasons Mably, therefore
good laws do not, either. "In truth," he exclaims, "wouldn't a

legislator do better to consult the sentiments of our hearts than a thermometer, to know what he should require or forbid? What matter plains, mountains, a soil more or less arid or humid, more or less fertile . . . and a hundred other similar accidents, in deciding the best laws for man's happiness? . . . Doesn't he everywhere have the same needs, organs, senses, inclinations, passions, and the same reason?" Everywhere, men's vices are the same.[32]

In another work, however, Mably advances the theory that children, at birth, are without any individual character or tendencies. The desire to feed is the only universal.[33] All the rest is formed by experience. This view, which is close to that of Helvétius, would seem to allow for a program of almost complete conditioning. However, no sooner does Mably expound it, than he tacks on a development which changes its entire meaning and direction. Quite erroneously, he dismisses as psychologically unimportant all that happens in childhood. The differences between men, he concludes, are due less to their experience than to the innate conformation and quality of their organs and senses. He then doubles back and admits the importance of physical and moral circumstances and accidents. It is therefore essential, he now urges, to start directing and conditioning a child from the early years on. Such a process, cleverly conducted, can make of a child anything we desire and change his original dispositions. We can make him "disagreeable, stubborn, ill-tempered, jealous, envious or teasing. . . ." There is then a "kind of creation" which we are capable of effectuating. But then Mably admits that if a child "has a decided character," it may be impossible to change him, *after all*. Mably, it appears, is of two minds, if not of more.

A few writers apparently denied the existence of a human nature in any form. We have seen this in Leroy's second theory. D'Argens and Sabatier de Castres offer two further examples. D'Argens states specifically that we cannot count on a universal human nature or mind. If there is such a thing, that is, a mind that is really constant, "it must be the same in all men, produce in them the same operations, and make them see things in the same way." [34] But the only universal law is diversity, and virtue

[32] *De la législation*, p. 21–23.
[33] *Principes de morale, Oeuvres*, X, 332–342.
[34] *Lettres cabalistiques*, IV, 42–48 (Lettre LXXXV).

and vice are words with no definite meaning. D'Argens, however, though an extreme relativist, would not deny universal tendencies such as self-love; his real purpose in this passage is to attack reason, or "natural light," and through it, revealed and absolute ethics. Similarly, Sabatier de Castres, some fifty years later, in attacking (apparently) Mably, declares that "if there were a primitive, invariable, universal reason, we should have to study that only, in order to make it the rule of all principles of morals, politics and arts. But, unfortunately, there is in the world nothing invariable, except the general laws of nature and the variation in human laws, nothing universal except the universe, and nothing primitive except the eternal." [35] The same restriction applies to this statement as to the preceding one. Sabatier, in his endeavor to carry out his consistent relativism and belief that men can be conditioned, is here forgetting his own posited principle of universal self-love. The basic level of structure and tendency remains, whether or not one chooses to dub it "human nature."

In evaluating eighteenth century thought on the question of a human nature, we must consider the prevailing opinions of our own day. Until recently, the concept of such a basic uniformity was looked upon with some contempt, as cultural relativism enjoyed an almost unchallenged rule. Recently, however, there has been a marked return (and, I may say, in more matters than this one) to a position much closer to that of the eighteenth century. Psychologists, archaeologists and anthropologists, all have swung in this direction. I can only indicate some of these movements in briefest fashion, taking an example from each of these fields.

Erich Fromm, the distinguished psychiatrist-philosopher, contends that the science of man rests upon the premise that there is a human nature characteristic of the species. Human evolution is rooted in man's adaptability and in "certain indestructible qualities of his nature which compel him never to cease his search for conditions better adjusted to his intrinsic needs." [36] Another im-

---

[35] *Pensées et observations morales*, p. 409.

[36] *Man for himself*, p. 20–24. Psychology and anthropology, remarks Fromm, must start out "with the premise that something, say X, is reacting to environmental influences in ascertainable ways that follow from its properties." Human nature is not fixed; but the mental and emotional reactions man develops in various cultures "follow from the specific properties of his own nature." In his

portant similarity with eighteenth century thought is this reminder of Fromm: "Human nature can never be observed as
such, but only in its specific manifestations in specific situations.
It is a theoretical construction which can be inferred from the
empirical study of the behavior of man."

An archaeologist, Noah Kramer, reaches this conclusion from
his investigations of Sumerian proverbs: "More than any other literary products, they pierce the crust of cultural contrasts and
environmental differences, and lay bare the fundamental nature
of all men, no matter where and when they live." Kramer's conclusion is related to what Jung and others have learned from a
study of myths. Regardless of the places or peoples in which myths
originated, the same basic themes are to be found all over the
world. This, it is now generally believed, is because they express
the underlying feelings and drives which motivate all of mankind.

We may look for a final confirmation of this renascence of
eighteenth century ideas in the words of a leading anthropologist,
Clyde Kluckhohn, who has in his own work veered from cultural
relativism to universalism. He has abandoned what was once the
orthodox view, because his study has convinced him that men,
in all times and places, have identical needs, find themselves in
similar situations, and have the same equipment with which to
face them. Birth and death; sex, food, illness and need of shelter;
fear of the supernatural; cooperation, communication, shared
values; the Oedipus complex, obligation, pride, hostility, love,—
and, "in broad outline, the simple but precious things that people all over the world and throughout historical time have wanted"
—all these are about the same for all men, while the modes and
means are, to be sure, quite different. The constants, for Dr.
Kluckhohn, are biological facts, universal conditions of life, and
the range of potentiality of human response. Logic is universal,
though the premises may differ. Certainly, this does not signify

article, "Ethical Relativism: *Sic et Non,*" Dr. Clyde Kluckhohn refers to numerous
other contemporary psychologists. Kolb speaks of that "universal emergent: human
nature . . . identical basic structures and functions organized around universal
psychic needs"; and another (Roheim) declares that "the psychic unity of mankind is more than a working hypothesis, it is so obvious that it hardly requires
proof." Roheim stresses the limitation of possibilities in the light of the fact
that human infants are dependent, have two parents of opposite sex, emotional
problems of competition with siblings, and similar neurological mechanisms for
defenses.

that similar stimuli will produce regular responses. However the broad outlines of all cultures are the same. Some factors are shaped by universals, others by historical accidents; but the variable features are secondary, and the permanent ones are primary. "Anthropology's facts," concludes Dr. Kluckhohn, "attest that the phrase 'a common humanity' is by no means meaningless." [37]

We may ourselves conclude, then, that René Hubert has erred in criticizing the *philosophes* for basing their moral and social investigations on the premise of a basic identity among all individuals. He is, however, correct in stating that their procedures often took them too far away from experience, into sheer speculation; and that those who followed the traditional view of a positive universal "content" in human nature made the error of regarding all deviations as pathological.

The consequences of the eighteenth century theories of man will be developed in the following chapters; but their implications will not fully manifest themselves until later parts of this study. The relations between ethics and politics cannot be understood except in the light of a theory of human nature and the degree of "conditioning" which a government and its mechanisms can properly, or potentially, perform. In ethical theory itself, we have seen the groundwork of several positions prepared. There will be a group of theories upholding absolute or revealed values, and connected with the concept of a universal human nature that is able to know or to intuit them. Here the problem of conditioning men is that of persuading them to overcome the non-moral aspects of the self which all recognized to be equally universal constants. Those whose concept of a universal human nature was physical and structural will either develop ethical theories that posit an objective system of universal values upon this common nature, or else expound various degrees of moral relativism, even to the point of nihilism. Where pleasure-pain

---

[37] "Cultural Anthropology," in Lynn White, *Frontiers of Knowledge,* p. 45–47; supplemented by notes on a public lecture delivered by Dr. Kluckhohn.

Particularly striking, in the light of these theories, is the modernity of Voltaire's concept. "There results from this tableau that everything that is intimately linked to human nature is alike from one end of the world to the other; that everything that may depend on custom is different, and that it is due to chance if it is alike . . . . nature spreads unity; it establishes everywhere a small number of invariable principles; thus the *fonds* is always the same, and culture produces different fruits." (*Essai sur les moeurs,* XIII, 177.)

is conceived of as the basic common motive, conditioning is expected to exercise maximum effect. Which of the latter positions was adopted depended upon how strictly and literally the sensualist psychology was adhered to. "If they were to limit themselves to sense data," comments Hubert, "it seemed they would not be able to get beyond the stage of indefinite multiplicity." [38] But by assuming identity of constitution, and therefore of sensations, one could infer an identity of needs and desires. The chain of being theory and the authority of Buffon and Leibniz supported the biological unity of the species, and held the characteristic of all animal species to be the faculty of feeling and desiring. It seemed to eighteenth century thinkers that similar faculties and tendencies, developing according to the same laws, would lead to a basic similarity of feeling, desire, and thought.

It is evident that such a theory was in itself no solution to the ethical difficulties of secularism. In fact, it made the problem of the genesis of ethical judgments particularly acute. It would also remain to be proved, at least by those who wished it, that a universal moral law results from this structural unity of a purely biological kind. The problem, in other words, was to reconcile a basically pluralistic view of man with the need for a constant moral law, a need that the older monism had satisfied more conveniently.[39]

A final difficulty—perhaps the most fundamental of all—was to justify the denomination of *human* in this concept of "human nature." A surface examination of some of the statements of the materialists might lead the casual reader to the conclusion that the qualifying adjective was not justifiable.[39a] At this point it would

---

[38] *Op. cit.,* p. 168.

[39] The materialists' admission of a basic uniformity in all men does not preclude their placing greater emphasis, when it suited them, on diversity. D'Holbach is a typical example. "There are not two individuals in the human species," he writes, "who have the same features, who feel exactly in the same way, who think alike, who see things with the same eyes, who have the same ideas and consequently the same system of conduct. . . . Thus, although men resemble each other in a general way, they differ essentially both by the tissue and arrangement of the fibres and nerves, as by the nature, quality, quantity of matter that activates these fibres. . . ." (*Système de la nature,* p. 129–135.)

[39a] We sometimes get the impression, especially in the materialist writings, that men are being studied as if they were things, to which one merely attaches certain attributes. Ortega y Gasset has written that to think about human life, we need concepts and categories "radically different from those which illuminate the phenomena of matter."

be interesting to turn back to the chapter, "Man's Place," and to recall how many of the followers of Condillac distinguished man by his unique possession of the power of abstraction and of the categories of moral judgment. These are traits that sometimes seem to be almost forgotten when the same writers discuss the question of a universal human nature. Yet, on a purely psychological and social basis, it is doubtless possible to discover certain characteristics and behavioral patterns that belong to all men, and to men alone. I am referring, for instance, to the Oedipus complex, the incest taboo, restitution and reciprocity, parent-child obligation, murder, and regulation of sexual activities. There are other unique compulsions, such as burial of the dead. The eighteenth century materialists were dubious about some of these matters, and ignorant of others. But even to them there was, within the apparent community of human behavioral needs with those of all animal life, at least one large sphere of the uniquely human. This distinctiveness was a peculiar manifestation of the ego-directed motivations: often summarized by the word "pride," it includes the need for esteem and for self-esteem, for prestige and for power. In this need, eighteenth century thinkers found a complex center of powerful motives arising from the singularly human power to objectify the self and to project an ego-image.

Some large questions remain. We shall discuss several of these in the next chapters, and leave others until we have reached a further stage in our investigations. Among the latter, there is one we must at least mention rapidly at this point. Is the doctrine of an immutable, universal human nature pessimistic and reactionary, as has been charged? [40] There is something to be said on both sides of this question, and we shall discuss it more amply in relation to the problems of law and justice, and Natural Law. It has been argued that a permanent, unchangeable nucleus within man consecrates the status quo, and blocks progress; and that Rousseau, therefore, was a liberal. This position has a specious appearance of logic, when considered in purely abstract terms. As the notion was developed concretely, however, in the eighteenth century debates, it did not reduce itself to so simple a conclusion. The pessimism about man was rescued—as we are about to see—by certain natural mechanisms of human vices, and by the possibility of artificially manipulating these same peculiarly

[40] A. Adam, "Rousseau et Diderot," p. 21–31.

human traits. Even abstractly, the possession of an impermeable nucleus of truly human characteristics may, from another viewpoint, be regarded as a "liberal" notion, as a safeguard against the "brainwashing" and dehumanization of men envisaged by the most reactionary and tyrannical political philosophies. In addition, Rousseau, at least in many of his writings, does hold to a constant human nature, necessarily developed when man is *in society*. This is why he distinguishes, in *Emile*, the things that are "natural to man in society." Vices may, then, be said to be *natural* to *social* man; and this statement may also be applied to certain moral judgments. As we have seen in this chapter, Rousseau believes in a universal human nature in much the same way as the sensualists. The agreement goes even deeper. Rousseau can say that vices are not natural to man, and that man is not naturally moral, only because he assumes a pre-social, isolated man. The other *philosophes*, most assuredly, would have agreed with his contentions, had they been willing, for the sake of argument, to postulate such an animal-state of early man.[41]

Finally, there is another problem, which even the wide limits of my subject do not permit me to expand beyond my earlier references to it. This problem is the nature of the personality, or self. Its relation to the subject of the present chapter is not difficult to perceive. If there is a universal human nature, there must be an innate structured self. But the sensualists denied the existence of any real, unitary, abstract self, outside the ebb and flow of experience and its recollection. What we have said concerning theories of freedom and determinism has perhaps cast some light on the diversity of viewpoints upon this matter.

[41] While Adam says that in society (according to Rousseau), men fight not because they are men, but because of inequality, I should rather say that Rousseau thinks they fight because of pride and emulation, which is to say, because they are men. While Adam claims that disorder, for Rousseau, does not therefore have a metaphysical but only an economic basis, it seems to me that he really assigns it a psychological cause.

Adam refers (p. 31–32) to a passage in which Rousseau declares that men have nothing in common, that there is no real collectivity, the "genre humain." However Rousseau is here eager to refute Diderot's concept of Natural Law as prior to society. We must never forget that Rousseau, like Voltaire, often argues in opposite directions according to the stimulus of the moment. Actually, what Rousseau here denies is a "genre humain" *existing as a natural moral or social collectivity*. He denies, not the possession of common qualities, but a common action, such as that of an organism, or a true collective unity. This, precisely, it is for man's will and reason to create. His politics rests on the belief that once it is created, what is common to all men is more basic and more important than the accidents of their differences.

$\mathcal{E}ight$

MAN'S DETRACTORS

BEFORE THE eighteenth century, there had not been wanting defenders of man, who assailed the proponents of his supposed innate wickedness.[1] Socrates had blamed evil on ignorance, and Pelagius had opposed St. Augustine. The early Renaissance was a period of optimism, of confidence in man's intellectual and moral possibilities. A high point was reached in the writings of Pico della Mirandola (1463–1494). It was followed by a period (sometimes called the Counter-Renaissance) of intense pessimism. Machiavelli, Luther, Montaigne, and many others deflated man, both in himself and in regard to his position in the universe. More often than not, he was likened to animals, or placed beneath them, his reason and his reasonableness derided. *Hamlet* and *Don Quixote* are the two great expressions in literature of this deep pessimism. The seventeenth century, especially in France, turned its rationalistic bent to analysis of human psychology. The works of Pascal, Boileau, Racine, La Rochefoucauld and La Bruyère paint man as irrational, ruled by passions and by egoism, motivated by prejudice, rationalization, vanity, hypocrisy and self-interest. Spinoza contended that we are *naturally* given to envy

[1] This chapter is not concerned with the view that men are presently evil, in society as it is constituted, but are not necessarily so.

and hatred, and derive pleasure and happiness from the misfortunes of others.[2] One result was the justification of political absolutism, not only in France, but in the influential writings of Hobbes, who in turn reflected Machiavelli. Pufendorf commented on man's inability to live without laws, since harm could only result from his acting according to his whims; men are weak, coarse, and "more wicked than beasts."[3] The political theme was not abandoned in the eighteenth century. Frederick the Great, as might be expected, held quite similar views. Nature produces evil men; "they cover the whole face of the earth; and without laws which repress vice, each individual would give himself up to the instinct of nature, and would think only of himself."[4] Even the so-called "optimists" of human nature, Morelly and Rousseau, betray themselves in their systems, which require rigid control of the individual.

In the eighteenth century discussion, the detractors of man include, in the first place, certain orthodox writers who maintain the traditional attitudes of the Church. It is significant that these are comparatively few in number, doubtless, in large part, because of polemical necessities, especially their opposition to the post-Cartesian, materialistic degradation of man to an animal level. Yet we do find a few Christian writers emphasizing man's defects in the older tradition of the seventeenth century. Thus Deslandes belittles our vaunted reason, limited in power, confused by sensations and desires, naturally borne towards error. Deception, wrath and injustice direct our actions. As a result, laws are designed to take the place of morals, but unfortunately they serve only to corrupt them more. Deslandes' conclusion, however, belongs to an eighteenth century current of thought: everywhere and always, some men will cruelly oppress and exploit others; abuses will always reign.[5] These words sound like a pre-echo of the marquis de Sade. Indeed, as we advance in our

[2] This aspect of evil in man will be treated more fully in Chapter 11. See *Ethic,* Third Part, Prop. LV, Scholium. Spinoza also affirms that men are naturally good, insofar as they are reasonable; but that they are not essentially reasonable. (Fourth Part, Prop. XXXVII, Schol. 1; Prop. IV, Corollary, etc.)

[3] *Le droit de la nature et des gens,* I, 161–166.

[4] Letter to Voltaire, in Voltaire: *Oeuvres,* XXXIX, 370 (1737). Frederick admits there are some "happy mortals" who love virtue for its own sake; but the sincerity of the admission is open to question.

[5] *Histoire critique de la philosophie* (1737), I, 272–275.

study, we shall continue to encounter situations in the thought of the apologists, such as we have already had occasion to comment on, that are either unexpected coincidences with the thought of their opponents, or lead unintentionally to their conclusions.

A few professional apologists stand alongside of Deslandes. Duhamel, in his *Lettres flamandes* (1753), argues logically. Since it is admitted by Voltaire, Pope and others that man must be both good and evil (evil resulting necessarily from the laws of motion); and since it is admitted also that self-love and passions must be checked, it is consequently admitted that man is radically evil. If we have a single evil passion, with which we are born, original sin is proven. The abbé Gauchat cries out against those who deny the innate tendencies "to seek one's own good at the expense of the whole species and of the whole universe." This is both Gauchat's reaffirmation of original sin, and part of his refutation of Morelly's *Code de la nature*. Richard's *Défense de la religion* (1775) is a page by page refutation of d'Holbach's *Système social* and *Politique naturelle*. It is important to note that it is in opposition to that detested atheist that Richard asserts man to be "naturally inclined to evil . . . radically vicious and corrupt" (although his free will enables him to resist his own corruption).[6] Finally, these views, and similar ones, are summarized in the verses of the religious poet, Louis Racine.

> Pour guérir la nature infirme et languissante,
> Ainsi que la Raison la Loi fut impuissante.[7]

Far more numerous are the *philosophes* or *incrédules* who proclaim evil to be radical in man. Two writers stand at the fount of this eighteenth century "philosophic" view, a Protestant Frenchman, Bayle, and a Protestant Englishman, Mandeville, who was influenced by Hobbes and Fontenelle.

In his earlier writings, Bayle establishes the existence in man of a moral reason, through which he knows the right, as a perception free of the taint of self-interest. "Reason dictated to the ancient sages that we should do the good for the love of the good itself, and that virtue should stand as its own reward, and it was

[6] P. 19. Richard was perhaps inclined to Jansenism. In another work, *La Nature en contraste avec la religion et la raison* (1773), he attacks Robinet's theory of equilibrium, and insists that evil prevails in human nature. Its origin is not a metaphysical necessity, but sin.

[7] *La Grâce* (1720), Chant I. Cf. the man-beast controversy, in Chap. 3.

only for a wicked man to abstain from evil out of fear of punishment." [8] But in the same work, *Pensées sur la comète*, Bayle's great thesis is that reason is not the spring of man's actions. He acts rather from his passions, which are evil. Consequently, as Bayle puts it elsewhere, "this proposition, *man is incomparably more inclined to evil than to good . . .* is as certain as any principle of metaphysics." [9] In spite of all ethical and religious teachings, "ambition, avarice, envy, the desire for vengeance, immodesty, the entire flora of vices flourishes abundantly in all centuries and in all countries." [10] Human nature, despite reason, is morally corrupt, and the disorder of human life stems from this essential corruption. "We are good and enlightened only insofar as we have been able to cure the natural sickness of the soul, and its consequences.[11]

Bayle's later writings reveal only a strengthened pessimism. In the article "Manichéens," he gives us a sweeping statement:

> Man is wicked and unhappy; everyone knows this by what goes on inside himself and by the commerce he is obliged to have with his neighbor . . . [We see] everywhere the monuments of man's unhappiness and wickedness: everywhere, prisons and hospitals; everywhere scaffolds and beggars. . . . History is, properly speaking, only an anthology of the crimes and misfortunes of the human race.[12]

Bayle's pessimism, which follows the Christian tradition, but deprived of the counterpart of grace, was quickly taken up by sceptical writers. An early *philosophe*, Baudot de Juilly, writes that we come into life with certain seeds of virtue; but scarcely are we born when we plunge into corruption, and the seeds are stifled. "It seems that we suckle error with our milk, and when from our nurse's breast we pass into the arms of our teachers, our

---

[8] *Oeuvres diverses*, III, 174.

[9] *Nouvelles Lettres critiques, Oeuvres diverses*, II, 248.

[10] Delvolvé, J., *Religion, critique et philosophie positive chez Pierre Bayle* (1906), p. 102.

[11] *Oeuvres diverses*, III, 220.

[12] "Remarque D." Cassirer has written well of Bayle's despair. "Bayle overcame the theological idea of an original corruption of the reason; but the other belief in the "radical evil" in empirical human nature he kept. . . . Thus the doubt about the reality of reason in Bayle is everywhere only the result and the necessary expression of despair about its empirical-historical realization." (*Das Erkenntnisproblem in der Philosophie und Wissenschaft der neueren Zeit*, I, 517.) On the other hand Bayle rehabilitates the independence of critical reason and the faculty of feeling. (Monod, *op. cit.*, p. 327-8.)

mind is already so imbued with false judgments that it is impossible to implant good doctrine in it." [13]

But it was an Englishman, Bernard de Mandeville, who was to give Bayle's doctrine its fullest development—both his theory of man, and his further deductions (which we shall discuss elsewhere) concerning the utility of vice. Mandeville's *Fable of the Bees* (1714–1729) was, in turn, widely influential in France, especially after its translation in 1740. It was written in reaction to the optimism of Shaftesbury, whose works also had deep influence on French thought, above all in the first half of the century. The *Fable of the Bees* provoked a furor among moralists, and a goodly part of their writings for the remainder of the century, especially in England, was but an effort to refute Mandeville and Hobbes. His system, Adam Smith was to say, taught vice "to appear with more effrontery, and to avow the corruption of its motives with a profligate audaciousness which had never been heard of before." [14] Mandeville's thesis consists, then, of two parts. First, men are held to be inherently vicious. We help others only to relieve our own unpleasant feelings of compassion, and all altruistic impulses may be reduced to selfishness. Second, vices are both necessary and productive of good. The "good" implied by Mandeville is not moral good, but the utilitarian good of practical social welfare.

> Millions endeavouring to supply
> Each other's Lust and Vanity . . .
> Thus every Part was full of Vice,
> Yet the whole Mass a Paradise. (1, 18, 24.)

Despite this "good," the fable relates, all the hypocrites pray for honesty. Jove finally grants their wish, and at once the arts and crafts decline, greatness is lost.

> Fraud, Luxury and Pride must live,
> While we the Benefits receive. (1, 36–37.)

We must likewise separate the impact of Mandeville's paradox into two branches. Its main part, the paradox of the utility of vice, became important principally in the controversy over luxury. It led also to the necessity of finding a way to utilize men's vices, to produce socially desirable, or "virtuous" behavior. We shall later observe how some French writers attempted to found ethical

[13] *Dialogues* (1701), I, 257–259.
[14] *Theory of Moral Sentiments* (1759), p. 459.

values on non-moral motives; Mandeville, however, makes no attempt to go beyond practical utility. But it is the first premise, that of radical evil in man, which influenced moral thinking directly, although it is true that his citation of the benefits of vice could not but predispose some skeptical minds to receiving his dictum with less horror. The editor of the classic edition of *The Fable of the Bees*[15] points out Mandeville's strategem in accepting the so-called "rigoristic" definition of virtue. Had he rejected this and merely espoused utilitarianism, that is, virtue as the socially useful, the rigorists could have defended their code. His acceptance of virtue as non-egoism made his display of the benefits of "vice" incontrovertible. There remained only two lines of reaction. One could denounce his description of human nature as false—a tactic adopted by some controversialists. Or else one could modify the rigoristic definition of virtue, admitting emotion and desire, even approaching a utilitarian position. There is some evidence of the second course in William Law and in Warburton's *Divine Legation,* and it becomes central to Hume's ethical thought. But it was primarily in France that we shall observe this second development.

In France, we find that the adherents of radical evil were mostly members of the atheistic group, although not all were atheists, and not all atheists adhered to this viewpoint. There is a logical association between their extreme ethical views, which deny virtue in a purely moral sense, and their evaluation of man's nature and capacities. To a certain extent, the French writers continue the pessimistic current of the late Renaissance, which had been prolonged by Hobbes. But the national turn of mind gives them a stamp of their own. French opinions tend to follow the seventeenth century tradition of "moral" analysis and find expression in psychological observations, often couched in epigrammatic style.

An early anonymous work that had extensive circulation in ms. form was the *Jordanus Brunus redivivus.*[16] Its main theme (de-

---

[15] Mandeville, *The Fable of the Bees:* or, Private Vices, Publick Benefits, ed. F. B. Kaye, I, cxxvi–cxxviii. (Page references are to the original pagination, reproduced in the margin.)

[16] See Ira O. Wade: *The Clandestine Organization and Diffusion of Philosophic Ideas in France from 1700 to 1750,* p. 234. The work was printed in a compilation, *Pièces philosophiques,* which bears no place or date. The *Jordanus Brunus,* however, and the preceding piece, have a separate title page with the date 1771.

signed to prove God's non-existence) is man's evil nature. The passage is perhaps not whole-hearted, since it makes some exceptions for savages. "There is no savage, no barbarian, who is not indignant at the sight of a man who, without any motive, attempts to kill a fellow-man. Even brutes show compassion for the pains their little ones show them." [17] Man has no innate idea of good and evil; he knows only pleasure and pain. A more moderate writer, Le Guay de Prémontval, was also more sweeping in his condemnation. "Men are usually so wicked," he avers, "and so deceitful, that there would always be a hundred degrees of probability in favor of the guilt of an accused person, were there not just as much probability that his accuser is a liar." [18]

La Mettrie was the most radical and consistent materialist in the middle years of the century. He attempts to discard illusions, treat man as he is, and draw the necessary consequences. The fact, according to La Mettrie, is that our natural disposition to evil is such that "it is easier for the good to become wicked, than for the latter to improve." We should not condemn man for this "human inclination," but rather excuse him. After all, we cannot help being what we are. Nor does it really matter; people can be happy in vice, since it is a natural tendency. They can even be happy in being cruel, and tearing their fellow-men like wild beasts. Can we do nothing about this? La Mettrie offers scant hope. Education can make a few people good—but very few. Man seems to follow the impetus of his blood and his passions, rather than the ideas he has received in childhood, which are the basis of natural law and remorse." [19] La Mettrie merely states these notions as necessary facts; in his mind they are not subject to approval or disapproval. Provided we have pleasure and happiness, nought else matters. The other materialistic *philosophes* either do not accept his unqualified estimate of man, or else refuse to accept the consequences (at least, in their published writings), and search for a way to the ethical life.

With Diderot, on the other hand, we must always remember that we are dealing with a *homo duplex*. In his case, as in Voltaire's, it is not precisely the same as with those who saw man as

[17] P. 112–113.
[18] *Le Diogène d'Alembert* (1755), p. 5.
[19] *Anti-Sénèque, ou Discours sur le bonheur, Oeuvres philosophiques*, II, 118–177.

a composite of good and evil. It is rather an alternation, intellectual or emotional, on the part of these writers, between moments of pessimism and of optimism. Diderot's pessimistic moods lead him to statements such as this: "He [man] absolutely insists on being wicked half by his nature and half by his social status." [20] He complains that we know how to hate, but not to love; he paints a frightening picture of how one individual, granted immortality, would treat his fellows.[21] His correspondence reveals that he is emotionally upset each time he hears of some instance of infamy. "Nothing shows so well how detestable human nature is as the facility with which people consent to the most wicked acts when suspicion is divided and nobody is personally responsible for the evil that is done." In such cases moral ideals go out of the window, and self-interest rules all.[22] In the article "Féroce," Diderot notes that man is the most ferocious animal, and the only cruel one. And he has Rameau say, "All that lives, without excepting man, seeks its welfare at the expense of whoever it may be." Diderot replies, in the dialogue, that this is true of the savage or "natural man," who would "twist his father's neck and sleep with his mother"—were it not for the development of his reason by education.[23] Diderot, in the *Neveu de Rameau,* and before him, Duclos and Rousseau (in the first *Discours*), were the only ones to point out the sharp cleavage that may obtain between a man's intellectual brilliance and his moral character.[24]

Voltaire is similarly torn. He will without exception reject the doctrine that man is innately evil. This is part of his quarrel with Pascal. To yield this point would be to accede to a cardinal dogma of Christianity, and that would be most abhorrent to him. He consistently maintains the reality of God-given, universal moral inclinations, and of an innate feeling of sympathy or benevolence. In his periods of philosophic calm, representing his deepest beliefs, he considers man a malleable creature, possessing capacities

[20] Letter to Dom Deschamps, in latter's *Le vrai système,* éd. Venturi (1939), p. 21. The Benedictine mocks him, finds him *"extrêmement peuple* in regard to ethics."

[21] *Lettres à Sophie Volland,* I, 56, 82.

[22] *Ibid.,* II, 84.

[23] *Neveu de Rameau,* p. 95.

[24] Duclos, *Considérations sur les moeurs de ce siècle,* (1751), p. 298 ff. Duclos even indicates that imagination and boldness in a brilliant man may be in opposition to moral "mediocrity." A like distinction is also implied in Voltaire's *Micromégas.* The idea recurs later in Laclos' *Liaisons dangereuses.*

for both great good and great evil.[25] Although, characteristically, he attacks Rousseau's doctrine that society has depraved human nature,[26] his own estimate is close to his enemy's. "Man is not born evil; he becomes it, as we become ill." We lose our goodness in contact with others because of the conflict of interests, because of customs, ways of living and the artificialities of society.[27] Men, says Jacques in *Candide,* have corrupted nature.

But time and again, Voltaire rejects his own moderation. Time and again, as he contemplates society or history, he is tempted to renounce the faith of the humanist. His letters and his tales, from *Memnon* to *Candide,* abound in pessimistic judgments on man's irreparably evil disposition. As he grows older, and especially after his period of emotional and intellectual crisis (1750–1756), the sphere of pessimism grows, while optimism shrinks. Shaftesbury's moral optimism, which had early influenced him, becomes linked in his mind with the metaphysical optimism he had abjured. When he thinks of human history, he now exclaims, he feels like changing his mind about men not being diabolic; they have an idea of right and wrong, but have ever flattered and worshiped evil. Nor can man be improved. The struggle is hopeless, and foolish. Human nature cannot be changed, and the scene of the world will always be the scene of human folly, cruelty and injustice.[28] Self-interest is to blame, and human stupidity, which prevents us from seeing where our real good lies. "And interest, that vile king of the earth," runs a verse in *La Pucelle* (c.1730); similarly another verse in the still earlier poem, *La Henriade:* "And interest, finally, father of all crimes." Like the cynics and materialists, Voltaire declares that even voluntary sacrifice, suffering and maceration arise from no other motive.[29] In another passage, he pictures the physical ugliness and grotesqueness of the human male and female, that animal who dared make God in his image.[30] In another he writes, "To know the character of a man

[25] Voltaire's *Notebooks,* I, 402; *Histoire de Jenni* (1775).

[26] *Oeuvres,* XIX, 378 ff.

[27] *Oeuvres,* XIX, 381–383; XX, 83–86; XXVII, 332; *Notebooks,* I, 382.

[28] *Oeuvres,* XXVII, 341–342, XLI, 52–53, XLII, 466; *Dictionnaire philosophique,* art. "Causes finales," "Droit," "Guerre."

[29] "Intérêt," *Dictionnaire philosophique,* XIX, 490. See the explanatory note, developing this theory, XXIII, 531. Elsewhere (e.g. *Les Questions de Zapata*), Voltaire recognizes that self-love has been given to us for our preservation. The two views are, of course, entirely consonant.

[30] "Homme," *Questions sur l'Encyclopédie* (1771), XIX, 373 ff.

is to know to what point he is capable of evil. Every heir wishes the death of his *testateur;* but not every heir will poison him." But he adds, "nobody is always evil, or always good." [31]

In the last analysis, there is probably no more crucial test than Voltaire's stand in the fundamental polemic on the values of truth versus deceit, falsehood and prejudice. "This is a touchstone for faith in man. Although his works abound with abstract defenses of truth, although he himself attacked prejudices, he none the less declared time and again that the cause of truth was hopeless. The deficiencies of human nature and the needs of society both make deceit, prejudice and superstition inevitable, and properly controlled, useful factors in governing men." [32] Yes, concedes Voltaire, shortly before his death, "the world improves a little; yes, the thinking world, but the masses (*le monde brut*) will long be a composite of bears and of monkeys, and the *canaille* will always be a hundred to one." [33] As with the problems discussed in the first chapter, we see in Voltaire a man divided between opposing intellectual commitments. He veers from a doctrinal opposition to pessimism about human nature, through a middle span of realistic balance, to the other extreme of bitter disappointment and defeat. He would love man and exalt him— did man only this allow!

Returning now to the *philosophes* who were committed to a radical materialism, we find that Helvétius, like La Mettrie, declares man to be evil. (We shall later see that he is not always consistent.) Man is a carnivore, vicious, cruel and bloodthirsty. "Self-preservation depends on the destruction of others . . . Habituated to murder, he must be deaf to the cry of pity." To the ears of the Inquisitor, cries of pain are sweet music. The closer we get to the state of nature the easier it is to murder.[34] Helvétius' picture of mankind is essentially similar to La Mettrie's, only it goes even further. The essential difference lies in the purpose of

[31] *Notebooks,* I, 402. In certain of Voltaire's plays, however, we find characters who reject the interest motive in favor of virtue and compassion (*Oeuvres,* III, 470, IV, 126–127). See VI, 67, IV, 210, VI, 427 for variations of opinion in other plays.

[32] L. G. Crocker, "Voltaire's Struggle for Humanism," p. 162. For a fuller discussion, see also my article, "The Problem of Truth and Falsehood in the Age of Enlightenment," p. 575–603.

[33] *Oeuvres,* XXX, 549 (1777).

[34] *De l'homme* (1776), p. 275 ff. Later in the work he defends Hobbes, and underscores the natural cruelty of children. Because men are social, that does not mean they are good: wolves are social, too. (P. 224–225 n., 228.)

the two materialists. Whereas La Mettrie blithely accepts his sketch and finds it not incompatible with happiness (which alone matters), Helvétius' aim is to develop a utilitarian ethics. To do this, he wishes to demonstrate the all-powerful effect of education. And so his theme is, "goodness and humaneness cannot be the work of nature, but solely that of education." Evil is the preliminary to good; the knowledge of it, the way to its conquest or limitation. The materialistic view does not see man's evil as a corruption of freedom, but rather, in accordance with the theory of determinism, as a natural necessity, one with which social forces must reckon, and on which they can also count, as on any physical datum.

Once more we find in the marquis de Sade the ruthlessly logical exploitation of radical views which had given their very proponents pause. A man of widest philosophical culture, Sade was thoroughly familiar with the writings of his century and of earlier times. He seems to unite the statements of Deslandes, La Mettrie and Helvétius: men will always oppress and exploit others; pleasure is most exquisite when it derives from cruelty; murder (preferably by torture) is the greatest source of pleasurable excitement. This is a law of nature, and man is incapable of extirpating it.

The weak is then right when, trying to recover his usurped possessions, he purposely attacks the strong and obliges him to make restitution; the only wrong he can have is to depart from the character of weakness that nature imprinted in him: she created him to be poor and a slave, he doesn't want to submit to it, that is his wrong; and the strong, lacking this wrong, since he preserves his character and acts only according to it, is equally right when he tries to despoil the weak and obtain pleasure at his expense. Let both now look for a moment into their hearts; the weak, in deciding to attack the strong, whatever his rights may be, will experience a slight struggle; and this resistance to satisfying himself comes from his trespassing against the laws of nature by assuming a character which is not his; the strong, on the contrary, in despoiling the weak, that is to say in enjoying all the rights he has received from nature, in giving them the greatest possible extension, finds pleasure in proportion to this extension. The more atrociously he harms the weak, the more voluptuously he is thrilled; injustice is his delectation, he enjoys the tears that his oppression snatches from the unfortunate wretch; the more he grieves him, the more he oppresses him, the happier he is. . . . Besides, this necessary gratification which is born from the comparison that the happy man makes between the wretch and himself, this truly delicious gratification never establishes itself better for the fortunate man than when the misery he produces is complete. The more he crushes that wretch, the more he intensifies the comparison and consequently the more he nourishes his voluptuousness. He has then two very real pleasures in the wrongs he inflicts upon the weak: both the increase of his physical resources, and the moral enjoyment of the comparisons which he makes all the more voluptuous in proportion as his injuries weaken the unfortunate wretch. Let him pillage then, let him burn, let him ravage, let him not leave the wretch more than the breath to prolong a life whose existence is necessary for the oppressor to establish his laws of comparison; whatever he does will be in nature, whatever he invents will be only the active use of the forces which he has received from her, and the more he exercises his forces, the more he will experience pleasure, the better he will use his faculties, and the better, consequently, he will have served nature.[35]

In fact, all a man needs is power, to make him more wicked than a tiger. This is nothing but the straining to godhood in him. To be like God is to be completely free, to act without limit. In man, action without limit can only be what is known as crime.[36] Everything that emanates from the womb of nature, "that is to say, from that of evil," is evil. "There exists no good being." The "good" man is only weak, and weakness itself is evil. Consequently, the more vicious men are, the more they are in harmony with nature, and the more virtuous.[37] In a note, Sade adds:

The first movements of nature are never anything but crimes; those which impel us to virtues are only secondary and never anything but the fruit of education, of weakness or of fear.

[35] *Histoire de Juliette*, I, 160–163. See also VI, 231, and *Les Infortunes de la vertu*, p. 154–155. It is to be noted that Sade, contrary to his own doctrines, is obliged to use words that have moral implications.

[36] "Yes," says the powerful and corrupt Saint-Fond, "we are gods; is it not enough for us, like them, to form desires only to have them satisfied immediately. Ah! who doubts that among men there is a class superior enough [to the weakest species] for them to be what the poets used to call divinities?" (II, 47). The analogy with Nietzsche, and with the Nazis, will be obvious. Compare also a modern recreation of this doctrine, in Albert Camus' *Caligula*. We shall refer later to Helvétius' theory of the power drive.

[37] *Ibid.*, II, 262–3.

An individual who would come out of the hands of nature to be a king, who would consequently have received no education and would become, in his new position, the strongest of men and immune to all fear, that man, I say, would bathe himself daily in the blood of his subjects and yet would be the man of nature.[38]

It is of more than passing interest that this striking last thought coincides with what Diderot had said about the behavior of a man who possessed the immunity of immortality. The coincidence is particularly significant because Sade was not merely echoing Diderot's idea, since he could not have read it. It indicates clearly that the climate of moral speculation about man, abetted by the materialistic view of the universe, was inherently bound eventually to produce this nihilism.

Drawing the ultimate conclusions from Condillac's psychology, Sade reduces the motive and goal of action to physical sensation —no other pleasure is admitted. Deliberately, he submerges man among the animals, and completes the integration of man into nature.[39] Sade's characters carry out his philosophy with most gruesome and repulsive efficacy, and with infallible good fortune. As we read his works, we shudder at the potentialities of hatred and destructiveness which lie dormant in the depth of every one of us.[40]

Once more, Sabatier de Castres turns out to be an interesting figure in the history of this discussion. In his earlier period, when he was somewhat attracted to the "philosophic" positions, he had defended self-love, in a rather conventional fashion. "It is permissible to love oneself as much as one wishes, when it is done right." We should desire, without limit, "the sovereign felicity";

[38] *Ibid.*, v, 238 n.

[39] *Ibid.*, I, 165, 227.

[40] Perhaps it should also be said, once and for all in our discussions of Sade, that many would excoriate and damn him (as indeed many have done) for attributing to all men pathological states that are not general. But others, including modern psychiatrists, would argue that, quite to the contrary, he has succeeded in his project of unmasking man; all that he says about us is true, even if we repress our instincts and urges in response to pressures. In this study, however, we are far less concerned with the merits or errors of Sade's psychology than with his place and significance in the history of Western culture and ethical thought. For the same reason, the assertion that Sade was a psychotic is not really of concern to us. If he was, we can only say that his mental pathology led to a philosophical statement of historic importance.

excess is only in the object of our desires, not in the desiring.[41]
Later, as we have noted, Sabatier was to develop out of his hatred
for the French Revolution a reactionary conservatism that was
less akin to Christian conservatism than to a pagan proto-fascism.
In 1794, he is in exile in Vienna. There he writes that man cannot
be qualified either as good or as evil, nature being morally indifferent. Egoism is the only characteristic he is born with. If a
babe had teeth, writes Sabatier tersely, he would bite off and eat
the nipple he sucks. All other passions are merely modifications
of this self-love. Life is "a search for pleasure and utility." Yet,
continues Sabatier, a man seems really to be more evil than good,
as the necessity and ineffectiveness of laws prove. The Biblical
story of the first man and woman, and of their first-born, confirms
this conclusion in his mind. Furthermore, as social relations grow
more complex, man becomes worse. Here Sabatier, writing during
the same years as Sade, adumbrates ideas that have an interesting
similarity. One person's happiness, he says, is obtained only at
the cost of another's unhappiness. "Civilization leads men to hat-
ing each other, to harming each other reciprocally." Because of
wealth, for instance, children wish for the death of their parents.[42]

This radical anti-moralism is developed still further in Sabatier's later *Lettres critiques*.[43] Men have needs and passions, he
there states, which they cannot satisfy except by tormenting and
devouring each other. They are not to be blamed for this:

[41] *Dictionnaire des passions* (1769), I, 68–69.
[42] While I have reserved discussion of Rousseau for two of the ensuing chapters,
it should be noted here that his criticism of man in society exercised a powerful
influence in support of this moral nihilism. Although Rousseau was speaking only
of man in society, his abstraction of man in the state of nature was not a
deterrent to the conclusions of a Sade or a Sabatier.
Primitivism, however, was also a persistent force in the eighteenth century.
Consequently, we are not entirely surprised to find Sabatier, at one point, at least,
affirming that Rousseau was right. Savage man has fewer needs, he desires only the
things he knows, and these, his only real needs, can be satisfied without hurting
others. "He knows neither the goods nor the ills of opinion [reputation]." He
has the natural *amour de soi-même*, but not *amour-propre*, and the former is not
egocentric, but may place its good in the happiness of others. It produces the
good and natural feelings of humanity, tenderness, virtue. Needless to say, these
remarks are not consistent with the descriptions of man given above and below.
(*Pensées et observations morales et politiques* (1794), p. 18–25.)
[43] 1802, p. 86–92.

. . . species and individuals, all are the children of necessity, that is to say, of those eternal laws which, because we are ignorant of their causes, are called Chance or Fatality by some, Providence or God by others, and Nature by most; in a word, beings destined to life are tigers or lambs, doves or vultures, monkeys or men, as they are placed by Fatality, Nature or Providence, in the chain of causes and effects, whose principle is beyond human penetration. . . . The nature of man is such, then, like that of all other animals, that he will love self above all, satisfy his needs at the expense of other animals, even of his species, as do certain savages who feed on human flesh.

There is no good or evil, Sabatier concludes, except pleasure and pain.[44]

We must remark on the fact that in proclaiming man and the universe to be evil, the moral nihilist was, in a sense, stepping outside the circumference of his proper universe of discourse. Where there are no moral values, there can be no evil. But this was obviously only a way of speaking, a way of referring and comparing their ideas to the generally held system of concepts, or a translation into those concepts. In other words, they considered man from the viewpoint of what others called evil, but which they could not properly call evil. And it should be emphasized, too, that extreme views, like those of Sade, were not typical. Indeed they would have been indignantly rejected by most of those who were their spiritual fathers. The value and importance of these extreme theories, however, is not diminished thereby, inasmuch as they are not unrelated to the premises of the others. They illustrate certain potentialities in those premises, which earlier authors (except, perhaps, La Mettrie) sought to fend off, and of which Christian apologists had warned. These potentialities are of special interest to our own age, in which they have been amplified in the theoretical world, and carried into concrete realization in the political world.

The case of Sabatier de Castres is a remarkable one, and a significant one. On the surface an anti-*philosophe* and a defender of the established order, religious and political, he ends by expressing the most radical conclusions of the atheistic materialists, and by condemning the *philosophes* for being too moralistic! He

---

[44] Rousseau, Sabatier now declares, was wrong. Men are *not* naturally good. All is necessary, and nature knows no moral distinctions.

is an outstanding example of the penetration of the new attitudes, and of their extreme implications. The beliefs that are central to Christianity (that man is an exception, a favorite creature of God, etc.) are discarded. By accepting the *philosophes'* view of man as a slightly differentiated, insignificant item in nature, Sabatier wrecks the whole inherited structure. But he fights with bitterness against their humanitarian, liberal conclusions in the realms of politics and human relations. It is a truth not sufficiently recognized, perhaps, that the *philosophes'* view of man and the world could, by a slight turn of logic, lead to anarchism, to the cruelest totalitarianism, or to humanitarian democracy.

Nine

REASON AND THE PASSIONS

"So convenient a thing it is to be a reasonable
creature, since it enables one to find or make a
reason for everything one has a mind to do."—
BENJAMIN FRANKLIN

"BY THE word [man], I understand an animal endowed with
a mind." [1] In writing this sentiment, Richard Cumberland was
following a tradition that had the authority of the Greek philosophers behind it. Many medieval philosophers, and the seventeenth century theorists of Natural Law, considered man as distinctively (though of course not entirely) a rational being. In the
eighteenth century man-beast controversy, which was in part an
evaluation of human nature, we have seen the claims of reason
asserted time and again. The importance of maintaining this distinctiveness was apparent to the apologists, who were defending
our spiritual soul. We are not surprised, then, to see the abbé
Gauchat taking Morelly to task for his semi-naturalistic view, that
reason is given to us to make us sociable creatures. No, he exclaims, reason is given to us so that we may be reasonable! "It is
astonishing that philosophers who give reason so many chimerical
privileges strip it of its true ones, and lower it to the vile and
coarse functions of feeling and satisfying needs." [2] Mably, an essentially conservative *philosophe* (despite his radical economic
theorizing), speaks against the materialists in similar terms. "It

[1] R. Cumberland, *A Treatise of the Laws of Nature*, p. 93.
[2] *Op. cit.*, XVI, 100–102.

218

is a strange folly . . . to dare to usurp the name of philosopher, at the same time that they abase themselves to the condition of animals, and to claim to reason while affirming that there is no reason." [3]

It was not only the religious issue that aroused debate on this subject. Eighteenth century thinkers were aware of a wider significance, which was the kind of ethics man could have, perhaps even the very possibility of his having any at all. Burlamaqui states explicitly that ethics depends on "whether man is susceptible to direction and rules in regard to his actions," and he defines man as a reasonable being, that is, one subject to rules, capable of moral direction, and therefore accountable.[4]

What then was the current against which these writers—and others, such as Shaftesbury and Vauvenargues[5]—were protesting? One phase of the psychological depreciation of man aimed to prove that reason is only a pretense and not the real spring of action. The subtle analyses of Pascal and La Rochefoucauld had carried further the opinions of Machiavelli and Montaigne in this regard.[6] The Protestant doctrine of Luther and Calvin, with its emphasis on the Fall and natural depravity, was another powerful reinforcement. The partisans of man's depravity explained apparently virtuous deeds as an unconscious hypocrisy, and vicious deeds as sanctioned by a perversion of the reason. Thus even Malebranche writes: "The passions always justify themselves and persuade us unconsciously that we have a reason for following them."[7] Abbadie also admitted that man, despite his powers of ratiocination, is unreasonable when his interest becomes involved. Reason produces knowledge, but does not affect will or action.[8] Spinoza, whose influence on the eighteenth century was profound, had also considered men to be irrational in their conduct, although the specific human characteristic and highest goal is rationality: ". . .

[3] *Oeuvres* (1789), x, 56.
[4] *Principes du droit naturel* (1748), I, 3–9, 49–51, 67.
[5] Shaftesbury also claimed reason as man's dignity, and as the source of good and happiness. (*Characteristicks*, II, 425.) Vauvenargues thinks man's reasonableness shows itself in his love of order; however, in other places, he deems our judgments to derive from pleasure and the passions.
[6] La Rochefoucauld wrote, "the mind is always the dupe of the heart." Pascal tells us we find the reasons afterwards.
[7] *Recherche de la vérité* (éd. Bouiller), Bk. VI, ch. 3, 8. Like Pascal, Malebranche considers imagination the means used by passion to overthrow reason.
[8] *Op. cit.*, (1692), Pt. 2, ch. 3, 10, etc.

we neither strive for, wish, seek nor desire anything because we think it to be good, but on the contrary, we adjudge a thing to be good because we strive for, wish, seek or desire it." [9] And elsewhere he is equally decisive: "Men are more led by blind desire than by reason . . . it is not in the power of any man always to use his reason." [10] This view was a part of Spinoza's determinism.

Fontenelle was a key figure in the transition to the eighteenth century. Time and again, in his *Dialogues des morts,* he paints men and women as irrational creatures, governed by the passions. No reasoning has ever made man better, he believes, for reason is only the tool of the passions. As J.-R. Carré has put it, "Madness and folly, power of the turbid forces of passion, uncertainties of the vacillating lights of reason, such is man in his entirety." [11] One of Fontenelle's interlocutors declares, "It is the passions that do and undo everything. If reason were dominant on earth, nothing would happen. . . . Passions in men are winds which are necessary to put everything into motion, although they often cause storms." [12] Fontenelle is not, then, entirely pessimistic. Our reason, after all, would not approve of our acting only by reason; "it knows too well that it needs the help of the imagination." [13] Fontenelle goes so far as to say that reason is a subtle poison that leads to unhappiness. Truth would make life unbearable.[14] Duty, founded on reason, is weak; but vanity and the illusion of glory lead us to great deeds. Fontenelle, though he sees the weakness of reason, does not, however, like Rousseau or Bernardin de Saint-Pierre, develop an alternative philosophy of feeling.

In the eighteenth century, this depreciation of the human reason was to achieve wide acceptance, and at least apparent predominance. Another important stimulus in support of the thesis that man is not a rational, or a reasonable being was contributed by the great sceptic, Bayle. We have seen that in the *Pensées sur*

[9] *Ethic,* Part III, prop. 9. Of course this was not the whole of Spinoza's ethics or theory of value. However, it must be remembered that eighteenth century writers usually pillaged Spinoza without taking the trouble to penetrate the significance of his philosophy as a whole.

[10] *Tractatus politicus,* ch. 1.

[11] *La philosophie de Fontenelle,* p. 49.

[12] "Hérostraste et Démétrius."

[13] "Lucrèce, Barbe Plumberge."

[14] "Jeanne I de Naples, Anselme," "Parménisque et Théocrite de Chio."

la comète (1682), his argument against a relation between religion and ethics was precisely that our acts are determined by our passions, not by our abstract opinions. Our passions, which are egoistic and brutal, are utterly independent of speculative or moral reason. Whereas for Descartes and Spinoza, the passions are a kind of imperfect or obscure understanding, which we should make clear, for Bayle human nature is fundamentally corrupt. Passion is an original principle of action, "foreign to and opposed to, intelligence." [15] If anarchy does not destroy the world, it is only because nature uses our vices to its own ends. As Fontenelle had previously shown, our vices produce both evils and their remedies. Social order, like physical order, is brought about through evil itself. This is a theme we shall amplify in the next two chapters.

In other writings, Bayle tells us that reason is the slave of passions and that the Stoics were insane to think we could escape their dominion.[16] Passions do not destroy our pure moral reason, but use it to their purposes, perverting our judgments. Bayle speaks (like Pascal) of "the chaos of man," and (like Paul) of "the intestine war that each feels within himself." Bayle is realistic. We must not dream of a utopian society, but accept men as they are.[17] After all (again Pascal!) prejudice and deceit are necessary and useful.[18] Delvolvé has pointed out that in the later phase of Bayle's work, he emphasizes the opposition between the passions and the conscience, and their prejudicial effect on the individual's self-interest. But despite the disorder they cause, the passions, he still holds, and not reason, make the world go 'round, and tend to prevent anarchy, even as they tend to cause it.[19]

We can mention only a few of the early eighteenth century writers who followed upon the traces of Bayle, and diminished the power, or value of reason. Saint-Mard mocks men for their vain pride in their reason. "I have seen some who, with wise reflections, had a mad conduct, others with mad reflections and a wise conduct." It is useless, then, to teach morals. (Bayle might well have drawn this conclusion.) "Teach men to think as you

---

[15] Delvolvé, *Religion, critique et philosophie chez Pierre Bayle*, p. 103. Hume was to adopt this viewpoint in his *Treatise*.
[16] *Dictionnaire historique et critique*, IV, 442–3 ("Ovide"). Cf. "Hélène," III, 263.
[17] *Ibid.*, III, 357 ("Hobbes").
[18] *Nouvelles lettres critiques, Oeuvres diverses*, II, 272. Cf. p. 278–283.
[19] Delvolvé, p. 377 ff. Cf. articles, "Hélène," "Eve."

will about virtues and vices, they will always act as it pleases their
heart; men are led by their hearts, the mind is only the spectator
of their actions." [20] Pope, though he assigns reason what he considers its proper place, emphasizes its weakness and limits:

> Born but to die, and reas'ning but to err; . . .
> Chaos of thought and passion all confus'd . . .
> Sole judge of truth, in endless error hurl'd . . .[21]

Fréret, proposing pleasure-pain as the universal law of all action,
qualifies reason's function as that of a scale on which to weigh
the greatest pleasure—"but it is always the appearance of greatest
pleasure that wins." [22] Jacques-François Bernard calls man a
creature "who in a way tortures reason to force it to justify all the
unreasonable things he does." [23] D'Argens points out that many
of men's follies are based on what they are pleased to call "reason"
—war and intolerance, for instance. "All believe they have an
equal share of it [reason], and all are equally steeped in error." [24]
The abbé de Saint-Pierre, finally, reduces all human motivation
to "a weighing of passion against passion, desire against desire,
desire against fear." [25]

These are among the early writers of the eighteenth century.[26]
Their opinions will be echoed throughout the years ahead.
Voltaire's constant torment is the abuse, or non-use of our reason;
he despairs of the herd ever becoming reasonable. Almost any of
his philosophic tales reveals his distrust of the human reason.
There is no more delightful portrait of man's rationality and irrationality than *Micromégas*. Rousseau does not think otherwise:
reason distinguishes man, feeling motivates him.[27] His "natural
man" of the second *Discours* possesses only the potentiality of
reason.

The materialists were unanimous in judging man a being

---

[20] *Op. cit.*, I, 303, 336–337.
[21] *Essay on Man*, II, 3–18.
[22] *Op. cit.*, p. 64–67.
[23] *Dialogues* (1730), p. 384–345.
[24] *Lettres cabalistiques*, IV, 48.
[25] *Projet pour rendre la paix perpétuelle en Europe*, II, 104. Action results from
a process which involves, in order, object, sense, imagination, memory, passion and
will. Reason, apparently, is not a part of this chain. (III, 42).
[26] Cf. also Lesage de la Colombière, *op. cit.*, p. 8–10; *Cours abrégé de philosophie*
(1711), p. 435.
[27] *La Nouvelle Héloïse* (ed. Mornet), III, 16.

actuated primarily by irrational self-interest. La Mettrie pointed the way. He deprecates reason:

> Cette fière raison, dont on fait tant de bruit,
> Un peu de vin la trouble, un enfant la séduit.

Ironically, he sympathizes with mankind. "Sigh, poor mortals! Who keeps you from it? But let it be at the brevity of your *égarements;* their delirium is of a far higher worth than that of cold reason which disconcerts and chills the imagination, and frightens pleasures away." [28]

Later in the century, Mably offers us an interesting debate in his *Principes de morale.*[29] Ariste, one of the interlocutors, despairs of any morality for men. We are the slaves and toys of powerful natural forces, among which are the passions. Reason is powerless.[30] Should we not then abandon ourselves to the wind and the waves? Théante counters that we have been endowed with an intellect capable of knowing virtue. But what good is this reason, asks Ariste, if it is the slave and dupe of the passions? In reply, Théante puts forth evidence of all the things men have accomplished through their intellect, and argues that we are capable of much more, even in our moral life. In a word, man—whatever else he also may be—is a rational creature. Unfortunately, rejoins Ariste, the few wise men Théante has referred to have spoken only to deaf ears. Reason, in most of us, is only "a miserable routine of the memory, a coarse instinct little different from that of animals." The multitude of men are stupid, brutal imbeciles, governed by the senses, gladly deceived by whatever flatters them. "It is this general stupidity which eternally halts the projects of reason, and which will eternally foil its finest enterprises. . . ." To this conclusive tirade, Théante can only reply that if most men are children, there are some—those who govern them—who can be fathers to them.

The question reached the Academy of Berlin. A paper read before that body in 1763 inquired why Christianity, like other religions, has not made men better. The author replies (rather

---

[28] *Système d'Epicure, Oeuvres* (1774), III, 227–228, 254.

[29] *Oeuvres,* x, 385–400 [1784].

[30] Earlier in the same work, reason is characterized even more pejoratively. "Reason hides like a fugitive slave, or reappears at times only to give us cowardly flattery, and to teach us to be unjust and wicked with a certain order, a certain method, and certain precautions." (P. 229.)

incorrectly) that it has appealed to the wrong motive—to reason. Man is more sensitive than reasonable; he will not be moved by philosophy or by the love of God.[31]

The marquis de Mirabeau admits that man is reasonable, but considers this the worse part of him. Nature and reason are at war in man; but nature (that is, natural impulse) is good, and reason is a perversion. "He [man] is avid for everything; and while nature on one hand forces him to unite with his fellow-man, the intellect, on the other, makes him feel that he is relying on his rival, on the natural enemy of all his desire." [32] Sociability and cupidity are the two poles of human nature; the one, natural and non-rational, is the bearer of virtues, the other, of vices.

Marat, in eloquent tones, exclaims, "o REASON! reason! boasted resource of the sage, what can your feeble voice do against the impetuous torrent of the passions? . . . to destroy the empire of the passions, we should have to destroy sensitivity itself. . . . Men are all slaves of their passions." [33]

Despite some apparent similarities, Rousseau would by no means have accepted Mirabeau's analysis of human nature. For him, sociability and cupidity are united, and opposed to nature. However he also held that the intellect is a source of perversion. Anti-intellectualism, which is the very theme of the first *Discours,* was sharpened in his mind (as we see in his *Confessions* and letters) by his break with the Encyclopedists, and by his conviction that their ratiocination was a perversion of "natural lights," or intuitive knowledge. This is clearest in the *Profession de foi,* where Rousseau indeed uses logical argumentation as long as it suits his conclusions, and denounces it as soon as it does not. Ironically, Rousseau was in this way a living exemplar of the common eighteenth century notion that reason is the servant, not the master. No better *mise-en-oeuvre* of this theory is to be found than in *La Nouvelle Héloïse,* where, throughout the work, reason is used now to favor passion, not to combat it, is now excoriated, now exalted by Saint-Preux and Julie. Rousseau does trust reason, in the sense

---

[31] *Histoire de l'Académie royale des sciences et belles lettres, Année* 1763, p. 341–355.

[32] *L'ami des hommes* (1756), I, 13–14, 20. Mirabeau is, of course, leading up to his theories of economic reform.

[33] *Op. cit.,* I, 311, 317, 322. Cf. also, Crousaz, p. 113; Delisle de Sales, *De la philosophie du bonheur* (1796), II, 43.

of intellectual intuition of right and wrong; but for him, as for Mirabeau, the confines of the "good" reason and the "harmful" reason are not clearly delimited, and the same word serves for both notions.

Kant's relation to the Enlightenment, on this issue, may be briefly indicated. Kant believes in a universal human reason, and he analyzes its peculiar characteristics and functions. Man, for him, is a creature of reason; that is, reason is normative for his acts and judgments. However man is not a rational being by nature. The rational life is a goal and an achievement. It is man's duty to make of himself the being of reason.

Although I shall have to make some reservations, we may, then, take it to be the consensus of opinion, in the eighteenth century, that men, despite their possession of reason, do not live like reasonable beings; instead of following their reason in some objective way, they prostitute it to their passions or interests.[34] Even those who believed that reason itself is sure thought that reason, in each man, is limited and unsure. This conclusion was often used by conservatives to defend prejudices.

Having discovered this about human nature, the very rationalistic writers of the time naturally proceeded to investigate the irrational conduct of their fellow men. Most particularly, they were concerned with the great force that held reason in thrall, the real spring of action, the passions. Since these writers—many of them, at least—were seeking in what is *natural* the sole justifiable and practical basis for religion, law and ethics, it was obvious to them that we have to accept man as he is. The greatest objection to Christian ethics was precisely that it ignored, or attempted to suppress, our natural needs and drives, in favor of some unreal and unrealizable image of what man (according to some deranged fanatics) should be. To accept man as he is means therefore to accept him as a being actuated by passions, not by reason. We should have to go on from there, and see what it was possible to do with such a creature, how he could be directed and handled.

[34] A recent book reviewer states that Freud brought man down from his pedestal, and "shattered the picture of man as a mere rational being." It was Freud who revealed the hidden bias in every man, the interdependence of body and mind, and the psychic life beneath the surface. While there is no denying Freud's great and revolutionary contributions, much of this was clearly anticipated in the eighteenth century.

In seventeenth century literature, passion had usually been described, or portrayed, in philosophy and literature, as a source of disorder and falsehood, to be dominated under pain of fearful consequences. The essence of the mind is thought; the passions are disturbances consequent to its union with the body. And this necessarily remained—despite the protestations we shall shortly observe—the traditional Christian attitude. The title of Chapter 5 of Book V of Malebranche's *De la recherche de la vérité* informs us "That the perfection of the mind consists in its union with God through the knowledge of truth and the love of virtue, and on the contrary, that its imperfection comes only from its dependence on the body because of the disorder of its senses and its passions." In 1728, Barbeyrac, in his *Traité de la morale des Pères de l'Eglise*, recalls that according to Clement of Alexandria, the perfect Christian is exempt from passions.[35] Père J. R. Joly warns that the passions chase Jesus from our heart, and that we must turn aside from "luxury, pomp, riches, pleasure," etc.[36] Quite explicitly, the passions are opposed, then, to virtue and to truth, and distinguished from the spiritual, as its foe. Virtue is precisely the use of reason and will to vanquish this enemy.

The eighteenth century naturalists, having decided to live with an image of man as he is and not as we should like him to be, and desiring to justify "natural" man, sprang to the defense of the passions—in varying degrees. This movement evoked opposition—also in varying degrees—in the traditionalist camp. The historian of this controversy is faced with a semantic obstacle. Although some writers were at great pains to analyze the several passions, their signs and their effects (a psychological analysis which is not the concern of this study), many others did not take the trouble to ask themselves, "What is passion?" or "What is a passion?" As a result, the partisans of either side—and, *a fortiori*, those who were debating on opposing sides—sometimes were not talking about the same thing at all. Defenders of the passions often confused them with sentiment or emotion, even using such vague words as "le coeur"; but it might conceivably be argued, in their defense, that they enlarged the concept of passion beyond

[35] v, 46 ff.
[36] *Dictionnaire de morale philosophique* (1771), I, 139–184.

the Christian idea of uncontrollable, disorderly impulse.[37] Perhaps this is nowhere more clearly evident than in Helvétius' *De l'esprit*, in which we find a general lumping together of needs, pleasure-pain reactions, *sensibilité* and violent emotions under the general concept of "passion," that is, whatever man receives passively.[38] Saint-Hyacinthe defines passions as "feelings of need, so keen that they triumph over any other feeling." [39] Robinet calls them "developments of sensitivity applied to different objects." [40] Several of the *philosophes'* opponents were keen enough to seize upon this lack of clarity. Thus Gauchat, in his refutation of Diderot's *Pensées philosophiques,* accuses him of confusing *sentiments et passions,* "in order to criticize religion and mix up everything in ethics." [41] More specifically, Chaudon, noting a similar confusion in Pope and Voltaire, comments that if by passions we mean only human feelings and desires, obviously they are necessary and morally indifferent in themselves. But if we refer to violent impulses that conquer reason and carry us away, then passions are vultures, and it is apparently in the latter sense that the *philosophes* make their apology.[42] The abbé Trublet tried to settle the question by admitting that passions are true and natural needs, but exaggerated to a degree beyond our needs.[43]

Vauvenargues took pains to present an analysis and classification of the passions. They have two sources, he explains, deriving either from the senses or from reflection. Also, they are of two kinds or species. "They have their principle in the love of being [and desire for its] perfection, or in the feeling of its imperfection or withering." [44] This definition is obviously based on Spinoza.

[37] The variety of meanings given to the word "passion" is evidenced by Descartes' inclusion of ideas which the mind receives without action on its part (such as the axioms), as well as of affections of the soul which relate to the soul itself. (*Traité des passions de l'âme,* Art. XVII.)

[38] P. 321 ff. For Helvétius, these are all forms of self-interest. Rivarol (*loc. cit.*) was of the same opinion.

[39] *Recherches philosophiques . . .* (1743), p. 242.

[40] *Op. cit.,* I, 102.

[41] *Op. cit.,* I, 107.

[42] *Anti-Dictionnaire philosophique* (4e ed., 1775), II, 362–364.

[43] "Du désir, de l'espérance, de la jouissance," in *Essais sur divers sujets de littérature et de morale* (1749), III, 306–307. I have not attempted, in this chapter, to treat theories of enthusiasm, a concept akin to that of passion, as developed by Shaftesbury and those whom he influenced.

[44] *Oeuvres,* I, 43–49.

From the experience of our existence, continues Vauvenargues, we develop an idea of greatness, pleasure and power, which we desire constantly to augment. But we also have an experience of the imperfection of our being, which gives us an idea of insignificance, subjection and wretchedness, that we try to stifle. "These are our passions." Happy people are those in whom the feeling of existence is stronger than that of their imperfection. "Thus I relate all our sentiments to that of our perfection." In a sense, it is all a defense of "our frail existence" from hurt. This is the source of all our pleasures and pains. Vauvenargues' analysis, although based on Spinoza, also seems to anticipate some modern systems of psychology. In its distinction between natural and acquired passions, and in its emphasis on the existence feeling, we are again reminded of another passionate and proud soul, Rousseau.

Rousseau, in his two *Discours,* separates "natural" passions from those created by social rivalry and emulation, calling the latter "artificial." His disciples followed suit, and the author of an anonymous *Essai de morale,* already quoted, defines the philosopher as one who "has only those of the passions that are natural, which are good for us."

Several of the *philosophes,* as is clear from the foregoing, could not be justly accused of having failed to try to define their concepts, though the results may not appear satisfactory. Condillac had been even more careful to distinguish among need, desire and passion. Need is a primary feeling, which occurs even before its satisfaction has been experienced or remembered. It is a type of animal restlessness. Desire is secondary, directed toward the object for which need is felt. Passion is a sensation transformed, or a modification of love or hate for an object, deriving from the feeling of pleasure or pain. A passion is "a desire which does not allow us to have others, or which at least is the dominant one." [45] As Ernst Cassirer has remarked, Condillac adopts Locke's principle of

---

[45] *Traité des sensations* (1754), ch. 3, par. 3, *et passim.* Condillac's analysis is so similar to Hume's, in the earlier *Treatise of Human Nature* (1739), that one is tempted to suspect an influence, although Hume was not translated until 1759–1760. At any rate, Condillac's ideas are much clearer than Hume's. (Cf. *Treatise,* Part III, Sec. 9). Kant was later to speak of a "faculty of desire," dividing its action into three classes: propensities (or predispositions), inclinations (which are acquired), and passions, which are "inclinations that exclude self-control." (*Op. cit.,* p. 335 nb.). We might call the latter "compulsions."

uneasiness and extends it to all the mental operations. "The will is not founded on the idea, but the idea on the will"—a theory which was to go through Schopenhauer to pragmatism.[46] Reason plays a subordinate role even in the mental processes.

The defense of passion begins in the seventeenth century. The influence of Descartes, despite his cautiousness and the brevity of his remarks, was doubtless important in this direction.[47] The apology continues in a repetitious crescendo, merging at the last with the swelling tide of romanticism. "Nothing," wrote Alès de Corbet in 1758, "is more *à la mode* today than to declare yourself an apologist of the passions; it is the title of a *bel esprit,* of a *philosophe,* of an *esprit fort.*" Declaiming against them is properly left, he continues, to the theologians: "they are left to preach their sad morality under the flag of Pascal." [48] The ancient Stoics, in particular, were ridiculed and roundly condemned. The remarkable, and highly significant character of the eighteenth century defense is its almost exclusively utilitarian viewpoint, in contrast with the later romantic exaltation of spirit and soul. This evaluation prefigures the utilitarian ethics that the period will, by and large, evolve as a replacement for the Christian. A second noteworthy feature of the apology of passion—again in sharp contrast to the romantic mood and also to the later nineteenth century glorification of will—is that its tone is not really, with a few very important exceptions, anti-rational. It is rather as if, man's rationality having been disproved, compensation were found in asserting the values and necessity of passions.

Toussaint is among the exceptions. Contrary to the moralists, he condemns reason. "It is our passions that are innocent, and our reason that is guilty." The passions are presents of nature, that is, of God; since God does not make his creatures poisoned gifts, they are good. The latent danger of such a radical defense of the passions is illustrated in another statement of Toussaint's: "Every feeling which is born in us from fear of suffering or love of pleasure is therefore legitimate and in conformity with our in-

[46] *Op. cit.,* p. 103.

[47] Descartes expounds the uses of the passions, and makes "all the good and evil of this life" depend on them. *Traité des passions,* Art. LII, LXXIV, CCXII. The eighteenth century view, however, was not Cartesian. For Descartes, passions are modes of thought, and may be valuable in fortifying useful thoughts. He held that we are able to acquire complete control of the passions.

[48] *Op. cit.,* I, 60 ff.

stinct." [49] Although Toussaint adds that reason is necessary to enlighten instinct, partisans of moral nihilism could find food in
such a phrase, and pious Christians were outraged by it. Toussaint's doctrine is pregnant with radical naturalistic implications,
and his book was condemned.

One of the early and influential defenders of the passions was
Alexander Pope. In his *Essay on Man* he considers the passions to
be merely "modes of self-love." Human nature is an equilibrium,
or partnership between self-love and reason, both equally necessary in the pursuit of pleasure, which is our goal.[50] Passions, then,
are not to be condemned out of hand. Pope's conclusion is logical,
once we grant his premise, the identity of self-love and passions.
The opposition to reason and virtue fades.

> Passions, tho' selfish, if their means be fair,
> List under Reason, and deserve his care;
> Those, that imparted, court a nobler aim,
> Exalt their kind, and take some Virtue's name . . .
> The rising tempest puts in act the soul,
> Parts it may ravage, but preserves the whole. (II, 96–106)

At this point, Pope proposes his famous theory of counterpoise,
or *concordia discors*:

> Passions, like elements, tho' born to fight,
> Yet, mixed and softened, in His work unite:
> These 'tis enough to temper and employ;
> But what composes Man, can Man destroy?
> Suffice that Reason keep to Nature's road,
> Subject, compound them, follow her and God. (II, 111–116)

Pope also introduces the fertile notion of a ruling passion, to
which reason and all the other faculties and powers are submitted.

> Reason itself but gives it edge and pow'r;
> As Heav'n's blest beam turns vinegar more sour. (II, 147–148)

But reason may still have the limited power of changing or
determining the direction of this passion; it may educe "good from
ill":

---

[49] *Op. cit.*, p. 38–49.
[50] Self-love, the spring of motion, acts the soul,
  Reason's comparing balance rules the whole.
  Man, but for that, no action could attend,
  And, but for this, were active to no end. (*Essay on Man*, II, 59–62.)

The surest Virtues thus from passions shoot . . .
Reason the byas turns to good from ill,
And Nero reigns a Titus, if he will . . .
The same ambition can destroy or save,
And makes a patriot as it makes a knave. (II, 183–202)

The utilitarianism of the apology of the passions asserts itself in a variety of shapes and guises. Biologically, passions are shown to be an essential part of our constitution, given, as Toussaint says, "the union of the soul with the body." Their function is the avoidance of pain and the pursuit of pleasure.[51] Spinoza, we recall, had written, in similar vein, that passions are not vices, but "properties just as pertinent to [human nature] as are heat, cold . . . to the nature of the atmosphere." [52] Voltaire defends the passions on this very basis, in his *Traité de métaphysique,* and as necessary to life. So do d'Holbach and Delisle de Sales.[53] Further, passions are the springs of all human activity. Saint-Mard asserts that the pursuit of knowledge is as much a passion as love. All passions are good. "They are too precious to waste any of them . . . we should rather dare to complain of not having enough." [54] Probably the most frequently employed metaphor—we find it over and over again—was to compare our lives to a sailing ship and the passions to the winds that move it on its course—or to its shipwreck, according to some.[55] The tide of romantic feeling is evidently rising.

The passions received most fulsome praise, as the stimulus of great art and great deeds, from Diderot, in his first original work, *Pensées philosophiques* (1746). His ideas contain no novelty; but he defends the passions with such *passion* and epigrammatic force, that the influence of his *pensées* was far more widespread than that of many other apologies.[56]

---

[51] *Ibid.;* also Anon., *L'âme mortelle,* p. 80–81; Morelly, *Essai sur le coeur humain* (1745). The idea is Cartesian.

[52] *Tractatus theologico-politicus,* ch. 1.

[53] D'Holbach, *Système social,* I, 89; Delisle de Sales, *Philosophie du bonheur,* II, 42–56.

[54] *Op. cit.,* I, 99–101. Saint-Mard does distinguish passions that profit only onself, commonly called vices, and those that profit others, called virtues. His opinions on the subject vary; cf. p. 303–309.

[55] E.g., the abbé Terrasson: "Passions are the winds that make our vessel go, and Reason is the pilot who directs it. The ship would not go without the winds, and would be lost without the pilot." (*La philosophie applicable à tous les objets de l'esprit et de la raison,* 1754). Cf. Fontenelle, *supra.*

[56] See Robert Niklaus' perceptive introduction, in his critical edition of *Pensées philosophiques.*

Muffled passions degrade extraordinary men. Constraint annihilates the greatness and energy of nature. Look at that tree;
it is to the luxuriousness of its branches that you owe the fresh-
ness and spread of its shade: You will enjoy it until winter
comes and despoils it of its hair. No more excellence in poetry,
in painting, in music, when superstition will have done the
work of old age on temperament.[57]

The theme was common. Dupuy (1717) had likened the passions to a torch "that throws off more light in proportion to its
agitation." [58] According to Dubos, they are the élan of intellectual
and esthetic activity, as well as the only way of avoiding boredom.[59]
And Vauvenargues: "We owe to the passions, perhaps, the greatest
accomplishments of the mind. . . . Would we cultivate the arts
without the passions? Would reflection by itself make known to
us our resources, our needs and our industry? . . . The passions
have taught men reason." [60] Helvétius (after Diderot) goes even
further. "The passions are capable of anything. There is no idiot
girl whom love does not make clever. . . . The man without passions is incapable of the degree of application on which superiority
of mind depends." [61] There is no more extravagant exaltation of
the passions, in the eighteenth century, than the one we find in
chapters 6, 7 and 8 of the third discourse of *De l'Esprit*. Since
Helvétius' system was centered on the notion that we are born
with approximately equal dispositions, differences supervening
only under the influence of interest and self-interest, he found it
necessary to make passion the stimulus of our attention, and thus
the efficient cause of our intelligence, or lack of it.[62]

Several other forms of utility are adduced by defenders of the
passions. Their social utility was early maintained by Bayle and
Mandeville (as forms of self-interest), and later, by the Physiocrats.
To destroy passions, cries Helvétius, would be the suicide of any

[57] *Pensée*, III.

[58] *Op. cit.*, p. 32–45. There is a pre-romantic tone in some of Dupuy's lines. "I
love the storm; I take a keen pleasure in seeing the waves of the sea in anger, its
calm bores me; the state of a soul without passion seems to me insipid and languish-
ing."

[59] *Réflexions critiques sur la poésie et la peinture* (1719), ch. 1.

[60] *Oeuvres*, III, 151–154.

[61] *De l'homme*, VIII, 136.

[62] Helvétius took no note of Abbadie's observation that while passions give us
esprit (which is possessed by many), they do not give us judgment (which is possessed by few). In fact, the two qualities are probably incompatible. (*Op. cit.*, Pt. 2,
ch. 18.)

nation.[63] Helvétius was defended by the extremist, Sylvain Maréchal.[64] Hume had already shown in his *Treatise of Human Nature* that reason, in the absence of passion, cannot motivate us to act either for our own good or for society's. D'Holbach also affirms that useful work and interest in others depend on them.[65] D'Holbach actually follows a view that characterized the large body of moderate thinkers. The passions are morally neutral in themselves; they are merely the necessary consequences of natural physical movements and desires. They always aim at happiness; "therefore they are legitimate and natural and cannot be called good or evil except in relation to their influence on beings of the human race." D'Holbach does not, then, consider passions as possibly contrary to self-interest; his eye is fixed on the social criterion.[66] Père André, in a detailed analysis of the nature of passions, declares that if human society is possible, it is only because the passions necessary to such a union are manifested externally (love, desire, joy), and because our emotions, like the cords of a stringed instrument, are naturally communicative. True, we have other, anti-social passions (André mentions hatred, desire of separation and sadness, but omits fear); even these are the necessary instruments of personal survival, and indirectly, by the incitement of compassion, serve a social purpose. "Everything then is marvelous in man, even his passions." [67] At least two writers find the utility of passions to lie in their contribution—a very necessary one—to the formation of the secular ideal, the *honnête homme*. They are Lemaître de Claville and the unknown author of the article "Philosophe" in the *Encyclopédie*.[68]

The social argument seems not to have been the most popular, perhaps because it was rather vulnerable to counter-attack from the moralistic viewpoint. Thus Voltaire declares Mandeville to be

---

[63] *De l'Esprit*, p. 164.

[64] *Examen des critiques du livre intitulé "De l'Esprit"* (1760), p. 219 ff. Maréchal is here defending Helvétius against attacks in the *Journal de Trévoux*.

[65] *Loc. cit.*

[66] In his *Morale universelle*, d'Holbach explains that passions are not diseases of the soul, any more than hunger is. They are the movement towards a pleasurable object, away from (or against) painful objects. (I, 17–18. For a longer defense, see p. 33–37.)

[67] "Discours sur les passions," *Traité de l'homme, Oeuvres* (1766), II, 1–36.

[68] Lemaître de Claville, *Traité du vrai mérite* (1737), I, 33, 39, 110. For the article "Philosophe," consult the excellent edition and introduction by Herbert Dieckmann, especially p. 92–94.

in error. Vices, such as vanity and avarice (and why not say crimes?) are not necessary to society. "It is quite true that a well governed society profits from all vices; but it is not true that these vices are necessary to the happiness of the world. Good remedies may be made out of poisons, but it is not poisons that make us live." [69]

An unabashed and unashamed eulogy of the passions was made by the two most radical and consistent materialists of the eighteenth century. La Mettrie, in his *Anti-Sénèque, ou Discours sur le bonheur* and especially in his scandalous *L'Art de jouir,* revels in the pleasures served by our passions. The second of these two writers, as may have been expected, is the marquis de Sade. Many of the arguments of the time are summed up by one of his characters:

> They dare to declaim against the passions; they dare to chain them by laws. But let us compare them both; let us see which, of the passions or the laws, have done men the most good. Who doubts, as Helvétius says, that passions play in the moral realm the role of movement in the physical? It is only to the passions that we owe the inventions and marvels of the arts; they must be regarded, continues the same author, as the productive germ of the mind and the powerful spring of great actions. Individuals who are not animated by strong passions are only mediocre beings. . . . Granted this I wonder what could be more dangerous than laws which hinder passions? Just compare the centuries of anarchy with those during which laws have been most effective, in any government that you choose, and you will easily be convinced that it is only at the moment when laws are silent that the greatest actions burst forth. As soon as laws recover their despotism, a dangerous lethargy lulls the soul of all men. . . . The springs become rusty and revolutions ferment.[70]

Sade leaves to another character, and to a footnote of his own, the praise of passions as the source of all our pleasures and all our happiness, and as the "motive forces of our being . . . so inherent to us, so necessary to the laws that move us, that they are like the first needs that conserve our existence." [71]

Finally, we must again make mention of Sabatier de Castres. Consistent with the total outlook he developed after the French

[69] *Oeuvres,* XVII, 30 ("Abeilles").
[70] *Histoire de Juliette,* IV, 180–181.
[71] *Ibid.,* V, 177–178 and nb.

Revolution, he accepts the passions as useful and necessary, and then turns his attention to the principal object of his interest—the art of using men's passions to control them. Here, as throughout the eighteenth century, we can see how political theories were closely dependent on the theory of human nature accepted by a given writer.

This first group of writers represents the most ardent defenders of the passions; their reservations are few, and sometimes *pro forma*. A second group, probably somewhat more numerous, was composed of moderates who joined in the apology, but rather strongly urged caution. Their viewpoint may be rapidly summarized. The passions do all the good things claimed for them; their role is quite as essential to the individual and to society as it is said; but they are also dangerous. They can be the source of devastating vices and disorders. Montesquieu's words may be taken as typical, Chamfort's as the most forceful. The former, after according them their due, warns of endless disorders when they are not directed towards their "true objects." If laws did not control our passions, "the earth would be only a den of tigers and lions, who would join every imaginable finesse to their cruelty." [72] Writes the epigrammatist Chamfort:

> The philosopher who wishes to extinguish his passions resembles the chemist who would like to put out his fire. . . . The greatest ill result of the passions lies not in the torments they cause; but in the faults, in the turpitudes they lead us to commit, and which degrade man. Without this bad effect, they would have very many advantages over cold reason, which does not make us happy. Passions make man *live;* wisdom only makes him exist.[73]

D'Alembert also warns that passions may be contrary to virtue. Thus love, the most natural of all, can produce the same effects as inhumanity, and degrade the individual. Even when the object is praiseworthy, a passion may be injurious by its mere excess. We must therefore make an effort to subordinate our natural passions to a rational ideal, the love of mankind.[74]

[72] *Essai touchant les loix naturelles, Oeuvres,* III, 183. See also the *Lettres persanes* (LXXXIII). Recent history has unfortunately borne out the truth of Montesquieu's prediction.

[73] *Maximes,* II, 17.

[74] *Elémens de philosophie, Oeuvres* (1821), I, 212.

Voltaire, while falling in with the general current, also exhibits a certain caution. In the fifth part of his *Discours sur l'homme* (written in 1739) he declares:

Oui, pour nous élever aux grandes actions,
Dieu nous a, par bonté, donné les passions.
Tout dangereux qu'il est, c'est un présent céleste;
L'usage en est heureux, si l'abus est funeste.
. . . .
Le ciel nous fit un coeur, il lui faut des désirs.

In the *Questions de Zapata* (1767), he agrees that passions "lead us to great deeds." But there and elsewhere he warns again that they need a moral brake.[75]

We have seen Diderot's ardent apology of the passions. Diderot, however, despite his enthusiasm, really belongs with the moderates; and his attitude toward the passions became, if anything, more cautious and reserved in later years, in regard to both their esthetic and moral functions. His esthetic judgments will be found in the *Paradoxe sur le comédien* and the *Rêve de d'Alembert*. For his moral views, let us give some consideration to his lengthy article on passions in the *Encyclopédie*. Although the first part of it is admittedly based on Levesque de Pouilly's *Théories des sentimens agréables,* Diderot paraphrases him with obvious approval. Passions are explained as related to inclinations, joined to "a troubled sensation of pleasure or pain, occasioned or accompanied by some irregular movement of the blood and animal spirits." An inclination is incited by the feeling of a great good or harm present in some object.[76] Pleasure and pain are thus at the base of all passions. Although passions are admitted as necessary to the individual and to society, as legitimate and pleasureable, the note of caution is strongly accented. Passions, by their very nature, deprive us of our freedom, make us *passive*. Under their influence we are like men acutely ill. This opinion is further emphasized in the section of the article which is Diderot's own. Passions, he writes, may become obstacles to knowledge and to happiness. "They are tinted glasses which spread their own color over all we see through them. They seize possession of all the

---

[75] *Oeuvres,* XXVI, 86.

[76] There is a lack of clarity in this regard: in one place, passions are reduced to the general "passion" of self-love; in another, they are held to be movements excited by a specific object.

powers of our soul; they leave it only a shadow of freedom; they numb it by so tumultuous a din that it becomes impossible to listen to the sweet and peaceful admonitions of reason." [77] Pleasures of the body are especially powerful, and likely to enslave us; but even the nobler pleasures of the mind may be deceitful sirens, turning us away from those of the heart, and particularly of virtue, which are the true road to happiness. The passions accomplish their evil work by corrupting the imagination, which then represents objects to the mind not as they really are, "but as they are in relation to the present passion, so that it may judge in its favor. . . . The clearest ideas become confused, obscure." Diderot's description savors of Malebranche. He then goes on to describe in detail how the workings of the mind become confused and distorted under the influence of passion. Fortunately, he concedes, we are able to moderate the passions by the influence of reason and rules of conduct.

It is noteworthy that Diderot, unlike Rousseau (or, later, Kant), denies man the power of "giving" himself a character. If we possessed such a power, he argues, we should be likely to form our character without passions. But they are a necessary part of our being, and so we must learn to live with them. This view is also in agreement with Diderot's opinion that we are *"heureuse-ment nés"* or *"malheureusement nés."*

Bonnet, in a sense, summarizes this general position. His opinion contains nothing original, except its impassioned tone.

> Admirable instruments, set to work by the WISE AUTHOR of nature, fortunate passions which like beneficent winds cause the animated Machines to float on the ocean of sensitive objects! It is you, who, by inducing the two sexes to draw near each other, preside over the conservation of Species; it is you who by secret knots tie Fathers and Mothers to their Children, Children to their Fathers and Mothers; it is you who provoke the industriousness of Animals, and that of Man himself: it is you, in a word, who are the Soul of the sentient World. Impetuous Passions, frightening and destructive hurricanes! It is you who cause the tempests which submerge Souls: it is you who destroy

[77] It is interesting to see these notions taken up and reformulated by psychiatrists of our own day. Erich Fromm writes: "Among the most powerful sources of activity are irrational passions. The person who is driven by stinginess, masochism, envy, jealousy, and all other forms of greed is compelled to act; yet his actions are neither free nor rational but in opposition to reason and to his interests as a human being." (*Op. cit.*, p. 87.)

Individuals in desiring to conserve Species: it is you who set up Parents against their Children, Children against their Parents; it is you who change industry to pillage, to ferocity, to banditry: it is you, in a word, who upset the sentient World.[78]

It is the conclusion of this group of writers that the passions, a dual-headed monster, must be simultaneously encouraged and controlled, and repressed when they pass beyond control. Such is the opinion of Frederick the Great, of Morelly, Boulainvilliers, Saint-Lambert, Lévesque, Rivarol, Raynal, Delisle de Sales, and many others.[79]

But how can the passions be controlled? We have seen that some would rely on the sanction of laws. A more common proposal was the attainment, through self-discipline and principally under the direction of reason, of a harmony, balance or counterpoise among the passions. It was said that only one passion could check another, as fire can fight fire. Diderot gives a typical expression to this idea.

It would then be a fortunate thing, you will say to me, to have strong passions. Yes, assuredly, if all are in unison. Establish an exact harmony among them, and fear no disorders from them. If hope is balanced by fear, the point of honor by the love of life, the inclination to pleasure by interest in health: you will see neither libertines, reckless persons nor cowards.[80]

This idea, which goes back to Descartes, Pascal and La Rochefou-

---

[78] *Contemplation de la nature* (1764–1765), *Oeuvres*, 1784, IV, 146–147.

[79] Frederick II, *Anti-Machiavel, Oeuvres*, VIII, 79; Morelly, *Essai sur le coeur humain*, p. 28; Boulainvilliers, *Réfutation des erreurs de Benoît de Spinoza* (1731), p. 164; Saint-Lambert, *Catéchisme universel, Oeuvres philosophiques*, II, 22–23; Charles Lévesque, *op. cit.*, p. 202–222; Boudier de Villemaire, *op. cit.*, p. 113–114; J.-H. Meister, *De la morale naturelle*, p. 69–70; Coyer, *op. cit.*, III, 275; Rivarol, *De l'homme* in *Oeuvres choisies* (éd. Lescure), I, 134–144. Raynal, *op. cit.*, IV, 165; Livre 8, ch. 6, sees the disruption of reason as the principal danger, barring which passions are good and legitimate. Delisle de Sales declares that all passions are good, if controlled, evil if they enslave us (*op. cit.*, II, 42–56). Rivarol attributes to the passions the origin of moral evil: "Nature has put man on the earth with limited powers and limitless desires." But he admits the good results, too, especially when passion is directed towards public welfare. In a later work, Boudier de Villemaire seems to regret his defense of the passions (*L'irréligion dévoilée*, 1774, p. 84–85). He decries emphasis on their impulsion to great things, and asks, "Cannot healthy reason, which points out the good, be as powerful a principle of activity? Such a spring is more suited to the dignity of a free being," who is not merely *moved*, like material beings. Moderate views are also expressed in the early eighteenth century manuscript, *De la conduite* (fol. 117) and in a paper read to the Académie de Caen (*Mémoires de l'Académie des Belles-Lettres de Caen*, 1754, Séance du 4 juillet).

[80] *Pensées philosophiques*, Pensé IV.

cauld, we have seen developed by Pope.[81] It was also urged, after Diderot, by Toussaint and Lévesque.[82]

One particular worry of several writers was the possibility of a man's life falling under the unconquerable sway of what the nineteenth century was to call a *passion dominante*. We have seen Pope refer to this danger. We find it, too, in Spinoza.[83] Seventeenth century French tragedy and comedy also offered numerous instances of such a phenomenon, as in *Phèdre* or *L'Avare*. Vauvenargues theorized about it. "The interest of a single passion, often *malheureuse*, sometimes holds all others in captivity; and reason bears its chains without being able to break them." [84] "We must observe," notes Helvétius, "that among the passions with which each man is animated, there is necessarily one that principally presides over his conduct, and which, in his soul, wins out over all the others." [85] Marat, who was a physician, paints the terrors of this "mistress of the soul which tyrannizes it with fury," and Delisle de Sales develops this theory in still greater detail.[86] The danger of the "ruling passion" lay in its disruption of the supposed harmony or balance we were to strive for. "Passions," writes Vauvenargues, "are opposed to passions, and may serve as a counterpoise; but the ruling passion cannot be led except by its own interest, true or imaginary, because it rules despotically over the will, without which nothing can be done." [87]

[81] Cf. La Rochefoucauld's Maxim 182: "Vices enter into the composition of virtues, as poisons enter into the composition of remedies. Prudence combines and tempers them, and uses them beneficially against the ills of life."

[82] *Loc. cit.* Several French writers may also have been struck by Hume's paradox, in his *Treatise of Human Nature*. Hume argues that reason, being unable to cause volition or action, can never prevent it. "Reason is, and ought only to be, the slave of the passions." The French did not accept his consequence, that reason and the passions can never be in opposition, except insofar as the passions "are accompanied with some judgment or opinion." (Book II, Sec. V). Kant was to nullify Hume's paradox by his dual concept of reason. Reason, in one sense, is grounded in the will and is thus merely instrumental to the realization of subjective existence; in another sense, it transcends the will and provides principles and laws for it to follow.

[83] *Ethics*, Fourth Part, Prop. XLIV.

[84] *Oeuvres*, III, 112 (Maxime 498); also p. 229 (Maxime 369).

[85] *De l'Esprit*, p. 372.

[86] Marat, *op. cit.*, I, 201–214, (1775); Delisle de Sales, *De la philosophie du bonheur*, p. 153–155 (1796). It is also mentioned in Philippe Fermin's *Dissertation sur la question, S'il est permis d'avoir . . . des esclaves . . .* (1770), p. 76–78.

[87] *Introduction à la connaissance de l'esprit humain* (1746), p. 77. Trying to preach to strong passions, Vauvenargues goes on, is like telling a deaf man to enjoy music. "Those who believe men to be the sovereign arbiters of their feelings do not know nature." The similarity with some of Hume's ideas in the *Treatise* (1737) is striking.

We have not yet mentioned one segment of the "moderate" group whose attitude is of particular interest. It includes a fairly large number of *dévots* who preferred realism to intransigence. The apology of the passions was like a flood-tide, and to these men it seemed foolhardy to toe the traditional line and yield no ground. Their defense was, first, to protest in great indignation against the typical attack of the infidels: that Christianity sought to make men inhuman, by demanding that passions be stifled. We may let the abbé Hayer act as spokesman for this group of writers, which included also Abauzit, Formey, Para du Phanjas, Paulian, Chiniac, and Hoin, and perhaps the abbé de Saint-Pierre.[88] The *philosophes,* complains Hayer, distort the true Christian position. Of course passions are necessary, and may be useful. Nobody tells Christians not to love, hate, fear and desire—*au contraire!* Apathy cannot make a good Christian out of a man, for he would lack moral ardor. What the Christian is against is not passions themselves, but their vicious aspects. Passion in itself is indifferent, "a movement of the soul towards an object"; it may even be a passion for truth or for virtue. The fact is simply this: passions become good or evil according to the value of their object—and the manner of their use.[89] Since this was the moderate and most widespread view throughout the land, the apologists felt that here they were treading on safe ground.

If some good Christians were willing to make such tactical concessions, there were many more who refused to budge from the traditional line. So much has been written by scholars about the revaluation of the passions in the eighteenth century that there is a tendency to think that its proponents had the field quite to themselves. This is far from the true situation. From one end of

[88] Saint-Pierre, *Réflexions,* quoted by G. Chérel, *De Télémaque à Candide* p. 239; Abauzit, *Oeuvres,* I, 44–76; Para du Phanjas, *op. cit.,* p. 222 (Para goes particularly far, for an orthodox *abbé,* in praise of passions), *Les principes de la saine philosophie* (1774), II, 192 ff.; Paulian, *op. cit.,* p. 130–132; Chiniac, *op. cit.,* III, 38–42; Hoin, *Discours sur l'utilité des passions* (1752), p. 44 ff. These writers seem practically to repeat each other.

[89] *Op. cit.,* VI, 310–314, 323–329. Formey concedes that the passions are the work of nature, and blames excess on man. "Passions are therefore innocent for we have received nothing from the Author of Nature" that is bad and fatal in itself, independently of its abuse. "I say more: the passions are useful, they are necessary to man." Without passions, man would be indolent and society would not exist. (*Le philosophe chrétien,* II, 105–106.) Formey thus departs from the definition of passion as excess, and veers toward the Aristotelian ideal of the mean, rather than the popular notion of counterpoise.

the century to the other, strong voices spoke up to condemn equally the passions and their ill-advised apologists. We shall look at their main objections.

In 1726, when France was still strongly Cartesian and Malebranchiste, Père Buffier urged men to be governed by reason, and to beware of reason's enemies, passion and imagination. It is useless to divide passions into kinds and groups, he argues; "we must be on guard against all." Since they are opposed to reason, they are also opposed to happiness, both of the individual and of society. To follow unbridled passions would be to make of society a permanent state of war.[90] (Materialists like Diderot and Sade, reformers like Morelly and Rousseau, said that society was just that.)

Camuset replied to Diderot in his *Pensées anti-philosophiques*. The sublime, he asserts, comes precisely from imposing *control* on the passions, both in life and in the beaux-arts; "great passions make dangerous men."[91] It is somewhat ironical that Diderot was later to adopt a rather similar viewpoint.

The abbé Guidi represents the uncompromising theologian. In a dialogue, this Christian apologist insists quite firmly that to be Christians, we must sacrifice our proud reason and embrace irrational mysteries. This is hard enough, he admits; but what irritates non-believers even more, is that religion demands an even more difficult sacrifice: that of passions.[92]

Others were more specific in their rebuttals. Père André, despite the concessions he makes elsewhere, writes that all passions are "misanthropic" and tend to our total destruction: anger, to that of life; ambition, to liberty; avarice, to property; envy, to reputation; and "the lowest of all, so low I can not name it," to the destruction of virtue.[93] Bergier points out that the apologists of passions have confused them with our "natural inclinations." The latter are indeed innocent; but as soon as they become excessive —passions, precisely—they become both unnatural and destructive, "the most fatal of all sicknesses." If passions are the voice of nature, what about conscience, that tells us not to yield to them? Surely, both cannot be the voice of nature. Bergier, obviously,

[90] *Traité de la société civile . . .* , p. 1–4, 29–38.
[91] 1770, p. 3–7.
[92] *Op. cit.*, I, 335–338.
[93] "Sur le beau," p. 51–52.

wishes to pre-empt that title for the conscience, and in so doing, reverses the thesis of the materialists.[94] Another apologist, Chaudon, follows Rousseau (without acknowledgment, of course): man's wickedness rises from his passions, especially for wealth, prestige and pleasure. He calls the apology of passions a "strange system born on the banks of the Thames," popularized by Pope and Voltaire.[95]

It is ridiculous, writes Nonnotte, to say that "great passions make great souls." Rather should we say they make great disasters and unhappiness, and degrade humanity by sacrificing justice, mercy, honor and right. Nonnotte attacks Diderot in particular. Yes, the passions give pleasure; but many pleasures lead to crime. Yes, they produce great deeds—great crimes and cruelty. Diderot himself admits they are the rival of reason. "Tell us, *Philosophe,* what are the great things to which the soul is elevated by the passions?" Socrates did not think that men degenerate when their passions dull. We should say, "Great passions make men of great vices, sober passions, men of lesser vices." As for harmony among passions—isn't that to speak of harmony among diseases? [96]

The abbé Pey aims his shafts at Toussaint and Helvétius and ridicules their defense of passions. Who can seriously accept Helvétius' dictum, "We become stupid as soon as we stop being passionate"? The rationalistic apologists of the passions do not

[94] *Principes de métaphysique et de morale* (1780), p. 207–220, 159. In his *Examen du matérialisme,* Bergier attributes all the ills of society to the passions, and declaims against the *philosophes'* "obstinate apology." Morality depends on self-discipline, and only religion supplies the motive.

[95] *Op. cit.,* I, 33, 37. Love is the worst of all passions, "tyrant of the soul, father of grief and dissension, source of disorders, darkness and error. It is not a simple error; it is the compound of all evils; it corrupts; it ruins society; it induces scorn for virtue and lays traps for wisdom."

[96] *Dictionnaire philosophique de la religion* (1774), III, 241 ff. The poet, Louis Racine, had earlier used his lyre to defend Christian hostility to passion (*La Religion,* Chant VI).

> Et le Dieu des Chrétiens n'est-il pas trop cruel,
> Quand il veut que pour lui renonçant à moi-même,
> Pour lui, mettant ma joie à fuir tout ce que j'aime,
> J'étouffe la nature, et maître infortuné,
> Je gourmande en tyran ce corps qu'il m'a donné?

But the pagans had said exactly the same thing, in their moral systems.

> Quoi! je trouve partout la morale cruelle.
> Catulle m'y ramène, Horace m'y rappelle.
> Que m'ordonne de plus, à quel joug plus pénible
> Me condamne le Dieu qu'on m'a peint si terrible?

realize, asserts Pey, that irrationalism, or anti-rationalism is their inevitable fruit. As proof, he cites a phrase from Toussaint, "our passions are innocent . . . it is our reason that is guilty." [97]

It would be fruitless to pursue further this polemic of the anti-philosophic Christian writers, and I shall merely list some additional references, for the reader who may wish to make use of them.[98] There remains to note briefly the important fact that a number of writers who were certainly not professional Christian apologists—some of them, indeed, belonging quite to the opposing camp—agreed by and large with the viewpoints of the apologists. This should again dispel the notion that defense of passion won a well-nigh universal victory.

Bayle, despite his recognition of the motivating power of the passions, had not approved of them from the standpoint of abstract morality, which must, he thought, be based on reason and the idea of justice and perfection. He had no doubt that passions were intrinsically inimical to that ideal.[99] The abbé de Saint-Pierre and Burlamaqui also follow the Cartesian opposition of reason and passion.[100] Duclos establishes an opposition that is really as typical of the eighteenth century as the tendency to unite the two contraries: they are pleasure-passion, on the one side, duty on the other.[101] Turgot urges us to "extirpate the passions" before

[97] *Le philosophe catéchiste,* p. 85–90.

[98] Richard, *Défense de la religion,* p. 17–18; La Luzerne, *Instruction pastorale* (1756), p. 64–65 (passions are inevitably opposed to morality, being insatiable; no compromise with the enemy); Sigorgne, *Le philosophe chrétien* (1765), p. 21–22; Gauchat, *op. cit.,* I, 106–112 (against Diderot, whom he accuses of confusing feelings and passions), p. 238–240, 253–257; Hennebert, *Du plaisir* (1764), p. xi; Polignac, *op. cit.,* I, 51, 67–69 (to suppress all passions is against nature and all the more worthwhile); Ilharat de la Chambre, *op. cit.,* II, 77.
Two Academies have left records of pieces read to them against the passions. One was read to the Académie de Rouen in 1750, and concludes, "Happy is he whose heart is open only to mediocre passions!" (Gosseaume, *Précis analytique des travaux de l'Académie . . . de Rouen,* I, 243–248. The Académie de l'Immaculée Conception de Rouen, in 1774 had a *concours* on the subject, "Les passions." The winning poem had for its motto, "There are no passions from which one can expect anything except madness and crimes." Both pieces are interesting reflections of common opinion.

[99] Cf. Delvolvé, *loc. cit.*

[100] Burlamaqui, *op. cit.,* I, 20–21 (1748); Saint-Pierre (*Ouvrages de morale et de politique,* 1737, XII, 350 ff.) calls passions "diseases of the imagination, picturing future pleasures greater than they are." He admits that "the ordinary interest of men is the satisfaction of their passions." But this is not necessarily in accord with genuine self-interest: "There is nothing he will not attempt even against his greatest interest, risking his own life to kill his enemies, which is the only remedy he imagines to put an end to his own suffering." (*Projet de paix,* II, 104, III, 42).

[101] *Madame de Luz, Oeuvres,* III, 218.

they work their ravages.[102] Mme de Lambert advised her daughter
to beware of the fatal consequences of the passions. "Nothing
lowers you so much, and puts you so much beneath yourself, as
the passions; they degrade you. Only reason keeps you in your
place." [103] Buffon defines *sagesse* as "intervals between passions." [104] For St.-Hyacinthe they are perverters of moral instincts.[105] Leroy declares them fatal to happiness.[106] They destroy
the natural tendency to compassion and goodness, and thus tend
to degradation and degeneration. They corrupt the reason and
may even destroy it. "But the passions bring us back to childhood,
by strongly presenting to us a unique object with that degree of
interest that eclipses all else." Leroy seems to combine arguments
taken from both d'Alembert and Rousseau. He sees the passions
in violent enmity both to the "better" part of our nature, and to
our reason. Marat, in the same work in which he derides reason,
also condemns the passions—from the viewpoint of a physician.
He describes in detail how passion "agitates our organs, alters and
troubles their economy, until they are totally destroyed." [107]

It is Mably who goes to particular pains to set matters straight.
In his dialogue, *Entretiens de Phocion,* the young Aristas expounds
the doctrine of the *philosophes,* praising passions as the call of
nature and instinct (which are always good), decrying reason as a
pale torch, uncertain, prejudiced and "the work of our vanity."
For this he is sternly taken to task by Phocion. If reason is only a
prejudice, then so is all virtue and morality. (Several of the
materialists, to be sure, proposed precisely this doctrine!) Passions
are the source of all our ills, personal and social, for nothing is
sacred to them in their wild stampede.[108] In another important

---

[102] *Premier Discours aux Sorboniques* (1750), *Oeuvres,* I, 200.

[103] *Avis d'une mère à sa fille, Oeuvres,* I, 172–175.

[104] Buffon, *Oeuvres* (Corpus général), p. 304A, ·330B.

[105] *Op. cit.,* 242.

[106] *Op. cit.,* p. 165–167, 270–271, 282–283.

[107] *Op. cit.,* II, 44 ff. But later he makes passion the spring of all mental activity,
very much like Helvétius.

[108] *Oeuvres complètes,* x, 44–47, 57. However in a much longer discussion, in his
Principes de morale, Mably takes the viewpoint of the "moderates," and urges
regulation of the passions, which are sometimes useful and necessary, but far more
often dangerous and destructive. The debate is a good summary of arguments on
both sides. (*Ibid.,* p. 205–279, 385 ff.). See also, xi, 42 ff. Other writers who condemn
passions are Richer d'Aube, *Essai sur les principes du droit et de la morale* (1743),
p. 8; Gérard, *Le comte de Valmont, ou les égarements de la raison* (1774), I, 278–

work, *De la législation,* Mably admits that passions are universal motives, productive of happiness or unhappiness. The obvious conclusion to be drawn from this psychological fact, it seems to him, is that men need a brake and a guide.[109]

On this issue of the passions, J.-J. Rousseau clearly cuts himself off from the philosophic group with which he had, at the outset of his career, associated himself. It is true that in this, as in most other matters, one can discover isolated statements that tend to make his position confused or obscure, unless they are viewed in a broader perspective. Thus in a letter to Ustéri, he writes, "only great passions lead to great deeds," and he defends them as necessary to society.[110] This is Rousseau's opinion, and never does he deny the status of the passions as natural, necessary, and as good in some of their potentialities. How close Rousseau's opinion is, in this regard, to the sensualist philosophies, may be seen in an important passage of the *Discours sur l'inégalité.*

> Regardless of what the moralists may say, the human understanding owes a lot to the passions . . . it is by their activity that our reason perfects itself; we never seek to know except out of the desire to enjoy; and it is impossible to conceive why he who had neither desires nor fears would give himself the trouble of reasoning. The passions in turn originate in our needs, and their progress, in our knowledge. For we can desire or fear things only in accord with the ideas we may have of them, or by the simple impulse of nature: savage man, without any kind of enlightenment, experiences only the latter kind of passions. His desires do not go beyond his physical needs.[111]

Rousseau's cultural dynamics entails a progression from needs, to passions, and thence to intellectual progress. Needs are conceived of, in the fashion of Montesquieu, as determined by natural and accidental circumstances. The essential fact is a point of stability,

283; Philippe Fermin, *op. cit.,* p. 76–78; Antoine Thomas, *Réflexions philosophiques . . . sur le Poème de la religion naturelle,* in Voltaire, *Oeuvres* (1822), IV, 443 ff. Thomas calls defense of passions "a branch of the great system of Tout est bien." Sabatier de Castres, in his pre-Revolutionary work, *Dictionnaire des Passions, des vertus et des vices* (1769, II, 181), writes that "passions are the vices and deep affections of our soul." There was also a *Danger des passions,* by J. H. Schneider, published in two volumes in Amsterdam (1758) which I have not been able to consult.

[109] P. 22–23.
[110] *Correspondance générale,* X, 39 (1763).
[111] *Political Writings,* p. 150–151.

preceding the formation of society, out of which men can be led only by some kind of a revolutionary "break-through." When this has been accomplished, however, there goes into effect a reverse dynamism; intellectual progress continues on its own, needs and passions are artificially multiplied without a fixed limit. But despite this, despite his scorn for reason (of a certain type), despite, also, his direct influence on nascent romanticism, Rousseau's basic thought berates the passions.

One part of Rousseau's reaction against the *philosophes* was against their concept of human nature, insofar as it was deemed to be essentially physical, requiring and legitimizing physical pleasure as a goal, and in consequence, minimizing, when not entirely denying, a relation between virtue and self-repression. For the essence of Rousseau's system is to point out the various ways in which we may form a "social man." The "social man" is conceived to be quite different both from "natural man," and from the unhappy hybrid of our present state, who is torn by conflicting demands, corrupted in his original nature by society, and yet imperfect in his achievement of the status of a social being. Of the hybrid state Rousseau speaks in a fragment, saying that "the laws of justice and equality are nothing for those who are living at one and the same time in the independence of the state of nature and submitted to the needs of the social state." [112] The chief cause of this imperfection (and we may take the word in its literal, etymological meaning), is the passions which are aroused by social living. Rousseau conceives of man as originally unsocial, and largely free of what may properly be called passions, though he possessed simple physical needs. However, as I have pointed out, Rousseau clearly tells us that what is "natural" to man in society is quite different from what is "natural" to man in the state of nature. Passions, precisely, are natural to social man; but so is a rational, spiritual and moral sphere of his being. Without the peculiarly human rationality, a major part of those passions could not exist. Conflict is produced by the clash with the spiritual and moral demands of the self. Conflict is further abetted by the opposition between the demands of the structures of social life and the resistance of the freedom-loving, self-centered drives of the natural or original man we bear within us—a self-centeredness which (as

[112] *Political Writings*, I, 323.

we shall see particularly in the next chapters) is exacerbated, distorted and corrupted by the passions. This is a large part of Rousseau's thesis in almost all his writings, and is initially expounded in the *Discours*. It is expressed most epigrammatically, perhaps, in a fragment which found its way into the first version of the *Contrat Social:* "our needs draw us together even as our passions divide us; and the more we become enemies, the less we can do without each other." [113]

In the *Lettre à d'Alembert sur les spectacles,* Rousseau condemns tragedy on the ground that it excites the passions. Again, this is consistent with the *Discours sur l'inégalité,* in which he had written of love that it is the most frightening of all passions, seemingly "suited to destroy mankind, which it is supposed to preserve." This thought leads him to a fundamental conclusion: "We must first agree that the more passions are violent, the more necessary are laws to restrain them." [114]

The question of the passions is most crucial in *La Nouvelle Héloïse.* This work contains the most stirring passions of any novel in the eighteenth century. It is, as critics have noted, ambiguous in several ways. It has been shown, by Schinz and other scholars, that Rousseau's own intentions varied during the composition of his long novel, for personal reasons that do not enter into our subject. Furthermore, while passion is the very theme and problem of the novel, it is also a subject of overt discussion by the characters themselves, in their epistolary exchanges. This obviously complicates the interpretation of the book, as is shown by the fact that most contemporaries understood it as a condemnation of passions, while readers of the Romantic generation took it as their exaltation. The characters' rational arguments are one thing; their actions and the results of their actions may have a quite different effect. One instance will suffice to illustrate this point. At the outset of the story, Saint-Preux passionately reassures Julie that he is beyond the criminal impulses of passion; her person inspires in him only the love of virtue. But unless he is playing the role of a seducer, or a Valmont *avant la lettre,* his very words abjuring passion reveal what the French would call *les égarements*

[113] *Ibid.;* also, p. 447.
[114] *Ibid.,* p. 163. For further condemnation of the passions in the *Lettre à d'Alembert,* see *Oeuvres,* I, 203, 216.

de la passion. Reasoning reaffirms the way of honor and virtue; but the affirmation is nature's way of beguiling us, by leading us into confidence in our good intentions and an underestimation of natural impulses.[115]

Although Julie forgives her seducer, on the ground that great passions characterize noble souls—a belief which is unquestionably that of the author[116]—the progress of her moral understanding, under the impact of the inalterable circumstances and blows to which life submits her, leads her to an even deeper realization of passion's fatal dangers. The chief direction of Rousseau's thought is towards a rational reconstruction and a rational reordering of the individual personality, and of the inter-relationships of individuals within the social structure—this despite the inner tension in Rousseau himself, between reason and intuition or sentiment. The very point of *La Nouvelle Héloïse* is to prove that passion, and especially sexual passion, is the element most destructive of our attempts at a rational ordering of our lives.[117] It may be said that the sexual drive now replaces emulation and esteem, which (as we shall see in the following chapters) were Rousseau's chief targets in the second *Discours*. In no way does the end of the novel—as critics frequently assert—contradict, confuse or belie its intent. It is true that Julie is aware of the imminent failure of her heroic effort to order her life in accord with a rational concept of virtue. Like Phèdre, she can no longer resist the unconquerable force of natural instincts when an unforeseen turn of circumstances surprises her with her guard lowered; though she is so fortunate as to be able to find death before rather than after her downfall. But is not this very outcome the most dramatic rendition of the dangers Rousseau sees in passion? Against a powerful and triumphant passion, Rousseau has erected a powerful, rational will to virtue. The plot line of the novel, after Julie's marriage, is nothing but the conflict between these two forces: the attempt to harmonize reason and nature, to

---

[115] Première Partie, ch. 5 (II, 19–21).

[116] II, 273, and note by Daniel Mornet.

[117] From an entirely different viewpoint, Montesquieu's *Lettres persanes* is another example of the defeat of the human will by the sexual forces in the harem; here, however, it is the male who seeks to impose a pattern of order and woman who defeats him, while in Rousseau's novel the positions are reversed. Perhaps it is this fact which explains the somewhat virile character of Julie and the somewhat effeminate character of Saint-Preux.

make them live together in peace, an attempt which, if successful, would really be a defeat of nature by reason. But the first fall is ultimately fatal. Passion, once triumphant, is never completely defeated.

It is here (though Rousseau, of course, indicates no such linking), that the reorganization of the personality, as programmed in *Emile,* appears as the logical complement to *La Nouvelle Héloïse.* Perhaps Rousseau intended us to see in Claire d'Orbe—to whom Julie mistakenly writes, "know and pity the madness of your wretched friend, and thank the heavens for having preserved your heart from the horrible passion that gives it [i.e., madness] to us" —the less unhappy (though less romantic and novelistically less interesting) alternative to Julie.[118] For Claire, though she suffers, preserves her integrity, by a strong will at the service of a concept of virtue which involves self-repression.

Other characters in the novel form an important part of this picture. Julie's husband, Wolmar, is the model of the sage, imperturbable and rational. Doubtless Rousseau was torn between self-identification with this projected model of himself and the picture of the weak, passionate, but noble Saint-Preux. Wolmar recognizes both the values of passion and the urgency of controlling it. In his concept of control, he echoes the common eighteenth century notion of a harmony or counterpoise of the passions.

> How can we restrain even the weakest passion, when it is without a counterweight? That is the disadvantage of cold and tranquil characters. All goes well, as long as their coldness guarantees them from temptations; but if one suddenly reaches them, they are vanquished as soon as they are attacked, and reason, which governs while it is alone, never has strength to resist the least effort. I have been tempted only once, and I succumbed. If the intoxication of some other passion had made me vacillate again, I should have fallen as many times as I stumbled: only souls of fire are able to fight back and win. All great efforts, all sublime actions are their work; cold reason has never done anything illustrious, and we triumph over passions only by opposing them one to another. When the passion for virtue happens to arise, it dominates by itself and keeps everything in equilibrium.[119]

[118] III, 29.
[119] III, 253.

Actually, Wolmar begs the question, as the final lines clearly show. For the "passion for virtue" of which he speaks is not a passion in the "natural" sense of the word (i.e., referring to what is original or instinctual), but rather involves commitment to a rationally accepted ideal, or value system. This is again Rousseau's attempt to reconcile reason and nature. Finally, the Englishman, Lord Bomstom, may be considered as a confirmation of Wolmar's pronouncement. Unlike Wolmar, he is too indifferent and world-weary to have a passion for virtue, man of honor though he be. He is unprepared for the assault of passion which overtakes him in Italy, and comes close to ruination at the hands of a skillful prostitute.

We need not analyze *Emile* in detail. Its program is, first, the avoidance of passion in early years, and, second, the building of self-discipline so that later passion can be not avoided, but mastered. "What is forbidden to us by conscience," says Emile's tutor, in the Fifth Book, "is not to be tempted, but to let ourselves be conquered by temptation. It does not depend on us to have or not to have passions, but it depends on us to rule over them." [120] Passions, because they are never satisfied, do not lead to happiness. Because they have no law but themselves, they lead to wickedness. Since virtue is, by definition, the overcoming of passions, they are opposed to virtue. The virtuous man "is able to conquer his affections; for he follows his reason, his conscience." Consequently, concludes Rousseau (quite inconsequently), passions are all good when we remain their master.

Rousseau's political writings are in harmony with this view of man. Political liberty is substituted by the social contract (properly understood and implemented) for the natural freedom which obtains both in the state of nature and, to a certain extent, in present society. Natural freedom operates through permissive behavior, that is, through the appetites, passions and instinctive drives. Political liberty, on the other hand, involves the "self-imposed" discipline of rational moral conduct, in submission to the general will. The passions are also repressed by social controls. The realm of the individual is severely restricted, for he must become a citizen, a social being, a unit in a higher collectivity, even as an organ in the body, says Rousseau, is submitted to a harmonious

[120] *Oeuvres*, II, 417.

role in the total organic economy. But the individual should be a willing participant in this process (—and this is of some importance in distinguishing Rousseau from modern totalitarians). Here again he falls back on reason, that is, a theory of human nature which places confidence in man's reasonableness.

> . . . Let us strive to take from the ill itself the remedy which is to cure it: . . . let our violent interlocutor[121] be himself the judge of our work; let us show him in art perfected the reparation of the evils which art, begun, did to nature. Let us show him . . . in a better understood constitution of things the reward for good actions, the punishment for bad ones and the happy accord of justice and happiness; let us illuminate his reason with new light; . . . let him learn to feel the pleasure of multiplying his being by uniting it with that of his fellows. Let him become for his own enlightened self-interest, just, beneficent, moderate, virtuous. . . .[122]

The debate over the passions had an important and direct bearing on the evaluation of human nature and of the phenomenology of moral experience. Is man reasonable? On this first question depends the nature of the moral solution. It appears from our investigation that in the "Age of Reason," most thought he was not —at least, not in the sphere of his behavior—however impressive might be his ability for abstract thought. It was also concluded— very often by the same thinkers—that man is not good. Then he must either be considered essentially evil, or inclined to evil when swayed by passion and self-interest, or seduced into evil by cultural circumstances. The logic of such a conclusion would be to condemn the passions; and all this, at least, is logically consistent. A much greater difficulty was incurred by those who defended the passions, and yet held man to be evil. This pitfall could best be avoided by taking the position that man is a composite of good and evil. The passions could then also be classified as good or bad, according to their nature, or their degree. But if some passions are bad only because of degree, that must signify that they are bad because they escape the control of reason. Reason would thus have to be accepted as man's defining characteristic, at least insofar as he

---

[121] Rousseau is referring to Diderot's nihilist in "Droit naturel."

[122] *Political Writings*, I, 323–324. It is true that Rousseau elsewhere opposes the theory of enlightened self-interest, but the contradiction is, at least in part, only apparent. In the first version of the *Contrat Social*, for instance, he is referring to the existing social state, and not to future possibilities (cf. ch. 2).

is a good and moral being. Others, however, avoided this difficulty by following an entirely different path. Reacting against the Christian doctrines of the natural depravity of man (after the Fall) and the corruption of the passions, they defended the passions and concluded, with some logical consistency, that man is naturally good. We shall meet this theory again in our twelfth chapter.

These, however, are inferences which we now may draw from a historical perspective on the entire discussion. Not all of them were clear to those engaged in it. The liberal or radical thinkers of the time were chiefly concerned with constructing the desired ethical system—that is, a realistic and workable one. In view of the over-all evaluation, it seemed clear to many that non-rational solutions were most suitable to human nature. The devout, of course, found in this conclusion added support for religion, as the only efficient control. But we shall observe other alternatives coming to the fore. Less religious conservatives (although they admitted the practical value of "superstitions") will rely more heavily on repressive social forces of various kinds.[123] Some will suggest a third way, the method of "counterpoise," a notion that had some popularity, especially in the first part of the century. But wherever such a counterpoise was suggested as a task for the individual to perform, it was a notion which, in the last analysis, involved *rational* control by a reasonable being. Still a fourth possibility lay in the effective manipulation of the passions by the State and by education, particularly by using the powerful impulses we shall see united under the name of "esteem" or "pride." On this point we may refer, for instance, to an important statement of d'Holbach's. Holding man to be moved only by self-interest and the passions, he relies not on rational means, but on compulsive social forces to establish a counterpoise. "By opposing passions to other passions, fear to the impetuosity of unruly desires, hatred and anger to harmful action, real interests to fictitious and imaginary ones . . . we can promise ourselves that we shall be able to make an advantageous use of the passions; we shall direct them to the public good. . . ."[124]

[123] On the question of superstitions, see, for instance, Mably, "De la superstition," in *Oeuvres*, 1794–1795, vol. xiv, and my article, referred to above, on Truth and Falsehood.

[124] *La Morale universelle*, I, 33.

In these various ways, it was hoped that despite the almost irremediable defectiveness of human nature, a "moral" society might still be created; that from selfish motivation might be rescued a large measure of general good, and from irrational beings might arise a rational polity.

And yet, it would be a distortion to leave the matter there. The eighteenth century is not called "The Age of Reason," or "The Age of the Enlightenment," without some justification. Our view of the total picture will show us that human nature had many defenders. The more optimistic esteemed man to be more good than evil, and many held him to be rational, or at least capable of rational behavior, given a rational society and education. In fact, as the century waned, although there was little change in the proportion of optimism and pessimism regarding man's innate dispositions and character, there apparently was a marked upswing in faith in his malleability, and in the efficacy of social mechanisms and pressures. Even more significant, the ethical approach that was probably most characteristic of the eighteenth century, the ethics of enlightened self-interest, necessarily assumed the potential rationality of mankind. It was predicated on the belief that men were capable of weighing and calculating the ultimate returns of alternate courses of action, and thus would choose (necessarily "choose," for the determinist) the sacrifice of immediate good for the "enlightened" good. And so Mably, in supporting the superiority of reason to the passions, rejects the latter as self-centered in an immediate, unenlightened fashion; while reason, "minister of the author of nature among men and organ of my will, cries to me to be just, human, *bienfaisant;* . . . it teaches me to seek my personal happiness in the public good, and to unite men by the virtues which inspire security and confidence." To put the matter somewhat differently: the predominance of the self-love motive indicated that men are not rational beings, that is, motivated by reason; but it did not prove that they might not be reasonable beings. A reasonable being, according to this theory, might, by calculation, overcome his passions and conclude that virtue is the best way to serve self-interest.

Thus the general attitude towards reason was not a simple one. In the field of epistemology, reason was exalted for its ability to discover nature's laws and to make order out of the apparent chaos of phenomena. At the same time, it was devaluated, and even derided, for its incapacity to grasp first and ultimate things. In the moral realm, reason was most frequently granted the power of discerning the right and the wrong. But, subject to error and to seduction by prejudice, self-love and passion, it was not deemed capable, purely by itself, of controlling behavior.

The problem was more complex than this, of course. Not until a later section of this study shall we be able to see how all we have examined thus far is interwoven with the direct ethical question of the origin and nature of our moral experience. And we shall have to bear in mind the possibility of significant inconsistencies, or perplexities, as a given writer may adopt a certain position on one of the basic questions, and not take the expected, consequent attitude towards another. Helvétius, a writer whose work is that of a cold rationalist, praises the passions; while Rousseau, a passionate sentimentalist, emphasizes their dangers. The belief that man is not rational, for instance, may clash with a philosophy that is eminently rational, forming the dichotomy of a non-emotional or rational approach to a being considered as primarily emotional or irrational. Or else it may be the contrary: one who professes a decent estimate of man may suggest purely non-rational or coercive means for governing his behavior. We might say that some rationalists use an empirical approach, some empiricists, a rational approach. Finally, there are even a few—a few very consistent and uncompromising thinkers—who will urge us to overthrow the whole sham and pretense of a moral existence, and to live honestly, like the irrational beasts which, they tell us, we really are.

The problem of the passions in human nature opens up into the widest perspectives. All but the moral nihilists agreed that human urges and drives must be limited by social law. Are the laws God-willed and ordained, and so to be obeyed as we obey our superior? Or are they necessary derivatives of a unique human organism and experience? If the latter, are they objective realities, inhering in the nature of things, or pragmatic decisions having local validity? Are they, perhaps, arbitrary tyrannies possessing no ontological status and no compelling authority for the individual strong enough, or clever enough, to evade them? Finally, if we are neither rational nor free, are we responsible for our inability to conform?

From another viewpoint, the most significant of the dilemmas was that of the normative value of nature and of reason. Buffon, better than anyone else, crystallized a notion that was well-nigh universal in eighteenth century ethical thinking: the secular version of the Christian view of man as a dual being. This, for Pascal, underlay his *grandeur* and his *misère*. The eighteenth century phrased the dualism in terms of spiritual and animal, rational and natural (or passionate), social and egoistic. All were agreed on this. The disagreement lay in the relation between the pairs. Was the social more natural or more rational? Did reason, as well as nature, justify egoism? To what extent were the rational and the natural in conflict, to what extent did they coincide? As we apply these uncertainties to the controversy over the passions, we see in retrospect that some writers either favored "nature," or thought it invincible; others refused to abjure reason. Some sought to use "nature" alone, as the ethical fundament; and while few opted for reason alone, most wished to reconcile, even to identify the two. All this, I hope, we shall see in a much sharper light as this study unfolds.

Ten

FORMS AND VALUES

OF SELF-INTEREST (1)

THE UPHOLDERS of radical evil in man, in their endeavor to buttress their position, often had recourse to an analysis of human nature that reduced all motivation to more or less disguised impulses of self-interest. Not all proponents of this *reductio,* however, concluded from it that man is evil. The development of eighteenth century thought on this question is somewhat complex. It follows three trails that are partly distinct and partly overlapping: the Christian, the seventeenth century secular tradition, and a new turn given to the latter by eighteenth century materialism. Furthermore, the question is envisaged in varying perspectives of wider or narrower scope. Self-interest is often treated in its most general terms; but concentration on smaller, particular spheres of self-interest is peculiarly characteristic of the period. The first smaller sphere is the happiness motive; a second and still smaller sphere, the pleasure-pain motive; a third and more amorphous sphere, the congeries of ideas associated with esteem and self-esteem. Since the latter subject is more particularized and was often treated rather separately from the general notion of self-interest, we shall reserve our discussion of it for the following chapter.

Self-interest, happiness and pleasure—the first two, especially

—were often considered by eighteenth century writers to be identical as motivating forces. Others, however, realized that self-interest is not necessarily to be equated with happiness, and still less with pleasure, since it may require the sacrifice of pleasure and the pursuit of duty. The distinction is important. A number of writers will attempt to derive an ethics from self-interest; few will essay the more difficult task of deriving it from pleasure.

The Christian tradition is itself twofold. The Augustinian and the Reformation theologies insisted on man's utter depravity. The relatively few writers who follow this tradition, in the eighteenth century, found in the invincibility of self-interest an important cause (or manifestation) of this moral worthlessness. Thus J.-Fr. Bernard—a Protestant—comments that the workings of self-love are devious and disguised in our conscious minds, so that we are really activated by motives we do not believe we have. So-called virtue is, then, largely of non-virtuous or of evil origin.[1] Bernard denounces man as a creature thoroughly corrupt and condemned to error.

The French Catholic writers, following by and large the tradition of the Jesuits, and influenced perhaps by the analysis of La Rochefoucauld, were inclined to be less harsh in their condemnation, even while agreeing on the universality and the deviousness of the self-interest motive. In the transition period between the two centuries, we find the influential apologist, Abbadie, insisting on the all-pervasiveness of self-love.[2] He terms it natural, primary and necessary; a feeling destined by God to direct our intelligence —whose function is, in turn, to rule feeling. To have proper self-love is to love God, and to see our true interest, which is in the life eternal. None the less, the fact is admitted that self-love "is the general principle of all our movements"; and love of others is only love of ourselves. "Self-interest is all powerful over minds," and virtue is attractive only when it flatters our *amour-propre*. In other words, there is no disinterested love of virtue, or even of God. *Amour-propre* and the desire for happiness, says Abbadie, are one and the same thing. He finds Epicurus "quite reasonable," provided we seek noble, and not voluptuous pleasures. It is true

[1] *Réflexions morales, satiriques et comiques sur les moeurs de notre siècle*, (1733), p. 157.
[2] His distinction between two forms of self-love: *amour de soi* and *amour-propre* will be developed later in this chapter.

that we are made for different kinds of pleasure—but we are all made for pleasure.[3]

The origin of some of Abbadie's ideas may be sought in the writings of Nicole, although the Jansenist moralist did not go nearly so far as his successor, nor was he so indulgent. For Nicole, our incapacity to love except in relation to ourselves is a "corruption" that spreads "in the search of sensual pleasures and honors." But even he admits an "enlightened *amour-propre*" that is not unlike Abbadie's.[4] We shall have more than one occasion to return to Nicole; his influence, while perhaps indirect, was by no means negligible.

Abbadie's phrase, "love of ourselves is the only source of all our other loves," signaled the start of a fierce controversy within the Church. In 1694, Père Lami, in his *Traité de la connaissance de soi-même*, replied to Abbadie that we have "a purely reasonable love," which requires no self-interest or pleasure in order to be excited. Fénelon's *Sur la vie mystique* also expressed the Quietist doctrine that we are capable of a pure and utterly disinterested love of God. But Bossuet attacked him, fearing the spread of Quietism, and insisted that the natural desire for beatitude is a necessary motive for our love of God. Malebranche's *Traité de l'amour de Dieu* sided with Bossuet, and the Catholic Church finally pronounced itself in his favor.[5] The question grew popular; it was debated in the *salons* and became the subject of essays in the schools. In short, as long as condemnation of human nature

[3] *L'Art de se connaître soi-même* (1692), p. 102–107, 206–216, 223, 238, 252–275. Abbadie's views were strongly supported by La Placette, in his *Nouveaux Essais de morale,* (1697), II, 1–40. Self-love, the spring of all our acts, is innocent, and receives moral qualification only in its use.

Compare Freud: ". . . the force behind all human activities is a striving towards the two convergent aims of profit and pleasure." The egoistic instincts are "at the bottom of all the relations of affection and love between human beings—possibly with the single exception of that of a mother to her male child." (*Civilization and its discontents,* p. 57, 89.)

[4] *Essais de morale* (1713), II, 40–41, III, 111 ff. See also Sylvain Régis: *Traité de morale* (1690), III, 403 ff. Self-love is "reasonable" when it leads to choice of spiritual good, "the sovereign good," "beatitude," etc.

[5] See also Malebranche, *De la Recherche de la vérité,* p. 401–402. "Pure charity is so above our strength, that far from being able to love God for himself, human reason cannot easily understand our being able to love except in relation to self, or to have any other end except our own satisfaction." Contrast Spinoza: "he alone lives by divine law who loves God not from fear of punishment or from love of any other object . . . but solely because he has knowledge of God . . ." (*Tractatus theologico-politicus,* p. 60).

followed such a traditional line of denouncing the sin, corruption, vanity, pride and selfishness in man, the Church saw no danger in it; in fact, as we see, its adherents participated in it.

Paralleling these developments in Christian writings, the secular school, continuing the Renaissance tradition, added ever greater emphasis on the theory that all motivation is reducible to self-love.[6] We have seen that some, from La Rochefoucauld on, utilized this analysis to proclaim or to condemn the immoral nature of human beings. A concomitant development, however, led others to a different evaluation of self-interest, as a purely natural phenomenon, as a characteristic that is non-moral and necessary, and susceptible of moral evaluation only in its applications.

Among foreign writers who strengthened the secular stream of thought were Spinoza and Pope. The entire development in the Third Part of Spinoza's *Ethic,* from Proposition X on, is a profound (and devastating) naturalistic analysis of human nature and motivation. Humility is associated with weakness, self-love with power and self-realization. The analysis is far too long for adequate discussion here, and I shall only quote a few pertinent excerpts.

> But desire is the essence itself or nature of a person in so far as this nature is conceived from its given constitution as determined towards any action, and therefore as a person is affected by external causes with this or that kind of joy, sorrow, love, hatred, etc., that is to say, as his nature is constituted in this or that way, so must his desire vary and the nature of one desire differ. . . . Since reason demands nothing which is opposed to nature, it demands, therefore, that every person should love himself, should seek his own profit—what is truly profitable to him—should desire everything that really leads man to greater perfection. . . . The more each person strives and is able to seek his own profit, that is to say, to preserve his being, the more virtue does he possess; on the other hand, in so far as each person neglects his own profit, that is to say, neglects to preserve his own being, is he impotent. . . . It appears, therefore, that men are by nature inclined to hatred and envy. . . .[7]

[6] Parallels among the ancient Sophists and Epicureans are obvious. Cf. Epicurus: "No one gives to another except for his own interest."

[7] *Ethic* (ed. *cit.*), p. 260, 301, 303, 258. See also *Tractatus politicus,* ch. 2. Spinoza's philosophy, as I have said before, ultimately surpasses this limited viewpoint, but it was his naturalism that was powerful in eighteenth century French minds.

Pope tells us,

> Two principles in human nature reign;
> Self-love, to urge, and Reason to restrain.[8]

Neither is good or evil; each has its proper operation, and if they function, good will result.

> Self-love and Reason to one end aspire,
> Pain their aversion, Pleasure their desire.[9]

Bayle's account of human behavior, in the *Pensées sur la comète,* embodies similar viewpoints, in its attribution of all motivation to passion or desire. He agrees with Bossuet that we are not capable of disinterested love.[10] Bayle's depreciation of human nature, and Mandeville's, were based half on the concept of invincible self-interest, half on that of man's irrationality.[11]

The first generation of *philosophes,* largely moderates, were inclined to follow this path. However, we must bear in mind that their apparent unanimity conceals a disparity of outlook. "Men want to be happy," notes Fontenelle, "and they would like to be happy with little effort (*à peu de frais*). Pleasure, and tranquil pleasure, is the common object of their passions, and they are dominated by a certain laziness." [12] In this purely naturalistic view, Fontenelle sees no straining for perfection—and no need of it. Man loves only his pleasure, declares another early writer, Lesage de la Colombière, and "loves nothing else except in proportion to the good he can get out of it." He is incapable of a disinterested action—but fortunately, he may sometimes find pleasure in virtuous deeds.[13] This evaluation is repeated almost exactly by a number of writers in the first half of the century, including Fréret and Vauvenargues. The atheistic Fréret, not satisfied with affirming that all our acts are intended to procure

[8] *Essay on Man,* II, 59–60.

[9] *Ibid.,* p. 87–88. Pope's opinions, however, vary. Similar ideas characterize the Natural Law school. Cf. Burlamaqui, *Principes du droit naturel* (1748, I, 71–73, II, 58 ff.). Morelly (*Essai sur le coeur humain,* p. xx–xxi) quotes Pope approvingly, and emphasizes the importance of education.

[10] "The most devout Christians, if they wish to be sincere, will admit that the strongest link that unites them to God is looking at him as beneficent, and considering that he distributes infinite rewards to those who obey him, and that he punishes eternally those who offend him." (*Dictionnaire,* "Epicure," II, 743).

[11] See Chapter 9.

[12] "Sur la nature de l'églogue," quoted by Chérel: *De Télémaque à Candide,* p. 52.

[13] *Le mécanisme de l'esprit, ou la morale naturelle dans ses sources* (1712), p. 10–11.

pleasure and avoid pain (and indeed, that it is utterly impossible for us to act in any other way) insists on the adjective "the greatest" before each of those nouns. From the differences in individual constitutions, he draws the further consequence of relativism in valuation—one that will be carried over into ethical theory.[14] Toussaint defines self-love as "that sort of affection for ourselves which pure nature inspires in us." He terms it "innocent, legitimate and even indispensable." If we are to love others as ourselves, we must love ourselves. No love can be disinterested, not even our love of God.[15] And Montesquieu declares that self-love and the desire for happiness are inseparable from human nature, and are "truly born with us, influencing all our actions, and are their prime, or to be exact, their only motive." [16] Voltaire summarized the accepted view in verse:

> Chez de sombres dévots l'amour-propre est damné,
> C'est l'ennemi de l'homme, aux enfers il est né.
> Vous vous trompez, ingrats; c'est un don de Dieu même,
> Tout amour vient du ciel: il nous chérit, il s'aime.[17]

That Voltaire's opinions were to vary, and to become more and more pessimistic, we have already seen.[18]

Still another parallel or tributary current that was to swell the naturalistic view of man's behavior—one that tended to view him more optimistically—was the demand for justification of legitimate pleasures and worldly satisfactions.[19] This was already an important aspect of the changing intellectual climate at the end of the seventeenth century. Bossuet had said that the Christian must not seek happiness on earth, and this was the "pure" Christian doctrine, against which the growing Epicurean current was

---

[14] *Op. cit.*, p. 64–67.

[15] *Les Moeurs*, p. 69–73, also Chap. 1. Unlike many others, Toussaint is careful to separate self-love from pride and vanity, which he condemns. This is similar to the self-love condoned by the Christians.

[16] *Essai touchant les loix naturelles, Oeuvres*, III, 188.

[17] "Cinquième Discours sur l'homme." The first line quoted was not added until 1752, the other three in 1751. In his *Remarques sur les pensées de M. Pascal* (c. 1728), Voltaire had written: "It is as impossible for a society to be formed without self-love as it would be to make children without concupiscence. . . . It is by our mutual needs that we are useful to mankind; it is the foundation of all commerce, the eternal link among men." (XXII, 36.) Cf. Mandeville.

[18] Cf. his letter to Frederick II (1770): "Yes, self-love is the wind that fills the sails, and which drives the vessel to port. If the wind is too strong it sinks us; if self-love is disordered, it becomes frenzy." (46:547.)

[19] See the discussion in the chapter, "Ethics and Christianity."

rising. The legitimacy of mundane happiness (conceived of as pleasure), and of the worldly ethical ideal of the *honnête homme* forms in fact the burden of many *libertin* writings during the seventeenth century, as we see in Saint-Amant and Saint-Evremond. Its defense grows into a louder chorus in the early part of the eighteenth. Mme de Lambert's writings were a typical and influential example, one which expressed the spirit of her milieu.[20] In the characteristic approach, however, the idea of pleasure is rather gingerly handled, the limits are stressed, and often the entire motive is still subordinated to heavenly imperatives and ultimate goals. Many of these earlier writers were deists, and significantly, even more were Christians. The devout writers felt a need to liberalize rigid attitudes in order to meet the unconquerable exigencies of the new drift of things. One reference will, I think, suffice to portray this group. The abbé Desfourneaux published in 1724 his *Essai d'une philosophie naturelle applicable à la vie, aux besoins et aux affaires.* He is willing to make reasonable concessions. We have, he tells us, two basic interests, which are (in order of time), "The first, a degree of happiness in this life, which does not prejudice what we must do in regard to the other life. . . . The second . . . is that we have to do, in regard to another life, all that reason requires." But the good abbé is afraid this may sound too forbidding to his worldly readers. He hastens to explain that reason does not demand anything excessive or unpleasant.

> I do not expect that reason should exclude, in favor of useful truths, those that have no merit other than to please. We need pleasant things (*l'agréable*) in life, provided we can enjoy them like *honnêtes gens.* . . . Besides, the useful is sometimes found in the pleasurable. At any rate, we need to have both. Don't we have need of some *douceurs* in our lives? Can we be always occupied with the useful, always working to help others, to heal or forestall needs and ills? Isn't there one, I mean, one ill, to which intelligent people are most subject, which would follow them everywhere if they didn't remedy it, and which serious work would increase in a way, instead of diminishing? I am speaking of boredom. . . . We are obligated to remedy this ill,

[20] See also A. R. Desautels, S. J., *Les Mémoires de Trévoux et le mouvement des idées au* xviiie *siècle (1701–1734),* p. 89–98; J. P. Zimmerman, "La Morale laïque au commencement du xviiie siècle," *RHL,* 1917; Lanson, "La transformation des idées morales . . . ," *R. du mois,* 1910.

both because it is one in itself, and because it makes us unable to prevent others . . . Reason commands that we prefer an urgent utility to one that can be put off, and the agreeable is useful when it heals us of boredom. . . .[21]

The abbé Desfourneaux really never doubts that happiness is the legitimate goal of men on earth. To induce them to live the Christian life, his tactic is to argue that we can never succeed in this goal. "We cannot reasonably think that God has made man capable of making himself very happy by the goods of this life." [22] In like fashion, he cheerfully admits that there are "rather great pleasures" of the body, as well as of the spirit, and that "at bottom, it is quite indifferent whether we feel pleasure through the body or through the spirit, since it is all pleasure, and that of the soul is not different in its nature from that of the body." It is somewhat startling to find, under the pen of the good abbé, a thesis that La Mettrie and Sade were to develop, with quite different ethical consequences. But he qualifies the statement, it is true, by assuring us that spiritual pleasures last longer and are better for the health.[23]

As the century proceeds, we find the majority of the Catholic writers maintaining the universal primacy of self-interest, and inclining more and more to indulgence.[24] The rise and spreading influence of the "philosophic" movement doubtless reinforced both these tendencies. The considerable number of orthodox writers who admit the unique motivation of self-interest and happiness is impressive. We find it explicitly stated in the apologetics of Pluche, Gauchat, the abbé de Saint-Pierre, and Ilharat

[21] P. 261–266. See also Le Maître de Claville, *Traité du vrai mérite* (1734), I, 100–101, 297–299.

[22] P. 334.

[23] P. 345–346. The qualification is itself qualified by the admission that many people "are incapable of being happy except through the body, or, so to speak, through the animal." (P. 348.) Another typical statement is that of Dupuy (*Dialogues sur les plaisirs,* 1717, Préface, Dialogue I). Man changes in everything except his unique motive, which is pleasure. Pleasure is necessary to the existence of the individual and of society. But we must manage wisely, or else the pursuit of pleasure is self-defeating.

Even earlier, Abbadie had written that it is impossible to desire happiness too strongly; the only wrong is in the methods used to attain it. (*Op. cit.,* p. 252 ff.) The abbé Descoutures finds much good in women and gold, when properly used. Pleasure, properly controlled, is the "source of wise conduct and heroic acts, of health and calm." (*La morale universelle,* 1687, p. 85 ff., 170 ff.)

[24] For a similar (though narrower) tendency on the part of seventeenth century Jesuits, see Pascal's *Lettres provinciales.*

de la Chambre, and by Pestré and Mallet in articles in the *Ency-clopédie* ("Bonheur," "Charité," respectively). These writings are more than a prolongation of the dispute over the question of "disinterested love of God," although that matter is still some-times referred to. They reveal a conscious effort to blunt the at-tack of the new secularism, with the result that, in a sense, they were obliged to absorb it. Thus Gauchat specifically assails the *philosophes'* utilization of this theme as a weapon to attack a supposedly "inhuman" Christian morality. He assures us Chris-tians recognize that God has put the desire for happiness into us, as an ineffaceable necessity in a thinking being.[25] The impact of the new secularism is seen even more palpably in the open adop-tion, by these writers, of utilitarian and non-moral motivation for being virtuous. We do not, cannot—and even should not—love good for its own sake, but because it is the path to greater happiness, here and in the hereafter. It is because Paradise offers us the perspective of more and greater happiness that we should cultivate the virtues that lead to it.[26] The point is frequently made by apologists—a point usually associated with the Reformation, with the seventeenth century cynics or with the eighteenth cen-tury materialists—that all apparently virtuous acts, as well as "indifferent" acts, are in reality motivated by the happiness prin-ciple. The ethical conclusion is that we are incapable of a dis-interested action, or of love of the good for its own sake. "Let us listen to our internal feeling," writes the abbé Mallet; "and we shall see that the aim of happiness accompanies men in the occasions most contrary to happiness itself. The ferocious Eng-

[25] "If it is self-love, the desire to make ourselves happy by legitimate means, re-ligion, far from condemning it, approves and orders . . ." (*Lettres critiques*, 1755–1763, XVI, 118–120). He reconciles this to Christian doctrine by stating that though we must love ourselves, we should also despise ourselves. (*Ibid.*, I, 238–240, 244.) See also Chiniac, *op. cit.*, III, 10–13 ("Man loves himself and loves himself legiti-mately: that is the foundation of his morality. This love is founded on the good-ness of his being.") Formey, *Le Philosophe chrétien*, II, 105–107 ("Only fanaticism can preach disinterestedness. . . . For whom should I work, if I do not deign to work for myself?"); Joly, *op. cit.*, p. 52–54; Para du Phanjas, *op. cit.*, p. 255–256; Christian Wolff, *op. cit.*, p. 47 (self-love is not only innocent, but a duty).
[26] Ilharat de la Chambre, *Abrégé de la philosophie*, 1754, II, 53–66; Yvon, "Bon" (*Encyclopédie*); Pestré, "Bonheur" (*Encyclopédie*). L. Le François calls the desire for happiness the only limit to our freedom of will. (*Examen des faits*, in *Oeuvres complètes*, I, 66.) Ilharat goes so far as to declare that self-abnegation is both ex-travagant and impossible. "Let us proclaim a morality that men can practice. . . . To avenge self-love is to re-establish man in the enjoyment of his rights."

lishman who slays himself wants to be happy; the brahmin who macerates himself wants to be happy; the courtier who enslaves himself wants to be happy; the multiplicity, diversity and *bizarrerie* of means show only better the singleness of happiness." [27] In a later chapter, we shall see that some Christians foresaw the dangers of this doctrine, in the eighteenth century context, and fought against it.

There can be little doubt that many Christian stalwarts, in their eagerness to absorb and to blunt the force of the new secularism, went beyond the "purest" Christian doctrine. This doctrine calls upon us to attain to self-forgetfulness in the love of God and of our neighbor; or, to adopt a less extreme formulation, to realize ourselves through sacrifice of self and through the love of others. We need go no further back than Malebranche, for a denunciation of the dangers of self-love, which he finds to be almost always in opposition to virtue and to love of order.[28] Christianity, moreover, aspires to raise man distinctly above the animal realm of nature, through participation in the Divine Nature. But the eighteenth century replaced man in nature and vindicated his animal instincts. The apologists hedged and compromised, were willing to settle for limited and controlled pleasure, passion and self-love. One apologist, late in the century, in protest against this tendency, took the opposite stand. "It is not surprising," writes Boudier de Villemaire, "that worldly people are so little attached to religion; it is a different order of things from that in which they live; it annihilates everything they lean on: nobility, fortune, even talents—it counts all that as nothing . . . What attraction could there be, for a sensual man, in a state from which corporal voluptuousness is excluded, where there is neither sex nor carousal—it is enough to disgust the animal man." [29]

Actually, what many apologists did was to give the appearance of accepting the new doctrines, while subtly twisting them to a religious purpose. This is precisely what Leibniz had done, too. Leibniz reduces altruism to pleasure and self-love, but he makes

[27] "Charité" (*Encyclopédie*). The passage seems imitated from a similar statement of the abbé Pluche, *Le Spectacle de la nature*, 1746, v, 164–5. See also, abbé de Saint-Pierre, "Un projet pour perfectionner l'éducation," *Ouvrages de morale et de politique*, v, 12.

[28] *Traité de morale*, p. 30–33, 62, 71–72, 264.

[29] *Pensées philosophiques* (1784), p. 147.

a significant distinction. "We do everything for our own good"—true enough. But there is a vast difference between seeking the good of another because of some advantage to ourselves, and making "the happiness of those in whose happiness we take pleasure . . . a part of our own happiness." In the second case, we desire a good for its own sake, it pleases us *in itself,* not for any ulterior advantage. Leibniz also declares that "wisdom is nothing but the very science of happiness." But it turns out that this idea is related to greater freedom of the mind, higher degrees of appetition and apperception, and that what he really means is the reverse of his statement, namely, that happiness is the "science" of wisdom.[30] He attempts both to appropriate the naturalistic explanation of conduct, and simultaneously, to interpret it rationalistically, in such a way that men *can* really love good for its own sake. He endeavors thus to "save the phenomena," and to save morality.

Even Malebranche concedes that self-love can be in agreement with "order"—when it turns away from self-satisfactions to embrace salvation through love of God. And the abbé Yvon: "For what is it to love ourselves as we should? It is to love God; and what is it to love God? It is to love ourselves as we should." [31] In justifying self-love, in this very special sense, and in using such a term really to mean self-abnegation, these writers were in fact adopting a tactic of confusion. The essential point for us to note is that this attitude of the Christian defenders tallies with that of the detractors of man, in the total denial of altruism; they do not condemn man, but only because they find a way to condone self-interest, by turning it away from the natural direction of its fulfillment.

About the middle of the century, a new current of empirical thought joined the older stream of Renaissance secularism, giving it not only fresh vigor, but a new basis, a new direction and new implications. This influence stemmed basically from Locke, but it was Condillac and Helvétius who gave it significant form for the age. Locke had attributed the origin of our ideas to sensa-

[30] *Monadology,* p. 285–287, 141, 146.
[31] *Encyclopédie,* "Amour." See also La Placette, *op. cit.,* chapters on the "défauts de l'amour-propre." Père Buffier, in his *Traité de la société civile* (1726) aims frankly at earthly happiness, which is a natural right, but finds its realization possible only through domination of self-interest and the passions.

tions; at the same time, however, he admitted an irreducible and independent series of psychological faculties which perform the processes of judgment.[32] Locke's influence was strongly reinforced by the tides of thought, stemming from the chain of being principle and from biological investigations, which led to the belief in the continuity of man and the lower animals. It seemed that the general and basic principle of all animal life was to feel and to desire.[33]

Condillac's great contribution, in his *Traité des sensations* (1754) was to focus the implications of this ideological background on the functioning of the mental process, and to construct therefrom a consistent and complete sensationalistic interpretation of psychic phenomena. The key step in his system was the reduction of all mental processes to a mere composite structure, derivative from sense data and the single experience of sensation. By means of his famous "statue," whose senses gradually awoke into action, Condillac attempted to show how the most complex mental phenomena are built up out of the simplest sense perceptions.

The impact of Condillac's theory was profound and revolutionary. Materialism received from it a new impetus and a new ground of certainty. Condillac's psychology tends to eliminate any autonomous psychic or spiritual reality.[34] All is reduced to the physically caused sensation, on which everything else is strictly dependent, including the operations of the understanding and the practical activity of the organism. The moral implications were no less radical. If all our ideas and judgments derive solely from sensations, if we exclude all *a prioris,* all ideas generated (as the Natural Law theorists held) by an innate psychological structure, then the intrinsic characteristics of sensation must inhere in the judgments which ensue from it as mental constructs. It follows, further, that the dictates of sensation become the direc-

[32] Locke distinguishes between ideas and knowledge. His criterion of knowledge is rationalistic: the perception by the mind of agreement among its ideas. Aside from mathematics and morals, we do not have knowledge in the strict and proper sense, other judgments being only empirical. The sensualist doctrine of the origin of ideas had received some diffusion, even before Locke, through Gassendi.

[33] For Leibniz, perception and activity are the attributes of all substance.

[34] Condillac himself, we remember, does not deny the existence of a soul. It seems to be nothing else, however, than the naked capacity to receive sensations, to remember and compare them, and to perform certain other related processes. For the role of language in his theory, see Frankel, *op. cit.,* p. 52–53.

tive forces of all action, since our judgments are only compounds of sensation and there are no autonomous psychic forces to counter them. "If we consider," writes Condillac, "that there are no absolutely indifferent sensations, we shall further conclude that the several degrees of pleasure and pain are the law, in accordance with which the germ of all we are has developed . . . for we are always moved by pleasure or by pain. . . . Indeed, our first ideas are only pain and pleasure." [35] Here, then, is the psychological basis of materialism and all the materialistic ethics of the eighteenth century.[36]

In point of time, however, d'Alembert had actually forestalled Condillac in several of his conclusions. The impact of Locke and his genetic method of psychological analysis was so profound that the adherents of his sensualism were almost bound to follow the track he had laid out. In the great *Discours préliminaire de l'Encyclopédie* (1751), d'Alembert asserts that the first step to be taken in an exploration of human knowledge is to examine "the genealogy and filiation of our knowledge . . . to go back to the origin and generation of our ideas." [37] D'Alembert still adheres closely to Locke, and divides all knowledge into two categories, direct and reflective. "All our direct knowledge can be reduced to that we receive from the senses; from which it follows that we owe all our ideas to our sensations." Proceeding genetically, he discovers that the first thing our sensations teach us is our existence; the second is the existence of outside objects, which affect us so powerfully, they force us to leave our world of inner experiences. The most important of these objects is our own body. Its needs, its exposure to the action of other bodies make us concern ourselves with its conservation. Sensations produce not only perceptions, but affections. Our reaction to other objects is either pleasurable or painful. "But such is the misfortune of the human condition that pain is the keener feeling in us." The memory traces left by sensations become the motives of future actions, whose purpose is to satisfy the object of desire—whatever yields the reward of pleasure. We need follow d'Alembert no further.

[35] *Traité des sensations,* ed. Picavet, p. 235–236.
[36] Parallel developments came through the theory of vibrations, sketched by La Mettrie and Diderot, systematized by Hartley. The basis is the same. See D. Hartley: *Observations on Man* [1749], I, 471 ff.
[37] Ed. Picavet, p. 13 ff.

The entire subsequent development is predicated on this premise: "The need to guarantee our own body from pain and destruction causes us to examine among outside objects those that may be useful or harmful to us, in order to seek after the former and to avoid the latter." [38]

Neither d'Alembert nor Condillac developed the extreme ethical conclusions that inhered logically in this psychology, although they are already adumbrated in Locke.[39] This task fell to Helvétius. In his notorious work, *De l'Esprit* (1758), he accepted the challenge; and he returned to the theme in his posthumous work. *De l'Homme* (1772), to develop it in more ample detail.

In the earlier treatise, the principal consequence of the new psychology is clearly presented. There is no separate realm of "moral facts," we are assured, or of "moral experience." The classical dualism, accepted by most eighteenth century writers, the tradition of *homo duplex,* torn between natural egoistic and altruistic motives or tendencies, is swept away. In its place, Helvétius erects his system of radical monism. Our psychic life rests entirely on a mass of sensations; all intellectual activity is reduced to judgment, which is merely a perception of similarities and differences between sense qualities: "to judge is simply to perceive," and there is no "faculty of judgment distinct from the faculty of feeling [sensation]." [40] Our judgments and our acts are motivated only by our self-interest, a necessary consequence of the pain or pleasure caused by our passive reactions to sensations.[41] In *De l'Homme,* Helvétius shows in even greater detail than in *De l'Esprit* the development of self-interest into its more complex

[38] The influence of Locke's emphasis on "uneasiness" is evident. Even before d'Alembert, Morelly, in his *Essai sur le coeur humain* (1745), deduced the need for happiness from physical sensitivity. He attributed to it a peculiarly human characteristic, restlessness *(inquiétude)*: "Our nature always lets us feel that we are lacking something." (P. 1–11.) Morelly's book, however, was little read, and scarcely any copies of it can be found today.

[39] In refuting solipsism, Locke denies that we have any disinterested concern for knowledge; beyond "pleasure or pain, i.e., happiness or misery . . . we have no concernment either of knowing or being." *An Essay Concerning Human Understanding, ed. cit.,* p. 368–369.

[40] *De l'Esprit* (1758), pp. 9, vi. The first chapter of the work contains an outline of its major theories. As proof of his ethical thesis, Helvétius attempts to show how the judgment, as to whether justice or goodness is preferable in a king, is determined by physical sensation.

[41] P. viii, 110 ff. We see here how the self-interest psychology fits in with the theory of determinism, and becomes the determinism of self-interest.

forms of ambition and pride, and its concealment in the falsely altruistic guise of virtue, justice, self-sacrifice. He outlines the following sequence: physical sensitivity, love of pleasure and aversion to pain, self-love, desire for happiness, desire for power. The latter produces, in turn, envy, avarice and ambition. The following sentences from *De l'Homme* illustrate Helvétius' system.

> All comparison of objects presupposes attention; all attention presupposes effort (*peine*), and all effort a motive to do it. . . . Now this interest, necessarily based on the love of our happiness, can only be an effect of physical sensitivity, since all our pleasure and pain has its source in it. . . . I conclude that physical pain and pleasure is the unrecognized principle of all the actions of men. . . . Remorse is only the foresight of physical suffering to which crime exposes us. . . . It is similarly from physical sensitivity that spring the tears with which I water my friend's urn. . . . I weep for the one who . . . wished to give greater extension to my happiness. . . . Pleasure and pain are and will always be the unique motives of men's actions. . . . Virtue to the clergy means only the idea of what is useful to it. . . . This feeling (of self-love), the immediate effect of physical sensitivity, and therefore common to all, is inseparable from man. I offer as proof its permanence, the impossibility of changing it, or even altering it . . . we owe to it all our desires, all our passions. . . . Everyone loves justice in others, and wants them to be just to him. But who could make him desire to be just to others? Do we love justice for its own sake, or for the esteem it procures us? . . . Man, uniquely concerned with himself, seeks only his happiness. If he respects equity, it is because he needs to . . . without an interested motive for loving virtue, no virtue. . . . The same opinions appear true or false according to the interest we have in believing them one or the other. . . . Interest makes us esteem in ourselves even the cruelty we hate in others. . . . Interest makes us honor crime. . . . Interest makes us daily violate this maxim: Do not do unto others what you would not want them to do to you. . . . Physical sensitivity is man himself and the origin (*principe*) of all he is.[42]

Ernst Cassirer has clearly set forth the implications of Helvétius' system. "Here, as one sees, both the edifice of ethical values and the logically graded structure of knowledge are demolished. . . . Differences in form as well as in value vanish and

[42] *De l'Homme* (1776), p. 78 ff, 81 ff, 96, 119 ff, 190, 210, 216, 252 f., 483, 578.

prove to be delusions. . . . Everything is on the same plane—equal in value and in validity." [43]

That happiness and self-love are the unique human motivations is, by 1760, so commonplace an assumption—though not an unchallenged one, as we shall see in another chapter—that we need not devote more space to it.[44] What deserves some emphasis is the further narrowing of primary motivation to the pleasure-pain reaction. It is true that for writers in the first half of the century, both Christians and skeptics, happiness and pleasure were sometimes interchangeable words.[45] Both could be twisted, in the fashion we have observed, to a Christian or a moral sense. In the second half of the century, however, the apologists became more wary. The fact that the pleasure-pain concept had become a part of the materialist reduction of mental phenomena to sensation, that is, to the irritability or contractility of living tissue, gave pause to many who were concerned with the idea of happiness. It became clear that it was, in effect, a step further in the reduction of man to the physical, a final narrowing of the spiritual sphere, or rather its complete elimination. Moralists began to point out that pleasure is not at all equivalent to happiness.[46] Even Diderot, in his *Réfutation d'Helvétius*, protested vigorously. And it is not surprising that we find practically no professional Christian apologist, in the second half of the century, who will risk such a confusion.[47] Because of the distinct connotative possibilities of the more general concept of self-interest or happiness, on the one hand, and those of the narrower concept of pleasure-pain, on the other, adoption of the latter as the key to motivation, by Christian apologists, would have marked their complete defeat by the tides of secular thought and feeling. And only rarely do

[43] *The Philosophy of the Enlightenment*, p. 27, 26.

[44] For further references, see Maupertuis, *Essai de philosophie morale, Oeuvres*, I, 383; Saint-Hyacinthe, *Recueil de divers écrits*, p. 241; Morelly, *Code de la nature*, p. 262; Coyer, "Plan d'éducation," *Oeuvres complètes*, III, 275; Delisle de Sales, *Philosophie de la nature*, II, 160–162; Sade, *Histoire de Juliette*, I, 191–196; Duclos, *Histoire de Mme de Luz* in *Oeuvres morales et galantes*, III, 263.

[45] Although Malebranche had warned against this confusion: "We must flee pleasure, even though it makes us happy." *De la Recherche de la vérité (ed. cit.)*, Livre IV, ch. 10; see also Livre V, ch. 5.

[46] Eighteenth century concepts of happiness will be investigated in a later section of this study.

[47] The only exception I have found is Para du Phanjas, who affirms pleasure is the instrument of Providence that attaches us to God and our fellows. (*Op. cit.*, p. 256.)

we come across it among some Christian writers who were less expert in the in-fighting of polemical warfare. In these cases, however, the apparent acceptance of the pleasure principle is again a false front, a false concession to the mood of the times, designed as a stratagem to lead the reader to a *renunciation* of pleasure.[48]

From the time of d'Alembert, then, the pleasure-pain motive is attached by the materialists to the very nature of sentiency, indeed of existence itself.[49] "Is not all self-interest," inquires Helvétius, "reduced in us to the search for pleasure?" D'Alembert, on the other hand, following Locke, had thought the avoidance of pain to be our supreme motive, the "sovereign good" (*summum bonum*). The supreme value is for him a negative one, and thus is in total opposition to the good of earlier philosophers. Voltaire put the matter in his usual felicitous fashion. What is the first perception we receive? "That of pain; then the pleasure of food. That is all of life: pain and pleasure." [50] Bonnet also affirms, at a later date, that the entire manifold of ideas we term "self-love" is nothing but the desire to "feel pleasantly"; there is no other source of action.[51] The same assumption underlies the economic and political doctrine of the Physiocrats. "Men are moved to action," affirms Le Mercier de la Rivière, "only to the extent to which they are impelled by the desire for gratification . . . nature, as I have already said, meant them to know two mo-

---

[48] Stanislas Leszczynski, founder of the Académie de Nancy, does give this explanation in his book, *Le philosophe chrétien* (1749, IV, 310–315). He admits that love of pleasure is more powerful, "more absolute than reason." But actually his purpose is only to warn against the dangers of pleasure, in words reminiscent of Plato: "Thus life is spent running from pleasures to boredom, and in returning from boredom to pleasures that bring it back ever anew." A provincial priest, Père Cerutti, also entertained the Académie de Montauban, on Aug. 25, 1760, with the words, "Pleasure is the goal of our lives, the motive of our heart, the center of all our thoughts, of all our feelings, of all our actions." But again, the title of his discourse, "Les vrais plaisirs ne sont faits que pour la vertu," will serve as a summary for the remainder. (The discourse was printed as *Discours qui a remporté le prix d'éloquence à l'Académie de Montauban, le 25 août 1760.*)

[49] The very interesting (anonymous) article "Existence" in the *Encyclopédie* deduces our awareness of existence and the self from pleasure-pain sensations, which are "never related to any other point of space."

[50] *Oeuvres*, 28:525 (1772).

[51] *Essai analytique sur les facultés de l'âme, Oeuvres*, VI, ch. 18. Bonnet goes on, it is true, to add that a *thinking* being can conceive of the love of perfection; but perfection is defined as that in which our happiness lies. It can lie in altruism— if that is how we can conceive our perfection. See Vauvenargues, *Oeuvres*, I, 42–3, Marat, *op. cit.*, II, 153.

tives only, a craving for pleasures and an aversion to pain." [52]
Pleasure lies in gain; gain demands laissez-faire capitalism. The
pursuit of this "natural law" can lead only to the general good.[53]

The logical fallacy in this position is illustrated in the first section of Diderot's article "Passions," which is based on Pouilly.
The premise there maintained, that all we do is accompanied by
pleasure or pain, does not necessarily lead to the conclusion that
these reactions are the only motives of action.[54]

For the materialists the pleasure-pain concept furnished an important link in the chain tying man to the rest of nature and
enabled them to round out a general theory of materialism. That
it did not, in the eyes of most of them, exclude a human ethical
life, we shall observe in a subsequent part of this study. In fact,
it may safely be asserted that Helvétius' analysis of human nature
and motivation forms the basis of the naturistic ethical theories
(with their several variations) developed by the eighteenth century materialists.

It is, at least, the point from which they start. D'Holbach ridicules the maxim, "Love thy neighbor as thyself." We are incapable, he claims, of loving others, except in proportion to their
contribution to our own good. Altruism is utterly impossible, egoism is the law of men.[55]

Diderot's opinions vary somewhat with his mood, at least in their
consequences. The article "Plaisir," in the *Encyclopédie,* is a
moderate statement of his views.[56] As he frequently does elsewhere, he here attempts to establish his ethical concepts on a
quasi-scientific foundation. He relates pleasure to any exercise of

[52] *L'ordre naturel et essentiel des sociétés politiques* (1767), éd. Depitre, p. 25.
[53] Cf. M. Albaum: "The Moral Defences of the Physiocrats' Laissez-faire." This
theory was to influence Adam Smith and his followers.
[54] *Oeuvres,* XVI, 207–208.
[55] *Le Christianisme dévoilé,* p. 215–216. See especially *La Morale universelle,* I,
23–32. This chapter is a systematic development of the thesis, "It is therefore
indubitable that all individuals of the human species act and can act only out of
self-interest." One of d'Holbach's main arguments, obviously connected with the
Condillacian psychology, is that "to act without interest would be to act without
motive." To assert that this principle of action is ignoble and vile "is to say that
it is ignoble and vile to be a man."
For a similar view, in modern dress, see Freud, *Civilization and Its Discontents,*
chap. 5. Freud, however, also goes "beyond the pleasure principle" and sets up a
"death instinct."
[56] *Oeuvres,* XVI, 295–302.

an organ that does not tire or weaken it. Thus the eye finds green the color most productive of pleasure. A similar application is made to sounds.[57] This physiological theory is then transferred to psychological experience, to the chess player and to the thinker. In the purely moral realm, Diderot holds that we derive pleasure from whatever "conspires with our inclinations." This is variable with age and character; but he finds pleasure formally connected with virtuous deeds: "pleasure is born from the womb of virtue." In the *Rêve de d'Alembert*, Diderot was to establish even more firmly the connection between the moral and the physical. Not only is each animal a system of "tendencies"—toward persistence in being and satisfaction of needs—but each separate organ is almost an animal, subject to the comfort it necessarily seeks and the discomfort it must avoid.[58] If the "soul" exists, he declares in the *Eléments de physiologie,* it is not important.[59] Diderot's dynamism of "tendency" and goal-seeking completes the biological foundations of the sensualist psychology of Condillac. Man is explained by these two words, sensation and tendency.[60]

In these more radical writings, Diderot presents the extreme view of the materialists. He reduces sympathy to a cover for egoism. "Believe me," says Jacques the fatalist, "we never pity anyone but ourselves." [61] Rameau, in the *Neveu de Rameau,* embodies these attitudes. He rejects cosmic viewpoints. "I am in this world, and I stay here. But if it is natural to have an appetite— for I always come back to the appetite, to the sensation that is always present in me—I think it is not a good order not to have enough to eat." [62] In morals, there is nothing absolutely true or false, "except that we have to be what self-interest requires us to be: good or bad, wise or mad, decent or ridiculous, honest or vicious." [63] This view is graphically illustrated at the end of the

[57] No application of this theory is made to sexual activity. The pleasure of being lazy (*il dolce far niente*) is not conceived of, either.

[58] *Oeuvres*, II, 139. Also *Eléments de physiologie:* "Interest is born in each organ, in its position, in its construction, in its functions; then it is an animal subject to comfort and discomfort, to the comfort it seeks, and the discomfort of which it tries to free itself." (IX, 375.)

[59] We have already referred to the statement, "Its power is less than that of pain, pleasure, passions, wine. . . ." (*Ibid.,* p. 377.)

[60] Hubert, *op. cit.,* p. 177. The influence of Spinoza and Leibniz on Diderot's concept is obvious.

[61] *Oeuvres*, VI, 25.

[62] *Neveu de Rameau* (ed. J. Fabre,) p. 103.

[63] P. 61.

work by Rameau's "pantomime of the positions," after which
Diderot comments, "My word, what you call the beggars' pantomime is the great dance of the world." [64] Man cannot escape from
his nature, or from nature. "In nature, all species devour each
other, all classes devour each other in society. . . . Everything that
lives, without excepting [man], seeks its good at some other's
expense." [65] The theme is taken up again in the *Supplément au
Voyage de Bougainville* (1772). The naive savage, Orou, addresses
the convention-bound chaplain. "Put your hand on your conscience; quit that display of virtue. . . . Tell me whether, in any
country whatsoever, there is a father who, without the shame that
restrains him, would not rather lose his child, a husband who
would not rather lose his wife, than his fortune and the comfort of
his life." [66]

The opinions of Diderot are evidently forerunners of the ultimate radicalism of Sade. This line of development is present in
the philosophical disquisition on man by Jean-Paul Marat. The
famous Revolutionary considers self-love essential to being, and
even anterior to sensation or ideas. Its motivating force, he declares, is irresistible; it dictates ends and means, and submerges
all others, even our friends, to our selfish good. When it meets
with opposition, it annihilates or denatures all other feelings. It
turns fraternal love into hatred, and causes the mother, in a be-
sieged city, to devour the fruit of her womb. It is true that love
of self makes us love other things and persons; but this love is
neither altruistic nor morally good. It manifests itself in two
forms. One is "preferential love," desire for whatever gives pleasure, without any idea of merit being attached to the object. The
second is "self-love," which does attach such an idea to the object.
The former excites us to work out our well-being, though to the
prejudice of others. The latter "causes us to contemplate with
pleasure the privations of others." [67]

Sade proclaims the final words. That part of nature which is
good impulse is simply excluded by him ("All that comes from
the heart is false; I believe only in the senses . . . in egoism, in

[64] P. 105.
[65] P. 37–38, 95.
[66] *Supplément au Voyage de Bougainville* (éd. Chinard), p. 171. "Shame" is apparently to be taken as an artificial accretion to nature.
[67] *De l'Homme* . . . (1775), I, 158–160, 25 ff.

self-interest.")[68] or else reduced to hidden forms of egoism. "And
what indeed is pity? A purely egoistic feeling that leads us to pity
in others the ill we fear for ourselves. Give me a being in the
world who by his nature can be exempt of all of humanity's ills;
not only will that being not feel any kind of pity, he will not be
able even to conceive of it." Like Diderot, in the *Lettre sur les
aveugles,* Sade points out the correlation between compassion and
distance.[69] Pride and pleasure are the motives of charity, so that
no obligation is owed by the beneficiary, whose humiliation is an
additional payment.[70] Sade, finally, goes back to Carneades' notion
that justice is the supreme folly, because it bids us attend to the
interests of others, not our own.

We must bear in mind that we are dealing not only with variations in the psychological analysis of self-love, but with differing
conclusions and consequences. When Abbadie, Fréret, Montesquieu and Sade agree on the motive, they differ in the evaluation
of man and the ethical conclusions. Confronted with such an
analysis, it was not difficult to conclude, especially, that man was
evil. If you were a Christian, you would consider this something
to be overcome, by will aided by grace. If you were a moral
nihilist, you would affirm this nature as something to be exploited
and enjoyed; egoism is the law of nature, the rest is an artificial
and invalid construct of reason. But these extreme responses did
not represent the mainstream of secular thought, or even of the
modified Christian attitudes.

The fact was there. This was man, uncovered. The question
was how to provide and substantiate an ethics in the face of it.
How could we fill the moral vacuum? To do this, it seemed necessary to many to avoid both extremes and yet to begin by accepting nature; from there we might go on to see how human
nature might be made to agree with what reason tells us is the

[68] *Histoire de Juliette,* II, 33.

[69] *Ibid.,* II, 99–100. Similar ideas had been developed by Buffon and Hume.

[70] *Les Infortunes de la vertu,* p. 20, 151–153. Sade affirms that not only is virtue
not a primary impulse, but that it is a vile and selfish one which says, "I give to
you so that you should return to me." This proves that vice is inherent and the
first law of nature. Man "is vicious when he prefers his interest to others; he is
vicious in the midst of virtue itself, since this virtue, this sacrifice to his passions
is in him only an impulse of pride or only the desire to attract upon himself a
quantity of more tranquil happiness than the way of crime offers him. . . . It is
absurd to say that there is a disinterested virtue whose object is to do good without
any motive." (*Histoire de Juliette,* I, 191–192.)

good and proper way for human beings to live together. Self-love must be considered as a mere natural fact, as a pre-moral motive. Morality must in some way include it and build upon it, but not attempt to deny, condemn or destroy it absolutely.

The first step, then, was to re-establish the legitimacy of the self-interest motives. As Aristotle and Spinoza had shown, they were, in a sense, even virtues, insofar at least as virtue is the pursuit of an individual's obligations to himself. But virtue, it was admitted by all except the moral nihilists, consists even more of the obligations we have to others. The problem was to get around the rigoristic Christian view, that self-love and love of others are exclusive alternatives. If this could be done, it would simultaneously solve the social aspect of the problem. For, as Addison put it in *The Spectator* (no. 588, 1714), "could a society of such creatures, with no other bottom but self-love on which to maintain a commerce, ever flourish? Reason, it is certain, would oblige every man to pursue the general happiness as the means to procure and establish his own; and yet, if, besides this consideration, there were not a natural instinct prompting man to desire the welfare and satisfaction of others, self-love, in defiance of the admonitions of reason, would quickly run all things into a state of war and confusion." In other words, if self-love is the unique principle of action, if benevolence does not co-exist beside it (*homo duplex*), what prevents the dissolution of society? (We shall shortly observe Montesquieu echoing and developing this argument in the *Lettres persanes*.)

But the *philosophes* who believed in the unity of nature and the singleness of its laws adopted two other directions. One was to show that love for others implies and favors love of self, and the truest pleasure and happiness. This was to be the ethics of enlightened self-interest, which does not enter into the present phase of our investigation. The other was to demonstrate that the pursuit of self-love brings about, or can be made to bring about, the good of others. This resulted partly from the natural checks and balances inherent in the interplay of individual egoisms. The Physiocrats believed strongly that natural law works through private good to the general welfare. Turgot exclaims, in an ironical phrase, "Oh, what a fine and wise project was that of Lycurgus, who [would abandon] that wise economy of nature by which she uses the interests and desires of individuals to carry out her general views and accomplish the happiness of all . . . !" [71] Adam Smith, in *The Wealth of Nations,* declares that when a man is guided by self-interest, he is "led by an invisible hand to promote an end which is not his intention"; this end is a natural process by which the conflicts of self-interest flow into a natural social harmony of mutual service. And Frederick the Great also exclaims, "What could be finer . . . than to draw, even from a principle that can lead to vice, the source of good, happiness, and public felicity?" [71a] We saw in the last chapter that a similar process of checks and balances, sometimes called that of "counterpoise," was conceived of as taking place within the individual. There are, then, natural and artificial processes which can lead us out of the moral impasse.

The natural process might be called "the self-interest reversal." While the detractors of man, in the seventeenth and early eighteenth centuries, had demolished virtue by showing it to be really of non-virtuous or evil origin, the eighteenth century moralists, from Bayle and Mandeville on, turned this about, and endeavored to show that non-virtuous, selfish impulses are really the origin of virtue. How this was done, and how it was thought that the natural process could be abetted by artificial conditioning, will be made clearer in our next chapter. But it must be carefully noted, in reference to our later discussion of ethical theory, that this reversal was really a reversal of ethical viewpoint and definition, from that of motive (or an absolute good will) to that of effect, or utility. This is quite evident, to take one example, in d'Holbach's recipe for a universal morality:

> Man is everywhere a sensitive being, that is to say, susceptible of loving pleasure and fearing pain; in every society he is surrounded by sensitive beings, who, like him, seek pleasure and fear pain. The latter contribute to the welfare of their fellows

[71] *Premier discours aux Sorboniques, Oeuvres,* I, 207.

[71a] Burke, toward the end of the century, admonishes the French: "you had all that combination, and all that opposition of interests, you had that action and counteraction, which, in the natural and in the political world, from the reciprocal struggle of discordant powers, draws out the harmony of the universe." (*Reflections on the Revolution in France,* p. 33.) For further study of the English phase of *concordia discors,* see E. R. Wasserman, *The Subtler Language,* especially chapters 3 and 4.

only for the sake of the pleasure they get out of it (*qu'on leur procure*); they refuse to contribute to it as soon as it hurts them. These are the principles on which a universal morality can be built. . . ." [72]

Nevertheless, the theorists of this self-interest reversal could not elude the fact that self-love and the passions it produced often led to unsocial, harmful or vicious acts. It was necessary to explain how the same motive could eventuate in both desirable ("moral") and undesirable ("immoral") consequences. The most common approach to this difficulty was to distinguish between proper and exaggerated, or licit and illicit degrees of self-love. Thus Bishop Butler favored "cool self-love" and Shaftesbury approved of the "self-affections." The more traditional writers in France usually put it this way: self-love is in itself morally indifferent, and acquires the names of virtue or vice according to the nature of the objects to which it is applied. This was extremely convenient for these writers, as it implied an objective order of values (natural or divine), which the will either adhered to freely or rejected.

There was one particular formulation of the notion of two different kinds or degrees of self-love which we must mention briefly before closing this chapter. Abbadie was among the first to express it. He advances the theory that it is really necessary to distinguish *amour de soi* (love of self) from *amour-propre* (selfishness, excessive craving for self-esteem and praise). There are certain original passions, or "first affections," such as the love of esteem, happiness and self-preservation, which in themselves are essential, legitimate, and conducive to good. When turned to objects that are "false goods" (that is, creatures, instead of the Creator), they yield only evil. Abbadie then offers this definition: "Love of self is that love, insofar as it is legitimate and natural. *Amour-propre* is that same love, insofar as it is vicious and corrupted." [73] One or the other of these feelings is the source of all our affections and the principle of all our acts.[74]

Abbadie's distinction had widespread influence.[75] We find it,

[72] *La morale universelle*, xix–xx.

[73] *L'art de se connaître soi-même*, 1692, p. 263.

[74] *Ibid.*, ch. 7, 8. There is a similar distinction in the anonymous ms. "Sur l'amour-propre," but it is impossible to date this piece.

[75] It may well have influenced Shaftesbury, in his distinction between "self-affections" and "unnatural affections."

in more felicitous language, in Vauvenargues.[76] In the *Encyclo-pédie,* abbé Yvon's article, "Love," is a paraphrase of Vauve-nargues and Abbadie. Both precede Rousseau's second *Discours.* Near the close of the century, we encounter an identical distinction in Rivarol and in the apologist, Chiniac.[77] Love of self is attributed by Chiniac to benevolence, which is man's greatest and distinctive virtue, and which is "the effect of natural benevolence for our-selves. By thinking ourselves worthy of performing virtuous acts, we become more virtuous." [78]

It was Rousseau, however, who made of this distinction a key notion in his moral and social system. He would have liked to prove human nature to be naturally or originally good; and yet, at the same time, to justify self-love, and the quest for happiness which appeared to him the chief purpose of life.[79] The separation between a legitimate self-love and a corrupted *amour-propre* struck him as the perfect device for maintaining these desiderata, and at the same time offered a precise explanation for the cor-rupting effects of civil society and progress. Rousseau, conse-quently, endeavored to sharpen the distinction, emphasizing the factitious and social origin, and the devastating results of *amour-propre.* Probably the chief evil effect, in his concept, is the re-placement of man as "sole spectator" of himself by the observa-tion of others. We end by "always asking others what we are, and never daring to interrogate ourselves." [80] This leads to emulation and a whole further train of evils, which we shall examine more closely in the next chapter. The distinction between love of self and selfishness persists throughout Rousseau's writings. We need only refer to his last work, his *Dialogues,* to observe how the notion remains an essential one in his thinking. In the first dia-logue, he asserts that the primitive passions having *amour de soi* as their principle, are gentle. But when they are blocked, they

---

[76] *Amour-propre* "subordinates everything to its convenience and well-being"; it is its own single object and its sole end: "so that instead of the passions which come from love of self giving us to things, *amour-propre* wants things to give themselves to us and makes itself the center of everything." (*Oeuvres,* I, 49–50, 70.) Cf. Louis de Beausobre: "Self-love might have been the source of all our virtues; it has become that of all our vices, and perhaps of almost all our ills." (*Le Pirrhonisme du sage,* p. 94–95.)

[77] Rivarol; *De l'homme,* p. 169–170.

[78] *Op. cit.,* III, 10–13. See also Diderot's article, "Passions," *Oeuvres,* XVI, 216.

[79] See Chapter 12 for a more exact analysis.

[80] *Discours sur l'inégalité,* Vaughan, I, 195–196, 174–5, 178–9, 217.

become irascible, and turn into *amour-propre;* thus a feeling which is "good and absolute" becomes relative, preferential and hurtful to others. *"Amour-propre,* the principle of all wickedness, is inflamed and exalted in the society that gave it birth, and in which we are at every moment forced to compare ourselves; it languishes and dies, for lack of food, in solitude."[81] *Amour-propre,* for Rousseau, is a restless, gnawing feeling that makes contentment ever impossible, requiring unceasing self-aggrandizement and self-assertion over others, almost inevitably to their detriment.

These were, then, the various approaches to a solution of the problem posed by the hypothesis of the invincibility of self-interest. The thinkers of the Enlightenment were making an effort to be, above all, realistic; to recognize human nature for what it is, and to determine how ethical behavior could ensure itself a legitimate status in the new secular view of things—a secularism that refused to base values on divine imperatives which humiliated men, and told them that their self-love was sinful and offensive to their Creator.

[81] *Oeuvres,* IX, 185, 197. This was Rousseau's answer to Diderot's accusation: "Only the wicked man is alone."

Eleven

FORMS AND VALUES
OF SELF-INTEREST (2):

APPROBATION, ESTEEM AND PRIDE

"Nor Virtue, male or female, can we name,
But what will grow on Pride, or grow on Shame."—POPE

THERE WAS one congeries of ideas, centered around the notions of esteem and self-esteem, that acquired particular importance, in the eighteenth century interpretation of human nature
and its moral components. Pride, the desire for approbation and
self-approbation, and their more special forms, such as the search
for reputation, glory and immortal fame, are present in most of
these evaluations. They appear sometimes as a generalized concept, sometimes as a commentary on one of the more particular
manifestations. By a few, this impulse was treated as one of the
passions; by many more, it was held to be a form of self-love, or
of affirmation of the self, peculiar to the human species.[1] As
Delisle de Sales was later to express it, the desire for fame, reputation, wealth and other forms of distinction is related "to an
innate love of greatness; it is as essential to the soul to extend
itself as to exist: that is what distinguishes man from the Supreme
Being, and from the lowest elements of matter." [2]

[1] See, for instance, "Note O" in Rousseau's *Discours sur l'origine de l'inégalité*.
Those who made the distinction between *amour de soi* and *amour-propre*
identified it with one or the other of these, according to their approval or disapproval of it in human nature.
[2] *Op. cit.*, III, 362–366.

Whatever its origin, this desire was universally judged to be an irrational, or a pre-rational spring of action. And since it was, simultaneously, marked as a chief distinguishing feature of mankind, the obvious conclusion (often but not always drawn), was that human conduct is not governed by human rationality. Yet, at the same time, there is a curious complexity of thought involved here, since the esteem motive could only have arisen—this was implied, to be sure, more often than it was stated—from the development in man of a certain kind of rationality. I refer to the objectifying activity of the mind, from which all essentially human traits are derived; that is, the continuous process of objectifying both the outer world, and the ego and all its states, with the result that man is aware of his own ego, of his opinions and feelings concerning it, and of the attitudes of other egos towards it.

If we may for a moment jump to the latter part of our period, we shall find Kant bringing to a focus the full implications of the subject we are about to investigate. Kant recognized the esteem motive as belonging to man's *"humanity* as a living and at the same time *rational* being"; and as involving a necessary comparative activity "which requires reason." [3] This comparative process impels us to estimate ourselves as happy or unhappy only in comparison with others. Its result is "the inclination *to obtain a worth in the opinions of others,* and primarily only that of *equality:* to allow no one a superiority over oneself, joined with a constant apprehension that others might strive to attain it, and from this there ultimately arises an unjust desire to gain superiority for ourselves over others."

Let us now return to the beginning, and trace the course of this concept and its role as an active factor in eighteenth century thought. The recognition of our deep need for approval and for self-approval, or for praise and distinction, as a powerful and omnipresent motive in human behavior was bound to exercise a profound influence on ethical speculation.

Here again we must distinguish the traditional, Christian atti-

[3] From *The Philosophical Theory of Religion,* in *Critique of Practical Reason and other works on the theory of ethics,* translated by T. K. Abbott, p. 332–334. Italics in the original text. Kant makes it clear, in the *Preface to the Metaphysical Elements of Ethics,* that man's power to objectify himself is the source of his conscience and his moral life. (*Ibid.,* p. 322).

tude from the new, secular analysis. The first, of course, did not cease at once to exercise a continuing impact on the second; but, as we have already had several occasions to observe, it was itself, to a larger degree, affected and modified by the upsurge of rational analysis. In the Christian view, the group of motives we are studying was generally summarized under the name of "pride"—a word that in itself conveys the disapproval that was bestowed on it.[4] Some of the earlier eighteenth century deists, notably Pope and Voltaire, prolonged this moral condemnation of individual pride; they were, however, more interested in censuring the "generic pride" of mankind.[5] Medieval Christianity had condemned pride in the corrupt individual, but had, within limits, fostered the idea of man's dignity in the universe. The heliocentric theory, and the chain of being concept (as well as the other intellectual developments of the late Renaissance to which we have already referred) were blows to this comforting illusion. In a sense, the censure of pride in the species amounted to a return to the Old Testament tradition of the Fall of Man, the tower of Babel, and the revolt of Job. A few lines from Pope's *Essay on Man* will serve to characterize this outlook:

> What would this Man? Now upward will he soar,
> And little less than Angel, would be more, . . .   (I, 173–4)
> While Man exclaims, "See all things for my use!"
> "See man for mine!" replies a pampered goose.   (III, 45–6)

Voltaire, in the sixth section of his *Discours sur l'homme*, reflects both the thought and tone of Pope's *Essay on Man*. Mice and donkeys replace the geese, and the analogy is drawn out; but the conclusion is the same:

> 'D'un parfait assemblage instruments imparfaits,
> Dans votre rang placés, demeurez satisfaits.'
> L'homme ne le fut point.

These eighteenth century denunciations of pride express, then, a disillusionment with mankind, even more than the traditional

---

[4] In the seventeenth century, according to Paul Bénichou, "The worth attached instinctively to glory, far from saving the honor of man, is . . . the most striking sign of his wretchedness." (*Morales du grand siècle*, p. 108.) Even in the eighteenth century, Père Joly preaches humility, the love of abjection, hatred for one's own excellence. (*Dictionnaire de morale philosophique*, 1771, I, 224 f.)

[5] See also Formey, *Le philosophe chrétien* (1752), I, 159–170, II, 100–115. For the best discussion of this phase of the subject, see A. O. Lovejoy, "Pride in Eighteenth Century Thought."

castigation of a cardinal sin. This disillusionment largely concerned man's rationality, as regards his behavior; and implied the consequent unlikelihood of his improving, or of his impelling himself to a nobler destiny. It became customary "to berate and satirize all forms of intellectual ambition, and to ascribe to it a great part in the corruption of the natural innocence of mankind." [6]

> Trace Science then, with Modesty thy guide;
> First strip off all her equipage of Pride;
> Deduct but what is Vanity or Dress,
> Or Learning's Luxury, or Idleness;
> Or tricks to shew the stretch of human brain,
> Mere curious pleasure, or ingenious pain;
> Expunge the whole, or lop th'excrescent parts
> Of all our Vices have created Arts;
> Then see how little the remaining sum,
> Which serv'd the past, and must the times to come!
> (Pope, II, 43–52)

Voltaire preferred to satirize the pretension to know beyond our power.[7] The primitivist literature seconded this whole tendency; so that Rousseau's *Discours sur les sciences et les arts* (1750) was, in one of its central ideas, a commonplace by the time he wrote it. Ethically, too, man was warned not to attempt to transcend the limits of his nature—not to seek perfect virtue, or perfect happiness.

> Contentons-nous des biens qui nous sont destinés,
> Passagers comme nous, et comme nous bornés . . .
> Et sachant qu'ici bas la félicité pure
> Ne fut jamais permise à l'humaine nature.[8]

"Moderation in everything" is the title of Voltaire's fourth *Discours*.

This phase of the question of pride is not, however, our concern here, although it does reflect a general view, which we have previously analyzed, of man's position, rationality and possibilities. Let us, then, turn to our principal subject: that need for approval, self-esteem and distinction (or, using the modern terminology, for "prestige"), which was outlined at the opening of

---

[6] Lovejoy, *op. cit.,* p. 35.
[7] *Discours sur l'homme,* "Quatrième Discours."
[8] *Ibid.,* "Sixième Discours."

our discussion, and which so arrested the attention of Kant.[9] We are faced with two questions: the analysis of this complex drive, and its import for ethics.

Once again the eighteenth century writers found the ground already broken and well cultivated by several of their seventeenth century predecessors. The first important challenge had been issued by Hobbes, particularly in the seventeenth chapter of the second part of *Leviathan* (1651).[10] In his picture of a state of nature, he represents men as at war with each other, precisely because of unique qualities which set them apart from other social animals. Among bees and ants, for instance, "the common good differeth not from the private; and being by nature inclined to their private, they procure thereby the common benefit. But man, whose joy consisteth in comparing himself with other men, can relish nothing but what is eminent." Add to this, a sense of injury that beasts do not possess, language (which permits deception), critical reason, the lack of a natural social agreement—and war among all men becomes inevitable. To this we must add what Hobbes had said in the thirteenth chapter of the first part of *Leviathan*. Men soon learn there is a pleasure in conquest, beyond the mere requirements for security. Each desires that "his companion should value him at the same rate he sets upon himself." The result is war; "and such a war as is of every man against every man." [11]

With Hobbes, then, the need for approbation turns into a compulsive power-urge, with no trace of a requirement to accommodate the demands of the ego in order to effectuate a conciliation. As in so many other matters, Hobbes aroused the ire of his contemporaries and successors. Richard Cumberland was to point out, quite correctly, that he had not shown why comparison and the desire for eminence are necessary.[12] Later, Rousseau was to assert

[9] Pope, it should be stated, was not unaware of this aspect of the question, as the following verses attest:

> That, Virtue's ends from vanity can raise,
> Which seeks no int'rest, no reward but praise. (II, 245–246)

Pope's statement of our need for approbation does not relate it to pride (IV, 39–49).

[10] See also, *De Cive*, ch. 5, par. 5.

[11] Hobbes also gives a pithy description of what is now known as "cold war."

[12] *A Treatise of the Laws of Nature* (1727), p. 137–141. Cumberland also protests that men *know* that their private good depends on the public weal. He believes that man is eminently a rational being. Agreement from reason is, then, properly called natural.

that Hobbes was entirely mistaken in painting as the state of nature what was really a primitive social state. In the true state of nature, he declared, men have no language with which to communicate and deceive, and no companion with whom to vie and to quarrel.

In France, it was Pascal who, briefly, but with a deeper perceptiveness than Hobbes, crystallized the psychological phenomenon and its ambivalence. The ego, he writes in *Pensée* 100, in its self-love, wants to be great and perfect, but sees itself small and imperfect. It therefore craves love and esteem, and even prefers esteem based on falsehood to the truth that diminishes it. In *Pensée* 404, he declares that the pursuit of glory is both a mark of baseness and of excellence; the need for esteem is "the most indelible quality of man's heart." Elsewhere, without referring to this motive, he enlarges on its psychological basis; "description of man: dependency, desire of independence, need" (*Pensée* 126). And in *Pensée* 131, he emphasizes man's "nothingness, his forlornness, his insufficiency, his dependence, his weakness, his emptiness . . . [his] despair." The result of this striving of the ego is inevitably an effort to secure power over others. Each self, Pascal concludes in *Pensée* 445, making itself the center of everything, "would like to be the tyrant of all others." Pascal's concentrated analysis contains the seeds of all the ensuing developments, even of moral nihilism.

After Hobbes, Locke stated what he called "the law of opinion or reputation." [13] Virtue and vice are words which are supposed to stand for actions "in their one nature right or wrong." But in actuality, they are everywhere given

> to such actions as in each country and society are in reputation or discredit. . . . I think I may say that he who imagines commendation and disgrace not to be strong motives on men, to accommodate themselves to the opinions and rules of those with whom they converse, seems little skilled in the nature or history of mankind: the greatest part of which he shall find to govern themselves chiefly, if not solely, by this law of fashion; and so they do that which keeps them in reputation with their company, little regard the laws of God or the magistrate. . . . There is not one of ten thousand, who is stiff and insensible enough to bear up under the constant dislike of his own club.

[13] *An Essay concerning Human Understanding* (1731 ed.), I, 326–331 (Bk. II, ch. 28, Sec. 10–12.)

Contrary to Hobbes, then, Locke emphasizes the accommodation, or socializing effect of the need for approbation; although the moral relativism to which it is conducive does not win his approval.

Spinoza (like Pascal) supplied the metaphysical, and in part, psychological, substructure that Cumberland later found lacking in Hobbes. Throughout the third and fourth parts of his *Ethic,* he develops a ramified concept of negative emotions, which diminish our being and which he deplores. He sees in man the need to increase or augment his being, and he encourages those impulses which lead, in this sense, to greater perfection. Thus we seek to increase our power of action, which is to increase our being.[14] We are disturbed when others hate what we like, or like what we hate. We tend to overestimate ourselves, and to underestimate those we dislike. Emulation is a correlate of sympathy; it is "nothing else than the desire which is engendered in us for anything, because we imagine that other persons, who are like ourselves, possess the same desire." [15] Consequently, we are moved to do what others will look upon with approval, and to avoid doing what they hate; this impulse is related to ambition, praise and blame. Furthermore, when we have so acted, we also look upon ourselves with joy, as we imagine the joy felt by others. "We will call this kind of joy which is attended with the idea of an external cause *self-exaltation,* and the sorrow opposed to it we will call shame." [16] The former experience leads to contentment with oneself, and thence to pride. It follows that everyone endeavors to make others love what he loves, and to hate what he hates; this is ambition, which is the natural desire "that other persons should live according to his way of thinking." [17] Man's nature is to envy those who are in prosperity.[18] Apprehension, anger and vengeance are inevitable, and cruelty may follow. The contemplation of our weakness yields only humility and sorrow, which feelings the

[14] For Spinoza this involves increase in the rational power which approaches us to God; but again, this part of his doctrine was disregarded in the eighteenth century.

Pascal's *Pensées* were published in 1670; Spinoza's *Ethic* appeared in 1677, but had probably been finished by 1665. Both were posthumous publications.

[15] Part III, Prop. xxvii and Scholium.

[16] Prop. xxx.

[17] Prop. xxxi.

[18] Prop. xxxii.

mind must endeavor to remove, either by diminishing the value of others or by "giving as great a luster as possible" to its own. "It appears, therefore, that men are by nature inclined to hatred and envy." [19]

Spinoza's picture is one of an irrational creature. But man's nature, he believes, is rational. Many of our affects, when properly guided, are in entire accord with reason. Reason, after all, demands that a person should seek what leads to his true profit and perfection. But fickle and false is the hunger for fame and the praise of others. It was doubtless in the following lines that Rousseau found the clue for one of his powerful criticisms of society, in the *Discours sur l'origine de l'inégalité:*

> As every one, moreover, is desirous to catch the praises of the people, one person will readily destroy the fame of another; and, consequently, as the object of contention is what is commonly thought to be the highest good, a great desire arises on the part of every one to keep down his fellows by every possible means, and he who at last comes off conqueror boasts more because he has injured another person than because he has profited himself.[20]

The Jansenist theologian, Nicole, too often neglected by historians of ideas, also has an important place in the development of our concept.[21] Beginning with a distinction between proper and corrupt self-love, he denounces the latter as exclusive and cruel, and the father of "pride." That, he cries, "is the monster we harbor in our breasts." The worst of the matter is that we hate the same feeling in others, because it opposes and limits ours. Therefore, as Hobbes had said, men tend to destroy each other. And yet, *amour-propre* is productive of good, as well as of ill. It enables men to live together in peace, for though they love domination, they love life and comfort even more. Here Nicole draws an important conclusion. Through this effect of self-love, all the needs of social life are taken care of, without charity (i.e., altruism) having a hand in it. In fact, men can live with as much peace, safety and comfort—even if they have no religion—"as if they were in a republic of saints." [22] (This latter statement is

---

[19] Prop. LV.
[20] Part IV, Prop. XVIII, Scholium.
[21] *Essais de morale* 1671, (1713 ed.), p. 111–160.
[22] P. 116.

particularly significant as a possible source of Bayle's paradox.)

None the less, what Nicole calls the "tyrannical inclination" subsists in our hearts, and produces a rivalry for power within society. Everyone pushes himself towards the top. In every occupation, in every rank, one always strives to acquire some sort of preeminence, authority, command, consideration, jurisdiction, and to extend one's power as far as possible. But here, too, the effect is ambivalent. The "most general inclination" inhering in *amour-propre* is the desire to be loved, though it is often less powerful than pleasure or other forms of interest. On the one hand, we want others to satisfy our thirst for domination by treating us as great and powerful, and exhibiting their own abasement; on the other hand, we want them to admire and love us. We dislike people who have an aversion to us, as much as we dislike their having contempt for us. The desire to be loved is more easily satisfied than the desire for power. This is most fortunate. Because of it, pride and self-love are transformed into *imitations* of charity. We avoid crimes out of fear, and do good to please men; but we do neither for love of God.

For the uncompromising Jansenist this is only another sign of man's utter depravity. Human honesty, he remarks, conceals *amour-propre;* while "Christian virtue destroys and annihilates" it. But he does admit that "enlightened *amour-propre* could correct all the exterior faults of the world, and form a well regulated society." Men, imperfect beings, must count on enlightened self-love to take the place of charity, and to show itself in its guise, even while "within, and in God's eyes," all would still be corruption.

Analysis of the desire for prestige and self-esteem was carried a step further by Malebranche, in his principal work, *De la recherche de la vérité* (1675). Admitting both the universality and the value of well directed self-love, he separates that feeling into two branches, love of greatness and love of pleasure, that is, love of being and love of well-being.[23] His analysis of the former is strikingly modern. It produces in us, he says, a desire

for power, elevation, independence, and for our being to subsist by itself. We desire in some way to have necessary being; we

[23] He holds the love of well-being to be stronger than that of being, since lacking the first, we sometimes desire non-being.

want, in some sense, to be like gods. For it is only God who truly has being, and who exists necessarily, since all that is dependent exists only by the will of him on whom it depends. Men therefore wish for the necessity of their being, wish also for the power and independence that makes them safe from the power of others.[24]

It is obvious that Malebranche, like Spinoza, but quite independently,[25] has built partly upon Hobbes and attempted to account for this powerful "drive" in us. Malebranche foreshadows Rousseau in two of his ideas: that greatness and independence do not make us happy in themselves, and that they are learned reactions, acquired from "the relation we have with the things that surround us." The workings of this impulse are thus described by Malebranche, in terms which were doubtless also to make an impression on Rousseau:

> All things which give us a certain superiority over other men, by making us more perfect, like knowledge and virtue, or which give us some authority over them, by making us more powerful, like honors and wealth, seem to make us in some sort independent. All those who are beneath us respect and fear us; they are always ready to do what pleases us for our self-preservation, and they dare not harm us nor resist us in our desires. Thus men always strive to possess these advantages which raise them above others. . . . But men do not desire only the effective possession of knowledge and virtue, honors and wealth; they also bend all their efforts to making others believe at least that they really possess them. . . . So men hold to their reputation as a good which they need to live comfortably in society.[26]

Malebranche warns men that they are embracing a phantom, since all being, well-being and true greatness depend on God, and not on other men's imaginations; but this part of his discourse was not to strike a responsive note among eighteenth century thinkers.

Abbadie, writing not long after Malebranche, seems more troubled about the deeper origins and effects of this complex of motives. He agrees with Malebranche's division into two forms of self-love, that of pleasure and that of greatness. Doubtless the latter is desirable to us, he speculates, because it produces the

---

[24] *De la recherche de la vérité,* p. 401.
[25] The *Ethic* was not published until two years later.
[26] *Op. cit.,* p. 403–404.

former; yet it is really somewhat different, and we seem actually to desire it for itself. "At least it is certain that it is not easy to find the first and most ancient reason why we like to be esteemed." [27] Why does this esteem, "which is something foreign to our selves," cause such satisfaction? It is not a principle of utility, or else men would not sacrifice their lives for it. "Someone," says Abbadie (who does not care, or perhaps dare to mention the name of Spinoza), has written that our self-love likes to think of our perfections; it cannot bear what disturbs this idea (scorn or insult), and passionately seeks what flatters and augments it (esteem and praise). The utility of esteem would thus lie in its confirmation of our self-approval. However, to Abbadie this explanation appears to be quite insufficient, inasmuch as men almost always care more for "the apparent merit which the esteem of others confers on them than for the real merit which earns this self-esteem." Abbadie thus clearly separates the need for approval from that of self-approval. Doubtless he underestimates the force of rationalization in the mind. Apparently he sees the relation of self-esteem to the need for security, but not that of self-respect to the moral conscience.

Abbadie next proceeds to cast doubt on a second explanation, the desire to raise ourselves above others. (It is probably Hobbes whom he has in mind now.) This is really to put the cart before the horse, he argues. It is not because we want to distinguish ourselves that we seek esteem; but rather, we desire distinction because we have a need of esteem. Abbadie here touches on the deepest point. But he only skirts it, and proceeds to a denial of a third explanation, which, apparently, is that of Malebranche. Our motive is not that self-idolatry "which makes us seek to be eternal and immense like God, creating an imaginary eternity for ourselves in the memory of men to save ourselves from the shipwreck of time . . . and striving to stretch ourselves and fill the world." Finally Abbadie deigns to reveal the "real explanation." God uses our love of esteem to prevent us from falling into vice and to impel us to praiseworthy actions. If men were reasonable beings, this recourse would not be needed. But since men use their reason to justify their pleasure, God has given us another judge, the reason of other men. This was, in fact, the traditional

[27] *L'art de se connaître soi-même* (1692), p. 410–494.

theory of an irrational motive instilled by God in his irrational creature, to make him behave the way his fellows wanted him to behave.

Abbadie's "real explanation," although it will be extensively utilized, is psychologically less interesting than his other analyses. Later writers were to realize that he had himself reversed matters, and discerned the *effect*, and not the cause. In another part of his analysis, Abbadie does indeed describe the forms and effects of "pride," in a passage that amplifies certain ideas of Spinoza and Malebranche, and that was destined to exercise a deep influence on Rousseau. He divides it into five branches: love of esteem, presumptuousness, vanity, ambition, and arrogance. Since there is in each man, Abbadie now concedes, an instinct "that makes him sensitive to whatever shocks the idea he has of his perfections," we pretend to qualities, fear to have faults, build a false image of ourselves, puff up our idea of our value. Vanity, pomp and display assume endless forms. We are possessed by ambition, rivalry, scorn for others. "Our superiority demands preference of consideration and esteem for ourselves." So we aspire to public recognition and honors, we like our rivals to court us and become dependent on us. We are delighted by the power that submits them to us. They, in consequence, feel hatred towards us. In fact, we desire so much not to be confused with others, that we naturally tend to despise them, and to lower them, "in order to appear the greater by their abasement." When we do not succeed, we are filled with envy, "an implacable sentiment." Abbadie thus finds that the excess of the needs which God had given us as a moral mechanism becomes highly immoral and injurious to society. It is, he says, "a reversal of nature." But his distinction between the natural, good love of esteem, and the "unnatural," harmful love of distinction is most tenuous, and in fact, untenable.

Abbadie may be considered one of the transition writers whose thought flows into the mainstream of eighteenth century rationalism. In the same group we may place Fontenelle, Bayle, Shaftesbury, Mandeville, and several lesser names.

Fontenelle's *Dialogues des morts* (1683) actually preceded Abbadie's book. In several subtle and witty dialogues, Fontenelle emphasizes the pervasiveness of vanity and fame as the sources of human works. "That chimera is the most powerful thing in the world." [28] He finds human nature such, that we are made unhappy by the good qualities of another, and we are not happy unless others are witnesses to our joy. Fontenelle's importance, however, is not in his contribution to the psychological exploration, but rather in his explication of the ethical import of this side of human nature. Like Nicole, he points out that the esteem motive compensates for our deficiency in rational and moral behavior. "At the end, all duties are performed, although not out of duty." Since imagination is stronger than reason, "what Nature would not have obtained from our reason, she obtains from our folly." In a word, virtue would not in itself attract men. "Morality also has its chimera; it is disinterestedness, perfect friendship. We shall never reach it. . . ." [29] From this, we arrive at a more general conclusion: man's good qualities derive from his bad ones. The delightful dialogue on love and vanity, "Soliman et Juliette de Gonzague," leads up to this thought: "Is it difficult for you to conceive that a man's good qualities depend on others which are bad, and that it would be dangerous to cure him of his faults?" J. R. Carré has pointed out that Fontenelle was the first to see in vanity, ambition and greed the source of activity, creative emulation and wealth. He had a marked influence on Mandeville and on Voltaire (*Le Mondain*).[30] To Bayle, too, he was important, enabling him to account for the enigma of how moral evil and anarchy did not produce (as they logically should) universal destruction. Although Fontenelle wrote several years before Abbadie, he already belongs to the eighteenth century. He uses the word "Nature" instead of "God."

Bayle was brought to our question by the need to justify his scandalous assertion (inspired perhaps by Nicole) that atheists could be moral, and form an orderly society. His *Continuation des Pensées sur la comète* (1707) reflects his reading of Fontenelle. More incisive and outspoken, Bayle formulates clearly a concept that was to be important throughout the century. "Human nature itself produces the *repressive principle* which they [men] need." [31] Reputation plays this essential role: "a man without faith may be

---

[28] "Lucrèce, Barbe Plomberge," "Hérostrate, Demétrius de Phalère," "Candaule, Gigès."

[29] "Artémise, Raymond Lulle."

[30] J. R. Carré, *La Philosophie de Fontenelle*, p. 62.

[31] *Oeuvres diverses*, III, 358. Italics added.

very sensitive to social honor, very avid for praise and adula-
tion. . . . The fear of passing in society for a villain and a knave
will win out over love of money. . . . For it is to the esteem of
other men that we above all aspire." [32]

Quite another subject, evil, leads Bayle to comment elsewhere
on the power of our desire for glory. We must excuse conquerors,
he says, for their illusion of universal renown and eternal fame;
they would be intolerably unhappy if they were reduced "to the
sole testimony of merit they would render to themselves." It
would be one thing if we could say that their only purpose was
to serve humanity, to establish justice, peace and morality on
earth—but this is characteristic of God, not of men, whose nature
"is too limited to suffice unto itself." Of course, continues Bayle,
with a trace of irony, true merit loves virtue for its own sake; but
we forgive the heroes their love of praise and fame, "because we
know that our nature, inseparable from its imperfection, cannot
itself fill up all its emptiness, nor tolerate itself without a foreign
sustenance, and that the love of virtue would not be an active
enough spring if the love of praise did not move it. . . . I need
not add that experience shows that receipt of praise fills our
hearts with joy, and its privation is an unhappy state (*un état
chagrinant*)." [33]

The weakness of Bayle's theory is its failure to relate approval
to self-approval, and its neglect of the latter. Its strength is in its
realism. His speculations lead him to the important conclusion
that our passions form a balance, or a system of counterpoise, in
which the factor of reputation, or the need for praise and esteem,
plays a vital part. Society, to be sure, increases vices of all sorts.
But it also imposes "a greater necessity to have a care for the
qu'en dira-t-on, and it excites a greater sensitivity for *la belle
gloire.* . . . It would be easy to show you in detail that each thing
has its counterweight in society, and that the difficulties are met
by the very constitution of governments and the opposition of
private passions. I need not add that in one and the same person
vices quite often work against each other." [34]

[32] *Ibid.,* p. 110.

[33] *Réponse aux questions d'un provincial, Oeuvres diverses,* III, 650.

[34] *Continuation des Pensées diverses,* III, 354. We need give only brief mention to
one of Bayle's adversaries, La Placette, who advanced a traditional Christian view.
To have pride is "to establish oneself as the center of everything. It is to wish to be

In England, too, the theme of pride and prestige was soon to be taken up anew. We must give a short account of the views of three writers, Shaftesbury, Mandeville and Hume, who were widely read in France.

One has the impression that Shaftesbury was uncomfortable about the whole question. While recognizing the force of these universal motives, he was, perhaps, apprehensive that they might not fit well into his system. Were they "natural affections," leading to public good, "self-affections," or "unnatural affections," productive neither of public nor of private good? He groups envy and excessive pride or ambition with tyranny, treachery, ingratitude and cruelty. The joy experienced from the suffering, blood or torture of others is for him "wholly and absolutely unnatural, as it is horrid and miserable." [35] Indeed, it is only an appearance of joy, one that ends with fears, aversions, insecurity.[36] These last emotions, which Shaftesbury terms the consequences of emulation and pride, were considered by the earlier writers we have discussed to be the *causes* of those phenomena. There was as yet no complete theory to unite both concepts into a linked, or unitary form.[37]

A quite different position was taken by Shaftesbury's contemporary, Bernard de Mandeville. Building upon Hobbes, Fontenelle and Bayle, he advanced a view of human nature, the candid and naked pessimism of which was the greatest shock experienced by eighteenth century moralists. It is doubtful whether, without the preparatory work of Mandeville and the further developments of certain of the French materialists, the marquis de Sade, at the terminus of the Age of Enlightenment, could have plunged man to the bottommost pit of the lower depths, and enveloped him

---

the final, or more exactly, the only end of all things, relating all to self, and relating self to nothing else." It is self-love without grace, an illusion—as is worldly reputation. *Nouveaux Essais de morale* (1697), I, 1–43.

[35] *An Inquiry Concerning Virtue and Merit, Characteristicks*, II, 163–164.

[36] *Ibid.*, p. 157–169.

[37] In another part of his essay Shaftesbury warmly accepts the desire for admiration and esteem, and accounts for it, in a way that was outside of the main stream of ideas, as one of the natural affections leading to fellowship, the need for "sharing contentment and delight with others," a need which enters even into our vices, such as vanity, ambition and luxury. Shaftesbury thus puts together, in a unique fashion, two reactions: the "community or participation in the pleasures of others," and "the belief of meriting well from others." These two branches of "social love" account for nine-tenths of life's pleasures. *Ibid.*, II, 108.

in utter moral and metaphysical nihilism. In Mandeville's doctrine of "private vices, public benefits," we have a theory of human nature, a theory of society, and a theory of morals. Man's vices, instead of being the signal of his depravity, are made the fount of his virtues—provided we give to the latter word a purely social, utilitarian value.[38] Chief among these beneficial vices is self-esteem, or pride. Because of it, praise and contempt are the legislator's chief support.[39] If private passions can be subordinated to the general good, it is through the desire (which distinguishes man from beast) to believe we are acting rationally. We need to think well of ourselves, and cannot easily do so without confirmation in the opinion of others.[40] This is the way, from the time of early childhood, that morality is taught. Pride and shame are "the two passions, in which the seeds of most virtues are contained." [41] Mandeville gives us a graphic description of the physical, rationally uncontrollable effects of these "passions." He concludes that pride, the faculty by which man overvalues himself, "is so inseparable from his very essence . . . that without it the compound he is made of would want one of its chiefest ingredients";[42] and that "we are possessed of no other quality so beneficial to society." [43]

The corollary of pride, riveted with equal firmness in the depths of human nature, is envy, which Mandeville also considers a salutary and cherished passion, for it relieves us from the uneasiness we necessarily feel when we see others possess what we should like. It produces emulation, and without it we should forego doing many things that require labor and pains. "As everybody would be happy, enjoy pleasure and avoid pain if he could, so self-love bids us look on every creature that seems satisfied, as a rival in happiness; and the satisfaction we have in seeing that felicity disturbed, without any advantage to ourselves but what springs from the pleasure we have in beholding it, is called loving mischief for

---

[38] See the letter from A. O. Lovejoy, quoted by F. B. Kaye in his edition of the *Fable*, II, 452.

[39] *Fable of the Bees*, "Enquiry into the Origin of Moral Virtue," I, 28–29, 32.

[40] ". . . for that we have such an extraordinary concern in what others think of us, can proceed from nothing but the vast esteem we have for ourselves." (I, 56, original pagination.)

[41] *Ibid.*, I, 31.

[42] I, 56.

[43] I, 105 ff. (The analysis continues throughout Remark M.)

mischief's sake." [44] Mandeville's main ideas, it is obvious, were not original. His development of their psychological and social implications, however, was so brilliantly cynical and uncompromising, that he gave those ideas a new potency in the eighteenth century intellectual ferment.

Probably the most refined psychological analysis of the esteem motive was supplied by Hume, in his *Treatise on Human Nature* (1739). Pride and its adjuncts he deems original properties or impulses of the mind, that is, "such as are the most inseparable from the soul and can be resolved into no other." It is in our primary constitution (as "an original and natural instinct") that pride cannot look beyond self.[45]

Investigating the causes of pride or shame, Hume stresses the urge to power as central to his concept.[46] Property, for instance, is an exclusive power; its possession by another is an implied threat to us. Wealth is a power for pleasure and comfort; with it we can satisfy our desires; without it, we are subjected to wants, mortifications and the will of others. Power over other beings— especially beings like ourselves—gives us deep pleasure and pride. "Comparison is in every case a sure method of augmenting our esteem of any thing. A rich man feels the felicity of his condition better by opposing it to that of a beggar. . . . There is a peculiar advantage in power, by the contrast which is, in a measure, presented to us, betwixt us and the person we command. The comparison is obvious and natural."

This is the original cause of pride and humility. A second cause, of equal weight, is the approbation of others. "Our reputation, our character, our name are considerations of vast weight and importance; and even the other causes of pride: virtue, beauty and riches, have little influence, when not seconded by the opinion and sentiments of others." Why should this be so? Hume's answer to the enigma is his principle of sympathy, which involves our receiving from others their inclinations, interests and opinions; an influence, most difficult to resist, which is founded on the universality of human nature, there being no passion or principle in others "of which, in some degree or other, we may not find

[44] I, 140 ff (Remark N).

[45] In *Works*, IV, 76–92. I am obliged to omit the interesting analysis of the experience of pleasure through pride.

[46] *Ibid.*, p. 92–117.

a parallel in ourselves." [47] When another person utters praise, it is natural for us to embrace his opinion.

The same constitution and relationships produce envy. Since all objects appear greater or lesser by a comparison with others, and we so judge of their value, and since our satisfaction or uneasiness in reflecting on our circumstances varies

> in proportion as they appear more or less fortunate or unhappy . . . it follows, that according as we observe a greater or less share of happiness or misery in others, we must make an estimate of our own, and feel a consequent pain or pleasure. The misery of another gives us a more lively idea of our happiness, and his happiness of our misery. The former, therefore, produces delight; and the latter uneasiness. Here then is a kind of pity reversed. . . .[48]

Thus another's pleasure gives us, first pleasure, by sympathy, and then pain, by comparison. "His pain, considered in itself, is painful to us, but augments the idea of our own happiness, and gives us pleasure." Similarly, as envy is excited by some present enjoyment of another, malice is "the unprovoked desire of producing evil to another, in order to reap a pleasure from the comparison."

The analyses of these English writings were woven inextricably into the pattern of French thought. Mandeville was translated in 1740, Shaftesbury in 1744, Hume in 1759–1760; but many among the more advanced French thinkers knew their work in the original. Their full impact, to be sure, manifested itself during the great upsurge of scientific and rationalistic thought that took place in France between 1745 and 1770.

Several French and continental writers, in the meantime, had continued independently the line of discussion which had originated in France. Actually, with the possible exception of Rousseau's theories, little remained to be said. The work to be done was rather one of diffusion, and most important of all, the incorporation of the consequences of the earlier speculation into the corpus of the new philosophies. We shall give only briefest mention, then, to the writers of the first half of the century. Rémond de Saint-Mard may have been known to Mandeville; he

---

[47] Compare Spinoza, above.
[48] *Ibid.*, p. 158–162.

had earlier written that "glory is an artifice which society uses to make men work for its interests." [49] Lesage de la Colombière anticipated Shaftesbury's theory that our need for esteem (our "most deeply rooted" inclination) derives from the need for others which we experience as social beings. Like children, we imitate others, and like to be imitated. The offspring of this desire is envy, jealousy and ambition.[50] Levesque de Pouilly explained our desire for the esteem of others as a need for "a security for our happiness." We want to believe in our perfection. Desire for glory, he concludes, is the source of great deeds, and fear of scorn prevents vice.[51] Vauvenargues, the sensitive and proud epigrammatist, was enthusiastic about the desire for glory; but, rather strangely, he condemns pride, after defining it in words that paraphrase La Placette.[52] Following a casual reading of Spinoza, he insists on our urge to persist in being, at all costs. "Would the weakest of beings be willing to die to see himself replaced by the wisest?" [53] All our feelings are related to that of the perfection and imperfection of our being. Ambition is part of "the instinct that leads us to enlarge our being," and may be either laudable or despicable.[54] The counterpart is boredom. It comes from the feeling of our emptiness, and of the insufficiency of our being.[55] Vauvenargues is content with a psychological analysis.

Mme de Lambert stands almost alone, in her linking of the honor or esteem motive to that of self-approval, and consequently,

[49] Quoted in *Fable of the Bees*, p. xcii, nb. The editor, F. B. Kaye, goes with considerable thoroughness into the background in the Renaissance and seventeenth century. It must be remembered that only in the eighteenth century was there a thoroughly developed theory of pride and esteem, integrated into a new moral, economic and social philosophy.

[50] *Le Mécanisme de l'esprit* (1700), p. 99, 263–264, 435. Among these earlier writers, the older tradition is maintained by Protestant writers, such as J.-F. Bernard. Bernard treats of pride as part of human corruptions and self-dupery (*op. cit.,* p. 158). In France, moral condemnation is to be found in Lemaître de Claville (*op. cit.,* 1734, I, 103–104), and in Toussaint (*Les Moeurs,* 1748, Pt. II, ch. 1.)

[51] *Op. cit.,* p. 117, 184.

[52] "Glory fills the world with virtues, and like a beneficent sun, it covers the whole earth with flowers and fruits." Quoted by F. Vial: *Une philosophie et une morale du sentiment,* p. 198. Glory impels us to make ourselves estimable, in order to make ourselves esteemed. (*Introduction à la connaissance de l'esprit humain, Oeuvres,* 1821, I, 54.

[53] *Ibid.,* I, 49, 78.

[54] P. 51–53.

[55] P. 74, and note. In Chapter XXIV, Vauvenargues brings out the fact that nothing is more pleasing to us than ourselves, and since we esteem most what pleases us most, we are always making unjust comparisons with others.

to the moral conscience. It is for this reason that she opposes the humility of Christianity.[56] The more usual approach was that of d'Argens, who prefers the power of shame and infamy to that of conscience. "There always remains in men's heart, no matter how villainous they may be, an *amour-propre* which makes them sensitive to the horror they feel others have for them." [57]

In an obscure early piece, Morelly, foreshadowing his political system, bases justice on equality, and considers pride as its chief violator. Pride, he says, "leads us to pass beyond the prescribed bounds by raising ourselves above our equals." Morelly delves deeply into the origin of this impulse. "The feeling which the soul has of its weakness causes it to see in others something capable of counterbalancing its desires and re-establishing the original equilibrium between it and its fellows; this thought produces in it an impulse of hatred, a violent desire to see what equals or surpasses it depressed as low as it sees it enhanced." [58] Fortunately, there is a limit to an individual's power over others. While the marquis de Sade was to see in the effort to attain this power the best goal of life, Morelly, like Mandeville, considers these vicious feelings to be of use only insofar as, by a reverse effect, they become the chief social bond. Men are certainly not held together by love of virtue. "They do each others service in order to acquire over them a degree of superiority and regard." Yet, by a curious paradox, we may say that Sade, almost despite himself, reaches a similar conclusion. His desire is for absolute independence and power; but these cannot be effective except in opposition to (and so, in conjunction with) other people, who must be the "victims." [59]

By the time Montesquieu publishes *De l'esprit des lois* (1748), the lessons of Mandeville and his predecessors have been well learned. Though Montesquieu condemns pride (from a political

[56] *Avis d'une mère à sa fille*, (1728), in *Oeuvres*, I, 108 ff.

[57] *Lettres juives* (1738), v, 232. Elsewhere he comments on the pain men experience on seeing others happier than they (II, 21–22). However he considers this "a preference for equality."

[58] *Essai sur le coeur humain* (1745), p. 117 ff, 184 ff.

[59] Rousseau realized this more clearly. He writes that hatred is conducive to social existence; the more inimical men feel towards each other, the greater their need for each other, in order to gratify their feelings. (See Charles W. Hendel, *Jean-Jacques Rousseau, moralist*, I, 69.) For other passages expressing Rousseau's belief that men's psychological needs increase their need for each other, see *ibid.*, p. 76–77, 126.

viewpoint), he eulogizes vanity as an excellent spring of government. He asks us to imagine "the innumerable benefits which result from vanity: luxury, industry, arts, fashions, politeness, taste." While pride, as Spain bore witness, produced idleness and poverty, vanity, as could be seen in France, stimulated activity and wealth.[60] But we see the lesson strike deeper roots in an earlier section of the book, in the discussion of the principle of the three kinds of government. Virtue is the principle of democracy. While Montesquieu pays lip service to it, it is obvious that he regards the love of virtue (or public good) for its own sake, as a shaky and easily corruptible support. The honor principle of monarchy, less noble and idealistic, is a better, surer motive, since it realistically pretends to derive the public good only from private advantage. Honor "can inspire the loftiest deeds; joined to the force of the laws, it can lead to the ends of government just as virtue itself." [61] This is because the nature of honor "is to demand preferences and distinctions." [62] In a monarchy, then, ambition is what gives life to the government, gives motion to all its parts, and withal links them in harmony; so that it turns out that "each one works to the common good, believing he is working to his private interest." Philosophically speaking, this is, to be sure, a false honor. But what matters? "This false honor is as useful to the public as true honor would be to individuals who might possess it." And is it not a great deal, inquires Montesquieu in his parting question, "to oblige men to perform all kinds of different actions, and actions which demand strength, with no other reward than the report (*bruit*) of those actions?" Montesquieu was the first writer, in the eighteenth century, who envisaged the manipulation of individuals in a State through a deliberate use, by the government, of the drives for esteem, reputation and public distinction.

It was inevitable that the themes of prestige should thread their way through the pages of the *Encyclopédie*. That *magnum opus*, although it offers us no original developments on the subject, is none the less valuable for intellectual history, as the great reflector of eighteenth century French thought. We need not discuss one group of articles ("Orgueil," "Vanité," "Fierté," "Hau-

[60] Livre XIX, ch. 9.
[61] Livre III, ch. 6.
[62] *Ibid.*, ch. 7.

teur," etc.) which are traditionally moralistic, and decry the vices announced in their titles. Under "Estime," we have the scholastic type of analysis, apparently imitated from Pufendorf.[63] Marmontel approaches our subject more closely, in the article "Gloire," where he echoes Vauvenargues' praise of that aspiration, and foreshadows the great development of this theme in Diderot's epistolary debate with Falconet. "The desire to make our fame eternal," he notes, "is an enthusiasm that magnifies us, lifts us above ourselves and our time." Diderot, however, was to penetrate more deeply into the psychological foundation of our desire for immortality. He sees its relation to human distinctiveness—a belief that was, in his mind, in constant tension with some of the basic assumptions of his materialistic naturalism.

> The animal exists only in the present moment, sees nothing beyond. Man lives in the past, the present, the future; in the past, to learn; in the present, to enjoy; in the future, to prepare a glorious one for himself and his descendents. It belongs to his nature to prolong his existence by views, projects, anticipations of all kinds. Whatever helps to raise the esteem in which I hold myself and my species pleases me, and should please me.[64]

Jaucourt—to return to the *Encyclopédie*—can almost always be depended on to reflect accepted opinion. In "Renommée," after endorsing reputation and shame as excellent levers of moral conduct and great deeds, he goes further, and condones them even when they are excessive or faulty in their "principle." [65] We must accept them as ineradicable springs of the heart, and animators of great men. In the article "Honneur," however, Jaucourt criticizes Montesquieu's theory, on the ground that honor may be attached to extravagant or wrong things. "We must remember here David Hume's great principle of utility: it is usefulness that always determines our esteem. The man who can be useful to us is the man we honor; and among all people, the man without honor is the one who by his character is held to be unable to serve society." [66] As we shall doubtless again observe, there is more than a touch of naive optimism in this eighteenth century utili-

---

[63] Cf. Pufendorf, *op. cit.*, I, 34, 269, 364.

[64] *Oeuvres*, XVIII, 175.

[65] Jaucourt may be attempting here to refute Abbadie.

[66] There is perhaps some confusion in Jaucourt's mind between "honor" in the sense of the desire to be honored by others (a motive which is useful to society), and "honor" in the sense of a certain code of personal integrity.

tarianism. Jaucourt, putting everything into the stew, next turns to his still fresh recollections of Rousseau's second *Discours*.[67] Society, he now tells us, changes the objects of our esteem from strength and courage to knowledge and talents. There are other ill effects.

> As society gradually spreads and becomes polished, there arise a multiplicity of relations between an individual and others; rivalry is more frequent, passions clash. . . . Men, forced to fight perpetually, are forced to change weapons. Trickery and dissimulation become current; there is less aversion for falseness, and prudence is honored."

To complete Jaucourt's pattern of disintegrated reflections, it suffices to mention the article "Emulation," which sentiment, in contrast to envy, he lauds as courageous, sincere, inspiring and morally good.[68]

Finally, the abbé Yvon's article, "Athées," is in part a commentary on Bayle. Personal interest, reasons the abbé, working through hope and fear, is the mainspring of human actions; it should produce social disorder. Fortunately, it has provided its own remedy. Such a powerful passion could be combatted only by another of equal strength. The only recourse, then, is to turn it against itself, and to use it for a contrary end. It is certain that the moral sentiments are insufficient to control men. So society uses religion to stimulate both hope and fear. Bayle, continues Yvon, called on another motive, "supposing that the desire for glory and the fear of infamy would suffice to rule the conduct of atheists." Yvon is quite willing to admit "that the desire for honor and the fear of infamy are two powerful motives to induce men to conform to the maxims adopted by those with whom they converse." Unfortunately, it is possible to get this prestige almost as surely, and more easily, by clever hypocrisy. Consequently, the atheist, not bound by conscience and religion, will do it just that way.

Yvon's analysis cuts right to the heart of the eighteenth century

[67] The eighth volume of the *Encyclopédie*, in which this article appeared, was readied for the press in 1758, shortly before the revocation of the printing license. The *Discours sur l'inégalité* had been published in 1755.

[68] Like Marmontel, Jaucourt exalts the urge to glory ("Temple de la Gloire"). The ancients, who did not believe in immortality, "regarded their actions as seeds sown in the immense fields of the universe, which would bring them the fruit of immortality across the flight of the centuries."

ethical dilemma. Can man be a rational and moral being? If not, what extra-moral means must be used to divert and to cheat his selfishness? The *philosophes* rejected religion partly because it was *unreasonable*. But they found it none the less necessary to make a purely natural passion serve a rationally conceived mode of judgment, or goal. Nature and reason must be brought into a functional harmony. So they proposed another "unreasonable" mechanism, instead, to control an irrational, or insufficiently rational being. But was this method good enough? Yvon lays bare its weakness; and his judgment was confirmed by the amoralism which was developed by the extreme materialistic school, and which permeates the eighteenth century novel.

This dilemma, and Yvon's justification, are seen in most dramatic form, in these middle years of the century, in Diderot's great dialogue, *Le Neveu de Rameau,* which pits the two viewpoints against each other. Diderot, the "I" of the dialogue, maintains that pride, reputation and the desire for immortality are sufficient promptings to virtue and sufficient rewards for self-sacrifice. Rameau (the "He" of the dialogue) paints a cynical picture of society, stripping the mask off men in a way that anticipates the uncompromising brutality of Sade. Esteem, reputation and power are indeed pervasive motives; but the first two come as the result of the third, and nowhere does virtue or morality enter into the equation. A virtuous man is a fool, and is likely to be a victim of the sharks.

Diderot sees the abyss, skirts its edge, but refuses to let himself be drawn in. To grasp the complexity of the problem in his mind, we must go back a few years, to the time when it first assumed concrete form, in his reply to the bitter moral nihilism of a friend, the lawyer and dramatist Paul Landois.[69] Self-sacrifice, he assures Landois, brings its own reward. "We take on in our own eyes so much greatness and dignity. Virtue is a mistress to which we become attached as much by what we do for it, as by the charms we see in it." Here Diderot is significantly concerned with self-approval and self-esteem. He does not at the moment see, or does not indicate, its relation to the moral conscience. This is because he is drawing up a materialistic ethics, deprived of moral

---

[69] The letter was written on June 29, 1756. Cf. *Correspondance de Diderot,* éd. Roth, I, 209–217.

freedom, grounded on utility and social repression. Consequently he passes almost at once to the motive of reputation and self-interest. Virtue, he now tells us, is only a special kind of vanity, "and nothing more." We make a show of sacrifice, but we are only seeking a satisfaction. The question thus presents itself in a new light—precisely in the form that the *Neveu de Rameau* was to explore. "There remains to decide whether we shall give the name of madmen to those who have made for themselves a way of happiness which appears to be as bizarre as that of self-immolation." Diderot's answer is stoutly given. If happiness is the end, why should a way of happiness, which creates happiness for others, be insane? He next throws into the balance the heavy weight of esteem. "Do not forget to evaluate the esteem of others, and that of oneself—and for all they are worth." The punishment of bad actions is inevitable; they lead to "the contempt of our fellow-men, the greatest of all evils." In Diderot's mind, the relation between esteem and self-esteem is not clear. This is so, because he was never able to work out his concepts of virtue and self-interest into a unified ethical theory, clearly moralistic, or, clearly utilitarian and pragmatic. His weakness is the weakness of the pleasure theory, and it was widespread in his time. It is the failure to distinguish between the satisfaction of a pleasurable act, which is one kind of motive; and the living up to a model of oneself—and this is what is involved in self-esteem. The latter implies a quite different motive, often requiring an unpleasurable act of self-sacrifice. It may be productive of pleasure as a concomitant of the act; but that pleasure itself is not the motive. On this view, self-approbation is confirmed by approbation, but is prior and superior to it. Diderot, however, defends virtue as a system of prudence.[70]

Voltaire contributed no new ideas to the currents of discussion. He early adopted the views of Mandeville, and they go throughout his writings, alongside a persistent traditionalistic condemnation of pride which we have already noted in the beginning of this chapter. Typical of the latter is a statement such as this: honor is "an empty phantom which we take for virtue; it is the love of glory, and not of justice." [71] But later, criticizing Montesquieu's

[70] For a more conventional statement by Diderot, see art. "Passions," *Oeuvres,* XVI, 215–216.

[71] *Alzire, Oeuvres,* III, 422.

separation of honor and virtue, Voltaire claims there can be no virtue without honor.[72] It is true that "honor" means "glory" in the first instance, and that in the second, he seems to take self-approbation as its chief component. But in another article, he again defends glory, defining it as "reputation joined to esteem." [73] And elsewhere: "Honor is a natural mixture of respect for men and for oneself." [74]

In his social thinking, however, Voltaire simply accepted Mandeville's thesis. In the *Traité de métaphysique* (1734), he set forth a view he was not to change. This is his belief that the passions have led to social order. "Pride is the principal instrument with which this beautiful edifice of society has been built." Men make a great pretense of sacrifice to social welfare, but pursue their own private good. "The desire to command, which is one of the branches of pride," is universal. It is a powerful exciter of industry and leads men to obedience; it is almost as good a mechanism as their avarice. But most important and efficient of all is their envy, "a very natural passion which men always disguised under the name of emulation." [75] Voltaire concludes his treatise by stating that honor is a universal and inextinguishable feeling which is the pivot of society. "Those who would need the help of religion to be decent people are indeed to be pitied; they would have to be social monsters, if they did not find in themselves the necessary sentiments for that society, and if they were obliged to borrow elsewhere what should be found in our nature." [76]

---

[72] *Dictionnaire philosophique*, "Honneur," XIX, 386–388.

[73] *Ibid.*, p. 264.

[74] *Pensées*, XXXI, 123. This is not a unique instance of Voltaire's variability. In one place he writes, "Si l'on dédaignait trop la gloire,/On chérirait peu la vertu" (IV, 276); and again: "La gloire n'est qu'une importune/Qui fait ombre à notre bonheur" (XLV, 87). See also, XVIII, 180 and X, 291.

[75] *Traité de métaphysique*, ed. H. T. Patterson, p. 53–54. Later he states that the Roman republic was based on a balance of private interests, on a desire to dominate "which does not allow another to dominate" (XXXIII, 387). But cf. XXIII, 530, for a different view.

[76] *Ibid.*, p. 63. Before leaving Voltaire, it is worth taking brief note of an observation in one of the refutations of his *Poème sur la loi naturelle* (1752), by Antoine Thomas. It attempts to account for man's restless, never satisfied need for "glory." The explanation, for Thomas, lies in "the frightful emptiness he experiences within himself; and, flattering himself that it (i.e., glory) will be able to fill up this emptiness, he looks upon it as a remedy for his ills and a resource for his needs. (In *Réflexions philosophiques*, quoted in Voltaire, *Oeuvres complètes*, 1822, IV, 397–398.) Another disbeliever in glory was Chamfort. He sneers at the idea that love of glory is a virtue. "A strange virtue indeed, whose helpers are all the vices, whose stimuli are pride, ambition, envy, vanity, sometimes even avarice!" *Maximes* CI, CII (*ed. cit.*, p. 37–38).

Probably the most important utilization of the esteem motif, by an eighteenth century French writer, was that made by Jean-Jacques Rousseau. As with several other notions, his originality lay in standing up against the mainstream of his time, returning first to the purest Christian tradition, but then making his own modifications and applications to society. In point of fact, however, there are two distinct and apparently opposing developments in Rousseau's writings.

The first of these contrasts man in the state of nature with man in society, and attempts to explain the vices and unhappiness of the latter condition. The focal point of the explanation is that the new relationship between men necessarily produces emulation, envy and pride. In the state of nature, contacts between men were few and fleeting. The situation was as Pope had described it:

> Pride then was not; nor arts that pride to aid;
> Man walked with beast, joint-tenant of the shade.[77]

While I cannot here perform the task of a biographer, it must be noted in passing that Rousseau's personal revolt against society was in large part centered on the importance of esteem and the opinion of others. He desired fervently to be independent and to be his own judge, and not to have to think of anything he did in the light of how others might regard it. After his "change of life," in 1751, this is what he tried to do, as he tells us in the *Confessions:* "I applied all the strength of my soul to breaking the chains of opinion and to doing with courage whatever appeared good to me, without worrying the least about the judgment of men." [78] To this, Diderot, at the height of their *démêlé,* took exception: "I know well," he wrote to Jean-Jacques in October of 1757, "that whatever you do, you will have the testimony of your conscience for you; but is that testimony, by itself, sufficient? Is it permissible to neglect to a certain point that of other men?" [79]

Rousseau's theory of human nature is based on the assumption that in the state of nature the seeds of later developments were present. Pride, in fact, was already experienced, not towards other men, but towards animals; and thus, "considering himself first by his species, he was preparing himself from afar to aim for it as

---

[77] *Essay on Man,* III, 151–152; *Discours sur l'inégalité,* in Vaughan, *op. cit.,* I, 163.
[78] *Oeuvres,* VIII, 257.
[79] *Correspondance,* éd. Roth, I, 249.

an individual." [80] In the second pre-civil stage, Rousseau's "Golden Age," the very first social intercourse and games produced just this result.

> Each began to look at the others and to want to be looked at, and public esteem acquired value . . . and that was the first step towards inequality, and simultaneously, towards vice. From these first preferences arose vanity and contempt, on the one side, shame and envy, on the other; and the fermentation caused by these new leavens produced at last compounds that were fatal to happiness and innocence.[81]

As metallurgy, agriculture, division of labor and property entered into and changed this pattern of life, all these vices became exacerbated. Only qualities esteemed by others were now of value. "To be and to appear became two different things; and from this distinction sprang imposing pomp, deceitful trickery, and all the vices which form their train." [82] They are summarized by the phrase "devouring ambition." After civil society is organized, comparison of prestige becomes a constant procedure. This would be less evil, if the comparison were made on the basis of real merit; but it was almost always made on the basis of wealth, which is most obviously useful. The result is our "prestige drive," which Rousseau describes in the following terms:

> I should observe how much this universal desire for reputation, honors, and preferences, which devours us all, exercises and compares talents and strength; how much it excites and multiplies the passions; and how much, by making all men competitors, rivals, or rather enemies, it daily causes reverses, successes and catastrophes of all kinds, by making so many contenders enter into the same joust. I would show that it is to this eagerness to have ourselves talked about, to this rage to distinguish ourselves which keeps us almost constantly outside of ourselves, that we owe the best and the worst things there are among men; our virtues and our vices, our knowledge and our errors, our conquerors and our philosophers; that is to say, a multitude of bad things for a small number of good ones. I would prove, finally, that if we see a handful of the powerful and rich at the summit of greatness and fortune, while the masses crawl in

[80] *Discours sur l'inégalité*, I, 170. Rousseau himself shares this pride, in the *Profession de foi*, in his doctrine of man as king of the created universe and principal object of providence.

[81] *Ibid.*, p. 174–175.

[82] *Ibid.*, p. 78.

obscurity and misery, it is because the former esteem the things they enjoy only as much as the others are deprived of them, and that, without changing their position, they would stop being happy, if the people stopped being wretched.[83]

Men, then, strive frantically to place themselves above others; they are filled with "a dark inclination to hurt each other," with a "secret desire to obtain their good at the expense of others." Hypocrisy follows.[84] The power drive, to subjugate and command, rules all; for men become "like those famished wolves who, having once tasted human flesh, reject all other sustenance, and want only to devour men." *Homo homini lupus*—yes, but only *after* man has been corrupted by society!

We cannot doubt that Sade found food for his own conclusions in these lines, and in several other eloquent passages to which I can do little more than refer. One such passage is a frontal attack on the theory of Mandeville and his followers (among whom we must not forget to include the Physiocrats), that everyone advances the happiness of others in trying to secure his own. There would be a measure of truth in this, counters Rousseau, were it not that he gained far more by hurting others.

> There is no profit so legitimate that it is not exceeded by the profit we can make illegitimately, and the wrong we do our neighbor is always more lucrative than the services [we render him]. It is only a question of finding the means of assuring oneself immunity; and it is to that end that the powerful use all their strength, and the weak all their ruses.[85]

In still another passage, in the *Préface de Narcisse* (1752), he continues the attack on Mandeville. Men cannot live together in our society, Rousseau again declares, without deceiving and hurting each other, for our good lies in others' hurt. "We must therefore take care never to let ourselves be seen as we really are." We must never reveal "all the horrors required by a state of things in which each, feigning to work for the fortune or the reputation of others, seeks only to enhance his own above theirs and at their own expense." [86]

[83] *Ibid.*, p. 192.
[84] P. 195–6. All is appearance, and we end by being proud of our very vices. Rousseau returns to Nicole's conclusion: we have honor without virtue.
[85] "Note i," I, 202–203.
[86] *Oeuvres*, v, 105–106.

Rousseau's great aversion is to a competitive society, and in fact, to competition itself, in any form. We can see this clearly in the "Septième Promenade" of his *Rêveries d'un promeneur solitaire.*[87] Speaking of the charm of botanical study, he declares that as soon as a motive of interest or vanity is mingled with it, "all this sweet charm vanishes; we no longer see our plants except as instruments of our passions . . . and in the woods we are only in the theatre of the world, occupied with the care of making ourselves admired." Personal pride and rivalry immediately enter into the game. "From them [come] the hatreds, the jealousies which competition for fame excites in writers on botany. . . ." While some might object to Rousseau that this excision of *amour-propre* is a denial or a shrinking of the self, to him it is the true self, or the best self, that can thus flower. For pride, in short, is the corruption, peculiar to human beings, of a simpler animal egoism and survival impulse.

There are frequent references in Rousseau's later writings to this point of view.[88] But a new attitude makes its appearance when he works out his system of a good society, although it is, to be sure, far less emphasized or developed than the first. To build Emile's structure of good habits, the tutor must utilize the child's desire to please and win approval. And in the *Contrat social* Rousseau not merely admits of "opinion" (a word which in the eighteenth century French usage signified "reputation"), but terms it the most important spring of government, "graven neither in marble nor in bronze, but in the hearts of the citizens . . . I am speaking of manners, customs, and above all of opinion."[89] It seems clear that this public opinion is useful insofar as it exercises an unconscious coercive force through the mechanisms of esteem, approbation and their contraries. Even in *La Nouvelle*

---

[87] Ed. J. S. Spink, p. 141–142.

[88] In *La Nouvelle Héloïse*, Rousseau emphasizes conscience over the opinion of others—although, paradoxically, he also makes conscience appear deceptive and dangerous. He contrasts the vain and fickle prejudices of honor which rests on public opinion with the honor that derives from self-approbation (éd. Mornet, II, 88–89; see also, IV, 44). He criticizes worrying about appearing ridiculous or being ashamed before others, as the source of our vices and the enemy of conscience (*ibid.*, II, 193 ff., 413–414). In *Emile*, he repeats the latter opinion, and calls "le ridicule" the weapon of thoughtless emulation (*Oeuvres*, II, 304). It is better not to learn at all, he advises, than to learn by envy or vanity (II, 155). Love, especially, produces emulation and hatred. Again and again he attacks the conformism produced by the fear of mockery and the tyranny of ridicule (II, 304, 324).

[89] Part II, ch. 12 (éd. Halbwachs, p. 223–224).

Héloïse, the motive of winning or losing esteem is actually as decisive, in the two protagonists' behavior, as that of conscience, and finally becomes the recommended corrective to conscience— thus bearing witness to the rightness of Diderot's words in his letter to Rousseau.[90] It is the desire to keep the esteem of Julie (and of Claire d'Orbe, or of Lord Bomston) that leads Saint-Preux to the greatest of personal sacrifices; it is Julie's esteem for Wolmar, and the desire not to lose his, as much as her conscience, that conserves her virtue, despite her passion. In fact, certain passages of the novel have a touch that is almost reminiscent of Corneille.

It is not surprising to find statements of a similar tenor in Rousseau's personal correspondence. In 1763 he writes to his friend Ustéri that as men's vices make civil society necessary, so do passions alone conserve it: "take away all the human passions, the link immediately loses its spring; no more emulation, no more glory, no more ardor for distinctions, private interest is destroyed, and for lack of a proper support, the political State falls into decay.[91] And later, he writes to M. de Saint-Germain, "One does not aspire to get through crime the reward that one can get through virtue. . . . Do we not know that a fine reputation is the most noble and sweetest reward of virtue on earth?" [92]

There are, then, two currents in Rousseau's thought. The first utterly rejects the supposed moral value of pride and reputation, and sacrifices esteem in favor of self-esteem. This embodies his desire for independence from others, and reliance on conscience rather than on conformity. The second current evinces some distrust of self-approbation and lays weight upon the approbation of others, as a dike to the pitfalls and selfish tendencies inherent in self-esteem. Despite his own theory, then, that emulation, pride, reputation and the like are the chief causes of vice, hatred and corruption in society, Rousseau is forced at times to have some recourse to these same motives, both in self-justification, and in his plans for governing men. Conscience and self-approval are not enough; for as Saint-Preux shows, we are rationalizing beings far more than reasonable beings.

Writing at the same time as Voltaire, Rousseau and Diderot,

[90] Cf. III, 3, 7, *et passim.*
[91] *Correspondance générale,* X, 37.
[92] *Ibid.,* XIX, 246–247 (26 Feb. 1770).

were two important materialistic theorists of social ethics, Helvétius and d'Holbach. The second is the less interesting of the
two. He repeats the by now accepted position that pride is necessary to social virtue. With his usual polemical intent, he opposes
it to Christian humility, but relates it instead to the self-approval
of conscience which we find in Rousseau. What other motive does a
man have to be virtuous, he inquires, especially in a society in
which the virtuous are scorned as dupes, in which crime and vice
are rewarded and esteemed?

> To annihilate in him so just a feeling of legitimate self-love
> would be to break the most powerful spring that impels him
> to doing good. . . . Man requires motives to act; he acts badly
> or well only in view of his happiness; what he judges to be his
> happiness is his interest; he does nothing gratuitously; if you
> withdraw the salary for his useful actions, he is reduced either
> to becoming as wicked as the others, or to paying himself with
> his own hands.[93]

In a later work, *La morale universelle*, d'Holbach is less bitter,
and partly replaces the *amour-propre* of self-esteem with the esteem of others.

> The desire for esteem and reputation is a natural feeling which
> cannot be blamed without madness: it is a powerful motive to
> excite great souls to apply themselves to objects useful to man-
> kind. This passion is blameworthy only when it is provoked by
> deceitful objects, or when it uses means destructive to social
> order.[94]

Helvétius was interested in the particular aspect of the esteem
complex which Nietzsche was to call the will to power. This
component, which had been emphasized by Hobbes and Hume,
was present in some degree in most of the current analyses. For
Helvétius, it is simply a manifestation of self-interest, or the
passion for pleasure. Power enables us to make others contribute to
our happiness.[95] Taking up this theme again in *De l'Homme*,
Helvétius calls power "the unique object of men's search." The

[93] *Système de la nature*, I, 350–355.

[94] I, 118. D'Holbach advises modesty for the same reason as Fontenelle: the opposite
would affect the self-esteem of other men and draw their hatred (p. 116). But he
also warns us, not without some inconsistency, of the imaginary needs created by
accepted opinion; we can be happy only with needs we ourselves can satisfy (p. 21).
See also p. 35–36.

[95] *De l'Esprit* (1758), p. 380.

easiest and most obvious form of power is wealth; the second is glory. "The love of glory, of esteem, of respect, is then really only a disguised love of power." It produces envy, avarice, ambition and all other "artificial passions." Intolerance, which is ineradicable, is also a form of the impulsion to power, since it is the desire to control opinions and minds. For others not to think like us is a limit to our authority.[96]

Only in this last comment does Helvétius begin to touch on the deeper roots of the power drive, which others had seen before him —the need to affirm our existence. He did not have a deep enough understanding of it to realize that it is akin to what Sade was to call the desire for godhood—a desire to which Malebranche and Abbadie had long before alluded. The pleasure motive is surely a very limited explanation, especially when it envisages power only as a source of other pleasures, instead of being, as Sade was to see, a pleasure in itself. Helvétius does perhaps glimpse something like this, in what he has to say of envy. That most detestable of all passions, which causes us to find pleasure in others' ills, he terms universal. "Nature has made man envious. To want to change him in this, is to want him to stop loving himself." [97] In other words, love of self requires the lowering, even the hurting of others. But instead of whipping this up into a condemnation of man or of society, as a Christian, or a Rousseau, would have done, Helvétius declares quite blithely that this disposition is most favorable to virtue. If we had to love virtue for itself, few indeed would be virtuous (Diderot would say, only those who are "fortunately born"). Laws would be powerless. But the power drive and its accompaniments can be utilized. "Heaven, inspiring in all the love of power, has made them the most precious gift. What matters whether all men are born virtuous, if all are born susceptible to a passion which can make them so?" [98] This works out through the need for esteem, and according to the system of counterpoise. Like the other followers of Bayle and Mandeville, Helvétius finds that in society man escapes disaster and destruction, because opposing drives cancel each other out, and result in a contrary good.

[96] P. 190–193, 222, 252–253.
[97] P. 194–195.
[98] P. 221. For further exposition of Helvétius' theories, see *De l'Homme,* pp. 85 ff., 190–194, 211–225.

Mirabeau, in the opening chapter of his *Essai sur le despotisme* (1775) seems to combine Rousseau and Helvétius. The desire for unchecked power he deems to be natural to man in society, where passions develop, that of domination being "one of the first to germinate in the human heart, as it is the fastest in growth." After painting what we should today denominate "the master-slave complex" Mirabeau concludes: "The desire for superiority is the most active passion in the human heart. . . . The desire to lower others is then inseparable from that of raising oneself." It would be interesting to explore the relation between these theories and Mirabeau's activity during the French Revolution.

A subtler view of the power drive was expressed by Charles Leroy, in his *Lettres philosophiques* (1768). It is conditioned and limited, he affirms, by the feeling of powerlessness. Its consequences are harmful.

> From it there results in each man only a restless desire to raise himself which stirs him, torments him, and often keeps him agitated all his life, although his deepest principle is the love of rest. The idea of distinction once established, it becomes dominant, and this subsequent passion annihilates the one that gave it birth. . . . His real needs are no longer the object of his attention or his acts.[99]

Under the influence of this drive, appearance and show assume overriding importance; those who are weak become envious and criminal. Clearly, Leroy follows Rousseau in assigning to the urge to power and esteem a negative origin and a baneful result. But he delves still more deeply into the psychological foundation. It would seem, he declares, that this desire to climb stands in contradiction to "an inclination to slavery that we notice in most men, which, however, is again only a consequence of the love of power." Courtiers are an example of those who crawl in order to have security and rest.[100]

[99] *Ed. cit.*, p. 187–191.

[100] I can only mention rapidly several other figures. Saint-Lambert criticizes Hume and Helvétius for their praise of glory. Like Rousseau and Mably, he fears popular evaluations. Among the crowd, success is what wins esteem and respect, and they worship even those who oppress and deceive them. But glory founded on virtue is good, and is encouraged by the longing for esteem and fame and by fear of shame. Emulation is fine, if it doesn't become jealousy. He decries calumny, whose purpose is "to deprive merit of the esteem of men, its due reward," but, unlike Rousseau, fails to make a connection between envy, calumny and the other ideas. (*Le catéchisme universel, Oeuvres*, II, 368–378, 42–43, 29.)

In *De la législation* (1776), his most radical work, Mably follows Rousseau in

The Physiocratic group, with its eyes fixed on other approaches to social problems, paid somewhat less attention to the various forms of the pride motif. Yet they did not neglect it entirely, since they also accepted the uniqueness of self-interest as a moving force. Le Trosne was particularly impressed by its value.[100a] "Although men are guided only by self-love and personal interest, which is the soul of society and the active principle that puts it into motion, they are capable of the most disinterested feelings, the most heroic devotion and sacrifices, and these generous actions are none the less dictated by love for themselves." This comes about, Le Trosne explains, because the individual is not isolated, in society; he places part of his existence in the mind of others, "in their esteem, in their opinion." This is a kind of moral existence, creating a type of self-interest which can surpass that of his physical existence. "What a treasure for society! . . . the most powerful and useful instrument of a wise administration." And Le Trosne goes on to claim the possibility, and the advisability, of the un-limited conditioning of human behavior—a most curious paradox, coming after the defense of self-interest as nature's mechanism for producing social good!

Ethical thought in England, as we shall several times have occasion to observe, was engaged in the same problems, but tended toward somewhat different solutions on a number of points. The theory of Adam Smith will serve as a good point of comparison with the French writers. Smith's *Theory of Moral Sentiments*

condemning artificial needs that create disorder and divide men. "When society is only an assemblage of envious, avid citizens, jealous and eager to hurt each other, because they cannot satisfy themselves except at each other's expense, can the legislator hope to restore unity . . . ?" The secret of government is to make laws that will control the private lives of citizens, "in such a way that we find our happiness without the help of avarice and ambition." (*Oeuvres*, ix, 26, 95.) In his *Principes de morale*, however, Mably seems to come closer to the more current view: emulation favors virtue, though envy hurts it; desire for esteem and aversion to contempt lead us to actions useful to all. We admire those who win such distinction without it hurting our *amour-propre*, because we identify our-selves with them. (x, 222, 234–235.) But then he excoriates those who urge manipula-tion of the passions for the public utility. This can only produce moral corruption, egoism, vanity, ambition, hatred, deceit and the desire to devour one another. (P. 261–276.)

Raynal urges the legislator, on the contrary, to utilize the precious instruments of honor and shame (*Histoire des Deux Indes*, 1781, I, 76). Dupont de Nemours finds that wicked men are hated and therefore unhappy, and vice versa (*Philosophie de l'univers*, 1792, p. 91).

[100a] Le Trosne, *De l'ordre social* (1777), p. 290–296.

(1759) seems to have been widely read in France, and was twice translated, in 1764 and again in 1774. Yet it is difficult to find many traces of its having exerted an influence. A brief account of his theory will indicate why. Smith's system derives from those of Shaftesbury and Hume, and the French had, for the most part, embraced Bayle and Mandeville.

Smith has a profound insight into the distinctiveness of man.[101] One important manifestation of his uniqueness centers around the need for approbation. This need is connected with sympathy, which is a pleasurable projection of ourselves resulting from the observation of "fellow-feeling." This is Smith's explanation of emulation and the desire for luxury and wealth. All are forms of vanity, the desire "to be observed, to be attended to, to be taken notice of with sympathy, complacency and approbation"—a desire which is conditioned by the fact that, because of the nature of the psychological phenomenon of sympathy, men sympathize with and approve of our joy, not our sorrow. In other words, we need a confirmation for our self-satisfaction. A man wishes to be the object of attention in order to feel that "mankind is disposed to go along with him in all those agreeable emotions with which the advantages of his situation so readily inspire him." The poor man is ashamed and distressed for lack of this "fellow-feeling" and approbation, "the most ardent desire" of human nature. Thus far, Smith's theory is not particularly original, but follows Hume (and probably Spinoza).

But why should we be so in need of approbation? Smith does not fail to reply to this basic question. The answer is the need for self-approbation. Because of the human trait of self-consciousness, we cannot form a judgment of our sentiments and motives except by projecting ourselves and viewing ourselves objectively, "with the eyes of other people." Our judgment must always "bear some secret reference, either to what are, or to what, upon a certain condition, would be, or to what, we imagine, ought to be the judgments of others." Adam Smith is thus in direct opposition to Rousseau, who urges that self-approval come from an independent conscience, and be separated from the approbation and esteem of others, which follow fashion and not right. For Smith, on the other hand, we are inseparable from our

[101] *Theory of Moral Sentiments*, p. 70–76, 161–223.

"mirror"—the faces, reactions, behavior of others. We are thus a double self: the agent and the spectator.[102]

Smith seeks to avoid Rousseau's argument by an optimistic postulate that Rousseau, a pessimist about men, was not able to make. Virtue is protected in this process, he thinks. We will love virtue, not for its own sake, but because it excites approval and love in others (since it is useful to them). "What so great happiness as to be beloved, and to know that we deserve to be beloved? What so great misery as to be hated, and to know that we deserve to be hated?" So that, by a slightly different route and with a different explanation, Smith arrives at the egoistic, utilitarian mechanism of social morality which characterizes the century.[103] One difference, however, is that (contrary, for instance, to Abbadie), he optimistically declares that we desire not only praise, but praiseworthiness, and in fact, desire the former only for the sake of the latter. Similarly, we dread blameworthiness, as well as, and more than blame. This is the essence of self-approbation. Emulation is only another aspect of the same process.

Adam Smith's reasoning involves a logical circularity. He began by arguing that we desire self-approbation because it assures us of approbation by others; he ends by reasoning that we need approbation because it is the only way we can confirm our self-approbation. He began by declaring, in effect, that we want praise-worthiness because it assures us of praise, and ends by asserting that we want praise because it marks our praiseworthiness. The love of self-approbation, writes Smith, "is the love of virtue." But is it certain, from the demonstration, that it is anything more than the desire for the approbation of others, and an imaginary bestowing of it upon ourselves? To be sure, he indicates that self-approbation is more important than approbation, since we are not satisfied with unmerited praise. But if we want the self-approbation only in order to be really deserving of approbation, we are still within the circle.[104]

[102] Yet the possible source of Smith's idea of the spectator may well have been "Note O" of the *Discours sur l'inégalité*. The notion of requiring confirmation of our self-approval is found in Abbadie, Mandeville and Hume.

[103] For utility, see p. 273–274. Smith, as we shall see elsewhere, does not accept Hume's utilitarianism as a sufficient explanation of moral judgments.

[104] For Burke's reflections on this subject, see *On the Sublime and Beautiful* (1757, translated in 1765); in *Works* I, 83–84. Adam Ferguson's "theory of emulation" does not seem to have had much influence in France. It appears in the

We may fittingly close our discussion with a brief summary of Sade's position. As we should expect, it is logically consistent with the body of his doctrine. His anarchism is not concerned with either political mechanisms of control or a fictitious virtue. In his earlier novel, *Les Infortunes de la vertu* (1788), the unfortunate heroine is advised by Sade's *porte-parole* that ignominy cannot matter to one who has no principles, for whom "honor is no longer anything but a prejudice, reputation a chimera, the future an illusion," and for whom death is death no matter where or how it is met. One is either successful in the great desire [for power and absolute freedom], and all is gained, or else one fails, and death can bring no other loss.[105] In the *Histoire de Juliette* (1791), the heroine's first lesson is that concern for the "opinion" of others must be overcome and totally destroyed in order to win and enjoy the freedom of vice.

> 'Oh Juliette! remember this well: reputation is a possession of no value; it never recompenses us for the sacrifices we make for it. She who is jealous of her glory undergoes as many torments as she who neglects it. . . . If there are then as many thorns in the career of virtue as in that of vice, why should we torment ourselves so much over the choice, and why not rely fully on nature for the one she suggests?'[106]

In fact, continues the wicked Mme Delbène, a bad reputation becomes itself a source of pleasure, far greater than the pleasure derived from a good one.

The latent irony in Sade's immoralism is that it unwittingly confirms the theory of the earlier materialists, that the motives of esteem and reputation—part of our pride—are deterrents to vice which the evil person must, as Sade makes clear, overcome. The irony is further carried forward in Sade's own career, which bears witness to the ill results of absolute and short-sighted egoism.

It was clear, in the minds of most eighteenth century writers,

---

Institutes of Moral Philosophy (1769, translated, Genève, 1775. See p. 93–105.). He rejects the motives of emulation and pride, bases approbation on the quality, in a character or action, of being excellent and just. This is the principle of ambition: "it is an ultimate fact in the nature of men, and not to be explained by anything that is previously or better known. Excellency, whether absolute or comparative, is the supreme object of human desire. Riches, power, and even pleasure are coveted with extreme ardor, only when they are considered as the badges of eminence or rank, and become the subjects of distinction and emulation."

[105] P. 174.

[106] I, 15–16.

that passion, pride and self-love were the three interconnected vertices of a triangle which confined human behavior, self-love being the base. These might be considered simply as necessary motives, or else as vices; but to most, it seemed that they were, or could be made to be, in some measure, self-correcting vices, and thus, eventually, useful mechanisms of social life.

Psychologically, if we add up the sum of seventeenth and eighteenth century contributions, we must admit that the moralists of that age achieved a deep understanding of human nature, although the view of any one writer may appear quite limited. Esteem and self-esteem were found to be concomitants of an objective consciousness of the self, and to distinguish man from other animals. At the same time, these motivations represent deep needs. They are, moreover, essentially comparative in their nature; self-esteem was held either to exist as a means of self-assertion in the world, or as a feeling which needs external confirmation for its subsistence and enjoyment. This comparative quality was, in turn, viewed in two different ways. By a few, it was seen as a form of sympathy and natural sociability, involving almost a cooperative and mutual approbation. By most, however, it was seen as the source of rivalry, emulation and envy (not to mention intolerance and arrogance), which, initially at least, are divisive and disorderly. One principal manifestation, viewed either as cause or as result, is a power or prestige drive, which a few writers properly understood to be a profound compulsion of the personality. The need to think well of ourselves, to increase or augment our being, to fill an inner emptiness, even to be like God, who alone has complete independence—all these are aspects of what was often called "pride." [107] Still another conclusion resulted from this analysis. Although the very possession of this power of objectifying the self indicates attainment by man of the highest stage of animal rationality, this power is itself a highly irrational, "passionate" and rationalizing function.

In twentieth century psychology, the need for approbation and for self-approbation is viewed as a basic and complex part of the personality. It involves the need for affection, which in Freudian psychology includes the libido; the need for security, which em-

---

[107] Another particular phase, luxury, will be discussed separately in a later section of this study.

braces the desire for safety and for power; and not least of all, the urge to self-fulfillment, or realization of the ego-image. Erich Fromm, in *Man for Himself,* emphasizes that the intensity of passions and strivings are not merely expressions of the life and death instincts. Many of man's drives and compelling problems begin beyond the organic, including his need for love, fame and power, and his humane ideals. Other metaphysical writers of our day, often of the Existentialist school, have also been attracted by our need to feel power, independence, and our own importance. They, too, have often interpreted this as a drive to surpass the contingency or absurdity of our existence, as an aspiration to godhood.[108]

The eighteenth century analysis of "pride," brilliant though it was, had some notable shortcomings. It did not succeed in reaching a clear, integrated concept of the interrelated motives of approbation and self-approbation. The need to believe in our own worth, in accordance with a projected ego-image, and the need for approbation, esteem, praise or submission on the part of others are two manifestations of the same need to affirm our importance and our existence, and to achieve some security in the face of nothing-

[108] Freud has related the drive for prestige and power to sadism. Distinguishing ego instincts and object instincts, he writes: "One of these object instincts, the sadistic . . . clearly allied itself in many of its aspects with the ego instincts, and its close kinship with instincts of mastery without any libidinal purpose could not be concealed." The truth, writes Freud, "is that men are not gentle, friendly creatures wishing for love, who simply defend themselves when attacked, but that a powerful measure of desire for aggression has to be reckoned as part of their instinctual endowment. The result is that their neighbor is to them not only a possible helper or sexual object, but also a temptation to them to gratify their aggressiveness on him . . . to humiliate him, to cause him pain, to torture and to kill him. . . . This aggressive cruelty . . . also manifests itself spontaneously and reveals men as savage beasts to whom the thought of sparing their own kind is alien." (*Op. cit.,* p. 85–86, 95.) Freud wrote these lines before the unparalleled sadism of the Nazis gave even more conclusive confirmation to his words than earlier episodes which he cites.

Of equal interest is the analysis of Hans Morgenthau (*op. cit.,* p. 13). "This lust for power manifests itself as the desire to maintain the range of one's own person with regard to others, to increase it, or to demonstrate it." Although related to selfishness, the two motives are not identical. The typical goals of selfishness are related to survival. The desire for power concerns itself rather with a man's position among his fellows once his survival has been secured. "Consequently, the selfishness of man has limits; his will to power has none. For while man's vital needs are capable of satisfaction, his lust for power would be satisfied only if the last man became an object of his domination . . . that is, if he became like God." Sadism is a perfect example of "this limitless and ever unstilled desire which comes to rest only with the exhaustion of its possible objects." As Blake put it, "More! More! is the cry of a mistaken soul: less than all cannot satisfy man."

ness. Eighteenth century naturalism gradually turned aside from the deepest psychological and metaphysical implications, into which the earlier writers had begun to delve, turned more and more towards a functional and utilitarian exploration of the role of "pride" in ethics and social life. As a result, the eighteenth century naturalists were not able to integrate the analysis of pride into their world-view, except on the insufficient basis of the competitive struggle of egoistic vitalities, which seemed an aspect of the universal competition among living forms. Yet they did recognize that the manifestations of the prestige-power drive are natural in a uniquely human way, transcending and dominating the biological impulses which largely govern the egoistic vitalities of beasts. They may not have been unaware of the phenomenon of anxiety, which is basic to this whole complex of motives; certainly the seventeenth and early eighteenth century writers had glimpsed what Kierkegaard was to call "Angst," or the dread of nothingness. But, for the reasons we have noted, eighteenth century naturalism was as yet too narrow to grasp the full import and implications of the essential fact that the roots of pride, and of anxiety, are in a distinctive freedom, as well as in a distinctive rationality.

The psychological analysis became, then, a means; its social utilization, the end. Man being what this analysis indicates, the eighteenth century writers concluded that he is incapable of loving virtue and social good for their own sake. This is the important fact; and the chief ethical consequence of the long discussion was the complete divorce of morality from good will, and the frank acceptance of utilitarianism. Most writers, however, found the vices of pride to be self-correcting ones. In this they were unique vices, and performed a unique function. It was on this account that they engaged the attention of moral and social thinkers. Just what was the role of these vices—this is the question they set out to explore. A few, like Rousseau (in his major phase) and Mably, considered the divisive and corrupting effects of pride to be its terminal effect. This was particularly true in regard to the desire for power and for self-affirmation at the expense of others, a desire whose ultimate terminus was sadism. The majority did not concur with this opinion. They also disagreed with the few who, like Shaftesbury, thought that esteem, when properly limited, was an *essentially* social feeling. They believed that the need for approbation and self-approbation, in all its forms, ultimately, but not intrinsically, is a force uniting men, and ministering to the general welfare.

This process of the reversal of the effects of egoism was conceived of as taking place in several distinct ways, which we shall now summarize. It could be looked upon as a social process of counterpoise among men. The Physiocrats, and other writers we have discussed, believed that as each man works for his private good, a process of mutual checks and cancellations prevents excessive egoism and assures the welfare of all. It was also conceived of as a moral process occurring within each individual: the passions (as we saw earlier) may form a harmony, while the need for approbation and the fear of ill-repute serve to correct motivation even before it finds expression in overt action. Again, from a different point of view, the process could be regarded as either an automatic and self-effectuating mechanism, or as one that could be manipulated by certain social institutions. The unique self-interest basis of motivation, and the power of the esteem or prestige drive could be used as a lever for government, legislators, and even for the Church and educators, to condition the behavior of individuals. In the latter view, the mechanisms of the self-interest reversal were conceived of as offering what we should now call an instrument of repression and manipulation, or of social control. Both processes accomplished the same eventual end. Reason perceived certain behavioral requirements from the viewpoint of social needs; nature, egoistic and irrational, was forced into an imperfect and unstable harmony with these needs. Thus pessimism about man was not exclusive of meliorism, which allowed the possibility that men could be made to obey moral laws despite contrary natural instincts—indeed, we may even say, because of them. Nothing is more characteristic of eighteenth century thought than this combination.

There was, however, the more pessimistic view, which we must not overlook in closing. It is present in Rousseau, and in some extreme radical works, such as the *Neveu de Rameau*, the novels of Laclos and of the marquis de Sade. Their pessimism stems partly from their answer to this question: To what does the world give its approbation, esteem and admiration? To follies, or to sheer success and power, was the reply. Fame and esteem come only from pleasing others, in doing what they themselves would like to do, but cannot. In this view, the mechanisms of pride were not self-corrective, since esteem was accorded to people of vicious and anti-social character. Even beyond this, it seemed to the same group of writers (Rousseau, perhaps, excepted), that a man could have complete self-esteem and self-approbation without being virtuous and without having the esteem of others. In fact, he could derive pride, joy and affirmation of his being precisely through the development of his most vicious and anti-social qualities.

This was the latent weakness of the eighteenth century emphasis on pleasure and social utility as the criteria of moral judgment. Had the moralists of the Enlightenment been more rigorous in their thinking, they would perhaps have contented themselves with a less inclusive, and wholly different assertion: that it is only pride in the sense of *moral* esteem and *moral* self-esteem that is productive of *moral* virtue. But this is conscience; and we must await a later point in our investigation to determine the meaning and role of conscience in eighteenth century ethical thought.

Twelve

MAN'S GOODNESS

THE DETRACTORS of human nature, those who "lowered" it to non-moral or to immoral impulses, strong though they were, did not have the field to themselves. The champions of man rose in firm, often angry rejoinder—though all did not reply in the same way, with equal confidence, or from the same motives. To a certain extent, defense of man was a form and a factor of the revulsion against the anti-humanistic dogma of original sin and toward Pascal's analysis. To a certain extent, it was a reaction to the cynicism of La Rochefoucauld, Hobbes, Mandeville and their eighteenth century followers.

To many of the defenders of human nature, it seemed that the first issue at hand was to refute the reduction of motivation to self-interest (in any of its forms). This concerned the English, who were faced with Hobbes and Mandeville, as well as the French, who had the challenge of Bayle. Some of the denials, it is true, were rather half-hearted,[1] but others were firm.

[1] Cumberland's influence on Shaftesbury was important, and via the latter, it undoubtedly reached Voltaire and Diderot. He argues, first, that in voluntary actions in which animals promote the good of others, but receive some benefit themselves, it cannot be claimed that they do not "alike intend and will both"; second, that to please others is pleasant to ourselves. (*A Treatise of the Laws of Nature,* 1727, p. 69 ff., 129–130, 174.)

Chubb argues that happiness being the proper end of action, it is reasonable for

The more vigorous refuters of the self-interest school attempted to advance alternative motivations. The abbé Desfourneaux, despite the concessions on happiness which we have noted, proposed the paradox that self-love is really lacking in most men. Do they not surrender themselves to a dominating passion or to enterprises in which they suffer real disadvantage?[2] (Other writers called this mistaken self-love.) Vauvenargues was similarly to suggest that "Love is more violent than self-love, since one can love a woman despite her scorn." [3] But again, love may be considered a form of self-love. A finer distinction was made by Père Gerdil. Attacking the very basis of the opposing ideology—the philosophy of sensation—he argues that "well-being" has an entirely different scope in an intelligent creature than in a purely sensitive one.

> He is not confined like the latter to the simple impression of felt pleasure. Men have been seen to be unhappy in a flood of delights. Contentment of the spirit contributes even more than pleasurable sensation to man's happiness. . . . A man needs to be in harmony with himself, that is, with his own reason. Such is the excellence of intelligent nature, that his happiness depends more on his ideas, than on his sensations.[4]

Gerdil, in these lines, has attempted a sweeping outflanking movement, which rests on the assumption that man is essentially and distinctively a reasonable, spiritual being. The quest for happiness may therefore be self-denying. Self-love and love of others become indistinguishable and unselfish. The assumption of his opponents was implicitly the contrary.

Equally sweeping, in its ultimate reach, was the well-known argument, proposed by Vauvenargues, the abbé Yvon and others, that it is absurd to call the sacrifice of one's life for another person an act of self-interest. "For," writes the former, "if the object of our love is dearer to us without our existing than our existing is

an intelligent being "to forego some low degree of pleasure to himself, when he can greatly heighten the pleasure of another, and more especially of a multitude thereby." Thus the happiness motive and the principle of greater good lead to self-denial. (*The Ground and Foundation of Morality*, 1745, p. 6–9.)

One of the most brilliant defenses of man's moral nature is sketched by Sade (*Histoire de Juliette*, III, 202–205). However he proceeds immediately to demolish it. For other weak refutations, see Frederick II, *L'Anti-Machiavel, Oeuvres*, VIII, 205, 276; Volney, *La loi naturelle, Oeuvres*, I, 262 f.

[2] *Op. cit.,* p. 81–82.

[3] *Oeuvres*, III, 251.

[4] *Discours philosophique sur l'homme* . . . (1769), p. 125–126.

without the object of our love, it seems that it is love that is our dominant passion and not our own person." With life we lose all. If we are still considering ourselves, then we are considering ourselves as the least part of the whole.[5] Vauvenargues goes on from there to broaden his argument. As we have already seen, he makes the distinction between *amour-propre* and *amour de nous-mêmes*. The latter allows us to seek happiness outside of ourselves, to love ourselves outside of ourselves more than in ourselves; "one is not his own unique object." There is obviously a difference between the satisfaction of *amour-propre* and its sacrifice.[6]

One of the stoutest refutations of the self-interest reduction was offered by Père André, who is better known as an aesthetician. He begins his "Premier Discours sur l'amour désintéressé" (1744)[7] by quoting several of the ancients. He recalls Zeno's statement: love of virtue is independent of love of ourselves; we can love others without interest, out of esteem, justice or duty. He next assails Abbadie for reducing all love to self-love, and for the stratagem he had used to make it acceptable, that is, the separation of *amour de soi* and *amour-propre*. Following other criticisms, André advances his own arguments. The "love of good," which is admittedly our motivating force, is not merely love of happiness, but also "love of what is termed honest, of order, virtue or the beautiful in manners." We are, in fact, divided between these two loves. Each is natural, each has its sphere. However it is also natural to our moral judgment to value the second kind of love above the first. This is the basis of personal esteem, which would obviously be impossible if our love of the moral good could not function independently of interested love of self. While we cannot help loving both *le bien honnête* and *le bien délectable,* in cases of conflict it is clear to all that we must sacrifice the latter.[8] But is it not obvious that this would be impossible if *le bien délectable* were our only motive, and that such a sacrifice implies the independent existence of the two motives? While we may sometimes make this sacrifice for the sake of a greater satisfac-

---

[5] Other writers used a similar argument. Chamfort, for instance, brings forth the example of people who help others at their own risk or disadvantage and refuse all recompense. (*Maximes, Oeuvres complètes,* II, 28.)

[6] See Ch. 4, note 76 and *Oeuvres,* I, 46–49, also p. 70.

[7] *Oeuvres philosophiques,* p. 360 ff.

[8] This assumption was of course denied by many naturalists.

tion, we may also prefer the virtuous act solely because it is reasonable to do so, or because we have a love of order. While duty may give us greater pleasure, it may also be unpleasurable, repugnant or dangerous. We may follow a purely intellectual perception; we may choose to lose the reputation of being a good man in order really to be one.

André next proceeds to make some important distinctions concerning pleasure, which indirectly answer the possible objection that in doing an unpleasurable duty, the idea of doing it is still pleasurable. We love only objects that please us. But "to please" and "to give pleasure" are not precisely the same thing. An object may evoke our approval without producing in us "a delectable modification." And when such a pleasurable sensation is produced, it may either precede our experience of the object, accompany it, or follow it. In the first case, it pleases us *because* it gives us pleasure. In the last case, the object pleased us before it gave us pleasure, and only as a consequence of rational approval. In other words, "spiritual objects"—truth, justice, order—please us by their intrinsic merit "before pleasing us by the feeling of pleasure they give us." [9]

A not unrelated distinction concerning pleasure was made by the deistic poet, Saint-Lambert. He expounded a theory that may possibly be an echo of the English writer, Chubb. "There is a pleasure attached to *bonté,* to generosity; a simple pleasure, independent of reflection and of reference to oneself." In fact, this instinct of *bienveillance* can be exaggerated beyond justice.

> I have seen some take on the feelings, espouse the interests of others, and enter into their situation to the point of losing their own feelings, of forgetting their own interests and situation. I have seen some repent of having yielded to their kindliness and generosity, and admit to me that they had been swept away by an irresistible force. This benevolence, this humanity, is connected with a feeling of love more than it is the effect of pity. . . .[10]

The importance of this statement, like that of Père André, lies in its distinction of pleasure as the accompaniment or result of an

[9] Bishop Butler, writing in 1726, had also contended that we have some disinterested motives, which we pursue in patent violation of our welfare (*Five Sermons* . . . p. 12–17). Butler, however, was never translated, and it is hard to find evidence of an influence in France.

[10] *Les Saisons,* "Eté," note, p. 118–119.

action, from pleasure as motivation; or between the pleasantness of a motivating idea and that of the act itself. It affirms our ability to break out of the circle of self and self-interest. Saint-Lambert also realizes that altruism is not in itself intrinsically moral, but may, like egoism, be right or wrong.

Quite germane at this point is Hume's essay, "The Dignity or Meanness of Human Nature." [11] In refutation of the Hobbesian contention that all human motivation is basically selfish, Hume asserts that unselfish acts produce pleasure, rather than arise from it. Again, while it is true that virtuous men like praise, it is a fallacy to claim that love of praise is their motive. Here we see that Hume's reasoning lies athwart the common trend, which proposed the esteem motive as a fulcrum to sway men towards virtue.

The vindication of human nature in still wider and more general terms by no means suffered from lack of proponents. It scarcely sufficed to assert that man was not ruled entirely by selfishness. The apologists were bound to offer a more positive defense, and to point out precisely where man's goodness lay. There were three principal approaches in response to this challenge. It was proposed that men naturally love the good, that pity and sympathy for others are a part of their nature, and that they are moved by moral considerations. These three qualities appear sometimes as distinct concepts, and sometimes shade off into each other.

There were a number of writers who maintained either that man is essentially good, or that he is a moral creature. There is a difference between these two descriptions, at least in some writings. With the first, we may have a general exaltation of man's inclination to do good to his fellows. Thus Leroy, moderate as always, describes man as endowed with a disposition "that inclines him to *bonté* when contrary passions do not overcome this natural tendency." True, he admits, there are "degenerates" in whom this disposition is warped. But man is not the less good because there are atrocities, as he is not the less reasonable because many people lack good sense. As proof, Leroy (perhaps in imitation of Hume) cites the effect of tragedies on the stage, and our sympathy with good heroes in novels. "It is enough to make men forget their

[11] *Essays, literary, moral and political*, p. 45–49.

private interests which isolate them, in order to bring them back to nature, consequently to compassion." [12] Perhaps Leroy belongs with the group of writers who judged men to be half-good, half-evil; but he does give the impression of a solid, though tempered optimism.

Leroy's evaluation had already been proposed, in somewhat varying measure, by others who wrote before him. As early as 1717, N. Dupuy—one of the defenders of hedonism and a partisan of secular morality—proposed that while men may like evil things, they do not like evil. One of the interlocutors in his dialogue inquires, "If we do not love evil more than good, why is the practice of virtue more difficult than that of vice?" The answer is that "We all have an inclination toward the good," but we imagine good where it is not, especially because of the forces of our senses. And, after all, wherein would lie the virtue of virtue, if it were the easier path? [13]

The pattern is clear. Man would fain be good—only there is something—an error of some kind—that turns him astray. So Leroy and Dupuy. So also Toussaint and Samuel Formey. "Man is naturally virtuous and great," is Toussaint's reassuring appraisal; "remove the base affections he contracts when he lets himself be swept away by his senses, and he will recover his original nobility by himself." [14] Formey generalizes, seizing upon an argument that reaches back through the Middle Ages to Aristotle. The will cannot possibly choose evil (cannot "love evil as evil," is the formulation of Ilharat de la Chambre[15]); a man does evil only when it presents itself to his mind as a good—therefore out of error.[16] Formey's argument is unfortunately not very strong. To begin with, it contains a confusion we shall find characteristic of eighteenth century ethical speculation, between good and right. There is a fundamental ambiguity in a phrase such as, "what presents itself to the mind as a good." In the second place, Formey's own definition of good, as that which leads to happiness, makes mock of his own argument. But let us continue with

[12] *Op. cit.*, p. 270–278 (1768).

[13] *Dialogues sur les plaisirs, sur les passions, sur le mérite des femmes* (1717), p. 70–78, 96.

[14] *Les Moeurs* (1748), p. 160.

[15] *Op. cit.* (1759), I, 461.

[16] *Le bonheur, ou nouveau système de jurisprudence naturelle,* (1754), p. 90–92.

Formey's reasoning. What causes our confusion, he explains, is the "voluntary enslavement to the senses" (apparently the will is sadly deceived here).[17] No, he urges us, let us not confuse corruption with nature. "Nature is that inner voice of reason, which calls us to search for truth and the love of happiness." Thus Formey has reconciled nature and reason—to his own satisfaction, at least.

Arguments in this pattern of natural love of good blinded by error were advanced by Robinet, Vauvenargues, Alès de Corbet and others.[18] Vauvenargues, who often enough satirizes man, feels that the prevalence of order is proof "that reason and virtue are the stronger forces" in him—an attribution that many others, in the eighteenth century, would have made to fear and to pride.[19] Bernardin de Saint-Pierre, like Voltaire, Rousseau and many other writers, held that man's natural goodness is deviated only by the conditions of social life and by improper up-bringing (*éducation*).

> It is our European education that corrupts our nature. . . . Wherever I have seen unhappy children, I have seen them ugly and wicked; wherever I have seen them happy, I have seen them beautiful and good. . . . Insane teachers! Human nature is corrupt, you say; but it is you who are corrupting it by contradictions, vain studies, dangerous ambitions, shameful punishments.[20]

Bernardin again raises to the fore a central problem of eighteenth century ethics, the relation between happiness and virtue. Make men happy, he tells us, and they will be good. Little does he realize all the hidden implications and problems contained in that statement!

Among our defenders of human nature is a group of particularly enthusiastic believers in human potentialities and goodness. We might well place Shaftesbury first among them, and then Hutche-

[17] *Mélanges philosophiques* (1771), p. 48–49. See also, *Principes de morale* . . . (1762), II, 39–40, 47.

[18] Robinet, *Dictionnaire universel* (1777–1783), "Amour de soi-même," "Bon." Authorship of the articles in this work is not certain; consequently, contradictory opinions are sometimes found.

[19] *Réflexions et maximes.* Alès de Corbet, in a lengthy refutation of Bayle, also insists on our natural love of order, of the good and the true, and on erroneous choice as the cause of evil; this is so true, he says, that we disguise our vices under the mask of the pleasurable or the useful. *De l'origine du mal* (1758), I, 56–59.

[20] *Etudes de la nature, Oeuvres*, IV, 407–427.

son. Both acknowledge self-love, but see no necessary contradiction with virtue, inasmuch as we may identify our own good with that of others. Shaftesbury adopts the "rigoristic" concept of virtue from which Mandeville was to profit so adroitly in order to prove men evil. To refrain from vice because of punishment, or to do good for reward, is not, according to Shaftesbury, virtue. But men, in addition to "self-affections" and "unnatural affections," also possess a general love of the good of all, which he pleasantly terms "natural affections." " 'Tis no more natural for the stomach to digest, the lungs to breathe, the glands to separate juices," than for men to have an affection toward the good of the species. Without it, the young would not survive. The heart, "in all disinterested cases, must approve in some measure of what is natural and honest, and disapprove what is dishonest and corrupt." Consequently, it is clear that man, God's highest creation is naturally good, even noble; though corrupted by unnatural affections, he may again regain his purity. That is why moral sense, rather than authoritarian repression and fear, is the best guide for conduct.[21] Human nature, confirms Hutcheson, seems incapable of "malicious, disinterested hatred, or a sedate ultimate desire of the misery of others, when we imagine them in no way pernicious to us. . . ." [22] These lines present a dramatic clash with the view that our happiness thrives on the misery of others, through the comparative process and the need for superiority.

There were French writers who had even fewer reservations. The anonymous deistic manuscript, *Examen de la religion, dont on cherche l'éclaircissement, de bonne foi,* declares that since we were created by God, it is impossible for us to have evil proclivities.[23] A statement such as this has its roots in the principal fount of belief in man's natural goodness—the whole current of primitivism in the seventeenth and eighteenth centuries, which was, in turn, nourished by the voyages of discovery and travelers' accounts of primitive peoples. We cannot here trace the history of this current of thought; nor is it necessary to recapitulate the ex-

---

[21] *Inquiry* . . . Bk. 1, Part 3, and *passim.* For Butler's defense of human nature, as benevolent and adapted to virtue, see especially, his first Sermon.

[22] *An inquiry into the original of our ideas of beauty and virtue,* p. 151, 174–5.

[23] P. 102–104. First published in 1745. See Wade, *op. cit.,* p. 152–158, for rejection of attribution to La Serre and Dumarsais. The B.N. copy bears after the title, "Attribué à M. de St. Evremond," which is also unlikely, as Wade points out. For the same argument used by Delisle de Sales, see *op. cit.,* II, 154–155.

cellent work which has already been done in that field by Gilbert Chinard and Geoffroy Atkinson.[24] We may, however, glance briefly at the characterization of man traced by Lahontan, who is typical in many respects of this outlook. In his *Mémoires de l'Amérique* (1703), Lahontan recounted his personal experiences with the Huron and other Indians. He paints a persuasive picture of a society that is free and self-disciplined, uncorrupted by knowledge, property, luxury and the arts, and by the train of artificial needs and vices, which are their inevitable product. In addition to the economic aspects, Lahontan emphasizes the prevalence of "free love" and divorce, with the result that sexual jealousy and crime do not exist. Rivalry, deception and hypocrisy, consequently, are also absent. In the subsequent *Dialogues,* the apparently untendentious picture of the *Mémoires* was made pointedly polemical. The wise savage, Adario—who was to become a prototype for many who followed him—replies to Lahontan, who is weakly defending European culture. "When you speak of man, say 'Frenchman'; for you know well that these passions, this selfishness, and this corruption, of which you speak, are unknown amongst us . . . I term a man, he who has a natural inclination to do good and who never thinks of doing evil." [25]

In Lahontan and other primitivists, we see some of the formative influences which were later to work deeply in the mind of Rousseau, and also to affect certain phases of the thought of Voltaire and Diderot. Both Rousseau and Voltaire realized that the goodness of the primitives (as described in travelers' accounts), was the goodness of innocence. It was the absence of vices, rather than resistance to them.[26] We cannot help thinking, too, of Rousseau's second *Discours,* and even of his concept of "negative education." Some of Adario's speeches remind us as well of Diderot's Orou (in his *Supplément au Voyage de Bougainville*), who, however, has the gift of eloquence which was that of his author. This is how Orou urges the white man to leave his people undisturbed in their state of bliss:

[24] See Chinard, *L'Amérique et le rêve exotique,* especially Part II, ch. 3, 4, Part III, ch. 3, Part IV, ch. 2; Atkinson, *Les relations de voyages du XVIIe siècle et l'évolution des idées* . . .

[25] Lahontan, *Dialogues curieux et Mémoires de l'Amérique septentrionale,* publiés par Gilbert Chinard. Cf. p. 96, 173–174, 184, 111–112.

[26] See, for instance, the good savage in the seventh chapter of Voltaire's *Histoire de Jenni.*

And you, chief of the brigands who obey you, remove your vessel promptly from our shore. We are innocent, we are happy; and you can only hurt our happiness. We follow the pure instinct of nature; you have tried to efface its imprint from our souls. Here everything belongs to everyone; and you have preached to us I know not what distinction between *thine* and *mine*. Our daughters and our wives belong to all; you have shared this privilege with us; and you have kindled an unknown fury in them. . . . They have begun to hate each other; you have slaughtered each other for them; and they have come to plant in our soil the title of our future slavery.[27]

The essential point of separation between Rousseau and the primitivist writers is that he places the time of man's goodness and innocence in a pre-social state of isolation. For him, society and the loss of innocence are synonymous. For the primitivists, however, man's goodness finds its natural expression and development, as brotherly love and cooperation, only in the community of men. The writers who are influenced by the primitivists tend, in consequence, to communism and anarchism—as we see in the works of Morelly, Dom Deschamps, Meslier, Robinet and Rétif de la Bretonne. This is the result of their belief in man's natural goodness. Rousseau, on the other hand, was to go in a different direction, and outline an ideal state that is authoritarian in its emphasis on the discipline and suppression of individual instincts.[28]

The primitivist influence is also evident in Raynal's widely read *Histoire des Deux Indes,* and especially in the third revision (1780), in which Diderot had a large hand. Here again man is proclaimed to be good in his nature:

For too long a time they have sought to degrade man. His detractors have made a monster of him. In their ill-temper they have overwhelmed him with insults. The guilty satisfaction of lowering him has alone guided their black pencils. Who are you then, who dare to insult your fellow-man thus? What womb gave you birth? Is it from the bottom of your heart that you drew so many blasphemies? If your pride had been less blind, or your character less ferocious, barbarian! you would have seen

[27] Ed. Chinard, p. 119–122. For the goodness of the Tahitians, see p. 126 f.
[28] We have seen that Morelly also goes in this direction, allying communism with absolute control.

only a being always weak, often seduced by error, sometimes led astray by imagination, who sprang from the hands of nature with honest inclinations. . . .[29]

In society, however, admits Raynal, self-interest rules all, and authority is necessary. Neither the demands of peoples nor the decisions of governments are determined by moral considerations.

We may give rapid mention to several lesser writers. Maupertuis is firm. "If we reflect on man's nature, we shall believe him capable of anything, provided we propose him great enough motives: capable of braving pain, capable of braving death." He finds his proofs among primitive peoples who calmly bear torture and die rather than be enslaved.[30]

The marquis de Mirabeau, though perhaps less influenced by the primitivist current, was no less eulogistic.

> Man is not a perverse race. We are a race with honor and feeling. An internal law impels us to the good without even the help of reflection. . . . No, man has a different kind of entrails: he is a being urged in substance and by nature towards justice and charity. . . . Man, I say, loves light and virtue . . . he realizes that error and vice are only misery and contagion . . . injustice only disorder, unenlightened self-interest only seduction, only straying (*égarement*), only delirium. That is what our heart tells us all, if we deign to listen to it in the silence of our inner being.[31]

As the century draws towards its close, this romantic sentimentality increases. The eccentric Rouillé d'Orfeuil, blasts all who have spoken ill of humanity.

> Man is, according to me, the most noble and most perfect of all beings, in his form and in his good qualities; alone capable of judging beauty, of loving it with awareness, he is naturally borne to the good. His passions make ceaseless and violent efforts to turn him aside from it; but he has received from the Supreme Being arms to fight them and the strength to conquer them. His countenance is pleasant, his air noble, imposing and gentle; his mind takes a thousand forms and procures him a thousand resources of all kinds. Woman is the masterpiece of

---

[29] Wolpe, *Raynal et sa machine de guerre*, p. 159. The picture of the "good savage" did not exclude ferocity, but this was not considered moral vice. In all these accounts, freedom and equality were emphasized. See *ibid.*, p. 81–82.

[30] *Essai de philosophie morale, Oeuvres* (1752), p. 392.

[31] *Philosophie rurale* (1764), I, 241, III, 253–254.

nature; her gentleness, finesse and delicacy, conjoined to the strength of man, form of these two moieties a perfect whole.[32]

This is essentially the faith of Bernardin de Saint-Pierre, and it seems that his master, Jean-Jacques Rousseau, often believed it to be his.

In this circle of romantic eulogists, we could possibly include one Christian apologist—the abbé Denesle—but him alone. He is the only Christian we find denying that it is at all in man's essence to do evil—for if it were, the abbé asserts, he could not wish not to do it any longer; and this is the secret wish even of evil men.[33] But even Denesle, despite his horror for the materialists' assessment of man, notes that we have perverted our nature.

This natural goodness of man—still taking the word "goodness" in the sense of unselfish motivation—was often brought to a focus in the impulses of compassion that all men experience towards each other. This was the positive counterpart to the denial that self-love is our sole motivation. Some of man's defenders, especially Shaftesbury, Rousseau and their respective disciples, denied the claim of the cynics and materialists that our feeling for others is no more than a disguised egoism, a projection of the self. They insisted on the reality of other-directed impulses. But even if the cynical analysis were correct, the possibility of altruistic acts, at least, and their value, remained unshaken.[34] Pity was frequently given a quasiscientific basis in the universality of human nature and human reactions. It is a physical reaction, asserted Buffon, and does not belong to the soul.[35] For Hume it is based on sympathy, a phenomenon that plays a vital role in his ethical thought.[36]

[32] *L'alambic moral* . . . (1773), p. 320–321. Another eulogistic defense of human nature was the *Essai de morale,* published anonymously, under the initials Ca . . . Mi, in 1791. The author proves vices are not natural, since it would then be natural to hurt ourselves, for others would have the same rights towards us. Implicitly separating man from nature, he declares that iron is in nature, but not swords, or the use we make of them; so with all corruption. (P. 4–35.)

[33] *Examen du matérialisme* (1754), II, 112.

[34] This defense was particularly strong in England. Adam Ferguson, for instance, in his *Essay on the History of Civil Society* [1767] p. 20–25, inveighs against the confusion between the words "benevolence" and "self-gratification" that identifies a parent's taking care of a child with a parent's neglecting him. If we do not have completely disinterested behavior, we often act in such a fashion that our own interest is lost, swallowed up in that of the *other*. The common sense of the words, for Ferguson, is a sufficient distinction. His argument recalls that of Vauvenargues.

[35] *Oeuvres philosophiques*, p. 367.

[36] "Now it is obvious that nature has preserved a great resemblance among all human creatures, and that we can never remark any passion or principle in others

Rousseau presents the "original man" as possessed of two native impulses: the one leads to the preservation of his own well-being, the other "inspires in us a natural repugnance to seeing any sensitive being, and especially our fellows, perish or suffer." [37] In the *Encyclopédie*, as René Hubert has pointed out, both attitudes run side by side.[38] Some articles reflect the Hobbesian, materialistic current, and maintain that men's egoism leads them to ruthless opposition. But other writers, such as the abbé Yvon, insist on the natural sympathy which leads to pity and generous deeds. To be sure, we love the "other" only because we consider him as another self, but the explanation does not destroy the reality of altruism.

The themes of the state of nature and the origin of society are obviously connected with those of pity and compassion. Both of these subjects presently stand in need of full-length studies, and we cannot hope to do them justice in a general synthesis such as the present one, especially since their ramifications would carry us far afield. We shall only note that the feeling of mutual sympathy was commonly held to be an important factor in the origination of society; or else (by those who considered society to be natural and co-existent with man), to be an essential spring of its maintenance. "At all times and in all climates," declared Delisle de Sales, "the sight of a suffering person moves us despite ourselves, and our soul automatically puts itself in harmony with this pain; pity is the cry of nature which summons to the conservation of beings all those who are near them." [39]

Rousseau, on the other hand, held the feeling of compassion to be both prior to society and unrelated to it, a mere animal reflex. Yet, also in the *Discours sur l'inégalité*, he contends that pity is the unique source of all social virtues, including generosity and friendship. He then proceeds to dispose of the commonplace objection.

Even if it were true that commiseration is only a sentiment that puts us in the place of him who suffers, an obscure and keen sentiment in savage man, developed but weak in civil man, how would this idea affect the truth of what I say, except to

of which, in some degree or other, we may not find a parallel in ourselves. . . . These two principles of authority and sympathy influence almost all our opinions . . . sympathy depends on the relation of objects to ourselves. . . ." (*Moral and Political Philosophy*, ed. Aiken, p. 6–9.)

[37] *Discours sur l'inégalité*, ed. Vaughan, I, 138.
[38] *Op. cit.*, p. 184–185.
[39] *De la philosophie de la nature* (1770), III, 376.

give it greater force? . . . It is then quite certain that pity is a natural feeling which, moderating in each individual the activity of self-love, tends to the mutual conservation of the whole species.[40]

Rousseau goes on to claim that pity, in the state of nature, takes the place of laws and virtue (an idea doubtless derived from travel books such as that of Lahontan), takes the place, too, of Voltaire's Natural Law, by inspiring in all hearts not the Golden Rule, but the more useful moral maxim (*sic!*), "Seek your own welfare with the least possible harm to others."

To redress the balance and present a fair picture, it must be emphasized that the more cynical and radical writers—d'Holbach and Sabatier de Castres, for instance—continued to disparage pity, or sympathy, not only as disguised forms of egoism, but also as ineffective motives. "Several philosophies," remarks d'Holbach, in open opposition to Shaftesbury and Rousseau,

> have founded morals on an innate benevolence, which they have thought to be inherent to human nature; but this benevolence can only be the result of experience and reflection, which shows us that other men are useful to us, and in a position to contribute to our own happiness. A disinterested benevolence, that is, one from which there would result for us, from those who inspire it in us, neither tenderness nor a return, would be a feeling deprived of motives, or an effect without cause. It is relative to himself that man shows benevolence to others. . . . We shall perhaps be told that virtuous people push disinterestedness to the point of showing benevolence to ingrates, and that others show it to men they have never known and whom they will never see. But this benevolence itself is not disinterested; if it comes from pity, we shall soon see that the compassionate man relieves himself by doing good to others.[41]

As for the marquis de Sade, we need scarcely say that pity of any kind is rigorously excluded from his naturalism, as a form of weakness and degeneracy.[42]

I have suggested that there is a difference in implication be-

---

[40] *Op. cit.,* p. 162. However, this passage was apparently written for Rousseau by his friend, Diderot. Cf. Diderot, *Oeuvres,* IV, 101. Since the same thought is repeated in the 1774 revision of Raynal, in words that in one place are identical (cf. Wolpe, p. 80), we may again see Diderot's hand here. The Raynal passage adds: "This sweet compassion has its source in the [physical] organization of man, for whom it is sufficient to love himself in order to hate the suffering of his fellows."

[41] *La morale universelle,* I, 26. For the chapter on pity, see p. 100 ff.

[42] E.g., *Histoire de Juliette,* III, 41–42.

tween the argument that men are naturally inclined towards good (love of order and justice, sympathy with others), and the assertion that man is ruled by a moral realm within him. The second statement necessarily implies the existence in his constitution of a non-physical, "spiritual" component, which may supply the determining motivation of his acts. Love and sympathy (in themselves) are on a pre-moral level, and are found among animals. Moral experience, however, is the intuition of an "ought," or an obligation. And the two may be in conflict. But in this regard, a further distinction is necessary. We must not confuse the belief, held by almost all eighteenth century writers, that man is a moral being, that is, one who necessarily makes moral judgments, with the belief that man is virtuous, that is, capable of and willing to do the good he perceives and to execute the judgments he makes. This the first does not necessarily imply, although it would be so maintained by men like Bernardin de Saint-Pierre. An even deeper ethical implication of the assertion that man is ruled by a moral experience concerns the reality and determinacy of suprapersonal values of a purely moral nature; whereas the first statement confines man and his moral life to the plane of inter-personal relationships.

It was Helvétius' reduction of all motivation to the physical that united much of the opposition on this point. Most of the refutations were made by Christian apologists.[43] Several of the humanistic *philosophes,* including Diderot and Marat, also rose in protest. Both the latter insisted that there were passions that relate only to the mind. "Let us leave it to the sophist author of *De l'Esprit,*" thunders Marat, "to try to deduce, by intricate reasoning, all passions from physical sensitivity; he will never deduce from it the love of glory, of that vain incense which ignorance and weakness offer to power, to courage, to knowledge, and for which fine souls are avid." Where is physical sensitivity in the life of Zeno, Cato and Socrates, in willing sacrifice and suffering? Beyond all doubt, there is "a love of the *beautiful* and the *good* which becomes for the heart of the wise man an unquenchable spring of delightful feelings, and lets him experience in the midst of alarms that sweet peace which misfortune cannot disturb." [44]

[43] E.g. *La religion vengée* (1757–1760), X, 149, VII, 10–12.
[44] Marat, *De l'Homme* (1775), I, 201–214. Diderot will be taken up later in this chapter.

It is on this basis that a considerable group of Christian apologists were able to support the existence of an invincible sphere of goodness in human nature. They were impelled to this advocacy by their overriding preoccupation with combatting the advance of materialism, with its reduction of motivation to pleasure-pain sensations, that is, to the physical, the organic, the animal. This doctrine menaced the Christian view of the soul, of man's place, and of his relation to God. Consequently, while some apologists, as we saw in the last chapter, continued to emphasize original sin, the larger number chose to lay stress (without excluding the former doctrine, of course), on the existence of a moral component in man, or in other words, on non-physical motivation. This question connects itself with the existence of a spiritual soul; we shall avoid this subject and hue to the line of ethical thought.[45] To the interlocutor who suggests that physical needs require physical goods, and that happiness is therefore physical, the abbé Pey's mouthpiece replies that conscience rebels against pleasure: "I do not know how it is I experience within me a natural feeling that forces me to esteem virtue as a real good . . . the instinct of pleasure is that of the brute and the instinct of reason is that of humanity." [46] The abbé Pichon, declaiming against Helvétius, points out that if the latter is right, if humaneness comes from the senses, then virtue is only "a special disposition of the muscles, fibres, etc."—an idea which he of course ridicules. "You calumniate man, M. Helvétius, when you say that men conceive of force before they conceive of justice, and follow the latter only out of fear of greater force. If there existed a man with absolute power, would he then be a ferocious beast? Do you not see that your philosophy makes real *moral* virtue impossible?" [47]

These, then, were the defenders of man; and it is clear that they

[45] For the distinction between feeling or thought and the physical see, for instance, Camuset: *Principes contre l'incrédulité, à l'occasion du Système de la nature* (1771), p. 23–26; Paulian, *Le véritable système de la nature*, p. 64–65.

[46] *Le philosophe catéchiste* (1773), p. 79–80.

[47] *Les arguments de la raison . . .* (1776), p. 99–106. We have seen how Diderot and Sade answered the question about the man with absolute power. Gauchat, together with his insistence on original sin, also argues for man's moral nature. *Op. cit.*, XVI, 13, 66. For similar opinions of the abbé Barruel and Pierre Fabre, see Hester Hastings, *op. cit.*, p. 166–167, 119 n.l. Other defenders of man in the man-beast controversy, who claimed the moral sphere as a distinctive human attribute, have been noted in the first chapter. Of course, not all were men of the cloth (e.g. Delisle de Sales, *op. cit.*, II, 7, III, 37).

were outnumbered and outweighed by his detractors. There remained, however, still another approach to the evaluation of human nature. This was to turn away from the affirmation that man is inherently either good or evil, and to assert instead, that he is both, or that he is neither. As this attitude was developed in the eighteenth century, the two formulations sometimes appear not to be far apart, but they are essentially quite different; and at the hands of certain *philosophes,* the latter formulation received a special implication, that of social rather than individual responsibility.

That man bears within him, at birth, both good and evil inclinations was, of course, the fundamental belief of all orthodox Christians, although polemical excitation often prevented a clear enunciation of this doctrine. The real distance that separates the statement, "Man is both good and evil" from "Man is neither good nor evil," is revealed in Hayer's denunciation of Helvétius for proclaiming the latter formula. Hayer first declares that as man is made in God's image, he has "traits of justice and virtue engraved on his soul," although these are disfigured by "the stain of our origin." Hayer thus realizes that it is the very heart of the Christian doctrine that Helvétius has denied. He then continues, denouncing the second important implication of Helvétius' ethics, the social criterion of moral value, which denies the inherence of right and wrong in acts. For Hayer, values are determined by imperatives that are outside of man, and superior to him. "It is certain, sir, that men are *good* and that they are *evil,* independently of a *common interest.* They are evil in surrendering to passions which have no connection with the common interest. They are good in repressing these same passions. The relations of man to God are absolutely independent of the common interest of society." [48] A further consequence of the Christian view, however, as developed by Hayer, approaches somewhat that of the *philosophe's* negative formulation. Man having dual possibilities, the determination of his character lies in what happens *after* his birth. It is not true, as Voltaire says, that men are "determined by their instinct" and "never change character." They have the power to conquer themselves, by force of will.[49]

[48] *Op. cit.,* VI, 315–316. Italics in text.
[49] *Op. cit.,* VIII, 282–284.

The concept of the simultaneity, or balance of good and evil in human nature, runs through the century, in more or less Christian terms. Two popular English writers, Pope and Wollaston, had set the tone.

> Virtuous and vicious ev'ry Man must be,
> Few in th' extreme, but all in the degree;
> The rogue and fool by fits is fair and wise;
> And ev'n the best by fits, what they despise.
> 'Tis but by part we follow good or ill
> For, Vice or Virtue, Self directs it still . . .[50]

At this point (though not at others), Pope—like the orthodox Christian—also separates sharply the two aspects of human nature; passion ("nature" in the sense of physical needs or what is common to all animal life), and reason, which is man's peculiar domain. Wollaston's outlook is similar: we may follow either passion (or pleasure, or profit), or else act reasonably, out of a sense of duty. The moral realm is attached to reason, the other motives are called "inferior springs." [51]

In France, as the seventeenth century drew to its close, the widely read Abbadie reaffirmed the Pascalian view of man, as both great and abased.[52] Rémond de Saint-Mard, an early proponent of *morale laïque,* was one of the first to set forth a type of analysis which was to become rather widespread. Man's nature, it proposes, destines him to conflict between the two main springs of his action: self-love, necessary to life, and love of others, necessary to society. The second makes us work for the social good, despite ourselves, but ultimately turns to our own profit.[53]

This doctrine of man's dual nature, as it traversed the century, became the basis of much of the speculation concerning ways of conditioning behavior so as to encourage tendencies which favor the general good and to minimize the self-centered impulses. The independent subsistence of both motives was the moderates' answer to the despair of the pessimists. Even though to some of these moderates, like Buffon and Voltaire, it seemed that the selfish motives were too powerful to be dominated, many, from Morelly to Condorcet, had faith in the possibilities of social con-

---

[50] *Essay on Man,* II, 231 ff; cf. 41, 59–60.
[51] *Op. cit.,* p. 173.
[52] *Op. cit.,* p. 1–21.
[53] Still a third spring is pleasure, at least in Saint-Mard's formulation, which in the act of reproduction unites the first two. (*Nouveaux dialogues des Dieux,* 1714.)

ditioning, while still others, like Hume, and some of the more optimistic writers we have encountered, believed the altruistic impulses were not so weak as was often supposed.[54] Among this second group, Mably was one of the strongest believers in the possibility of shifting the balance.

> What! because the passions have done much ill, we must allow them to do still more! Most men's reason is astray, blind and corrupt. . . . The feeling of virtue (*honnêteté*) which you still find in their hearts, the virtuous men who still subsist in the midst of corruption, and whose race will never be extinguished, shouldn't all that bring you back to a more human and consoling philosophy . . . ? Society itself, by its laws, its institutions and its discipline, can give us all the virtues we need to be happy. When we say that we were born with an inclination to the good, and that our sociable qualities prepare and invite us to find our private happiness in the public good, we must . . . be careful not to believe that we can abandon ourselves without danger to these virtuous affections. . . . Why? because nature has not done everything, and because she has left something for our reason to do.[55]

We must keep in mind that at this point we are dealing with purely moral assessments of human nature, that is, with the springs of action. Few would have denied that men's actions in themselves may be judged both good and evil; but we have seen to what egoistic origins the majority of writers ascribed even the good actions. The writers we are discussing in this chapter were concerned with establishing the reality of non-egoistic motives, and the love of good for its own sake. Consequently, those who believed that man, from this viewpoint, is both good and evil, might also believe in the predominance of evil in his actual behavior, either because of its inherent strength, or because of the conditions of social life. Marivaux's position is particularly interesting, in this regard, because he was aware of the ubiquity and dominance of evil, but found in this fact the very proof that man is also ineradicably good.

> The most astonishing thing in the world is that there is always on earth a mass of virtue that persists despite the affronts it suffers and the encouragement given to iniquity itself; for it

[54] For Hume, see, for instance, "Of the Obligation of Promises," in Aiken p. 87. For Buffon, see *Oeuvres* (ed. Piveteau), p. 337 ff.

[55] *Principes de morale, Oeuvres*, x, 229 ff. The natural motives are pleasure and pain; but these are not safe guides to our true interest.

[i.e., iniquity] receives all the honors, when it can escape the laws that condemn it. And assuredly, there are more guilty who are honored in the world than punished. How many times is the crime redeemed by the gain from the crime itself? Men must bear in the depths of their soul a colossal fund of justice, and they must have in their original nature a powerful vocation for following order, since there are still honest people among them.[56]

If men were all wicked, continues Marivaux, who rejects the Hobbesian explanation, they would abolish laws against wickedness. A society of wicked men could not even agree, in order to prevent mutual slaughter, to kill the perpetrator of a murder; one thing would be lacking in such an agreement: "that is, being made among creatures capable of observing it." Marivaux's conclusion is similar to that of writers who regarded men as evil. Fear of punishment is needed to balance iniquity and to reach "a certain mediocrity of peace, such as we have in this world." So we have a world of hypocrites, of "wicked men who will not dare to be as wicked as they would like." This is the best we are capable of, and it is up to each man to watch out for himself. Although Marivaux does not condemn men absolutely, his pessimism is supreme, and his conclusions are not too distant from those of Diderot's Rameau or of Sade. It will be interesting to see how Marivaux's concept of human nature is reflected in his novels.

This evaluation of human nature is again apparent in Leroy's important *Lettres philosophiques* (1768). To the defense of human goodness which we saw earlier in this chapter, he adds a qualifying statement. "When I maintain," he writes, "that man is born good, I do not imply that this quality is a habitual principle of action in men." This is so, simply because personal interest is the most powerful motive in life. The most we can say is that "they usually do not reject opportunities to do good to others," and that when not preoccupied with themselves, "they yield gladly to pity." [57]

---

[56] *Le Cabinet du philosophe* (1734), p. 75–80. In an earlier work, Marivaux had emphasized the feeling of dignity and excellence we experience in *not* following self-interest. (*L'Indigent philosophe,* in *Le Spectateur français* (1728), II, 80–82.)

[57] P. 277–278. Leroy also expresses his thought as follows: "Man may then be considered as a good being, or at least endowed with a disposition that develops simultaneously with the other faculties and which inclines him strongly to goodness when he is not agitated in a contrary direction." Passions may produce a de-

A particularly interesting example of the difficulty of defending man's goodness in the eighteenth century intellectual climate is provided by Mirabeau, in his *Essai sur le despotisme* (1775). He opens the essay with a stout affirmation of the optimistic position, based on the thesis that men are necessarily, if not naturally sociable. Sociability, he argues, is itself a virtue, and involves justice, which includes all other virtues, even benevolence. Society, then, does not need to postulate wickedness to explain its origin: "man, whom an irresistible instinct attracts to society, is not a wicked being. . . . I promise only to prove . . . that social man is essentially and naturally good, that he can be happy only in fulfilling this necessary condition of his being, and that he will always be just and happy when he will be enlightened about his true interests, which are always in conformity with justice and with his happiness." Consequently, all passions can be easily directed to the general good; otherwise nature (which obviously cannot be contradictory), would not have made man social.

A more optimistic statement would be hard to find. But then Mirabeau gradually becomes entangled in a web of his own spinning. Man, he must admit, has a natural desire to dominate, enslave and exploit his fellows. This is not really a contradiction, Mirabeau argues, since goodness and justice (which, we remember, are his natural disposition) consist in subordinating these passions to the general interest. Of course, the existence of despotism shows that abuses are possible, but only when the despot is not *éclairé* as to where his true happiness lies. Still, Mirabeau is honest enough to admit it is true that egoism has always been, and will continue to be humanity's greatest flaw. This is so be-

generation of this original nature. See also his *Examen des critiques du livre intitulé De l'Esprit.*

Similar opinions, in the writing of J.-Ph. Varennes, Duclos, Boudier de Villemaire, Vauvenargues, Rivarol and Marmontel contain little that requires special mention. Duclos stresses the influence of education, while Marmontel points out the fact cooperation is equally, with competition, a law of nature that extends to many species. Bonnet, on the other hand (like Rivarol) lays emphasis on "physical organization" as the important determinant, though not refusing all influence to education. In effect, he denies the transcendent value of good will, claiming that right understanding—which "resides in the organization—will induce right choice; once again, the moral sphere is assigned to reason. See Bonnet, *Essai sur l'âme*, ch. XXIX; Varennes, *Les hommes* (1727), p. 3–10; Duclos, *Considérations sur les moeurs de ce siècle* (1751), p. 8, 28–29; Boudier de Villemaire, *L'Andrométrie, ou examen philosophique de l'homme* (1753), p. 127–150; Vauvenargues, *Oeuvres*, III, 12, 33, 71; Rivarol, *De la philosophie moderne*, p. 57–58; Marmontel, *op. cit.*, p. 149 ff.

cause men, to whom *nature* "prescribed the desire and need to love themselves more than all else, tend to love themselves exclusively." Unfortunately, this is an irremediable condition.

> Now, it is not possible to remake humanity; the whole trick consists in doing the best we can with it: we have to be governed by our prejudices and our passions. The science of political education is to inspire in us prejudices which tend to the general welfare, and to direct our passions to it; and these passions, these so active interests, apparently so opposed, eternal sources of human divisions, will be the basis of the citizens' unity, the link of their fraternity when they will be enlightened. . . . One should therefore speak to men . . . only of their own interest. . . . Generosity, *bienfaisance*, justice are only words to them.

So, "enlightenment" is indefinitely postponed and gives way to "useful prejudice," or falsehood, and to effective social conditioning! No wonder Mirabeau in later years ruefully admitted that he had "mutilated his subject"! But it is probable that he never realized why. It is doubtful that he ever realized that he had confused "nature" and "reason"—the natural (or animal) demands of human nature, and its rational demands (which stem from his being as a child of culture); and that, in refusing to allow nature to be contradictory, he was trying to avoid an admission of that unique transcendence of nature which makes it impossible to explain man in purely "natural" terms.

The counterpart of this first current, namely, that we are born neither good nor evil, but morally neutral in our inherited dispositions, was to receive its first important exposition in the writings of Morelly. Following Locke, and before Condillac or Helvétius, he develops a fairly comprehensive theory of sensualism, in a book that was little read, *Essai sur l'esprit humain, ou principes naturels de l'éducation* (1743). The mind is essentially passive, "like a mirror that one takes out from behind a curtain." All men have essentially the same mental powers; all differences are caused either by different degrees of sensitivity of the receptor organs, or by the experiences to which they are exposed.[58] If a man is only what he is made to be, *la conclusion s'impose:* he is indefinitely malleable, morally neither good nor evil in his inherent nature. His moral judgments, like his intellectual judgments, are extraneous to his nature; and he does not, primarily,

[58] P. 2–11, 364.

have the responsibility for them. Responsibility devolves on the people among whom he is brought up, thus most importantly of all, upon the society or culture, its ideals and its faults. In his later *chef-d'oeuvre, Code de la nature* (1755), Morelly not only enlarges and perfects his basic theory, but tells us the specific flaw which is the cause of all human evil. It is the unlawful and unnatural institution of property. Without the hatreds, rivalry and vices engendered by property (and it is the origin of all vices), men would live together in cooperative and loving fraternity, in simple and perfect harmony.

Morelly does not deny that men are actuated by love of self; but, without making Rousseau's distinction overtly, he uses the phrase *amour de soi* (although he also uses the more common term, *amour-propre*). In his mind, self-love definitely refers to a pre-moral motivation.[59] However men also possess an equally natural love of their fellows, which only our competitive society distorts and suppresses.[60] But Morelly, far from believing (as it has been claimed) that the free play of individual interests would result in their harmony—a theory that belongs rather to Helvétius (with reservations) and to the Physiocrats—reveals his fundamental distrust of human nature and of "amour de soi." The society he sketches, here and in earlier pieces, *Le Prince* (1751) and *La Basiliade* (1753), relies upon a complete repression, a complete totalitarianism.[61] In this, Morelly merely confirms what many egalitarian Utopias foresaw, and what history has confirmed, that a state of true communism and "fraternal love" can exist only at the price of total regimentation. Human nature, it would seem, is not what Morelly pretends to believe it is. In Newtonian fashion, he had described men as actuated by laws of attraction and repulsion—love of self, fraternal love. The suppression of prop-

[59] It is only the desire of self-preservation, by innocent means. The import of Morelly's theory is that a good society will prevent the necessity of other means. However, the means of prevention he urges betray a fear of the evil in human nature. Gauchat (*op. cit.*, xvi, 116–123) properly criticizes Morelly's theory for reducing man to physical motivations and satisfactions, "without supposing in man feelings, desires, superior to those of his animal part." Morelly, to be sure, would use repression to keep it that way.

[60] Neither of these motivations, however, is innate; both develop naturally from experience. This seems to be Morelly's thought, though he does call self-love an "inclination."

[61] Note, however, that (in contrast with Rousseau's *Contrat social*), Morelly supposes no constituted *State*, but a *res publica* in which citizens govern by turns.

erty, he avers, will secure economic equality, and simultaneously cause the "love of self" motive (at least in the distorted phase of *amour-propre* or competitive self-love) to wither away, leaving only fraternal love. But Morelly must assure the working of this theory by an Inca-like regime of benevolent totalitarianism.[62]

The second great system to incorporate the "neutral" evaluation of human nature was that of Helvétius. It is true that we have also classified Helvétius among man's detractors, and in a certain sense that was appropriate. He is always more eager to depreciate men than to elevate them, always ready to take up arms against the theory of *bonté naturelle,* and to point out the tendency to wickedness. All this is in accord with his naturalistic view of the world. But Helvétius could not accept the theory that men are inevitably, or irremediably evil in conduct; for that would be to ruin his major thesis, which is the complete modifiability of men. Consequently, as he states his position in *De l'Esprit,* he maintains

> that men, sensitive to themselves alone, indifferent to others, are born neither good nor evil, but ready to be one or the other, according to whether a common interest unites or divides them; that the sentiment of preference that each feels for himself, a feeling to which the conservation of the species is attached, is engraved by nature in an ineffaceable way; that physical sensitivity has produced in us the love of pleasure and the hatred of pain; that pleasure and pain have then planted and made bud in all hearts the seed of self-love, whose development gave birth to passions, from which all our vices and virtues have come forth.[63]

This theory represents a terminus of the sensationist psychology of the *tabula rasa.* It is taken up again in *De l'Homme.* The wickedness or virtue of men, Helvétius there proclaims, is purely "the product of their good or bad laws." He rejects both the Hobbesian theory that men, because of their desire to possess the same things, are born in a state of war, and, on the other hand, the "original goodness" and moral sense of the English. Men want only to be happy. They are not necessarily bad, for the simple reason

[62] Morelly's writings had at first little influence; not so much because of their moral notions [as Delisle de Sales claimed], but mainly because current moral and political theories, and the theory of man, were based on the idea of property as a natural instinct and right. The best edition of *Le Code* is that of Professor Gilbert Chinard.

[63] P. 238.

that their happiness is not necessarily attached to another's harm. (Here is where Sade went far beyond his master.)[64] We do love others, when we feel or know it will be good for us to do so. But the necessity for laws proves that men are not. *naturally* good. Even Rousseau, charges Helvétius, admits, in the first book of his *Emile,* that we must experience suffering before we can pity others. The child has all the vices of the man. The great examples of virtue are found not among savages, but among civilized peoples; in any society, the most detestable person would be the natural man, obeying only his caprice and passing feeling. Here it is obvious that Helvétius, unlike Rousseau, confuses goodness with virtue. For him there is only one criterion, the general welfare, and only one way to attain it, through "sound education" and the proper political arrangement, which must unite self-interest with public interest, largely through the mechanism of esteem.[65]

If Helvétius inclined to the pessimistic side, another great materialist, d'Holbach, tended toward optimism. Applying physics to human life, he conceived of history as an inevitable advance towards truth, an advance determined by the law of egoism (or the desire to better ourselves), and by the harmony of nature. His central tenet is again that of the sensualist-materialist school. "Man by his nature is neither good nor evil. He seeks happiness at each instant of his duration." [66] Passions are determined by the pleasure-pain reaction, which is merely necessary, and pre-moral. A man becomes moral if he complies with these impulses and satisfies his needs in a way useful to himself and his fellow-men.[67]

[64] Helvétius does say that "one necessarily becomes the enemy of men when one can be happy only by their unhappiness" (p. 373).

[65] *De l'Homme,* p. 137 ff., *De l'Esprit,* 371 ff. Whereas Condillac's own reasoning left man a prisoner of experience, Helvétius and other materialists thought man could make environment, and, by determining experience, determine behavior, through the pleasure-pain motives. Helvétius, as we know, believed that character, as well as ideas and reactions, could be thus formed. Another "optimist" in this regard was the marquis de Chastellux, who also proclaimed the malleability of human nature and the power, through environment, to manipulate it. The constancy of human nature in regard to its needs and motives could be counted on to produce the desired results, with the certainty of physical determinism. (Cf. Ch. Frankel, p. 57 ff.)

[66] *Système social, ou principes naturels de la morale et de la politique* (Londres, 1773), I, 9.

[67] See the long development in *Système de la nature,* I, 161 ff. "The heart of man is a field which, according to its nature, is equally suited to produce the thistles or useful grains . . . according to the seed that will be sown in it, and the culture that will have been given it."

(But if the need and the impulse are *necessary*, will he not be inclined to satisfy them at any cost? This is one of the ethical problems the materialists had to face! [68]) This summary statement could be attributed equally to Helvétius or to d'Holbach.

What determines a man to fulfill the conditions of virtue? Like Morelly and Helvétius, d'Holbach gives full weight to "circumstances," emphasizing examples, habits and above all government. "You can make of man whatever you want." [69] The greatest scoundrel could have been a model of virtue, the most virtuous man an arrant villain. "Our conduct, good or bad, always depends on the true or false ideas we fashion or which others give us." This will determine *how* we go about satisfying our necessary needs—in egoism, or in *bienveillance*.[70]

Optimism infiltrates d'Holbach's theory when he objects to man being "unjustly considered" as inclined to evil, and as an enemy of his fellows; and when he declares, "No man is evil gratuitously." [71] Passions are natural; but the bad use of them is not.[72] Also optimistic is the implication of d'Holbach's whole theory, that men are reasonable, and will, if properly enlightened, choose the way of virtue. Virtue is the choice of reason.

We shall close this section of our discussion with the mention of several lesser writers who upheld the "neutral" theory, and with a brief consideration of the *Encyclopédie*. One of these lesser, but fascinating figures, is the anarchist Dom Deschamps—an eccentric but powerful thinker. In the primitive state, he believes,

[68] In *Le Christianisme dévoilé*, d'Holbach writes that man does good when it is to his interest, and evil only when he would otherwise be obliged to give up his welfare.

[69] *Système social*, p. 12. D'Holbach does not deny a temperamental penchant towards what society qualifies as good or evil, but believes it can almost always be overcome.

[70] "It is our parents and our teachers who make us good or evil. . . . Their examples and their lessons modify us for our entire lives." (*Système de la nature*, *loc. cit.*) In his refutation of d'Holbach, Richard attacks this whole theory. "Experience proves that we cannot make of man whatever we wish, and that our vices are born with us." Bad men often spring from the best upbringing, and vice versa. (*Op. cit.*, p. 9 ff.) The malleability theory was defended, however, by the abbé Coyer, who was interested in refuting Hobbes' description of man as evil. "If education had no effect, man would be less perfectible than the brute we put to sleep by discipline." (*Plan d'éducation publique, Oeuvres* (1782–1783), III, 116–119. Diderot's refutation of Helvétius, consequently, is simultaneously a refutation of d'Holbach.

[71] P. 24. See note 68, *supra*. This belief ties in with d'Holbach's uncompromising defense of truth, in the controversy over the values of truth and falsehood.

[72] P. 117.

men were only slightly inclined to evil. In the "state of laws," they are necessarily evil, because laws contradict their desires. But in the anarchic state, or *"état de moeurs,"* of which he is the proponent, there would be none of the rivalry or factitious passions which "make of us the most unreasonable animal species," and we could not be evil. The results of these factitious appetites have been the development of man's intelligence and everything excessive that he does. "His morality is so insane, that, physical being though he is, he seems to form a *genre à part* and to be of another nature than the physical. Whence the idea which we have, that he is indeed of another nature." [73]

A second figure is Charles Lévesque, who in 1775 published a book entitled *L'homme moral.*[74] Lévesque was clearly influenced by Rousseau, as well as by the sensualists. Man, according to him, is born *ni bon ni méchant,* since he is born without ideas. In the state of nature, he thought only of satisfying his needs—or rather, he *felt,* since he could not reason. He had therefore no moral notions, no respect for property, no relationship with others. Then he acquired ideas, and mostly false ideas. Once he has reached that point, a man's inclinations will always be determined "by the way in which he considers his interests." Consequently, to make man good *again* (*sic*), what we have to do is rid him of his imaginary self-interest. Lévesque concludes that men must either give up living together, or give up their freedom and submit to repression—such are the vices of their nature. "Men infect each other, when they touch each other too closely." Like Rousseau and Morelly, Lévesque blames an acquisitive society—but he envisages no other.

Rivarol also fits within the logic of this position. Natural goodness is an imaginary entity.

Man is born with physically good organs and useful needs; but there is nothing moral in that; if he were born good or evil, he would be born a man fully made and determined; nothing could convert him or pervert him. But man is born able to become just or unjust, and especially to be both, and in general, to be good and evil in mediocrity.[75]

[73] *Le vrai système,* p. 105–106.
[74] P. 33–40, 106.
[75] *De l'homme intellectuel et moral* (1800), in *Oeuvres choisies,* ed. de Lescure, I, 212. Rivarol does not deny that men are capable of virtuous deeds (I, 135).

Rivarol, with little confidence in man, nonetheless reserves a wide field to the powers of conditioning and coercion, thereby justifying his political authoritarianism.

The belief that men are born neither good nor evil by a necessary and natural predetermination dominates in the *Encyclopédie* and was shared by a large number of writers. René Hubert has shown that to a certain degree the *philosophes'* primitivism is deceptive. Many writers, including Jaucourt and Diderot, acknowledged or even emphasized the vices and aberrations of primitive peoples. They could not really believe in man's *bonté originelle,* because they did not believe in an "original" human nature which "fell" and was corrupted. Primitive society, no matter how primitive, is already conducive to vice and corruption, to a greater or lesser extent, and there is no earlier human nature to talk about. In other words, man in himself is not a rigidly defined being, but rather, as Diderot wrote in the *Rêve de d'Alembert,* an ensemble of faculties and tendencies. It means nothing to speak of these as developing "normally," since they will respond to precise situations that differ widely, and will conflict among themselves, as self-interest and compassion, for instance, are bound to do. Yet, paradoxically perhaps, we may properly speak of human nature as being depraved or corrupted, when this development is harmful to the self or to others, or contradicts what we feel man might have been.[76] As Gilbert Chinard has noted, the problem for Helvétius and d'Holbach, for instance, "is not to bring man back to a [moral] goodness which he never knew in the state of nature, but to the innocence from which he has strayed, under the influence of charlatans who have invented religion and ambitious men who have invented government. . . ."[77] Thus Morelly satirizes philosophers who have given men innate vices and virtues, as well as innate ideas of virtue and vice, and who have put within his breast "the fateful seeds of depravity which impel him to seek his good at the ex-

[76] Although I do not agree with all of Hubert's analysis, his summary of this concept of man's nature is excellent. "He is only a faculty of receiving impressions, a tendency to seek them and retain them. Morally man is capable of justice and virtue, but the tendency of a being to affirm itself, which is the principle of all forms of life, may lead equally to egoism, to rivalry among individuals, to inequity and to vice." (*Op. cit.,* p. 173–174.) The influence of Spinoza and Condillac is particularly evident in this summary.

[77] Morelly, *Code de la nature,* p. 162 n.

pense of all his race and the entire universe, if it were possible."
Man, he contends, is born only with faculties enabling him to
acquire all of these.[78] This is also Rousseau's basic opinion, though
it is not possible to harmonize all his statements. Hence, for all
these thinkers, the molding and conditioning powers of society
are of supreme importance—a view which Diderot, in his *Réfutation d'Helvétius,* was to criticize because of the limits imposed
by heredity.

Although the names of the four most famous of the *philosophes*
have frequently come into this discussion, it would be well, at this
point, to examine some of their ideas more closely. This is particularly important in regard to Rousseau. His opinions on man's
goodness, frequently debated, have frequently been misunderstood, and I have reserved a general discussion of them until this
point in our survey.

Montesquieu's principal statement comes early in his work, in
the episode of the Troglodytes.[79] The story is developed by Usbek,
in reply to his friend's request for a justification of his earlier
opinion, "that men were born to be virtuous." There is, then, a
fusion of two separate questions in this episode. Montesquieu not
only paints men as naturally good, but contrary to the distinction
Rousseau was later to make between goodness and virtue, he attributes to them a concomitant knowledge of moral distinctions
and obligations. We must further emphasize the fact that Montesquieu presents us two groups of Troglodytes. The first are a
supposed incarnation of the Hobbesian concept of human nature
(or, *mutatis mutandis,* of Sade's). Montesquieu, in this part, shows
how utter selfishness leads to self-destruction; a society based on
pure egoism is not viable. The annihilation of the Troglodytes
spares two families, who were "very strange." They were innocently good, affectionate and benevolent; they worked willingly
for the common good, and found their pleasure in virtue, of which
they had a natural knowledge and perception. These Troglodytes,
possessing both moral knowledge and moral will, form a happy
and prosperous society, one which proves that all virtues do not
derive from selfish motives, and that happiness never does. But

---

[78] *Ibid.,* p. 161–162.
[79] *Lettres persanes* (1721), Lettres XI–XIV. For an excellent study of this question,
see A. S. Crisafulli, "Montesquieu's Story of the Troglodytes."

Montesquieu shows, as Rousseau was also to do in his *Discours sur l'inégalité,* that the state of innocence is a temporary one.[80] As social and economic structure becomes more complex, the Troglodytes find it necessary to develop at least mildly coercive political mechanisms, and to add utilitarian motivations to their natural propensities toward altruism and social welfare. With these aids, it is possible for natural virtue to survive in an artificial society.

The apologue of the Troglodytes does not really pretend to prove that men are naturally good. Its first purpose is to show that the concept of human nature as radically evil is not the only possible assumption; that it is, in fact, an impossible one. In view of the persistence of functional societies, it is equally *possible* to assume an original human nature that is innocently good and altruistic—even though present reality indicates degeneration from such a state and the need to cope with human selfishness. The episode of the Troglodytes is an abstract reconstruction, a lesson in what might be, or what might have been. Another alternative is set up against Hobbes, as an equally plausible, or perhaps a more plausible assumption to explain the origination and the continuance of societies. Most important of all, perhaps, Montesquieu, before Rousseau and Morelly, emphasizes the possibility, and indeed the necessity, of a society based on cooperation, in preference to a society motivated by competition and self-seeking. This outlook stands in opposition to the theories of Mandeville, to those of the Physiocrats, and to the tide of nascent laissez-faire capitalism.

Montesquieu is essentially a realist. In the Troglodyte apologue, he does not lose sight of the power of self-interest, and of its struggle against good and moral impulses. In a later part of the *Lettres persanes,* he emphasizes this conflict, and especially the separation between knowing the good and willing it. Men will not do evil gratuitously, for its own sake, but they will do it for *their* own sake.

It is true that men do not always see these relations; often, even when they see them, they turn away from them; and their in-

[80] "This is clearly recognized by Montesquieu in 'Letter 83' where he states that if men are not always just, it is because the voice of justice is often drowned by passions and by stronger feelings of self-interest." (Crisafulli, p. 387.)

terest is always what they see best. Justice raises her voice; but she has difficulty making herself heard in the tumult of passions . . . nobody is evil gratuitously: there must always be a determining reason; and that reason is always a reason of self-interest.[81]

The *Esprit des lois* (1748) reveals no significant change in Montesquieu's realistic views on the combination of good and evil in human nature. He admits men may be good in an abstract state of nature, or in a primitive relationship. But as soon as they form an organized society, "they seek to turn in their own favor the principal advantages of that society, which produces a state of war among them." Laws and government become necessary.[82] Montesquieu thus reverses Hobbes. Society favors the development of certain selfish tendencies that become evil because of the harm they do to others. Because the combination of good and evil in men is shifting, and because they are malleable, Montesquieu sees the necessity of different forms of government based on different moral principles. Democracy, relying on virtue, assumes that they are capable of far more than self-love, that they are capable of living in a cooperative society. Monarchy, depending on honor, that is, on the desire for distinction, utilizes self-love for the betterment of a competitive society. We have already noted that Montesquieu considers this form of government to be the most practical, because non-selfish virtues are not to be depended on, though it is ideally inferior to democracy. The system of checks and balances, which he considers necessary to liberty (and which he perhaps intends to apply to democracies also) relies not on the goodness of human nature, but on competition among rather selfishly inclined men. "Ambition," James Madison was to say, "must be made to counteract ambition." [83] As for despotism, which relies on fear, it can only be considered as destructive to all virtue, and even, in a sense, to self-interest.

We have followed the general course of Voltaire's thought, as well as the oscillation of his feelings, in regard to the evaluation of human nature. However, since the general tenor of my earlier analysis laid considerable weight—and properly, I think—on his increasing pessimism, it would not be inappropriate, in this chap-

[81] P. 213.
[82] Livre I, ch. 3.
[83] Havens, *op. cit.*, p. 155.

ter, to emphasize a bit further the more optimistic aspects. Again, what we are considering is not man's moral knowledge, but his will and capacity. The most important element of optimism in Voltaire's evaluation is his persistent rejection of the doctrine of original sin, and consequently, of natural depravity. This is a central point in his humanistic opposition to Christianity, and to Pascal in particular. To be sure, Voltaire's own pessimistic pronouncements often sound perilously close to this very doctrine, but there is an important distinction to be made. Voltaire's unalterable opposition is to the absolute derogation of human nature implied in the theological doctrine, with its consequent dependence on divine grace, mediated through the Church. In society, Voltaire would hold, men are evil, because they become so. It is not impossible that under other conditions they might become good. "Man is not born evil; he becomes it. . . . You have at most on earth, in the stormiest times, one man in a thousand who can be called evil, and even he is not always so." [84] And again: "Man is not born evil; he becomes it, as he becomes ill." [85] Evil is a pathological state, to which men are, indeed, very prone. Unfortunately, the depth and import of Voltaire's philosophy suffer from his defense of the prevailing society and its basic values (notwithstanding his attack on particular abuses), and from his failure to take up the ultimate challenge implied in his defense of human nature. His attitude was essentially pragmatic; he was anxious only to bring about those reforms which seemed feasible within an immediately foreseeable future.

With Diderot, too, we have seen the alternating moods, and examined his pessimism. We should not forget that he wrote that man is the most ferocious animal, and the only cruel one.[87]

---

[84] *Dictionnaire philosophique*, Art. "Méchant," *Oeuvres*, xx, 53–56. Also, xxvii, 338.

[85] Art. "Méchant," xx, 83–86. A more complete and definitive statement of the good and evil Voltaire sees in men is contained in the article "Homme" (xix, 373–385). He specifically blames "education, example and the government" into which men find themselves thrown, and chance, which often determines a man one way or the other. He repeats the same judgment in his *Notebooks* (i, 382), referring here to the innocence of children and the generosity of young people. "Pity is in all hearts." In an earlier work, the *Traité de métaphysique* (1734), Voltaire asserted that *bienveillance* for others of his species is one of man's three natural instincts, self-love and reproduction being the others; it is a distinctively human trait.

[87] Art. "Féroce."

His emotional nature, however, led him to moments of enthusiastic rapture such as Voltaire was not inclined to. Much depended on the stimulus of the moment. On hearing a tale of heroism, he exclaims,

> No, my dear, nature did not make us bad; it is bad education, bad examples, bad legislation that corrupt us. If that is an error, at least I am satisfied to find it at the bottom of my heart, and I should sorely regret it if experience or reflection ever disillusioned me. What should I become? I should either have to live alone, or else believe myself continually surrounded by wicked men.[88]

Voltaire and the deists began their defense of man by rejecting outright the dogma of original sin. Diderot scarcely considered it worth refuting.[89] He was more concerned—when not pursuing materialistic paradoxes—with establishing his belief that man loves the good. This was for him an article of faith. He gives it most revealing expression in a letter to Sophie Volland describing a heated discussion among the encyclopedists.

> We tore each others' eyes out, Helvétius, Saurin and I. Last night they claimed that there were men who had no feeling of rectitude and no idea of immortality. . . . I admitted freely that fear of resentment was indeed the strongest dike against wickedness, but I insisted on joining to this motive another which arose from the very essence of virtue, if virtue was not to be a word. I insisted that its imprint was never entirely effaced, even in the most degraded souls; I insisted that a man who preferred his own interest to the public good must feel more or less that there was something better to be done, and that he must esteem himself less for not having the strength to sacrifice himself; I tried to say that, since a person could not make himself mad at will, neither could he make himself wicked; that if order was something, one could never succeed in ignoring it as if it were nothing; that however one might pretend to scorn posterity, there was no one who would not suffer a little when assured that those whom he would not hear would say of him that he was a scoundrel.[90]

---

[88] *Correspondance,* éd. Roth, III, 226. It is likely that, in this last thought, Diderot had Rousseau in mind. He goes on to blame religion for human cruelty.

[89] He makes only a mocking reference to it in an early work, *La Promenade du sceptique* (*Oeuvres,* I, 201), and elsewhere in a footnote (II, 98).

[90] 1er décembre 1760, *Correspondance,* ed. Roth, III, 281.

This optimism about human nature is recurrent in Diderot's writings.[91] Lying in between it and the pessimism we observed earlier, is an adherence to a middle ground. Men do feel pity and sympathy, and this is a great source of happiness for them.[92] But at the same time, rivalry and competition are inevitable in the pursuit for self-fulfillment, and men can therefore desire the hurt of those who are most like themselves.[93] This view, which we noted in Saint-Mard and others, is a secular version of the Christian dualism. For Diderot, too, the balance can be turned by social factors. In his Dedication of the *Père de famille*, Diderot declares his belief in two equal forces in man, self-love and benevolence. Both are proper, and the great ethical problem in life is to establish "a just relationship between these two motives of our life." Men are evil, but are capable of good: "Remember . . . that men would not need to be governed if they were not wicked; and that, consequently, the purpose of all authority must be to make them good." [94] But in either direction, there are limits; man can go, or be led, only so far.[95] We have seen that these opinions were held by a large group of writers.

Diderot's moralistic reaction against his materialistic comrades, La Mettrie (from whom he borrowed many ideas), and Helvétius, is at times dramatic. In his last major work, *Essai sur les règnes de Claude et de Néron* (1778–1782), he excoriates La Mettrie's character and writings, accusing him of vilifying mankind in his *Traité du bonheur*, which holds that "man is perverse by his

[91] See article "Passions," xvi, 211 f., and the following from the Second *Entretien sur le Fils naturel*. "When I see a scoundrel capable of a heroic action, I remain convinced that good men are more truly good than wicked men are truly wicked; that goodness is more inseparably a part of us than wickedness; and that, in general, there remains more goodness of heart in the soul of a wicked man, than wickedness in the soul of good men." (vii, 127–128).

[92] *Lettres à Sophie Volland*, ii, 280. Diderot's faith has deep roots in his early study of Shaftesbury. Although he later spurned the latter's moral sense theory and innatism, the distinction between man and animal in motivation remains strong in his heart. Shaftesbury maintained that sympathy or compassion is not a physical reaction of pleasure or pain. Diderot comes to believe that sympathy is an accompaniment of self-love, but he never ceases to praise acts of altruism and self-sacrifice.

[93] Art. "Droit naturel," "Homme."

[94] vii, 181 f.

[95] Art. "Hobbisme," xv, 122–123. Both Hobbes and Rousseau go to improper extremes, he asserts. "Between the system of one and the other, there is another, which is perhaps the true one. The fact is that although the state of the human species is in perpetual change, its goodness and wickedness are the same: its happiness and its unhappiness circumscribed by limits it cannot cross."

nature, and which makes of the nature of beings, moreover, the rule of their duties and the source of their happiness." [96] The significance of these lines should not be overlooked. Faced with a choice between naturalistic materialism and morality, Diderot, in the last analysis, sacrifices the former.

The most important and original statement of Diderot's position is the one he had developed in the *Réfutation d'Helvétius*.[96a] We have already observed how he was repelled by the materialistic reduction of man to the physical. Without abandoning materialism, he seeks to enlarge it and to surpass the narrow eighteenth century concepts. In the article "Fin," he had written, "Take a man from motive to motive, and you will find that his personal happiness is always the final end of all his purposeful acts." Diderot's refutation of Helvétius does not contradict this basic position. His entire purpose is to argue that man acts and exists on a truly moral level, as well as on a physical level, and that the first is not reducible to the second. There are two orders of pleasure: these are not moral and immoral, but physical and moral. It is not, then, the reduction to pleasure and pain to which he takes objection, but rather the reduction of these motives to the physical, or to the lowest common denominator.

> . . . I am a man, and I insist on causes appropriate to man . . . Of what use is a series of consequences which are equally applicable to the dog, the weasel, the oyster, the dromedary? . . .
> Is it certain that physical pleasure and pain, perhaps the only principles of action in the animal, are also the only principles of the actions of man? . . . I would be taking the condition of all animal action in general to be the motive of the action of an individual of an animal species called man. All that I do, I do assuredly in order to feel agreeably, or for fear of feeling painfully; but does the word feel have only one meaning? Is there only physical pleasure in possessing a beautiful woman? Is there only physical pain in losing her by death or inconstancy?
> Isn't the distinction between the physical and the moral as solid as that between an animal that feels and an animal that reasons? [97]

---

[96] *Oeuvres*, III, 217.

[96a] Written at intervals between 1773 and 1776.

[97] There is an interesting parallel between Diderot's refutation of Helvétius, and Spinoza's argumentation in Prop. XVII of the third part of the *Ethic*. After establishing that all affects are related to desire, joy and sorrow, Spinoza, in the Scholium, asserts that the affects of animals "differ from human affects as much as the nature

Like most others in his time, Diderot was impressed with man's duality, his capacity for great good and great evil. We see in Diderot's work his belief that men could not escape the knowledge of good and evil, or love for the one and aversion for the other. But this belief is an aspiration, unable to free itself from the reality of the human situation. Man is immersed and entangled in nature, whose only right is of the strong, only value success, and only law selfishness. If Diderot's logic often cast him on the side of the beasts, his heart and his humanism always put him on the side of the angels. To the point where, in moments of primitivism, his faith in man's goodness leads him to favor a Lahontan-type of semi-anarchism, in which the impulses of nature would alone prevail, trusting that these impulses would not be the ones that society has nourished (impulses typified in his portrait of Rameau's nephew), but rather those of innocence.

With Rousseau's attitude, or attitudes, towards man's goodness, we enter into a problem that has understandably perplexed innumerable readers and critics. Part of the difficulty derives from confusing the idea that man is naturally good with the idea that man is naturally moral. Rousseau himself took some care to separate these two notions; yet, it must be confessed, he at times writes in such a way as to lead others to confuse them, if indeed, he did not do so himself. The deep sense of his whole work is to separate them.[98] Consequently Delvolvé errs in concluding that "the optimistic finalism of Shaftesbury . . . will end up, in Rousseau, with the rehabilitation and exaltation of sensitivity, with faith in primitive instincts, with the perfection of the state of nature." [99] Rousseau does not trust the feelings or passions, does not believe the state of nature to be the perfect state, and will not let individual instincts have their sway in society. This is why his work, though it deceptively sets out from a similar criticism of society as that

of a brute differs from that of a man. Both the man and the horse, for example, are swayed by the lust to propagate, but the horse is swayed by equine lust and the man by that which is human. . . . Finally, it follows from the preceding proposition that the joy by which the drunkard is enslaved is altogether different from the joy which is the portion of the philosopher. . . ."

[98] Compare Shaftesbury, who on the contrary, had made no such distinction, holding that man's nature is good and so tends spontaneously to virtue and social harmony.

[99] *Op. cit.*, p. 104–105, n. 3.

of Dom Deschamps and certain primitivists, terminates at the opposite pole, and bears more analogy to that of Morelly.

Rousseau's principal writing on the subject is his *Discours sur l'origine de l'inégalité*. It is the most developed, the most original, and the most clearly thought out. In contrast to later statements that are often brief, emotional and defensive, this one is reasoned, systematic and part of a total philosophical view.

Let us first examine what Rousseau says in regard to the goodness of man in the original state of nature, which he conceives of as a pre-social state of individual isolation and independence. Since society, according to Rousseau, is a deformation of man's original nature, we cannot judge of this nature until we go back in our minds to a hypothetical uncontaminated man. Such a man is not, properly speaking, a human being, but beast-like. He lacks speech and abstract thought, which develop from social relations. He is incapable of moral judgments, since these, too, derive from social relations, as well as from reason.[100] Original man is not, therefore, a moral being by nature; he is only what Dr. Lovejoy has called "a non-moral but good-natured brute." He owns all the qualities of a moral being only *in potentia,* eventually to be awakened when the principal human trait he does presently possess is set into motion: that is, perfectibility, an attribute of intelligence which is associated with his unique freedom and consciousness of freedom. The fact that the moment at which man leaves the state of nature is the moment at which this distinctive quality comes into play signifies that the state of nature is a condition in which man is like other animals.[101]

Like other animals, this original of man is not what *we* should call evil. That is, although his actions are motivated by exclusive concern with his own comfort, safety and well-being, he will not

[100] In the *Préface,* Rousseau defines a moral being as one who is "intelligent, free, and considered in his relations with other beings." *Discours sur l'inégalité,* in Vaughan, I, 137. Rousseau will later reaffirm his belief that men become moral in society.

[101] Dr. Lovejoy concludes, with perfect logic, that one cannot therefore speak of a "degeneration" from this state. Rousseau, however, does ("thinking man is a depraved animal"), for reasons that will become obvious in this discussion. See A. O. Lovejoy, "The Supposed Primitivism of Rousseau's *Discourse on Inequality.*" In this article, Dr. Lovejoy has already pointed out, in a somewhat different fashion, Rousseau's emphasis on the evil in human nature. My own conclusions were reached independently.

purposely hurt others; whereas social man, as Rousseau goes on to show, necessarily finds his self-interest and pleasure in so doing. On the other hand, he does possess a second human trait: a biological reaction of pity for his fellows in distress. Both these qualities, self-interest and compassion, are pre-moral.[102] There is no judgment of right or wrong, no impulse whatsoever to sacrifice one's own good for the sake of another. This original man will, without hesitation, hurt others when it is necessary for his advantage—though Rousseau assures us that such occasions would be rare. He will, as Rousseau puts it, do his own good with the least harm to others. He will help those who need him, when he can do so with no cost to himself.[103]

Much of the difficulty in understanding Rousseau's thought lies in a double semantic confusion. The first confusion inheres in the words "good" and "virtuous." While Rousseau separates these two qualities (though not so sharply in the *Discours* as in later writings), it is very difficult for us to think of man as "good" without thinking of *moral good*. On the other hand, Rousseau's natural self-love is not evil; but it does turn evil, under social conditions, when knowledge of right and wrong, unnecessary hurt to others, and moral effort or struggle become involved. In consequence of this chain of definitions and postulates, Rousseau can

---

[102] Mandeville had said that pity resembles virtue, "but as it is an impulse of nature, that consults neither the public interest nor our own reason, it may produce evil as well as good." (*Fable of the Bees*, 1, 42.) The same idea is found in Condillac. "Through instinct alone men asked and gave help to one another. I say, 'By instinct alone,' because reflection could not yet play any part in it. The one did not say, 'It is necessary for me to act in such and such a manner in order to make known what I need, and in order to get him to help me,' nor the other, 'I see by his movements that he wants such and such a thing, I am going to give him possession of it,' but both acted in consequence of the need which urged them on." (Quoted by Ch. Frankel, *op. cit.*, p. 53.)

[103] Anthropologists properly reject Rousseau's concept of the state of nature, and affirm that men have always been social animals. Aristotle states that man is a social animal more than any bee or ant, because without living in community with other human beings he cannot even become a human being. Rousseau is consistent and logical, in the sense that the creature he paints is not really man, but a pre-human being. He is illogical, in taking this pre-human creature as the point of reference to judge the nature of "fully" human beings, since the implication is perfectly clear that men do not become human beings until they develop consistent relationships. Rousseau doubtless means that this is what men would be, even now, if they were to grow up in isolation, or if the nature with which they are born were left to blossom by itself. Fundamentally, Rousseau is wrong, inasmuch as the evolution of animals testifies to the fact that social living preceded even the pre-moral qualities of which he speaks.

assert that man is "naturally good," and that he becomes evil in society, the reader taking him to mean (in fact, Rousseau later sometimes seems to take himself to mean) that man is *morally* good by nature; whereas both the qualities he has postulated (self-love and pity) are *pre-moral*.

The second semantic confusion enters at this point. While we may set up two words for Rousseau's concepts of "good" and "morally good" ("virtuous"), we have only one word for "evil," with no pre-moral analogue. Consequently, when Rousseau asserts that man becomes evil in society, he leaves the assumption that there was no correlative of evil in man's original nature, corresponding to the pre-moral "natural goodness" that is the correlative of moral goodness. This is a fallacious impression. Evil has its analogous correlative, in pre-moral self-love.

The following diagram will perhaps help to clarify the true relationships of ideas. (The solid arrows represent the proper progression implied by Rousseau's theory. The broken arrow represents Rousseau's partial, or fallacious formulation which is apparently implied when he says "man was good, society has made him evil.")

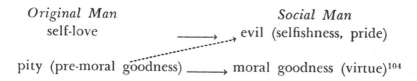

Original Man *Social Man*
self-love   ⟶ evil (selfishness, pride)

pity (pre-moral goodness) ⟶ moral goodness (virtue)[104]

To say "man was naturally good and society has corrupted him" is as illogical—and as meaningless—as to say, "man was evil and society has made him good." Both statements are meaningless, because they lack a common element, and exist in two separate frames of reference, the pre-moral and the moral. What Rousseau could properly say, according to his own account, is that man has progressed from one frame of reference to the other. To be rigorous, we should have to formulate his theory somewhat as follows. The original nature of man (or of the clever primate which he was originally), being devoid of moral judg-

---

[104] Rousseau does not trace the psychological origin of moral goodness in the *Discours*. In the *Profession de foi*, however, he makes it clear that the impulse to moral goodness springs from innate good will, a "voix intérieure." This is not unrelated to ego-satisfactions; but the latter are moral satisfactions, and not those which belong to innate (pre-moral) self-love. (*Emile*, p. 348–354).

ments, is neither morally good nor morally evil. It has egoistic and altruistic tendencies, self-directed and other-directed motives. Evil is inevitably developed by society, through the processes of self-consciousness, the habit of comparison and the cultivation of *amour-propre* as distinguished from *amour de soi*. The significant point is that hurting others comes into being as soon as a man has to deal with other men. Equally important is the fact that this condition does not exclude men's having good impulses towards each other, as well: social relations lead also to judgments of right and wrong, and to the moral conscience. In society, virtue is also developed; that is, the suppression of the egoistic impulse (which must necessarily achieve its goal at others' expense), in the light of moral law. But it is rarer and more difficult to cultivate, requiring special care and favorable circumstances. Since man is *naturally* social ("naturally," not in Rousseau's sense of "originally," now, but in the implied sense of "inevitably" [105]), Rousseau's real thought is that man is "naturally" (but not "originally") evil. He is also, in the same sense, "naturally" moral; but the evil is dominant, and therefore men in society are predominantly evil. "Men are wicked, a sad and continual experience makes the proof superfluous." Rousseau several times assures us, in his writings, referring both to others and to himself, that we can be "good" (i.e., admire and desire the good), even as we do wrong, and act as wicked men.[106] This is not moral goodness, then; and man does not naturally possess it, since, to achieve it, he must conquer himself. To put it succinctly, men in society are necessarily wicked, and men must be in society. Man, as soon as he becomes man, is evil; but he is a moral being, aware of good *and* evil. It is this idea alone that can explain the meaning and direction of Rousseau's work.

Consequently, the central problem and principal subject of his writings will be the ways of diminishing and controlling this evil, and of changing the balance by artificial means. Sade's philosophy is truly implicit in Rousseau's; but Jean-Jacques shunned his conclusions and desperately sought a way out, through perspectives

[105] This is clear not only in the *Discours,* but in later writings, e.g., the *Profession de foi (ibid.,* p. 354): "Man is sociable by his nature, or at least made to become it."

[106] "I see the good, I love it, and I do the wrong." (*Emile,* II, 249 ff.)

on the past and on the future.[107] From Rousseau's point of view, the important thing is that there is not an absolute or ontological identity between the "original nature" and what it becomes. The child does *become* something. Even if evil is a necessary outcome of virtual and latent characteristics, the fact that an intermediate developmental *process* is involved allows the possibility of intervention—of conditioning—so that a wide latitude for character-formation exists. (This is also the basis of modern psychoanalytic theory.)

Natural man, then, is not what Rousseau thinks man should be. Jean-Jacques harbored some sentimental, primitivist regrets for a lost state of innocence; and, as Dr. Lovejoy has written, "he was not emancipated from the assumption of 'natural' as excellent *per se*," nor from the eulogistic, deistic usage of the word to indicate an uncorrupted model. Nevertheless, there is no doubt that he preferred the state of inner conflict which impels us to live on the moral level. Civilized man is at least capable of acting as a rational being, determined by justice, while the original man was

[107] It seems that Rousseau would often wish us to conclude from his thought that while man in society is evil, this is not his true nature. What he has demonstrated, however—accepting his premises—is that wickedness is not his *original* nature, but that it is his *true* nature, since his true nature is specifically the freedom and perfectibility that produce the wickedness. Or else we must admit that man must be *defined* as an amoral, or premoral creature, which Rousseau himself would never have allowed. As Dr. Lovejoy has put it, "It is therefore as true to say that Rousseau teaches the *méchanceté naturelle*, as to say that he teaches the *bonté naturelle* of man; and the former teaching is the more significant of the two since it alone relates to what is 'distinctive' in man's nature" (*op. cit.*, p. 178). Of course, we must not forget the compassion which is also natural and distinctive. Nonetheless, the source of evil is in human nature.

Morelly, writing in the same year as Rousseau (1755), points out the essential identity between the view that men are born wicked, and the view that, because of their nature and the circumstances of life, they inevitably become wicked. Rousseau, like Morelly, pins his hopes on the "freedom" or malleability of human nature, and on the possibility of developing more favorable circumstances. (See *Code de la nature,* p. 159 ff). Morelly also sees the basic human nature as premoral, therefore not evil. The view of man's detractors, especially Sade, like the later theory of Freud, is the contrary. They held, as Morelly puts it, that man "bears within his breast the fatal seeds of depravity that impel him to seek his good at the expense of his species, and of the entire universe, if it were possible." Both Rousseau and Morelly err in thinking they have succeeded in escaping the noose by attributing this wickedness to a social development, general in the case of the former, specific in the case of the latter. As Reinhold Niebuhr has remarked, if man believes himself essentially good, and attributes evils to social and historical causes, he is begging the question. These causes are "no more than particular consequences and historical configurations of evil tendencies in man himself." A capacity for, and an inclination toward evil are presupposed. (*Op. cit,* I, 2.)

"a stupid and limited animal," a slave to his impulses. For man to place himself on the level of beasts, "which are the slaves of instinct," would be "to degrade human nature." [108] What Rousseau longed for most of all was to prove that man is not born wicked in his given nature. He would then be able to refute both the doctrine of original sin and the cynicism of certain *philosophes*. In opposition to the Church's original perversity, he proposed original innocence, to which is added "inevitable perversity," but one which may yet—in view of the original innocence—be checked or modified. He thought he could then, like the Christians, free God from the onus of evil and preserve faith in divine providence. At the same time, man, and his own conscience, were also to be relieved, by this new theodicy, of their burden of guilt. And the dream of a better world, of happiness, was not shut out.[109]

All his life, Rousseau was haunted and depressed by the evil in man—in others, and in himself. To begin with, he could not completely escape the grip of Calvinism. But the effective confirmation came in his own life; the injustices (genuine and fancied)

[108] Important confirmation of this view is given in the first version of the *Contrat Social* (Vaughan, I, 448–449). There has never been an ideal society in the past; this is for us to create.

[109] It seems, then, that "naturally good," in one sense, is similar to the Christian idea, in its concept of an innocent, non-historical past, before the Fall, and in another sense—that of the unspoiled babe—is opposed to the Christian doctrine of innate depravity. When Rousseau speaks of man being naturally good, he refers to this ontologically "real" human nature, innocent, unmindful of evil. He must insist that this man is not a social being, or else the ontological basis of a non-evil human nature disappears. Rousseau's theory also agrees with Christian doctrine in affirming that man, in the context of history and society, is inevitably evil (omitting, of course, the help of grace). Dr. Lovejoy excludes the psychological meaning of "naturally good" from Rousseau's hypothesis, and considers it a later confusion in his thinking between an anthropological culture stage and the native psychological endowment of infants. A passage in the *Préface*, however, seems to indicate that he had both ideas in mind: "it is no light enterprise to disentangle what is *original* from what is artificial in the *present* state of man, and to know well a state which exists no longer, which perhaps never existed, which probably will never exist, and about which we must nonetheless acquire accurate notions *in order to judge properly of our present state*." [Italics added.] Assuredly, it would not be necessary to know the past, or original, condition of man in order to understand his nature now, and what is "natural" in it, unless the pre-social man in the state of nature and the pre-social child were equivalent transpositions, the former being a useful hypothesis to illuminate the latter. Rousseau's frequent "natural-artificial" antithesis, in writing about social man, also indicates the transposition. Assuredly, the child, like "original man," is both self-interested and innocently amoral. Rousseau is thus enabled to contemplate man free of the historical and contingent, in his "essential" nature. It is, of course, dubious that man, in infancy, is "man as he really is"; this qualification belongs rather to what he becomes, when his virtualities are developed.

which he suffered, and his unhappiness, had, he was convinced, no other cause. Man has spoiled everything. Man's nature is such that he had to become civilized, and thus to corrupt himself and all about him. At the same time, Rousseau was oppressed by his own guilt. This wickedness in himself, this guilt, he could not understand, for he felt his own good impulses and his love of virtue. There was only one explanation, one way out. He had to prove that man is not inherently or essentially evil, but has been made so. Consequently, he imagines him outside of society, an unsocial creature, a human animal who has not yet tasted of the tree of knowledge of good and evil. Thus man (including Jean-Jacques) is innocent, yet destined by his own virtualities to fall, when he commits the "original sin" of society. "As soon as I lost sight of men, I ceased to despise them; as soon as I lost sight of the wicked, I ceased to hate them. . . . I became again shy, courteous and timid, in a word, the same Jean-Jacques I had been before." [110] If Rousseau had not been obsessed with man's wickedness, he would not have pursued the dream of a state, past or future, in which man is a different being from the one we know. His struggle was to escape from the Calvinist idea of depravity, and from his own sense of guilt. Hence the desperate flights from original sin, from society, and from his own vices and failures, through the hypothetical state, and hypothetical nature, of men who existed free of the corruption which living with other men must bring about.

The ground for Rousseau's optimism lies only partly in his belief that man, considered in a situation prior to society, has no wicked impulses towards his fellows (which is all his theory really asserts). His optimism is grounded also in this other belief: it is only what might be called "natural society" that depraves man— by which term I mean the society which is formed in the inevitable course of history under the pressure of men's evil instincts. This "natural society" is the society which Rousseau calls "artificial," because he is contrasting it with the "original," pre-social state. Because this "natural society" inevitably depraves man, as described in the *Discours sur l'inégalité*, Rousseau deems it essential to create a *truly* artificial society—that is, one designed with intention and forethought—in order to dominate the natural evil in

[110] *Confessions,* Livre IX.

us, and favor the good. Men grow more evil and unhappy as
society grows more complex, and as artificial needs increase. But
they are not fatally condemned to this. They may yet control their
own cultural evolution. This is the faith of Rousseau, and it is the
faith of the Enlightenment, with which Rousseau seems so often
to quarrel.

Because of his concept of human nature, Rousseau opposed the
moral and political program of the Encyclopedists, which was based
largely on frank exploitation of invincible egoism, and that of
the Physiocrats, which held that egoistic forces, if allowed free
play, would work out to a natural harmony. His purpose was to
attenuate the force of egoism, to annul its social effects, by the
creation of an artificial, or "social" man. Precisely as he had rejected the sensationist reduction of the personality and insisted
on the distinctively human, so he felt that such qualities as
spontaneous sympathy, fraternal cooperation and moral feeling,
which were as real as the motives of pleasure and pain, could
become dominant social factors. But this would never come about
naturally. To achieve it, a complete social, political and educational reorganization was necessary. Individual rights, as an immutable concept of Natural Law, had to be abandoned, and powerful coercive and conditioning forces put at the disposal of the
collectivity, to be used from earliest childhood onward. Rousseau's
theory, though it is more complex and far-reaching than the more
naïve doctrines of Morelly, Helvétius and their compeers, although it traces out an entirely different road, proclaims essentially the same lesson. Our hope lies in conditioning and repressing natural instincts, which are selfish, wicked or unsocial, by
creating the proper societal environment. Since there is no fixed
human nature, since man is malleable, he will respond to the
stimuli of these processes.

Rousseau's opinions on man's goodness, in his other writings,
are usually more fragmentary, and consequently are sometimes
confusing. The majority of his statements, duly considered, do
not infirm our interpretation. In the *Discours sur les sciences et
les arts,* he tells us that in primitive times "human nature, at
bottom, was not better"; and that "men are perverse; they would
be worse still, if they had had the misfortune to be born

learned." [111] By "perverse," Rousseau means that their impulses lead them to desire those things in the denial of which virtue consists—a situation which can exist, of course, only in society. If primitive men had fewer vices, it was only because conditions did not lead to temptation and to destruction of their innocence. Rousseau's *Réponse au roi de Pologne* contains this remark concerning curiosity, which is already pregnant with the whole system he will develop: "He [man] should thus strive to repress it, like all his other natural inclinations." [112] Natural inclinations, harmless in a state of isolation, are dangerous to virtue in society. In the *Lettre à d'Alembert* and in *Emile,* Rousseau's strictures on Molière and La Fontaine again testify to his belief in the wickedness of human nature; for he is certain that both adults and children will, in each case, put the worst, the most vicious interpretation upon the situation presented, regardless of the author's intentions.

In the *Lettre à d'Alembert* Rousseau also declares that love of moral beauty is as innate in us as self-love. "Man's heart is always right about what does not concern him personally. . . . When our self-interest gets involved, our feelings are soon corrupted and it is only then that we prefer the evil that is useful to us to the good that nature makes us love." Obviously, however, *nature* makes us love ourselves first and most.[113] Rousseau's social reform is designed with the hope of a state of things in which there will be no advantage to evil-doing; consistently, he stresses our weakness in love of the good, and the necessity of avoiding temptation. His assertion of man's "goodness" is, as I have said, principally an effort to prove that man is not naturally *perverse;* that is, he does not naturally love evil for its own sake, and derive pleasure from it. Social man, it is true, develops inevitable perversity, but to be good is not *against nature.* It is significant that contrary to the statements of Diderot and Sade which we noted in an earlier chapter, Rousseau exclaims, "He who could be all-powerful (*celui*

---

[111] *Discours sur les sciences et les arts,* ed. George R. Havens, p. 105, 126. See Prof. Havens' explanatory note, p. 184–185.

[112] *Oeuvres,* I, 35.

[113] I, 191–192, 236. Again in the *Confessions* (VIII, 38), Rousseau tells us that we will be naturally evil any time conditions conflict with our own interest. Cf. *Dialogues* (IX, 209), "let nature be still. . . ." In the latter work, he tells us that men should always do the opposite of their desires, "because of the very fact that they desire it."

qui pourrait tout) would never do evil." [114] In other words, assuming natural "goodness" in such a creature, he would do no evil, having no *need* to.

Rousseau's theory also holds, however, that when man becomes fully human, in society, he becomes a moral being; he knows good and evil, and is capable of good, even though evil is dominant. All this is clearly seen in *La Nouvelle Héloïse*. To be sure, when we do good, we are in the deepest sense doing it for ourselves, since it makes us happy to follow our natural longing for the good. The same instinct for happiness carries us to love of the good and to passions that destroy it. Left to ourselves, the passions will triumph over virtue; "for what can all that do against my personal interest, and in the end which matters most to me, my happiness at the expense of the rest of mankind, or the happiness of others at the cost of mine?" Our feelings mislead us; nor can we count on our reason; for reason, corrupted by egoism, corrupts the conscience itself.[115] We must fight, Rousseau warns us, not only against the artificialities and corruptions of society, but against penchants and passions which, non-moral in the state of nature, are vicious in society—even though they are "natural." But here, and elsewhere, Rousseau does not fail to insist on men's compassion and humanity, on his impulsive (or "natural") love of the good purely for its own sake. Julie learns that self-interest is not the only motive of action;[116] and that self-love may be made either good or bad "by the accidents that modify it, which depend on customs, laws, ranks, fortune, and our whole human polity." [117] All this is consistent with the main drift and tenor of Rousseau's work: that virtue is necessary to happiness; and for men to be virtuous, the good in them must be fortified, and the wickedness deterred, by such recourses as belief in a personal, provident God, by proper ways of living, by education and by the institutions of a rationally constructed State.

In *Emile* we read, "It is not true that the inclination to evil is

---

[114] *Emile, Oeuvres*, II, 235.

[115] *La Nouvelle Héloïse*, ed. Mornet, II, 297–298, n. 2; III, 65–85.

[116] In the *Profession de foi*, Rousseau repeats the common argument, "What does it mean, to go to one's death for one's own interest?"

[117] *La Nouvelle Héloïse*, III, 250–251, II, 297–298. All the ideas referred to are stated by Julie de Wolmar, who is Rousseau's *porte-parole* in these parts of the work.

invincible." The word "invincible" implies both the innateness, or inevitability of wickedness, and the belief that it can be overcome. Rousseau's "negative education" similarly implies that although goodness is an innate potentiality in the child, so is evil.

The reader of Rousseau, as is well known, will not obtain from his writings such an impression of logical consistency. As the years advanced, he tended more and more to fragmentary, epigrammatic statements, to the effect that man is naturally good and society has corrupted him. Whether it be due to impatience and reluctance to explain the intricacies of his thought at each moment, or to an increasing polemical sharpness, or even to a confusion in his own thinking, such isolated, facile phrases distort the deeper meanings of his philosophy. And yet, quite understandably, they have been generally taken as its final formulation, and have been the carriers of his influence.

That there are some changes, or divergences, in Rousseau's opinions, is undeniable. He will even occasionally confuse the concepts of man as naturally good and naturally moral, by making conscience, which is (in some of his formulations) the faculty of knowing good and evil, or (in others) the innate love of moral good, a part of *bonté naturelle*. He will stoutly maintain that all our first impulses are *"droites,"* oblivious that this means nothing in view of their absence of context; for innocence cannot exist in a social context, but only morality and immorality. There is, perhaps, no more typical or succinct statement, than the one which occurs in his *Lettre à M. de Beaumont* (1762): ". . . that man is a being naturally good, loving justice and order; that there is no original perversity in the human heart, and that the first impulses of nature are always *droits*." [118] All of this statement, except the phrase "loving justice and order," is consistent with the *Discours sur l'inégalité;* but a casual reading leaves a quite different impression. Rousseau's awareness of the contradiction, and his desire for consistency, are apparent when he asks, almost in objection to his own lines, how man can be called naturally good if his sole innate passion, *amour de soi*, is "indifferent to good or evil." And his explanation is precisely that man is not originally good, but pre-moral; and that his goodness, his moral and spiritual

[118] *Oeuvres,* III, 64.

being, develop only from his relations with others, even as his wickedness does. The rest of the explanation follows the three cultural stages of the *Discours*.

It would be most interesting to follow in detail the vagaries of Rousseau's opinions in all his works. We do not have space for this, and we can afford to spare ourselves the task, in view of the notable series of articles on this subject by George R. Havens.[119]

The real import of Rousseau's "theory of natural goodness," is, then, that social man (i.e., *man*) is naturally wicked; and that he also has knowledge of the moral good and rather weak inclinations to it which it is our problem to encourage in every way. Man is good, but that is not enough; he is also so wicked, that we must look forward to his learning to be virtuous—by which is meant his learning to overcome his wickedness. Thus, in a roundabout and unique way, Rousseau belongs with those who considered man to be both good and evil. His accent is often on the goodness; but paradoxically, this was because he was so profoundly convinced of the evil.

In closing our discussion of this subject, we should take brief note of Kant's chapter, "On the Radical Evil in Human Nature" (1792).[120] It is not my intention to analyze Kant's moral philosophy; but there are several points of relationship with the thought of the French Enlightenment that are worthy of mention.

In his essay, Kant poses the problem of man's nature in the dual form we have examined: "the question is, whether a mean is not at least possible, namely, that man as a species may be neither good nor bad, or at all events that he is as much one as the other, partly good, partly bad?" Kant rejects both formulations. In answering this question, he eliminates the two criteria that were most characteristic of the writers we have studied. On the one hand, he rejects the criterion of actions, since their adherence to or violation of objective moral laws does not necessarily correspond to subjective motives, or "maxims." On the other hand, he rejects equally those impulses or inclinations, altruistic or egoistic, usually called "natural," which determine the elective will (e.g., compassion, or Rousseau's pre-moral "goodness"). De-

---

[119] "La théorie de la bonté naturelle de l'homme chez Jean-Jacques Rousseau."
[120] From *First Part of the Philosophical Theory of Religion*, in T. K. Abbott, *Kant's Critique of Practical Reason and other works*, pp. 325–360.

spite the use of different vocabulary, Kant follows the drift of Rousseau's distinction, and limits moral goodness, or the decision as to whether a man is morally good or bad, to "the rule that the elective will makes for itself for the use of its freedom," that is, its maxim.[121]

For Kant, as for Rousseau, the test of moral goodness comes in a situation in which our knowledge of right, or objective moral law, is in conflict with pleasure, passion, self-interest. A person is good if he follows the former out of free preference—free of coercion, of fear of punishment or remorse, and of desire for reward. We have seen that only a minority of French thinkers considered this possible, and almost none considered it a consistent likelihood, in view of their estimate of human nature. Many believed men were not free, many more believed men could follow only self-interest, and some did not believe in an objective moral law. Men, they concluded, had to be conditioned, coerced, or lured by ultimate self-interest. They were good if their actions coincided with positive law or what was held to be public good; or if they possessed natural (i.e., necessary) altruistic impulses, and followed them. We can apply to them Kant's statement, that they are satisfied "to call a man good who is a bad man of the average class."

We shall not try to follow Kant in his interesting analysis of human nature, but merely note the points of reference to our earlier discussion. Included in his analysis is the non-moral concept of "mechanical self-love," and that of the "vices of culture," which derive from man's rational nature and bring in the peculiarly human characteristic of "estimating oneself as happy or unhappy only in comparison with others." Jealousy, rivalry, and fear of superiority in others result from the latter. A third factor is man's moral nature, his ability to choose the moral law as spring of his will.

In discussing man's propensity to evil, Kant makes some distinctions that are related in interesting fashion to the thought of the French writers of the Enlightenment. He sees three degrees in this propensity: frailty, or weakness in following maxims (Rousseau's "I see the right, I love it, but I do the wrong"); im-

---

[121] That. Rousseau, however, was not able to free himself from an admixture of enlightened self-interest, we shall see later in this study.

purity, or mixture of non-moral motives even in good purposes ("dutiful acts are not done purely from duty"); depravity, or the propensity to adopt bad maxims—which is perversity, as it reverses the moral order, even when the actions performed are legally good.

> For if other springs besides the moral law itself are necessary to determine the elective will to actions conforming to the law (*ex. gr.*, desire of esteem, self-love in general, or even good-natured instincts, such as compassion), then it is a mere accident that they agree with the law, for they might just as well urge to its transgression. The maxim, then, the goodness of which is the measure of all moral worth in the person, is in this case opposed to the law, and while the man's acts are all good, he is nevertheless bad.

Contrary to Rousseau, Kant declares that in the state of nature men do evil for its own sake, without the excuse of advantage. In civilization, they are more vicious: we find conquerors taking satisfaction merely in their superiority; secret falsehood in the most intimate friendship; hatred for benefactors; secret joy in the misfortunes of those we love. Here, then, is the picture we found sketched by man's detractors, the same evaluation which led Sade to draw the conclusion: this is the way men are, therefore this is the way they must be, and should be.

For Kant, however, this badness cannot be imputed, as was usually done, to inclinations springing from sensibility (pleasure and pain). These have no direct reference to badness, and we are not responsible for them. Nor does the cause of wickedness reside in the Reason, for such a malignant Reason would then be the spring for action; it would disown its own moral law and abolish obligation.[122] The first of these two imputations would make of man a mere animal being; the second, a devilish being. Man can never abandon the moral law, as it is part of his essential nature; but it is opposed by his physical nature (sensibility, and self-love, which are blameless in themselves). The evil lies, then, in his subordination of the first to the second, in making self-love the condition of his obedience to moral law. This is Kant's conclusion, and we see how contrary it is to the general drift of eighteenth century

---

[122] This, of course, was precisely Sade's attempt.

French thought, which held that self-interest is the legitimate, best and only way for man to adopt the moral maxim.

There is, then, in human nature this radical propensity to evil; a natural propensity, corrupting the source of all maxims, which cannot be destroyed, and which is rooted in the free elective will. Yet it is possible to *overcome* this propensity. Human depravity is not so much a disposition to adopt the bad as bad (this would make man devilish, as Sade did); it is rather perversity, which makes us look, at best, at the conformity of actions to moral law, not to their derivation from it. Like Rousseau, Kant wonders at the original moral capacity within us:

> What is that in us (we may ask ourselves) by which we, who are constantly dependent on nature by so many wants, are yet raised so far above it in the idea of an original capacity (in us) that we regard them all as nothing, and ourselves as unworthy of existence, if we were to indulge in their satisfaction in opposition to a law which our reason authoritatively prescribes; although it is this enjoyment alone that can make life desirable, while reason neither promises anything nor threatens.

While we shall not try to go into the complexities of the relation between Rousseau and Kant, the following few lines from the *Profession de foi* strike significant echoes:

> The origin (*le principe*) of all [moral] action is in the will of a free being; we cannot go back any further . . . There is then at the bottom of our hearts an innate principle of justice and virtue, by which, despite our own maxims, we judge our actions and those of others as good or bad . . . in meditating on the nature of man, I thought I discovered in it two distinct principles, one of which raised him to the study of eternal truths, to the love of justice and moral beauty, to the regions of the intellectual world whose contemplation is the delight of the sage, the other of which lowered him into himself, enslaved him to the empire of the senses, to the passions which are their ministers, and through them frustrated all that the first feeling inspired in him.

On the basis of a rigorously logical development, Kant has rejected the formula that man is both good and evil. But his theory works out in such a fashion, that many of the French moralists we have discussed would have reached precisely that conclusion from his presentation of the basic phenomena of man's indestructible moral capacity which is always at grips with an innate propensity to pervert it. Like the majority of the French thinkers, Kant finds this propensity both radical and generally triumphant. Unlike them, he will not admit the pragmatic evasions on which they pinned their hopes for making man a "moral being." In all this, we can see how close Kant is to the French Enlightenment—and yet how far beyond it he has gone.

The analysis of human nature performed by eighteenth century moralists left ethics and the problem of values in an impasse. The struggle of these moralists to find a way out, which we shall examine in the second part of this study, was unsuccessful. Its failure left as other possibilities the moral nihilism of Sade, Kant's return to ethical rigorism, or the Romantic return to Catholic absolutes. The choice was between authoritarianism or dogma, and the absurd. The revolt of Western man was to become a concrete reality; but the middle road, the humanistic quest for the realm of justice, was unable to maintain itself against the two extremes, the absolute of the sacred and the absolute of violence. It is significant that Kant and Sade were writing in the same years, at the very close of a century of *philosophie*.

Thirteen

ETHICS AND CHRISTIANITY

THE CONTROVERSY over the relation between ethics and Christianity is of peculiar interest to us at this point of our study. It embodies both a particularized phase of our earlier discussion of man's relation to God, and the results of the reassessment of human nature which we have investigated in the preceding chapters. Its emphasis was less on the theoretical aspects, as in the former controversy, than on the practical. The practical aspect concerned the means of controlling human behavior and of ensuring a moral society. Atheists, and many deists, now claimed that institutional religions were unnecessary, and even harmful to the moral life. These deists, although they dreaded the chaos of any further step (fearing there could be no ethical certitude without a universe that was not itself a moral structure resting on a divine absolute), wished to liberate man from a false "Revelation." But other, more conservative deists, and all who were opposed to the new philosophies, saw in the attack on Christianity a crisis that threatened the moral basis of society. Even if the reality of vice and virtue could be theoretically upheld, would men, without religion, have motive enough to follow the thorny path of virtue?

As the eighteenth century dawned, men began increasingly to resist submission to authority, to insist on the evidence of facts and the approval of critical reason. The pertinent fact which many observed (and which Bayle brought out to those who had not) was that men were no better after seventeen centuries of Christianity than they were elsewhere, or in earlier times. Savages and Siamese, they learned from their travel books, had discovered sane moral truth by their unaided natural reason. It was the rise of critical rationalism that made the great factual discrepancy— that people do not live according to their Christian principles— meaningful. The fact itself had always been known; indeed, had it not been, the sermons of the preachers could scarcely have failed to make it known. Critical rationalism thus became the directing force of an evolution of feeling that depended, in the last analysis, on the multiple sociological factors that were transforming the French *mores,* and turning men away from transcendent goals to immanent aims. To advanced thinkers it began to appear that it was going to be necessary to have to undo the course of European intellectual history, and to divorce religion and morality.

The purport of eighteenth century humanistic thinking was consistently to demand the satisfaction of natural desires (confined by rational and social limits, to be sure), within the duration of this natural life. As d'Holbach phrased it, "Several sages of antiquity have pretended that philosophy was only a *meditation on death;* but ideas more in conformity with our interests and less lugubrious will make us define philosophy as a *meditation on life.* . . . A morality that conforms to nature can never displease the Being who is revered as the author of that nature." [1] But the preference for an ideal of pleasurable living was not itself (as Lanson maintains) the characteristic of this crisis of the European conscience. The novelty lay rather in the open and declared defense of this preference, which contravened the basis of Christian ethics.

The question of the relation between ethics and Christianity resolved itself into the attitude that ought to be taken to the "fact" which Bayle had brought out, that behavior is motivated by pleasure, passion, or self-interest, and not by rational principles. What is the relation between this fact and the Christian ethics? According to Bayle, it proves that Christian ethics is inefficacious, because it is against nature; where religion does influence conduct,

[1] *La morale universelle,* I, xviii–xix.

it does so in an undesirable direction, inspiring "anger against those who are of a different opinion . . . and especially a certain zeal for the practice of external ceremonies, in the thought that these external acts, and the public profession of the true faith, will serve as a rampart for all the disorders to which [man] abandons himself, and will some day procure him forgiveness for them." Christianity is, then, harmful to the moral life. Since all men, idolaters and Christians, act upon the same principles, a republic of atheists is quite conceivable, for civil punishment, concern for reputation, and the natural inclination not to go against the group are the effective protectors of society. Certainly, atheists would need strong laws, but so do we. "Would we dare to leave our homes, if theft, murder and other violent crimes were permitted by civil law?" [2]

Anonymous manuscript writers were quick to take up Bayle's corrosive arguments. Later they were restated and embroidered on by almost all the *philosophes;* for the controversy—contrary to the impression that is given (perhaps unwittingly) by most histories —was destined to wax unabated until the very end of the century, as religious scepticism grew more widespread, and resistance to it grew fiercer.

Nowhere is it clearer than in Montesquieu's *Lettres persanes* (1721) how Bayle's powerful reasoning was to become the theoretical basis of "secular morality." For Montesquieu finds all our duties inscribed in our natural condition as men, citizens and parents.[3] Obviously, these do not stand in opposition to reasonable satisfaction of natural desires. In the later and more conservative *Esprit des lois* (1748), however, Montesquieu openly attacks Bayle's paradox. In his important statement on this subject, he perceives at once the central issue. "From the idea that [God] does not exist ensues the idea of our independence; or, if we cannot have this idea, that of our revolt. To say that religion is not a repressive motive, because it does not always repress, is to say that civil laws are not a repressive motive either." [4] It is evident throughout the twenty-fourth book of the *Esprit des lois,* as elsewhere, that

---

[2] *Oeuvres diverses,* III, 86–114, 174, 399 ff. Cf. Delvolvé's summary of Bayle's views: "Religion is not a repressive principle that can overcome man's bad instincts. Perhaps it is even an agent of their corruption." (*Op. cit.,* p. 388–389.)

[3] P. 31, 115, 117, 213–214.

[4] Livre XXIV, ch. 2.

Montesquieu's consideration of religions is carried out from the empirical viewpoint of their effect on society and conduct; and except for the conventional bow, he treats the Christian religion like any other. Religion can be of service; it can also be harmful and itself need correction by civil law.[5] He points out the danger of "a religion" that judges morally indifferent acts as wrongdoing, or that turns its adherents away from love and pity for men.[6] Continence is a noble virtue, but socially harmful.[7] In his discussion of homosexuality, he counts not on religion, but on social factors and on natural pleasures to discourage it.[8] He proclaims the perfection of the ethics of Stoicism. "Never has there been any whose principles were more worthy of man, and more suited to forming virtuous men." [9] Finally, he declares resolutely that "we must not decide according to the precepts of religion, when it is a question of those of Natural Law." [10] Perhaps the *mot de l'énigme* is given us in his private *Pensées,* where he writes that "a small present pleasure affects us more than great, distant punishment," so that punishment in another life is a weaker restraint than fear of punishment in this life. He agrees, however, that it is ineffective to appeal to men through their reason, instead of through the senses and imagination.[11] It is clear that Montesquieu, though not a partisan of Christian ethics, would not, after his youthful writings, care to dispense with the social safeguards of religious sanctions.

Montesquieu's hesitancy is symptomatic. The separation of religion and morality, and the ethical sufficiency of Natural Law are themes that run throughout the anti-Christian writings of the eighteenth century. They were based on two fundamental suppositions. The first is optimism about man himself and about his

[5] Nothing is more revealing than the opening statement in chap. 19. "The truest and most holy dogma may have very bad consequences, when they are not linked with the principles of [a] society; and on the other hand, the falsest dogma may have admirable results, when they are in relation to the same principles." See also chap. 20.

[6] Livre XXIX, ch. 22.

[7] Livre XXIII, ch. 21.

[8] Livre XII, ch. 6.

[9] Livre XXIV, ch. 10.

[10] Livre XXVI, ch. 7. In making points like this one, Montesquieu of course uses the example of pagan religions; but the transposition, in the eighteenth century intellectual climate, was easy. That this was done is evident in the attacks on the *Esprit des lois,* and in Montesquieu's reply (*ed. cit.,* IV, 250–3).

[11] *Oeuvres,* II, 168, 2.

future, an optimism which stands at times in apparent contradiction to the estimate of human nature proposed by some of the same writers, when they were not attacking Christianity. This implication was apparent very early. We see it in the polemical manuscript (published in 1731) of Boulainvilliers, *Réfutation des erreurs de Benoît de Spinosa*.[12] Moral truths, we are assured, are engraved in all hearts, are evident to the reason of all men; those who follow them are happy; culprits are rejected by other men and their own conscience. Rewards and punishments are effectuated right here, on this earth. To say we need a religious motivation is to say virtue "is not appealing enough to win the heart by itself," and vice so delightful, only fear keeps us from it. Diderot, in his moralizing moments, was to make essentially the same points.

The second attitude is a boundless confidence in the secular conditioning of human behavior by education and by a rational, realistic system of laws. This attitude, though contradictory to the first, really supplements it. With this confidence, Helvétius and d'Holbach thunder against the vested powers that keep men in ignorance.[13] For these two materialists, all that is needed is the pressure of an educational and a legal system that are realistic, that is, built on the one actual motive of conduct, which is self-interest. If we recognize this fact, they maintain, and utilize it to direct men, we shall find that aside from this natural, non-moral and malleable motive, they are not evil.[14] This approach also involves a certain confidence in man's basic rationality, at least as regards his self-interest.

We have proven [claims d'Holbach] that it suffices to meditate on the essence of a sensitive, intelligent, reasonable being in order to find motives to restrain one's passions, to resist one's vicious penchants, to flee criminal habits, to make oneself useful and dear to beings of whom one has a continual need. These motives are certainly truer, more real and powerful than those some think we should borrow from an imaginary being, who shows himself in different form to all who meditate on him.

[12] P. 46–48.

[13] *De l'Esprit*, Discours II, ch. 24; *Système de la nature*, ch. 9.

[14] *De l'Esprit*, loc. cit.; *De l'Homme*, Sect. IX, X, *passim. Système de la nature*, II, 254–255, I, 374 ff. It will of course be remembered that many writers (including Helvétius) believed that man derives greatest pleasure from the disadvantage, or the hurt of others.

Atheists can of course be moral. (Is he not one?)[15]

The opponents of Bayle's views may be divided into two groups, the Christian apologists, and the moderate deists.

The apologists challenged Bayle's logic. They appealed to practical considerations. It is fallacious, declares Hayer, to conclude that because some religious people are wicked, the motives of hope and fear have no influence on conduct.[16] Bergier calls attention to the fact that the Natural Law (even if understood by the masses) provides in itself no motive for its observance. Reason has never been enough to govern men. "The people need a religion; if they do not have a true one, they will make for themselves a false one." [17] To this Boudier de Villemaire added another realistic consideration, which the atheists, in their estimate of human nature, had themselves proclaimed. Without religious sanctions, men are disposed to urge observation of moral laws by others; "but each individual will be tempted to weaken them in his own favor." [18] Le Franc de Pompignan levelled his attack against still another bastion of the non-believers. He repudiates d'Holbach's contention that desire for esteem and approval is a sufficient stimulus to virtue, and fear of hatred and scorn a deterrent to vice. This is wrong, as it overlooks ignorance, error, injustice and partiality. Remorse fails with hardened criminals, and earthly immortality is a will-o'-the-wisp. Religion, on the other hand, provides definite judgments, backs them up with rewards and punishments. Le Franc goes still further, attacks the heart of the materialists' moral system. It is ridiculous to say that laws can modify passions, direct them in such fashion that public and personal interest are combined. "Personal interest is not a spring that public power can manipulate as it wills . . . How will you persuade men, whom you have let believe that this life is the end of their existence, that they should be satisfied with the portion of satisfactions that the republic allots them, that their merit does not entitle them to more . . . ?" Such a philosophy,

---

[15] In his *Système social* (1773), d'Holbach assures us that no divine punishments are needed, since the motives associated with the "prestige drive" are more powerful. (I, 4, 72, 159–160).

[16] *Op. cit.*, VI, 132.

[17] *Apologie* . . . (1769), 19–20, 204–213. In his *Examen de la religion chrétienne* (1771), Bergier devotes some seventy pages to proving that atheism is incompatible with morality (II, 391–459).

[18] *L'irréligion dévoilée* (1774), p. 113–114.

he thinks, can only exacerbate the eternal war between personal and public interest.[19]

The Protestant, Samuel Formey, was one of the most clever and prolific of the apologists. He insisted that without belief in the after-life, with its rewards and punishments, laws lose their authority, and violence becomes legitimate. "Since universal annihilation will soon confuse the impious and the devout in the horror of the tomb, virtue and vice, the good man and the wicked become equivalent." [20] (With this the marquis de Sade will agree! [21])

The second group of writers who stood up against Bayle consisted of moderate deists and liberal abbés who were sympathetic to certain of the new ideas. In this matter, however, they stood very close to the most conservative theologians. Their concept of human nature was alike. D'Argens, who fought relentlessly against Christian "superstition," sees Bayle's thesis as possessing only a very limited value. "Unfortunately these precepts may well be of some use to philosophers, already good and virtuous by temperament; but they are of no use to the common people, and I should gladly say to three-fourths of men." [21a] As the abbé Yvon put it in the *Encyclopédie* ("Athées"), our disposition is such that moral instinct and knowledge will not, by themselves, without the

---

[19] *La religion vengée* (1772), p. 251–286.

[20] L'Anti-Sans-Soucy (1761), p. 5, 174.

[21] Emphasis on the insufficiency of reason and the corruption of human nature can also be found in the abbé Pluche (*op. cit.*, VI, 15–16), in La Luzerne (*Instruction pastorale*, 1786, p. 100–130), Holland (*op. cit.*, II, 176, 206–217), Sigorgne (*op. cit.*, p. 116–119), the monk Thomas Jacob (*Essai sur la jurisprudence universelle*, 1779, p. xiv, 4, 174–207). Gérard (*Le comte de Valmont*, 1774, I, 494–513). Holland, accepting d'Holbach's thesis that nature tells man to be happy, adds that it tells the good man to be happy by being good, and the evil man to be inhuman; nature is not an ethical guide. (It is obvious in what sense Holland takes "nature" here). In a society in which crime is rewarded and fortune worshiped, how can reason alone be sufficient, when reason and religion together are not? Sigorgne also holds that civil restraint only "sharpens the cleverness of scoundrels." Gérard emphasizes that virtue often requires heavy sacrifices, with no apparent reward, and virtue's charms are not powerful enough to effectuate such sacrifices. La Luzerne argues that the instinct of self-preservation stops short of moral feeling: "it allows what is only harmful to others."

[21a] *Lettres chinoises*, quoted by Bush, *The marquis d'Argens and his philosophical correspondence*, p. 139. Cf. Lanson (*Histoire*, p. 332): "I don't know whether it has been noticed often enough, the most fragile or false ethics have always been proposed by very moral people who have taken the fundamental rule of life from instinct and pleasure, because their instinct and pleasure did not lead them noticeably away from those actions without which there can no longer be any morality, therefore any society: such was Helvétius, such was Montaigne."

stimuli of fear and hope, lead us to morality. Virtue must not merely be loved; we must consider it a personal good, "part of our own happiness." Precisely because Bayle was correct in pointing to passion rather than reason as our motivating force, a counterweight is necessary. Precisely because we are ruled by self-interest, by fear and hope, the same motives must be used as a remedy. Religion provides them, more effectively than any other agency. The abbé Raynal, friend and collaborator of the *philosophes,* was to go even further. He considers the social function of religion as more important even than its salvation of souls.[22] There is no hope here that men will ever make the moral law the "maxim" of their actions.

Duclos even warns against enlightening men. Prejudices that produce social good are *ipso facto* truths. And why try to make men do by reason "what they have followed out of feeling and honest prejudice?" Prejudice, "the law of the common man," is a surer guide.[23] In a similar but much broader vein, Turgot declared that men are so meanly self-interested, so divided and opposed in the natural pursuit of happiness, that Christianity is needed to conciliate and to direct them.[24] All these writers are typical of the "moderate" group. Like Montesquieu, they fear human nature even more than they dislike Christianity.

Dom Deschamps offers us—as usual—a strange assortment of ideas. In his attack on d'Holbach, he warns (like Formey) that the destruction of religion would leave only force as the basis for law. Force without religion will produce its own destruction, and revolution will result. Such a revolution will be useless; for no *société policée* can exist without religion. It is rather, he urges the whole moral and social structure that must be destroyed; and then, in a state of complete community and equality, religion will wither away.[25]

Like Montesquieu, Voltaire may be said to have belonged, with some reservations and regrets, to the moderate camp. In the early

---

[22] Wolpe, p. 139.

[23] *Considérations sur les moeurs de ce siècle* (1751), p. 37–40. See my article, previously referred to, on the debate over truth and falsehood. See also, P.-Ch. Lévesque, *L'homme moral* (1775), p. 74–84.

[24] "Discours aux Sorboniques" (1750), *Oeuvres,* I, 200–210.

[25] *La voix de la raison* (1770), p. 18 ff. These ideas are developed more fully in the work which he left unpublished, *Le vrai système,* p. 53–4, 86, 102–103, 106 nb., 137–138, 199, 202, 203.

Traité de métaphysique (1734), he was inclined to rely on Natural Law, love of virtue and the natural spring of pride and desire for approbation. "This is perhaps the greatest brake that nature has made for human injustice. . . . Those who would need the help of religion to be good men would indeed be to be pitied."[26] Voltaire's optimism and faith in man waned after the mid-century. In the *Traité sur la tolérance* (1763), we find him declaring that any superstition is better than no religion. "Man always needs a brake. . . . An atheist who would be violent, powerful and a reasoner, would be as disastrous a scourge as a sanguinary fanatic. . . . Wherever there is an established society, laws watch over known crimes, and religion over secret crimes."[27] These opinions Voltaire was to repeat often in his later writings.[28] But his hatred of Christianity was so great that it took all his distrust and fear of the *canaille* to impel him to such a position. Religious dogma, he declared time and again, are poisons that divide men. Christianity and reason are not reconcilable; "we must teach men, not deceive them."[29] In his private notebooks, he commented, "Religion is not a brake, it is on the contrary an encouragement to crime. All religion is founded on expiation." But a few pages later, he notes that it is socially useful to have a church cult and a fear of the after-life. And a bit later he again changes his mind: "Natural religion can suffice against solitary and secret crimes; but positive religion has no brake for crimes committed together with others. . . . Religion even encourages them; it blesses a hundred thousand men who are going to slaughter each other."[30]

[26] P. 62–63.

[27] *Oeuvres*, xxv, 100.

[28] The "Homélie sur l'athéisme" (1765, xxvi, 322–329) largely rephrases the same ideas. In the article "Athéisme" of the *Dictionnaire philosophique*, he takes open issue with Bayle (xvii, 474); see also "Enfer" (xviii, 544); "Dieu, Dieux" (xviii, 376–377). Cf. the famous lines from the "Epître à l'auteur des Trois Imposteurs" (x, 402–405):

> Ce système sublime à l'homme est nécessaire.
> C'est le sacré lieu de la société,
> Le premier fondement de la sainte équité,
> Le frein du scélérat, l'espérance du juste.
> Si les cieux, dépouillés de son empreinte auguste,
> Pouvaient cesser jamais de le manifester,
> Si Dieu n'existait pas, il faudrait l'inventer . . .
> Ah! laissons aux humains la crainte et l'espérance . . .

[29] Cf. xx, 506; xxvi, 444, 550–552.

[30] *Notebooks*, ii, 313, 321, 375, 390.

To Voltaire it was obvious that there is no necessary relation between virtue and speculative opinions, including religion. But he came to the conclusion that men must be forced or tricked into being virtuous by motives that are completely non-moral, and related only to the non-moral aspects of their self. And—bitterly for him—the most powerful force in repressing evil is an institution which is itself the principal generator of evil, the established church. If there is indeed a real basis for ethical values (and Voltaire never will give up this conviction), men, unfortunately, are not moral beings, and will not do the right for the sake of right. They will do it only for their own sake—and society can exist only if we make them believe, or make them act as if they believed, that it is for their own sake they must be virtuous.

Rousseau also found himself in an intermediary position, but for somewhat different reasons than Voltaire. One cannot doubt that he was fundamentally a humanist—unless indeed we were to define that word in such narrowly rationalistic terms that the place of sentiment and intuition be denied. For Rousseau man is the only end, and he must always be treated as an end. "Man . . . is too noble a being to have to serve merely as an instrument for others. . . . It is never permissible to deteriorate a human soul for the advantage of others. . . ." [31] His writings are concerned, above all else, with the problems of self-fulfillment during this life. This goal, plus his own experience with Catholicism and Calvinism, left him with a strong dislike for dogma and ritual, and with a firm aversion to restrictions or duties which seemed unrelated to a rational morality based on human desires and needs. He warns, in *Emile,* against exaggerated puritanism and urges free expression for youth in legitimate forms of "fun." "By exaggerating all duties, Christianity makes them vain and unobservable," and sours the human disposition.[32] "A society of true Christians," he writes in the *Contrat social,* thinking of other-worldliness, "would no longer be a society of men." [33]

On the other hand, we know that Rousseau looked upon human nature, at least in its historical realization in society, with the pessimism of Calvin, intensified by his own unhappy experiences.

[31] *La Nouvelle Héloïse,* IV, 22.
[32] P. 468.
[33] Ed. Halbwachs, p. 423.

He also was impregnated with an emotional religiosity, accompanied by a deep need to believe in a God concerned with his personal destiny and in an anthropomorphically just universe. For all these reasons, his political and moral philosophy, which are in many ways inseparable, postulated, as we saw in an earlier chapter, man's subservience to a Creator who rewarded and punished. In *La Nouvelle Héloïse,* Julie, after many torments, reaches a note of mysticism which contravenes natural desires and which is in perfect accord with the most severe Christian morality.[34] It is true that natural desires obtain their revenge, in a sense, at the end of the tale. But where self-discipline fails, the discipline of the State takes up.

The same basic considerations apply, then, to the *Contrat social.* We must not forget that Rousseau's purpose is the re-conditioning of man, so as to change the "natural man," who cannot function properly in the artificiality of social structures, into a "social man"—to force man to be free, to force him to be what he really wants to be. One proper mechanism for obtaining this result is censorship. A second mechanism is what Rousseau calls "civil religion." "It is essential to the States that each citizen have a religion which will make him love his duties." Rousseau's position is, then, that religion is essential to ethics in society.[35] Compliance cannot be expected from the individual's moral will, but must be compelled. The Christian religion, however, is the least suited and the most contrary to this purpose. Instead, he proposes a State religion which is in perfect accord with the deism of the majority of the *philosophes,* and includes belief in a just, provident and personal God, in rewards and punishments in the future life, and in the sanctity of the laws.[36] However he gives this State religion a total and compelling force of which the *philosophes* would not have dreamed, but which must be understood as essential to his proposed "re-conditioning" of man. Whoever refuses to accept the dogma is to be banished. "Whoever, having accepted them, acts in such fashion as if he did not believe in them, let him be

[34] III, 65–68.
[35] See also the "Lettre sur la Providence," where Rousseau admits that without an after-life in which justice is done, there is no motive, or reason, to be virtuous.
[36] *Ibid.,* p. 426–429 and p. 427 nb., 387. Cf. *Profession de foi,* "As for the external cult, if it must be uniform for good order, that is purely *une affaire de police;* no Revelation is needed for that."

punished by death." In a word, Rousseau, on the issue of religion and morality, is in agreement with the Christians and the more conservative *philosophes;* but he rejects the religion of the former and demands a social control unimagined by the latter, with consequences that point to a new radicalism and repression. Law, writes Paul Vernière, becomes the measure of morality; "there is no longer but one sin, social sin." [37] The sources of Rousseau's idea are in Spinoza; its first fruits, in Robespierre.

The torments of Voltaire and the solutions of Rousseau plunge us once again into the central dilemmas of the age, as revealed by its more radical thought. The materialists were not, for the most part, immoralists, but seekers for a truer and more effective moral system. Yet their philosophies—as Voltaire and many others feared —opened the door to moral relativism and anarchism. On the other hand, many who defended religion on the social grounds we have seen, were also, without realizing it, skirting the same abyss. A good instance of this difficulty came to light at the very beginning of the century, in Bayle's reply to a sermon preached at St. Paul's Cathedral by William Harris, on January 3, 1698.[38] For the atheist, the preacher had said, the only motive for doing good is not hatred of evil acts, but *amour-propre:* fear of the law and concern for his reputation. The conclusion imposes itself: if atheists are not stupid, they should use any means to get pleasure that they can with impunity.

These words seem almost like an invitation for the atheist to reject the existence of any moral order. They allow no natural or objective criterion of good, once God's existence is denied, other than the value of individual pleasure or happiness. On the other hand, the moral order Harris proposes rests on the very same happiness principle, with its locus shifted to a future world. It assumes that God has set up a moral order; but that, without rewards and punishments (i.e., the *happiness* motive), it would be no order to man, since it would not satisfy his only criterion of value. Consequently, happiness *is* the only value, and there is no natural moral order, only an arbitrary order set up by the authority and power of God (or the State). This, of course, Harris does not say; he affirms only that the atheist, guided solely by

[37] *Spinoza et la pensée française* . . . II, 484.
[38] *Continuation des Pensées diverses, Oeuvres diverses,* III, 410–415. Also ch. 172.

happiness, finds no action *naturally* better than any other—that is to say, as long as happiness results, all acts are equal (and the only "better" act is one that is conducive to greater happiness). However, following Harris' reasoning, there is no way in which the Christian, either, could judge an act to be *"naturally,* or inherently better," except also that inasmuch as God has commanded it, reward or punishment ensues. We have, then, a purely authoritarian morality, or restraint; and, if one should ever overthrow the authority, the morality and the restraint must go, too.

In his own refutation of Harris, Bayle concedes that fear and hope are stronger motives than right reason. But atheists who act morally, purely out of right reason, perform a more truly moral act, "inasmuch as it will not appear to them attached to divine rewards." Many women would not be unfaithful, even if they could be, unknown to man or God; nor would sons poison their fathers and mothers. Thus Bayle, the unbeliever, is more rigorously moral than the Christian.

The marquis de Sade, however, was to confirm Harris' view. Sade's literary sons do poison their fathers, mothers, and children. We have noted that the apologists foresaw such a consequence, and warned against it. "And in good faith," asks the cardinal de Polignac, "if there were no God, is there a motive strong enough to determine [a man] to make himself wretched, by fighting his inclination . . . without hope of reward . . . ?" None at all, if he can get away without reproach from others, since from conscience there will be none: "when one enjoys without scruple, one must be insensitive to remorse." Only religion, then, represses vice.[39] While to most *philosophes* this would signify false fears and hope producing false virtues, Sade, once more, agrees with the Christian: the words "vice and virtue" have no status in reality; there is only passion and pleasure. Both Harris and Polignac are right, in Sade's view of things:

As soon as one no longer believes in religion, and consequently, in the imbecillic confidences made by God to men, all that comes

[39] *L'Anti-Lucrèce* (1769, I, 29–30). Thomas Jacob similarly asks, "But what can virtue do for him who believes that God does not exist, or that he disdains to lower his looks to the earth, that death is for man the end of his existence . . . ? Virtue is in his eyes only an illusion, a vain idea. It promises him nothing after this life; it leaves him unhappy in this one. . . . He will cry, like Brutus on the plains of Philippae. . . . 'Why did I not rather flee your sterile and unhappy ways, to devote myself to injustice . . . ?'" (*Op. cit.,* p. 325.)

from these same men must be . . . treated with the vilest scorn. . . . No being has the despotic right to submit me to what he has said or thought. And no matter to what point I trample on these human reveries, there is no individual on earth who can acquire the right to blame me or to punish me. . . . And by what incredible injustice will you name *moral* what comes from you, *immoral* what comes from me? To whom shall we have recourse to know on which side is right? [40]

The acceptance of moral nihilism is implicit in the writings of two arch-conservatives who had absorbed the lessons of the whole century, Sabatier de Castres and Antoine de Rivarol. Both had flirted early in life with the liberal trends, both were to become bitter anti-*philosophes*, but on premises that were inherent in some of the positions of the *philosophes* themselves.[41] Thus Sabatier (who is the less interesting on this point) defends the necessity of religion and public cult purely as an instrument of social utility, and with no interest in their truth.[42] The French Revolution had taught him this. Rivarol, writing to Necker the year before the Revolution, admits that if there is no God who punishes, then there is no reason not to do anything which we can do with impunity. But here is precisely where Rivarol differs from the apologists. In their somewhat naive reasoning, the formula, "no morality without God and religion," was an argument for the truth of God and religion, as well as for their necessity. In Rivarol's mind, however, the formula only tends to prove that there is no morality, or, as he puts it, "accredits the dangerous sophism." Clearly, the same march of ideas leads both to Sade and to Rivarol and Sabatier; only the former embraces the anarchism, while the latter turn to a proto-totalitarianism to stifle it. Rivarol is aware of the danger: "as you will resist in vain the 'march of enlightenment,' and the number of unbelievers will increase, they will remain unbridled." What, then, is Rivarol's proposal? We must rehabilitate morality, he urges Necker, "by basing it no longer on heaven, but on earth," that is, on enlightened self interest. But religious morality will still be needed for the ignorant and stupid masses:

[40] *Histoire de Juliette*, VI, 168–169. An outline of a theory of moral nihilism follows; we shall return to it in a later chapter.

[41] Perhaps there is some analogy here with a twentieth century intellectual politician, Benito Mussolini.

[42] "Lettre aux Français républicains," in *Lettres critiques* (1802).

. . . a lie that makes them happier and better is no longer one . . . The people would mock a man who offers as the moral rule only the general utility of societies, and as motive, the interest and pleasure of doing good. This system is so bare, it speaks so little to the imagination, it supposes so much reflection and knowledge, so much nobility and rectitude of soul, that it will never suit the multitude.[43]

In writing to Necker, Rivarol is somewhat circumspect. He is more brutally frank in a post-Revolutionary work, *De la philosophie moderne.*[44] Here he writes that God is always present in the physical order, always absent in the moral order. "Therefore it has been necessary to make up for him, to make him intervene in this order where he is not." It has been necessary to invent religions, to have God send a representative down here "to prop up the insufficiencies of morality, to settle the perplexities of conscience. . . . If all that had really existed, if morality, like the physical world, had been founded on visible and invariably effective laws, the intervention of God, and consequently of religion, would have been unnecessary." If we take poison, we die, but if we lie, our tongues are not frozen in our mouths. Nature punishes our errors, the civil police can punish open crimes, but religion must take care of passions and hidden crimes. Furthermore, religion is free to promise rewards, while justice can only punish. Nonetheless, crime will always prosper, provided the criminal is an "artist." Nature's only contract is the eternal laws of motion, which form a definite order. It is for us "to form a conspiracy in the moral world, in favor of virtue and against vice, in favor of order and against anarchy." Only religion can do this. Only religion can preach to man equality and fraternity—without danger.[45]

Not very distant from these two writers is a third, the abbé de Mably, who combined a theoretical economic radicalism with an authoritarian political philosophy that became exacerbated in his

[43] "Seconde Lettre à M. Necker," 1788, (summarized in A. Le Breton, *Rivarol,* p. 254–256).

[44] N.d., n.p., p. 23–34.

[45] Rivarol boasts of having been the first to attack the French Revolution, a year before Burke. On July 30, 1789, he had written, "Woe to whoever stirs up the dregs of a nation! There is no century of enlightenment for the populace. . . . The populace is and will be the same in all countries, always cannibalistic, always man-eating" (p. 47–48 n).

later writings.[46] Mably, too, lays weight on the secret crimes argument, and on the impossibility of bringing sufficient motivation to bear to induce men to follow reason, instead of passion, when they are safe from the sanctions of political laws. Religion, no matter how false or absurd, stands guard in this breach. Are not false rules of justice and duty better than none at all? A republic of atheists, to be honest and consistent, would have to teach the young that there is no real virtue or vice.[47] By implication, Mably seems willing to admit that Christianity may be false and that there is no "real virtue or vice." Six years later, in 1783, Mably wrote his *Observations sur le gouvernement et les lois des Etats-Unis d'Amérique* and addressed it to John Adams. He warns Adams that indifference in matters religious, harmless in enlightened and rational individuals, is fatal to the *mores* of the herd. A government must control and direct the thought of these "children," as fathers do before their young have reached the age of reason. When they lose fear, they lose shame, remorse and honor.[48] One would almost say, a Parable of the Grand Inquisitor *avant la lettre!*

The *philosophes,* shunning both extremes of anarchism and total repression, were bound to reply to the counter-assault of the *dévots.* In doing so, they adopted several tactics. Reputed facts, such as the historical existence of virtuous atheists and the virtue of the Chinese people, were frequently brought into evidence. The universality of morality, consequently its independence from religion, was of course constantly maintained from the early years of the century when, for instance, the author of the widely circulated manuscript, *Le Traité des trois imposteurs,* pointed out that in the Christian ethics there was nothing new, nothing divine, nothing unknown to the pagans.[49]

Nature, and nature only, cry a multitude of writers, is the valid basis of moral values. The unknown author of the important article in the *Encyclopédie,* "Philosophe," maintains these must be founded on love for man "not *qua creatura,* not *qua imago*

---

[46] "Choose," he cries in *De la Législation,* "between revolution and slavery, there is no half-way house." (Quoted by K. Martin, *French Liberal Thought in the Eighteenth Century,* p. 249.)

[47] *De la législation* (1776), in *Oeuvres complètes* (1789), IX, 232 ff.

[48] *Ibid.,* VIII, 346–347, 357–358.

[49] Folio 136.

Dei, but simply as a human being." This meant freeing "the conception of man and his duties from all that is out of proportion to human nature itself." [50] Religion was accused of giving short shrift to the mainsprings of human nature. As Montesquieu noted in his *Pensées,* "It is in vain that an austere morality wishes to efface the traits which the greatest of all workmen has imprinted in our souls. It is for morality, which seeks to work on the human heart, to regulate its sentiments, not to destroy them." [51] Religious morality was also held to be harmful to society; not only in specific, anti-social valuations, but in its general spirit, which shrugged off the miseries and injustices of this world, and led to an underestimation of one's duties as a citizen. This argument also traverses the century, in manuscripts, in Fréret, Meslier and d'Holbach, as well as in Rousseau. The Hollander, Hemsterhuys, put it in these words: "A great part of the imperfections of the present form of society derives from the difference between the purpose of religion and that of civil virtue: the one aims at the eternal happiness of each individual, the other at the temporal happiness of society. Some have tried to reconcile religious and civil virtue: that is impossible." [52]

These comments lead us into what was to be the principal course of argumentation developed by the *philosophes,* after Bayle, in their continuing attack upon the Christian outlook. Not only is ethics independent from religious dogma and cult; there is, they argued, an essential opposition between them. If ethics is to grow out of human nature and tend toward individual and social good, then it may be asserted that religion, and Christianity more than all other religions, has actually perverted ethics. On the one hand, then, the devout cried out against the danger latent in the position of the *philosophes,* the danger that it made all acts equivalent, without real moral value. On the opposite side, the *philosophes* exclaimed that as soon as the other-worldly becomes the directive and the end, all else must be subordinate to it. This assertion was correct, at least to the extent that such a current of thought and feeling has always existed in Christianity. What Pascal reproached the casuists for was essentially their substitution of a

[50] Herbert Dieckmann, *"Le Philosophe," textes et interprétation,* p. 76.
[51] *Oeuvres,* II, 2.
[52] *Oeuvres philosophiques* (1792), I, 222–223.

human, reasonable ethics for a divine ethics whose principles exist not in our corrupted human nature, but only in our original nature. The Church itself, however, for this very reason, had never expected perfect purity and saintliness of most men; but the *philosophes* preferred, in the heat of combat, to ignore this, to exaggerate the Christian attitude, making it equivalent to the line of Don Alvaro, in Montherlant's drama, *Le Maître de Santiago:* "Every human being is an obstacle to one who reaches for God." Don Alvaro's antagonist, precisely like the eighteenth century *philosophes,* accuses him of being dangerous to society.

The *philosophes* were basically right, too, inasmuch as, in important forms of Christianity, morality is essentially a matter of pleasing God. For the *philosophe,* morality was something quite different: the best way to the fulfillment of human nature, which, in society, involves its "proper" regulation. They were unable to approve, or even to conceive of the Christian ideal, which aspires towards a surpassing of nature. The latter phrase, to be semantically precise, meant the depreciation or even the suppression of "nature" in the sense of certain biological and egoistic survival instincts, and the exaltation of those aspects of human nature that were, in the same sense, un-natural—the altruistic and the spiritual. The Christian would hold that the first group of instincts are really the anti-social ones. The *philosophes* claimed that they were necessary to society, and in fact its very basis; and that the second group, when exaggerated out of their proper place in the total human harmony, distorted the personality, with consequences that are injurious to ethics and to society.

The question of chastity turned out to be one focus of this issue. Monasticism, for both males and females, became a concrete bone of contention. As the century advanced, attacks against the conventual system, in particular, grew ever more thunderous. It was condemned on a diversity of grounds; among them were the suppression of natural desires, perversion of character, and injury to society through parisitism and impoverishment of the population. In a broader way, the ideal of chastity itself was attacked on the same counts, and as typical of a false ethical system. As d'Argens wrote, "To be a perfect Christian, one must be ignorant . . . renounce all pleasures, honors, wealth, abandon his family and friends, keep his virginity, in a word, do all that is contrary to nature." [53] All that is contrary to society, later writers would have added. In chastity, the *philosophes* saw the inversion of moral values, as well as the perversion of character. As the author of an early manuscript wrote, keeping one's virginity becomes more important than being a good father or mother; the virtues of religion are imaginary virtues, even vices.[54]

From the standpoint of the *philosophes*, then, Christianity was proposing absolutes, with no regard to their effect on the welfare of individuals and society—an accusation that has been renewed in the twentieth century, in the campaign for birth control. In the eyes of the Catholic, the *philosophes* were incapable of understanding the religious spirit. As a later apologist put it, the eighteenth century, imbued with the criterion of utility, "was poorly disposed to appreciate the beauty and moral usefulness of absolute renunciation, of mastery exercised over oneself, of the flesh conquered and sacrificed to the ideal." [55] Because of the Fall, virtue lay in struggling against our corrupt nature, and in triumphing over it. No view could have been more opposed, or more repulsive to the new spirit of the times.

The accusation of perverting ethical values, which was levelled against Christianity, assumed from the outset a much broader scope than the particular subject of chastity. Thus the writer of one early manuscript claimed that whereas atheism leaves man free to follow his "philosophical feelings" as a guide to moral virtue, religious people are guided by superstition, which leads to discord and violence, and to such cruelties and immoral acts as Christianity is shown by its history to abound in.[56] There is no atheistic writer in the eighteenth century who does not repeat this charge, and many deists, especially Voltaire, joined in the chorus.

The basic requisitories were drawn up early in the century, and no writer was more important in their composition than Fréret. How can we establish ethics, asks Fréret, on an enthusiastic, mys-

[53] *Thérèse philosophe* (1748), p. 114–115.
[54] *Difficultés sur la religion*, Pt. IV, fol. 16 ff. Humility and forgiveness of all offences are cited as two additional examples. The writer compares the doctrine with the edifices and sumptuous living of those who preach it (Pt. III, fol. 63–85). Also the ms., *Dialogues sur l'âme* (later printed in *Pièces philosophiques*, n.d., n.p., p. 105–111).
[55] H. Potez, *L'Elégie en France*, p. 61–62.
[56] *De la conduite* . . . , fol. 137 ff.

terious, contradictory religion, on the concept of an unjust and malignant Being who tempts man (for whom he created the world), in order to have the right to punish him? How can we know the will of a God who says "Thou shalt not kill," and exterminates whole nations? If we are to love God above all else, we must love him more than our fellow-men, and so exterminate the latter if they offend him. Humility destroys energy, harms not only ourselves but also society, inasmuch as pride, reputation and desire for others' esteem are necessary motives for public good.[57]

The penetration and diffusion of ideas such as Fréret's are evidenced not only by their frequent expression in France, but also in England. Thus a paragraph of Hume's conclusion to his *Enquiry concerning the Principles of Morals* could be fitted word for word into one of Fréret's pages, or into one of Helvétius or d'Holbach.[58]

Diderot was deeply concerned with this question. In his earlier writings (*Essai sur le mérite et la vertu, Promenade du sceptique*) he follows the deistic current, considering morals to be independent of religion and related only to man's passions, interest and happiness in society. Like many deists, however, he holds religion to be a very useful mechanism of moral discipline, and in the *Promenade du sceptique* (1747), he tells a story of an atheist who is robbed by a servant to whom he had imparted his doctrine. What seems to have changed Diderot's thinking, some time after this, was his conversion—very likely effectuated by the influence of d'Holbach—to the view that religion actually perverts moral values and is inimical to the humanistic ethics towards which he was working. In 1759 we find him writing to Sophie Volland, in regard to his brother, who was a narrow-minded zealot, "He would have been a good friend, a good brother, if Christ had not commanded him to trample on such trivialities. He is a good Christian who proves to me at every moment that it would be

---

[57] *Lettres à Eugénie, Oeuvres complètes,* III, 75–84. For Fréret's charges made on the basis of human nature and needs, see *ibid.,* p. 1–26. This section also contains a sweeping attack on the assumed relation between "obscure dogma" and "evident moral ideas" and on the motivation of immortality. Cf. the later broadside of Naigeon: "They tell us we must love our neighbor like ourselves; and on the other hand, they ceaselessly repeat as the most beautiful and essential thing, that we must hate ourselves. Must we then hate our neighbor?" (*Le Militaire philosophe,* 1768, p. 35.) See also Mirabeau, *Des Lettres de cachet,* in *Oeuvres,* VII, 41–63.

[58] *Moral and Political Philosophy,* p. 251.

better to be a good man and that what they call evangelic perfection is only the fatal art of stifling nature. . . ." [59] In the
crystallization of this opinion, in the minds of Diderot and
of innumerable contemporaries, the martyrdom of Calas, Sirven
and La Barre, in the 1760's, was undoubtedly a decisive factor,
leading to conclusions such as the one expressed by Diderot:
"Everywhere a God is admitted, there is a cult; wherever there
is a cult, the natural order of duties is reversed and morals corrupted. Sooner or later, there comes a moment when the notion
that has prevented the stealing of an *écu* causes the slaughter of a
hundred thousand men." [60]

We may perhaps attribute to Diderot the intercalation, in the
third edition of Raynal's *Histoire des Deux Indes* (1780), of the
following opinion: "More than two thousand years ago, Socrates,
stretching a veil over our heads, had declared that nothing that
went on above that veil mattered to us, and that men's actions
were not good because they pleased the gods, but that they pleased
the gods because they were good: a principle that isolated morality
from religion." [61] This may be said to represent the conclusion of
Voltaire and of all the *philosophes*.

At the head of the polemicists was d'Holbach. His writings
were the most numerous, the most widely diffused and the most
complete. All the wrongs and harms of the Christian religion, all
its incompatibilities with a social and humanistic morality and
the demands of human nature were broadcast by him, in volume
after volume. I shall beg off from the task of following the course
of his ideas here. They are not only repetitious from book to book,
but repeat the arguments we have already expounded, though
often in more dramatic and effective phraseology. [62] One passage
must suffice to illustrate his presentation.

What, indeed, results from the confused alloy that theology has
made of its marvelous chimeras and reality? . . . religion wished

[59] *Correspondance* (éd. G. Roth), II, 218.
[60] *Lettres à Sophie Volland* (éd. Babelon), II, 298–299. For a particularly bitter
denunciation of the Christian inversion of values, see Diderot's *Entretien d'un
philosophe avec la Maréchale de ****, Oeuvres*, II, 517–518. See also Naigeon, *op.
cit.*, p. 153–193.
[61] 1781 ed., X, 280.
[62] For his principal statements, see *Le Christianisme dévoilé* (1756), p. 8–26, and
especially ch. 11, 12, 13; *Système de la nature*, I, 164–165, 349–386, II, 284–311, 374 ff;
Système social, I, 24–40.

to command nature, to bend reason under its yoke, to submit man to its own caprices; and often in the name of the Divinity, it forced him to stifle his nature and violate out of piety the most obvious duties of morality. When this same religion wanted to repress mortals, whom it had taken care to make blind and unreasonable, it had nothing to give them but brakes and ideal motives; it could substitute only imaginary causes for real causes, marvelous and supernatural motives for natural and known ones, fiction and fable for reality. By this reversal, morality was deprived of sure principles; nature, reason, virtue, evidence depended on an indefinable God, who never spoke clearly, who stilled reason, who explained himself only through zealots, impostors and fanatics, whose delirium or desire to profit from men's aberrations interested them only in preaching abject submission, factitious virtues, frivolous observances, in a word, an arbitrary morality, in conformity with their own passions, and often very harmful to the rest of the human race.[63]

We may fittingly close our history of this controversy with another quotation, taken from that bizarre figure of the Revolution, Anarcharsis Cloots:

. . . morality is the result of social interest, which itself is the result of private interests. We weaken human motives by inventing divine motives. Society tells me: thou shalt not steal. I can conceive that, and I obey a law that is formally or tacitly consented to . . . Nature has put into me the feelings of shame, pity, love. . . . I cannot gainsay these affections without feeling the remorse of a timorous conscience. . . . But by invoking the voice of God, we deprive the law of the motive of consent, without which we cannot be accused; we muffle the sonorous voice of nature and of society. We put all sins and crimes under a single tariff: fornication and gluttony are both damnable sins, just like stealing and murder; the same ablution washes away the stains of the weak and the atrocities of the wicked. . . . But all morality is founded on reason, and an arbitrary heavenly order makes us lose sight of the real interests of this world. The habit of virtue, that is, obedience to our laws, is a powerful deterrent to secret crimes. The fruit of a good up-bringing, the vanity we derive from fine deeds, the pride of honor, the instinct of justice, the horror of ignominy resemble that modesty, as praise-

---

[63] *Système de la nature*, II, 293–294. Mention should be made, in passing, of the deist, Saint-Lambert, who defends the necessity of religion to morals, since men are governed by imagination ("astonish by the marvelous, master by threats or promises, make passionate those you cannot convince"), but who also argues that the development of a clergy produces inevitable perversion, useless or harmful "duties" being placed above real virtues. (*Oeuvres philosophiques*, I, 4–5).

worthy as it is inexplicable, that would prevent us from walking naked in the Tuileries, even if the police would not oppose it. . . . When man has reconquered his dignity, he will fear that the walls will reproach him for his faults.[64]

In looking back over this controversy, certain generalized antitheses suggest themselves. Both Bayle and the Christian apologists agreed on the moral insufficiency of reason in the motivation of human behavior, but drew opposing conclusions from that opinion. The moderate liberals agreed with the apologists, but the extreme thinkers showed either a greater optimism or a greater pessimism than either of these. Both sides thought they could establish the objectivity of moral value, but differed as to whether they could do this without religion. A few extremists on the right or left denied any objective reality to moral distinctions. Both the *philosophes* and the apologists used the ambiguous criterion of nature, but again in opposing ways, either as the standard of virtue and value, or as something to be feared and repressed. The few writers I have labeled proto-totalitarians, holding that we arbitrarily create values, felt it necessary to project them through a God and a religion, and to create fictitious divine imperatives in accord with the established social order.

One conclusion we may draw from this chapter is that the deepest cause of the *philosophes'* resentment of Christianity was their desire to replace consciousness of sin by consciousness of evil. The implications of such a substitution were revolutionary, in regard to the content of ethics, the sources of moral judgment and the stimuli to adherence. The Church quickly perceived the danger and reacted vigorously. The more timid liberals, while agreeing with the new view in theory, feared it, too, in practice.

In the heat of polemics, the *philosophes* naturally judged the Church by its worst practices only, and by the "purest" (or least humanistic and palatable) aspect of its doctrine. Thus Fréret wrote that "to deserve to be happy in that unknown world, religion teaches us that we can do no better than to make ourselves unhappy in the one we know," and especially "to forbid ourselves the use of reason." [65] In vain the apologists retorted that Christianity desired men's happiness on earth as well as in heaven, that

[64] *L'orateur du genre humain* (1791), p. 118–124.
[65] *Lettre à Eugénie, loc. cit.*

it was not opposed to legitimate natural pleasures, and was in fact the surest way to earthly happiness.[66] The *philosophes* paid no attention and kept on hammering home the same points.

The chief weakness in the reasoning of many of the *philosophes* was their vague optimism and trust in man's natural moral impulses. This was evident from the first. "Self-love, humaneness, finally nature will restrain us more than religion . . . vanity and passions restrain men." [67] But it was never clear how these mechanisms would be more effective than the religious motives which Bayle mistakenly dismissed as abstract and unrelated to action, and which later followers of his deemed unnecessary or harmful. The same *philosophes* placed their trust, too, in man's rationality. "Man has only to contemplate himself to feel that his own happiness depends on that of others, that the most hidden vices can tend to his own ruin, that his crimes will infallibly make him despicable in the eyes of his associates, in a word, that public opinion, better than religion, will show him his duties." [68] But do men contemplate themselves in this way, and judge each other in this way? It seems that the *philosophes* were the ones who were guilty of violating Bayle's maxim and his realistic analysis of motivation.

We have, then, a paradoxical situation. Many who expressed a dim view of man's goodness and who reduced his motivation to pleasure, passion and self-interest, optimistically insisted, when it came to the issue of ethics and Christianity, that the Christian appeal to these motives was superfluous, or futile. On the other hand, some who opposed the extreme pessimistic evaluation of human nature insisted, in refutation, that men could not be trusted and had to be repressed by the force of religion.

Only a few eighteenth century writers went beyond a hedonic calculation and held men to be capable of governing themselves

---

[66] Abbadie, for instance: "For Jesus Christ did not come to annihilate nature, but to perfect it. He does not make us give up the love of pleasure, but he proposes purer pleasures. . . ." (*Op. cit.*, p. 252 ff.) Schweitzer emphasizes the eighteenth century triumph over the world- and life-negation of Christianity, but points out that the Christian world-view had been changing since the Renaissance. "It gradually begins to be accepted as self-evident that the spirit of Jesus does not renounce the world, but aims at transforming it." In fact, this was a wrong interpretation of the world-view of Jesus, which was pessimistic about the natural world and looked forward only to its end. (*Civilization and Ethics*, p. 62, 66.)

[67] *Examen de la religion*, p. 139.

[68] Fréret, *loc. cit.*

by true moral feelings, by a sense of right and wrong, and of obligation. The failure of most of the group to take such a position actually placed them on the same ground as the apologists, that of relying on non-moral motivations. This being so, the Christian position was obviously the stronger, since it added additional motivation, of a type that required neither innate virtue nor rationality. The apologists were accused of opposing and perverting human nature; but in a sense it was the former who misjudged our nature. This was their fatal weakness. Their own frequent restriction of their views to a select élite, their own frequently expressed distrust of the common people, was a confession of this failure. Even Fréret, after all his attacks, admits as much.

> The common man is too corrupt and too unreasonable not to have to be led to the practice of virtuous actions, that is, those useful to society, by the hope of reward, and turned away from criminal actions by the fear of punishments; that is what gives rise to laws; but as laws do not punish or reward secret crimes, and as in the best regulated societies powerful and influential criminals find a way of eluding the laws, it has been necessary to imagine a more redoubtable tribunal than that of the magistrate. . . . This belief is without doubt the firmest foundation of societies. . . . As long as it is used only for public welfare, I shall regard it as a useful error that good people should respect. . . .[69]

The devout writers, on the other hand, accepted human weakness and depravity. "It is impossible to offer man sufficient motives," wrote Mably, "to persuade him to follow his reason rather than his passions; and he will be just only insofar as he will be unable to escape the vigilance of laws and magistrates." [70] It is no wonder then, that a Voltaire was torn between allegiance to a philosophy of whose truth he was convinced and fear of mankind, whose nature he despised and distrusted.

It is true that the *philosophes*, in their theoretical optimism, were thinking not of men as they were then, or as they are now. Their effort was a total one, towards a new view of man in nature,

[69] *Op. cit.*, 145-146. La Mettrie had also admitted that religion, "that marvelous work of politics," is necessary for the *vulgus*, that "imbecillic, low and crawling species, which society has deemed it can use only by captivating the motive of all minds, self-interest: that of a chimerical happiness." (*Système d'Epicure*, p. 252.)
[70] *De la législation*, p. 323.

towards a new humanistic society. With prejudice and superstition swept away, with government and society organized on just and rational lines, with an economic and moral system based on an acceptance of so-called "laws of nature," reason, they thought, would be free, self-interest would be rational, natural desires would receive proper and harmless satisfaction. Some *philosophes,* notably Voltaire, despaired of any radical improvement; but many more believed that man needed only to be conditioned to this new way of living by a suitable education and a proper social and legal climate. Many of those who were pessimistic about human nature—or at least relatively pessimistic, in their attribution to men of the unique motive of self-interest—also recognized the necessary existence, in human beings, of moral experience and moral judgments. Their optimism was not about man left to himself, but about what he might be made into.

A faint shadow of collectivist control thus arises from the humanistic writings of the eighteenth century, and from those of Helvétius, d'Holbach and others. It raises its head even in Montesquieu, when he writes on democracy.[71] We can understand why Rousseau's *Contrat social* crowns the century's political thought. In fact, the meaning of that work requires the illumination of this intellectual background for its full understanding.[72] While a Sabatier de Castres or a Rivarol tended towards totalitarianism as an oppressive system to assure the *status quo* (man not being capable of better, but only of worse), other *philosophes* were driven towards collectivism as the necessary mechanism of man's reconditioning. Perhaps only Morelly and Rousseau went so far as to realize clearly that to make men into what we should like them to be, more or less complete control and conditioning are necessary; but even they certainly did not realize the implied destruction of human values that was ultimately involved, a destruction far beyond that which they attributed to Christianity. At the other pole, the liberation from superior directives was to lead a

---

[71] Precisely because democracy requires a type of conditioning that will control the egoistic motives of behavior; and this is what Rousseau was to develop. See *De l'Esprit des lois,* Livre IV, ch. 5, 6.

[72] Rousseau's espousal of what we would consider totalitarian conditioning comes out most openly in his *Considérations sur le gouvernement de Pologne,* see especially Vaughan, II, 427 ff., 437.

few men, like Dom Deschamps and the marquis de Sade, to a complete anarchism.

We have here our first wide view of the failure of eighteenth century ethical thought. It is not enough to show man his true position. We must, in Mably's terms, find another way, offer him sufficient motives. The humanistic *philosophes*, as we shall see more clearly in later parts of this study, sought what they considered to be the way of reason, or the way of nature, or a way that reconciled these. But nature was never only what they took it to be; and the failure of reason has had its continuing and widest reverberations in the crisis of our own age. And yet, the humanist of today, like those of the eighteenth century, cannot turn back. Bronislaw Malinowski has shown that among primitive peoples, religion and ethics are always inseparable.[73] The humanist of today cannot consent to such a regression, but feels that man must march bravely into his future, be it a brighter day or a starless night.

[73] See Malinowski, *The Foundations of Faith and Morals.*

Fourteen

HUMAN NATURE IN THE NOVEL

BECAUSE literature is more than art, because it is embedded in the emotional and intellectual climate of its time, the attitudes towards man and his behavior that characterize a period are inevitably illuminated, in a context of life itself, in the novels of its great writers. This is true even though the novel may not be expressly concerned with the philosophical speculations of the age, but spring simply from a realistic view of human nature as observed in society. A full-length study of the eighteenth century novel (from this viewpoint, as well as from others) is still to be written. While such a task is obviously not germane to the present volume, we cannot completely neglect a connection between thought and art which is bound to throw light on both. I propose, then, to limit myself, after a brief reference to the most important novel of the seventeenth century, to an examination of nine of the major novelists of the eighteenth century: four (Lesage, Marivaux, Prévost, Crébillon) belonging approximately to the first third of that period; two (Duclos, Diderot) to its middle stage; and three (Laclos, Rétif de la Bretonne, Bernardin de Saint-Pierre) to the eve of the French Revolution.[1]

[1] Rousseau and Sade are excluded, since their novels are discussed throughout the other chapters of this study.

That a novel reflects and participates in the values and the prevailing outlook of its age is clearly borne out in the master-work of seventeenth century French fiction, Mme de Lafayette's *La Princesse de Clèves*. This finely worked love story is not only a brilliant example of the aesthetic ideals of French classicism, but a mirror of the moral life of the most influential segment of French society. Realistic in its social observation and its psychology, *La Princesse de Clèves* does not conceal the cruelty of human beings in their rivalries and intrigues, political or amorous. But what stands out above this objectively uncovered panorama is the moral stature of its heroine, who stands up for her ideals against the *mores* of her class and her time. Beset, like all of us, by the necessary urges of the instincts or passions, by the need for pleasure, she refuses to accept the naturalness or necessity of these urges as qualifications of value, or as evidence that they are not controllable. Against natural passion, the Princess of Clèves holds fast to a human and rational value system, in which personal honor, self-respect and integrity add up to an ideal of virtue that is placed above happiness. Pleasure is not our only motive, nor the most legitimate one. The heroine is impregnated with a Cartesian belief that the will can conquer passion and reason can guide our lives. Her ideal does not, in fact, bring happiness either to her, to the husband to whom she is faithful, or to the one she loves. But this, as Kant was to say much later, belongs to circumstance; and it is not in what life does to us that lies our worth, or worthlessness. Life is not absurd, precisely because the human personality has worth, which it *creates* by its transcendence of nature in the moral life. At the end of her drama, the Princess maintains her self-approbation, and the esteem of the author and the reader. If being men is a situation of tragedy, this book seems to say, then let us still be men.

The picaresque stories of Alain René Lesage form a transition to the eighteenth century climate. Lesage, to be sure, is more a satirist and a story-teller than a novelist; but there is sufficient character and sufficient relation of character to its human environment, in his writings, for him to retain the title. From the seventeenth century, Lesage carries on the Molièresque satire of the vices and follies of men and women, but with a cynicism *à la Rochefoucauld* that reflects the immoralism and loss of ideals of the Regency. Lesage's intention is to uncover men as they are, and to laugh at them, not to moralize or to reform.

In 1707, Lesage wrote his *Diable boiteux,* based on *El diablo cojuelo* of Guevara.[2] It is a series of tales and vignettes held together, in picaresque fashion, by the person of its hero, Don Cleofás, who is less important in the story than the characters he sees or hears about from a friendly devil whom he has rescued. In *Le diable boiteux* we already glimpse what is destined to be the most common theme of the eighteenth century novel: the great game of love, in which the male's role is ruthlessly to seduce and to enjoy, that of the female to conquer and enslave—or, to use a word that was to become the fashion—*fixer* the male. This game calls up the most ingenious resources of which both sexes are capable. The more difficult the barriers erected by law or vigilance to the natural urge to pleasure, the more ingenuity they summon forth, as they seem driven on to satisfy it. It is a game with many dangers, in which the weak must perish. Thus one lady, surprised by her husband in bed with his valet, cries that she is being raped, and the luckless valet pays the penalty.

But Lesage's field of vision is much broader. He sees men and women as ruled by a menagerie of vices, among which the sexual are only the most entertaining, and not necessarily the most powerful. This is symbolized by the defeat and crippling of Cleofás' devil, Asmodée, who is the devil of love, by Pilladorc, the devil of interest. In episode after episode, we are shown that money and vanity are the two dominating motives of human behavior, and that virtue is the mask used to protect the designs of vice. Thus the first step in the seduction of Leonor is to lure her duenna by a false act of generosity from which she will profit. The enticement of further profit completes the subornation of the formerly virtuous duenna. Indeed there are few whose virtue does not have its price. The acceptance of evil is clear-sighted and freely willed, a calculation of gain. From here on, it is enough "that nature take a hand," relates Asmodée. "She is not less dangerous than I; the only difference there is between us, is that she corrupts hearts gradually, whereas I seduce them suddenly." And the course of Leonor's seduction is slowed less by her sense of obligation to virtue, honor and her father, than by fear of losing the esteem of her lover by a rapid capitulation.

If this is men and women as they usually are, it is not however, all of their nature. Lesage recognizes that they also have good impulses, and that good impulses occasionally find fruition in virtuous acts. He has even enough of optimism to admit that not all virtuous people are naive dupes, and that virtue is sometimes esteemed and rewarded. The seduction of Leonor has a happy, romantic ending. The villain is overcome by her virtue and by remorse for the gratuitous harm he has wreaked. Good and evil struggle in his heart, and he freely embraces the good. It is true that Cleofás restricts such an ending to Spain, and excludes similar honorable conduct from French *mores*. But it is clear that though men are beset by devils within them, they admire the good and are occasionally capable of it. This optimism is even stronger in a later episode, in which two men put friendship above love for a woman, valuing a platonic or spiritual relationship above a physical one. "Can a lover give up the adored object by whom he is loved in order not.to make a friend unhappy?" asks Cleofás. "I thought that was possible only in novels." The devil replies, "I admit that it is not very usual; but it is not only in novels, it is also in man's finest nature; and since the flood, I have seen three examples of it, not counting this one." The irony undoubtedly conveys Lesage's final assessment. He has wanted to tell a good story, and he knows his readers like to read about the virtues they do admire, and do not practice. In fact, the 1726 revision adds an even rosier ending. Lesage stresses first the altruistic pity for human suffering, as Cleofás witnesses a fire in which a girl is trapped; and then, Cleofás' basic honesty, as he refuses to profit illegitimately from a stratagem. The devil, disguised as Cleofás, saves the maiden. Her grateful father later offers Cleofás both his beautiful daughter, with whom he has of course fallen in love, and great wealth. But shame and honesty—or an innate and invincible good will—make him freely confess the truth. The father, however, is even more impressed by the confession than by the earlier heroism, and all ends happily.

Lesage's *Gil Blas* (1715–1735) is a technically more accomplished novel. This time the narrator is himself the subject of most of the action; and, despite the fantastic nature of his adventures, we get to know him thoroughly as a human being as we follow him through the course of his life. A vast panorama of human character, which cuts across the spectrum of classes and occupations, is unfolded in the smoothly narrated adventures that succeed each other with vertiginous rapidity. Gil Blas is the model of a *picaro*, a youth abandoned on the sea of life, a rough ocean of unforeseeable storms and treacherous currents. His history may be considered as having three logical divisions, which we might entitle, "Innocence," "Corruption," "The Triumph of Virtue."

The naive and uncorrupted Gil goes out into the world. His nature and impulses are fundamentally good. He has a normal provision of *amour de soi;* but he wishes to hurt no man, and is not possessed by *amour-propre*. He soon discovers that the world is a hunting wood, where the innocent and virtuous are the natural prey of the rapacious and unscrupulous, in a pitiless struggle for survival. The outlaw Don Raphaël remarks. "We are only trying to live at the expense of others; if stealing is an unjust act, the necessity of it corrects its injustice." Food and money appear as the greatest driving motives in this "human" commerce, but as the book advances, they are supplemented by sex, vanity and the lust for power. As Gil Blas moves higher up in the social scale, the latter two become most important. But even in the very beginning, it is through adroit exploitation of Gil's vanity that he is fleeced, and it is his vanity, or self-esteem, that is most hurt by the loss. Whenever trickery and deceit are insufficient, violence and brutality are used. All that matters is satisfaction of "natural" pleasure and egoism; any successful means is a good means.

There is one episode in the first book, in which Gil Blas and a lady are sequestered and enslaved by highwaymen, supposedly for life, that foreshadows a type of absolute immoralism and destructiveness which Sade, at the other end of the century, was to exploit in his Justine novels. Sex and lasciviousness, however, are only referred to by Lesage, never represented "on stage." Indeed, the novel is almost puritanical. In the matter of love, Lesage displays a nicely balanced realism. While sex is most often a crude physical enjoyment or a lure to the unwary, several of the characters, including the hero, experience sincere and romantic love.

It takes some time and many rude blows, but Gil Blas eventually learns to play the game. Each time that he is honest—as when he tells one master how his mistress is deceiving him, and another (in answer to the latter's plea for sincerity) that his last sermon was below his usual standard—he suffers the consequences. Soon Gil finds himself tricking, fleecing and abusing others, whenever the opportunity arises. When the wheel of fortune spins him upwards, and he becomes a favorite of the prime minister, the Duke de Lerma, he enters fully into the corruption of human life. In the higher social strata, the methods and ends are the same as among the petty, but the activities are conceived on a grander scale. Lust for money, or perhaps a combination of greed and ambition, perverts Gil's original goodness. He loses his natural feelings of pity and charity. Friendship and gratitude become motives for fools. In fact, gratitude, as Sade was to say, is a source of pain: "the services he had done for me weighed upon me." He turns his back on his parents and refuses to help them.

The heights of fortune, with their giddy intrigues, are followed with capricious suddenness by fall from favor and imprisonment in the Tower of Segovia, as Gil Blas is ruthlessly sacrificed by the Duke. A serious illness brings him to the edge of death. He now has time to meditate and to develop a new perspective on what is valuable in life. He realizes many things: that the lure of money and vanity is hollow, that he has been a tool for others and has sacrificed the better part of himself; most of all, that there are true friends and decent people who refuse to "play the game." He leaves the Tower sincerely despising wealth and honors: "wealth is good only to corrupt morals." He accepts a small property from a true friend whom he had helped, but refuses a pension. With another true friend, his valet Scipio, he retires to a tranquil country life.

But Gil's career is not yet at an end. The Duke de Lerma is in turn disgraced, and Gil becomes an even more powerful favorite of the new prime minister, the count Olivares. This time he resists corruption, and prospers all the more because of his virtue. Most of all, he is content, for his resources within himself and with others are on a sound basis. This time, the minister's fall is a relief, not an anguish. And Gil, now a noble, returns to the country to marry and raise a family—to live, in fact, very much as Rousseau was to propose in *La Nouvelle Héloïse*.

In *Gil Blas,* as in *Le diable boiteux,* Lesage portrays men and women as a compound of good and evil, animals in the main, but having truly human potentialities that are sometimes realized. Lesage's lesson, one is tempted to say, is that society has perverted men, and that to be virtuous, it is necessary to rise above the corruption of competitive social existence. This is a lesson that Rousseau may conceivably have read in *Gil Blas*. Nevertheless, Lesage's pessimism is probably somewhat deeper. Even in the most favorable circumstances, the majority of men, rapacious and aggressive, will act so as to bear out Hobbes' phrase, *homo homini lupus*. This short-sighted egoism is, however, self-defeating and even self-destructive. The only sure happiness lies in overcoming the passions, and in living under the discipline of virtue.

With Prévost's *Manon Lescaut* we have another masterpiece of the novel, one that returns to the pure and simple lines of its classical forebear, *La Princesse de Clèves*.[3] But the tone of the work, with its first person narration, its romantic moods, exclamations and fits of emotion, with its youthful recklessness and abandon, uncovers the gap between the generations. The picture of human nature and motivation has been quite turned about. Here passion and pleasure are shown to be the directing forces of behavior, before which reason and the Cartesian will are baffled and humbled.

Manon Lescaut is a variation on the theme of a man's enslavement to a woman by an *amour fatal*, a theme which reaches back to Tristan and Yseult and continues on through the Romantic period to such recent works of fiction as Somerset Maugham's *Of Human Bondage*. The peculiar accent of *Manon Lescaut* is the unworthiness of the object of this love (rather than frustration by external circumstances, although this, too, is present), and the consequent moral degeneration of the protagonist. The story-line is cleanly rectilinear, tracing this deterioration in eleven steps, or actions, which are the dramatic hinges of the story.

The pattern of forces that shapes the history is geometrical, having a rectangular construction. Des Grieux is the man who is led by invincible passion. Manon is motivated by the non-rational and amoral pleasure motive. Her brother, Lescaut, is the immoralist, for whom there is no valid moral law, but only the natural law of egoism. The forces of rational morality and discipline,

---

[3] *Manon Lescaut*, published in 1731, was probably written as early as 1728.

finally, are represented by Des Grieux's friend, Tiberge, with the
occasional supplement of other episodical characters.

Rousseau's distinction between natural goodness and virtue,
twenty-five years before he developed that theory, is incarnated
in the person of Des Grieux. Prévost himself, in his Preface to
the novel, speaks of "a perpetual contrast between good feelings
and bad actions." [4] Des Grieux has a fine moral sensitivity and
never loses his clear view of the right; he experiences pungent,
if fleeting shame and remorse after each descending step; and
often, especially in the early stages, he is beset by hesitation and
inner conflict before the act. He is aware of his degradation, of
his growing loss of self-respect, and of his fall from innocence.

> I found myself with divided feelings, and consequently in an
> uncertainty so difficult to terminate that I remained a long time
> without answering a large number of questions which Lescaut
> asked me about both of them. [5] It was at that moment that
> honor and virtue made me feel again the barbs of remorse and
> that I turned my eyes, sighing, towards Amiens, towards my
> father's house, towards Saint-Sulpice, and towards all the places
> where I had lived in innocence. What an immense distance
> separated me from that happy state! [6]

But the hesitation is vanquished, the remorse repressed, the degradation accepted, because reason loses its Kantian transcend-
ency, its law-giving function, and becomes that other reason which
the seventeenth and eighteenth century detractors of man had
stigmatized as self-deception, and which Freud was to call rationalization. Or, to put it simply, passion subjugates reason and
makes it a slave to its purposes. Almost inevitably, Des Grieux's
moral personality, exhausted by the struggles and defeats, finally
gives value to the reprehensible course of action it is obliged to
follow. This is a natural defense mechanism. From time to time
we find him attempting self-justification by a concept of values
that fringes on moral nihilism. He calculates that moral probity
in a person makes it easier to victimize him. [7] He reasons that if
his way of life makes him unhappy, the way of virtue is not a

---

[4] *Histoire du Chevalier Des Grieux et de Manon Lescaut*, éd. M. Allem, p. 2.
[5] This refers to Manon and the rich rival with whom Lescaut proposed that Des
Grieux share her.
[6] P. 75.
[7] P. 59.

surer road to happiness; and that happiness can be found in vice.[8]
There is no happiness, he argues, other than pleasure.[9] His pleasure is to have Manon; this is the sole value, and in losing all else, he has lost nothing of real value.[10]

Of Des Grieux we may say, then, as Rousseau said of himself, that he sees the right, loves it, and does the wrong. The source of evil is passion, which trespasses violently on the order established to regulate behavior and particularly to control the passions, an order we call morality. The passion involved is sexual love, which the experience of human history shows to be notoriously rebellious to control. Prévost himself qualifies his hero's life as "a terrible example of the force of the passions." [11]

This is the source of evil, and it brings us to the more complex question of responsibility. Many people love, but not all are degraded by their passion. Des Grieux himself wonders about this. "Love is an innocent passion; how has it changed, for me, into a source of wretchedness and disorder?" [12] Doubtless the force of circumstances—Manon's character and social position—were important causative factors; but they were only occasional causes, and the decisions were made by Des Grieux. The latter may be viewed as inevitably determined in his actions by the unusual power of his passion. Love is a natural phenomenon which, in his case, becomes a pathological psychic state, a sickness of the mind, deranging the force of reason and conscience, though not destroying the mind's perception of them. This naturalistic determinism, though logically applicable, would seem to be historically inappropriate (if we wish to approach literature in this way) because of Prévost's personality and the still incomplete ideological evolution of the period.

But there is another type of fatalism, one which would also accord with Des Grieux's *amour fatal:* that of Jansenism. This would be much closer to Prévost's beliefs and his milieu. There are indeed several clear traces of Jansenism in the novel.

If it is true [says Des Grieux] that heaven's succor is at each moment of a strength equal to that of the passions, I should like

[8] P. 96–97.
[9] P. 99.
[10] P. 204.
[11] P. 2.
[12] P. 75.

to understand then by what fatal ascendency one suddenly finds himself carried off far from his duty, without being capable of the least resistance and without feeling the least remorse.[13]

Oh, dear friend, I answered him, it is here that I recognize my wretchedness (*ma misère*) and my weakness. Alas! yes, it is my duty to act as I reason! but is the action in my power? What help would I not need to forget Manon's charm? [14]

In the lines that follow, Des Grieux admits to believing in the truth of the Jansenist doctrine. From this viewpoint, then, we must look upon our corrupt nature as the source of evil, which takes the form of passions destructive to reason, to order and to life itself. Reason alone, or even aided by good will, cannot overcome this rampant corruption. It is only divine grace that can make reason the stronger, as it does in the instance of Tiberge, who is the antithesis of Des Grieux.

I had as much penchant as you [he says] for lasciviousness, but Heaven had given me, at the same time, a taste for virtue. I used my reason to compare the fruits of each and I was not long in discovering their differences. The help of Heaven joined itself to my reflections.[15]

For the inscrutable reasons of Jansenist predestination, this grace has been denied to Des Grieux. The help he asks for is never given. Even when he resolves to follow Tiberge's example, and devotes himself for many months, with complete sincerity and wholeness of will, to a Christian life, to the point where he believes he has at last conquered his fate—all he has done melts away into nothingness when Manon comes again to destroy his edifice of reason. Even in seeking God and abjuring sin, he is destined to fail, lacking the grace of God. From the standpoint of human logic, Des Grieux is God's victim. Little wonder that the Jesuits feared such a concept of an irrational cosmos! And who knows whether the marquis de Sade, reading *Manon Lescaut,* may not have been helped to his conclusions that the operative law of the universe is evil and that God, if he exists, is also evil? [16]

[13] P. 42.

[14] P. 99–100. See Paul Hazard, *Etudes critiques sur Manon Lescaut,* p. 47–69.

[15] P. 48.

[16] Prévost himself seems to have been somewhat entangled in the Jansenist paradox of free will and predestination. In his Preface he declares Des Grieux to be morally responsible, since he acted "by choice" and foresaw his misfortunes *"sans vouloir les éviter"* ("without wishing, or trying, to avoid them"). He does not ask

For the purpose of this study, Manon is of less interest than her lover. We should indeed remember that the correct title of the novel is *Histoire du chevalier Des Grieux et de Manon Lescaut.* Des Grieux is the protagonist, and we know Manon only through him. It is in him that the inner drama takes place. And yet it is Manon, perhaps because of the mysterious power of her femininity and the latent romanticism in all men, who has captivated the imagination of subsequent generations of readers. If Des Grieux represents the failure of the moral reason, and Manon's brother, Lescaut, the deliberate rejection of moral values, Manon may be taken as a representation of "natural man," in whom the moral feelings and judgments (for some reason unknown to us) have never been cultivated.[17] This "natural man" (presented here in his feminine counterpart) is not naturally virtuous. Manon is *good,* in Rousseau's sense of wishing to accomplish her own good with the least possible harm to others. She wishes to hurt no one, and takes no pleasure in so doing. But she is cowardly, perverse, lascivious and frivolous. Until the very end of the book, she is incapable of love in the spiritual sense, which involves the desire of self-sacrifice for the beloved. There is no disapproval of conscience for any of her betrayals, and no remorse. She is both guilty, and innocent. The moral conscience, it would seem, is not innate. All that is innate is what we would term the impulse of the *id* for pleasure of all kinds (what Tiberge calls "the poison of pleasure"), and for the avoidance of pain; a natural impulse which is aggravated by what Rousseau was later to call the "artificial needs" of an effete civilization, for luxury and satisfactions of vanity. Manon is, then, the archetype of the female who is destructive of the rational ordering of the world which the male imposes on the chaos of natural impulses—a model that goes back at least as far as Greek epic and tragedy.

It is of little matter, for our purposes, that the unity of the portrait is broken, at the very end, by a romantic twist as aesthetically outrageous as any to be found in the nineteenth century. Manon is finally touched by the endless devotion and self-sacrifice

whether Des Grieux was free so to will, or to try. But in his own analysis of *Manon Lescaut,* in *Le Pour et le Contre,* he describes Des Grieux as the victim of "an insane passion," and as a "wretched slave of love, who foresees his misfortunes without having the strength to take measures to avoid them." (*Manon Lescaut,* p. 267, n. 3.)

[17] The reason may be a traditional concept of woman as amoral, or morally inferior to man.

of Des Grieux. Through him, and his suffering, she discovers the spiritual dimension of love, and the superiority of self-sacrifice over egoism. The fallen woman is redeemed, the sinner is saved. Des Grieux's destiny is indeed unchanged. But is Prévost trying to tell us that this may be the very meaning of that inscrutable will of God which so baffles human understanding? If God has elected Des Grieux to be his victim, was it not so that, in his mysterious and unfathomable ways, a great sinner might be saved? And Des Grieux, the unwitting hand of God, will surely not be the loser when the accounts are reckoned up.

Let us turn next to Marivaux. Although his fame as a comic writer has eclipsed his novels and journalistic essays, Marivaux is the author of two popular and not insignificant novels, *La vie de Marianne* (1731–1741) and *Le paysan parvenu* (1735–1736). The first of these was serially published and was left unfinished.

Despite serious deficiencies *La vie de Marianne* is a work of considerable interest and importance. In its innovations in narrative technique, which were to influence Sterne and Diderot; its realistic portrayal of daily life and customs; its criticism of the convent as a cruel and unjust social institution within the eighteenth century system of family and marriage: in these, and in several other ways, Marivaux blazed a path which others were to imitate and develop.

More germane to our purpose are several other values of this novel. In general, it is of interest to us for its broad picture of human nature and its subtle psychological analyses of motivation. In particular, it introduces two themes which are related to the eighteenth century preoccupation with the problem of evil, and which were destined to play a significant role in the novel. First, Marivaux introduces the character of the wicked and willful seducer, and the theme (secondary, here) of seduction of a virtuous and innocent girl. Second, the central theme of the book is that to which Sade was to give the title, "Les Infortunes de la vertu" —though there are important differences to which we shall come in our discussion. It is this second theme which has the broader moral implications.

Marianne's life begins in the style of what the Romantics would later have called "the ill-starred heroine"; but Marivaux's presentation, though romantic in its incidents, is naturalistic in its picture of motivation. Noble in birth and noble (within the limits

we shall observe) in character, Marianne starts life as a nameless
waif, after the murder of her parents on a road in France. It is
as a beautiful and forlorn maiden that we soon find her, utterly
alone in the heartless world of Paris. Here we see human nature
in the raw. Men and women are wolves to each other, all too
ready to devour the helpless prey. They are rapacious, lustful and
heartless. Rushing desperately from those who seek to swindle her,
and perhaps do even worse, Marianne is sent by a naive monk
(which is to give him the benefit of the doubt) to a Tartuffe named
M. de Climal. It is this gentleman who is a prototype of the
eighteenth century seducer. He lures Marianne to the shop of a
Mme Dutour, a *lingère,* who is quite willing to favor his designs,
while pretending to be utterly unaware of them. He offers Marianne wealth, tries to corrupt her moral notions, in short, does
his best to seduce her. In several respects, however, Climal is not
typical of some of his successors. He is fifty years old, and more
odious than seductive. His motive is physical enjoyment, and is
therefore not perverse, but results from the natural passions or
evil in human nature. Most particular of all, after his plans are
foiled, and he has been mortally embarrassed, and is on the point
of death, he repents. In fact, he even leaves Marianne a tidy in-
come, in order to win God's forgiveness.

To follow the endless details of Marianne's history would take
us far too long. She finds a protectress, Mme de Miran, like her
a "noble" character, who is willing to overlook Marianne's economic and social status in favor of the beauty of her soul, and
even to favor marriage with her son, Valville. The latter *galant*
is a thoughtless *petit-maître* who becomes enamored of Marianne's
physical beauty, and then drops the precious jewel for some more
attractive, and more suitable damsel. This intrigue occupies the
main part of the book. Throughout it, we find the virtuous, "helpless" Marianne meeting obstacle after obstacle, defeat after defeat,
but marching steadily onward. The difficulties arise from the
cruelties, prejudices, jealousies and rivalries of those who oppose
her marriage. When Marivaux's story ends, she has lost Valville,
but there is another suitor on the horizon, and indications are
that all will yet turn out well—indications which are strengthened
in the clever continuation which Mme Riccoboni later provided
for the unfinished story.

This is the important reservation I referred to, in suggesting the theme of "Les Infortunes de la vertu." Marivaux's book contains a number of good people, who help Marianne to overcome the wicked. There is compassion for suffering, as well as hardness and cruelty. Several of the wicked even repent, and several others are punished for their wrongs. We have, as I say, the impression that virtue will not make out too badly in the end. In a word, virtue in this world must undergo many trials and tribulations. As Marivaux writes, "the earth must be a land where virtue is a stranger, for it only suffers on it." But its cause is not utterly hopeless. Perhaps "The Trials of Virtue," then, would be a more accurate sub-title.

On the other hand, Marianne's story leads into the relation by a nun of her own unhappy life history. This interminable history, which finally bested even Marivaux's endurance, is a repetition, save for the literal detail, of Marianne's autobiography. Like hers, the nun's tale is unfinished. (Mme Riccoboni quickly eliminated it as hopelessly boring, and left it forever unfinished.) Like Marianne, the nun is given to a slightly nauseating sentimentality and weepiness, thus announcing the *comédie larmoyante* and similar middle-class literature. Again like Marianne, the good sister has undergone every persecution at the hands of a selfish, ungrateful, perfidious, grasping, heartless and depraved humanity. She, too, has had her benefactors. However, from the fact that she is presently unhappy, deprived of her freedom and sexually frustrated, we must assume that in this case, at least, "Les Infortunes de la vertu" would be the appropriate title.

Marivaux's picture is thus profoundly ambiguous. I have suggested a reservation, in the name of the "good" and "noble" characters of the book. But how good are the "good" people? Let us proceed to examine this matter. We have called the virtuous Marianne "helpless," but this is not entirely so. Like so many other heroes and heroines of French fiction, she is gifted with an unusually lucid insight into her own secret motives, and into other people's.[18] This is certainly an advantage, and she makes

[18] This point has been noted by Pierre Trahard, in his definition of *sensibilité:* "To be *sensible*, for Prévost, Diderot and Jean-Jacques, is not to limit oneself to feeling, it is to be aware of feeling, to study sensation, to reflect on one's emotions when the first flame has fallen; it is, if necessary, to provoke sensation in order to analyze it with cruel refinement. . . ." (*Les Maîtres de la sensibilité française*, I, 18–19.)

use of it. She also makes skillful and calculating use of her virtue and nobility of soul, as well as of her physical endowments.[19] Even the undeserved misfortune of her destiny becomes a powerful weapon in the hands of this very adroitly virtuous maiden. It is not that she is not sincerely virtuous; but rather that she is very vain about her virtue, very self-conscious about it, and not a bit loth to put it to fruitful use in attaining her ends. She will fight against the most powerful forces in order to keep her lover —using her helplessness and her virtue as weapons. She will agree instantly to surrender her lover, when it is a matter of showing gratitude to Mme de Miran, her benefactress. But who can say to what degree this is naive impulse, and to what degree the calculation to which even she confesses? She is quite aware that she is using her self-sacrifice as a strategy of conquest. She claims to realize its practical advantage only after the spontaneous impulse. But although Marivaux always remains overtly neutral, there is ample ground to suspect the self-deception with whose workings he was so familiar.

In all of Marianne's actions (even in the deeds of virtue), the satisfactions of her ego, her need for the esteem of others and for self-esteem, are decisive. In the simplest form of activity, she has the proper feminine vanity of coquetry, that of being admired and desired by men, admired and envied by women. Marianne goes to church. "I enter, I am seen, and all those other faces become nothing at all." On another level, it is the sensitive ego: "Slights, the exposure of one's personal affairs, slander, even indelicacy in extending aid," writes Dr. Ruth K. Jamieson, "all these, whether real or imagined, are forms of torture to the sensitive ego." [20] This sensitivity also provides its own cures and compensations, real or imaginary. The ego cannot long tolerate a wound to its self-esteem, so basic is the need of it (as we have

[19] About the latter she says "It is good in such occasions to please the eyes a little; they recommend you to the heart." About the former, she candidly admits that her virtue is partly a calculation, and that she would not be so strongly inclined to be virtuous without the admiration with which she was rewarded. (See *La Vie de Marianne*, éd. "Cent Romans français," pp. 187–188, 280.)

[20] *Marivaux. A Study in Sensibility*, p. 54. The fourth chapter of Dr. Jamieson's study offers an excellent analysis of *amour-propre* in Marivaux. My own viewpoint on *La Vie de Marianne* is, however, quite different, being (among other things) much less optimistic. I am more inclined to favor the definition given by Marcel Arland of Marianne (in his Introduction to the edition I have used) as "a being who starts from nothing to conquer the world and who creates her destiny."

seen in an earlier chapter) to the safety and well-being of the self.

On still another level, there is the *amour-propre* of virtue and self-denial. In the final analysis, Marianne's virtue may be only the compensation for her inferiority in other respects (which she keenly feels and which others make her feel). Her ostentatious virtue, constantly displayed to others and to her own conscience, is the salvation of her intense need for self-esteem and prestige. It is not surprising that the ending of the story, as Mme Riccoboni conceived it, is "an interplay between two *amour-propres*," that of Marianne and Valville.

The other eminently virtuous character is Mme de Miran, Marianne's benefactress. She desires her virtue to be recognized as often as possible. "Any other mother but me would not act the same way," she exclaims. "All difficulties are overcome with a bit of patience and skill, especially when one has a mother like me for a confidante." Here, precisely, is Marivaux's outstanding quality. His ability to see through sham and pretense, even when unconscious, results in a pitiless portrayal of human beings that is all the more cruel for its apparent good humor and ingenuousness, and its lack of sarcasm. Marianne herself comments, "Don't you know that our soul is even more proud than virtuous, more attached to glory than integrity, and so, more delicate about the interests of its vanity than about those of its true honor?" And again, she writes,

> We attend to the most urgent thing first; and the most urgent for us, is ourselves, that is to say, our pride; for our pride and we are only one, whereas we and our virtue make two . . . This virtue must be given to us . . . this pride is not given to us, we bring it on our birth; and we have it so strongly, it cannot be taken away from us . . . Nature has the advantage over education. . . . In life, we are more eager for the regards (*la considération*) of others than for their esteem. . . . Oh! we love ourselves even more than our morals. Honor my good qualities as much as you please, all men would tell you, you will please me, provided that you honor me, me who have them, and who are not they. . . .[21]

These samples will suffice to indicate what is in fact a continuing theme. *Amour-propre*, or vanity, in which is included the desire

[21] P. 96–97. Marianne comments about a sermon: "it was with the vanity of preaching elegantly that the vanity of worldly things was preached to us." (P. 200.)

to be approved, liked and esteemed, and the pleasure derived from feeling superior to others—this is the ineradicable motive in human beings and the motor of society. Does not the pleasure of charity, or a large part of it, lie for most in crushing the *amour-propre* of the beneficiary and in enjoying the feeling of superiority? Such is Marianne's experience. And should we be surprised if we are repaid with ingratitude? [22] Mme Riccoboni, who grasped Marivaux's concept of things, has Marianne say,

> Although *amour-propre* seems sometimes to neglect its interests, it is being none the less zealous in pursuing them. It is the soul of all our movements, it acts in secret; we do not even perceive it, and often we sacrifice to it within us at the very instant when we think we are immolating or destroying it.[23]

The vanity of virtue is at least better than wickedness. It is a far lesser degree of aggressive self-interest; and its hypocrisy, unlike that of M. de Climal, or of Mlle Varthon (who steals Valville away) is at least unconscious. These at least try to *do good;* the others do evil. And they do evil consciously and willfully. They are not, like Des Grieux, fatally impelled to it, nor, like Manon Lescaut, amoral and innocent. They calculate the harm they do, and will it. Nevertheless—and this is a point to be noted carefully—it is not for evil's sake that they do evil; but rather for the satisfaction of passions, pleasures and self-interest, all of which are needs that inhere in the miserable human frame. The satisfaction of these needs, in the case of individuals who are not "fortunately born," requires hurting others, and in some instances, is intensified by the comparative process. The only way to avoid it would be to be virtuous, in Rousseau's sense of virtue-sacrifice. But there are almost no Christians in Marivaux's portrait gallery, almost none who are capable of sacrificing their interest to help others, or to avoid hurting them. Those few who do are ruthlessly taken advantage of. And this, in itself, is enough to indicate Marivaux's opinion of human nature. Although all this is clear in the history

---

[22] "The humiliation [a person] has suffered has closed his heart to you in that regard. His heart keeps a rancor which it does not itself know it has, as long as you ask only for feelings which are your just due; but do you ask for affection, oh! that is another matter: its self-love recognizes you then; you are irremediably its enemy, it will never forgive you." (P. 52–53.) Here again we have one of the rivulets that will feed the stream leading to the Sadian psychology.

[23] *Ibid.,* p. 564.

of Marianne, it is emphasized in the nun's story. In order for the nun's mother to achieve her ends as a social climber she must abandon and disown her; in order for those who wish to defraud her of an inheritance to achieve theirs, they must break up her marriage and ruin her reputation. There are no alternatives. At the same time, there is nothing to make us think that the wrong-doers would not have preferred virtue, or not hurting others, were that possible. In other words, hurting others is not, in itself, the very source of pleasure. If Mlle Varthon is ungrateful to Marianne, it is only because jealousy and vanity are stronger human motives; and if the woman saved by the nun is even more shockingly ungrateful to her, it is only because the nun unfortunately stands in the way of her greed and her ambitions.

Taken all in all, the sum of the picture is most unfavorable to the human race. The picture of "virtue" in *La vie de Marianne* is a perfect example, or application, of Kant's analysis, which we examined at the close of the twelfth chapter. It makes us think that perhaps Rousseau was right when he said that the best possible rule for mankind is not the Golden Rule, but to accomplish our own good with the least harm to others. As Marianne says, "men's virtues accomplish no more than their exact duties . . . only vices have no limits. . . . We have to stiffen up to be great; we have only to remain as we are to be small." All this Mme Riccoboni understood, too; and she only continued Marivaux's view of the world when she commented, "Aside from the real pleasure we feel when we do right, I don't see what good virtue is. The wicked take advantage of it, are not grateful to us for it, and think themselves more in debt to their own cleverness than to our goodness." [24]

The same pessimism applies to *Le paysan parvenu,* which I am not able to discuss because of limitations of space. *Le paysan parvenu* is a picaresque novel, with rather savage overtones, as the title suggests. Its *picaro* rises, like Julien Sorel, by using (and abusing) women. Marcel Arland's comment is *à propos*. Replying to Larroumet's assertion that Jacob, in contrast to Gil Blas, is not vicious, he writes:

> But that is precisely the audacity of the book, its perfect amoralism, and even, if you will, its danger. Jacob, the stout, dark

[24] P. 571.

lad, the peasant Gilles de Retz, is not given to us as a scoundrel; he overflows with good sense and health; he feels compassion; he can be generous. Le Sage paints a rogue . . . but try and guess what Marivaux thinks of his hero! With what complaisance he follows him from conquest to conquest! . . . No, decidedly, Jacob is not repugnant to him. His shrewd innocence lets him see everything with a fresh eye, to say everything as if in spite of himself.

Vanity, ambition and pleasure are, without any doubt, Jacob's directing motives. Like Marianne (and like Stendhal's hero), he is determined to "create his destiny." It is his weapons that differ, as he relies only on his physical attractiveness.[25]

To the Existentialist philosophers of the twentieth century, the characters of Marivaux are outstanding examples of "bad faith." And Marivaux's purpose is strikingly like that of Sartre, in his novels: to make the reader, deceived by the innocence and ambiguity of the portrait, identify himself with the characters, and then discover his own bad faith, which is identical with theirs. Marianne, Jacob, Mme de Miran make the reader uneasy, by their combination of evil and innocence. They see lucidly into the evil in the motivation of other people, but not into themselves. Even Marianne's lucidity stops at a certain point. She decides not to accept expensive clothes from M. de Climal, but finds a way of doing so without injuring her feeling of virtue. Arland, precisely, speaks of a "perverse innocence," and of "the triumph of the lucidity of the equivocal." [26]

We can see, then, how closely Marivaux' novels (and his theatre, as well) are connected to that phase of eighteenth century ethical and psychological exploration which emphasized self-deception and the prostitution of reason by the deeper vitalities: a line of

[25] Dr. Jamieson mistakenly treats the theme of *Le paysan parvenu* as the development of moral sensibility in its hero. Arland has correctly seen the more subtle intent: "What a school of softness, of voluptuousness, of corruption, and consequently, of sentiment! For the soul becomes refined in proportion as it becomes corrupt."

[26] Cf. Nietzsche: "Do not deceive yourself: what constitutes the chief characteristic of modern souls and modern books is not the lying, but the innocence which is part and parcel of their intellectual dishonesty. . . . The real lie, the genuine, determined honest lie . . . would prove too tough and strong an article for them by a long way; it would be asking them to do what people have been forbidden to do, to open their eyes to their own selves, and to learn to distinguish between 'true' and 'false' in their own selves." (*Genealogy of Morals*, third essay, par. 19.

thought which was to culminate, though only after a leap, in the work of Sade.

But let us balance the picture. Marivaux believes that some chosen people are "fortunately born," with a delicate moral sense and a propensity to virtue. They do the generous and noble thing by a *mouvement naturel*. This virtue inevitably produces pleasure, in the form of self-satisfaction or a satisfied conscience, or self-approval. It also produces the admiration of others; for, though many are not eminently virtuous themselves, they are touched by virtue in others, even as Shaftesbury had said that when our self-love is not involved, we naturally approve of virtue and abhor vice. The satisfactions and advantages of virtue become stimuli to continued virtue, and, in fact, its principal motivation —with the accompaniment of self-deception. To a certain extent, virtue always becomes calculated self-interest. To a certain extent, it also remains impulse—that natural impulse of which Rousseau said, it is always "droit," or true; provided we may interpret "true" as meaning not only sincere and moral, but also the well-aimed, unconscious instinct or intuition, to hit the mark. Love of virtue, then, such as it is, is persistent in the human race; and reference to Marivaux's statement, quoted earlier,[27] confirms this opinion.

On the other hand, the majority of men and women are not so "fortunately born." The strength of their *amour-propre* and self-directed motives leads, as we have seen, to cruelty and viciousness, to the law of the jungle. Still others, who are inclined to virtue, like Valville, are weak, vacillating and changeable. Once again, the knowledge of good and evil, or moral conscience, which all men possess, is seen to be quite different from the *will* to justice and virtue, which few possess, or the will to virtue-sacrifice, which only a chosen few—if any—possess. Society is the place of temptation and trial, in which weak virtue succumbs, strongly rooted virtue rises, in an ambiguous way, to noble deeds, and the egoism of most men, exacerbated, condoned by custom and the struggle for self-advancement, runs rampant.

[27] See above, p. 343. Compare the following lines, written in the *Spectateur français* after Marivaux had lost his fortune in the "Mississippi Bubble": "It is true that we are all born wicked; but we bring this wickedness with us as a monster that must be combatted." (Quoted by Jamieson, p. 120.) In *L'Isle des esclaves*, Marivaux portrays a return to innocence in an artificial utopia.

We need not dwell quite so long on our next three novelists. Their contribution to our subject, though by no means insignificant, is less complex, and less debatable than that of Marivaux.

Crébillon-*fils* is widely known as the author of erotic stories and novels. Most of them pall with the monotony of the game of seduction, endlessly repeated. They are none the less valuable as a panorama of upper-class society, of its *mores* and values. Ideals and moral credos are no longer given even lip-service by characters in Crébillon's novels. Pleasure, and the vanity of "the kill" are the sole motivations in their relationships. "Love" is a purely physical satisfaction, deprived of any emotional dimension; it is distinguished from animal eroticism only by its intimate association with the complex of feelings we have called "pride," and by the highly stylized gestures and formulas of a ritual. The male and the female are engaged in a pleasant game of warfare that has its mortal aspects. One of the two must be the victim of the other's egoism. Physical pleasure is, in fact, secondary to what Helvétius was to call the need for power, the need to placate and to affirm the ego by the subjugation of another ego. In this pleasant and deadly game no holds are barred.

Les égarements du coeur et de l'esprit (1736) is Crébillon's most ambitious and least licentious work. It, too, is an unfinished novel; but there is enough of it to make it easily his best. The theme of the story is simple. It is that of innocence pitted against a corrupt world, and destroyed by it. Meilcour and Hortense, two innocent (i.e., uncorrupted) young people, fall in love, in a way that, in other circumstances and in another milieu, might lead to a romantic, idyllic love. But they are never given even the opportunity to declare their love. Between them stands the society in which they have the misfortune to have been born: not only the temptations it presents, but the will of corrupt people who cannot tolerate innocence, but are drawn to it, as to a natural victim. The corrupt people are two middle-aged women who compete to obtain Meilcour's virginity, in order to re-establish their prestige and to satisfy their vanity. In this project, they are aided by Meilcour's friend, Versac, a model of the corrupt masculine ideal of Crébillon's world, whom Meilcour admires and aspires to imitate. The methods used include unscrupulous deceit, ruthless calumny, and coquetry of the most complex and subtle kind (so subtle, in fact, that it often passes over the victim's head, and the lady is forced to go beyond the rules of the game and speak forthrightly—that is, with hypocritical honesty). Meilcour, after much struggling and torment, is ruined, morally and spiritually. As for Hortense, who remains in the background of the novel, we can foresee that she will eventually be like the others.

Hyprocrisy, placed always at the service of vanity, dominates this corrupt society. Formal politeness and expressions of friendship and feeling are stratagems and routines which mask the one purpose of getting the intended victim, of either sex, into bed. Society is painted, *sur le vif,* with lines and colors that confirm and carry out the worst accusations that Rousseau was to level against it. It is a school of shame, of in-fighting, of corruption. Vanity and reputation (what Rousseau was to call "opinion") are the principal directors of behavior. The nub of the lesson is given to us in Versac's private talk with Meilcour, initiating him into *le monde comme il va.* He pleads with Meilcour to realize that it is impossible to be virtuous, *dans le monde,* without suffering in reputation and in fortune. He urges him to be ruled by pride and by the will to assert his superiority over others. Most important of all is to remember that, "in all events, it is safer to subjugate others than to sacrifice to them the interests of our *amour-propre.*"

As Meilcour becomes rather painfully initiated, he discovers the power of vanity and pride. At one point, for instance, he is piqued because his would-be seductress, whom he has treated brutally after his vanity has been injured by her deceit, may have "thought so soon of another engagement." Actually, she is still baiting her hook for him.

> Yet I could not say that what she inspired in me was love: I was carried away by impulses that I did not recognize and which I could not have defined: they were violent without being tender; no desire was mingled in them and I was piqued without being in love. If she had appeared *sensible* a single moment, if I had seen her jealous again, angry, if she had made efforts to bring me back, the charm would have vanished; my vanity, once satisfied with the humiliation in which I would have seen her, my heart would have found in her only an indifferent and perhaps a scorned object.

By now Meilcour has learned what "love" is. "What the two sexes called 'love' then was a kind of relationship (*commerce*) in which they engaged, often even without taste for it, in which convenience was always preferred to mutual attraction (*sympathie*), self-interest to pleasure, and vice to sentiment."

The busy round of pleasure and intrigue is unable to fill the boredom and inner emptiness which it hollows out more and more deeply. "In the midst of the tumult and the brilliance that constantly surrounded me," admits Meilcour, "I felt that my heart was missing everything; I longed for a happiness of which I did not have a clear idea. . . . I wanted in vain to close my eyes to the inner *ennui* with which I felt myself overwhelmed." But precisely at that point, Meilcour decides to seek a remedy in the pursuit of women, which is to lead him to further degradation.

There are several passages, in the *Discours sur l'inégalité,* which are so perfectly applicable to the world of *Les égarements du coeur et de l'esprit* that, had they not sprung from Rousseau's own thought and experience, one might take them for a commentary.

Charles Duclos, another keen observer of the social scene, was the author of several tales and two novels. In his best fictional work, *Histoire de Mme de Luz* (1741), he does not attempt a portrayal of contemporary society. In imitation of Mme de Lafayette, he goes back to the time of Henry the Fourth. While he is too far from that period to recapture the realistic immediacy of *La Princesse de Clèves,* the temporal distance does help him to create a classical effect of universality and timelessness, in his own fashion. The theme of *Mme de Luz* is also related, in an ironical way, to that of *La Princesse de Clèves.* Like the latter, its heroine is an admirable woman of Cartesian stamp, willfully committed to a life of the highest moral standards. Like Mme de Clèves, she is married to a man she respects, but does not love; and, after meeting the man whom she does love, one who is worthy of her love, she resolutely dominates her passion and sets her course in the path of duty.

But Duclos' view of life is ironical. In fact, the story of Mme de Luz becomes a reversal, almost a parody, of that of Mme de Clèves. While Mme de Luz succeeds in guiding her actions by will and moral reason, she discovers that this is contrary to human nature and to the conditions of life. In most other people, and especially in the powerful, reason is dominated by passion, when it is not actually prostituted to it. All this is explained to Mme de Luz—though she will not heed it—in these clear terms:

> . . . do you imagine that a rebel's pardon can be bought by a virtue which is of no value to the State? This virtue, so precious in your eyes, is only a chimerical prejudice, which men, by another prejudice, demand in their wives or their mistresses, and which they scorn in others. It may sometimes evoke a sterile esteem; but as it is contrary to their pleasures, which is their dearest interest, they do not believe they owe it much gratitude.

As a result of these existential conditions, Mme de Luz, in the course of her history, is seduced or enjoyed, despite herself, by three men; while the man she loves, to whom she virtuously refuses herself, and who virtuously respects her refusal, is the only one of her admirers who is unrewarded by her possession. She is the victim, in turn, of ruthless cruelty, of physical violence, and of perfidious hypocrisy. In the first instance, she is forced to sacrifice her virtue, out of her very sense of duty to her husband, to M. de Thurin, a powerful magistrate. Thurin had believed "that his prestige (*sa gloire*) would be untouchable if he could let it be known that Mme de Luz was his." But his vanity turns into a mad, uncontrollable love. When M. de Luz is implicated in a conspiracy against the king, and his life is placed in the hands of M. de Thurin, the magistrate obliges Mme de Luz to yield to him. "And Thurin was," comments Duclos, "at that moment, the happiest of men, if it was possible to be it in crime and when his heart should have been torn by remorse."

Not long after this episode, two other courtiers, the count de Maran and the chevalier de Marsillac, both fall passionately in love with Mme de Luz, and become bitter rivals. Both are treated by her with fierce scorn. Marsillac is a gentleman, but Maran is only a courtier, and he is determined to have his way. One day, when Mme de Luz is bathing, quite unclothed, in the stream adjoining her country house, she is momentarily left alone. Maran, who has been observing her from his hiding place, goes quickly towards her. She sees him, runs out of the bath, pursued by her determined ravisher, who soon catches up with her and prepares to do her violence. At that moment, Marsillac chances to pass by, hears Mme de Luz's outraged screams, rushes to her rescue, and after a brief but vigorous duel, runs Maran through. During this incident, Mme de Luz has been discreetly hiding in a grove, and in fact, has fainted. Marsillac, coming now to comfort and help her, is so overcome by the sight of her beauty that physical passion and lust conquer his will to virtue. Losing control of himself, he rapes her. But he, at least, feels remorse.

This second defeat of her virtue leads Mme de Luz to reflect upon the matter. An idea dawns upon her, which she quickly rejects. "She looked at herself with horror. How could she, with so much virtue in her heart, have become so criminal? But how, with so much misfortune, could she still be innocent? It would be to accuse heaven of injustice. She preferred to condemn herself."

Grieving over her twice-offended virtue, Mme de Luz turns to religion for solace. She falls under the influence of an adroit and perfidious priest, M. Hardouin. Unlike the first two villains, this one is a moral nihilist, and foreshadows the great creations of Laclos, Rétif de la Bretonne, and Sade. He, too, develops a violent physical desire for the irresistible and unfortunate lady. With deliberateness and calculation, he captures her confidence, undermines her feeling of remorse for the two earlier misfortunes, and insinuates (after her husband's death) that a further sin would be an inconsequential peccadillo compared to her previous adulteries. But Mme de Luz is not to be shaken. Finally Hardouin's need becomes so urgent that he decides to use more direct measures. He gives opium to both Mme de Luz and to her chambermaid. When the former is asleep, he possesses her. "Let us turn aside," comments Duclos, "from the image of so frightful a perfidy, worthy of all the human and divine vengeances." In the midst of this act, Mme de Luz recovers her senses, and then gives way to violent rage and utter despair. Already she had suspected that there is a plot against virtue in the universe of God, but her Christian patience had stifled that impious doubt. Now, however, raped by the very servant of God, she knows no bounds, and cries out to the heavens. "To what peaks of horror was I then destined? Cruel heaven! In what way have I deserved your hatred? Can it be that virtue is hateful to you?"

Mme de Luz falls mortally ill. On her death-bed, the one she loves, the one she had avoided, returns to her bedside in time to console her. "Thus died the most beautiful, the most unfortunate, and I may also say, the most virtuous and most respectable of all women."

In the *Histoire de Mme de Luz,* Duclos touches Mme de Lafayette with one hand, and the Marquis de Sade with the other. The second aspect is, of course, the more original and the more interesting. We have already mentioned the fact that from *Mme de Luz* Sade took the subject of his two great novels. While Duclos does not, like his last villain, embrace and urge moral nihilism, there is nothing to prevent others from drawing that lesson from the picture he offers. There are good men and women, to be sure, ruled by moral law and decency. But they fall into two equally lamentable groups. In some, reason and the will to virtue become the easy prey of passion and the animal drives. The others, who persist in virtue, find themselves inevitably in a position of weakness. They are destined, by nature's laws or those of "whatever gods may be," to be what Sade was to call "victims." The world has no regard to desert, only to strength and to weakness. Whether it be from a free will, as it is with some, or from weakness and against their rational will, men are devoted to evil, and evil rules the world.[27a]

The picture drawn by Diderot offers some curious similarities to the one Duclos has shown us. This is despite the fact that his fictional writings, rich though they are in other respects (and doubtless for that very reason) are concerned only secondarily with the questions that are pertinent to our inquiry. In the tale, *Les Deux amis de Bourbonne,* it is the devotion of friendship that moves us primarily. Secondarily, however, the story involves several

[27a] Paul Meister takes Duclos at his word, when the latter writes that his purpose was only to show that a woman can be dishonored without being criminal. He disposes of Duclos' statements ("Baroness de Luz is one of the strangest examples of the misfortunes which follow virtue," and "It seems that a woman's virtue is in this world a foreign being, against which everything conspires") by asserting that they represent only the victim's viewpoint (although she does not utter them). But Duclos' own protestation, the amplitude of the development and its obvious metaphysical implications indicate the contrary. Meister is himself compelled to enlarge the theme to include the idea that fate "is not concerned with punishing or rewarding; it is blind and, in fact, not deserved or undeserved"—a theme which is already perilously close to the one he rejects. At the end, however, Meister admits that the reader is right in retaining the thesis which may not have been Duclos'. He is more accurate when he says that Duclos wants to "denounce by its absurdity the presumptuousness of which the Princess of Clèves was guilty." Why should a woman refuse the man she loves, when she may reach the same end with one she does not? But it is almost always an error to reduce a work of art to its smallest and narrowest terms. (*Charles Duclos,* p. 136–140, 201–202.)

other assumptions. It is possible for two men to be superior to all the instincts of egoism and self-interest, to be completely and truly altruistic in their relations. But these two friends, more by a chance concatenation of circumstances than by anyone's willful maliciousness (though there is a little of that, too), meet misfortune after misfortune, and bring unhappiness to those they love, until their miserable deaths. *Les Deux amis* may thus be viewed as forming a part of the current we are studying. The accent is metaphysical. Virtue, we conclude, is a stranger in this world, unwanted and punished. Diderot, however, makes no overt reference to such a conclusion; and one feels that his interest lies perhaps as much in another problem, one which concerned him in several of his writings: the possibility that virtuous conduct may be in opposition to the requirements of religion and the laws.

Another of Diderot's tales, *Ceci n'est pas un conte,* may be described by two of its lines. "You must admit that there are very good men and very wicked women. . . . And then, if there are wicked women and very good men, there are also very good women and very wicked men." The story proceeds to prove both assertions in romantic and touching terms. Here the accent is on human nature, with only passing metaphysical overtones. But Diderot's principal interest, as in much of his other work, is in the psychology of sexual behavior, and the relations between the sexes. Within this field of human behavior, then, it is shown that the good and true lover may be the weak and helpless victim of the partner who does not love, and who is therefore strong, and heartlessly evil in his (or her) egoism. The victim is treated only as a means, or an instrument, to further his needs and ends. This time the conclusion is made overtly, and it is generalized, in ironical terms. "But that too is just about within the order of things. If there is a good Tanié, it is to a Reymer that Providence will send him; if there is a good and honest [Mlle] de la Chaux, she will become the lot of a Gardeil, so that all may be for the best." [28]

Diderot's best novel is *La Religieuse.* We need not go into the details of the plot, as it touches only incidentally upon our themes. In a variety of figures, we see the perverted outlets taken

[28] *Oeuvres,* v, 331. The names in the quotation are those of the characters. The facts of this story were taken from life. The editor notes that Mlle de la Chaux suffered a miserable death while still young, and that the wicked Gardeil lived on to the age of eighty-two.

by the sex drive when its natural expression is dammed up by confinement in the convent. Though there is goodness in human beings, that goodness is destroyed when their animal needs are thwarted. Physical and moral cruelty, and sexual perversion, always latent in human nature, become rampant under the driving force of sexual energy which has been turned aside from its normal expression. Once again, the good and virtuous nun, who refuses to be a compliant victim, becomes instead the object of savage torture for those who have the power to satisfy their deep, though perverted needs at her expense. Diderot clearly anticipates Sade's *Justine* in his willing emphasis on the nun's virtue and on the sadistic cruelty and pleasure provoked by its persecution and attempted corruption.

When we come to Laclos, we take a step forward in time, and a much larger step forward in the history of the ideas with which we are dealing. The consequences of the materialistic revolution in morals, about which the traditionalists had warned, begin now to reach their fruition. *Les Liaisons dangereuses* (1782), the greatest French novel of the eighteenth century, is remarkable from a multiplicity of viewpoints, many of which, including structure, style, psychology and tragic poetry, do not enter into the plan of this chapter. It is also remarkable for its uncompromising boldness in the realization of a concept of human nature and human relationships; and with this aspect of the work we are concerned.

Les Liaisons dangereuses is the story of two seductions; but these seductions, though told with a concrete realism, both physical and psychological, that had never been approached before, are only the mechanisms of a deeper study. Most other "lascivious" novels of the eighteenth century are half-humorous, half-grotesque tales of seduction and amorous feats, that still bear the stamp of Boccaccio. But Laclos' novel, precisely, is not lascivious; it is, to be sure, partly concerned with *human lasciviousness,* and that is a quite different matter. It is much more deeply concerned with the inner drama, the moral drama, of certain individuals of heroic stature. Their driving force is not animal desire, but human desire; sex, yes; but pride, conquest and revenge, the fascination of evil, and the revolt against moral compulsion: these are the vital springs. The theme is worked out in a multiple action, interconnected as in life, and woven into a skillfully constructed plot.

The multiple action produces a plurality of viewpoints, which act like the focussing of mirrors to illuminate the phenomena of the soul.

The antagonists of this drama are drawn up on two sides. On the side of Satan are Valmont and Mme de Merteuil. It is hard to say which of the two is more satanic; but Valmont, as the seducer, is the effective agent and has the center of the stage, while Mme de Merteuil is the actuating impulse, and is probably superior to her ally in hard principle and consistency. Both are unusually intelligent and lucid; but their reason—and this is in accord with one important view we have analyzed—is not a guarantee of moral goodness, but a weapon placed at the service of an evil will.

"Natural" desires and needs are only a secondary motive in Valmont's actions, though he makes use of them to conquer his victims. Vanity and pride are the efficient causes of the actions of both conspirators. Thus far Laclos follows his predecessors. The vast difference between Laclos' concept of human nature and those of his predecessors lies in the fact that Valmont and Merteuil do not do evil merely to satisfy other motives of pleasure. Their chief pleasure in doing evil comes from the fact that it *is* evil. The psychology of the "detractors of man" (including that of Rousseau) had emphasized our need for power and for superiority, in order to satisfy the ego's hunger for self-affirmation—some had even called it an aspiration to godhead.[29] They had pointed out, time and again, that our pleasure is comparative, and increases with the misfortune of others. The aspiration to godhead was the ultimate logical conclusion of a philosophy which, excluding values from the objective universe, set the ego and its demands at the origin of ethical experience and closed the circle by making the ego and its demands the sole ends of conduct. The *philosophes* (as we shall see in a later part of this study) tried to short-circuit this progression by interposing social criteria between the origin and the end. But, as electricity takes the most direct path, so did the logic of the radical materialists, from La Mettrie to Sade. Now

[29] Mme de Merteuil, who is profiting from the confidence of Mme Volanges and her daughter to destroy them both, writes to Valmont: "There I am like the Divinity; receiving the opposed prayers of blind mortals, and changing nothing in my immutable decrees." (Lettre XXIII.) Later, Valmont exults at the prospect of Mme de Tourvel pleading with him to retard her fall. "The fervent prayers, the humble supplications, all that mortals, in their fear, offer to the Divinity, it is I who receive them from her." (Lettre XCVI.)

godhead, in human beings, cannot be exerted by an absolute of creativeness. It can only be exerted (as twentieth century Existentialist literature has again demonstrated) by an absolute of destruction.

In Laclos' novel, the ultimate implications of the sensationist reduction of human experience and values are transposed from philosophy to fiction, from theory to life. In the mentality of Valmont and Mme de Merteuil, the satisfactions of the ego, or pleasure in its various forms, are the only real values. And the greatest pleasure comes from achieving complete power over other human beings, and destroying them; that is, from evil. Reversing Rousseau's formula, Valmont wishes to accomplish his own good with a maximum of harm to others. But over whom can such power be obtained and wielded? Who are the *natural* victims of the ruthlessly strong? They are, in the first place, the innocent and uncorrupted; and, in the second place, those who are committed to the moral structure which the protagonists of evil seek to destroy. Both of these, for the respective reasons of innocence and 'morality, are the weak, whom nature has intended to be the victims of the strong, according to the workings of the *natural* laws and forces of the universe. However, triumph over the second type of victim is more difficult, more challenging, and represents the acme of satanic achievement, even as the godly are the choice victims of Lucifer.

The plot of *Les Liaisons dangereuses* revolves around a series of carefully planned campaigns and battles, the objective of which is to hurt, corrupt and destroy innocence and virtue. For Valmont, the victims are naturally women. One of them is in fact warned that "to be cruel and wicked without danger, he has chosen women for victims." The antagonists on the other side (or the victims) are Cécile Volanges and Mme de Tourvel. The former incarnates innocence, the latter, virtue. Mme de Merteuil, as a moral nihilist, has used the tactics of hypocritical virtue in order to secure sexual pleasures, satisfy her vanity and conserve her reputation, it matters not at whose cost.[30] Because of outraged vanity, she decides to

[30] We find out that she has taken pleasure in ruining the life of another man, simply for the pleasure of so doing.

It has not been noted, I believe, that Laclos may have found the prototype for his Mme de Merteuil in "Madame C." of D'Argens' novel, *Thérèse philosophe* [1748]. Since this book is difficult to obtain, a brief outline may be of interest.

avenge herself on a former lover, by having another ex-lover, Valmont (whom she is secretly trying to win back) seduce Cécile Volanges. Cécile, the daughter of a friend who trusts her, has just left the convent and is completely innocent. Valmont accomplishes this minor feat with little difficulty, but with much skill and relish. His pleasure comes not only from the experience of seduction, but from complete mastery of the girl, and the destruction of her innocence and moral restraints. He blackens her mother's reputation to her, since this is necessary, he says, if you do not wish merely to seduce a girl, but to deprave her. He debases her to all kinds of practices, and impregnates her, in order to complete her destruction and also to obtain the added pleasure of having her bear his child after marrying another man.

Valmont, however, is far more interested in seducing Mme de Tourvel, a woman of truly noble character, sincere virtue, strong will, and religious faith. Here we see that French literature is again haunted by the memory of Mme de Clèves, and that she has become a symbol which defies the naturalistic view of man. Her image, in the figure of Mme de Tourvel, is a challenge to both Valmont and Mme de .Merteuil; they can have no peace, no security, while it exists. Valmont, recognizing in her conquest the fulfillment of his destiny, or as he says, his glory, lavishes his most consummate talents on her. "But what fatality attaches me to this woman?" he exclaims; "do not a hundred others desire my attentions?" Again, the pleasure is not that of mere seduction. Valmont is not interested, he tells Mme de Merteuil, in the insipid desire of a young man to add another woman to his list; he wishes to pro-

---

Madame C. is a woman of virtuous and pious reputation. She is a friend of Thérèse's mother, who is grateful to her for giving friendship and counsel to Thérèse. The mother recommends to her daughter that she be more friendly with Mme C., who has determined to be the instrument of her seduction. Madame C. receives the innocent admissions of Thérèse without surprise or reproof. Up to this point, the situation in the two novels is closely similar, but from here on the action diverges. Mme C. confides Thérèse to the direction of her lover, the abbé T. The abbé advises onanism, but Mme C. prefers to have the abbé seduce her, though it might be dangerous as yet. "Il y a de quoi faire par la suite un bon sujet," she says. Thérèse overhears this conversation, and also observes them engaging in "strange exercises." However the seduction is not completed. Thérèse goes to Paris, where she is taken in hand by another "good" woman, Mme Bois-Lamier, who tries to arrange her fall, and meanwhile initiates her to Lesbianism. Then Thérèse meets a count, who is really a good man (that is, according to d'Argens' philosophical principles). She becomes his mistress for life, and both enjoy "legitimate" natural pleasures.

long the agony, in order to relish "the charms of long struggles and the details of a painful defeat." [31] Most of all, he seeks to destroy the model of virtue she represents and which has resisted him. He desires, he says, to enslave her; and this is only to show, to others and to himself, his omnipotence. He intends to demolish her virtue and her self-esteem so completely, that she will thank him for her defeat and beg him for the happiness which only his love can bring her, and devote all her life to the one purpose of pleasing him.

The principal drama of the book is the mortal struggle between this angel and this devil. For Valmont conceives of himself as Satan, pledged to "snatch her from God," and to make himself "the god she shall prefer." Mme de Tourvel declares to him that there is no greater pleasure than the tranquillity of a good conscience. Valmont's task is to prove to her that there are greater pleasures in physical sensation heightened by sin and wrongdoing. The angel, attracted by evil as the moth by the flame, falls, but the devil is destroyed by his victory. At the end, he falls in love with her. Only the persistence of the integrity of his will and character—helped, it is true, by the devilish promptings of a humiliated Merteuil—enables him to complete the seduction. This integrity of character is one of the aesthetic highlights of the novel. The same persistence obliges him to complete his triumph by abandoning her and degrading her, by humiliating her and destroying the integrity of her self. Mme de Tourvel will die, a truly pathetic victim. But Valmont has enslaved her so completely that even in repentance and at death's door, she dreams only of his love.

Now Valmont finds himself engaged in another mortal combat with an unexpected foe, one more redoubtable than innocence or virtue. All along, Mme de Merteuil and Valmont, partners in evil, had really been engaged in a secret war on each other, each trying to reduce the other under his power. She had successfully manipulated him, through his vanity and the promise of surrender, and made him break off with Mme de Tourvel. Only then does he find out that she has seduced Danceny, the young man with whom

---

[31] Lettre XXIII. For a similar, and more detailed declaration, see Lettre LXX, where he speaks of "making her virtue expire in a slow agony," and promises to make her beg him to take her. Also, Lettre XCVI.

Cécile was originally in love. As the price of "sacrificing" Danceny, Mme de Merteuil now demands complete submission from Valmont: this, the conquest of her only equal, is to be her greatest triumph. This conquest is all the more necessary, since she knows that Valmont has really preferred Mme de Tourvel, a woman whom she already hated because of her sincere virtue. After an exchange of threats, they declare open war on each other. The forces of evil are now turned on each other. After a brief, but savage combat of great dramatic intensity, they destroy each other.[32] The tragic irony is that Valmont, near his end, sincerely regrets the loss of Mme de Tourvel's love; and Mme de Tourvel, in her last gesture before death, prays God to forgive him.

Laclos has explored not only the forms and manifestations of evil in human behavior; he has delved into its nature and its source in the personality. Evil is radical in human beings, though it can be overcome, since in some individuals the personality is integrated by the moral self, not by the egoistic self.[33] Evil is attached to some of the deepest, pre-rational needs of the personality, and as such provides the most intense sensations of pure pleasure. In a philosophy which made ego-satisfaction the sole value, in a psychology which reduced the self to a succession of sensations, one logical terminus was, as I have said, the exaltation of evil as the highest value. None of this is explicitly proclaimed by Laclos, as it will be by Sade; and he, personally, is utterly opposed to it. His characters, to be sure, are lucid in all their acts, and their conduct is rationally planned and directed; the evil they do comes from the commitment of a free will, not from a passion or impulse that overwhelms the reason.[34] But they neither proclaim a philosophical theory, nor act to illustrate one. They are among the most intensely *living* creations of literature. If they have any abstract philosophy, it appears only in their behavior and feelings. This is one way in which Valmont differs from Molière's Dom Juan. Valmont may consider himself to be, like Dom Juan, a rebel against the gods and against man, the standard-bearer of the

[32] Laclos does call on the assistance of a *deus ex machina* to complete Mme de Merteuil's punishment.

[33] According to Valmont, all men are equally evil in their intentions, but most are weak in executing them, because of moral scruples; a weakness which they call probity. (Lettre LXVI.)

[34] See Lettre LXXXI, in which Mme de Merteuil proclaims her consistency to fixed principles: "I created them, and I can say that I am my own work."

limitlessness of the absurd, but he gives no expression to such a feeling. He appears, rather, as a man of heroic stature, committed to evil, because he is seeking unlimited self-fulfillment through the sensations that only evil can provide. His nihilism is an aspiration to the existence or will without limits which is godhood. He must, then, like god, control the destiny of others; and this he can do only to women, and only by destroying them. (Mme de Merteuil can play the same role only by controlling the destiny of Valmont.) His drama is a psychological one. It is also a tragic one. Evil destroys good, but also itself. As in *Hamlet,* we learn that evil is a limit to the good, and also to itself. An evil world can never be a viable world, because it devours itself.

Rétif (or Restif) de la Bretonne was one of the strangest characters among eighteenth century writers. His most noted work is the novel, *Le paysan perverti* (1776) and its sequel, or complement, *La paysanne pervertie* (1784), which were fused into one in a 1785 edition. Although Rétif's novel is historically interesting, it has been overrated by some critics. It is diffuse, repetitious and tedious; to the modern taste, its drenched sentimentality and heavy "melerdrammer" are ridiculous.

The theme of *Le paysan* is once again the evil in human nature, and its struggle with the good. Rétif, in a sense, stands on two sides. In his presentation of willful wickedness, he goes a step beyond even Laclos. At the same time, however, he also represents a loud reaction to philosophical materialism and its moral consequences. Whereas Laclos, primarily a superb artist, was objective in his picture of the struggle between good and evil, and its consequences, Rétif is a verbose preacher. The punishments of vice occupy a large part of the book, and the blessings of the right way are tediously and emotionally described. In Laclos, Rétif and Sade, the corruption of French society and the moral nihilism latent in its materialism came to a head. Laclos thought that the best way of exposing the corruption was to paint it with psychological realism and in the tones of tragic drama. Rétif turned it into melodrama, picturing fiendish vice receiving its just desserts. Sade, on the other hand, with the same vision, accepted and embraced the nihilism, as the enduring truth of the human condition.

Following Rousseau, Rétif centers his story about the corruption of life in the cities, compared with the simple innocence of the country. We shall not go into the details of the long and loosely-knit story. Edmond and his sister, Ursule, are corrupted, and corrupt others. Virtue is so strong and natural in them that it dies a long and hard death. When it dies, the descent into immoralism, debauchery and crime is rapid and complete. Rétif, before Sade, includes incest and homosexuality in his picture; but he brushes past them with dark references, and does not linger to paint them, as he does depict seduction. Crime and vice bring their own hideous punishments. Then Ursule is redeemed, and goes on to live a moral life with her illegitimate child, until she is assassinated by Edmond, in an accident which is obviously decreed by fate. Edmond is also redeemed, but too late. He drags his miserable existence through many countries and several hundred pages, losing first an arm and then an eye, ranting endlessly about the dangers of vice and the happiness of virtue, and the mark of Cain which is on him, until he dies, just as happiness is rewon. But even this is not enough. The sins of the father are visited upon the sons; and two of Edmond's illegitimate children enjoy an incestuous marriage.

Edmond and Ursule are victims. Their virtue has been overcome by the force of circumstance, by *la forza del destino,* and by their own weakness in resisting seduction. They succumb to the passions associated with physical pleasure and vanity, in the conquest of which virtue consists. The men in the story all derive a feeling of power from seducing or violating women, from making them pregnant and leaving them to suffer with their ruined lives —though Edmond's enjoyment is frequently interrupted by swift pangs of remorse.

The real antagonists are the virtuous, angelic Mme de Parangon (a name which means "paragon"), and Gaudet, the *méchant par principe.* It is unfortunate that the "paragon's" perfection is slightly sullied by a Lesbian attraction to Ursule; but it is strong enough to overcome even a moment of weakness which results in her giving birth to one of Edmond's four illegitimate children. It is also unfortunate that the two antagonists remain in the wings, and scarcely come into direct conflict, while the major part of the story is enacted by Edmond and others, who are manipulated by Gaudet. In the character of Gaudet, Rétif advances beyond Laclos and towards Sade. For Gaudet is a philosophical nihilist. He is moved primarily by an intellectual revolt against rationalism and religion, which have given us the morality of altruism and self-sacrifice. In a universe without moral value (an "absurd" universe), egoism and its pleasurable satisfactions are the only truth.

Gaudet's philosophy is expounded (with calculated reservations) in his letters and in those of his disciples. We can summarize it synthetically by selecting certain ideas that run through the volumes. Rétif himself suggests, in his preface, that in the competitive life of the cities, the successful are the ones without moral scruples. This is borne out by the tricked Edmond: "Will virtue always be the dupe of hypocrisy?" Later, having become a trickster himself, Edmond cries, "See how the Gods favor the stratagem of crooks!" Gaudet's ally, Father d'Arras, dispels Edmond's prejudices about sexual jealousy, referring to writings of the *philosophes,* works which had also corrupted Manon, Edmond's first wife, whom he married although she was pregnant by M. Parangon (whose wife Edmond was later to violate with similar consequences). As Edmond puts it (but in relation to another of his victims), "Tit for tat; every man for himself." Manon, incidentally, brings home the lesson of self-esteem, "that salutary brake which controls us better than religion and laws, which are always powerless, if it doesn't give them all their force."

Under the tutelage of Gaudet, Edmond learns that honor, virtue and modesty are platitudes devoid of meaning; "the proof is that each man feigns to respect them in regard to others, and to destroy them as soon as he can in the heart of any woman, in regard to himself." Virtue has "denatured" love. He reaches a point of debasement at which he concludes that "pleasure ennobles all it touches," and that there is no difference between good and evil except as pleasure determines. "Who says nature, says reason *par excellence.*" The two contraries of eighteenth century thought, reason and nature, are thus united under the mastery of the latter. As a consequence, all our supposed vices are now shown to be "the height of wisdom and the perfection of moral welfare." The only free man is one who lives idly, in a state of nature. But society is only a disguised state of nature: slavery and cannibalism have assumed more refined forms. "All that is admirable! . . . Let us try, then, my dear Leader, to keep in the ranks of the eaters; the role of the eaten is only for the weak and the fools." (Had Diderot's Rameau said anything different?)

Although Gaudet devotes himself willfully to crime, he declares that it does not depend on us to avoid crimes, since we are only passive machines. The good man and the evil man merely do what pleases them best, and there is no merit or blame, except as society may decide. Nature, indifferent to our judgments, produces both good and evil men indifferently, as it produces predatory animals and poisons. Man can recover his dignity only by ridding himself of all prejudices and breaking the bonds of his education, under which he is yoked. "My friend, there are only two classes in the world, that of slave, and that of master." Gaudet urges Edmond to be guided only by logical reason, which dispels "prejudices." We must distinguish, he says, men's laws, which are all conditional and relative, from nature's, which are absolute; and nature is purely physical. Rape, for instance, is a social crime, but a natural virtue.[35]

Gaudet, it is clear, despite a shadowy and disunified portrayal by Rétif, seeks power and absoluteness, rather than evil for its own sake. His quest requires freedom from all obstacles set up by men. It takes the particular form of a desire to be creative, like God. Edmond is to be his creation. Desire for godhead in men, as I have noted, can only manifest itself destructively, at least until we are able to create life, and worlds, and be immortal. There is no other issue for the man who wants to affirm the self-sufficiency of his ego, to make his being be centered on himself, as is the being of God, if he exists. Gaudet gives himself the illusion of being a creator; but his creation, to be absolute, can only function through evil. He shapes Edmond for the freedom of evil and destruction; and in this he, too, must participate, whether or not he loves evil, in his process of "creating" Edmond in his own image.

We shall succeed, and I shall have, in raising you, the inexpressible pleasure that the Creator has in contemplating his

---

[35] Gaudet does say that those human laws which are necessary for society (not to kill or steal, to give each his due, etc.) must be observed. However, unless this is an unlikely inconsistency, we must take this to be part of his tactics of gradual indoctrination, especially as he is later involved in two passion-murders. On the other hand, the supposed editor's note (*Paysanne pervertie*, III, 167–168) calls Gaudet a noble soul who has gone astray because of his loss of faith in God. "He is not a scoundrel, although he is a corruptor."

creature. . . . Let us then, like the characters of a play, go firmly to our goal, without worrying about the dagger-thrusts we shall have to give in order to bring about the dénouement; let us make ourselves feared, loved, admired; let all means appear good to us: after all, what do we risk?—giving ourselves a happy destiny. The laws, that vain scarecrow of timid souls, what can they do to us? The worst they can give us is death; but, I ask you, is death in our beds not as painful and as frightening?

The remainder of the letter from which this passage is taken develops a philosophy of nihilism and sensation, and taxes the *philosophes* for having gone only half-way.

Gaudet recognizes Mme Parangon as his chief antagonist. He urges Edmond to possess her in order to destroy her self-esteem and virtue, and lures him by describing the pleasure of loving and perverting such a woman as the most exquisite of all. He even engages in an indirect epistolary debate with Mme Parangon, over their respective philosophies. Little wonder that Ursule, whom he has ruined, cries to him, "Wretch! You are not a man, you are the devil sent on earth to do evil!" An outburst which reminds the reader of what Edmond had written to Gaudet himself: "There are in the world two beings who astonish me, my cousin [Mme Parangon] and you. One is an angelic creature; the other is a devil, but so worthy of being an angel that I hope he will become it."

Le paysan perverti may from one viewpoint be considered the ultimate reduction or terminus of the picaresque novel, of a *Gil Blas,* after it has become suffused with materialistic nihilism (which is already dawning in Lesage's novel) and with post-Rousseau romanticism. Both Laclos and Rétif, as I have said, portray the ultimate consequences of the eighteenth century moral impasse which resulted from the destruction of objective ethical universals by the new materialism. Each of them, in his own way, tries to show the danger and to warn against it.

In point of historical fact, Rousseau may properly be considered the initiator of the revolt against the *philosophes.*[36] We are not considering *La Nouvelle Héloïse* in this chapter, although it may be said to belong here, because we have already included it in the analysis of Rousseau's philosophy. It will be remembered, how-

[36] I am speaking now of literary men, not of the Christian apologists, who had never ceased to warn against the dissolution of moral values.

ever, that Rousseau, in that novel, condemns the moral consequences of the doctrines of sensationalism and materialism, and
urges the validity and the necessity, for both the individual and
society, of a *human* rather than a natural ethics; one which derives
from reason, conscience and moral will, and which rests ultimately
on the authority of the superhuman commands of God, as revealed through the moral conscience.

We may close our view of the eighteenth century French novel
with Bernardin de Saint-Pierre's *Paul et Virginie* (1787). This
slender work, which enjoyed tremendous popularity for a century
after its publication, is still widely read, and appreciated for the
beauties of its style. Yet it is tedious and flat as a homily, and
insipid and false as a novel, despite the delicate sense notations of
its descriptions and several passages of narrative power. *Paul et
Virginie* is obviously a fictional translation of parts of the *Discours
sur l'inégalité* and parts of *Emile*. Two children, reared far from
civilization and with only occasional contacts outside the family
group, live according to nature, in the innocence of the Garden of
Eden. But this "nature" is quite different from that of the
materialists. Its chief characteristic is virtue, the desire to do good
to others, even at one's own cost, and to follow God's moral laws.
And when adolescence comes, there is no serpent, and no Fall.

The author's immediate purpose in this idyll is, then, to vaunt
the goodness of the natural life in contrast to the corruption of
civilization, and he labors his contrast with a heavy pre-romantic
hand. Out of his counterpoise there also emerges a clear view of
human nature and of values. Happiness, the goal of behavior,
comes only from "nature and virtue"—these two words not being
dissociable. Virtue is defined as "an effort made on ourselves for
the good of others, in the intention of pleasing God alone." Friendship, sincerity, hospitality and a desire for the good, characterize
the natural man. In civilization, on the other hand, there is only
rivalry, hypocrisy, vain reputation, and cruelty. People seek others
only to use them, and to acquire advantage over them. Commerce
(contrasted with agriculture) is at the heart of this pernicious
rivalry which degrades man. As an inevitable result, civilized men
never find the happiness they are seeking. Natural man, on the
other hand, in his semi-solitude, is beautiful in soul and contented
in heart, relying on God's providence in all things, and guided by

the testimony of his conscience, rather than the "opinion" of others, or fear of their ridicule.

It is somewhat unfortunate, for the persuasiveness of this picture, that our little family group requires the help of negro slaves, and even contemplates the acquisition of additional slaves, in order to make their lives easier. What becomes of these as human beings? That is not worth considering; they are apparently designed, in God's providential plan, for maintaining the material well-being of the chosen ones. It is obvious that God's providence does not succeed in taking equal care of every one. Certain men are born to serve as means for the ends of others. There are poor families, living in misery, close by. But perhaps this, too, may be considered providential, since it affords Paul and Virginie the opportunity to be *bienfaisants*. Part of their happiness is also due to their ignorance. There are no useless sciences here, no reading or writing to poison their minds. This is good, because happiness is the highest goal, and it can be reached only through innocent virtue. Thus we see that Bernardin de Saint-Pierre embraces Rousseau's *Discours sur les sciences et les arts,* and implicitly rejects Voltaire's parable of the *Good Brahmin,* who preferred being a man to being happy. Unfortunately again, it is not clear how this tallies with the eulogy of books as a prime source of virtue and happiness, and of writers as benefactors of mankind who deserve public esteem.

All is well in the garden of Eden. Then comes the Fall—but not the same kind as in the Bible. In Bernardin de Saint-Pierre's version, it takes the form of succumbing to the pernicious influences of society and commerce—even though they are forced upon the heroine by her family—expressed in the desire for the comforts and security which wealth can provide. The innocent lovers are separated, to meet again only in death.

In the perspective of the earlier development we have traced, *Paul et Virginie* appears as an attempted defense of man against the basic concepts of motivation and nature which had been advanced by those novelists who were following the main currents of the new philosophy.[37] Man's evil tendencies, it is acknowledged by

[37] ". . . *Paul et Virginie* is . . . the novel which, forming a dyptich with *Les Liaisons dangereuses,* its antagonist, closes, on the eve of the Revolution, the glorious course of a genre which won, in that century, its full dignity." (Jean Fabre, "*Paul et Virginie,* pastorale.") Professor Fabre also points out that, in contrast to its predecessors, *Paul et Virginie* does not present lovers who are divided, hesitating,

Bernardin de Saint-Pierre, are inevitably developed in a competitive society. But it is wrong, he proclaims, to judge man by the men we see around us. Passions, vices and egoism do not necessarily rule their behavior, in all situations. If they would live as nature intended them to, they could be happy and good again.[38]

But Bernardin is also forced, in a way despite himself, to write a pessimistic book, another version of the misfortunes of virtue in the world as it is. Setting out to counteract the licentious novels that painted and accepted the corruption of the human heart and the supremacy of evil, he is obliged to admit the corruptibility of the one (not our heroine's, but her mother's), and to demonstrate the power of the other. The ignorance and the isolation from civilization which he proposes were certainly not constructive remedies, but a weak utopianism, a flight from life and reality, that could do nothing to halt or turn aside the onrushing tides of thought.

The basic optimism of *Paul et Virginie* is a symptomatic reaction against the depths to which man had been depressed in eighteenth century literature. Perhaps men will always refuse to be pushed back into the bleakness of utter despair and absurdity, and will always rebel against that rationalism which destroys all rational meanings and values. This had certainly been the course of the most significant part of eighteenth century thought, and its progress has been clearly visible in the novels we have examined. These novels are a concrete, psychological counterpart of the speculative discussion. Starting from a naturalistic view of man as actuated by calculated self-interest or uncontrollable passion, and as devoted only to pleasure and worldly happiness, the eighteenth century novel became more and more involved in the problem of evil. The progression was from naive evil, latent in human instincts and drives, to conscious and willful evil. In one way or another, evil was seen to be inevitable and dominant in human behavior, and to be tolerated, if not protected, by the gods, or by nature. Its psychological roots were explored with acumen and finesse. Man was viewed as, in essence, an irrational and immoral

or enemies. He emphasizes the pessimism which shows that love and purity cannot exist successfully in the social context.

[38] Moralizing novels were common throughout the century; but, aside from those of Rousseau and Bernardin de Saint-Pierre, they are undistinguished and unimportant.

animal, whose superior intelligence makes him all the more dreadfully wicked. To the evil protagonists (if not to the novelists), this seemed quite normal, as man is only a slightly differentiated part of a non-moral and valueless world.

In Rétif, the recognition of the absurd and the revolt against rationalism and its restraints become an explicitly formulated philosophy. In Sade, we reach the acme of this development. In Sade alone, the wicked are made, with logical consistency, the winners. In the other novelists, there is, to be sure, no reward for virtue; in Sade, there is also no punishment for the wicked and the strong (or, at least, for the strongest of the strong). Finally, Sade takes still another step beyond all the others, by making the instincts of perversion and cruelty ineradicable motives, even if they are often repressed, in all human beings. Although he sets up a few virtuous characters as foils, it would seem that the only difference he sees between men is that between the strong and the weak, the exploiters and their victims. For Sade, this was stripping off the mask, and his concept of human nature is one of the most revolutionary aspects of his work.

The preoccupation with eroticism, illicit love and seduction which characterizes so large a segment of the eighteenth century novel was more than a reflection of manners. Both the manners and the novels were an expression of the break-up of values in general —of which sexual discipline had been the epitome, as the expression of a rational, moral control of natural impulses, in the name of an ideal. The past, to be sure, had never succeeded in living up to such an ideal; but never before had there been such a willful declaration of its impossibility, and even more, of its undesirability. This stand betokened a willingness to give up trying to reconcile reason and nature, the human and the animal, and a resignation to living life on the lower natural plane. It led to a fundamental anti-rationalism, and to a romantic anarchism which, it may be noted in passing, are not unlike those we can observe in the United States (and probably elsewhere) today.

There is little doubt that some of the *philosophes,* notably Diderot and d'Holbach, were aware of the ultimate nihilism to which their doctrines might lead. They fought hard against it, and sought a new basis, in nature and reason, for a humane ethical life. I have already suggested that their effort was to fail. One proof of its failure lies in the history of the eighteenth century novel, which marches on inevitably to the marquis de Sade. Another sign is the reenactment of this progression in our own day, in the recent history of Western culture and in the sadistic nihilism of Nazism. But what in the eighteenth century was theory and dream was to become, alas, in the twentieth century, an unspeakable reality of human depravity and suffering.

CULMINATIONS

"Bliss was it in that dawn to be alive,
But to be young was very heaven."—WORDSWORTH

THE ONSET of the French Revolution was greeted with joy
and hope by those *philosophes* who were still living. The old
order was to be changed at last. Reason was to have its day, its
chance to reorganize society and to re-direct men as natural laws
and social utility dictated. Unfortunately, both joy and hope were
to be ground into the ashes of disillusion, as nothing worked out
the way it should have. Wordsworth returned to England, eventually to become a Tory and an opponent of the Revolution.
Condorcet, the child of the *philosophes*, a noble idealist who tried
to maintain his principles, became the victim of the happy mil-
lenium whose arrival he had applauded. A fugitive from the
Terror, half-starved, he took his own life in despair, yet not before he had reaffirmed his belief in an unlimited vista of human
progress, in the "Dixième époque" of his *Esquisse d'un tableau
historique des progrès de l'esprit humain.* Mirabeau, a follower
of the *philosophes*, who had jumped into the fray with ardor,
perhaps was saved by death from a similar fate. Robespierre, too,
greeted the Revolution with joy. On July 23, 1789, he wrote to
Buissart, "The present Revolution, dear friend, has let us see
within a few days the greatest events that the history of men has to
show." [1] Robespierre, within four years, was to travel a road that

[1] *Correspondance*, p. 42.

led to the Terror, to the opposite extreme from his starting point.

One of the aspects of the marriage or liaison between the French *philosophes* and the Goddess of Liberty was the practice of electing non-French philosophers or other writers to honorary citizenship in the French Republic. Bentham, Wieland and Klopstock were among those so honored. Many of the recipients of this honor later sent back the diploma in which it was conferred—a fact which again testifies to the widespread disappointment with the constructive accomplishments of the Revolution, with their lack of correspondence to the hopes and dreams aroused in the hearts of those who had been nourished on the writings of the *philosophes*.

While the failure of the Revolution was in no way *caused* by the ideas of the eighteenth century, it nonetheless casts light on the weakness of those ideas. The Revolution was a critical, extreme moment of crisis. But it was the culmination of the crisis that had been building up during the century; and it is in such moments that the implications of a philosophy and the contents of a culture are revealed. Has not European history, moreover, been one of increasing crisis and extremism ever since then? The course of the Revolution was determined, to be sure, by tensions due to conflicts, fears, hatreds and animosities, and by the dynamics of revolution itself. But the Revolution was also an attempt to implement ideas of the eighteenth century; and its failure reflects in some measure, at least, upon the inadequacies of those ideas and the outlook they embodied. While it would be patently absurd, then, to cast any responsibility on the *philosophes* for the complex circumstances which determined later happenings, it is nevertheless true that the intellectual climate which they helped to create was an important part of those circumstances, insofar as men's ideologies and outlooks affect their decisions and their behavior. What had been in the realm of mind came to life in the realm of political events. The French Revolution was the crowning of a hundred years of struggle to free men's minds and institutions from a thousand years' dead weight of medievalism. The men of the Revolution tried to create the rational society of which the *philosophes* had dreamed.[2] It is significant that Sade was to see

---

[2] See Henri Peyre, "The Influence of Eighteenth- Century Ideas on the French Revolution," and B. Groethuysen, *Philosophie de la Révolution française*. The latter work must be read with caution, as the author generalizes far too easily, fails to estimate properly the character of eighteenth century pessimism and the antin-

in the Revolution and in the Terror which climaxed it the failure of rationalistic attempts to reform society, and of the rationalizations that defended society with the pretense of morality; the failure, in fact, of society and culture themselves.

Although our study is still incomplete, let us turn back to that part of eighteenth century thought which we have explored, in order to review the new directions that were taken and the promises that were held out—many of which accompanied the revolutionary tide.

The eighteenth century was in several ways a turning point in our cultural history. It was an age in which the streams of the past were gradually infiltrated by new facts, new meanings and new attitudes. Turbulence and confusion resulted. The absolute, the essential and the rational swerve toward the relative, the existential and the empirical, in a disordered mixture. A new positivistic outlook denounces hypotheses and mathematical *a prioris;* yet, unable to find explanations and solutions according to its own methodology, this positivism supposes and imagines what it cannot observe, and uses the very rationalistic approach it condemns. The supernatural is submerged by the natural. Science allies the empirical and the rational, seeking, in the historical particular, the essential of law. Anthropology triumphs over metaphysics, psychology over logic. Reason and sentiment are locked in endless debate, the more entangled because a sentimentalist, like Rousseau, believes in the value of human reason, properly used, while a supposed empiricist, like Diderot, is suffused with pre-romantic sentiment.

Whereas the physical sciences had already, in the seventeenth century, broken the shackles of the ancient and medieval worldviews, and looked at nature objectively, in ethics the inherited faith in an immutable moral order, supported by the Divinity, continued to struggle vigorously, backed by the fear of many men that mankind was about to become entirely lost in a strange and alien world it had not dared to conceive of before. The physical sciences had expelled from the universe considerations based on value and purpose; a cosmic revolution which inevitably had to

omous values of "nature." Cf. also the statement of Burke (a prejudiced observer, to be sure): "I hear on all hands that a cabal, calling itself philosophic, receives the glory of many of the late proceedings; and that their opinions and systems are the true actuating spirit of the whole of them." (*Reflections* . . . , p. 86.)

penetrate into the world of man. The security that came from the consciousness of being sheltered by an inviolable order, an order designed for man and embodying a meaning that in turn gave meaning to human life and aspirations, was forever shaken. This trend was abetted by a nascent revolution in the biological sciences. Life, it appeared, was only an accident of matter's endless transformations, and its changing convolutions were determined by its own built-in dynamism. Already, in the minds of some, the notion of organic evolution was dawning. This discovery was to complete the rout of faith in man's majesty and security, and in the whole inherited conceptual framework in which he had pictured himself, by ironically changing his origin from God-sprung to a humiliating unfolding of lower forms.

But other men were not afraid. They were determined to face the naked reality of their true place. They were further resolved to apply the empirical method to ethics, and to find a way in which they could live without illusion, and yet live as moral beings, convinced that in the long run a moral order must be of man, and for man. A new courage was now necessary, for whether or not they realized it, mankind was now embarked on a dangerous journey that would take it to the end of the night.

The defense of suicide was one dramatic manifestation of this revolution, and of the intellectual dilemmas it created. It uncovered the bifurcation between a humanistic and an authoritarian view of man's estate. Its chief significance was precisely the establishment of the specific character of moral law as a function of man's specific nature. It was a recognition of a distinctive human rationality. For this act, no matter which attitude one took towards it, epitomized every man's isolation, and his independence in value creation: either by his legitimate mastery over his own destiny or by his very rebellion against a supposed order in which he had been assigned his proper place. At the same time, the effort to subsume the act of suicide into the universal natural order was both a part of the attempt to unify nature and human reason, and a move to withdraw man from his supposedly privileged status.[3]

[3] The debate over suicide had a parallel, with some of the same overtones, in the controversy over inoculation. See A. H. Rowbotham, "The 'Philosophes' and the Propaganda for Inoculation of Smallpox in Eighteenth Century France." The opponents of inoculation said that smallpox was a *natural* risk sent by providence, inoculation an *unnatural* risk. Inoculation is a kind of moral probabilism. "The most direful consequences," wrote Chais, "never authorize us to commit moral evil." Dubois declared that "Inoculation forces Nature, tempts God, attacks the perfection of his work. . . ." Professor Rowbotham concludes: "On the one hand is a

For man to have a moral life, three conditions are prerequisite. First, there must be an accepted distinction between good and evil, and an obligation to do the good. Second, man must be capable of knowing the good. Finally, he must be capable of doing it. Part of the eighteenth century crisis was the re-discovery and triumph of the idea (at least, in many minds) that moral good and evil exist only for man, and in man, and have no other ontological status or support. To these minds it appeared evident that the essential truth which had to be accepted is that "the ethical is not to be discovered in any form of the world-process." [4] This fact, which may be considered as humanity's greatest title to dignity and to glory, was greeted with dismay in many quarters. Christians denied and denounced it. Deists tried desperately to conserve a moral principle in an infinite, undifferentiated Newtonian universe that had no structure in the medieval sense of a rational and hierarchical cosmos. But even they, for the most part, knew that man now had to find his way without God's help. And the debate over evil showed that the march towards divorcing God and the universe from human values could not be halted. The upshot was that no significant purposes for life could be found in the history of the universe, but only within the life of man himself. The depth of the crisis is at once evident. Man found himself utterly without significance, lost in endless space and time, and simultaneously, the center and end-all of his own little universe, ready to annihilate the world, as Schopenhauer says, to maintain his own self a little longer. The very existence of moral good and evil—that is, of good and evil outside of mere individual sentiency—was challenged, and it became necessary to substantiate their objective reality in other ways. This most of the *philosophes* were confident they could do. But if we put together two of the basic postulates of eighteenth century radical thought, that all acts are indifferent in a universe without an objective or absolute order, and that man, as a non-transcendent element of nature, is solely a part of this order, then the foundations of moral nihilism are assured, and the

morality which is absolute, based upon the immediate relation between the soul and God and sacrificing the welfare of the individual to those immutable laws of dogma on which the spiritual salvation of the individual rests; on the other hand, the view that the temporal happiness of the individual (and consequently of society) is the great aim of social endeavor . . . The sole test of any practice or institution . . . is its social efficacy."

[4] Albert Schweitzer, *Civilization and Ethics,* p. xi.

effort of rational solutions becomes very difficult. Of course the *philosophes* did not stop at these two postulates, and in the third part of this study we shall examine and evaluate the solutions which they did propose.

In the second place, believing, for the most part, in the objective reality of right and wrong (though not in their absoluteness), the *philosophes* did not doubt that men, as moral beings, know the right and the wrong. But can they do the good which they know, and will they do it? This was the heart of the matter. The difficulty lies not only in man's egoism, but in his unique intelligence and freedom, which enable him to circumvent and overcome any restrictions, often even those of nature. He is different from other animals, many agreed, inasmuch as his behavior is not determined by inherited instincts, and he does not always have to do the same things, in the same way. This concept was particularly in accord with the materialists' belief that it is man who created the moral world, and added it to a value-less universe—a view they entertained despite their denial of transcendence, on a purely natural basis. But there is another freedom, which conflicted with the resistance to Christianity and with the desire to integrate man into the purely natural realm. Therefore these thinkers denied man moral freedom and limited his power to fulfill the obligation he might perceive. Yet it is doubtful that those who denied him freedom would have given him a definite essence, a fixed potentiality and specific modes of expression, like other natural things. On the other hand, a few extremists went even further, and denied obligation itself; for man, they reasoned, is of nature, and nature knows only life and death, pleasure and pain.

Either moral judgments and values are innate and natural, and man is an exception; or he creates them, by reason and experience, and he is still an exception. Most of the *philosophes* did not deny this. What they tried to do was to make the moral realm part of the natural realm, as in their attitude to suicide, and to justify its validity. Their rejection of man's separateness was, at bottom, the desire to sever him from a providential God and a chimerical supernaturalism, and (for some of them) the desire to establish physical nature as the sole and universal reality. They were guided by humanistic motives, and did not wish to debase human dignity. But here again rose a dilemma, and a danger.

Was man to be freed from servitude to God, only to be enslaved to nature? Does not man transcend, even deny nature, in his rational and social activities, or are these only disguised and complex forms of needs and drives which he shares with other animals? On this fundamental issue independent thinkers divided into two groups. Some, notably Rousseau, and Diderot in his later writings, recognized that for the human animal, culture transcends nature in many respects, and that man transcends culture. The more radical disciples of La Mettrie and Condillac, following the new thought in science and psychology, developed the monistic conception that there can be only one form of being and of law; both the physical and the moral order are reducible to matter and motion. Man, as Cassirer has put it, has no existence except in nature; even in thought he can only apparently transcend nature's law and the world of sense, since the mind's only power consists in the combining of sense data. But can the total nature of any complex phenomenon be "explained" by the irreducible elements from which it has originated?

The question of man's capacity to do what is right has another aspect. It depends also on the springs of his behavior. It was not enough to shift from a revealed body of moral laws, having their sanction in God's will, to an ethics that proclaimed its allegiance to needs and directives of human nature. What is human nature? Can morality be established on human rationality? Or if men are, on the contrary, irrational in motivation, what irrational components of their nature can be utilized, and in what way, in order to secure the desired behavior? To what extent is human nature naturally inclined to moral virtues? To what extent does living in society provide such motivations, or can it be used to build a new and valid authority, replacing God and religion, to control human egoism? How can one reconcile the fact that man is a moral being with the commonly accepted belief that the desire for pleasure and the fear of pain are his only motives, without falling into the Christian dualism?

Many other questions and problems haunted the minds of eighteenth century moralists. They rose, like ghosts, from the graves in which they had been conveniently, but prematurely buried. What is the genesis in men, and the character, of moral judgment and of moral experience? What is conscience? How could obligation be justified, and justified in such a way that men would want to make it the guide of their conduct? In other words, what is good, and why should a man want to be good? If self-interest is the only motive, a way must be found of filling the moral vacuum that suddenly appears in man, as well as in the universe; unless, that is, we are to resign ourselves to Rameau's nephew and his like proliferating in a culture with no sure values. These, and other matters, will be the subject of the next part of our investigation.

The problem of the eighteenth century was, then, as much one of re-interpreting man himself, and the functions of his social institutions, as it was one of re-interpreting his place in the universe. We have seen how the evaluations of man and the interpretations of his motivations run the entire span from optimism to pessimism, with a heavy concentration falling somewhat left of center, towards the pessimistic side. There were those who held men to be essentially selfish, and even malicious, driven on by the craving for a comparative superiority. Many more esteemed them to be good, except when their own interest was involved. And a few even proclaimed the paradoxical doctrine that man is essentially good, or would be, were he not corrupted by human society. The extremes, in one sense, cancelled each other out through their internal contradictions. Rousseau finds men theoretically good, but actually evil. Sade finds them theoretically evil, but implicitly acknowledges that they are also good (in the conventional sense), since he assigns the fools who are good to be the victims of the strong.

Although self-interest was often defended as not intrinsically evil, being a natural and necessary effect of the desire for survival, its corruption in society, in its peculiarly human forms of rivalry, pride and lust of power, was recognized even by the most optimistic; and these were seen to be its characteristic, if not its original or essential forms of expression. Paradoxically, some of the most pessimistic thinkers emphasized the beneficial social effects of self-interest; cynics like Mandeville perceived direct good effects, others believed self-interest was a convenient lever which could be manipulated to produce desired behavior.

To be sure, man had his apologists; and the upsurge of pre-romantic sentimentality kept alive, in certain sections of society, the belief in his goodness. Many who criticized him, moreover,

were convinced of his excellence, in some regards, and of his
potentialities. The opinion entertained by some writers, that he is
neither good nor bad innately, may even be considered a kind of
optimism, since it implies that his natural egotism can be shaped
and directed, by outside forces, to the collective and moral good.
But nothing could be more erroneous than to speak, as has often
been done, of the "simple, naive optimism" of the Age of Enlightenment, and of its belief in "the fundamental goodness and
rationality of man"; or of its unawareness that "civilization was a
thin and precarious crust," and of its superficial view of human
nature that ignored "so many of the deeper and blinder passions
both good and bad which inhabit the human heart." [5]

The optimism of the Age of Enlightenment was, for the most
part, not about human nature, but about what could be done
with human beings, through the progress of science, through education and government, and in general, through the rational
reconstruction of society. Its confidence was less in man's reasonableness, than in the power of reason to devise ways of coping with
such a creature. This was the hope, but it overlay a substratum of
pessimism about man himself. We have seen that many of the
writers, on both sides, were aware of man's basic irrationality, and
of the reality of radical evil in him (that is, of evil in the core of
his personality, his will).[6] We have observed the "will to evil"
which forms so strong a current in the novel, and the competitive
power drive which underlies Rousseau's philosophy of man in
society. Even if men know what is right, the force of their natural
instincts is such that they often cannot do the right, or do not
want to. The thinkers of the Enlightenment were acutely conscious of the corruption of self-interest in all ideal pretensions of
human culture; consequently, their major and continuing effort
(except for a few nihilists and anarchists) was to control the workings of that spring of action, by using it to control itself. They did
not, as is often claimed, undervalue the power of self-interest;

---

[5] See especially chapters 8 and 9 of this section.
[6] Some of the phrases I have quoted come from a review in the London *Times*.
But many others have expressed similar views, including Carl Becker (*The Heavenly
City of the Eighteenth Century Philosophers*), R. L. Ketcham ("James Madison
and the Nature of Man"), and even R. R. Palmer, in his excellent book, *Catholics
and Unbelievers in Eighteenth Century France*. Monod's statement, "the idea of
man's goodness . . . the deep and most fervent faith of the century," is founded
on a superficial view of the defense of the passions. (*Op. cit.*, p. 291.)

they overestimated the ability of social institutions to effectuate such a control. Perhaps it would be more exact to say that they underestimated the amount of conditioning and coercion that would be required, once a society embarked on such a scheme; and this is what the French Revolution, and later, the Communist revolutions, were to show.

It is true, on the other hand, that they also frequently over-estimated—in defiance of their own analysis—the power of rationality to distinguish ultimate self-interest and to give it a greater weight than immediate self-interest and thus to achieve a limited control of egoistic propensities. In other words, their hopes of what could be done with man rested partly on an assumption of rationality and good will which much of their own theory denied.

This is nowhere clearer than in Chastellux's *De la félicité publique*. History, declares Chastellux, shows that governments have always been founded on force, ambition and jealousy. But this is a matter of ignorance and error. "It is therefore for enlightenment, for true philosophy, to change men's fate." If Rome and Christianity failed, it was because they did not follow truth, but "blind passion, sordid interest, odious rivalries." And if the progress of knowledge did not work out among the Greeks, it was because pride, love of glory and vanity produced political divisions, instead of unity. His hope was essentially that of Robespierre, and it foundered on the same reef—human nature.[7] Condorcet was another writer who tended towards extreme optimism. Men can be enlightened, he declares; and by that he means, they can be made to realize that their true interest lies in acting in harmony with the general interest—it is merely a matter of true or false calculation. But this is an obvious admission that men are not morally motivated. Hence Condorcet's further assurance that justice and generosity are in all hearts, and "await only the gentle influence of enlightenment and liberty to develop in them." This effect is "in the necessary order of nature," as much as physical laws. There is only an apparent opposition between the private and the general interest; and "the purpose of the social art" is to destroy it.[8]

[7] P. 79, 210–216. We recall the phrase of Mirabeau, quoted earlier. Man "will always be just and happy when he is enlightened about his true interests," and also his contrary theory that political education consists in inspiring prejudices and passions which are conducive to the general welfare.

[8] *Esquisse*, p. 289–293.

The failure of the *philosophes'* hopes and plans may thus be attributed to their unwillingness to view pessimistically their pessimism about human nature. They were entirely wrong, as La Mettrie, Diderot (at times), Rousseau and others had known, about men being willing to sacrifice concrete, immediate self-interest for a vague, ultimate self-interest. They were at least partly wrong about conditioning, in underestimating the degree of control that would be requisite to make them willing to do so.

The reasons for their attitude are not hard to find. They lie in the great surge of optimism and affirmation· which rose from the discovery of the uniformity of natural laws, such as that of cause and effect, which the *philosophes* believed could also regulate human affairs, since man was now seen to be wholly a part of nature's realm; a concept which was abetted by unwillingness to recognize man's unique freedom and transcendence of nature, even in matters most natural.[9] The same discovery blinded the *philosophes* with the limitless perspective of scientific advances—a triumph of man's rational powers—which they sometimes mistook for a perspective of rational progress. We again see that the weakness was less faith in man's rationality—they recognized fully the biological forces in man, and their peculiar cultural sublimations —than the reduction of man to a simple and universal type of natural law, based on sensation, expressed in human terms as

[9] This despite the fact that many writers pointed out that moral laws do not work with the same regularity as physical laws. For a typical example, cf. d'Holbach, "Nature is ruled by simple, uniform, permanent laws that experimentation enables us to know. . . . Consequently in all his investigations, man must turn to physics and experimentation: such must be the source of his information in religion, ethics, legislation, government, in the sciences and the arts, in his search for happiness and avoidance of pain." (*Système de la nature*, I, ch. 5.) This view leads both to the Idéologues and to positivism and behaviorism. It is a distortion of man, by reducing him to fit a Procrustean bed of sensationist psychology and available techniques. It obviously cannot account for man's creative and destructive achievements, which derive from motivation that transcends biological needs and separates his dissatisfied life from the harmonies of nature as seen in the impulses of animals. Pride and power, it has been said, are more important factors in economic life than hunger and survival. The same transcendence is expressed, in different terminology, by F. S. C. Northrop, who distinguishes between natural entities "whose behavior is completely the expression of their essential nature *qua* fact," and men, "whose judgments are in part at least the expression of what they think all first-order facts are *qua* theory." ("Ethical Relativism in the Light of Recent Legal Science," p. 659.) In all this we see the danger of a too narrowly conceived naturalism. We must also remember that in the eighteenth century context, and from the prospect afforded by atheism or even an impersonal pantheism or deism, there was no longer any external or higher reference enabling man to believe he could transcend nature. There was only nature; which left the dilemma of what nature is, and the relation of reason to it.

egoism or self-interest, subject to experimental verification and to control by conditioning. Only Rousseau, among the major figures, recognized the fallacy of this approach. He called for a different, a more radical revolution; yet he, too, relied on educational and legislative repression, of an extreme kind. La Mettrie, a consistent materialist, would perhaps not have fallen victim to the error. Sade, Rivarol, Sabatier de Castres were aware of it. Sade knew what evil man was capable of; and the other two advised the use of all repressive means to crush it. But the thinking of most was directed by two unconscious intellectual assumptions of the rationalist-empirical philosophy—assumptions which, as Hans Morgenthau has pointed out, persist in our own age.[10] One was the notion that the physical and the social worlds are intelligible through the same processes; the other, that understanding in terms of these processes is all that is needed for control of these two worlds.

What did the *philosophes* mean, then, when they said that it was necessary to enlighten men? They meant, in the first place, that men could profit from enlightenment, because the freeing of the natural light of reason from the shadows of superstition and prejudice would strengthen the forces of rationality and reasonableness within them. However, few if any believed that this enlightenment would, in and by itself, make men virtuous. What they rather hoped was that the liberation of their rationality would enable them, as Condorcet put it, to perceive where their true self-interest lay. Given a universal, though not rigid human nature, the motives, but not the modes of behavior will always be the same. The best that can be done is to condition men and to provide the cultural milieu in which these motives can be directed so as to do the least evil, and the most good. This program did not signify that men were utterly devoid of good impulses and motives; but rather that these were secondary, fragile and insufficient by themselves. "Enlightenment," then, was a way of improving conditions. There is no point, for instance, in trying, first and directly, to make men tolerant. The first thing to do is to establish tolerance, in the constituted social institutions of Church and State, and then men might be made to be tolerant.

It must be remembered, however, that the ultimate reconcilia-

[10] Morgenthau, H., *op. cit.,* p. 3.

tion of self-interest and the general interest was not considered to be a practical and immediate program—although it sometimes sounded that way—but only an abstract and theoretical possibility. There is no real reason to assume that anyone (except, perhaps, extremist fanatics like Morelly and Dom Deschamps) thought that such an accord could be perfectly or permanently realized. It was, rather, a goal, an ideal, towards which some progress could be made, if society directed its efforts properly. As to how much progress could be made, there was a wide variety of opinions. The earlier writers, like Montesquieu and Voltaire, were most cautious in their hopes. But it is true that as the century drew towards its close, confidence in the power of conditioning processes increased, and this type of optimism became stronger in some minds.

Again, it is true that pessimism about human nature apparently clashes with the strong opposition to the Christian doctrine of man's native depravity. But if we look below the surface, we see that the *philosophes'* disapproval was not of the idea that man is evil, but rather of the theological dogma of original sin on which the Christian doctrine was based; and even more, of the anti-humanism of seeing in God's grace the only way of overcoming it. It was also a refusal to accept the condemnation of self-love and pride as evil *per se*.

That the *philosophes'* views contained their own inner contradictions, and serious, even fatal shortcomings has, I hope, been made amply clear throughout this volume. I should like merely to mention, at this point, two further contradictions which are particularly pertinent to the foregoing remarks. The first is an opposition found in many writers, including Voltaire and one phase of Diderot. It is between an ethical system based on the golden rule and Natural Law, on the one hand; and, on the other hand, a theory of human nature which indicated springs of action quite contrary to this law; a theory that was accompanied, moreover, by a social philosophy which contemplated using these same springs in its plans to achieve the ethical ends. This signified a reluctance to be rigorously consistent in the surrender to utilitarianism, and to sacrifice completely reliance on a moral good will. The second inconsistency was to proclaim—like d'Holbach and Helvétius, for instance—that men are not and cannot be disinterested and truly moral; while at the same time, their own assumed attitude and their own efforts, in teaching men the right way, disproves that very generalization.

If much of the dynamism of the eighteenth century crisis seems like a thrashing around in concentric whirls, it must be remembered that this is true of any period of revolutionary change. The minds of men are breaking out of a circle, and it is not clear which is the best direction to take. There is no perspective on the struggle in which one is engaged. Nevertheless, underneath the confusion of battle, there was meaningful movement, in clear directional lines. It forms a pattern of revolt against the traditional concepts of man, his life and his world, and a consistent search, which we have attempted to follow along part of the trail, for new explanations and for new aims and means consonant with a naturalistic and realistic outlook.

What practical conclusions, or programs were drawn, then, from the reassessment of the human condition? There were two extremes, radical fringes that claimed only a few adherents. One was anarchism, a doctrine which itself grew out of two contrary views of man: first, from the opinion (as among the primitivists) that he is naturally good, and has been corrupted by civilized society; second, from the moral nihilism which denied good and evil, and asserted only the right of the strong. On the other extreme is a clear foreshadowing of modern totalitarian doctrines, with reliance on conditioning and repression as the only means of controlling a creature who is refractory to non-egoistic motives. In between the two was a fluctuating and shadowy program which tried to take into account both the good and the evil in man. It preferred the certainty of the self-interest motive and of determinism, as elements that could be worked with, to a weak love of virtue and an uncertain freedom. It relied on enlightenment, on the esteem motive, on education and example, and on a political and social system that would—somehow—identify the personal and the social good. To the third of these three alternatives, we may apply Niebuhr's criticism of Marxism: its proponents, while discounting the pretenses of rational man, believe that it is possible to build a society governed by a remarkable "rational coherence of life with life and interest with interest." [11]

[11] *The Nature and Destiny of Man*, I, 21.

In this amorphous group of writers, however, there were wide differences. The most notable, perhaps, is seen in the two theories of self-interest: the one entertained by the Physiocrats (and some others), that what is best for each individual will work out for the best interest of the community—a theory foreshadowing nineteenth century capitalism; and the theory, more widespread, which held that what is best for all is also best for each—a theory underlying modern collectivist systems. In one way or the other, the *philosophes* hoped to solve the great problem of human societies: if we accept the *naturalism* of the self-interest reduction, how can we make it coincide with the *rationalism* of self-sacrifice or virtue?

Needless to say, the defenders of the established institutions and dogmas resisted all such interpretations and programs with every means at their disposal. For them, the Christian interpretation of human nature and destiny alone accounted satisfactorily for man's contradictory nature, and alone provided a sure, objective and efficacious ground for moral values and their implementation.[12] The tactical error of the conservatives was, in part, to reason and to trade blows, hoping to defeat the proponents of an invincible new scientific movement on their own terms. It was, even more, to give ground, and to try to reconcile their position to the new cry in favor of the "natural" instincts and needs of man, instead of frankly proclaiming an anti-natural aim and basis.

The makers of the Revolution were representatives of the moderate, deistic current, which had won the allegiance of the vast majority of liberals and thinking men, and not of the bolder, more original extremes of materialism, anarchism, or proto-totalitarianism. But it turned out that the pessimists about human nature had been right, after all; that social life is a struggle for self-interest and power; and that to avoid anarchism, the Revolution was obliged to go to the other extreme, and to forge the first model of totalitarian repression and terror. It is not surprising

[12] "They thought of man as a being created by God and subject to his judgment, who by his free will was capable of deviating, but whose true object in life was to conform himself to the realm of absolute righteousness from which he had come. . . . *Philosophes*, on the other hand, determined human nature empirically. They emphasized the facts of human behavior. What they perceived clearly in men was not their relationship to an objective world of absolute ends and values, but their actual needs, wants, feelings, inclinations and ideas." (R. R. Palmer, *op. cit.*, p. 184.)

that Saint-Just, in 1786, wrote a long poem which foreshadows aspects of Sade's outlook. In *L'Organt* we see scorn for reason:

> [La raison] n'est qu'un noir composé
> D'orgueil adroit et d'orgueil intéressé . . .
> . . . un grand monstre, appelé Raison
> Cet animal à la tête pointue
> Trois pieds noués et du crin sur la vue.[13]

Man is an animal: "Il n'est plus que la première bête/De ce séjour dont il se dit le Roi." And this bestiality is given free expression, in the poem, in the form of what we now know as sadism, the joy of humiliating and inflicting hurt on another human being. We know what Saint-Just's role was to be.

Like Condorcet, Robespierre, when the Revolution broke, represented the average liberal state of mind on religious, political and moral questions. A provincial lawyer and an intellectual, nourished on the writings of the *philosophes,* he became their spokesman, their definer and their preacher. His wide popularity grew partly out of the fact that he eloquently expressed the assumptions and the goals which the *philosophes* had made the common property of the middle class.

Robespierre considered himself a moralist. The science of politics, he declared to the Convention, is only that of "putting into laws and administration the moral truths found in the books of the philosophers. . . .[14] What was this morality? He defined it time and again in his speeches. Men are good or evil according to the direction they give their passions. We must conquer our egoistic passions in order to be good citizens. There are two kinds of self-love: one that is vile, "which seeks an exclusive well-being, purchased by the unhappiness of others; the other, generous, *bienfaisant,* which fuses our happiness with the happiness of all. . . ." These, and similar theories, we are by now well acquainted with. It was this Robespierre who, in 1791, demanded the abolition of the death penalty, as "essentially unjust" and as completely ineffective, "multiplying crimes rather than preventing them." Here is the heart of his plea: "Listen to the voice of justice and of reason; it cries to us that human judgments are never

---

[13] The quotations are taken from Ollivier, *Saint-Just et la force des choses,* p. 47.
[14] H. M. Stephens, *Orators of the French Revolution,* II, 392.

sure enough so that society can put to death a man condemned by other men who are subject to error." [15] And, even in 1792, he fulminated wrathfully against the "frightful doctrine of denunciation," warning the delegates not to raise a temple to fear.[16]

Let us glance at the origins of some of Robespierre's political ideas. From Montesquieu, he took the theory of representation and the definition of virtue in a republic. He declared that the Legislative Assembly represents "the essence of sovereignty" and was the highest power.[17] Virtue, he held, is love of the republic and of the general welfare, above all things; a love that will assure purity of morals. Rousseau gave him the doctrines of the social contract and of the general will. In the article, "Political Economy," Rousseau had written, "the general will is also the most just, and the voice of the people is indirectly the voice of God." Robespierre proclaimed time and again that the people were sovereign, that the State is a collective moral and political body, with absolute power over the individual. It is a common self, a single will: "the sovereign is above the laws." [18] The sovereign must dominate all individual wills. The goal of the social contract will thus be attained; men are to be submitted to their own wills, in such a way that Rousseau's dictum, "each uniting with all will nevertheless obey only himself," may come true. For already, in Rousseau, we see the merging of private and public interest turning into the same patriotic or nationalistic idea of the good citizen which the Revolution, and Robespierre in particular, were to consider its essential form.

Montesquieu and Rousseau had both stressed conditioning by a national system of education. Rousseau had written, "It is not enough to say to the citizen 'be good.' He must be taught to be so. . . . It is education which ought to stamp on the soul of your citizens the print of their nationality and so guide their tastes and opinions that by inclination, by passion, by necessity, they will be patriots." [19] This was precisely the declared aim of the system of national education instituted by Robespierre. As he said, "The people will become easier to lead as the human mind

[15] *Ibid.*, p. 299–300.
[16] *Ibid.*, p. 354.
[17] Deymes, *Les doctrines politiques de Robespierre*, p. 167.
[18] *Ibid.*, p. 23.
[19] Vaughan, I, 250, II, 437–438.

acquires greater activity, light and philosophy." [20] His hope was to "regenerate the nation," to make a "new people." Children, from the age of five, were to belong to the nation. Here it can be seen again that *éducation,* as the word was used by such eighteenth century writers, is not to be taken as a synonym of enlightenment, but is to be referred to its etymological meaning.

From Mably, Robespierre took the theory of a single legislative chamber, and the belief that the executive, necessarily the enemy of the legislative branch, must be submitted to it. Like Mably, Robespierre emphasized equality above all else, but as a bourgeois, did not dare to apply it to the distribution of wealth. He followed sound "philosophic" doctrine: the right of property is sacred, within vague limits of social responsibility. Extreme disproportion of fortune "is the source of many evils and many crimes," but equality is a chimera.[21]

Robespierre carried to totalitarian limits the process of conditioning that was implicit in some of the *philosophes'* theories, and furnished a model for modern collectivist systems. He caused popular clubs to be founded throughout France, in which, by speeches, songs and discussions, ideas and emotions could be manipulated and men trained to self-sacrifice for the public weal. His government sent "commissioners" throughout the land, to "propagate public spirit, watch over the enemies of the Republic, and establish Jacobin clubs. . . ." [22] He realized fully the power of the press, and insisted on effective propaganda, through that medium, in the theatre, and in the other arts.[23] Following Rousseau again, censorship was established. "All journalists who opposed his ideas were labeled as unpatriotic 'impostors' and hence to be suppressed." [24]

In an early speech Robespierre had said, "We must speak to the people in the language of justice and reason." [25] He proclaimed the absolute power of the legislature as the will of the nation,

[20] J. M. Eagan, *Maximilien Robespierre: Nationalist Dictator,* p. 75.
[21] Stephens, p. 367. Speech of April 24, 1793.
[22] Eagan, p. 86.
[23] *Ibid.,* p. 86–88. "Propaganda became a means of education, both at home and abroad, while the press and the stage became mere tools of the government and were forced to be patriotic. Robespierre envisioned a cultural society completely dominated by the State."
[24] *Ibid.,* p. 84.
[25] *Discours,* in *Oeuvres,* VI, 49.

saying that "it must necessarily have its sacred authority, superior to any individual will." [26] The development and happiness of the individual, Robespierre assured the nation, was the purpose of society. "The only way to reach that goal is the agreement of private interest and general interest." [27] No *philosophe* had ever said it better.

But all this was to change:

> Robespierre the humanitarian, liberal patriot and politician would have shuddered at the thought of an authoritarian or totalitarian state. Such a system of government would crush the very liberty and equality which he had argued for at such great length. This seemingly firm belief in the virtues of democracy and republicanism would hardly seem compatible with a nationalist dictatorship. Yet, in the brief period from 1789 to 1794, Robespierre turned from a liberal humanitarian pacifist into a nationalistic zealot eager to include all political, social and economic power within the state.[28]

The effective causes of this change were, of course, political and economic, and all who know the history of that stormy time are familiar with them. However, these causes might not have produced the same effects had Robespierre's ideology been different. The eighteenth century writers had announced themselves as moralists, and so did Robespierre. But, as we shall see (and have already glimpsed), it was a morality whose basis was social utility, and not ethical principle; or, to be exact, it made of utility, social and individual, the chief moral principle. Furthermore, a philosophy of totalitarianism was implicit in a political doctrine whose basic tenet was that the collective will was everything. A later day was to reveal even more fully what Niebuhr has called "the demonic fury of fascist politics in which a collective will expresses boundless ambitions," and which testifies to the result of surrender to the collectivity, as the means of securing individual happiness. As the deputy Courtois wrote in 1795, "they were killing individual happiness to create public happiness."

History shows us that in all such situations, the governing party, or group, and most particularly its leader, assumes that it

[26] *Ibid.*, p. 87.
[27] Deymes, p. 50.
[28] Eagan, *op. cit.*, p. 85.

(or he) is the true expression of the collective will.[29] All opponents are "mistaken," and are "enemies," if they persist. All must be conditioned to recognize the popular will, which is really the will which the leaders assert. They must be "forced to be free." Thus power, starting with a process of rationalization and continuing with one of persuasion, reaches the use of force and finally terminates in terror. Never did Robespierre doubt that he represented the true will of the people. In this way, Rousseau's great "solution" for the social-political problem, submission of the individual will to the general will only (that is, abstractly, to itself), instead of to another individual or to a group, turned out, in practice, to be illusory and self-defeating. At the same time, this course of events also proved again the general truth, that the will-to-power never fails to justify itself in moral terms and to claim the sanctity of pure principles; and the eighteenth century, which understood the egoistic corruption of ideals, might not have been unprepared for this. Twentieth century analogies are obvious. In particular, in our own time we see once more how such epithets as "capitalist conspiracy" or "communist conspiracy" tend to take on ever wider applications until they become identified with all opposition to those who hold power.

It is not surprising, then, that in 1793, only four years after the outbreak, Robespierre declares, "The people are sublime, but individuals are weak . . . There must be a center of operations. The people as a whole cannot govern itself." [30] All who oppose him are now traitors and conspirators, enemies of the people, and must be exterminated. Justice, whose sacred standard Robespierre had raised from the first days of the Revolution, becomes converted into a mockery far more cruel than anything that had existed under the Old Régime. The death penalty is now the order of the day. In 1788 Robespierre had said that relationship to a criminal was no crime; five years later, he guillotines not only a young woman suspected of wishing to assassinate him, but also all her relations. When Marat is slain, Robespierre seizes upon that incident to wipe out the Girondists, on the pretext that they are in sympathy with it. Like the aristocrats, Danton and his group

[29] Each of the many factions, at the end of 1793, were "denouncing their enemies as false patriots, and all asserting their identity with the people." (Palmer, *Twelve Who Ruled*, p. 255.)

[30] Eagan, p. 93.

are denied a fair trial. There are no proofs, and no evidence; they are even denied the right of self-defense, on the grounds that conspirators against the people have insulted national justice.

This, too, was logical. The safety of the people overrides all purely moral considerations. Rules relating to the treatment of individuals must be determined by social utility, by the general will, to which, according to Rousseau's doctrine, each individual has surrendered himself entirely, with all the rights which he had in the state of nature.[30a] Since the end—the general welfare—determines and justifies the means, conspirators must be exterminated even without individual responsibility, or absolute proof of guilt. They must be cut off, as we cut off a gangrened limb to save the body. Society cannot help its necessary wrath; and the ill results of their behavior, regardless of all else, make them responsible. How many *philosophes* had proclaimed just that moral doctrine in the free will controversy, over three long generations of disputation? [31]

[30a] Burke's rational analysis—despite the distortions of his fanatical prejudice—does uncover some basic truths. "On this scheme of things," he writes, "a king is but a man, a queen is but a woman; a woman is but an animal, and an animal not of the highest order. . . . The murder of a king, or a queen, or a bishop, or a father, are only common homicide; and if the people are by any chance, or in any way, gainers by it, a sort of homicide much the most pardonable. . . ." Burke goes on to describe "a principal actor weighing . . . so much actual crime against so much contingent advantage. . . . In the theatre, the first intuitive glance, without any elaborate process of reasoning, will show, that this method of political computation would justify every extent of crime. . . . Justifying perfidy and murder for public benefit, public benefit would soon become the pretext, and perfidy and murder the end, until rapacity, malice, revenge, and fear more dreadful than revenge, could satiate their insatiable appetites." (*Reflections* . . . , p. 74, 78–79.)

[31] In the totalitarian view, according to Hans Morgenthau, the discrepancy between morality and reality is sidestepped. The state is the source or manifestation of morality, and "whatever it does in the name of the state partakes of the ethical dignity emanating from it." The state is the repository of the common good, consequently its ends justify all means. (*Scientific Man* . . . , p. 4, 7). Following Professor Morgenthau's analysis, we should have to say that the *philosophes* did not realize that political action and doing evil are inevitably linked; an act cannot conform both to the rules of the political art, which are those of power and success, and to those of ethics.

The perversion of justice was described with cold irony by the marquis de Sade, who had himself experienced it. "The regime of despotism had created a judicial truth which was not moral and natural truth . . . evidence did not have the right to convince without witnesses or written proofs. . . . The indulgent counter-revolutionaries tried to subject national justice and the course of the revolution to these rules. . . . Everything was working to soften justice or make it go astray. . . . There was no surprise when shameless women asked that liberty be sacrificed to their family, their husbands, their friends. . . . The result has been that never has national justice shown the imposing attitude, or displayed the energy proper to it;

And so, Robespierre, who wanted to make private interest agree with public interest, found (as Morelly had tacitly assumed, and as Le Franc de Pompignan had forewarned) that it could be done only by absolute conditioning and repression—that is, by the crushing of private interest. The "language of justice and reason" became the language of terror and death. The submission of the executive to *vox populi vox dei* was reversed. Freedom of the press and of assembly, which Robespierre had announced as basic, became freedom only for those who spoke for the people, not for their "enemies." Whole classes were "vilified, intimidated, hunted." [32] Camille Desmoulins, in the *Vieux Cordelier*, "drew a gripping picture of society under the Caesars, a society driven frantic by suspicion, uncertainty, fear, delation, duplicity and violence." [33] But Robespierre, five years after the Bastille, was still the idealist, and still refused to accept, like so many others, disillusion. He still insisted on principle, still hoped to purge the nation of vice, hypocrisy and egotism. His theory was, as before, the liberalism of constitutional government and of individual rights, as he declares it in his speech of 5 Nivôse.[34] He was not acting under the pressure of circumstances only. His speech of February 5, 1794 makes clear that he still hoped (in his own words) "to make good the promises of philosophy." He was still, as R. R. Palmer expresses it, the "child of the Enlightenment." [35] His error was, at least in part, to ignore the evil in human nature,

that we have seemed to pride ourselves on being just to individuals without worrying overmuch about being just to `'` republic. . . . The life of scoundrels here is balanced with that of the peorle `e`re . . . every indulgent or superfluous formality is a public danger. The delay in punishing the enemies of the republic should never be longer than the time it takes to recognize them. . . . Indulgence towards them is atrocious; clemency is parricide." (G. Lely, *Vie du marquis de Sade*, ii, 467–468.) Lely quotes several articles of a Revolutionary decree, including the following:

"Art. ix. Every citizen has the right to seize and to hail before the magistrates conspirators and counter-revolutionaries. He is required to denounce them as soon as he knows them.

Art. xvi. The law gives calumniated patriots patriotic jurors as defenders; it gives none to conspirators."

Obviously, judgment was pronounced before trial. Sade himself was condemned to the guillotine in 1794 for having volunteered in 1791 for service in the Garde constitutionnelle established by the Assemblée nationale. Death was also decreed on suspicion of thinking wrongly.

[32] Palmer, p. 254.
[33] *Ibid.*, p. 259.
[34] *Ibid.*, p. 264.
[35] *Ibid.*, p. 276.

and not to realize *how much* coercion and conditioning would be required to attain his ends—a measure so great, that the humanity of human beings would be destroyed.

One of the most interesting episodes of the Revolution was the declaration of the Festival of the Supreme Being. Robespierre was not likely to neglect what Rousseau had so strongly emphasized, the establishment of a State religion to repress anti-social behavior. He knew, too, the importance of spectacles and of what we today would call mass demonstrations. The State religion was proposed in 1794. Robespierre explained what it was to do, in terms that will sound familiar:

> The masterwork of society would be to create in it a quick instinct for moral things which, without the tardy help of reason, would lead him to do good and avoid evil; for the individual reason of each man, bewildered by his passions, is only a sophist which pleads their cause, and the authority of man can always be attacked by the *amour-propre* of man. Now what produces or replaces this precious instinct, what supplements the insufficiency of human authority, is the religious feeling imprinted in our hearts by the sanction given to the precepts of morality by a power superior to man: thus I am not aware of any legislator who thought of establishing national atheism.[36]

The tenets of the new religion emphasized belief in a Supreme Being and a religion of social duties. Its cult consisted of mass festivals and dedications—less to the proclaimed Goddess of Reason than to the nation. Before the Convention Robespierre denounced atheism, on grounds of utility that recall the debate which ran throughout the eighteenth century: atheism leads to crime and vice; the belief in God and immortality is "a continual reminder to be just."

But are the existence of God and immortality truths? This is not important, to Robespierre. "Eh! How could these ideas not be truths? At least I cannot conceive how nature could have suggested to man fictions that are more useful than all realities, and if the existence of God and the immortality of the soul were only dreams, they would still be the most beautiful of all the concepts of the human mind." [37]

[36] Stephens, p. 402. See Rousseau, *Contrat social*, Bk. IV, ch. 8. The example of Soviet Russia has lately disproven Robespierre's last assertion.

[37] *Ibid.*, p. 400–401.

All this was not only Rousseau's doctrine; it was that of Voltaire, d'Alembert and many many others. The right and the true are identified with, or replaced by the socially useful. Had not Mably written, "If the truth is always useful, atheism is then not true"? [38] Here we see the danger of the *philosophes'* identification of the true and the useful; while they had often declared that all truth is useful, it is only too easy to reverse the equation, and declare false and iniquitous whatever impedes the chosen end.[39] It is not surprising, then, that the Religion of Reason became, in the hands of Robespierre, the worship of the nation and the particular protector of the Jacobin régime, and of himself. He declared himself, in fact, to be under the protection of the "Eternal Author of Things" and of his providence. Crimes and assassination threats were punished in the name of that Being. "Worship of the Supreme Being had become fanatical, the very crime with which it had charged Catholicism." [40]

The cruelty and bloodthirstiness of the Terror were due to revolutionary dynamics, not to any ideas of the *philosophes,* as the Reaction later charged. Yet there was a connection which made the development easier intellectually. The ideas of the Enlightenment were part of the context in which the Revolution evolved. In the revolutionary crises, certain extreme possibilities which those ideas contained, and which were not apparent under other conditions, were summoned forth; and the very failure of the moderate approach, which the creators of those ideas had in mind, is significant.

The *logical* outcome is partly revealed, mostly after the fact, in Sade's writings; the Revolution had already made it real. "We must attribute to Sade," writes Paul Klossowski, "the role of denouncer of the obscure forces camouflaged as social values by the defense mechanisms of the collectivity. Thus camouflaged, these social values can whirl in their infernal dance." [41] "If man, slave and torturer," comments Georges Lely, "had been willing to peer into the atrocious possibilities that his nature contains, and which our author, first, had the lucidity to conceive and the courage to

---

[38] *Oeuvres*, IX, 408.

[39] For a fuller discussion of this problem, see my article, "The Problem of Truth and Falsehood," especially p. 601 ff.

[40] Eagan, p. 176.

[41] *Sade mon prochain*, quoted by Lely, *op. cit.,* II, 522.

reveal, perhaps the unspeakable period of 1933 to 1945 might not
have come to brand forever the character of the human race." To
this we must add that what Sade lay bare with a merciless lucidity
utterly unknown before him had at least been pointed to in some
of the earlier eighteenth century analysis of human nature. This
we have had ample occasion to observe.

The ethical doctrine which the *philosophes* proposed to substitute for objective imperatives cut away both the metaphysical and
the moral supports from under itself. By affirming what they perceived to be man's true place in the universe, they loosed the
metaphysical moorings and set him adrift. In a piece in *La philosophie dans le boudoir,* "Frenchmen, one further effort if you
wish to be republicans," Sade—who was always, regardless of his
own errors, the destroyer of human self-delusion and self-blind-
ness—showed that the republic was founded on the murder of
Louis XVI, a king ruling by divine right. It was God who was
guillotined on January 21, 1793.[42] For Sade this meant that there
was no longer any right to forbid crime and evil instincts, or to
prevent his proposed universal society of crime. It was the monarchy that had maintained the idea of God, as the support for
laws. Sade goes on to justify calumny, theft and murder, and to
demand that they be tolerated.

The *philosophes* had drawn no such conclusion, though a few
perceived the danger of it. They believed that ethics can and
should be independent of the supernatural. Its necessity and justification, both natural and rational, lay within human life itself.
Unfortunately, as we shall later see in more detail, the moral
support for ethics was also weakened, as a result of their analysis
of human nature and their selected norms of value. They relied
on self-interest, on the private and public utility, which they
hoped to reconcile in a reconstructed society.

All of their hopes were to fail. The perfect social order could
never be created, precisely because of the self-interest and the
drive for power which they had understood so well. We have seen
where the methods of conditioning and repression were to lead.
And rationality, which they themselves so often doubted, was
not to govern men's actions. The history of the Western world
since the French Revolution bears ample witness to the truth of

[42] The phrase is that of Camus, in *L'homme révolté,* p. 58.

this analysis. The evidence is written in the minds of the men who came after the eighteenth century, in their continuing doubts, in the increasing confusion and pessimism that envelops them, as well as in the crimes and follies of history. It would be absurd, as I have said, to cast any responsibility on the *philosophes* for the complex circumstances which determined later happenings. They cleaned out the débris of the past and unblocked the roads to the future. They did not succeed in showing men the path to a new way of life, as they had hoped, nor in solving the problem which they helped to bring to a new crisis: the moral and political problem of the relations between individuals in a community, and between the individual and the community. But they took a fateful step forward, one which mankind, in the process of its growth, had to take. In so doing, they left a heritage for the future, both precious and dangerous. The old structure was forever broken. Mankind had to create a new one. The one they dreamed of, to put in its place, was built on faith in human potentialities, and on love for their fellow men. We know now what has happened to this glorious hope, which even then covered a basic pessimism about men themselves. When it crashed and burst, and the smoke of illusion was dissipated, all that remained was the pessimism, exacerbated by the Freudian psychology, intensified by an increased awareness of the metaphysical emptiness which the eighteenth century had indeed experienced, but from which it hoped to escape through an independent, humanistic affirmation.

History, and particularly the contemporary state of mind, as we observe it in our politics, literature and arts, show that the rationalistic solutions of the middle ground have not succeeded, and have lost their formerly powerful appeal. We are impelled to extremes—to those of Sade, of Morelly, of Kant, or of the Grand Inquisitor—towards absolutes of some kind. This is to say that today we are still engaged in the same struggles. Only the shadow of despair has grown deeper, and the conflict, more desperate, has entered into the concrete arena of politics and life. The liberals and rationalists of our own time—the true children of the *philosophes*—still hope for a reasonable and a secular solution to the problems of the individual and society. They are beset, more critically than before, by the two opposing forces which were their enemies in the eighteenth century crisis. Many, appalled by the failure of reason, seek refuge within the safe citadel of the supernatural, which points to the lesson of history for its justification. Many others, indeed, whole nations, for whom science is the inescapable force controlling the future, brush aside that citadel as one that is untenable and, in fact, already fallen. Embracing the nihilism, the philosophy of the absurd that was one child of the Enlightenment, they rebel against rationalism and objective standards, in the arts and in politics, in law and in morals, drift in aimless despair, in the liberal West, or follow some philosophy of naked power and amoral scientism. But the problems are the same as those we have discussed, and those we shall later examine: our existence, the nature of man, the organization of society and the integration of the individual within it, the direction of a moral life in a creature whom Pascal rightly understood as a monster of contradiction. And even though the failure of the *philosophes* to solve the moral and social problem is historically attested, other men will go on, avoiding both extremes of absolutism and nihilism, and continue to strive for a rational, humane way of life. The eighteenth century posed the problems. We are still groping for the solutions.

It was, clearly enough, an age of crisis. But the crisis was not only of that age. It was the crisis of man. Of man, who discovered his strangeness and his frustration in a world not made for him, a universe he has passed beyond in moral value, but which annihilates him and all his work. Man, the only dissatisfied animal, who must pay the penalty for his freedom and his intelligence, and strive ever onward into unsafe regions where, perhaps, he cannot live. Man, the only tragic being, because he would be more than he is, more, perhaps, than he can be.

BIBLIOGRAPHY

A. Manuscripts

Anon. L'âme matérielle, ou nouveau système sur les faux principes des philosophes anciens et modernes et des nouveaux docteurs qui soutiennent son immatérialité. Arsenal 2239.
———— L'âme mortelle. Mazarine 1189.
———— "De la conduite qu'un honnête homme doit garder pendant sa vie," Mazarine 1194, fol. 113–151. [End of seventeenth or early eighteenth century, judging by reference to Mathias Knuzen.]
———— Difficultés sur la religion. Maz. 1163.
———— Essai sur les facultés de l'âme, et Sermon du Rabin Akib, prononcé à Smyrne le 20 octobre 1761. Traduit de l'hébreu. Maz. 1192.
———— Recherches curieuses de philosophie, ou Dissertation sur les principes des choses naturelles. Par T.S.I.F. Imprimée à Londres aux dépens de la Compagnie 1713. Traduite en 1714. B.N. Fonds fr. 9107.
———— Recherche de la vérité. Arsenal 2558.
———— "Sur l'amour-propre, et sur la différence de ce sentiment avec celui de l'amour de soi-même." B.N. Fonds fr. 7510. Recueil de pièces sur les Etats-Généraux, fol. 69–76.
———— Traité des Trois Imposteurs. B.N. N. Acq. fr. 10978.
Boulainvilliers. Abrégé de l'histoire universelle [1700]. B.N. Fonds fr. 6363–6364.
Meslier. Fénelon, Oeuvres philosophiques. Première Partie. Démonstration de l'existence de Dieu, tirée de l'art de la nature, Paris, 1713 [volume containing autograph marginal notes by Meslier].
Lau. Méditations philosophiques sur Dieu, le monde et l'homme. Maz. 1190.

B. Printed Works*

Anon. L'Anti-naturaliste, ou examen critique du poème "De la Religion naturelle." Berlin, 1756.

* Where no place of publication is given, Paris is to be assumed.

474

—— Catéchisme de morale. Bruxelles, 1785.

—— "Dialogues sur l'âme, par les interlocuteurs en ce temps-là." In Pièces philosophiques. N.p. n.d. [For original ms., see Wade, *infra*. This piece has printed date, 1771.]

—— Epître à J.-J. Rousseau, Citoyen de Genève. Genève, 1769.

—— Epître à un ami sur la recherche du bonheur. 1765(?).

—— Essai de morale et de politique. By "Ca . . . Mi . . ." N.p., 1791.

—— Examen de la religion, dont on cherche l'éclaircissement de bonne foy. Londres, 1761. [For ms., see Wade.]

—— Histoire de l'Académie royale des sciences et des belles-lettres de Berlin. Berlin, 1746–1786.

—— Histoire de Mademoiselle de Brion, dite Comtesse de Launay. N.p., 1754.

—— Jordanus Brunus redivivus, ou Traité des erreurs populaires. Published in Pièces philosophiques, n.p., n.d. [This piece is dated 1771. For ms., see Wade.]

—— Journal de Trévoux, 1700–1780.

—— Le Philosophe. Texts and Interpretations, by Herbert Dieckmann, ed. Saint Louis, 1948.

—— Mémoires de l'Académie des Belles-Lettres de Caen. Caen, 1754.

—— "Réflexion sur l'existence de l'âme, et sur l'existence de Dieu." Nouvelles libertés de penser, Amsterdam, 1743, p. 153–171. [For ms., see Wade.]

—— Analyse de la religion chrétienne. N.p., 1792. [For ms., see Wade.]

Abauzit, Firmin. Oeuvres de feu M. Abauzit. Genève, 1770.

Abbadie, J. L'art de se connoître soi-mesme, ou La recherche des sources de la morale. La Haye, 1692; 1749.

—— Traité de la vérité de la religion chrétienne. Toulouse, 1864. 2 v.

Addison. The Spectator. Philadelphia, 1832, vol. 12.

d'Aguesseau. Oeuvres, 1865. 2 v.

Alès de Corbet. De l'origine du mal, ou Examen des principales difficultés de Bayle, sur cette matière. 1758. 2 v.

Ameline. L'art de vivre heureux. 1667.

André, Père. Essai sur le beau. Amsterdam, 1759.

—— Documents inédits. Publiés par A. Charma and G. Mancel. Caen, 1844, 1856. 2 v.

—— Oeuvres. 1766. 4 v.

—— Oeuvres philosophiques. Avec une introduction par Victor Cousin. 1843.

d'Argens. Lettres cabalistiques, etc. La Haye, 1767, 2 v.

—— Lettres juives. La Haye, 1738. 6 v.

—— La Philosophie du bon sens. La Haye, 1737; also 1755; also 1746. 3 v.

—— Songes philosophiques. Berlin, 1746.

——(?) Thérèse philosophe, ou Mémoires pour servir à l'histoire du P. Dirrag et de Mademoiselle Eradice. La Haye, n.d. [1748].

d'Artaize, H. Prisme moral, ou quelques pensées sur divers sujets. 1809.

Aube, Fr. Richer d'. Essai sur les principes du droit et de la morale. 1743.

Barbeu Du Bourg. Petit Code de la raison humaine, ou exposition succinte de ce que la raison dicte à tous les hommes, pour éclairer leur conduite et assurer leur bonheur. n.p., 1789. [1774].

Barbeyrac. Traité de la morale des Pères de l'Eglise. Amsterdam, 1728.

[Barrin, l'abbé]. Vénus dans le cloître, ou la Religieuse en chemise. Nouvelle édition. Dusseldorf, 1746. [Cologne, 1683].

[Billardon de Sauvigny, L. E.]. La religion révélée, Poème, en réponse à celui de la "Religion naturelle." Genève, 1758.

Baudot de Juilly. Dialogues entre Monsieur Patru et D'Ablancourt sur les plaisirs. 1701. 2 v.

Bayle. Dictionaire historique et critique. Cinquième édition. Amsterdam, 1734, 5 v. [1697].

—— Oeuvres diverses. La Haye, 1737. 4 v.

de Beausobre, Louis. Dissertations philosophiques. 1753.

—— Essai sur le bonheur. Berlin, 1758.

—— Le pirrhonisme du sage. Berlin, 1754.

Bergier, N. Apologie de la religion chrétienne, contre l'auteur du Christianisme dévoilé, et contre quelques autres critiques. 1769. 2 v.

—— Examen du matérialisme: ou Réfutation du Système de la Nature. 1771. 2 v.

Bergier (et Bouchaud). Principes de métaphysique et de morale, à l'usage des élèves de l'école royale militaire. 1780.

Bernard, J.-Fr. Dialogues critiques et philosophiques. Amsterdam, 1730.

—— Réflexions morales, satiriques et comiques sur les moeurs de notre siècle. Liège, 1733.

Boisguillebert. Le détail de la France. In Economistes français du XVIIIe siècle. Ed. Eugène Daire. 1843. [1697, 1707].

Boismont (de). Lettres secrettes sur l'état actuel de la Religion et du Clergé de France . . . n.d., n.p. [1781].

Bonnet, Charles. Oeuvres d'histoire naturelle et de philosophie. Neuchâtel, 1781, also 1782. 7 v.

Borde, Charles. Profession de foi philosophique. 1763.

Bossuet. Traité du libre arbitre. In Oeuvres philosophiques. 1843.

Boudier de Villemaire. L'Andrométrie, ou Examen philosophique de l'homme. 1753.

—— L'Irréligion dévoilée, et demontrée contraire à la saine philosophie. Londres, 1774.

—— Pensées philosophiques, sur la nature, l'homme, et la religion, 1784.

Boufflers, Stanislas. Discours sur la vertu. Prononcé à l'Académie des sciences et Belles-Lettres de Berlin le 25 janvier 1797. An IX–1800.

Boulainvilliers. Réfutation des erreurs de Benoît de Spinosa. Bruxelles, 1731.

Boulanger, N. A. Oeuvres. En Suisse, 1791. 10 v. Also, Amsterdam, 1794.

Boullier. Discours philosophiques. Amsterdam, 1759.

Brissot de Warville, J. P. Correspondance universelle sur ce qui intéresse le bonheur de l'homme et de la société. Neuchâtel, 1783. 2 v.

Buffier. Traité des premières vérités. 1843 [1724].

—— Traité de la société civile. 1726.

Buffon. Corpus général des philosophes français. Buffon. Edition Jean Piveteau. 1954.

—— Oeuvres complètes. 1884–1885. 14 v.

Burke, Edmund. Reflections on the French Revolution. London (Everymans Library), 1950 [1790].

—— Works. London, 1897, v. 1.

Burlamaqui, J. J. Principes du droit naturel. Genève, 1748. 2 v.

Butler, Joseph. Five Sermons preached at the Rolls Chapel and A Dissertation upon the Nature of Virtue. New York (Liberal Arts Press), 1950 [1726].

Camuset. Pensées anti-philosophiques. 1770.

—— Principes contre l'incrédulité, à l'occasion du Système de la nature. 1771.

Carra, J. L. Système de la raison, ou Le prophète philosophe. Londres, 1782.

Castel, Père L. B. L'Homme moral opposé à l'Homme physique de M. R . . . [Rousseau] Toulouse, 1756.

Castilhon, L. Essais de philosophie et de morale. Bouillon, 1770.

Cerutti, Père. Discours qu'a remporté le prix d'éloquence à l'Académie de Montauban, le 25 août 1760. "Les vrais plaisirs ne sont faits que pour la vertu."

Chamfort. Oeuvres complètes. 3e éd. 1812. 2 v.

Chastellux. De la félicité publique. Amsterdam, 1772.

Chaudon. Anti-Dictionnaire philosophique. 1775. 2 v. (4e éd.).

Chiniac, Pierre. Essais de philosophie morale. An IX (1801). 5 v.

Chubb, Th. A Collection of Tracts. London, 1730.

———— The Ground and Foundation of Morality. London, 1745.

———— A Vindication of God's Character. London, 1726.

Clarke, Samuel. A Collection of Papers, which passed between the late Learned Mr. Leibnitz and Dr. Clarke, etc. London, 1717.

Cloots, A. La république universelle, ou Adresse aux Tyrannicides. L'an quatre de la Rédemption.

———— L'orateur du genre humain. 1791.

Collet. Traité des devoirs des gens du monde. 1763.

Collins, Anthony. A philosophical Inquiry concerning Human Liberty. London, 1717.

Condillac. Oeuvres. An VI (1798).

———— Oeuvres philosophiques. Corpus général des philosophes français, 1947.

———— Traité des sensations. Introduction de G. Lyon. 1886. Also éd. Fr. Picavet, 1928.

Condorcet. Esquisse d'un tableau historique des progrès de l'esprit humain. 1822.

———— Oeuvres. Publiées par O'Connor et Arago. 1847–49.

Coyer. Bagatelles morales. Londres, 1759.

———— Oeuvres complètes. 1782–83. 7 v.

Crébillon, fils. Les égarements du coeur et de l'esprit. A La Haye, 1764.

Crousaz. Examen de l'Essay de Monsieur Pope sur l'homme. Lausanne, 1737.

———— La logique, ou système de réflexions, etc. 2ᵉ éd. Amsterdam, 1720.

Cudworth, Ralph. A Treatise concerning eternal and immutable morality. London, 1731.

Cumberland, Richard. A Treatise of the Laws of Nature. London, 1727.

Daire, Eugène, ed. Physiocrates. 1846.

d'Alembert. Discours préliminaire de l'Encyclopédie. Publié par Fr. Picavet. 1894.

———— Oeuvres. 1821. v. 1.

Delandine. Ouvrages académiques, ou Recueil des prix proposés par les Sociétés savantes. 1787.

Delille, J. L'homme des champs, ou les Géorgiques françaises. Strasbourg, An VIII, 1800.

———— Les trois règnes de la nature. 1832.

Delisle de Sales. De la philosophie de la nature. Amsterdam, 1770, 3 v.

———— De la philosophie du bonheur. 1796.

Denesle. Examen du matérialisme. 1754. 2 v.

Descartes. Oeuvres philosophiques. Publiées par A. Garnier. 1835. 4 v.

Deschamps, Dom. La voix de la raison contre la raison du temps, et particulièrement contre celle de l'Auteur du Système de la nature, par demandes et réponses. Bruxelles, 1770.

———— Le vrai système, ou le mot de l'énigme métaphysique et morale. Ed. Jean Thomas et F. Venturi. 1939.

Descoutures. La morale universelle. 1687.

Desfourneaux. Essay d'une philosophie naturelle applicable à la vie, aux affaires. 1724.

Deslandes, A. F. B. Histoire critique de la philosophie. Nouvelle éd., Amsterdam, 1756. 4 v.

Diderot. Correspondance. Ed. Georges Roth. 1955 et seq.

———— (ed.) Encyclopédie, ou Dictionnaire raisonné des sciences, des arts et des métiers, par une société de gens de lettres. 1751–1765. 17 v.

———— Le Neveu de Rameau. Ed. critique par Jean Fabre. Genève, 1950.

———— Le Rêve de d'Alembert. Ed. critique par Paul Vernière. 1951.

———— Lettre sur les aveugles. Ed. critique par R. Niklaus. Genève, 1951.

———— Lettres à Sophie Volland. Ed. A. Babelon. N.d. 2 v.

———— Oeuvres complètes. Ed. Assézat et Tourneux. 1875–77. 20 v.

———— Pensées philosophiques. Ed. critique par R. Niklaus. Genève, 1950, 1957.

———— Supplément au Voyage de Bougainville. Ed. G. Chinard. 1935.

Domat. Les loix civiles dans leur ordre naturel. 1689. 2 v.

Dubos, Charles. Réflexions critiques sur la poésie et la peinture. 1740.

Dubuisson, Paul-Eric. Nouvelles considérations sur Saint-Domingue, en réponse à celles de M.H.D. 1780.

Du Châtelet. Lettres inédites à M. le Comte d'Argental. 1806.

Duclos, Ch. P. Considérations sur les moeurs de ce siècle. 1751.

—— Oeuvres morales et galantes, suivies de son Voyage en Italie. L'An V (1797). 4 v.

Duhamel, Joseph. Lettres flamandes. Lille, 1753.

Dulaurens. Imirce, ou la fille de la nature. Berlin, 1765.

—— Le Compère Mathieu. Londres, 1770. 3 v.

—— Le porte-feuille d'un philosophe, ou Mélange de pièces philosophiques, politiques, critiques, satyriques et galantes, etc. Cologne, 1770. 3 v.

Dumas, Jean. Traité du suicide. Amsterdam, 1773.

Dumas, M. L'Esprit du citoyen. Neuchâtel, 1783.

Dupont de Nemours, P. S. Opuscules morales et politiques, retirées de différens journaux. An XIII.

—— Philosophie de l'univers. 1792, also 1796.

Dupuy. Dialogues sur les plaisirs, sur les passions, sur le mérite des femmes. 1717.

Fabre, Pierre. Recherches sur la nature de l'homme, considéré dans l'état de maladie. 1776.

Ferguson, Adam. An essay on the history of civil society. 7th ed. Edinburgh, 1814.

—— Institutes of moral philosophy. 3rd ed. Edinburgh, 1785.

—— Principles of moral and political science. Edinburgh, 1792. 2 v.

Fermin, Philippe. Dissertation sur la question S'il est permis d'avoir en sa possession des esclaves, et de s'en servir comme tels dans les colonies de l'Amérique. Maestricht, 1770.

Fontenelle. Oeuvres. 1825. v. 3, 4.

—— Oeuvres diverses. Londres, 1721.

[Fontenelle]. "Traité de la liberté par M . . ." In Nouvelles libertés de penser, p. 112–151. Amsterdam, 1743. [1724? For ms. see Wade.]

Formey. L'Anti-Sans-Soucy, ou la Folie des nouveaux philosophes. Bouillon, 1761. 2 v.

—— Examen philosophique de la liaison réelle qu'il y a entre les sciences et les moeurs. Avignon, 1775.

—— Le bonheur, ou nouveau système de jurisprudence naturelle. Berlin, 1754.

—— Mélanges philosophiques. Leyde, 1754. 2 v.

—— Le philosophe chrétien. Leyde, 1752.

—— Principes de morale, déduits de l'usage des facultés de l'entendement humain. Leyde, 1762.

—— "Réflexions sur le goût," in Père André: Essai sur le beau, avec un Discours préliminaire par M. Formey. Amsterdam, 1759.

—— Systeme du vrai bonheur. Utrecht, 1771.

Fougeret de Montbron. Margot la ravaudeuse. Hambourg, 1800 [1750].

Frédéric II. "Essai sur l'amour-propre envisagé comme principe de morale." (1763). Hist. de l'Académie de Berlin, 19: 341–354.

—— Oeuvres. Berlin, 1846–57. v. 8, 9.

Fréret. Oeuvres complètes. Londres, 1775. t. 3.

Gauchat. Lettres critiques, ou analyse et réfutation de divers écrits modernes contre la religion. 1755, also 1763. 18 v.

Gérard. Le comte de Valmont, ou les égaremens de la raison. 1774. 3 v.

Gerdil, Père H. S. Discours philosophiques sur l'homme, considéré relativement à l'état de nature, et à l'état de société. Turin, 1769.

—— Recueil de dissertations sur quelques principes de philosophie et de religion. 1760.

Goguet. De l'origine des loix, des arts et des sciences. 1759.

Gosseaume, L. G. Précis analytique des travaux de l'Académie royale des sciences, belles-lettres et arts de Rouen. Rouen, 1821. 5 v.

Grimm, Melchior, *et al.* Correspondance littéraire. 1877–1882. 16 v.

Grotius. Le droit de la guerre et de la paix. Ed. par Pradier-Fodéré. 1867. 3 v.

Guidi (abbé). Entretiens philosophiques sur la religion; Suite des entretiens, etc. 1772. 2 v.

Haller, A. von. Lettres de feu M. de Haller contre M. de Voltaire. Berne et Lausanne. 1780.

Hartley, David. Observations on man. His frame, his duty, and his expectations. 4th ed. London, 1801. [1749].

Hayer. La religion vengée, ou Réfutation des auteurs impies. 1757–60. 21 v.

Helvétius. De l'Esprit. 1758.

———— De l'Homme. Londres, 1776. [1772].

———— Le Bonheur. Poème en six chants. Nouvelle éd. Londre, 1776.

Hemsterhuis. Oeuvres philosophiques. 1792. 2 v.

Hennebert, J. B. Du plaisir, ou du moyen de se rendre heureux. Lille, 1764.

Hobbes. The Moral and Political Works of Thomas Hobbes of Malmesbury. London, 1750.

Hoin. Discours sur l'utilité des passions, par rapport à la santé. Dijon, 1752.

d'Holbach. Ethocratie ou le gouvernement fondé sur la morale. Amsterdam, 1776.

———— Boulanger [*sic*]. Le christianisme dévoilé. En Suisse, 1791.

———— La morale universelle, ou Les devoirs de l'homme fondés sur sa nature. 1820.

———— Système de la nature. Londres, 1771. 2 v.

———— Système social, ou principes naturels de la morale et de la politique. Londres, 1773. 3 v.

Holland, G. J. Réflexions philosophiques sur le Système de la Nature. Neuchâtel, 1773.

Hume. Enquiry concerning human understanding. In The English Philosophers from Bacon to Mill. Ed. by Burtt. New York, Modern Library, 1939.

———— Essays, literary, moral and political. London, 1870.

———— Hume's Moral and Political Philosophy. Ed. by H. Aiken. New York, 1948.

———— Philosophical Essays. Morals, Literature and Politics. Georgetown, D. C., 1817. v. 1.

———— The Philosophical Works of David Hume. Ed. by T. Green and T. Grose, London, 1874. v. 4.

———— Two Essays. London, 1777.

Hutcheson, Fr. An inquiry into the original of our ideas of beauty and virtue. Third ed. London, 1729.

Ilharat de la Chambre. Abrégé de philosophie, ou Dissertations sur la certitude humaine, la logique, la métaphysique et la morale. 1754. 2 v.

Jacob, Frère Thomas [Bernard Lambert]. Essai sur la jurisprudence universelle. 1779.

Jamin, N. Pensées théologiques, relatives aux erreurs du temps. 1769.

Joly, J. R. Dictionnaire de morale philosophique. 1771. 2 v.

Kames, Lord. Essays on the Principles of Morality and Natural Religion. Edinburgh, 1751.

Kant, I. Critique of Practical Reason and other works on the theory of ethics. Translated by T. K. Abbott. London, 1954.

Laclos, Ch. de. Les Liaisons dangereuses. Publiées avec une introduction par Fr. Carco. 1931. 2 v.

Ladvocat. Entretiens sur un nouveau système de morale et de physique, ou La recherche de la vie heureuse selon les lumières naturelles. 1721.

La Harpe. "Fragments de l'Apologie de la Religion." Oeuvres. 1820. t. XVI.

Lahontan, Baron de. Dialogues curieux entre l'auteur et un sauvage de bon sens qui a voyagé et Mémoires de l'Amérique Septentrionale. Publiés par G. Chinard. Baltimore, 1931.

La Luzerne. Instruction pastorale. 1786.

Lambert, Mme de. Avis d'une mère à sa fille, Oeuvres. 1748.

La Mettrie. Histoire naturelle de l'âme. La Haye, 1745.

———— L'Homme machine, suivi de L'art de jouir, Ed. Maurice Solovine. 1921.

———— Oeuvres philosophiques. Berlin, 1764, also Amsterdam, 1774. 3 v.

Lamiral, D. H. L'Affrique et le peuple affriquain, considérés sous tous leurs rapports avec notre Commerce et nos Colonies. 1789.

Lamourette. Pensées sur la philosophie de la foi. 1789.

La Placette. Eclaircissemens sur quelques difficultés qui naissent de la considération de la liberté nécessaire pour agir moralement. Amsterdam, 1709.

———— Essais de morale. Seconde Ed. Amsterdam, 1716 [1695]. 4 v.

———— Nouveaux essais de morale. Cologne, 1697. 4 v.

Lassay, marquis de. Lettres amoureuses, et Pensées diverses. Ed. par M. Lange s.d.

La Touraille, comte de. Nouveau recueil de gaîté et de philosophie. Londres, 1785.

Lebrun, P. D. Oeuvres. 1811. t.2.

Le Franc de Pompignan. La religion vengée de l'incrédulité par l'incrédulité elle-même. 1772.

Le François, L. Oeuvres complètes. 1856–7. 2 v.

Le Guay de Prémontval. Le Diogène de d'Alembert; ou Diogène décent. Berlin, 1775.

———— Vues philosophiques, ou Protestations et Déclarations sur les principaux Objets des connoissances humaines. Berlin, 1761. 2 v.

Leibniz. Extraits de la Théodicée. 1878.

———— The Monadology and other philosophical writings. Translated by R. Latta. Oxford, 1898.

Lelarge de Lignac. Le Témoignage du sens intime et de l'expérience, opposé à la foi profane et ridicule des Fatalistes modernes. Auxerre, 1770. 3 v.

Le Maître de Claville. Traité du vrai mérite de l'homme. 3ᵉ éd. 1737. 2 v.

Le Mercier de la Rivière. L'ordre naturel et essentiel des sociétés politiques. 1910. [1767].

Léonard. Poésies. 1826.

Leroy, Ch. G. Examen des critiques du livre intitulé De l'Esprit. Londres, 1760.

———— Lettres philosophiques sur l'intelligence et la perfectibilité des animaux, avec quelques lettres sur l'homme. An X (1802) [1768].

Lesage, A. R. Gil Blas. 1836.

———— Le diable boiteux. n.d. [1707].

Lesage de la Colombière, G. L. Cours abrégé de philosophie par aphorismes. Genève, 1711.

———— L'esprit des loix. Genève, 1751.

———— Le mécanisme de l'esprit, ou la Morale naturelle dans ses sources. Genève, 1711. [1700].

———— Les principes naturels des actions des hommes. Genève, 1749.

Le Trosne. De l'ordre social. 1777.

Lévesque, P. Ch. L'homme moral, ou l'homme considéré tant dans l'Etat de pure Nature, que dans la société. Amsterdam, 1775.

Levesque de Pouilly. Théorie des sentimens agréables. Genève, 1747.

Linguet. Le fanatisme des philosophes. Londres, 1764.

———— Théorie des loix civiles, ou Principes fondamentaux de la société. Londres, 1767.

Locke, John. An Essay concerning human understanding. Ed. by A. C. Fraser. Oxford, 1894. 2 v. Also, London, 1731, 2 v.

Luzac, Elie. L'homme plus que machine. In La Mettrie, Oeuvres philosophiques, t.3.

Mably. Oeuvres complètes. Londres, 1789. 13 v. Also, 1794–95. 14 v.

Malebranche. De la recherche de la vérité. Ed. par Fr. Bouiller. n.d., 2 v.

———— Traité de morale. 1953.

Malouet, P. V. Collection de mémoires sur les colonies. An X, t.5.

Mandeville, B. The Fable of the Bees: or, Private Vices, Publick Benefits. Ed. by F. B. Kaye. Oxford, 1924. 2 v.

Marat, J. P. De l'homme, ou des principes et des loix de l'influence de l'âme sur le corps, et du corps sur l'âme. Amsterdam, 1775. 3 v.

Maréchal, S. De la vertu. 1807.

———— Examen des critiques du livre intitulé "De l'Esprit." Londres, 1760.

———— Mélanges tirés d'un petit porte-feuille. Avignon, 1782.

Maret, M. "Description d'un hermaphrodite," Mémoires de l'Académie de Dijon, 1774, p. 157–169.

Marivaux. La vie de Marianne, avec la suite de Marianne, par Madame Ricoboni [*sic*]. Préface de Marcel Arland. 1947.

———— Le cabinet du philosophe. 1734.

———— "L'indigent philosophe," in Le Spectateur français, t.2. 1728.

———— Le paysan parvenu. Ed. par A. Farges. n.d. [1939].

Marmontel. Leçons d'un père à ses enfants sur la métaphysique. Leçons . . . sur la morale. In Oeuvres complètes, 1819, t.XVII.

Maubec. Principes physiques de la raison et des passions des hommes. 1709.

Maupertuis. Oeuvres. Lyon, 1756. 4 v.

Meister, J. H. De la morale naturelle. Nouvelle éd. Londres, 1788.

———— Mélanges de philosophie, de morale et de littérature. Genève, 1822. 2 v.

Melon. Essai politique sur le commerce. n.p. 1734.

Mendelssohn, M. Phédon, ou Entretiens sur la spiritualité et l'immortalité de l'âme. 1772.

———— Recherches sur les sentimens moraux. Genève, 1763.

Mercier, L. S. L'an deux mille quatre cent quarante. n.p. 1791.

Merian. "Dissertation ontologique sur l'action, la puissance et la liberté," in Histoire de l'Académie de Berlin, 6:459–516 (1750).

———— "Examen d'une question concernant la liberté." In *ibid.* 9:417–430. (1753).

———— "Sur le sens moral." In *ibid.* 14:390–413. (1758).

Meslier. Le Testament de Jean Meslier. Ed. par Rudolf Charles. Amsterdam, 1864. 3 v.

Mirabeau, Honoré. Oeuvres, 1835, t.VII, VIII.

Mirabeau, V. R. L'ami des hommes, ou Traité de la population. Avignon, 1756. 3 v.

———— La science, ou Les Droits et les devoirs de l'homme. Lausanne, 1774.

———— Philosophie rurale, ou économie générale et politique de l'agriculture, etc. Amsterdam, 1764. 3 v.

Moncrif, Paradis de. Oeuvres de Monsieur de Moncrif. 1751. 3 v.

Montesquieu. De l'esprit des lois. Londres, 1757. 4 v. Also éd. par J. B. de la Gressaye. 1950–.

———— Grandeur et décadence des Romains. 1860.

———— Lettres persanes. Ed. par A. Adam. Genève, 1954.

———— Oeuvres complètes, publiées sous la direction de M. A. Masson. 1950–1955. 3 v.

Moreau, J. N. Mémoire pour servir à l'histoire des cacouacs. 1828.

———— Variétés morales et philosophiques. 1785.

Morellet. Mélanges de littérature et de philosophie du XVIIIe siècle. 1818. 4 v.

Morelly. Code de la nature. Publié par G. Chinard. 1950.

———— Essai sur le coeur humain, ou principes naturels de l'éducation. 1745.

———— Essai sur l'esprit humain, ou principes naturels de l'éducation. 1743.

———— Le Prince. Les délices des coeurs, ou Traité des Qualités d'un grand Roi, et Sistème général d'un sage Gouvernement. Amsterdam, 1751.

———— Naufrage des Isles flottantes, ou Basiliade du célèbre Pilpaï. Poème héroïque. Messine, 1753. 2 v.

Naigeon. Discours préliminaire pour servir d'introduction à la morale de Sénèque. 1782.

———— Le militaire philosophe. Londres, 1768.

Necker, Mme de. Nouveaux mélanges extraits des mss. de Mme Necker. An X–1801. 2 v.

Nicole. Essais de morale. 1713. 8 v.

Nietzsche, F. The Genealogy of Morals, in the Philosophy of Nietzsche. New York, Modern Library, 1954.

Nonnotte. Dictionnaire philosophique de la religion. Besançon, 1774. 4 v.

Nougaret, P. J. B. La voix du peuple, poème au sujet de la chute et de la diminution des grains. Amsterdam, 1769.

Para du Phanjas. Eléments de métaphysique sacrée et profane, ou Théorie des êtres insensibles. 1767.

—— Les principes de la saine philosophie, conciliés avec ceux de la religion. 1774. 2 v.

Pascal. Pensées et opuscules, publiés par Léon Brunschvicg, Hachette, n.d.

Paulian, A. H. Le véritable système de la nature. Avignon, 1788.

Pey. La loi de nature, développée et perfectionnée par la loi évangélique. Montauban, 1789.

—— Le philosophe catéchiste, ou Entretiens sur la religion. 1779.

Pichon. Cartel aux philosophes à quatre pattes. n.p.n.d.

—— La raison triomphante des nouveautés. 1756.

—— Les argumens de la raison, en faveur de la philosophie, de la religion et du sacerdoce, ou examen De l'Homme, de M. Helvétius. Londres, 1776.

Pluche. Le spectacle de la nature. 1746. 8 v.

Pluquet. Examen du fatalisme. 1757. 3 v.

Polignac. L'Anti-Lucrèce, Poème sur la religion naturelle. 1769. 2 v.

Pope. An Essay on Man, in The Works of Alexander Pope, Esq. London, 1787. v. 2.

Postel. L'incrédule conduit(e) à la religion catholique. Tournay, 1769.

Prévost. Histoire du chevalier Des Grieux et de Manon Lescaut. Ed. par M. Allem. 1927.

Price, Richard. A review of the principal questions in morals. Ed. by D. D. Raphael. Oxford, 1948 [1758].

Priestley, Joseph. A free discussion of the doctrines of materialism, and philosophical necessity, in a correspondence between Dr. Price and Dr. Priestley. London, 1778.

—— Institutes of natural and revealed religion. Birmingham, 1782, 2 v.

Pufendorf, S. Le droit de la nature et des gens. Traduit par Jean Barbeyrac. 5e éd. Amsterdam, 1734, 2 v.

Quesnay. Oeuvres économiques et philosophiques. Ed. par A. Oncken. 1888.

Racine, Louis. La Religion. La Grâce. 5e éd. 1747.

Raynal. Histoire philosophique et politique des établissements et du commerce des européens dans les deux Indes. Amsterdam, 1770. 6 v.; 1781. 10 v.

Régis, P. S. Système de philosophie. 1690. 3 v.

Reid, Thomas. An inquiry into the human mind, on the principles of common sense. 4th ed. London, 1785.

—— Essays on the Active Powers of the Human Mind, in Works. Ed. by Dugald Stewart. New York, 1822. v. 3.

Rémond de Saint-Mard. Oeuvres. Amsterdam, 1750. 3 v.

—— Lettres galantes et philosophiques. Cologne, 1721.

—— Nouveaux dialogues des dieux. Rotterdam, 1714.

Rétif de la Bretonne. Le paysan perverti, ou les dangers de la ville. A La Haie. 1776. 2 v.

—— La paysane pervertie, ou les dangers de la ville. A La Haie, 1784. 2 v.

Richard, Ch. L. Exposition de la doctrine des philosophes modernes. Malines, 1785.

—— La défense de la religion, de la morale, de la vertu, de la politique et de la société. 1775.

—— La nature en contraste avec la religion et la raison, ou l'Ouvrage qui a pour titre "De la Nature," condamné au tribunal de la foi et du bon sens. 1773.

Rivarol, A. C. De la philosophie moderne, n.d.n.p.

———— De l'Homme, de ses facultés intellectuelles, et de ses premières idées fondamentales. An Huitième (1800).

———— Pensées inédites. 1836.

Robespierre, M. Correspondance de Maximilien et d'Augustin Robespierre. Ed. par G. Michon. 1926.

———— Oeuvres. Ed. par Bouloiseau, Levèbvre et Soboul. Discours, t. 6, 7. 1950.

Robinet, J. B. De la nature. 3ᵉ éd. Amsterdam, 1766. 4 v.

———— Dictionnaire universel des sciences morale, économique, politique et diplomatique. Londres, 1777–83. 30 v.

Roucher. Les mois. Poème en douze chants. 1779.

Rouillé d'Orfeuil. L'alambic des loix, ou observations de l'ami des français sur l'homme et sur les loix. Hispaan, 1773.

———— L'alambic moral, ou analyse raisonnée de tout ce qui a rapport à l'homme. Maroc, 1773.

Rousseau, J. J. Discours sur les sciences et les arts. Ed. critique par George R. Havens. New York and London, 1946.

———— Emile, ou de l'éducation. Ed. par Fr. et P. Richard. n.d. [1951].

———— La Nouvelle Héloïse. Nouvelle éd., publiée par Daniel Mornet. 1925. 4 v

———— Lettre à Mr. d'Alembert sur les spectacles. Ed. critique par M. Fuchs. Genève, 1948.

———— Oeuvres complètes. Ed. Ch. Lahure (Hachette), 1865, 13 v.

———— The Political Writings of Jean Jacques Rousseau. Ed. by C. E. Vaughan. Cambridge, 1915. 2 v.

———— Les rêveries du promeneur solitaire. Ed. critique par M. Raymond. Genève, 1948.

Roussel. La loi naturelle. 1769.

Sabatier de Castres. Dictionnaire des passions, des vertus, et des vices. 1769. 2 v.

———— Lettres critiques, morales et politiques. Erfurt, 1802.

———— Pensées et observations morales et politiques, pour servir à la connaissance des vrais principes du gouvernement. Vienne, 1794.

Sade, D. A. F. Histoire de Juliette, ou les prospérités du vice. Sceaux (Pauvert), 1954. 6 v.

———— La philosophie dans le boudoir. n.p., 1948.

———— Les infortunes de la vertu. Ed. par M. Heine. 1930.

———— Morceaux choisis de D. A. F. Sade. Publiés par G. Lely. n.d. [1948].

Saint-Evremond. Oeuvres. Ed. par R. de Planhol. 1927. v. 1.

———— Oeuvres mêlées. Amsterdam, 1706. 5 v.

Saint-Hyacinthe. Recherches philosophiques, sur la nécessité de s'assurer par soi-même de la vérité, etc. Londres, 1743.

———— Recueil de divers écrits. 1736.

Saint-Lambert. Les saisons. 1823.

———— Oeuvres philosophiques. An IX (1801). v. 1, 2, 3.

Saint-Martin. De l'esprit des choses, ou coup-d'oeil philosophique sur la nature des êtres et sur l'objet de leur existence. An 8.

———— Tableau naturel des rapports qui existent entre Dieu, l'homme et l'univers. Edimbourg, 1782.

Saint-Pierre, Bernardin de. Etudes de la nature. In Oeuvres complètes, 1818.

———— Harmonies de la nature. In Oeuvres posthumes. 1833.

———— Paul et Virginie. Ed. par M. Souriau. Roches, 1930.

Saint-Pierre, Castel de. Annales politiques (1658–1740). Nouvelle éd. par J. Drouet. 1912.

———— Extrait du Projet de paix perpétuelle de Monsieur l'abbé de Saint-Pierre. Par J. J. Rousseau, Citoyen de Genève. n.p. 1761.

———— Ouvrages de morale et de politique. Rotterdam, 1737. v. 12.

———— Oeuvres diverses. 1730. 2 v.

———— Projet pour rendre la paix perpétuelle en Europe. Utrecht, 1713–1717. 3 v.

Senac de Meilhan. Oeuvres philosophiques et littéraires. Hambourg, 1795.

Shaftesbury. Characteristicks of Men, Manners, Opinions, Times. Sixth ed. n.p., 1737. 3 v.

Sigorgne. Le philosophe chrétien. Avignon, 1765.

Silhouette. "Préface du traducteur." Essai sur l'homme. Par M. Pope. n.p., 1736.

Sisson de Valmire. Dieu et l'homme. Amsterdam, 1771.

Smith, Adam. Theory of moral sentiments. London, 1892. [1759].

Spinoza. The Chief Works of Benedict de Spinoza. London, 1909. v. 1.

―――― Ethic. In Selections. Ed. by J. Wild. New York, 1930.

Stanislas I. Le philosophe chrétien. n.p., 1749.

―――― Oeuvres du philosophe bienfaisant. 1763. t.4.

Stephens, H. M., ed. The Principal Speeches of the Statesmen and Orators of the French Revolution. Oxford, 1892, v. 2.

Sulzer. "Considérations psychologiques sur l'homme moral." In Histoire de l'Académie de Berlin, 25:361–380 (1769).

―――― "Essai sur le bonheur des êtres intelligents." In *ibid.*, 10:399–417 (1754).

―――― "Recherches sur un principe fixe, qui serve à distinguer les devoirs de la morale de ceux du Droit Naturel." In *ibid.*, 12:450–458 (1756).

Terrasson. La philosophie applicable à tous les objets de l'esprit et de la raison. 1754.

Thomas, A. "Réflexions philosophiques et littéraires sur le Poème de la Religion naturelle," in Voltaire, Oeuvres complètes. 1822. t.4.

Toussaint. "Discours sur les avantages de la vertu." In Histoire de l'Académie de Berlin, XXII:461–486 (1766).

―――― Les moeurs. Amsterdam, 1748.

Trublet. Essais sur divers sujets de littérature et de morale. 1749. 3 v.

Turgot. Oeuvres. Ed. par G. Schelle. 1913. 4 v.

―――― Textes choisis. Préface par P. Vigreux. 1947.

Varennes, J. Ph. Les hommes. 1727. Also, 1735, 2 v.

Vauvenargues. Oeuvres complètes. 1821, 4 v.

―――― Oeuvres morales. 1874. 3 v.

Volney. Oeuvres complètes, 1821. t.1.

Voltaire. Candide. Ed. critique par A. Morize. 1913.

―――― Correspondance. Ed. by Th. Besterman. Genève, 1953 et seq.

―――― Oeuvres complètes. Ed. par L. Moland. 1877–85. 52 v.

―――― Poème sur la loi naturelle. A critical edition. By Francis J. Crowley. Publications of the Univ. of California at Los Angeles in Languages and Literature, v. 1, no. 4, p. 177–304. Berkeley, 1938.

―――― Traité de métaphysique. Ed. par H. Temple Patterson, Manchester University Press, 1937.

―――― Notebooks. Ed. by Th. Besterman. Genève, 1952. 2 v.

Wolff. Principes du droit de la nature et des gens. Amsterdam, 1758. 3 v.

Wollaston, Wm. The Religion of nature delineated. London, 1726.

C. Secondary References

Adam, Antoine. "Rousseau et Diderot," Revue des sciences humaines, 53:25–31 (1949).

Albaum, Martin. "The Moral Defenses of the Physiocrats' Laissez-faire," Journal of the History of Ideas, 16:179–197 (1955).

Alderman, W. F. "Shaftesbury and the Doctrine of Benevolence in the Eighteenth Century," Transactions of the Wisconsin Acad. of Sciences, Arts and Letters, XXVI:137–159 (1931).

Alverdes, F. The Psychology of Animals in Relation to Human Psychology. London, 1932.

Barber, W. H. Leibniz in France. Oxford, 1955.

Barker, J. E. Diderot's Treatment of the Christian Religion in the Encyclopédie. New York, 1941.

Bartholmess, Chr. Histoire philosophique de l'Académie de Prusse depuis Leibniz jusqu'à Schelling. 1850–51. 2 v.

Beauvoir, S. de. "Faut-il brûler Sade?" Les Temps modernes, 7:1002–1033, 1197–1280 (1951, 1952).

Becker, C. L. The Heavenly City of the Eighteenth Century Philosophers. New Haven, 1932.

Bénichou, Paul. Morales du grand siècle. 1948.

Besterman, Theodore. "Voltaire et le Désastre de Lisbonne," Travaux sur Voltaire II. Genève, 1956.

Burgelin, Pierre. La philosophie de l'existence de J. J. Rousseau. 1952.

Bush, Newell. The Marquis d'Argens and his philosophical correspondence. Ann Arbor, 1953.

Camus, Albert. L'homme révolté. 1951.

Carré, J. R. La philosophie de Fontenelle, ou le sourire de la raison. 1932.

———— "Voltaire philosophe," Revue des cours et conférences 39 (2), passim, 1938.

Cassirer, Ernst. Das Erkenntnisproblem in der Philosophie und Wissenschaft der neueren Zeit. Erster Band. Berlin, 1906.

———— The Philosophy of the Enlightenment. Princeton, 1951.

———— Rousseau, Kant and Goethe. Princeton, 1945.

Chauchard, P. "Evolution de la conscience et conscience de l'évolution," Rev. scientifique, VI:35–45 (1953).

———— "Physiologie de la liberté," Rev. scientifique, 1:408–18 (1948).

Chérel, Albert. De Télémaque à Candide. 1933.

———— La pensée de Machiavel en France. 1935.

Chinard, Gilbert. "Montesquieu's Historical Pessimism," Studies in the History of Culture, 1942, p. 161–172.

Collingwood, R. G. The Idea of History. Oxford, 1949.

Crisafulli, A. S. "Montesquieu's Story of the Troglodytes: its background meaning and significance," PMLA, 52:372–392 (1943).

Crocker, L. G. "Diderot and Eighteenth Century French Transformism," in Forerunners of Darwin, ed. Bentley Glass, Baltimore, 1959.

———— "The Discussion of Suicide in the Eighteenth Century," J. of the History of Ideas, 13:47–72 (1952).

———— "The Problem of Truth and Falsehood in the Age of Enlightenment," J. of the History of Ideas, 14:575–603 (1953).

———— "Voltaire's Struggle for Humanism," Voltaire Studies IV, ed. by Th. Besterman, Genève, 1957, p. 137–169.

Desautels, A. R. Les Mémoires de Trévoux et le mouvement des idées au XVIIIe siècle. Rome, 1956.

Delvolvé, Jean. Religion, critique et philosophie chez Pierre Bayle. 1906.

Deymes, J. Les doctrines politiques de Robespierre. Bordeaux, 1907.

Dieckmann, H. Le philosophe. Textes et interprétations. Saint Louis, 1948.

Dingle, Herbert. The Scientific Adventure. London, 1952.

Dumas, J. B. Histoire de l'Académie royale des sciences, belles-lettres et arts de Lyon. Lyon, 1839. 3 v.

Duncker, Karl. "Ethical Relativity? An Enquiry into the Psychology of Ethics." Mind 48:39–57 (1939).

Dupréel, Eugène. Traité de morale. Bruxelles, 1932. 2 v.

Eagan, J. M. Maximilien Robespierre: Nationalist Dictator. New York, 1938.

Fabre, Jean. "Une question de terminologie littéraire: Paul et Virginie, pastorale," Annales publiées par la Faculté des Lettres de Toulouse, 3:168–200 (1953).

Fellows, O. E., and Green, A. "Diderot and the abbé Dulaurens," in Diderot Studies, ed. Fellows and Torrey, Syracuse, 1949, p. 64–93.

486 *Bibliography*

Frankel, Chas. The Faith of Reason. The Idea of Progress in the French Enlightenment. New York, 1948.

Freud, S. Civilization and its discontents. New York, 1930.

Fromm, Erich. Man for Himself. New York, 1947.

Glass, Bentley. "Maupertuis and the Beginning of Genetics," The Quarterly Review of Biology, 22:196–210 (1947).

Gottschalk, Louis. "Reflections on Burke's Reflections on the French Revolution," Proceedings of the American Philosophical Society, 100:417–429 (1956).

Groethuysen, Bernard. Philosophie de la Révolution française. 1956.

Hastings, Hester. Man and beast in French thought of the Eighteenth Century. Baltimore, 1936.

Havens, G. R. "La Théorie de la bonté naturelle de l'homme chez Jean-Jacques Rousseau." Revue d'histoire littéraire, 31:629–642 (1924); 32:24–37, 212–225 (1925).

―――― The Age of Ideas. New York, 1955.

Hazard, Paul. Etudes critiques sur Manon Lescaut. Chicago, 1929.

―――― La Crise de la conscience européenne. 1935. 3 v.

―――― La pensée européenne au XVIIIe siècle, de Montesquieu à Lessing. 1946. 3 v.

―――― "Le problème du mal," Romanic Review, 32:147–170 (1941).

Hendel, C. W. Jean-Jacques Rousseau, moralist. London and New York, 1934. 2 v.

―――― The Philosophy of Kant and our modern world. New York, 1957.

Hermand, Paul. Les idées morales de Diderot. 1923.

Hobhouse, L. T. Morals in Evolution. New York, 1916.

Hubert, René. Les sciences sociales dans l'Encyclopédie. 1923.

Jamieson, R. K. Marivaux. A Study in Sensibility. New York, 1941.

Johnston, Elise. Le Marquis d'Argens. Sa vie et ses oeuvres. n.d. [1929?].

Klein, D. B. Abnormal Psychology. New York, 1951.

Kluckhohn, Clyde. "Ethical Relativity: Sic et Non," J. Philosophy, 52:663–677 (1955).

Koyré, Alexandre. From the Closed World to the Infinite Universe. Baltimore, 1957.

―――― "The Significance of the Newtonian Synthesis," Archives internationales d'histoire des sciences, 29:291–311 (1950).

Kramer, Noah. From the Tablets of Sumer. Indian Hills, Colorado, 1956.

Lanson, G. Histoire de la littérature française. 1912.

―――― "La transformation des idées morales et la naissance des morales rationnelles de 1680 à 1715." Revue du mois, 1910.

―――― "Le Rôle de l'expérience dans la formation de la philosophie du XVIIIe siècle," Revue du mois, 1910.

―――― "Origines et premières manifestations de l'esprit philosophique dans la littérature française." Revue des Cours et Conférences, 1908–1910.

Le Breton, A. Rivarol. Sa vie, ses idées, son talent. D'après des documents nouveaux. 1895.

Lely, Gilbert. Vie du marquis de Sade. T.1., 1952. T.2., 1957.

Lovejoy, A. O. Essays in the History of Ideas. Baltimore, 1948.

―――― "'Pride' in Eighteenth Century Thought," Modern Language Notes, 36:31–37 (1921).

―――― "Some Eighteenth-Century Evolutionists," Scientific Monthly, Sept. 1950, p. 162–178 (reprinted from The Popular Science Monthly, 65:238–251, 323–340 (1904)).

―――― The Great Chain of Being. Cambridge, 1948.

―――― "The Supposed Primitivism of Rousseau's Discourse on Inequality," Modern Philology, 21:165–186 (1923).

Lovejoy, A. O. and Boas, G. Primitivism and related ideas in antiquity. Baltimore, 1935.

Loy, J. R. Diderot's Determined Fatalist. New York, 1950.

Malinowski, B. The Foundations of Faith and Morals. London, 1936.

Maritain, Jacques. "Natural Law and Moral Law," in R. N. Anshen, Moral Principles of Action, New York, 1952, p. 62–76.

Martin, Kingsley. French Liberal Thought in the Eighteenth Century. Boston, 1929.

Mayer, Jean. "Illusions de la philosophie expérimentale au XVIIIe siècle," Revue générale des sciences, 63:353–363 (1956).

Meister, Paul. Charles Duclos. Genève, 1956.

Mitchell, E. T. A Systém of Ethics. New York, 1950.

Monod, Albert. De Pascal à Chateaubriand. 1916.

Morehouse, Andrew. Voltaire and Jean Meslier. New Haven, 1936.

Morgenthau, Hans J. Scientific Man vs. Power Politics. Chicago, 1946.

Mornet, D. Les sciences de la nature en France au XVIIIe siècle. 1911.

Niebuhr, Reinhold. The Nature and Destiny of Man. New York, 1941. 2 v.

—— The Children of Light and the Children of Darkness. New York, 1949.

Northrop, F. S. C. "Ethical Relativism in the Light of Recent Legal Science," J. of Philosophy. 52:649–662 (1955).

Ollivier, Albert, Saint-Just et la force des choses. 1954.

Palmer, R. R. Catholics and Unbelievers in Eighteenth Century France. Princeton, 1939.

—— Twelve Who Ruled. Princeton, 1941.

Peyre, Henri. "The Influence of Eighteenth Century Ideas on the French Revolution," J. of the History of Ideas, 10:63–87 (1949).

Piaget, Jean. "The Child and Moral Realism," in R. N. Anshen, Moral Principles of Action, New York, 1952, p. 417–435.

Pingaud, L. Documents pour servir à l'histoire de l'Académie de Besançon," Procès-Verbaux et Mémoires, Acad. des sciences, belles-lettres et arts de Besançon. Année 1892. Besançon, 1893. P. 234–311.

Polin, Raymond. Politique et philosophie chez Thomas Hobbes. 1953.

Potez, H. L'élégie en France, de Parny à Lamartine. 1898.

Rosenfield, L. C. From Beast-Machine to Man-Machine. New York, 1941.

Rosso, Corrado. "Il 'Paradosso' di Robinet," Filosofia, 5:37–60 (1954).

Rothbard, M. N. "A Note on Burke's Vindication of Natural Society," J. of the History of Ideas, 19:114–18 (1958).

Rowbotham, A. H. "The 'Philosophes' and the Propaganda for Inoculation of Smallpox in Eighteenth-Century France," Univ. of California Publications in Modern Philology, 18:265–290 (1935).

Rueff, Jacques. "L'ordre dans la nature et dans la société," Diogène, 10:3–20 (1955).

Sabine, G. H. A. History of Political Theory. New York, 1950.

Sartre, J. P. Literary and Critical Essays. New York, 1955.

Schlegel, D. B. Shaftesbury and the French Deists. Chapel Hill, 1956.

Schmidt, A. M. "Duclos, Sade et la littérature féroce," Rev. des sciences humaines," 1951, p. 146–155.

Schweitzer, Albert. Civilization and Ethics. London, 1946.

Seeber, E. D. Anti-Slavery Opinion in France during the Second Half of the Eighteenth Century, Baltimore, 1937.

Stephen, Leslie. English Thought in the Eighteenth Century. New York, 1949, 2 v.

Tisserand, Roger. Au temps de l'Encyclopédie. L'Académie de Dijon de 1740 à 1795. n.d.

Torrey, N. L. The Spirit of Voltaire, New York, 1938.

Trahard, Pierre. Les maîtres de la sensibilité française. 1933. 4 v.

Trilling, Lionel. Freud and the Crisis of our Culture. Boston, 1955.

Vartanian, A. "Trembley's Polyp, La Mettrie, and Eighteenth-Century French Materialism," J. of the Hist. of Ideas, 11:259–286 (1950).

Vial, Fernand. Une philosophie et une morale du sentiment: Luc de Clapiers, marquis de Vauvenargues. 1938.

Vernière, Paul. Spinoza et la pensée française avant le Révolution. 1954. 2 v.

Wade, I. O. "A favorite metaphor of Voltaire." Romanic Rev. 26:330–34 (1935).
—— The Clandestine Organization and Diffusion of Philosophic Ideas in France from 1700 to 1750. Princeton, 1938.
—— The Search for a New Voltaire. Philadelphia, 1958.
Wasserman, E. R. The Subtler Language. Baltimore, 1959.
Wells, G. A. "Herder's Determinism," J. of the Hist. of Ideas, 19:105–113 (1958).
Westermarck, Edward. The Origin and Development of Moral Ideas. Second ed. London, 1917.
Weulersse, Georges. Le mouvement physiocratique en France, de 1756 à 1770. 1910, 2 v.
White, Lynn. Frontiers of Knowledge. New York, 1956.
Willey, Basil. The Eighteenth Century Background. Studies on the Idea of Nature in the Thought of the Period. London, 1953.
Wolpe, Hans. Raynal et sa machine de guerre. L'Histoire des Deux Indes et ses perfectionnements. Stanford, 1957.
Zimmerman, J. P. "La morale laïque au commencement du XVIIIe siècle," Rev. d'histoire littéraire, 24:42–64, 440–66 (1917).
Zuckerman, S. The Social Life of Monkeys and Apes. London, 1932.

INDEX